This volume provides students and scholars with a text that examines, explains, and appraises contributions made by the United Nations to contemporary international law and the law-creating process. The authors consider how UN institutions have made the law, what law has been made, and the extent to which that law has been meaningfully accepted by and evidenced in contemporary state practice. The study first deals with processes and measures that cut across law-making, covering practical as well as conceptual aspects. Then the substantive law is addressed in terms of the different fields of activity that the United Nations has made subject to legal rules and processes. Some chapters cover prominent areas, such as human rights, use of force, and economic relations; others deal with topics that have not previously been examined with sufficient care, such as labor, the environment, refugees, and women. The book's final section deals with the internal law of the UN system itself – the international civil services and financial contributions.

THE UNITED NATIONS AND
INTERNATIONAL LAW

THE UNITED NATIONS AND
INTERNATIONAL LAW

edited by

CHRISTOPHER C. JOYNER
Georgetown University

A co-publication with the
American Society of International Law

ASIL • THE AMERICAN SOCIETY OF INTERNATIONAL LAW

CAMBRIDGE
UNIVERSITY PRESS

Published by the Press Syndicate of the University of Cambridge
The Pitt Building, Trumpington Street, Cambridge CB2 1RP
40 West 20th Street, New York, NY 10011-4211, USA
10 Stamford Road, Oakleigh, Melbourne 3166, Australia

First published 1997

Printed in Great Britain at the University Press, Cambridge

A catalogue record for this book is available from the British Library

Library of Congress cataloguing in publication data

The United Nations and international law / edited by Christopher C. Joyner
p.   cm.
ISBN 0 521 58379 9. – ISBN 0 521 58659 3 (pbk.)
1. United Nations.   2. International law.   I. Joyner, Christopher C.
JX1977.U42575 1997
341.23–dc20   96-43488   CIP

ISBN 0 521 58379 9 hardback
ISBN 0 521 58659 3 paperback

CONTENTS

vii

PREFACE

This volume is the revised, abridged product of the United Nations Legal Order (UNLO) project, a three-year multidimensional study sponsored by the American Society of International Law and funded by a grant from the Ford Foundation. The principal aim of the project was to assess the evolving importance, present competence, and future roles played by the United Nations system in shaping and enhancing the contemporary international legal order. As the study progressed, its timing became especially appropriate. Not only was the UNLO project conceived and carried out during the United Nations' declared "Decade of International Law"; its published product, *United Nations Legal Order*, also appeared on the eve of the celebration of the United Nations' fiftieth anniversary in 1995. Publication of that study hence took on even more significance as a retrospective assessment of UN law-creation at the Organization's half-century mark of life.

This volume embodies much of the UNLO project, although in abridged form. The fundamental purpose of UNLO was to examine, explain, and appraise contributions made by the United Nations System to international law and the law-creating process. The broad design of this condensed study, therefore, aims to analyze and assess contributions of the United Nations to the post-World War II international legal order, especially that law which has persisted into the present legal order. This involves a critical appraisal of how UN institutions have made the law, what law has been made, and the extent to which that law has been meaningfully accepted by and evidenced in contemporary state practice.

The main themes of the volume converge into several related questions: How is international law made, revised, or repealed by UN institutions? What contemporary operative international law owes its existence to the United Nations? How have UN bodies served as sources of international law? How do they create international law? What forms of law –

conventions, principles, customary norms – stand as evidence of this UN law-creating function, and to what degree can this law be said to work as an effective regulator of state conduct? In sum, have viable legal regimes been created or advanced by UN institutions for dealing with international problems? How so? And in what ways is that United Nations-produced law enforced, and how is compliance induced? By substantively addressing these questions, this study supplies a coherent and relevant appraisal of the ways and means in which the United Nations Organization has made concrete, salient contributions to the contemporary international legal order.

From its inception, the UNLO project aimed at bringing together a group of international lawyers and experts from different parts of the world, with different experience in United Nations matters. Completion of this substantially revised edition was equally challenging. Such a revision entails certain risks and difficulties. Early on, two obvious risks became apparent: First, events affecting the role of the United Nations in world affairs happened so rapidly and with such profound implications during the mid-1990s that considerable updating and revisions would have to be made. Would every selected author be willing to return to this project, undertake such tedious tasks, and do so in an expeditious manner? The second risk also grew from time considerations: Would some contributors be overly committed to other professional activities and thus be unable to complete abridging and updating their own pieces? Fortunately for the finished product, these concerns proved to be unfounded.

With respect to difficulties, it is not hard to appreciate the problems of communicating with fifteen colleagues located in several countries, and coordinating revision of *United Nations Legal Order* between the editor, staff at the American Society of International Law, and Cambridge University Press. These difficulties proved merely inconveniences, not impediments, thanks largely to smooth cooperation by all parties concerned.

It is customary and proper to thank people and institutions who have assisted in various ways to help bring this volume into being. In the case of the original UNLO project, special mention must be given to the Ford Foundation for its generous financial support and patience throughout the entire course of this project. Without this Ford Foundation support, the UNLO project could never have been as comprehensive in scope or authoritative in substance as it became. Nor would the present volume ever have emerged as its offspring. Likewise, a great intellectual debt is owed John Lawrence Hargrove, who in his capacity as Executive Director of the American Society of International Law personally wrote the grant proposal to the Ford Foundation. It was Larry who conceived of the UNLO project, who secured the funding for its promotion, and who personally worked to select several individuals who came to be contributing authors. His contribution was substantial and lasting.

Thanks are also due to the School of Law at Columbia University and to the American Society of International Law for hosting various meetings of the authors. The staff of the American Society of International Law in Tillar House, in particular Jill Watson and Sandra Liebel, greatly assisted in hosting two early committee meetings that discussed the substance and outlined the structure of the original United Nations Legal Order project.

Marilou Righini, ASIL Director of Publications, deserves special mention. The present volume is largely a product of her imagination and persistence. Marilou was instrumental in persuading this editor that such a revision was necessary and that it would be useful in the classroom setting. She moreover was especially helpful in facilitating publication arrangements with Cambridge University Press.

Special thanks are due to George Little and Tamara Wittes, my research assistants at Georgetown University, whose services were of considerable value in the production phases of editing the manuscripts. Likewise, a number of my former George Washington University students rendered valuable assistance in researching and cite-checking materials. Jocelyn Aqua and Douglas Miller were particularly helpful in that regard.

The production staff at Cambridge University Press has been superb indeed. Special gratitude is owed to John Haslam, Commissioning Editor of Social Sciences, for his courtesy, professionalism, and constant encouragement during the preparation of the manuscript. John's friendly nature was much appreciated. I also wish to thank Caroline Drake and especially Mary Starkey for their excellent editorial and copy services and Lyn Chatterton for keeping the publication production of this volume on schedule.

My greatest personal debts are owed to two special people who made the UNLO project happen. First, Oscar Schachter, co-editor of the volumes comprising *United Nations Legal Order*, made enormous intellectual contributions to the original manuscripts. His keen insights during the editorial review process helped all involved in the project to focus their analysis on substantive issues of international law. His extensive personal experience with the United Nations, coupled with an invaluable historical perspective of the institution, added a critical evenhandedness to the treatments. It was this balance that permitted the authors to more thoroughly weigh and objectively assess the process of law-creation through the United Nations Organization. We all learned much from his legal perspicacity.

The second person to whom particular gratitude is owed is Charlotte

Ku, Executive Director of the ASIL. Throughout the original UNLO project, she acted as liaison, facilitator, and coordinator, and became the engine that kept "UNLO" running on course and on time. I am especially grateful for her constant support, sincere dedication, and personal encouragement in helping to bring this project to fruition.

More than any others, though, thanks are due to the group of colleagues who generously gave of their intellectual resources and valuable time to make possible the completion of the original study, but most especially this updated, abridged revision. Their effort was truly a collective one. Their patience, cooperation, and legal insights are genuinely appreciated. My sincere gratitude to all.

Christopher C. Joyner
Editor
Annandale, Virginia

NOTES ON THE CONTRIBUTORS

Jose E. Alvarez is a Professor of Law at Michigan Law School. From 1989 to 1993 he was an Associate Professor at the National Law Center at the George Washington University. Prior to entering academia, he was an attorney-adviser at the US Department of State where he served on delegations to various international negotiations, including those involving bilateral investment treaties, the UN proposed Code of Conduct for Transnational Corporations, and the Canada–United States Free Trade Agreement. A graduate of Harvard College, Harvard Law School and Oxford University and a former International Affairs Fellow at the Council on Foreign Relations, he teaches and writes in the areas of international jurisprudence, international investment, and international organizations.

Rebecca J. Cook is a Professor and Director of the International Human Rights Programme, Faculty of Law, University of Toronto. She is a member of the Washington, DC Bar and is a co-founder of the International Women's Rights Action Watch. She serves on the Advisory Board of Profamilia Women's Legal Services, Bogotá, Colombia and as an occasional adviser on women's human rights to the Commonwealth Medical Association, Ford Foundation, and World Health Organization.

Hurst Hannum is Professor of International Law at The Fletcher School of Law and Diplomacy of Tufts University, where he teaches international organizations, international human rights law, and nationalism and ethnicity. His recent publications include *Autonomy, Sovereignty, and Self-Determination: The Accommodation of Conflicting Rights* (rev. ed. 1996); *International Human Rights: Problems of Law, Policy and Process* (3d ed., 1995, with Richard Lillich); and *Guide to International Human Rights Practice* (2d ed., 1992). He is General Editor of a multi-volume series of books on the Universal Declaration of Human Rights, which will be published by Martinus Nijhoff beginning in 1997.

Robert S. Jordan is Research Professor of International Institutions and Professor of Political Science at the University of New Orleans. He holds doctorates from Princeton University and from Oxford University, where he was a member of St. Antony's College. He was also the first Dag Hammarskjöld Visiting Professor of International Affairs at the University of South Carolina; Distinguished Visiting Professor of Strategy at the US Naval War College; and Director of Research of the United Nations Institute for Training and Research (UNITAR). He has been a Vice-President of the International Studies Association, chairman of its International Organization Section, and has served on the Editorial Board of *Public Administration Review*. His most recent books are *International Organizations: A Comparative Approach* and *General Lauris Norstad: Cold War Alliance Commander*.

Christopher C. Joyner, Co-Editor of *United Nations Legal Order* (1995) and Director of the American Society of International Law's Project on the United Nations Legal Order, is Professor of Government at Georgetown University, where he teaches courses on international law and international organization. From 1981 to 1994 he was Professor of Political Science and International Affairs at the George Washington University. He serves as Chair of the International Law Section of the International Studies Association and Vice-Chair of the ASIL's Antarctica Section. The author of numerous articles on international law and world politics, his most recent books include *Eagle Over the Ice: The US in the Antarctic* (1997); *Antarctica and the Law of the Sea* (1992); *The Persian Gulf War* (1990); and *The Antarctic Legal Regime* (1988). He has also taught international law at Dartmouth College, the University of Virginia, and the Johns Hopkins University School of Advanced International Studies.

Frederic L. Kirgis is Law School Association Alumni Professor at the Washington and Lee University School of Law. He is the author of publications on international law and organizations, including *International Organizations in Their Legal Setting*, now in its second edition. He is a former member of the Board of Editors of the *American Journal of International Law*, and was Vice-President of the American Society of International Law from 1985 to 1987.

Virginia A. Leary is Distinguished Service Professor, State University of New York, and Emerita Professor of Law, State University of New York at Buffalo. In 1986–87 she was the first holder of the Ariel Sallows Chair in Human Rights at the College of Law, University of Saskatchewan, Canada. Prior to joining the faculty of the Law School at Buffalo, she was an official at the International Labour Office, Geneva, Switzerland and practiced law in Chicago. She is the author of *International Labor Conventions and National Law, Ethnic Conflict and Violence in Sri Lanka,* and co-author of *Asian Perspectives on Human Rights,* as well as a number of book chapters and articles on international law, human rights, and international labor law. From 1990 to 1992 she served as Vice-President of the American Society of International Law.

David A. Martin is Henry L. and Grace Doherty Charitable Foundation Professor, University of Virginia School of Law, and the author of numerous works on immigration, refugees, and international law. He entered teaching after a period of private practice and service in the Bureau of Human Rights and Humanitarian Affairs at the US Department of State. At the Department he worked on both human rights and refugee issues, and was closely involved in the drafting of the Refugee Act of 1980. He has served in a variety of advisory capacities, including as a consultant to the Administrative Conference of the United States for a study recommending comprehensive reforms to the US asylum adjudication system. He is also co-author of *Immigration Process and Policy,* which received the annual book award (Citation of Merit) from the American Society of International Law in 1986. In 1995 he took leave from the University of Virginia to serve as General Counsel of the US Immigration and Naturalization Service.

John F. Murphy is Professor of Law at the Villanova University School of Law. Prior to going into teaching, Professor Murphy was an attorney with the Office of the Legal Adviser, US Department of State, and engaged in the private practice of law in Washington, DC and New York City. In addition to Villanova, he has taught at Cornell University, the University of Kansas, Georgetown University, and was the Charles H. Stockton Professor of International Law at the Naval War College. His publications include (with James D. Dinnage) *The Constitutional Law of the European Union* (1996); (with Alan C. Swan) *The Regulation of International Business and Economic Relations* (1991), which was awarded a Certificate of Merit by the American Society of International Law in 1992; and *The United Nations and the Control of International Violence* (1982).

Ved P. Nanda is the Thompson G. Marsh Professor of Law and Director of the International Legal Studies Program at the University of Denver College of Law and Evans Professor and Vice Provost for Internationalization at the University. He has served as President of the World Association of Law Professors, and is currently Honorary Vice-President of the World Jurist Association, US Branch, and on the Editorial Board of the *American Journal of Comparative Law* and the *Indian Journal of International Law.* He has authored a dozen books and numerous other publications on international law and was given the World Legal Scholars Award at Beijing in 1990 by the World Peace through Law Center.

Bernard H. Oxman is Professor of Law at the University of Miami School of Law. He received his A.B. and J.D. degrees from Columbia University. His association with the law of the sea commenced while serving in the International Law Division of the United States Department of the Navy Office of the Judge Advocate General. It continued at the Department of State Office of the Legal Adviser where he served as Assistant Legal Adviser for Oceans, Environment, and Scientific Affairs. During that period he also served as United States Representative and Vice-Chairman of the US Delegation to the Third United Nations Conference on the Law of the Sea. He has written extensively on the law of the sea and currently serves as a member of the Board of Editors of the *American Journal of International Law.*

Oscar Schachter, Co-Editor of *United Nations Legal Order* (1995) and Hamilton Fish Professor Emeritus of International Law and Diplomacy at Columbia University, has combined a scholarly and practical career in international law and regulations for over fifty years. He has worked for and with United Nations organizations in senior positions since 1944 and has written extensively on related legal and organizational topics. His professional honors include the Presidency (and Honorary Presidency) of the American Society of International Law, Co-Editor-in-Chief of the *American Journal of International Law,* membership since 1965 in the Institut de Droit International, and recipient of the prestigious Manley Hudson Gold Medal for preeminent scholarship and achievement in international law. His published writings include *International Law in Theory and Practice* (1991); *Sharing the World's Resources* (1977); *International Law: Cases and Materials* (Co-editor); *Law and Action in the United Nations* (Hague Academy) and numerous articles on various aspects of international law and institutions. He has also taught at Yale, Harvard, and New York University Law Schools and directed studies for the UN Institute of Training and Research.

Ralph G. Steinhardt is Professor of Law and Associate Director of the International and Comparative Law Program at the National Law Center of George Washington University. He has been a Faculty Associate of the Space Policy Institute since 1988 and has served as a legal consultant to the US Congress, Office of Technology Assessment, on space law issues. He is the author of numerous articles on international law and has served as legal counsel to the UN High Commissioner for Refugees, Amnesty International, the International Human Rights Law Group, and the ACLU

Foundation of Southern California, in a range of human rights cases. He is the founder and co-director of the joint Programme in International Human Rights Law at Oxford University.

Paul C. Szasz is an Adjunct Professor of Law at the New York University School of Law. Between 1959 and 1989 he served as a Legal Officer of the IAEA, the World Bank and ICSID, and the United Nations, retiring as Deputy to the UN Legal Counsel. Since retirement, he has been Legal Adviser to the UN's Namibia operation and to the International Conference on the Former Yugoslavia. He has participated in numerous codification and other treaty-making conferences and in several ICJ advisory proceedings, and has written extensively on the law of international organizations, especially in the environmental area and on the international legislative process. He has served as Vice-President of the American Society of International Law.

Stephen Zamora is Dean and Professor of Law at the University of Houston Law Center. He has served as Chairman of the International Economic Law Interest Group of the American Society of International Law, and is a member of the Bretton Woods Committee. His publications include a two-volume reference work (with Professor Ronald Brand) entitled *Basic Documents of International Economic Law,* as well as numerous articles on international economic law subjects. He is also a General Editor of a computer database on international economic law that is on-line with LEXIS and WESTLAW.

TABLE OF CASES

ABBREVIATIONS

General

CCITT	International Telephone and Telegraph Consultative Committee
CEDAW	Convention on the Elimination of Discrimination Against Women
CERD	Convention on the Elimination of All Forms of Racial Discrimination
CFR	Code of Federal Regulations (USA)
CITES	Convention on International Trade in Endangered Species
COLREG	Convention on the International Regulations for Preventing Collisions at Sea
COPUOS	Committee on the Peaceful Uses of Outer Space
ECOSOC	United Nations Economic and Social Council
EEC	European Economic Community
FAC	Food Aid Convention
FAO	Food and Agriculture Organization
GA Res.	United Nations General Assembly Resolution
GATT	General Agreement on Tariffs and Trade
GEMS	Global Environmental Monitoring System
IAEA	International Atomic Energy Agency
IBRD	International Bank for Reconstruction and Development (World Bank)
ICAO	International Civil Aviation Organization
ICJ	International Court of Justice
ICSC	International Civil Service Commission
ICSID	International Centre for the Settlement of Investment Disputes
IDA	International Development Association

IFAD	International Fund for Agriculture Development
IFC	International Finance Corporation
IGO	International Inter-Governmental Organization
ILC	International Law Commission
ILM	*International Legal Materials*
ILO	International Labour Organization
IMF	International Monetary Fund
IMO	International Maritime Organization
IOC	International Oceanographic Commission
ITU	International Telecommunications Union
LNTS	League of Nations Treaty Series
MARPOL	International Convention for the Prevention of Pollution by Ships
NATO	North Atlantic Treaty Organization
NGO	Non-Governmental Organization
NIEO	New International Economic Order
NPT	Non-Proliferation Treaty
OAS	Organization of American States
OAU	Organization of African Unity
PCIJ	Permanent Court of International Justice
SC Res.	United Nations Security Council Resolution
SOLAS	International Convention for the Safety of Life at Sea
TIAS	Treaties and Other International Acts Series
TNC	transnational corporation
UNAT	United Nations Administrative Tribunal
UNCED	United Nations Conference on Environment and Development
UNCITRAL	United Nations Commission on International Trade Law
UNCLOS	United Nations Conference on the Law of the Sea
UNCTAD	United Nations Conference on Trade and Development
UNDP	United Nations Development Programme
UNEF	United Nations Emergency Force
UNEP	United Nations Environmental Programme
UNESCO	United Nations Educational, Scientific and Cultural Organization
UN GAOR	United Nations General Assembly Official Records
UNHCR	United Nations High Commissioner for Refugees
UNIDO	United Nations Industrial Development Organization
UNIFIL	United Nations Interim Force for Southern Lebanon
UNRWA	United Nations Relief and Works Agency
UN SCOR	United Nations Security Council Official Records
UNTS	United Nations Treaty Series

UPU	Universal Postal Union
UST	United States Treaties and Other International Agreements
WARC	World Administrative Radio Conference
WFP	World Food Program
WHO	World Health Organization
WIPO	World Intellectual Property Organization
WMO	World Meteorological Organization
WTO	World Trade Organization

Journals and yearbooks

Ann. Français de Droit Int'l	*Annuaire Français de Droit International*
AJIL	*American Journal of International Law*
Amer. U. L. Rev.	*American University Law Review*
Am. Soc'y Int'l L. Proc.	*Proceedings of the American Society of International Law*
Am. U. J. Int'l L. & Pol'y	*American University Journal of International Law and Policy*
Annals Air & Space L	*Annals of Air and Space Law*
Austl. Y. B. Int'l L.	*Australian Year Book of International Law*
B. C. Int'l & Comp. L Rev.	*Boston College International and Comparative Law Review*
Brit. Y. B. Int'l L	*British Year Book of International Law*
Buff. L. Rev.	*Buffalo Law Review*
Bus. Law.	*The Business Lawyer*
Cal. W. Int'l L. J.	*California Western International Law Journal*
Case W. Res. J. Int'l L.	*Case Western Reserve Journal of International Law*
Colo. J. Int'l Envt'l L. & Pol'y	*Colorado Journal of International Environmental Law and Policy*
Colum. J. Int'l Aff.	*Columbia Journal of International Affairs*
Colum. J. Transnat'l L.	*Columbia Journal of Transnational Law*
Cornell Int'l L. J.	*Cornell International Law Journal*
Denv. L. J.	*Denver Law Journal*
Denv. J. Int'l L. & Pol'y	*Denver Journal of International Law and Policy*

Dep't St. Bull.	Department of State Bulletin
Duke J. Comp. & Int'l L.	Duke Journal of Comparative and International Law
Ecology L Q.	Ecology Law Quarterly
Ethics & Int'l Aff.	Ethics and International Affairs
Eur. L. R.	European Law Review
Fletcher F. World Aff.	Fletcher Forum of World Affairs
Fordham Int'l L. J.	Fordham International Law Journal
Ga. J. Int'l & Comp. L.	Georgia Journal of International and Comparative Law
German Y. B. Int'l L.	German Year Book of International Law
Grotius Soc'y Transactions	Transactions of the Grotius Society
Harv. Int'l L. J.	Harvard International Law Journal
Harv. L. Rev.	Harvard Law Review
Hastings Int'l & Comp. L. Rev.	Hastings International and Comparative Law Review
HRLJ	Human Rights Law Journal
Hum. Rts. Q.	Human Rights Quarterly
IAEA Bull.	IAEA Bulletin
ILO Official Bull.	ILO Official Bulletin
Immig. & Nationality	Immigration and Nationality
Int'l & Comp. L. Q.	International and Comparative Law Quarterly
Int'l Conciliation	International Conciliation
Int'l Economic Inst.	International Economic Institutions
Int'l Envt. Rep.	International Environment Reporter
Int'l Env. Daily	International Environment Daily
Int'l J. Refugee L.	International Journal of Refugee Law
Int'l Lab. Rev.	International Labour Review
Int'l Law.	The International Lawyer
Int'l Migration Rev.	International Migration Review
Int'l Org.	International Organization
Int'l Stud. Q.	International Studies Quarterly
Iowa L. Rev.	Iowa Law Review
Isr. Y. B. Hum. Rts.	Israel Yearbook on Human Rights
J. Developing Areas	Journal of Developing Areas
J. Int'l Aff.	Journal of International Affairs
J. Int'l Comm. Jurists	Journal of the International Commission of Jurists
J. Int'l L.	Journal of International Law

J. L. & Soc'y	Journal of Law and Society
J. Mar. L. & Comm.	Journal of Maritime Law and Commerce
J. Space L.	Journal of Space Law
J. World Trade L.	Journal of World Trade Law
Law & Contemp. Probs.	Law and Contemporary Problems
Law Library J.	Law Library Journal
McGill L. J.	McGill Law Journal
Mich. J. Int'l L.	Michigan Journal of International Law
Mich. L. Rev.	Michigan Law Review
NC J. Int'l L. & Com. Reg.	North Carolina Journal of International Law and Commercial Regulation
Neth. Int'l L. J.	Netherlands International Law Journal
Neth. Int'l L. Rev.	Netherlands International Law Review
Nordic J. Int'l L.	Nordic Journal of International Law
Notre Dame L. Rev.	Notre Dame Law Review
Nova L. Rev.	Nova Law Review
NYU J. Int'l L. & Pol.	New York University Journal of International Law and Policy
Ocean Dev. & Int'l L.	Ocean Development and International Law
Ohio St. L. J.	Ohio State Law Journal
Oregon L. Rev.	Oregon Law Review
Pub. Admin. Rev	Public Administration Review
RBDI	Revue Belge de Droit International
RCADI	Recueil des Cours d'Académie de Droit International
R. Int'l Arb. Awards	Report on International Arbitration Awards
San Diego L. Rev.	San Diego Law Review
Tex. Int'l L. J.	Texas International Law Journal
U. Chi. L. Rev.	University of Chicago Law Review
U. Miami Inter-American L. Rev.	University of Miami Inter-American Law Review
UNEP Env'l L.	UNEP Environmental Law
UN Jurid. Y. B.	United Nations Juridical Yearbook
UN Observer & Int'l Rep.	United Nations Observer and International Report
U. Pa. L. Rev.	University of Pennsylvania Law Review
U. Toronto L. J.	University of Toronto Law Journal
Va. J. Int'l L.	Virginia Journal of International Law

Vand. J. Transnat'l L.	*Vanderbilt Journal of Transnational Law*
Victoria U. Wellington L. R.	*Victoria University of Wellington Law Review*
Wm. & Mary L. Rev.	*William and Mary Law Review*
World Pol'y J.	*World Policy Journal*
Yale J. Int'l L.	*Yale Journal of International Law*
Y. B. Int'l L. Commission	*Year Book of the International Law Commission*
Y. B. UN	*Year Book of the United Nations*

PART I

THE UN SYSTEM AS A SOURCE OF LAW

CHAPTER ONE

THE UN LEGAL ORDER: AN OVERVIEW

Oscar Schachter

The end of the Cold War gave new visibility to the United Nations and raised hopes for a more effective international legal order. The new era also made it especially timely to examine and assess the structures and processes for creating and applying law by and within the United Nations system of organizations. To that end, this introductory chapter provides an overview of what is called the United Nations Legal Order. It presents some important features of legal processes in the UN system and notes trends and problems of general interest. It does not avoid value judgments.

1. Law-making in the UN system

Neither the United Nations nor any of its specialized agencies was conceived as a legislative body. Their charters and governing instruments contemplated that their objectives would be carried out mainly through recommendations aimed at coordinating (or "harmonizing") the actions of their member states. The authority to impose mandatory rules was limited (with some exceptions) to the internal administration of the organization in question. Member states were free, of course, to create new law or repeal existing law through the traditional processes of treaty and customary law. What was not fully realized at first is that the UN political bodies – though denied legislative power – could act like legislatures by adopting law-making treaties and declarations of law. Their recommendations did not have to remain merely requests or wishes if the collective will of governments supported more authoritative outcomes. In retrospect, it is not surprising that the major intergovernmental bodies have utilized their recommendatory authority to achieve binding law where that served their aims and had the requisite political support. Although it has often been emphasized that they are not legislatures, most UN organs have acted much like parliamentary bodies in their proceedings. Moreover, member governments and international officials often called for solutions to the world's problems through new law and legal regimes. Thus, demand stimulated supply, and in various ways texts of legal import were produced. The studies in this volume show the extent and significance of such law-making. They have affected virtually every area of human life that cuts across national boundaries and even, in some important ways, matters entirely within national states.

The processes of law-making have not been simple, nor free from serious controversy. Various procedures, methods, and techniques have been used by different UN agencies for law-formation in particular fields. There have emerged gradations and subtleties in conceptions of authoritative law, wavering lines between peremptory "hard" law and varieties of "soft" law. Rules have emerged from practice and from interpretations by officials, as well as through pronouncements of organs composed of member states.

The most obvious instrument of law-making in the UN system is the multilateral "norm-creating" treaty. Hundreds of such treaties have been concluded; they were initiated, negotiated, and adopted by UN organs or by international conferences under the aegis of a UN body. Their subjects have been as diverse as the functions of the UN organizations. Many deal with problems that are technical and seemingly arcane. Others address problems affecting ordinary people: health, food, education, human rights, pollution, transportation, television. All, even the most technical, are the products of a political process, usually marked by conflicting interests and concerns over grants of power.

Their genesis in the UN system involves an apparent "democratization" of law-making markedly different from traditional treaty-making and contemporary treaty negotiation by a few states. In the UN system the rule is that all member states have a right to participate in the negotiation and adoption process. They generally do so on the basis of "sovereign equality." Decisions are usually taken by simple or two-thirds majority vote. An obvious problem is that states are not, in fact, equal in population, capability, power, or interest. Weighted voting has been employed by a few institutions, especially financial bodies. Other solutions have also been found, as, for example, negotiating processes that take account of the uneven distribution of capability and impact. In many cases, voting has been dispensed with in efforts to achieve consensus. This is not always acceptable to majorities (as shown by the Law of the Sea Conference) and even the desirability of obtaining adherence to the treaty by important states may not overcome the weight of a firm majority.

A question of some consequence and subtlety is whether UN law-making treaties bind states that choose not to become parties and refrain from the acts that signify adherence. In a formal sense, those states are not bound by the treaties. However, some treaties such as codification conventions express preexisting customary law. Some "crystallize" emergent rules of law. Still others generate custom embodying the treaty rules, the treaty itself "attracting" practice. A much-cited example is the 1982 UN Convention on the Law of the Sea, which includes several important articles expressing "new custom" recognized during the period the treaty was negotiated. The UN Covenants on Human Rights and other major human rights treaties have also been regarded by some jurists as new customary law or recognized general principles of law with respect to some of the rights expressed. To support that conclusion, it is argued that government statements made in UN bodies and resolutions of UN organs are evidence of state practice and *opinio juris*. This departs from the traditional view of custom as requiring uniformities of state practice revealed in behavior and the claims of states against other states. Some writers and occasionally governments have maintained that some general multilateral treaties adopted by a UN body are strong evidence of "generally accepted rules" binding on all. These varied arguments have led a critical French jurist to observe that the requirement of consent to treaties has not been "frontally assaulted, but cunningly outflanked."[1]

A related problem of law-making is raised by resolutions that embody declarations of principles and rules of international law. They are especially cited when adopted without dissent. A leading example is the Declaration on Principles of International Law Concerning Friendly Relations and Cooperation of States in Accordance with the Charter of the United Nations.[2] This declaration was adopted without dissent in 1970, after a decade of debate and negotiation. While its language is quite general, it elaborates the major principles of international law in the UN Charter, particularly on use of force, dispute settlement, nonintervention in domestic affairs, self-determination, duties of cooperation and observance of obligations, and the principle of "sovereign equality." Generally referred to as the "Friendly Relations" Declaration, it is probably one of the most frequently cited resolutions of the United Nations.

Lawyers have argued that resolutions and various other declarations may be authoritative evidence of binding international law on one or more of the following grounds: (a) as "authentic" interpretations of the UN Charter agreed by *all* the parties; (b) as affirmations of recognized customary law; and (c) as expressions of general principles of law accepted by states. These reasons fit into the three sources of international law contained in Article 38 of the Statute of the International Court. The

---

[1] P. Weil, "Towards Relative Normativity in International Law," 77 *AJIL* 413, 438 (1983). For different perspectives, see J. I. Charney, "Universal International Law," 87 *AJIL* 529 (1993), and writings cited therein.   [2] GA Res. 2625 (XXV) (Oct. 24, 1970).

International Court has recognized the legal force of several UN declarations in some of its advisory opinions.[3] But some caution is called for. Even a UN declaration adopted unanimously will have diminished authority as law if it is not observed by states particularly affected. Negative votes by a few concerned states to a declaratory resolution also cast doubt on its authority as presumptive evidence of existing law. One cannot apply a categorical rule to all cases; distinctions must be drawn that take into account the nature and importance of the legal rule in question. Declarations that affirm the prohibitions against aggression, genocide, torture, or systematic racial discrimination would not be deprived of their legal value because they are not uniformly observed. On the other hand, declarations asserting or affirming legal rules of a less peremptory character would not prevail over evidence that such rules were not generally observed by affected states.

United Nations recourse to recommendatory authority to declare law is a reflection of the perceived need for more law in many fields. The traditional case-by-case process of customary law cannot meet the necessity for common action to deal with the numerous problems raised by technological developments, demographic and environmental impacts, changing attitudes as to social justice, or the many requirements of international business. While all of these matters could be dealt with by multilateral treaties, the treaty processes are often complicated and slow, whereas UN resolutions can be more readily attained. As we have noted, the curious result is that new law is often called "custom" or based on already recognized general principles. The law-declaring resolutions are not only a response to felt needs; they are also a consequence of the opportunity opened for the numerical majority of states in the UN system. The weaker states who constitute a numerical majority in UN bodies use their voting strength for law-making to improve their position *vis-à-vis* the more powerful states. However, these efforts are often limited by the realities of power and politics. It has now come to be recognized that resolutions by majorities on economic matters are likely to remain "paper" declarations without much effect unless genuinely accepted by states with the requisite resources to carry them out.

The role of the International Law Commission in law-making is rather more complex than its statute suggests. At its inception its role was described as "scientific" in contrast to the political role of governments. Its members were to be experts of distinction, serving in their individual

---

[3] See, e.g., Advisory Opinions on Western Sahara, 1975 ICJ 12 (Oct. 16); Legal Consequences for States of the Continued Presence of South Africa in Namibia (South West Africa) notwithstanding Security Council Resolution 276 (1970), 1971 ICJ 16 (June 21) (hereinafter Namibia).

capacities, though nominated by UN member states and elected by the General Assembly. Their dual task in accordance with the relevant UN Charter article was to codify existing law and "progressively develop" the law. Almost from the very beginning, it was evident that codification involved a measure of progressive development. Inconsistencies in existing law often had to be dealt with and gaps filled. Questions of policy and expedience could not be avoided in these cases. Still, the major codifying conventions produced by the Commission and adopted by plenipotentiary conferences were in large part "restatements" of major areas of customary law. Some of these conventions were widely accepted as law even before they entered into legal effect. They have been treated as authoritative by nonparties as well as parties. As a practical matter, lawyers in or outside governments relying on the codification no longer search through diplomatic history or scattered case law for precedents. Practice thus follows the texts. Only rarely have some provisions been questioned on the ground that they went beyond codification and therefore bound only parties to the convention.

At the present time, several new factors raise questions as to the Commission's law-making role. For one thing, the major traditional subjects of customary law have been "codified" except for state responsibility. The Commission itself has changed. Observers see it as more "politicized," most of its members now diplomats or government officials. Only a few are comparable to the influential scholars on earlier commissions. A more basic problem is whether the Commission can be expected to carry out its main tasks satisfactorily through multilateral conventions that require general acceptance. The prevailing practice of seeking consensus or near-unanimity to adopt a convention has led to highly ambiguous or vacuous provisions. Another important, if less obvious, factor is the contradictory element in the law-making process. On the one hand, the rapidity of change creates the demand for new law; on the other hand, it leads to doubts about adopting new rules for an indefinite future. We may also discern dissonance resulting from the consciousness of interdependence and a sense (or fear) of loss of autonomy. The consequence is hesitation to move toward new treaty obligations of universal application.

The Commission's law-making may move in a different direction as suggested by its work on state responsibility.[4] In that field the reports of the special rapporteurs (all eminent authorities) and the draft articles have become widely invoked evidence of general international law. In other fields, where the paucity of general practice makes it difficult to determine a clear line between *lex lata* and *de lege ferenda*, the Commission's studies and

---

[4] See *United Nations Codification of State Responsibility* (M. Spinedi & B. Simma eds., 1987).

7

the comments of its members and governments provide authoritative material that can be invoked by governments and their legal advisers when concrete issues arise. True, this falls short of a definitive treaty or agreed codificatory text, but it is not without practical effect.

In the end, the "law" is determined by the subsequent conduct of the states and their views of the law (*opinio juris*). The Commission's role is not insignificant insofar as its draft articles provide systematization and generalization that give coherence to prior practice and diverse views. Even if this does not meet a positivist conception of law, it is undeniably a step toward the formation of legal order.

Taking the UN system as a whole, we can see that a large area of international regulation has been developed by the specialized agencies, though this is not widely known. Innovative techniques have been used by many of these agencies to extend the range of international regulation. The techniques are of particular interest since they significantly relax the traditional principle that no state is bound without its consent. An example is a provision for amendment of treaties by treating silence as consent and allowing for "opting out." Another is an unusual provision that new decisions pursuant to a treaty may be binding on all members of the organization solely by virtue of their membership. Moreover, in practice, as noted, texts that are only recommendatory have as much effect as formal rules in channeling state conduct. "Codes" that lay down standards and prescribe action, but are not legally mandatory, may be incorporated into domestic law by states. An example is the Codex Alimentarius produced jointly by the Food and Agriculture Organization and the World Health Organization prescribing standards "for all principal foods."

A survey of UN law-making would not be complete without referring to the law governing the internal governance of the international bodies. Internal law also includes the rules of procedure governing the conduct of the principal organs and the rights of members in those organs, a highly important area of UN law. Other examples of special significance are the regulations applicable to the military forces engaged in peacekeeping or enforcement activities. These comprise rules of engagement, precepts of command and control, privileges, and immunities. They are appropriately considered as part of UN law since they are adopted by the competent political organs and by the Secretary-General. An analogous legal regime is made up of the rules, norms, and procedures governing the many thousands of officials and experts engaged in technical assistance, humanitarian activities, economic and social development, and administration of regulatory regimes. The term "internal law" does not mean that it is without consequences for those outside the institutions. The conduct of international officials and of others subject to the authority of the

8

international bodies may have considerable impact outside the institution. The expansion of peacemaking and enforcement measures in recent years has given much greater importance to these areas of internal law.

2. Interpreting and applying law

Applying and interpreting law take place continually throughout the UN system. In many fields, they are the main way in which law develops, whether case by case, or by new rules that add more specific meanings to existing law. Disputes about interpretation, especially of provisions in the UN Charter, have been frequent and at times intense. All bodies in the UN system are governed by written instruments, ranging from the Charter and general treaties to the specific resolutions and decisions prescribing terms of reference. Each expresses the objectives to be achieved in varying degrees of generality. They may also indicate the means to be used and the limits on competence. In practice, interpretation is generally required in applying text to actual cases. But, unlike judicial interpretation, UN interpretation does not usually have an adjudicative character. The task faced by most UN bodies is practical and instrumental – that is, to prepare a plan of action or to recommend state behavior to achieve a goal. These functions, like building a house or picking a football team, are not performed by deciding if a rule applies to a particular situation. Problems are analyzed, proposed solutions negotiated, decisions reached. Interpretation is implicit in the measures adopted, which are centered largely on the relation between means and ends in the specific contexts.

There are important exceptions, however, where interpretation of a more explicit adjudicative character is a matter of great concern. These cases have related mainly to the UN Charter provisions and to some major treaties. The most virulent controversies have involved the competence and powers of the Security Council and General Assembly, especially in respect of domestic matters. Other debates on interpretation have concerned the obligations of states under the Charter and general international law in regard to use of force, intervention, self-determination, and human rights. The positions taken by governments on interpretation have nearly always been predictably linked to their political views and alignments. The end of the Cold War brought an end to some of the old controversies, but new debates have arisen as a consequence of a more active Security Council and a marked increase in cases involving UN sanctions and internal conflicts. The application and interpretation of law have also given rise to differences in nonpolitical areas, but on the whole they have been solved through consensual procedures rather than by confrontational voting. This is especially evident where international cooperation is clearly essential, such as in activities affecting aviation, shipping, and telecommunications.

Disputes about UN interpretation of basic legal instruments, notably the UN Charter, are not merely about the meaning of words or legal maxims. They often raise basic issues regarding the relation of the international community to individual states and, beyond that, the responsibility of people to give effect to the aims and ideals enshrined in the Charter. The cases that arise require that content be given to abstract concepts and principles, for example, sovereignty, independence, threats to peace, self-determination, and development. The answers are not found in their "ordinary meaning" or in the dictionary. Choices have to be made, often between competing principles, each applicable to the particular case but pointing to different solutions. It is commonplace in UN debates to find each opposing side citing relevant Charter principles in support of its position. This is not the result of defective drafting or even of political compromise; it is, rather, a reflection of the plurality of values and aims in international society. Moreover, the competing principles have to be applied to concrete cases of varying content. For example, what is the appropriate territorial unit for self-determination in the particular circumstances? When is internal disorder or repression a threat to peace? These questions cannot be answered without regard to the factual context and to the consequences of a decision to the states concerned. Hence, interpretation involves fact-finding and also projection into the future.

Can we identify an overarching principle of interpretation to govern the choices of UN organs? Some have suggested the "principle of effectiveness," which would give priority to achieving the major purposes of the Organization overriding restrictive provisions of the Charter. Support for this may be found in the tendency of the principal political organs to adopt an expansive view of their competence and powers when a strong political case is made for their action. In contrast they have shown little interest in the views of the framers of the Charter as to its meaning and intent. They recognize that the world has undergone radical transformation since 1945 and that the expectations of the governments at that time cannot be controlling at present.

These tendencies, and indeed the entire history of the United Nations, support the common perception that interpretation in the UN is essentially political in the sense that conflicting interpretations are resolved mainly by what member states desire as a matter of policy. Alliances, coalitions, and bargaining affect those choices. The elasticity of the Charter language allows such choices to be relatively free of restraints. This is bolstered by the assumption that interpretations that are "generally acceptable" settle the issue. Of course, if all members agree, the question of the proper legal interpretation would rarely arise. When disputes do arise and the opposing views are each supported by textual references and other authority, the political organs will tend to decide "on the merits," that is, on the basis of their views as to what is desirable and politically feasible. Such decisions do not usually ignore relative power, but there are plenty of cases in which numerical majorities override the more powerful states.

Interpretation of Charter provisions by majority votes based on political considerations has understandably given rise to some concern by states that find themselves in a small minority and who fear that the "integrity" of the Charter may be impaired by political tendencies. They are not satisfied by the principle agreed to in San Francisco that the principal organs would "inevitably" have to interpret the relevant Charter provisions, but that such interpretation would not be binding unless generally acceptable. This statement has been turned around by commentators and some governments to state that interpretations generally acceptable are binding on all members. This proposition has indeed become a canon of UN interpretation. It does not, however, allay concerns, both political and intellectual, regarding the rights of dissenting states under the Charter. Some governments are troubled from time to time that in treating most interpretive decisions as acts of political choice, majority coalitions can play fast and loose with Charter precepts and limits on competence.

The end of the Cold War and changes in political alignments have given rise to new concerns over "political" interpretation of the Charter, particularly by a more active Security Council. Since the Council has mandatory powers and may impose sanctions, the issue of its conformity to Charter provisions has arisen more sharply in debates and in scholarly commentary. This has revived interest in the possibility of utilizing the International Court to render advisory opinions on the interpretation of the Charter by the political organs. In the past, the Court has been called on by the political organs in several cases for advisory opinions on Charter issues in controversy. While one might have expected that such requests would originate with outvoted dissenting states, in fact the references to the Court were favored by the majority in the belief that their position was well founded and that an advisory opinion of the Court would bolster the authority of the decision taken by the political organ. Examples are the several advisory opinions relating to South West Africa (Namibia) and the 1962 opinion concerning expenses of peacekeeping. Experience indicates that dissenting minorities are unlikely to have their requests for advisory opinions accepted by the organ.

Few would disagree with the idea of the Court as the guardian of legality if and when questions of law came before it for judicial determination. Nor would there be any serious doubt that the Court should apply juridical concepts and criteria of validity that would not be used by a political or

11

executive organ. Surely, there would be general agreement with Judge Weeramantry that the Court should "zealously preserve its independence of judgment." The key point, however, is that the International Court has not been given review or appellate power to pass on decisions of the political organs unless it is asked for an advisory opinion by the organ.

More difficult questions are raised in respect of Charter determinations by the political organs, i.e., the Security Council and the General Assembly. These organs established by the Charter are subject to the legal limitations expressly or impliedly laid down by that treaty. It is recognized that their criteria of validity and the bases of their decisions are not the same as they would be in a judicial body. The implication clearly is that while the political organs are bound by the Charter and therefore must apply and interpret it in particular cases, the criteria they use are not judicial criteria. The question then is whether "nonjudicial" standards may be identified as appropriate for a political organ to apply in judging the validity of a proposed exercise of competence. As Kelsen and others have suggested, this may mean no more than that the organ is free to make a political choice as long as its action falls within a "possible interpretation of the Charter." In view of the elasticity of the Charter and its abstract principles, this would leave the organ virtually a free choice in most important cases. Even explicit and concrete terms can be given new meanings, as shown by the Council's decision to treat abstention as a concurring vote or its decision to read the explicit reference in Article 23 to the USSR as meaning the Russian Federation after the dissolution of the Soviet Union.

A more controversial issue concerns the finding of a "threat to peace" in cases of internal affairs as, for example, civil disorder, severe deprivation, or race discrimination. Is the Security Council subject to a test of validity in respect of its judgments applying that Charter standard to situations that do not involve transborder violence or any reasonable likelihood of international conflict? The cases strongly suggest that the Council has regarded such determinations as essentially "political" in the sense that it has full discretion to decide on the existence of a threat to peace. On this view, even a decision clearly contrary to generally agreed facts would not be challengeable on legal grounds. This does not allay the concern of some member states that the political bodies, and the Council in particular, may be so dominated by political factors as to exceed the clear meaning of the Charter provisions.

As a general comment on the interpretation process, it is interesting to note that the arguments in the UN organs on interpretation fall, by and large, into two categories. One, the more common, lays stress on the aims and ideals of the institution as expressed in the Charter. The other argues mainly on the basis of practice and precedent. The fifty years of debate on the meaning of domestic jurisdiction exhibit these two lines of argument. More often than not, the proponent of one or the other point of view will claim support on the basis both of the constitutional purposes and state behavior. The criticism that these dual rationales lack coherence has not dissuaded government representatives from invoking both lines of justification. True, arguments that rely on the idealism of Charter goals and the realism of actual practice may clash with each other. But is it not essential to any legal system and certainly the United Nations that it include both lofty goals and a realistic appreciation of what is acceptable? The interpretive process in the United Nations reflects this essential polarity and the need for reasonable choices sensitive to the particular circumstances.

3. Compliance and enforcement

For a long time compliance and enforcement were on the margins of UN concern. Like somewhat backward members of a family, their place was vaguely recognized, but not much was expected from them. The busy world of UN law-making and law-applying carried on pretty much without serious consideration of means of ensuring compliance. Some international lawyers dismissively referred to enforcement as a political matter outside the law. Within UN bodies, comfort was taken in the pious hope that governments that acknowledged their legal obligations would carry them out, at least most of the time. It was far from evident that this was generally the case in some areas, but measures such as compulsory jurisdiction, mandatory fact-finding, or coercive sanctions were not considered acceptable or feasible. However, attitudes began to change as governments were gradually impelled to take precepts they had adopted more seriously. In large part, this occurred because public sentiment in some areas (notably, human rights) was brought to bear on governments. In other areas, fears and threats of violence had an impact. Terrorism and arms build-ups demanded responses that were more than appeals to behave. The lengthening list of economic and social ills brought pressures on international bodies to give more than lip-service to the principles they had adopted and urged on the states. All of these factors tended to move UN organs to take action that went beyond exhortation and admonition. The end of the Cold War and dissolution of the communist bloc accelerated these tendencies. It became possible to achieve agreement on a variety of procedures to induce and even compel states to carry out their legal obligations. The enforcement powers of the Security Council were reinvigorated, virtually overnight, and a new perspective on compliance opened up.

It is hard to think of a subject of international law more complex and nuanced than enforcement and compliance. Nonetheless, we can get a clearer view of the whole array of the various compliance and enforcement processes used by UN organs by classifying them into several categories.

First are the reporting and supervision procedures in a particular treaty or code of conduct. These procedures are most familiar in the human rights area, especially under the Covenant on Political and Civil Rights and the Convention against Race Discrimination. They have also been used by the International Labour Organization and by the treaty organs dealing with narcotic drugs. The following pattern is characteristic:

> periodic reports by states in accordance with detailed guidelines;
> review by a committee, accompanied by questions to the reporting states;
> in some cases detailed inquiry by a subcommittee or individual rapporteur;
> a committee report noting discrepancies between the states' conduct and the requirements of the treaty or applicable law

An important addition to the supervisory system is a procedure for individual or governmental complaints of violations such as those brought under the optional protocols to the covenants. The common pattern is for the complaints to be investigated by a committee or a special rapporteur who then makes their conclusions public or transmits them to a parent body. An essential element in cases of this kind is the fact-finding by an international authority. The ability to perform such fact-finding adequately depends on cooperation by the governments concerned, on material facilities and a high degree of probity and persistence on the part of the investigating body. Investigations of this kind range over the whole gamut of UN concerns. Very few receive wide public attention, but they are important to their particular audience. Two examples may be noted here. One is a working group of the Human Rights Commission that has investigated some 15,000 cases of "enforced or involuntary disappearances" each year for several years. The second is the on-site investigation of nuclear capabilities in Iraq by a UN group acting under Security Council mandatory authority, following the UN action against Iraqi aggression in 1990–91.

A second broad category of mechanisms for inducing compliance may be characterized as "facilitative." They include measures taken by the United Nations to assist states in carrying out obligations imposed by law or by specific decisions of the organs. A good example is the use of armed peacekeeping forces to assist governments to comply with transborder truce and cease-fire agreements or, in some cases, to help in maintaining internal law and order. Another example of some importance is the use of observers

14

for national elections; this is a means of facilitating compliance with legal undertakings to hold such elections. In some fields financial and technical assistance is provided to assist states to comply with legal requirements, for example, to reduce pollution or to cut down the production of narcotic drugs.

A third category of compliance measures directly penalizes a law-breaking state by expelling it from the Organization or from taking part in some of the latter's activities. The Charter provides for expulsion for persistent violations of the principles contained in the Charter. This may be done by the General Assembly only upon recommendation of the Security Council (Article 6). The lesser penalty of suspension of privileges of membership may also be imposed by the General Assembly on recommendation of the Security Council against a state "against which preventive or enforcement action has been taken by the Council." Neither of these provisions has been applied up to now. An indirect way to impose suspension of privileges has been the rejection of the credentials of a state. This penalty was applied in 1974 against South Africa for its apartheid policy by the General Assembly, a controversial decision that appeared to open the way for *de facto* expulsion. Other UN organizations also excluded South Africa from taking part in their principal bodies during the period when apartheid was in effect. Although many states have been charged with violating the Charter or other important legal obligations, the penalty of exclusion has rarely been imposed by an organ.

A fourth category of compliance measures is nonmilitary enforcement action taken by the Security Council under Article 41 of Chapter VII of the Charter. This applies only when the Council has found a threat to the peace, or a breach of peace or act of aggression. Sanctions under Article 41 have come to be seen as the quintessential type of international enforcement. Its language is broad enough to cover any type of punitive action not involving use of armed force. Typically it has been used to impose economic embargoes extending to trade and financial relations on either a comprehensive or selective basis. Severing communications (including air traffic) and breaking diplomatic relations have also been employed. Under its terms, Article 41 may be used by the Security Council to "give effect to its decisions." It was not meant to provide sanctions for enforcing international legal obligations as such. The Security Council may presumably apply it against a state that has not violated any legal requirement if the Council decides that it is in the interest of maintaining peace and security. In practice, however, the Council has generally applied Article 41 sanctions against a state that has not complied with a Charter requirement or a significant legal obligation. While the Council may impose such sanctions only when it has decided that a threat to peace, breach of peace, or act of aggression has occurred, its determination is considered discretionary and final. Article 41 was applied sparingly for many years, but after the end of the Cold War it was increasingly used.[5] Its effectiveness, even against weak states, was uneven and its use has caused hardship, at times extreme, to the general population of the targeted state, thus raising humanitarian concerns.

The fifth category of compliance measures – or more precisely, enforcement – is the use of armed force pursuant to Chapter VII of the UN Charter. It is noteworthy that the Security Council has applied its authority under Chapter VII by authorizing member states to use armed force as necessary to give effect to its decisions. The fact that member states have not concluded agreements with the Security Council to make armed forces available at its call (under Article 43) has limited the Council's power to mandate military action. It could do no more than authorize members to use troops as necessary to achieve the prescribed goals.[6] The difficulties in obtaining military forces required for enforcement (in contrast to consensual peacekeeping) have led to demands by some governments and public opinion for new arrangements to ensure the availability of forces when required. An independent force of volunteers (not unlike the French Foreign Legion) has been prominently advocated, along with the idea of governmental "stand-by" forces on call by the Security Council. By 1993, enforcement through armed forces had become a high priority for the UN, but practical implementation remained uncertain. It has remained unclear how far governments were prepared to incur the costs in lives and resources necessary for collective enforcement. The actions taken were selective and raised charges of double standards. Decisions taken under Chapter VII in respect of Somalia and ex-Yugoslavia failed to achieve their objectives and very few, if any, governments were prepared to incur the substantial costs in lives and resources necessary for collective enforcement. The optimistic belief that unanimity of the "Big Five" expressed in legally binding resolutions would in itself bring about compliance could no longer hold.

Judicial enforcement, our sixth category, is of particular significance for legal order. It is employed in both international and national tribunals. The International Court of Justice is potentially the most important. However,

---

[5] The remarkable increase in the use of Chapter VII by the Council is shown by the following statistics. In the forty-five years prior to 1990, the Council adopted only fourteen resolutions under Chapter VII. From 1990 through 1993, it adopted fifty-eight Chapter VII resolutions, twenty-five of them in 1993. These figures were supplied by the UN Secretariat.

[6] While the Security Council referred expressly to Chapter VII in the Iraq case, it did not mention any article in that chapter. Some commentators inferred that the Council's action fell under Article 42, some considered Article 51 on collective self-defense as the implied basis, whereas others considered that both Articles 42 and 51 applied: still others believed that Chapter VII alone was intended as the basis. See O. Schachter, "United Nations Law in the Gulf Conflict," 85 *AJIL* 452, 457–63 (1991).

it is limited in respect of binding adjudication to cases in which the parties have accepted the Court's jurisdiction. Actually states have done so in numerous treaties and (to a much lesser extent) through declarations accepting compulsory jurisdiction under the optional clause of the Statute of the Court. Two notable cases were brought under treaty clauses – one by the United States against Iran for the seizure of the US Embassy in Tehran and the detention of the US diplomatic staff; the other was the case brought by Nicaragua against the United States for its military and paramilitary measures against Nicaragua. Both cases were essentially actions to bring about compliance by the respondent states with fundamental legal rules. Also relevant is that several advisory opinions of the Court have been regarded as helpful in inducing compliance. The advisory opinions on the former South West Africa territory – now Namibia – are often given as examples. The indications in 1996 are that more cases are likely to be brought to the Court by states alleging breaches of international obligations.

United Nations bodies have devoted much discussion and study to proposals for international criminal jurisdiction to deal with "international crimes," especially "offenses against the peace and security of mankind." The International Law Commission, acting under General Assembly directions, has been the main body engaged in preparing a statute for a permanent criminal court. While the idea has much support in principle, it is uncertain whether it will come into existence in the near future. The Security Council has established an *ad hoc* tribunal to try and sentence individuals for war crimes and crimes against humanity committed in the former Yugoslavia in the conflict of 1991–94.[7] This would be the first international tribunal since the Nuremberg tribunal of 1945 to be used for enforcement of international law against individuals.

The foregoing account of the judicial and institutional processes for furthering compliance and enforcement should not lead us to conclude that the UN system and general international law have provided for mechanisms comparable to those in domestic legal systems. It is still true that on the international level governments usually seek to cope with violations through various means of dispute settlement or self-help, rather than through judicial or institutional enforcement. Violations of law are seen, on the whole, not as challenges to the authority of the system, but as causes of disputes between states to be settled by them. The Charter accordingly gives priority to the peaceful settlement of disputes, rather than to the

---

7 SC Res. 808 (Feb. 22, 1993); SC Res. 827 (May 25, 1993), reprinted in 32 *ILM* 1203 (1993). The statute of the tribunal is in UN Doc. S/25704 (1993), reprinted in *ibid.* at 1159. See J. O'Brien, "The International Tribunal for Violations of International Humanitarian Law in the Former Yugoslavia," 87 *AJIL* 639 (1993).

coercive enforcement of law or compulsory jurisdiction of the International Court. Chapter VII enforcement authority was meant to be limited and to be applied only in cases where peaceful means had failed.

As a consequence, states have recourse to "self-help," a broad if somewhat imprecise term, which covers a range of nonforceful actions that may be taken by a state injured by a violation of legal obligations owed to it. Analytically, it falls into the category of actions to achieve compliance or to enforce obligations. The term "counter-measures" has come to be used for self-help action in place of the older terms "reprisal" and "retorsion." But it is still relevant to distinguish between counter-measures that would be illegal if not for the prior illegal act of the state against which they are directed (i.e., reprisals), and counter-measures which a state could legally take against any state irrespective of that state's conduct (retorsion). Both may be regarded as sanctions against violations. Reprisals are generally permitted if they do not involve use of force contrary to the Charter and if they are directed to obtaining redress for the wrong committed. Moreover, they must not be disproportionate to the violations to which they respond. A tit-for-tat response would meet the requirement in most cases of treaty violation, but obviously this could not justify such reciprocal acts as denying human rights because the offending state did so.

Many counter-measures would be legal whether or not responsive to a prior illegal act. States are free to reduce trade, investment, or aid with another state, whether or not the other state acted illegally. Such "retorsion" may be more effective and coercive as a policing action than reprisals. It is difficult, of course, to assess the efficacy of counter-measures in an overall appraisal of compliance, but it is clear enough that they are, taken as a whole, an effective instrumentality for achieving compliance with international obligations.

A significant theoretical expansion of self-help has resulted from the concept of "*erga omnes*" obligations – that is, obligations in which the entire community of states has a legal interest, and therefore any state may apply counter-measures against the offender. In its advisory opinion of 1971 concerning Namibia, the International Court declared that all states must deny recognition to acts of South Africa relating to Namibia.[8] It also indicated that it may be the duty of all states to take counter-measures when the offending state has violated a Security Council decision or breached a fundamental legal obligation. There is room for debate on whether this principle is open to abuse by a majority, but this should not minimize its potential value as a means of strengthening respect for law of fundamental importance.

[8] Namibia, 1971 ICJ, at 55–56.

Finally, we take note of public opinion as an element in achieving compliance. This is an amorphous factor, but it may be given more concrete form through the activities of nongovernmental organizations that are dedicated to achieving implementation of one or more specific international norms. Their activities carried on within national states and to some extent on the international level have been a potent force in furthering compliance in various areas of UN concern. The advances in information technology and communications have greatly enhanced the ability of nongovernmental organizations to bring pressure to bear on governments. Public opinion is also manifested in institutions of civil society such as professional bodies, universities, religious and communal institutions. The influence of nongovernmental organizations has been particularly evident in support of peaceful settlement, human rights, and environmental measures.

A survey of means of enforcement and of inducing compliance is an answer to the charge that enforcement is a purely political matter. Legal processes are an important – indeed essential – part of enforcement which is a major element of the UN Legal Order. As this brief survey indicates, the legal techniques are no longer seen as unrealistic or as solely a function of power. On the other hand, it is undeniable that enforcement measures are dependent on the will of states and often on their relative power – that is, the ability to control the outcome of contested issues. But power, important as it may be, is not the only political aspect. The authority of a law-applying organ is also determined by its composition and behavior. A body that is not adequately representative of relevant interests or one that appears to apply double standards will forfeit respect. The problem of compliance thus leads deeply into challenges to the existing distribution of power on both the international and national levels. Reliance on the great powers to effectuate and enforce has given rise to concern on the part of lesser powers. On a different level, the turbulence within national states and the weakened loyalty to state institutions also create doubts as to enforcement of international rules and decisions. These issues go beyond the legal means for enforcement. They call for a broader concept of collective enforcement and its relation to the needs and grievances of ordinary people. It cannot be said that the United Nations has made progress in solving that problem.

4. Patterns and politics of UN law

We can be quite sure that when the UN Charter was adopted, its framers did not envisage that a vast and multifarious *corpus juris* would emerge from the new institutions. However, in today's perspective, it is not surprising that international legal regimes have proliferated in response to new needs and pressures. We are acutely aware of the impact of change through new technology, the population explosion, globalization of production and trade, the emergence of new actors, the claims of formerly submerged peoples – the list can go on. Matters once solely of local concern now have impact across national borders. Conflicts between states, or even within them, engage outside parties. Mass poverty, environmental dangers, shared natural resources are perceived widely as matters of global concern. Each of these problems and many others are perceived to require norms and procedures for resolving conflicts and for collective action to render them effective. The availability of international institutions and the permanent conference machinery makes it virtually certain that law (hard or soft) will be created, adapted, and applied to many of these problems.

An overview of the UN Legal Order reveals a complex pattern. We see a multitude of specialized bodies of law, each with its distinctive features, many intricate and dense. They are fully accessible only to specialists, versed in doctrine and procedure that often seem arcane to outsiders. We might envisage them as separate communities, on a terrain that includes cities, towns, villages, hamlets. Extending this metaphor, we note that they are connected to each other by roads, highways, and paths, that is, by concepts, principles, and processes. The communities differ, of course, in size, influence, and in their linkages to each other.

Two areas of UN law that stand out are human rights and the law relating to peace and security (i.e., force, arms, etc.). They would be metropolises on our imaginary map. Human rights, in fact, could be likened to a metropolitan area, since it embraces a large core city and many connected towns and villages.

The development of human rights in the UN system is of particular interest in an overview. Its beginnings were not auspicious. The Charter references are slight. It is listed only as one among many purposes (Articles 1 and 55) and mentioned as a subject for a commission of the Economic and Social Council. It was only briefly discussed in San Francisco, and few expected it to be important in UN activities. In 1948 the Universal Declaration of Human Rights, an extraordinary achievement at the time, was cautiously declared to express aspirations, but not binding law. A gradual, but nonetheless remarkable, development took place in the 1950s and 1960s. The erosion of the reserved domain of domestic jurisdiction was most conspicuous in relation to apartheid in South Africa. Numerous other instances of increased recognition of human rights can be found today, for example, as various protections for children, women, migration and refugees, labor standards, self-determination, education and culture, as well as prohibitions against torture, racial discrimination, and genocide. In other fields, it has an important place – as for example, in such different subjects as health, telecommunications, and international criminal law. It also crosses over into the legal regimes concerned with armed force and measures for maintaining peace and security. As we noted earlier, the key threshold concept of threats to peace in the Charter has been broadened to take account of mass violations of human rights. Moreover, democratic freedoms are more and more seen as critical supports of a peaceful world. Human rights conceptions have also had an impact on the large areas of UN activity devoted to economic and social development. The economic criteria originally applied to development have been supplemented with criteria of "human development" that incorporate many of the basic human rights, especially but not only those of an economic, social, and cultural character. The promotion of a many-sided human right to development and support for a nascent human right to a clean and safe environment aim to transmute social goals into the law of human rights. While the results of these efforts remain uncertain (and, to some, questionable), they do evidence the importance attributed to the human rights movement and ideology.

The other "metropolis" on our map is the law of peace and security. In contrast to human rights, this subject is solidly grounded in the UN Charter and supported by the enforcement authority of the Security Council. Here we find the leading cases, the great dramas of the UN, along with intense disputes about the interpretation and application of legal principles. This is the area of law in which the stakes are highest and the authority of UN law is on trial. Whether or not a United Nations Legal Order exists will be determined largely by the effectiveness of its efforts to maintain peace and security.

One example is the central importance of the veto in the Security Council. The veto (or principle of unanimity) is a legal rule embodied in the Charter for political reasons and used (or, some would say, abused) by the permanent members primarily in their national interests. Like other legal principles, the veto has generated subsidiary rules by usage and agreements. These constitute, so to speak, the "law of the veto." They are observed in practice even though many member states would prefer to change that practice for their own political reasons. In the meantime and for the foreseeable future, the "law of the veto" governs the decision process of the Security Council.

Another sector of UN "peace and security law" consists of interpretive resolutions on basic Charter concerns. Such resolutions or declarations have been adopted by the General Assembly by near-unanimity or consensus. The leading examples are the resolutions on the definition of aggression and that, referred to earlier, on principles of international law, the "Friendly Relations Declaration." The International Court of Justice in *Nicaragua* v. *United States* (1986) considered both resolutions to reflect international customary law.[9]

The International Court of Justice has also had a significant role in the development of "peace and security law." The *Nicaragua* cases are the most comprehensive exposition of many basic issues and constitute an authoritative pronouncement on several legal principles. Other decisions and advisory opinions of the Court have also contributed to the law in this area. We can expect more in the near future.

The metropolis of peace and security law, like human rights, has its suburbs. One of the most important is the regulation and prohibition of armaments, especially weapons of mass destruction. As Professor Murphy shows, the legal pattern in this area is predominantly made up of negotiated agreements, on a global or regional basis. It also embraces inspection to ascertain compliance with legal obligations such as those contained in the Treaty on the Non-Proliferation of Nuclear Weapons or Security Council decisions under Chapter VII as, for example, applied to Iraq. Efforts to outlaw mass weapons or their use on the basis of existing principles of customary law or the Charter itself persist in UN bodies but lack support by the major powers concerned.

Still another suburb in the peace and security area comprises the law developed by the Security Council and, to some degree, the General Assembly in respect of peacekeeping, peace enforcement, inspection, and control. However, as 1995 drew to a close, the lack of resolve on the part of major powers, along with weaknesses within the UN operations, augured a retreat from peace enforcement and perhaps from consensual peacekeeping. While the main legal principles are not likely to be abandoned, we can expect changes in legal arrangements bearing on rules of engagement, command, and control, and perhaps criteria for UN interventions.

I turn now to international economic law, the most varied area of UN-linked law. We can define it by its objectives: development, trade, stability, technical cooperation. Beyond that, generalization is limited. A survey of treaties and practices suggests that each is a *lex specialis*, to be understood on its own terms. One strand that runs through most of the agreements is recognition of the uneven interests of the states concerned. This is a reason for weighted voting in many institutions (for example, the International Monetary Fund and the World Bank) and also for group representation in the law-applying organs such as those concerned with particular commodities. Still another common element in UN-influenced law is the broad undertaking to give preferences to the less-developed

---

[9] Nicaragua, 1986 ICJ at 103, paras. 193, 195.

countries. We find such preferences in agreements on trade, investment, and technical cooperation. The general principle may be said to be part of contemporary international economic law, even though the practical effects have not satisfied many of the poorer countries. Efforts to create new fundamental legal rules on investment and trade in favor of the developing countries, as through the Charter of Economic Rights and Duties of States, have sharply revealed the obstacles to creating new economic law without the concurrence of the states with economic power.

Private international law should not be forgotten. It is more of a region with its own towns and villages. In the United Nations, it is characterized mainly by treaty law and uniform national legislation fostered by UN bodies. Like those in the other highly specialized fields, its participants include nonofficial specialists as well as governments. The traffic between them and the other areas of UN law is rather slight, but basic principles of international law apply on many issues. Globalization of trade and production will tend to stimulate new law in this area.

All of these subjects are part of the "terrain" of UN law since they were generated by UN organs or applied by them. Our metaphorical map reminds us that these various legal communities are not entirely separate, that highways and byways provide linkages in the form of common principles and processes. Without pressing the metaphor, we find interconnecting doctrine in the basic postulates of international law to which participants in the UN system, whatever the subject, profess adherence. States are regarded as the principal actors in creating and applying law. Their independence and formal equality are taken as axiomatic. The principles of territorial integrity and *pacta sunt servanda*, as well as the customary rules of diplomatic intercourse, are accepted in the UN system, as they are in general international law. Also accepted is the basic divide between the international and domestic domains, though, as indicated earlier, the line between them may change or blur in particular cases. All of these propositions are recognized as applicable to the legally relevant activities in the UN system. They are the connecting highways that run across the landscape and impart a degree of unity to the various activities.

These connecting highways – the concepts and principles of international law – are a conspicuous feature of UN debates. As the Secretary-General recently observed, "political discourse and the vocabulary of law mix cheerfully with one another . . . the dialectic between law and diplomacy is constantly at work."[10] Perhaps it is not always "cheerful." The Secretary-General went on to say that "the United Nations shows, better than any other organization, the competition States engage in to try

10 Boutros Boutros-Ghali, Statement to sixty-sixth session of the Institute of International Law (Aug. 30, 1993), UN Press Release SG/SM/5069, at 2 (Sept. 1, 1993) (trans. from French).

and impose a dominant language and control the juridical ideology it expresses." We are thus reminded that legal discourse is not divorced from political conflict. On the one hand, the concepts of international law provide a necessary code of communication, and therefore greatly facilitate the institutionalization of international society. On the other hand, international law is often relied upon by states to resist the transfer of their power to international authority. We have to look beyond international law itself to evaluate the likely consequences.

An overview of UN law reveals several other interesting characteristics of the UN system.

I would begin with the characteristic modes of decision-making in the UN system. These are essentially political processes, but they are shaped by the conditions of quasi-parliamentary procedures and the mandates of constituent instruments. What is perhaps most important in this respect is the central role of blocs and alliances in law creation and law application. State autonomy and equality are profoundly affected – that is, reduced – by the requirements of group cohesion. To be sure, these are not ironclad requirements. A member of the "77" (i.e., about a hundred and fifty developing states) or of the European group may cast an independent vote, but this is exceptional. Many groups coexist, some based on particular interests (for example, petroleum producers), others on regional or historical ties. The result is a degree of procedural complexity quite different from the processes of international law in the noninstitutionalized contexts.

The procedural complexity is matched by the substantive complexity of UN law-making and law-application. Their multilateral character presents issues to member states that are significantly different from the usual international legal problems faced by governments in a bilateral or small-group context. In the world of UN law, states are compelled to define their national interest in relation to the collective interests of various groups of states and, ideally, in relation to the common interest of the whole community of states. The UN consideration of the law of the sea – both in the negotiation of the 1982 Convention and in decisions on specific issues of law – is an instructive example of the complexity of multilateralism. Even narrow issues of law may have wide effects and conflicts of interest, and diverse perceptions of policy usually complicate the task of ascertaining or creating acceptable legal rules. Critics seem to delight in pointing to the contradictory provisions and vague terms in many UN resolutions. But such indeterminate texts can provide a basis for procedures in which situations are considered and resolved case by case. For example, in the field of human rights, legal principles in treaties or declarations that leave ample room for conflicting interpretation have been concretized in decisions of competent organs such as the Human Rights Committee under the International Covenant on Civil and Political Rights and the ILO Committee on the Application of Conventions and Recommendations.

We noted earlier that all the collective organs function under a governing instrument that explicitly declares the objectives of that particular body. This holds not only for the UN Charter and the other constituent instruments; it applies to every organ, committee, or *ad hoc* working group. The point may seem obvious, but it is not trivial. The practical effect by and large is that the organs have a dominant instrumental character. In consequence, the recognition by them of explicit ends tends to reduce the role of precedent and doctrine in formulating or applying law. This tendency is, of course, an aspect of the political character of the UN bodies. They are not expected to behave like courts or academic scholars when they apply or create law.

Still another characteristic of the UN system is its relative transparency and linkages to nonstate actors. This may surprise outsiders who feel excluded by its arcane language and somewhat elitist character. However, on a closer look at activities of legal significance, it becomes evident that member states are not the only participants, even if in a formal sense they are the designated players. In actuality most efforts directed to achieving new law or giving effect to existing law involve substantial participation by nonstate actors. Many enter as "experts" through governments or nongovernmental bodies. They are usually part of the "epistemic communities" that share and produce knowledge of particular subjects. They are necessary to informed decisions on seemingly technical questions. Although many are formally under governmental authority, their specialized expertise gives them a degree of independence and also raises the level of international cooperation.

A somewhat different role is played by groups and individuals outside governments who are dedicated to "causes" and take part indirectly in UN deliberations as "lobbyists" or "activists." While their influence varies with cause and case, it seems reasonable to suppose that their actual role in the political and technical aspects of UN law-making is increasing. The communications revolution, the spread of democracy, and the growth of transnational interest groups are factors that favor a larger role for nongovernmental bodies. As noted earlier, international lawyers have a special role and responsibility. As the work of experts, their commentary and proposals are likely to influence their professional colleagues in official posts. We hope that, as in the past, they will be responsive to the aims and ideals of the UN Charter.

As a final comment, I suggest an architectural metaphor. It views the UN Legal Order as a three-level structure:

On its ground floor, I place the actions of states – including the demands and goals of the governments and other organized groups in furtherance of their needs, wishes and expectations.

On the second level are the activities of a legal character – the formation and invoking of legal norms, and their application to particular situations.

On the third level, I would place the broad policy goals, aspirations, and ideals that influence governments and the other actors.

Each of these levels exhibits its own values and processes. But there is continuous movement from level to level. The sphere of law in the middle level is influenced by the interests expressed below and the ideals and policy manifested above. The connections run both ways. Legal norms have an impact on the perceptions of interest and needs in the lower level and on the policies of the top level. This image helps us to see that the UN Legal Order is influenced by the multitude of political demands and interests from below (as it were) and by the general ideals and principles on the higher level. It also reminds us that law exercises its influence in both directions, up and down. The stairways run both ways.

Our metaphors may help to avoid a deductive conception of law in the UN system. To appreciate what has been achieved, we need to comprehend the UN Legal Order in its full complexity and diversity. We may also envisage, as our metaphors suggest, the promise of new law responsive both to practical needs and shared ideals.

CHAPTER TWO

GENERAL LAW-MAKING PROCESSES

Paul C. Szasz

I. BASIC CONCEPTS AND INTERACTIONS

Just as domestic law constitutes the binding force of and finds its source in individual nation-states, so international law structures and is created by the international community. And just as there are important differences but also basic similarities between national and international law, so too there are both differences and similarities between the processes by which the respective legal systems are created and nourished. However, national legal systems and legislative processes are simpler and more transparent than their international equivalents.

National laws can generally be classified into "black letter"-type law such as constitutions, statutes, and regulations arranged in a strict hierarchical order and into less clearly articulated norms such as common law and the ever less important customary law.

By contrast, international law is manifested in a large variety of different types of instruments, such as treaties, nonbinding agreements, and declarations and decisions of international organs. All of these have the characteristics of "black letter" law in that the provisions can easily be read, although their binding force is widely differentiated and certainly cannot be defined by constructing hierarchies. There are also other manifestations of the collective, coordinated, or merely parallel will of states that can only be determined by studying their actions in the light of expressed or implied motives. Thus, in addition to the distinctions between black and increasingly light gray letter law, there is the distinction between binding or "hard" law and various "softer" forms. The international legislative or norm-making process is confusing in that there is no single legislature and no single source of administrative law. Instead, there is a multitude of norm-makers at every geographic "level" (i.e., global, regional, subregional, etc.), as well as inchoate processes that create and identify international customary and perhaps even general principles of law.

Furthermore, the rather clear-cut relationship that exists at the domestic level between processes and products (e.g., a legislative body produces statutes) is by no means as simple internationally, where all sorts of processes can produce, as direct outputs or as indirect by-products, various types of hard and soft, written and unwritten law.

It is vital to recognize that this confusion in no way masks a bankruptcy of the international legal system, in the sense that perhaps there is actually very little "real" international law out there. Instead, and this is a widely unappreciated fact, a great deal of international law exists and is very generally observed – usually without enforcement mechanisms. Moreover, all types of international law, especially treaty law, are being created at an ever-increasing rate – indeed at a rate that sometimes seems to exceed the capacity of the international community (and especially of its newer and less well-equipped members) to absorb and digest all the new norms. And in spite of the availability of increasingly sophisticated data-processing devices, little has yet been done to make readily available, and particularly to structure, the already existing large amount of international law. It is this lack of information that is probably more responsible than any other factor for the widespread underestimation of the quantity, quality, and import-ance of the legal tools that control and shape international interactions.

Although the source of practically all of international law is the will of states, acting jointly (e.g., by concluding treaties or by issuing solemn declarations) or severally (e.g., when creating customary law by a series of similar actions), these legislative activities are being expressed increasingly in or through international intergovernmental organizations (IGOs). These organizations exist and function at many different levels: global or universal, worldwide but not necessarily universal, and many are regional, subregional, and interregional. Although there are some strictly regional IGOs (e.g., the Council of Europe) that are legislatively very productive both quantitatively and qualitatively, as judged by the importance of the instruments produced, and even some similarly active unaffiliated world-wide IGOs (the Antarctic Treaty System or the Customs Cooperation Council), a predominant share of international law is being created under the aegis of IGOs of the UN system. It is the legislative or more generally the norm-making activities of the United Nations system that are the focus of this chapter.

It should be understood that while norm-making is an important activity of many UN system IGOs and organs, it is the exclusive task of only a few (e.g., of the International Law Commission [ILC] and the United Nations Commission on International Trade Law [UNCITRAL]). For most others, norm-creation is just one of many important tasks or perhaps merely an occasional or even exceptional one.

28

A. Forms of international law

As pointed out above, international law does not always come in a neatly labeled package, nor is the legal quality of what some may assert as law always noncontroversial. It may therefore be useful to survey various asserted manifestations of such law, as preparation for entering into the real subject matter of this study – the various means by which international law is created.

It is common practice to start, and sometimes to end, any listing of the various forms of international law by referring to the four subparagraphs of Article 38(1) of the Statute of the International Court of Justice (ICJ): conventions (i.e., treaties); international custom; general principles of law; and judicial decisions – but not by way of *stare decisis* – and authoritative teachings (though both of these are identified merely as "subsidiary means" for the *determination* of rules of international law). Considering, however, that this list was formulated some seventy-five years ago, it may now be useful to recognize also some other legal instruments or actions, such as the decisions of international organs, as possible manifestations or sources of international law.

International law comes in two flavors: "hard" or binding, and "soft" or not quite binding, which are technically non-binding norms that states actually do follow or at least subscribe to.

1. "Hard" law

(a) Treaties

Treaties originally constituted contracts between states – normally just two. It should be recognized, however, that, while maintaining their contractual trappings, the instruments that nowadays form the backbone of the law of nations and the bulk of both the "black letter" and the "hard" forms of that law are not contractual in the normal sense – as representing conventional bargains or arrangements between two or more states. Rather, they are "law-making" or "law-expressing." The international community, as yet lacking any straightforward legislative authority, has resorted to the multilateral contractual device to bind states to rules to which they are willing to conform, even in instances such as human rights treaties, where the element of reciprocity that is the basis of genuine contracts is almost entirely absent. These law-making treaties can perhaps best be compared to the hypothesized "social contracts" postulated by the Enlightenment.

At the beginning of the modern era of international law, at the time that the League of Nations was founded, there were only a handful of significant multilateral treaties that could be characterized as "law-making." Some growth took place during the inter-world war period, but the real bloom started only with the establishment of the United Nations and the many organizations that became its specialized and related agencies, together constituting the UN system. By 1993 there were some 1,500 multilateral treaties, both global and significant regional or subregional, and their number is growing by several dozen each year.[1] Although not all such treaties are "law-making," as they may instead create a military alliance (e.g., NATO) or settle a conflict (e.g., peace treaties), the great bulk of these agreements set out at least some norms binding on the parties, and for most that is their main purpose.

The formulation and promulgation of these multilateral law-making treaties is the principal and clearest legislative activity of the world community. There is an important though perhaps somewhat theoretical distinction between two types of such legislative activities: "codification" and "[progressive] development."[2] The former is the process of collecting, clarifying, systematizing, and restating existing law (which in itself can be less clear or less universal treaty law, but more often is customary international law, and more and more often "soft law"), while the latter means the creation of new law as required by the world community – which may be old needs not previously addressed legislatively, but more often constitute new demands arising from technological developments, scientific insights, or merely the ever-increasing number and complexity of international interactions.

(b) Customary law

International custom is the other great source of classical international law. Well before the development of law-making treaties, international law was based mostly on the customary behavior of states when motivated by the belief that such behavior was required by law (the so-called *opinio juris* [*sive necessitatis*]). Such "customs" remain a primary source of international law. New customary law is also still being established and that process is being increasingly mediated by IGOs.

Unlike treaty law that is binding only on the states parties to the treaty in question, customary law is normally binding on states generally.

Some rules of customary law, especially recent ones, reflect such a strong conviction of the world community as to their imperative nature that no derogation is allowed from them, either by the unilateral decision of a state to exempt itself from that custom, or by treaties between two or more states. These rules are called peremptory norms, or *jus cogens*, and have only relatively recently achieved recognition.

---

[1] See the treaties listed in M. Bowman & D. Harris, *Multilateral Treaties: Index and Current Status* (1984) and in the annual Supplements thereto.   [2] Cf. UN Charter, art. 13.1(a).

Normally, especially in the past, it took considerable time for a custom followed initially by a few states to harden into a rule of international law, since this requires evidence that the practice in question is widely followed or at least accepted, and that the necessary *opinio juris* exists. Due to the general acceleration of international interactions, however, and especially the activities of IGOs – which often succeed in coordinating the actions of their members and also are the means of articulating legal principles or demands that states act in a particular way – the speed by which new customary law is being created is also increasing, though naturally it is impossible to quantify this phenomenon in the same way as for treaty law. There is also a constant interaction between treaty and customary law. Codification through multilateral treaties is likely to draw heavily on prior customary law, while new treaty law and even the process of formulating it may stimulate states (even with treaties not yet in force or by nonparties) to behave in the sense of the new conventional rules and thereby create new customs.[3] Conventional and customary rules can also coexist.[4]

(c) General principles of law

The third source of international law referred to in the ICJ Statute is "the general principles of law recognized by civilized nations." Although this has not proved to be a particularly productive source, it is not to be excluded that certain principles emphasized repeatedly by the international community through organs such as the UN General Assembly, for example, the prohibition against torture, may through such repetition and sponsorship come to be generally accepted by all states and thus become part of international law even before customary law has developed in the same sense.[5]

(d) International administrative law

International administrative law is a recent addition to the panoply of forms of public international law. It is not mentioned in the ICJ Statute, in part because it barely existed at the time the League created the Permanent Court of International Justice (PCIJ), but also because administrative law is not likely to affect the outcome of interstate disputes (to which Article 38 of the ICJ Statute relates). Although perhaps still not fully matured, such law

---

[3] See, e.g., the US reliance on the 1982 UN Convention on the Law of the Sea, against which it voted at the Conference and which it had not signed, for the proposition that the limit of the territorial sea is now 12 miles. See US Presidential Proclamation on US territorial sea, 28 *ILM* 284 (1989).

[4] See Military and Paramilitary Activities in and against Nicaragua (*Nicar.* v. *US*), 1986 ICJ 14 (Merits Judgment).

[5] Although torture may still take place in a number of states, no accused government defends itself by asserting a right to torture, but rather by denying such activities. So, while it cannot be said that torture violates customary law, which reflects how countries actually behave, it can be said that all legal systems now condemn torture, which suggests a general principle of law.

has certainly greatly increased in quantity, as IGOs have grown both in number and in significance.

International administrative law is basically that which governs IGOs. Its principal manifestations are: the constitutional law of IGOs; procedural rules; the privileges and immunities of IGOs and their staffs; the rules governing the granting of assistance by IGOs to states; the rules governing various types of activities carried out by IGOs within states; and the personnel and financial regime of IGOs. Some of that law is created mostly by treaties; some by decisions of international organs; and some by the actions of these organizations, largely through their secretariats.

Although each IGO has its own administrative law, certain general principles have emerged, particularly as to privileges and immunities and personnel regimes.

(e) Judicial decisions and authoritative teachings

Although Article 38(1) of the ICJ Statute specifically refers to "judicial decisions and the teachings of the most highly qualified publicists of the various nations," it characterizes these not as a type or source of international law but merely as "subsidiary means for the determination of rules of law."

2. "Soft" law

Hard international law is, by definition, binding, at least on some international entities (states or IGOs), although not necessarily on all. By contrast, soft international law is not binding, though perhaps superficially it may appear to be so; nevertheless, international entities habitually comply with it, and it is this feature that makes it possible to characterize it as "law."[6]

Soft law manifests itself in various ways. One is in hortatory rather than obligatory language contained in an otherwise binding instrument, such as in a treaty when, for example, certain actions to be taken are introduced by "should" rather than "shall." More frequent are obligations clearly expressed as such but set out in an instrument that is not binding, such as a resolution of an international organ or an agreement understood not to be

---

[6] The term "soft law" is not much more than a decade old in the literature, but by now it has become the subject of a number of studies, among them: J. Gold, "Strengthening the Soft International Law of Exchange Arrangements," 77 *AJIL* 443 (1983); T. Gruchall-Hesierski, "A Framework for Understanding 'Soft Law'," 30 *McGill L. J.* 37 (1984); W. Riphagen, "From Soft Law to *Jus Cogens* and Back," 17 *Victoria U. Wellington L. R.* 81–99 (1987); C. M. Chinkin, "The Challenge of Soft Law: Development and Change in International Law," 38 *Int'l & Comp. L. Q.* 850–66 (1989); K. C. Wellens & G. H. Borchard, "Soft Law in European Community Law," 14 *Eur. L. R.* 267–321 (1989).

considered as binding.[7] Such nonbinding "precepts" (rather than "obliga-tions") are only to be considered soft law if international entities, particularly states, habitually comply with them.[8]

Soft law is usually generated as a compromise between those who wish a certain matter to be regulated definitively and those who, while not denying the merits of the substantive issue, do not wish to be bound by rigid and obligatory rules – perhaps because they fear they cannot obtain any necessary domestic legislative approval.

3. International "non-law"

Beyond the fringes of soft law, whose legal status is somewhat questionable and perhaps conceded only as a matter of grace, there are certain types of instruments, such as model laws[9] and guidelines,[10] that do not pretend to express international law. This is so because compliance is not done out of any sense of obligation *vis-à-vis* other states or international entities, but comes merely as a matter of national convenience: the perceived desirability of regulating certain matters similarly to other states or the convenience of having a ready-made set of useful technical norms that most states would be unable to develop on their own.

B. Fora and actors in the international legislative process

International law is increasingly being formulated within IGOs. This clearly applies to treaty law, as well as to international administrative law; but it is also true of customary law and general principles, which are often first articulated within international organizations before being inter-nalized in the practices and legal systems of states.

IGOs are complex compound structures that perform their various tasks through different organs and combinations thereof. These organs in turn are composed of individuals representing different constituencies, with correspondingly varying responsibilities, competencies, and degrees of freedom of action.

---

[7] The prime example of such an instrument is the 1975 Final Act of the Helsinki Conference on Cooperation and Security in Europe, which explicitly states that it is not a treaty and is not subject to registration under Article 102 of the UN Charter, but nevertheless is considered by the public, and is often cited by governments, as setting out legal obligations.

[8] See O. Schachter, *International Law in Theory and Practice* 129–30 (1991); O. Schachter, "The Twilight Existence of Nonbinding International Agreements," 71 *AJIL* 196 (1977).

[9] For example, the 1985 UNCITRAL Model Law on International Commercial Arbitration.

[10] For example, the 1985 FAO Guidelines for the Packaging and Storage of Pesticides.

1. Representative organs

All international organizations have at least one, and usually several, organs that are composed of governmental representatives. In the United Nations these include the General Assembly and the Economic and Social Council (ECOSOC), plus numerous subsidiary organs that they have established. In most of the specialized and related agencies there is a general plenary organ in which all members are represented and a governing organ of restricted membership, as well as subsidiary representative organs. While the constitutional or principal organs are of a permanent nature, the subsidiaries may be either standing or *ad hoc*, with the latter of long or short duration; a short-term, *ad hoc* plenary organ consisting of relatively high-ranking representatives is often called a conference.

The representative organs set the agenda for the IGO and determine which legislative projects are to be undertaken. While in the United Nations this is usually decided by the most representative organ, the General Assembly, in many other IGOs the task falls to a more restricted governing organ. The organ that decides on the initiation of such a project generally also decides in what organ or organs the work is to be carried out: by itself, by a standing or an *ad hoc* subsidiary representative organ, by a conference, by a standing or *ad hoc* expert body, or by the secretariat. It is mainly in representative organs – whether principal, subsidiary, or a conference – that the intergovernmental negotiations are carried out to determine the terms of the instrument (e.g., a treaty, or solemn declaration) in which the legislative project is to be embodied, and the formal adoption of the instrument in question is almost always a task of a generally representative organ.

While the composition of plenary organs is obvious, that of restricted organs requires some comment. Basically, the purpose of establishing organs in which only part of the membership is represented is normally twofold: (a) to create bodies of manageable size that can work efficiently and somewhat intimately; and (b) to adjust the distortion in power relationships caused by the one-state/one-vote rule by allowing a relatively greater number of "important" states to participate in the restricted organs. IGO representative organs, while generally composed of the representatives of some or all member states, are often open to observers appointed by non-member states, other IGOs, or NGOs. Such observers sometimes are permitted to participate quite actively in the proceedings and are able to influence the governmental representatives. These proceedings are generally also open to the media, thus enabling the latter and the public to exercise some pressure on the governments whose representatives act in these organs.[11]

---

[11] For example, national NGOs, and consequently the press and the public, generally observed quite critically the position of the US Administration in the final stages of negotiating the 1992 United Nations Framework Convention on Climate Change, and it would appear that

Normally, these representatives of governments are middle-level bureaucrats, but may occasionally include elected officials, cabinet members, and sometimes private individuals. In any event, representatives must be properly accredited by their governments, and thus their official actions, such as making proposals or statements and casting votes, are in effect actions of their governments. It is for this reason that decisions of IGO organs may represent, at least to a certain extent, actions of states, the legal consequences of which in terms of law-making correspond to other governmental actions.

Although these representatives receive instructions from their governments – detailed in case of large, well-organized states, more general in smaller, simpler ones – it is also important to recognize that the human factor can by no means be disregarded in understanding how international organs function and reach decisions. Some representatives are more skillful than others, and often those of small countries, suffering under fewer constraints, may be more effective in carrying out the negotiations required for almost all meaningful IGO actions. But, more important, the international legislature consists ultimately of people who interact, often for many years. This interaction breeds loyalties, both to persons and more often to causes, that may transcend a particular representative's instructions, especially vaguely expressed directives regarding international political enterprises far from home. In such an international community[12] leaders may develop whose standing in no way reflects the status of their countries. Often enough, faltering legislative projects have been rescued – and perhaps occasionally a promising one has been destroyed, weakened, or delayed – by individual representatives or occasionally a secretariat official.

Furthermore, it often matters precisely where and how the instructions to representatives are formulated. In FAO, representatives' instructions are most likely to be formulated in ministries of agriculture, and in WHO, by ministries of health. Tennyson's "Parliament of Man"[13] currently has many distinct manifestations, from the UN General Assembly (which itself has seven quite differently natured plenary Main Committees), to the World Health Assembly, to the IAEA General Conference, to the Board of Governors of the World Bank, and even to plenary conferences (such as the Third UN Conference on the Law of the Sea, UNCLOS III). It is not a

---

these pressures, in a presidential election year, had at least some effect in modifying the originally entirely obdurate stand.

12 Social scientists have characterized these as "epistemic communities." See, for example, J. Ruggie, "International Responses to Technology: Concepts and Trends," 29 *Int'l Org.* 557 (1975); P. Haas, "Do Regimes Matter? Epistemic Communities and Mediterranean Pollution Control," 43 *Int'l Org.* 377 (1989).

13 *Locksley Hall*, line 128. The current fragmentation, described in the text following immediately above, is no doubt due to the fact that the second vision in that line, a "Federation of the world," has not yet come to pass.

matter of complete indifference which of these takes up a particular legislative proposal.

2. Expert organs

Although the international legislative process is naturally (like its domestic equivalent) largely a political one and thus principally within the domain of the representative organs, certain norm-making projects require technical knowledge. The need for such occasional expertise may be satisfied by choosing a single consultant or establishing a committee or other organ made up entirely of experts. Such organs may be standing, as is the International Law Commission, or *ad hoc* for a particular legislative project.

The selection of experts may be done in several ways. In some cases this task is assigned to the IGO's executive head, who will generally make his choices in consultation with member states, though he might also seek advice from other sources. In other cases the competent representative organ may select a panel of states and have each one appoint an expert with the appropriate qualifications.

Whichever device is used, care is taken to achieve a certain political/ geographic distribution, taking into account considerations similar to those for establishing a restricted representative organ. The more political this process is – that is, the more the choice is made by a representative organ rather than by the executive head – the less assurance there is of the genuine expertise of the persons selected.

Experts are normally selected *ad personam* and serve in their "individual [or personal] capacity."[14] This means that regardless of their normal title or assignment as government officials, they are as experts not to be beholden to any government or other authority. What their actual independence from their national governments is depends on a number of factors: the method of their selection (i.e., what role individual governments play); their national background; their personal dispositions, which may depend in part on their international reputation; and the general expectations relating to the particular organ. It is thus quite likely that at least some of the experts serving on a panel are in fact, though not in law, representatives of their governments; others may be truly independent, having only nominal contacts with their governments. Because of the nominal independence of the experts, their actions are not considered those of governments, leaving the latter in a position to repudiate both the actions of their own expert and the collective conclusions of the entire body.

---

[14] See, for example, art. 3.1 of the Statute of the International Civil Service Commission.

3. Secretariats

In any IGO project, the executive head and the secretariat that s/he leads must play at least a minimal role. Sometimes that role is entirely passive, ministerial, and subaltern. Often, the secretariat makes substantive contributions to legislative projects, ranging from the preparation of background and other studies to the development of commentaries on drafts, and even to the formulation of initial drafts of the formal and sometimes the substantive portions of the legislative instruments under consideration.

All such secretariat work is carried out under the direction and responsibility of the executive head. The latter is chosen or approved by the senior representative organ and is ultimately responsible to it for the quality and political balance of his work and that of the secretariat.

4. Nongovernmental organizations

Nongovernmental organizations (NGOs) normally do not provide fora within which international law is formulated. However, these organizations are becoming more significant contributors to the international legislative process carried out under the aegis of IGOs.

These contributions are mainly made as participant observers in the work of representative or of expert IGO legislative organs. These are increasingly being opened to various types of observers, among which NGOs are often the most active and helpful. How observers, in particular NGOs, can participate in the work of IGO organs depends on their rules of procedure or on established or *ad hoc* practices. In some instances they are allowed to make oral contributions, while in others only written ones, subject to restrictions as to length, relevance, distribution, and so forth. Even if these modes of expression are precluded, observers at meetings are usually in a good position to lobby official representatives, and present their points of view, as well as arguments and even draft texts. NGOs can also exercise influence on the international legislative process within IGOs by lobbying or assisting the secretariat in carrying out functions assigned to the latter.

NGOs serve to introduce into the international legislative process, which is otherwise solely carried out at the governmental level (i.e., in intergovernmental organs staffed by governmental representatives and by secretariats and experts employed by an IGO), some direct contact with members of the public. For an NGO to be allowed to play such a role in a given IGO, it normally must receive some sort of recognition by the latter. Each IGO, and sometimes different organs within an IGO, have lists of approved NGOs and procedures for adding to such lists. On the other hand, for some recent conferences and in certain organs, there practically is no admission procedure. A mere request can suffice for an invitation.

The NGOs in "consultative status" with the ECOSOC, which have corresponding privileges with other UN System IGOs, are a varied lot. Heavily represented are human rights and environmental groups, but many other interest groups, from professional to political to economic to business, also enjoy observer status.

5. The media

Another form of indirect public participation in the international legislative process is coverage by the media.

Although the work of IGO secretariats is generally not open to the public, and thus to the media – and that of expert organs rarely is – most representative bodies conduct at least some of their proceedings in public, and their reports to senior organs are almost always public documents. The effect of such openness is that the public in democratic countries is enabled to intervene with its governments concerning the positions the latter take at successive stages of the legislative process.

C. IGO-mediated international legal processes

Having examined the various forms that international law may take, and noting that such law is principally created by the will of states, it is useful to consider through what sort of actions IGOs can perform their important catalytic functions in developing that law. This inquiry is by no means a simple one, for there is little one-to-one correlation between particular types of IGO actions and particular forms of law; rather, most types of action can produce or advance different forms of law.

1. Multilateral treaty-making

The most obvious and most direct form of international legislation sponsored by IGOs is multilateral law-making treaties. While it is not practical to make a complete count of such treaties, it should be noted that the UN Secretary-General is depository for about four hundred agreements, most of which fall into the category of UN-sponsored law-making treaties.[15] In addition, there are others falling into that category for which

---

[15] See *Multilateral Treaties Deposited with the Secretary-General: Status as at 31 December 1995*, ST/LEG/SER.E/14.

38

one or more states are depositories.[16] The ILO has formulated 160-plus such treaties, and many other UN system organizations (especially IMO and WIPO) are responsible for dozens of others. Altogether, of the some 1,500 multilateral treaty instruments, nearly half are attributable to the UN system, and the rate of production of new ones is steadily increasing.

As mentioned earlier, multilateral treaty-making generally has two difficult-to-separate aspects: codification and progressive development. When the emphasis is on the former, the work is assigned to bodies of experts in international law. Their task is to determine precisely what the existing law is, whether in the form of conventional, customary, or other types of hard or even soft law, so as to propose texts that will most cogently, coherently, and completely reproduce that law. Progressive development, on the other hand, primarily requires persons knowledgeable in the substantive problems of the matter to be regulated – a task that might be assigned to a suitably constituted expert organ or even a less expert representative organ.

The process of codification, the preeminent master of which is the UN's International Law Commission (ILC), requires at the outset a thorough study of the existing law. The results of such studies are normally reflected in reports submitted either by a specially designated rapporteur, or an expert consultant, or by the secretariat. Because of the reliability of the person or body that prepared them and the seriousness of the expert body that will consider them, these studies are often accepted as authoritative statements of the existing law. Thus the conclusion of such a report that a certain rule constitutes established customary law can be and frequently is accepted by courts, governments, and other scholars as relatively decisive. Such a conclusion can then serve to strengthen the customary nature of the rule, as governments act in conformity with the declared rule. A similar result may follow during the next step of the codification process, and to a lesser extent during the corresponding one of developing international law, when substantive texts are being formulated for a new treaty instrument. While these texts are still under consideration by expert and representative organs, they are likely to attain wide circulation in the interested parts of the international legal community, and will immediately start influencing the actions of international entities.

As to progressive development of international law, the senior representative organ responsible for a particular legislative exercise may issue a solemn declaration, often at the very beginning of the process to serve as a

---

[16] For example, the 1967 Treaty on Principles Governing the Activities of States in the Exploration and Use of Outer Space, Including the Moon and Other Celestial Bodies and the 1968 Non-Proliferation Treaty, for both of which the Soviet Union (now Russia), the United Kingdom, and the United States act as co-depositories.

guideline therefor, but which also has the effect of putting the international community on record that the declared new rules have at least in principle already attained a high degree of acceptance. While the strict legal force of such a declaration may be minimal, its effect is often to start conforming state conduct in the sense of the pronouncement; this then may be considered as constituting soft law. Furthermore, to the extent that the actions of states reflect their declared impression that the principle in question has, by reason of that declaration or otherwise, already attained a degree of legal force, this may constitute the necessary *opinio juris* required for the creation of new customary law.

Thus the multilateral treaty-making process may produce, in addition to treaty instruments, by-products in the form of soft law and new or strengthened customary law, or possibly even new general principles of law.

2. IGO decisions

The political or representative organs of IGOs act by taking decisions, usually in the form of "resolutions." These decisions can be divided roughly into two categories: (a) those that directly create legal facts or obligations; and (b) those that constitute recommendations.

For the most part the legally effective IGO decisions are those that relate to the organization itself. Thus, the competent representative organs can establish regulations and rules for the IGO, adopt programs and budgets, and direct that particular projects or tasks be undertaken by designated organs or officials of the IGO. In some organizations certain organs also have limited authority to impose substantive regulations on member states, though these usually are given the opportunity of opting out of such an imposed regime.[17] Furthermore, IGO representative organs are sometimes given authority by treaties to impose or modify regulatory regimes established under such treaties in regard to the parties thereto.[18]

One of the few IGO organs that has powers exceeding those just described is the UN Security Council. By Charter Article 25, UN members have undertaken to carry out decisions of the Council, and by Article 48(1), they have specifically agreed to carry out such decisions that are for the maintenance of peace and security. Article 2(6), to a limited extent, extends this obligation even to nonmember states. Because of the substantial

---

[17] See, e.g., WHO Const., art. 22.
[18] E.g., the IAEA Board of Governors was given the power, by Article I(2) of the 1963 Vienna Convention on Civil Liability for Nuclear Damage, to determine the maximum limits within which small quantities of nuclear material can be excluded by states parties from the application of the Convention.

paralysis of the Council throughout the Cold War years, the full extent of its powers has not yet been explored. In particular, it is not clear whether the Council can take general legislative decisions, as distinguished from those that relate to a particular situation. Thus, could the Security Council declare that certain types of weapons *per se* constitute a threat to the peace, and thereby proscribe or limit them? Could it perhaps even declare that certain nonmilitary-related activities, such as aggressive economic policies or behavior insensitive to the environmental needs of the world community,[19] constitute threats to world security and thereupon issue directives or perhaps even promulgate general norms? For the nonce, all this remains unexplored legal territory.

Insofar as IGO resolutions are addressed to states or to other IGOs, they constitute mainly "mere" recommendations. Such recommendations can be expressed with varying degrees of urgency or solemnity and can be coupled with various mechanisms calculated to encourage compliance, such as requests for regular reports. The question is whether these recommendations carry any legal force whatsoever, or whether they are incapable of establishing legal obligations. Though most clearly do not attempt to do so, in respect of the few that do the following should be noted:

1. In the first instance, while IGO recommendations may, almost by definition, not create any firm obligation to comply, all members of an organization whose organs have the power to address them in this manner probably have at least an obligation to consider such recommendations in good faith. In addition, certain IGO constitutions specifically require states to consider particular types of recommendations and even to report on the outcome of such consideration and on any obstacles to compliance.[20]

2. A further argument for compliance with or at least for good faith consideration of IGO recommendations takes into account that in order to be adopted, any recommendation must be supported by at least a majority of the states voting in the organ concerned. Often even higher qualified majorities are required for adoption, and in fact many recommendations are adopted by unanimity or consensus. The question then becomes whether a state whose representative formally voted for a recommendation addressed to all states is not estopped from

---

[19] In this connection it should be noted that in the note issued on behalf of the members of the Security Council by its President at the conclusion of the High-Level Meeting of January 31, 1992, the following was included: "The absence of war and military conflicts amongst States does not in itself ensure international peace and security. The non-military sources of instability in the economic, humanitarian and ecological fields may become a threat to peace and security" (S/23500, at 3). [20] See, e.g., ILO Const., art. 19.5–6.

disavowing its representative by simply disregarding the recommendation.

3. A further reinforcement of this argument comes from the consideration that most resolutions constitute negotiated compromises between different points of view. Is it then proper for a state whose representatives participated in and to an extent benefited from this bargaining by somewhat reshaping the text in its own sense, to disregard the results of that bargain entirely?

4. Because IGO recommendations are often based on purported legal rules:[21]
   (i) to the extent that states are more likely to respond positively to recommendations that purport to derive from existing international law, these recommendations and the legal sources that they cite may then be characterized as at least soft law;
   (ii) to the extent that states do act on the basis of such recommendations in the belief that they are thereby fulfilling international legal obligations, they create customary international law;
   (iii) the very expression in the IGO decision of the purported existence of certain international law may be considered as evidence of the existence of such law.

5. Not to be disregarded is the observable fact that IGO decisions have a strong precedential value, in the sense that once a senior IGO organ has taken a certain decision, it is apt to repeat or apply that decision by analogy, and so will other organs of the same IGO and even of other organizations. This is so because at such junctures the individual representatives who are called upon to approve the later decision are generally comforted by the fact that their governments had approved the earlier one, and thus it seems politically safe to do so again. Consequently, what may once have been a bold and therefore legally doubtful initiative after a while is voiced with increasing conviction by the various organs of the international community.

6. Finally, there are more practical considerations as regards those recommendations for which the IGO organ also adopts measures designed to promote compliance, e.g., to require the executive head to

---

[21] The eighth and ninth preambular paragraphs of A/RES/44/225 on Large-scale Pelagic Driftnet Fishing and its Impact on the Living Resources of the World's Oceans and Seas, in which the General Assembly asserts the duty of "all members of the international community" to cooperate in the conservation and management of the living resources of the high seas, as provided for in the United Nations Convention on the Law of the Sea, is an example (even though that instrument was not yet in force, and had been objected to by some important states).

inquire of each state as to compliance and to report thereon to a competent IGO organ. While nothing compels a state to respond, consistent failure to do so may itself be considered a negative response, which may expose the state to unwelcome criticism by others.

The result of these considerations is that certain IGO recommendations are indeed generally complied with. Therefore such recommendations appear to constitute at least soft law. Furthermore, to the extent that states generally take action to comply, and do so on the assumption that there is at least some legal obligation to do so, customary law may be created that eventually may bind states in general.

There can be no doubt that the decisions of IGO organs are the primary source of international administrative law. Although such law generally applies only to the particular IGO, to the extent many IGOs take similar decisions, whether by imitation or by conscious coordination, a certain common or customary international administrative law may be created.

Thus IGO decisions can lead to the creation of almost all the forms of international law: conventional, customary, administrative, and, perhaps to the greatest extent, soft law.

3. IGO activities

Aside from making political recommendations or taking other types of decisions through their representative organs, most IGOs engage in particular activities. Indeed, for some organizations this is the principal means of manifesting themselves. The United Nations, for example, engages in peacekeeping operations, succors refugees, gives technical assistance, registers and acts as a depository of treaties; financial institutions make loans and grants; others promote health, or agriculture, or education by giving or arranging for technical assistance, carrying out research, convening meetings, and so forth.

All these activities by international entities may, just like the activities of states, create international law if carried out – as is usual for organizations created by international law and subject to the scrutiny of many states – in a regular manner and in the conviction that even if not responding to positive requirements of international law they are at least authorized by and in conformity with such law.

Most IGO activities involve the conclusion of agreements – between the IGO and states, and sometimes among IGOs. Such massive participation in the conclusion of treaties cannot but influence the law and the practices relating thereto. Furthermore, as IGOs have become the predominant depositories of multilateral treaties, the rules for carrying out these functions are increasingly those set by the organizations. Finally, since most multilateral treaties are now developed under the aegis of an IGO, the practices relating to the format of these instruments are in the first instance determined by these organizations.

Aside from the formalities relating to treaty-making, the substance of an increasing number of treaties, particularly bilateral treaties between an IGO on the one hand and a state on the other, displays an understandable regularity (because an IGO cannot wantonly discriminate between states), which through a consistent repetition of certain legal obligations may tend to establish legal norms. These obligations include those relating to the privileges and immunities of the organizations, the settlement of disputes with them, the conditions for granting technical, financial or other assistance, and the arrangements for international meetings.

Going beyond these legal provisions, many IGOs have established patterns of carrying out certain functions: the granting of fellowships, the assignment and control of experts, the protection of refugees, the delivery of supplies, and the stationing of military forces. Taken together with the rules deriving from the bilateral agreements just referred to, these multifarious activities can be said to have created numerous pockets of IGO-related customary law.

II. DESCRIPTION OF UN SYSTEM-MEDIATED LEGISLATIVE PROCESSES

This section examines in greater detail the three principal norm-making procedures: multilateral treaty-making, which may also yield by-products in the forms of customary law and soft law; the process of adopting other types of IGO norm-making decisions, which for the most part are designed to create soft law or "non-law" or to stimulate adoption of customary law; and the processes by which IGOs elaborate international administrative regimes.

A. Multilateral treaty-making

From 1977 to 1984, the Sixth Committee of the General Assembly studied the multilateral treaty-making process.[22] The following description is

---

[22] See P. C. Szasz, "Reforming the Multilateral Treaty-Making Process: An Opportunity Missed?," in *International Law at a Time of Perplexity: Essays in Honour of Shabtai Rosenne* (Y. Dinstein ed., 1989). Much of the information gathered is set out in *Review of the Multilateral Treaty-Making Process*, UN Legis. Ser. No. 21, ST/LEG/SER.B/21 (1985).

based on that study and adopts the same overall analytical structure.[23] But in dissecting the process and presenting it as essentially the progression of four stages, it should be recognized that these are not always distinguishable or clearly separated.

The entire treaty-making process entails mediating different interests, public and private. It is therefore essentially one of negotiation, which may start even before the process is formally initiated and may continue after it has theoretically been concluded with the adoption and even with the entry into force of a treaty.[24] In this, it is no different from any other legislative process, such as national law-making, where different interests constantly review and attempt to modify important legal regimes, with such activity naturally most intense while new legislation is under current consideration by the legislature.

1. Initiation

Formally, the process of creating a new multilateral treaty is initiated in an IGO when a relevant proposal is introduced in one of its competent organs. Normally such a proposal will come from a member state, but it may also be submitted by another organ or IGO.

In certain basically linear organizations, such as the ILO, there is no doubt what the competent organ to initiate the treaty-making process is,[25] while in more complex ones, such as the United Nations, this is not always so. Although Charter Article 13(1)(a) gives a general mandate to this effect to the General Assembly, the law-making competence is not vested exclusively in that principal organ; indeed, the Assembly and the ECOSOC have delegated this function to numerous subsidiary organs, such as UNCTAD,[26] UNEP,[27] the quinquennial Crime Con-

[23] That structure derives from the Secretary-General's report to the General Assembly, A/35/312 & /Corr.1, largely reproduced in Part Two of the publication cited in note 22 above.

[24] This phenomenon is best exemplified by the establishment of the regime for protecting the ozone layer. From the time the problem was first recognized in the mid-1970s and the initiation of low-intensity discussions by UNEP soon thereafter, and starting particularly with the adoption of the 1985 Vienna Convention for the Protection of the Ozone Layer, through the adoption of the 1987 Montreal Protocol on Substances that Deplete the Ozone Layer, continuing through the meetings of the parties to both agreements in London (1990) and Copenhagen (1992) where important amendments to the Montreal Protocol were adopted, and thereafter in the institutions for operating the fund established by the London amendments, the pace of negotiations has ever quickened and is still continuing with considerable intensity. All but the latest stages are described by R. E. Benedick in *Ozone Diplomacy* (1991).

[25] The ILO's multilateral treaty-making process is described in Part Four II.D at 396-405 of the publication cited in note 22 above.

[26] Which generates, *inter alia*, the numerous commodity agreements.

[27] Which is responsible, *inter alia*, for eleven sets of regional seas agreements and for the several related instruments to protect the ozone layer mentioned in note 24 above.

gresses,[28] and the Regional Commissions,[29] many of which operate with scant or no supervision from New York.

Once the competent organ is formally seized of a proposal to initiate the process of creating an international treaty instrument, there are several points to be considered.

(a) The need for the proposed instrument
Whether or not a new instrument is needed depends on:

(i) whether it is agreed that a particular problem exists that may be susceptible of solution through the creation of a new or the improvement of an existing legal regime;

(ii) what other law already exists or is being formulated in the field.

(b) The optimum form of a new instrument
Although a multilateral treaty may be a method of resolving a perceived lacuna in the international legal fabric, various other devices may be better or simpler: a series of bilateral treaties, perhaps following a model that the IGO may formulate;[30] one or more regional treaties; a nonbinding agreement; a formal hortatory declaration by some senior international organ, such as the General Assembly or a specially convened conference; a set of detailed guidelines; and so on.

(c) The likelihood of success
It is not sensible to embark on a treaty-making project if the likelihood of success is slight because of either of two factors:

(i) the technical difficulty of the project;

(ii) the resulting product may not be acceptable to sufficient states.

(d) Anticipated schedule and costs
The international treaty-making process is usually not cheap and may be

---

[28] Such as the Eighth United Nations Congress on the Prevention of Crime and the Treatment of Offenders (Havana, 1990) which produced more than two dozen sets of rules, basic principles, guidelines, and model treaties, see A/CONF.144/28/Rev.1, ch. I, of which eight were specifically incorporated into General Assembly resolutions, A/RES/45/110–13, 116–19. See generally, 30 *ILM* 1357 (1991).

[29] Probably the legislatively most productive has been the Economic Commission for Europe (ECE), for many decades one of the few bodies linking East and West Europe as well as the United States and Canada; it is responsible, *inter alia*, for numerous transport and environment-related agreements, including the 1979 Geneva Convention on Long-Range Transboundary Air Pollution and its several Protocols.

[30] See, e.g., the Model Treaties on Extradition, on Mutual Assistance in Criminal Matters, on the Transfer of Proceedings in Criminal Matters, and on the Transfer of Supervision of Offenders Conditionally Sentenced or Conditionally Released, respectively A/RES/45/116–19, 30 *ILM* 1407–49 (1991), prepared by the Eighth Crime Congress. See note 28 above.

enormously expensive, both in monetary and especially in human resources. One of the principal motivations for the above-mentioned Sixth Committee study was the perception that the ever faster churning international legislative process was becoming unduly burdensome, both to the sponsoring organizations and especially to certain member states that disposed of only relatively few persons capable of participating actively in these negotiations and in assisting their governments in taking proper account of the flood of new treaty instruments.[31] Before embarking on each new legal project, it therefore becomes necessary to consider in what type of existing or *ad hoc* organs it will be carried out and also how long it is likely to take.

Although in some instances it may be possible to answer these questions quickly and without extensive debate or dissent, it is often necessary to engage in preliminary studies. These may be assigned to the secretariat, which in turn may be asked to survey the views of governments and/or of competent IGOs and NGOs; or an expert committee or a subsidiary representative organ may be asked to take up these matters. Then it must be decided:

1. Should the process be initiated, and with what tentative goal?

2. Should at least the initial work be assigned to an existing standing organ or to a specially created one?

These choices seem essentially technical, i.e., to decide which organ is most likely to complete the assigned task expeditiously and satisfactorily. In fact they are often highly political, in that various factions will strive to choose an organ politically responsive to them. Thus, even if logic and precedents might suggest assignment to an existing body, it may be decided to create an *ad hoc* organ whose composition and other features more precisely reflect the political balance of power on that issue in the originating body.[32]

3. Should any interim measures be taken, such as the adoption of a formal declaration that would both serve as a recommendation as to how to deal with the problem pending a formal treaty and constitute a guide to the designated negotiating bodies?[33]

---

[31] See Part Three II of the publication referred to in note 22 above.

[32] This was evidently the principal reason why the General Assembly in 1990 shifted the negotiation of the proposed climate convention from the Intergovernmental Panel on Climate Change (IPCC), established by UNEP and WMO in 1988, to the more inclusive Intergovernmental Negotiating Committee for a Framework Convention on Climate Change.

[33] These were evidently the purposes of the General Assembly resolutions respectively on the activities of states in outer space, which in 1963 initiated the preparation of what became the 1968 Space Treaty, and on the use of the seabed, which in 1970 launched the negotiations leading to the 1982 Law of the Sea Treaty.

2. Formulation of a multilateral treaty text

Once it has been decided to proceed with a treaty-making project, the organ(s) charged with formulating a text must take several steps.

(a) Preliminary studies

This involves surveying governments and other interested entities, performing research, convening expert organs, and ultimately preparing reports.

(b) Initial draft

The preparation of an initial draft of the proposed instrument is always an important step, since it tends to focus the necessary negotiations and further studies. Sometimes this is done by the sponsor; sometimes several states will present alternative drafts; sometimes the executive head of the IGO will be asked to undertake this task, perhaps with the help of designated consultants or a group of experts; sometimes a subsidiary representative organ may be tasked. And sometimes no full initial draft is prepared, but the organ concerned builds one, provision by provision, on the basis of its debates and of individual proposals considered in the course thereof.[34]

(c) Negotiations

The process of negotiation permeates the entire treaty-making process, from or before its beginning to and sometimes beyond its end. Negotiation is usually most intense and focused during the conversion of the initial draft into a text ready for adoption. This process is clearest when it takes place in a representative organ, where the advocates for different national, regional, or other interests openly confront each other. However, it is also present when the forum is a so-called "expert" group, and even when the task is assigned to an IGO secretariat.

It is in the dynamics of multilateral negotiations that the treaty-making process most resembles the national legislative process. In both processes, various interests, some directly opposed but many differing only in approach, must be reconciled through the earnest efforts of persons more or less directly representing and committed to these interests and approaches. Extraneous factors, such as the "power" of the various actors and the perceived need or desirability of meeting various artificial deadlines, often play a decisive part.

[34] That, in effect, was the procedure perforce followed (because no agreement could be reached on a procedure to develop an initial text) by the Third UN Conference on the Law of the Sea (UNCLOS III) in negotiating what is arguably the most complex, and certainly the longest, global treaty instrument.

The negotiation of multilateral law-making treaties in an IGO context is facilitated by the fact that both its staff and the national representatives who normally deal with the organization become familiar with the technical details of the negotiating process. Usually the techniques of wringing the maximum progress possible under the prevailing political circumstances are well established and generally understood. These include especially the many informal ways of exploring and signaling tentative and conditional concessions. Some of these are advanced in unattributed "non-papers," or as submissions that can only be put on the table as part of a package presented as the ostensible proposal of a third party. As successive drafts are prepared, brackets may indicate areas of continuing disagreement.

(d) Expert legal organs

Regardless of whatever technical expertise may be required in formulating a particular multilateral treaty, legal experts must always be involved. When an exercise is considered to be primarily one of codification, then the demand for legal expertise is the greatest. What is required is to determine precisely the state of the existing international law and to reformulate it so as best to respond to current requirements. However, some of the same skills are required for progressively developing the law in a given field since development implies a starting point well grounded in existing norms. Thus it is customary in treaty-making exercises to establish at least an expert legal organ.

Preeminent among such legal organs is the International Law Commission (ILC). Its role is special in that it has been entrusted by the UN General Assembly with the initial treaty-formulating task in certain fields, such as the law of treaties, of diplomatic intercourse, and of the legal interactions among states. Under the guidance of the Sixth Committee of the General Assembly, which gives the ILC the necessary political input, the Commission originates, negotiates, and drafts legal texts. These are formally considered by a political organ (the Sixth Committee or a codification conference) only at the pre-adoption and adoption stages.[35]

Another legal function that must be performed in developing a proposed treaty text is drafting, i.e., the conversion of political agreements reached during negotiations into legally satisfactory texts. This work is normally assigned to a drafting committee which, at the minimum, examines the

---

[35] The procedures of the International Law Commission are summarized in *The Work of the International Law Commission* (5th ed., 1996) and were described by the Commission itself in a report prepared for the above-mentioned General Assembly study of the multilateral treaty-making process, A/35/312/Add.2 & /Corr.1, reprinted in the publication cited in note 22 above, Part Four I.G. For a more critical view of the work of the Commission, see M. El Baradei, T. M. Franck, & R. Trachtenberg, "The International Law Commission: The Need for a New Direction," *UNITAR Policy and Efficacy Studies* No. 1 (1981).

texts that emerge from the general representative organ(s), coordinates them with each other, sees that their formulation is clear, consistent, and reflects the decisions of the organ accurately – and does so in all the languages in which the text is to be authentic. Often additional functions are assigned, such as formulating the final or formal provisions of the treaty and possibly also of the primarily legal ones (e.g., settlement of disputes; immunities).

(e) Consultations with governments

During the process of formulating a multilateral treaty the governments of all the potential parties are likely to be consulted, even if the negotiations are carried out within an organ where all interested states participate as members or as observers. This may be done by circulating a report to all states concerned indicating the progress so far achieved and signaling the remaining disagreements through the use of brackets in the latest draft text. Governments may be asked to submit comments, which are transmitted to the negotiating organ(s). Sometimes periodic reports are presented to the parent organ, which is likely to be plenary and to consist of representatives reporting to the central parts of each government, rather than to the special offices that may control the representatives assigned to the specialized organ in which the principal negotiations are being carried out. The debates in the parent organ will suggest whether the negotiations are politically on track, and their record will be transmitted to the subsidiary organs concerned. In whatever way such consultations are carried out, their purpose is to minimize the possibility that some specialized organ will develop a text that, while technically outstanding, still remains unacceptable to key governments.

(f) Participation by the public

The negotiation of international treaties remains an affair of governments and, traditionally, the public is not invited. At most, the public could have its say in national parliaments when a treaty is completed and considered for ratification by individual states. The seeds for a widening of public participation are contained in Article 71 of the UN Charter, which authorized the ECOSOC to make arrangements for consultations with international and, to some extent, with national NGOs. The practice soon spread to other representative organs of the United Nations, and by now the participation of NGOs in treaty-making bodies is well established.

3. Adoption of multilateral treaties

Once the principal organ charged with formulating a multilateral treaty reports to the parent organ that the process has been completed, or carried as far as possible, the initiating organ once again is faced with a number of decisions to be taken and arrangements to be made.

(a) Whether or not to proceed

If the decision to proceed with the treaty-making project was originally well conceived, then presumably the formulating process will have yielded a text that is responsive to the problems to which it is addressed and acceptable enough to states that it is likely to be adopted and enter into force for at least a sufficient number. But of course political decision-making is not an exact science; a project that may have been initiated with high hopes, or under the pressure of a powerful member or group of members, will not necessarily yield a satisfactory result. Furthermore, during the period of formulation, which may range from a few months to several decades, the problem may have changed, political alignments and interests may have shifted, or certain irreconcilable differences may have arisen that prevent agreement on a meaningful legal regime. At the end of the formulating process, the initiating organ will have to determine, usually by reaction of the governments represented therein, whether or not it is still worthwhile to proceed.[36]

(b) Choice of adopting forum

If it is decided to move to adoption of a multilateral treaty, the forum in which this is to occur must be designated. In some instances that decision is predetermined by the constitution or practices of the IGO.[37] If the decision is open, the choice is normally between a standing organ and an *ad hoc* conference and will be based on several considerations:

1. The adopting organ should, as closely as possible, consist only of the potential parties to the instrument – it being equally undesirable to have decisions as to the provisions of a treaty made by governments that may not become parties as it is to exclude governments that are expected to participate. If there is no standing organ that fulfills this specification, then it is preferable to convene a specially composed conference.

2. If all that remains to be done is to agree on the formality of the adoption, then this can usually be handled as part of the routine business of the competent standing organ; however, if extensive negotiations are still required, a specially convened conference may be preferable.

3. Depending on the nature and importance of the subject matter, either

---

36 For example, after the ILC labored for some fourteen years on codifying or developing the law relating to the most-favored-nation clause, and reported a set of draft articles to the General Assembly in 1978, the latter some years later in effect abandoned the project when member states showed little interest in concluding a convention on the subject.

37 This, for example, is true of the ILO, under whose constitution its conventions must be adopted by the International Labour Conference.

adoption in a high-profile, senior IGO organ, such as the UN General Assembly, or at a special conference may be considered as the better launching platform.

(c) Tasks of the adopting forum
At the conclusion of its work, the adopting forum should be able to approve the texts of one or more instruments, and therefore must complete whatever the formulating organ has not:

(i) complete the substantive negotiations – usually only on a few especially difficult points that the primary negotiating forum was not able to resolve;

(ii) perfect the text, which may require the addition of further languages and the use of a drafting committee;

(iii) formulate the final clauses that determine, *inter alia*, which international entities can become parties to the proposed instrument and on what terms;

(iv) consider potential reservations to be regulated either generally by a clause in the instrument itself or, in response to requests of particular states, in a Final Act; and

(v) make a formal record to enable all potential parties to announce and have preserved their interpretations of the instrument, as well as political statements and reservations.

The final product of the adopting forum, particularly if it is an *ad hoc* conference, will consist of one or more instruments meant for action by states. These instruments may include several coordinated treaties or a principal treaty and subordinated protocols, resolutions presenting the collective views of the adopting forum or making interim arrangements until the treaty enters into force, and a Final Act that pulls all of these together and supplies or refers to a sufficient record to put the entire exercise into context and to permit differing views to be preserved formally, whether for political or for eventual legal reasons.

(d) Decision-taking in the adopting forum
All the fora so far referred to, but particularly the adopting one, must take a series of decisions in advancing the legislative process and especially in completing each stage thereof. In principle all these decisions can be taken by votes, but in practice increasingly more of them are taken without this formality.

The gradual decrease in the frequency of voting in international organs is by no means a casual phenomenon. The one-nation/one-vote rule is today widely recognized as unrealistic, by pretending to equate in this single respect the influence of individual states that differ drastically in all others: population, size, military or economic power, and contribution to the international community. Since there is no immediate possibility of changing this rule, and since more powerful states are steadily more reluctant to subject themselves to this artificial type of "majority rule," it has become necessary to ensure the continued participation of these states in important political processes by avoiding voting as much as possible. This avoidance is expressed most frequently as an attempt to attain "consensus" or "general agreement."

If resort is had to voting, then it is useful to have in mind a dual count: one reflecting the formal majority requirements, which in most IGO organs and IGO-convened conferences requires that substantive matters be approved by two-thirds of those casting yes or no votes; the other relating to the importance, for the issue at hand, of the dissenters. So even if adoption in a formal sense can be attained, but it is clear that implementation will be crippled by the nonparticipation of important states, a sensible strategy might be to suspend the process until a more generally satisfactory solution can be secured through continued negotiations, or until pressures on dissenting governments bring them around.

4. Entry into force of multilateral treaties

The principal significant difference between the domestic and the international legislative process is obvious: once a domestic statute has been adopted, it automatically applies to everyone within the jurisdiction of that country, while the adoption of an international treaty does not by itself cause it to come into force. Rather, ordinarily, each potential party must specifically agree to its entry into force. Once enough of them have done so, the treaty enters into force, but only for those states that have consented; the extension of obligation to other states requires that they also consent individually.

(a) Formal requirements
The formalities required for a treaty to enter into force must thus be considered from two aspects: international and domestic.

1. The *international requirements* are set out in the final clauses of the treaty itself, which indicate, first, the method by which potential parties are to signify their consent to be bound. These methods normally include a choice of: a definitive signature; a signature followed by a ratification,

acceptance, or approval; or accession without prior signature. More important, the final clauses indicate how the treaty itself enters into force, which will normally be expressed in terms of a certain number of consents, though the number may be qualified by specifying that in any event certain states, or states that individually or collectively meet certain criteria, must be among the consenters.

2. The *domestic requirements* arise from national law, most likely from the constitution. These specify which treaties may be entered into on the sole authority of the executive, and which require some sort of legislative concurrence and, if so, by what house(s) and what majorities. They may also specify certain matters that a state may not do, and therefore which it cannot commit itself to by treaty.

Thus, for a treaty to come into force, a series of both domestic and international requirements must be fulfilled. This circumstance unfortunately is likely to result in delays, sometimes very long, in the entry into force of multilateral treaties – particularly of important treaties requiring numerous parties. Worse still, a number of treaties solemnly adopted and duly celebrated never enter into force at all for lack of sufficient participation.[38] Sometimes this may result from genuine political difficulties, which cause either the national executives or the legislatures to decide against participation; more often, nonparticipation may simply result from negligence or indifference, or from the inability of domestic authorities to process and reach decisions regarding all the multilateral treaties presented for their approval. On the other hand, sufficient international political pressure may result in extraordinarily rapid action with regard to certain instruments.[39]

A particular disadvantage of this method by which treaties enter into force for particular states is the inhomogeneity it creates in the affected international legal regimes. While relations among parties are governed by the treaty, relations between these and nonparties, or among nonparties, are governed by whatever was the preexisting law. Furthermore, concerning the extent that similar entry-into-force requirements might apply to amending and superseding treaties, each having different sets of parties, it

---

[38] The 1975 Vienna Convention on the Representation of States in Their Relations with International Organizations of a Universal Character, and the 1983 Vienna Convention on Succession of States in Respect of State Property, Archives and Debts are examples.

[39] For example, both the 1986 IAEA Conventions on Early Notification of a Nuclear Accident and on Assistance in the Case of a Nuclear Accident or Radiological Emergency, 25 *ILM* 1370, 1377 (1986), could enter into force with just three parties, and their commitment could even be provisional. One Convention consequently entered into force within a month, and the other within some four months – well before the first anniversary of the Chernobyl accident that had caused these treaties to be negotiated and opened for signature.

may happen that in effect multiple different treaty regimes become extant on the same subject matter. International law, instead of being a seamless web, often rather resembles an unfinished patchwork quilt.

(b) Reservations and options
The inhomogeneity of much multilateral treaty law is further aggravated by the right of states to make reservations to particular agreements and sometimes even by options incorporated into a treaty or flowing from facultative ancillary instruments (such as a disputes settlement protocol). The reason potential parties may be given such choices is to enhance the likelihood of their participation. Unless such differences go to the very foundation of the proposed treaty regime, it may be decided in formulating the treaty that it is preferable to accommodate them rather than to risk nonparticipation by a significant number of states.

Since the possibility of making a particular reservation or of exercising a particular option may ultimately affect the strength and quality of a treaty regime, consideration of the provisions that allow or disallow them may, to an extent, inform the entire treaty-making process. In some instances the initiating organ may from the beginning decree that no reservations or options are to be permitted, and the negotiations must proceed on the basis that every provision will become fully binding on all parties. More usually, only after the negotiations are largely completed in the adopting forum and the substantive provisions have all been decided is a decision reached and inserted into the final clauses regarding reservations and options that are to be permitted. But whether reached early or late, such a decision must balance the desirability of maximizing participation as against maximizing the homogeneity of the proposed regime.

(c) Technical difficulties in domestic decision-taking and potential international assistance
For a state to take a responsible decision to become party to a multilateral law-making treaty is by no means a simple matter.[40] Regardless of whether the decision is to be taken by the executive alone, or in collaboration with a legislative organ, a number of steps may have to be taken.

1. The proposed treaty and any ancillary instruments may have to be rendered into the national language(s).

2. A survey should be made of the state's existing international legal obligations to determine if the new treaty would contravene any of these.

[40] This was explored by O. Schachter et al., in *Wider Acceptance of Multilateral Treaties*, UNITAR/ST/2 (1969).

3. A similar survey should be made of the national legislation, and especially of any constitutional prescripts.

4. A determination should be made regarding whether the proposed regime is advantageous to the state, balancing the benefits and costs of participation against those of non-participation, taking into account any international or regional pressures likely to be exerted.

5. Finally, if participation is decided, it may be necessary to prepare changes in domestic legislation or in administrative regulations.

All this may be a formidable task for states with weak bureaucratic infrastructures, as is the case of many developing countries. This situation is particularly so, since it is not only a single instrument that must be considered, but an ever-increasing flow of perhaps two dozen instruments annually, in addition to any backlog that is likely to exist from the time of independence.[41]

In light of the foregoing, it has become clear to many IGOs that if their members are expected to become parties to treaties so painfully and painstakingly negotiated under the auspices of their organization, it will be necessary to provide them with relevant materials and technical assistance. Some organizations are already doing so, while others are considering how and from what resources to provide it.

5. Keeping multilateral treaties up to date

In today's fast-moving world, international law, just as its domestic counterpart, must be kept up to date, sometimes at almost breakneck speed. Treaty law traditionally has been adjusted from time to time by additional treaty actions, either by amending existing instruments, or by creating others to complement older texts, or by entirely superseding those that cannot easily be adapted to serve modern purposes. All these measures technically require full-scale treaty initiation, formulation, adoption, and entry-into-force procedures, with all the inherent work and complications. Furthermore, because each such amendment or new treaty is subject to the same domestic treaty-acceptance procedures as the original instrument, and because these procedures are accomplished with uneven speed and efficiency by different states, the pattern of ratifications becomes yet more complicated. This creates an entirely uneven and ultimately unintelligible pattern of obligations among states that are parties to the same agreement

---

[41] A study completed shortly before Namibian independence listed 160 multilateral treaties to which the new country was in a position to succeed. See *Independent Namibia: Succession to Treaty Rights and Obligations*, UN Institute for Namibia, Namibia Study Series No. 13 (J. Faundez ed., N. K. Duggal, 1989).

but with different amendments, or that may participate in different supplementary or superseding agreements. Instead of progressing toward generally applicable international regimes, the volume of international law may be growing at the cost of uniformity of coverage.

(a) Simplifying the treaty-updating process

It is for this reason that a number of devices have been developed to simplify the process of updating treaties, devices that concern one or both major phases of the legislative process just described. These devices include: (a) the use of framework or umbrella conventions that merely state general obligations and establish the machinery for the further norm-formulating devices described under this heading;[42] (b) the supplementation of such conventions by individual protocols establishing particular substantive obligations;[43] (c) the use of easily amendable technical annexes;[44] and (d) amending procedures that do not require the explicit acceptance of states that are parties to the basic convention in order to become binding.[45]

With respect to all these devices, the international phases of the treaty-making process – initiation, formulation, and adoption – can be simplified and accelerated by assigning them to specially designated expert or representative organs.

(b) Simplifying the domestic approval process

Another important saving in time and effort can be achieved during the domestic phase of the process. This may be done by providing in the basic convention that all or certain of these new instruments do not require ratification, but enter into force in some simplified way.

Evidently, such devices that remove the need for each state to act positively on any treaty instrument before it enters into force will be accepted only with great reluctance by many of them, and generally only if restricted to basically subordinated and technical matters; as already pointed out, it is usually necessary to preserve some method for the state to opt out simply, either from the new legislative feature or, perhaps, from the entire regime. Although these are instances of an IGO organ "legislating" directly for states, the legal obligation of each state derives ultimately from

---

[42] Framework conventions have proved to be particularly useful in the international environmental regulation field. They include the 1979 Geneva Convention on Long-Range Transboundary Air Pollution, the 1985 Vienna Convention for the Protection of the Ozone Layer, the 1992 UN Framework Convention on Climate Change and the basic agreement for each of the regional seas regimes, such as the 1976 Barcelona Convention for the Protection of the Mediterranean Sea against Pollution.

[43] For example, the 1985 Vienna Convention for the Protection of the Ozone Layer, arts. 2 & 8, pursuant to which the 1987 Montreal Protocol was adopted.

[44] See *ibid.*, art. 10(2)(a).   [45] See, e.g., *ibid.*, art. 10(2)(c).

its consent to the underlying treaty in which the particular empowerment of the IGO is set out; hence, one might refer to a "derivative treaty obligation."

B. Law-making by IGO decisions

1. Direct creation of binding international law

It is generally accepted that IGOs in general, and those of the UN system in particular, do not have any inherent legislative authority; that is, they cannot create international norms that are directly binding on states generally or even just on their members – though they can take certain decisions binding on their members *vis-à-vis* the organization (e.g., the assessment of contributions). There are a few, albeit rather limited, exceptions to this principle that are gradually becoming increasingly significant. Because these exceptions cannot be based on customary law they are necessarily derived from treaties – in some instances from the constitutional instruments of an IGO, but more frequently from later treaties, usually negotiated under the auspices of the organization, that assign certain functions to the latter.

As states are naturally loath to empower IGOs, even those of which they are members and which they can therefore control, albeit only collectively, these legislative mandates are not only quite limited in scope but also carefully circumscribed procedurally. The object is to make certain that any instruments developed will be both technically correct and politically tolerable. This combination may be attained by assigning the task of formulation to a carefully composed expert organ, and having the latter's work vetted by a strictly representative one.

The actual formulation of binding international norms in expert organs is basically the same as the formulation of treaty texts. In particular, the methods of preparing the initial draft, of quasi-negotiating an adequate and acceptable text, of obtaining governmental comments, and of the participation of NGOs are all essentially the same regardless of the nature of the legislative product.

Almost always consideration and approval by a representative organ is provided for, essentially to give the necessary political imprimatur. As nearly all texts so developed are essentially of a technical nature, consideration by the representative body is usually limited to a formal review of the work of the expert body, to make certain that all prescribed steps have been taken and that no politically unacceptable results have been reached.

2. Creation of soft law and other nonbinding instruments

The greater part of nominally normative international instruments – those that express textually rules of behavior – have at most the force of soft law, and often even less. They are being produced at an increasing rate by worldwide and regional IGOs.

As these instruments do not have any, or at most, qualified, legal force, the procedures for producing them often lack some or all of the political safeguards that generally inform the international legislative process. Indeed, one of the reasons for preparing nonbinding normative instruments is that it is much easier to do so than to formulate, adopt, and bring into force agreements that are intended to have binding effect. One can, however, distinguish between two sorts of nonbinding instruments: low-level, purely technical guidelines, manuals, model instruments, and so forth; and high-level, solemn declarations of senior IGO organs, in particular the UN General Assembly.

The former are normally prepared by expert bodies, or even by an IGO secretariat (often with the help of expert consultants or advisory bodies), and issued by the executive head of the IGO without any particular political approval. The representative organs content themselves with receiving reports about instruments issued, being worked on or being planned, and may through their debates and decisions, particularly budgetary ones, encourage certain lines of work and discourage others.

At the other end of the spectrum, when the UN General Assembly considers the pronouncement of a solemn declaration on some subject, it is likely to engage in an abbreviated version of its normal treaty-making process. After deciding to prepare such a declaration, it normally assigns formulation of the text to one of its Main Committees and perhaps also to some specialized representative or expert organs. When the Assembly deems that the work has been carried as far as feasible, it will itself consider the text and then take a decision to adopt it, if at all possible by consensus.

For either type of instrument, that completes the formal procedures. No signatures or other forms of formal acceptance by states are required, though they are free, and may even be encouraged, to take certain steps in regard to the new instruments: the adoption of model laws as part of their domestic legislation; the incorporation of guidelines and manuals into appropriate domestic regulatory instruments; or the further publication and dissemination of certain of these instruments, particularly important pronouncements of the General Assembly. The effectiveness of the process of producing these nonbinding norms is ultimately measured by the degree that these attain acceptance and compliance by states.

C. IGO actions with norm-making effect

Aside from the self-conscious norm-making processes just discussed, IGOs may also create certain types of international law by merely going about their normal business. Two principal forms of such processes are discussed below.

1. Creation of customary law

Although classically the only creators of customary international law were states, the growing activities of IGOs as international entities with recognized legal personalities have resulted in making these activities, either mediately through the corresponding reactions of states or perhaps even immediately since the actions of IGOs partake of the nature of collective state actions, potential sources of customary law. Such law normally does not pretend to govern state-to-state interactions, but merely governs the interaction of IGOs with states and perhaps that of the mutual interaction of IGOs, or IGOs with international NGOs.

Almost all substantive activities of IGOs, except for the preparation of studies and reports that have no inherent legal consequences, require the conclusion of agreements with states. These include agreements for granting assistance, loans, or credits by IGOs; for states to provide them with certain resources, personnel (including, for example, military units for peacekeeping operations) and facilities; and for IGOs to carry out activities within the territories of states, such as establishing headquarters or posts, operating facilities, holding meetings or conducting educational activities, stationing troops, and so forth. These agreements, some of which are concluded by the dozens or even hundreds, naturally tend to follow patterns – for each IGO in dealing with particular transactions and even for IGOs in general with respect to the same types of transactions. As legal relationships are thus largely uniform with respect to a multitude of transactions of a certain type, it can be said that a particular customary law has developed in respect of these.

How, then, are provisions of these agreements and legal relationships established and maintained? Although there are marked differences in the operations of different IGOs, certain general patterns can be recognized.

(a) The role of governing organs

The basic types of transactions carried out by an IGO are always authorized by a representative organ, sometimes by the plenary one but perhaps more often by a governing body of selected membership. That body will specify the principal parameters of these transactions, including the types of agreements to be concluded and perhaps some matters to be covered. Depending on the importance of these transactions, collectively and individually, the governing organ may reserve the right to approve a standard or model agreement, or even each agreement that is negotiated.[46]

(b) The role of secretariats

The executive head of the IGO and the secretariat under his direction normally play the principal roles in preparing any standard or model texts, whether or not these must be submitted for the approval of a representative body. The negotiation of individual agreements, whether or not based on a standard text or requiring approval of a governing organ, invariably becomes the responsibility of the executive head, who generally has extensive discretion to formulate individual variations to deal with particular circumstances.

2. Creation of international administrative law

The principal type of international law that IGOs create on their own authority is international administrative law. Although the bulk of that law remains entirely internal to the respective IGOs or family of IGOs (such as the UN system), certain aspects of it may create direct obligations on member states.

(a) Law binding on member states

As already noted, IGOs generally have no international legislative authority, i.e., the ability to promulgate norms binding on states, even on their own members. The only prominent exception is that IGOs can, to a limited extent, create obligations for member states relevant to the functioning of the organization itself.

One method of creating such obligations that most IGOs possess in principle, but that is only most rarely used for this purpose, is to amend its own constitution, which entails of course a binding international treaty among all the members. The reason why this possibility exists is that most such constitutional instruments can, unlike other treaties, be amended by a qualified majority of all the members, with the resultant amendments

---

[46] For example, as regards safeguards agreements, the IAEA Board of Governors has approved sets of standard clauses (in effect, model agreements), but also insists on approving each agreement, evidently because of their political sensitivity. The UNICEF Executive Board, however, having approved a Basic Standard Agreement, does not approve each agreement concluded pursuant to that model. The UNDP Council has not considered the Revised Basic Standard Technical Assistance Agreement formulated by the Administrator in consultation with the secretariats of the executing agencies, nor does it approve individual agreements concluded pursuant to that model.

binding on all. This departure from normal treaty practice reflects the recognition that: (a) it may be necessary occasionally to amend the basic instruments of an organization that is expected to function over many decades through changing circumstances; (b) this objective could often not be attained if it were necessary to secure the consent of every single member; and (c) an organization could not function if certain aspects of its basic law (the composition of its organs; the financial obligation of its members) were not binding uniformly on all members.

More routine are the financial assessments that most IGOs are authorized to impose on their members. The decisions that result in such assessments are normally of two types: (a) those that set items to include, and at what financial levels, in the budget of the organizations; and (b) the construction of a scale of assessments to distribute the budgeted expenses among the members. Although the individual budgetary and distribution decisions taken year for year lack the character of general norms, each organization over time creates a structure of general rules regarding how and of which items the assessable budget is formulated and the ways in which scales of contributions are constructed. Within the UN system this structure is to a considerable extent centralized in the United Nations and involves: the Secretary-General, the Committee for Programme and Coordination, the Advisory Committee on Administrative and Budgetary Questions, the Committee on Contributions, the Fifth Committee of the General Assembly, and finally the GA Plenary itself.

(b) Internal administrative law

Restricted as an IGO's powers are *vis-à-vis* the outside world, including even its member states, most of them have considerable freedom in taking internal administrative decisions and in creating norms for the taking of such decisions. These include matters such as the rules of procedure of representative organs, the establishment of subsidiary organs, the direction of the secretariat, the administration of personnel, and the financial administration. For each of these matters a hierarchy of norms prevails, which will have some or all of the following elements:

(i) constitutional principles – i.e., those set out in the IGO's constitutional instruments;

(ii) regulations adopted by the general representative organ or by a competent governing organ;

(iii) *ad hoc* resolutions by the competent representative organ;

(iv) rules promulgated by the executive head pursuant to the applicable regulations;

(v) administrative directives by the executive head; and

(vi) *ad hoc* decisions by the executive head.

Although evidently not all administrative directives and decisions constitute norms, those of general applicability may do so. Furthermore, to the extent that these norms demonstrate a regularity from organization to organization (whether resulting from a purposeful striving for uniformity as in the UN system, or from mere imitation, or from the natural logic of the matters dealt with), one may speak of either general principles or of customary legal rules.

III. CONCLUSION

The international norm-making or legislative process exemplified by the UN system defies easy analysis or even description. In part this is due to the highly decentralized and almost completely uncodified nature of the process, but largely it reflects the many and varied forms of international law and the often elusive and even controversial nature of the binding force of some of its manifestations.

It is, however, safe to generalize that states remain the principal actors and that IGOs have become the principal fora for almost all aspects of the norm-making process. It is also true that, in spite of the growing importance of regional organizations, particularly in Europe, the great bulk of international law is still being created by the organizations of the UN system, including their regional organs.

Partly because the record keeping of the international legislative process remains woefully fragmented and underdeveloped, it is difficult to establish anything like a complete catalog of all its accomplishments, or even to determine in which fields it has been most productive and effective. Certainly the areas best covered within the UN system include: human rights, labor regulations, protection of the environment, international trade, international transport, intellectual property, control of narcotics, and diplomatic relations and related privileges and immunities. In some areas, such as the law of outer space, the total body of law is not very large, but clearly almost all that exists is a product of the United Nations.

At present it does not seem likely that any major changes in or reforms of the process can be anticipated soon. For instance, one should not expect creation in the foreseeable future of an international organ with true legislative functions, or a centralized coordination of the diverse legislative activities, or even just greater centralization of multilateral treaty-making.[47]

The most that can be hoped for is that some means will be found, whether within the United Nations or by other, probably nongovernmental, initiatives, to catalog and publicize the rapidly growing body of international law more effectively – a task requiring probably only relatively modest resources and imagination, aided by modern technologies for storing, classifying, organizing, transmitting, and displaying information.[48] Such an effort would do much to facilitate better appreciation of the United Nations' wide-ranging contributions to the international legislative process.

SELECTED BIBLIOGRAPHY

Bokor-Szego, H., *The Role of the United Nations in International Legislation* (Elsevier, 1978)

De Cooker, C. (ed.), *International Administration: Law and Management Practices in International Organisations* (Kluwer, 1990)

Heere, W., *International Law and Its Sources* (Kluwer, 1988)

Higgins, R. *The Development of International Law through the Political Organs of the United Nations* (OUP, 1963)

Review of the Multilateral Treaty-making Process, UN Legislative Series, No. 21, ST/LEG/SER.B/21 UN sales No. E/F.83.V8 (1985)

Schachter, O., *International Law in Theory and Practice* (Martinus Nijhoff, 1991)

Schermers, H., *International Institutional Law* (Kluwer, 1981)

Sonnenfeld, R., *Resolutions of the United Nations Security Council* (Kluwer, 1988)

Szasz, P., "The United Nations Legislates to Limit Its Liability," 81 *AJIL* 379 (1987)

---

[47] This is suggested by the substantial failure of the review of the multilateral treaty-making process referred to in note 22 above and in its related text.

[48] See, e.g., the proposals ventilated by C. A. Fleischhauer in "The United Nations Treaty Series," pt. VI (The Future), in *International Law at a Time of Perplexity: Essays in Honour of Shabtai Rosenne* (Y. Dinstein ed., 1989).

CHAPTER THREE

SPECIALIZED LAW-MAKING PROCESSES

Frederic L. Kirgis

I. INTRODUCTION

A leading political scientist has said, "The primary aim of intergovernmental institutions is to produce some predictability about the behavior of their members."[1] Whether or not one agrees that this is the *primary* aim, it clearly is high on the list. A principal way to induce predictability is the promulgation of norms for the conduct of members.

This chapter focuses on the nontraditional ways in which organizations related to the United Nations promulgate these norms. Not all of the norms are binding, but all of them of interest to this study are more than hortatory. In general, they have the capacity to channel the conduct of members in ways that are designed to advance, or at least not impede, an organization's attempts to achieve its stated goals. They are promulgated or established by bodies recognized as legitimate by the members, and as a result they command the respect, even if not always the strict obedience, of decision-makers in national governments.[2]

The panoply of unorthodox means of promulgating norms is found not in the United Nations itself, but largely among its related organizations – the specialized agencies plus the International Atomic Energy Agency (IAEA). Consequently the discussion focuses on the related organizations. This means, among other things, that no analysis will be made of the normative aspects of UN General Assembly resolutions,[3] but attention will be paid to resolutions in discrete fields adopted by UN-related agencies.

We are concerned with measures that set standards of conduct, and that

[1] L. Gordenker, "International Organization in the New World Order," 15 *Fletcher F. World Aff.* 71 (1991).
[2] For a definition of "norm" in a slightly different context, see R. Higgins, "The Role of Resolutions of International Organizations in the Process of Creating Norms in the International System," in *International Law and the International System* 21 (W. Butler ed., 1987).   [3] For discussion and references, see chapter 2 of this volume.

– in most cases – have a recognizably legislative form. A measure of this sort has three major characteristics:[4] (a) it is adopted with some degree of formality by an authorized body of an organization, without the necessity of explicit consent by all members intended to be subject to it – except in the sense that members may have consented expressly to the norm-creating process itself; (b) it is intended to provide a channel for the conduct of entities, usually states and usually members of the organization, whether or not it is formally binding by virtue of an antecedent or contemporaneous treaty obligation; and (c) it is of general application, either to the membership at large (occasionally, even beyond the membership) or to some subgroup having common characteristics to which the norm applies.

II. FORMAL NORM-CREATING TECHNIQUES AND THEIR RESULTS

A. Nontraditional treaty-making

The United Nations and its agencies rely to a considerable extent on quite traditional treaty-making for the promulgation of international rules. For example, the International Labour Organization (ILO) relies heavily on treaty-making for its norms relating to the full range of employee and employer concerns, including such fields as worker health and safety, freedom of association, equal opportunity, protection of human dignity in the workplace, etc. The ILO treaty-making process is nontraditional in several significant respects:[5]

1. ILO conventions are adopted by the International Labour Conference, the ILO's plenary body, after a painstaking preparatory process that usually lasts more than two years. The Conference meets annually in Geneva. The representation of members is unique among UN-related organizations, in that it is tripartite: each member is represented in the Conference by two government officials, one workers' representative, and one employers' representative. Thus, unlike the usual process outside the ILO, the process of negotiating and adopting labor conventions is not entrusted simply to governments.

2. ILO conventions are not signed. They are adopted in plenary session by a majority of two-thirds of the votes cast. As will appear below, a member has obligations regarding an adopted convention even if all four of the member's votes have been cast against it.

[4] Cf. E. Yemin, *Legislative Powers in the United Nations and Specialized Agencies* 6 (1969).
[5] The formal process is set out in ILO Constitution, arts. 19 and 22, upon which the discussion in the text is based.

3. One such obligation for all members is to bring the convention before "the authority or authorities within whose competence the matter lies, for the enactment of legislation or other action,"[6] normally within one year after the Conference has closed. The competent authority is the domestic legislature.[7] "Other action" presumably refers (at least) to whatever executive or administrative action is needed under domestic law to make the convention effective and thus to enable the government to ratify it.

4. All members must inform the ILO Director-General of the measures they have taken to secure the approval of the domestic legislature.

5. If the domestic legislature approves the convention, the government is required to ratify it and to see that it is effective.[8]

6. Members may not attach reservations to their consent to be bound by ILO conventions.[9] The rigidity of this rule is tempered by the use of "flexibility clauses" in some conventions, permitting ratifying members some leeway in their application of the duties imposed.

7. If the domestic legislature does not approve the convention, the government is required to report to the ILO at appropriate intervals on the extent to which its law and practice are consistent with the convention, "stating the difficulties which prevent or delay the ratification" of the convention.[10]

8. If the member becomes a party to the convention, it is required to report periodically to the ILO on the measures it has taken to give effect to it. The reports are scrutinized by the ILO Committee of Experts, whose own reports are published[11] and reviewed by the International Labour Conference's Committee on the Application of Standards. It in turn reports to the full Conference.[12]

9. Copies of members' reports must be given to representative associations of workers and employers in the reporting state, and these associations may submit their observations to the ILO.[13] This, of course, enables

[6] ILO Const., art. 19(5)(b).
[7] See N. Valticos, "Fifty Years of Standard-Setting Activities by the International Labour Organisation," 100 *Int'l Lab. Rev.* 201, 222–23 (1969).   [8] ILO Const., art. 19(5)(d).
[9] See Written Statement of the International Labour Organisation, 1951 ICJ Pleadings (Reservations to the Convention on the Prevention and Punishment of the Crime of Genocide), 216, 225–36 (Jan. 12, 1951).   [10] ILO Const., art. 19(5)(e).
[11] See Report III, pt. 4A, of the documentation for each session of the International Labour Conference.
[12] The Conference Committee's reports are published in the Records of Proceedings of the International Labour Conference.   [13] ILO Const., art. 23(2).

these associations to apply pressure upon their governments to comply fully with their obligations.

10. The Conference often supplements ILO conventions with recommendations adopted contemporaneously. A recommendation frequently supplies details that give substance to the more general provisions of the companion convention.[14] In this respect, it may act almost as a protocol to the convention. Much like conventions, recommendations are subject to reporting requirements.[15]

By virtue of all this, a state – merely by being a member of the ILO – incurs significant responsibilities, and subjects itself to peer pressure, regarding not only conventions it ratifies, but also those of which it disapproves. In effect, the International Labour Conference, by two-thirds of the votes cast, channels all members' conduct in the direction of the norms embodied in an adopted convention. The members may not ignore it, and cannot costlessly ratify it.

The ILO's super-treaty system is more sophisticated than that of any other UN-related organization, but it is not entirely unique. In particular, the constitutions of the World Health Organization (WHO) and of UNESCO contain some parallels.

Before we examine quasi-legislative forms of treaty amendment, mention should be made of another nontraditional rule-making aspect of the treaty process. It has been recognized for some time that essentially legislative provisions in a treaty that enjoys widespread participation may quickly become binding on nonparties, even though the treaty has been adopted by traditional treaty-making methods.[16] This has occurred even before such a treaty enters into force. Well-known examples include the Vienna Convention on the Law of Treaties[17] and the UN Convention on the Law of the Sea.[18] ILO conventions have had this legislative effect in a

---

[14] ILO recommendations are not always tied to conventions. Some stand alone, and have significant impact.   [15] See ILO Const., art. 19(6)(d).

[16] See North Sea Continental Shelf cases (FRG v. Den. & Neth.), 1969 ICJ 3, 42 (Judgment of Feb. 20).

[17] 1155 UNTS 331. For discussion of its effect as custom, see I. Sinclair, "The Vienna Convention on the Law of Treaties: The Consequences of Participation and Nonparticipation," 78 AJIL 271, 273 (1984), and the cases cited therein.

[18] Dec. 10, 1982, UN Doc. A/CONF.62/122 (1982), entered into force Nov. 16, 1994. Most substantive provisions of the Convention, other than those on deep seabed mining, were regarded as either reflecting or generating custom even before the Convention entered into force. See Military and Paramilitary Activities case (Nicar. v. US), 1986 ICJ 14, 111 (Judgment of June 27); Gulf of Maine case (Can. v. US), 1984 ICJ 246, 294 (Judgment of Oct. 12); Continental Shelf case (Tunis. v. Libya), 1982 ICJ 18, 74 (Judgment of Feb. 24); GA Res. 44/225, UN GAOR, 44th Sess., Supp. No. 49, vol. I, Preamble, at 147, UN Doc. A/44/746/Add.7 (1989); Restatement (Third) of the Foreign Relations Law of the United States, II, 5 (1987).

number of instances.[19] Conventions adopted by specialized agencies without the ILO's super-treaty mechanisms could have similar effect, if they are normative and attract widespread participation. Unless they codify preexisting custom or reflect peremptory norms, states could opt out after they are adopted – just as states may opt out of other developing customs before they crystallize – but they would have to act promptly and make their intention clear, to avoid being bound.

B. Amendments of constituent instruments and related treaties

The constituent instruments of most specialized agencies contain amendment procedures that bind all members if some fraction – often two-thirds – of the total membership adopts and ratifies the amendment. Amendments adopted by these procedures often concern the internal workings of the organization, in which case it is essential that all members be bound once the designated number has completed the steps to bring the amendment into force.[20] But some constituent instruments contain substantive duties for member states, going beyond institutional matters. When those duties are subject to amendment by a process that binds all members upon approval and ratification by fewer than all, or when such a process adds new substantive duties (whether or not the original instrument contained any), the process is quasi-legislative.

The Chicago (ICAO) Convention is an example of a constituent instrument that contains substantive duties, relating to such things as air navigation, flight over the territories of member states, and the nationality of aircraft. It is also an example of a constituent instrument that may be amended only as to those members that actually ratify the amendment.[21] But some others with substantive duties are not so limited.

For example, the IAEA Statute sets forth rights and duties relating to safeguards for Agency-assisted nuclear energy projects.[22] Amendments enter into force for all members when approved by two-thirds of those

---

[19] See N. Valticos, "Nature et portée juridique de la ratification des conventions internationales du travail," in *International Law at a Time of Perplexity: Essays in Honour of Shabtai Rosenne* 987, 990–92 (Y. Dinstein ed., 1989).

[20] See, e.g., W. Morawiecki, "Legal Regime of International Organizations," 15 *Pol. Y. B. Int'l L.* 71, 96 (1986). But see Convention on International Civil Aviation, Dec. 7, 1944, art. 94(a), 61 Stat.(2) 1180, 1206, 15 UNTS 295 (hereinafter the Chicago Convention), reprinted in ICAO, Convention on International Civil Aviation, ICAO Doc. 7300/6, at 1 (6th ed., 1980) (amendment of ICAO constituent instrument enters into force only for member states that have ratified it).   [21] Chicago Convention, note 20 above, art. 94(a).

[22] IAEA Stat., art XII, reprinted in *International Organization and Integration*, pt. I.B.2.2.a, (P. Kapteyn et. al. eds., 2d rev. ed. 1981), and in IAEA Stat. (as amended to Dec. 28, 1989), at 25 (1990).

present and voting in the General Conference and accepted by two-thirds of all members under their constitutional processes.[23]

The Articles of Agreement of the International Monetary Fund impose several substantive duties upon members. The duties relate to such things as members' exchange arrangements, exchange controls, discriminatory currency practices, and furnishing of information to the Fund.[24] These duties, like most other provisions in the Fund Agreement, are subject to amendment binding upon all members by weighted majority vote of the Board of Governors and acceptance by three-fifths of the members having 85 percent of the total (weighted) voting power.[25] The Fund Agreement even contains an extraordinary authority that, in effect, allows the Executive Board to amend certain provisions temporarily, in an emergency.[26] So far, this provision has not been used.

C. Tacit-consent/opt-out procedures

Several specialized agencies have procedures that modify, without eliminating, the positivist principle that states are normally bound only by international rules to which they have consented. Under these procedures, an organ adopts or amends rules (often appearing as annexes to existing treaties), followed by a designated period during which a specified percentage – usually fewer than half – of the membership may block the rules from entering into force by objecting. This is normally combined with an escape hatch allowing individual members to object, and avoid being bound by the new rule, even if the total number of objections amounts to less than the blocking percentage. In some agencies, a member may even opt out after a new rule has entered into force.

The ICAO provides a prime example. The Chicago Convention authorizes the ICAO Council, currently a thirty-three-member body, to adopt international standards and recommended practices, as annexes to the Convention.[27] It has adopted both types of measure, except in the case

---

[23] *Ibid.*, art. XVIII(C). A member that rejects an amendment may withdraw from the Agency. *Ibid.*, art. XVIII(D). The United States Senate has said that the United States will not remain a member if the Senate refuses its advice and consent to an amendment that is nevertheless adopted. See P. Szasz, *The Law and Practice of the International Atomic Energy Agency* 76–77 (1970).

[24] Articles of Agreement of the International Monetary Fund, arts. IV, VIII, reprinted in IMF, Articles of Agreement of the International Monetary Fund 1 (1982) (hereinafter Fund Agreement).

[25] Fund Agreement, note 24 above, art. XXVIII. An amendment affecting members' right to initiate any changes in par values of their own currencies would require acceptance by all members. *Ibid.*, art. XXVIII(b)(iii).

[26] *Ibid.*, art. XXVII(1). The provisions that may be temporarily supplanted deal with such things as conditions for the use of the Fund's resources, and repayment obligations when members draw upon the resources.

[27] Chicago Convention, note 20 above, arts. 37(c) & 54(l). The Assembly has approved an

of rules of the air.[28] The measures cover a wide variety of matters related to the safety and efficiency of civil aviation. They become effective within a designated period after adoption by two-thirds of the Council, unless in the meantime a majority of ICAO member states disapprove of them.[29] A state that finds it impracticable to comply in all respects with an international standard may opt out by notifying the Organization of the differences between its own practice and that contemplated by the standard.[30] No international standard has ever been disapproved by a majority of the members, but not all members have found it practicable to comply with all standards.[31]

There has been a debate over whether international standards are formally binding on member states that do not have a convincing impracticability excuse or that have not notified the Organization of discrepancies in their own practices.[32] The ICAO Assembly has defined a standard as "any specification . . . the uniform application of which is recognized as necessary for the safety or regularity of international air navigation and to which Contracting States will conform in accordance with the Convention; in the event of impossibility of compliance, notification to the Council is compulsory under Article 38 of the Convention."[33] This sounds as though standards (not recommendations) are binding unless a state finds it "impossible" to comply. The *travaux préparatoires* to the Convention, however, contain a statement that "the Annexes are given no compulsory force."[34] The commentators are divided.[35]

The debate is largely academic. Whether or not ICAO standards are formally binding in the treaty law sense, they are highly authoritative in

amendment to the Convention, subject to ratification, that will increase the size of the Council to thirty-six members. See 1990 Annual Rep. of the Council, ICAO Doc. 9568, at 107.

[28] See pp. 77–78 below.   [29] Chicago Convention, note 20 above, art. 90(a).

[30] *Ibid.*, art. 38.

[31] See T. Buergenthal, *Law-making in the International Civil Aviation Organization* 98–107 (1969); G. Fitzgerald, "The International Civil Aviation Organization – A Case Study in the Implementation of Decisions of a Functional International Organization," in *The Effectiveness of International Decisions* 156, 173–76 (S. Schwebel ed., 1971). Members have not always notified the ICAO of their discrepancies.

[32] The debate does not extend to international standards comprising the rules of the air, at least over the high seas. Those standards clearly are binding. See pp. 76–77 below.

[33] ICAO Assembly Res. A297, app. A, reprinted in Assembly Resolutions in Force (as of October 8, 1992), ICAO Doc. 9602, at 111, 112 (1992).

[34] M. Whiteman, 9 *Digest of International Law* 404 (1968).

[35] Compare C. Alexandrowicz, *The Law Making Functions of the Specialized Agencies of the United Nations* 45–46 (1973); Buergenthal, note 31 above, at 98–101; Yemin, note 4 above, at 138–44, 149–50; and J. Erler, "Regulatory Procedures of ICAO as a Model for IMCO," 10 *McGill L. J.* 262, 263–65 (1964) (all arguing that ICAO standards are not formally binding), with D. Bowett, *The Law of International Institutions* 145 (4th ed., 1982); B. Cheng, *The Law of International Air Transport* 68–70 (1962); J. Naveau, *International Air Transport in a Changing World* 54 (1989); P. Sand, *Lessons Learned in Global Environmental Governance* 18 (World Resources Inst. Report, 1990); and K. Skubiszewski, "Enactment of Law by International Organizations," 41 *Brit. Y. B. Int'l L.* 198, 211 (1965–66) (all contra).

practice. This reflects their recognized importance for the safety and efficiency of civil air travel, and the thorough process by which they are promulgated.[36] Moreover, they are grounded in authority in the Chicago Convention that explicitly distinguishes them from recommendations. Even if they are not at the fully binding end of the spectrum running from the purely precatory to the formally mandatory, they are close to it for states that have not opted out.

The International Maritime Organization has adapted the tacit-consent/opt-out procedure to its own uses, taking the ICAO procedure as a model. An IMO-related treaty, the Convention on Facilitation of International Maritime Traffic, 1965,[37] illustrates the usefulness of the procedure as compared with more traditional forms of international rule-making. The Convention is designed to promote uniformity in states' documentary requirements and in their health, customs, and immigration procedures for ships calling at their ports. The body of the Convention is a bare-bones affair, with standards and recommended practices in an annex. The Convention defines standards as those measures the uniform application of which is "necessary and practicable" in order to facilitate international maritime traffic.[38] Parties were given a chance to opt out on grounds of impracticability or "special reasons."[39]

As in the analogous ICAO situation, there is some uncertainty about whether or not the standards are binding.[40] At a minimum, the standards establish more authoritative limits on parties' freedom of action than do recommended practices.[41]

The primary rule-making significance of the Facilitation Convention lies in the amendment procedures for its annex. As these procedures now stand, any party may propose an amendment to the annex; it is considered by the IMO Facilitation Committee (which is open to all IMO members); if adopted by two-thirds of the Facilitation Convention parties present and voting in the Committee, it is sent to all parties; it enters into force fifteen months later, unless within twelve months one-third of the parties object; if it enters into force, all parties are bound except those that notify the IMO Secretary-General of differences between their own practices and the

---

[36] Member states have ample opportunity to influence the form and content of international standards as they are being prepared. See, e.g., Fitzgerald, note 31 above, at 170–71; Skubiszewski, note 35 above, at 213–14.

[37] (Apr. 9, 1965), 18 UST 411, 591 UNTS 265, reprinted in *International Maritime Law Conventions*, IV, 3118 (N. Singh ed., 1983), as amended, Nov. 19, 1973, TIAS No. 11,092, at 4–5, reprinted in *International Maritime Law Conventions*, IV, 3148 (N. Singh ed., 1983).

[38] *Ibid.*, art. VI(a).   [39] *Ibid.*, art. VIII(1), 18 UST at 416, 591 UNTS, at 272.

[40] See IMCO (IMO) Docs. FAL/CONF/C.1/SR.3, at 7, and FAL/CONF/C.1/SR.4, at 38 (1965). See also Alexandrowicz, note 35 above, at 65–67.

[41] IMCO (IMO) Doc. FAL/CONF/C.1/SR.3, at 7 (1965).

amended standard.[42] This procedure seems to have worked satisfactorily.

IMO also administers important conventions dealing with safety at sea and marine pollution from ships. With variations tailored to the subject matter, these conventions follow the basic pattern of the Facilitation Convention: a brief main convention supplemented by detailed regulations in annexes, with an implied-consent/opt-out procedure as one alternative, at least, for amending annexes that are likely to need frequent reexamination.[43] In 1994, IMO used this procedure to add three new chapters to the annex to SOLAS, the convention on safety at sea.[44]

The annexes to the marine safety and pollution conventions have been made unequivocally binding for parties to them.[45] The amendments are formulated within either the Maritime Safety Committee or the Marine Environmental Protection Committee of IMO.[46] The decision-making process, either in one of these committees or in the Assembly, is expanded to include any non-IMO members that are parties to the relevant convention.

These procedures represent a major tool currently in use for adapting marine safety and environmental regulations to changing needs and technologies. They may well affect even nonparties to the conventions they implement, and even nonmembers of IMO by virtue of the 1982 UN Convention on the Law of the Sea. The 1982 Convention's several references to "generally accepted" norms (variously described as rules,

---

[42] Facilitation Convention, note 37 above, art. VII (amended). Article VIII(2) requires notification "as soon as possible after the entry into force of such amended or newly adopted Standard." *Ibid.*, 18 UST, at 418; 591 UNTS, at 272. It is unclear whether notification before an amended or new standard enters into force would suffice.

[43] See Convention on the International Regulations for Preventing Collisions at Sea, Oct. 20, 1972, art. VI, 28 UST 3459, 1050 UNTS 16 (hereinafter COLREG); International Convention for the Safety of Life at Sea, Nov. 1, 1974, art. VIII, 32 UST 47, 1184 UNTS 2 (hereinafter SOLAS); Protocol Relating to the 1974 International Convention for the Safety of Life at Sea, Feb. 17, 1978, 32 UST 5577, TIAS No. 10,009; Protocol of 1978 Relating to the International Convention for the Prevention of Pollution from Ships, 1973, Feb. 17, 1978, reprinted in 17 *ILM* 546 (1978), incorporating with modifications International Convention for the Prevention of Pollution from Ships, Nov. 2, 1973, 12 *ILM* 1319 (hereinafter MARPOL 73/78).

[44] See IMO, SOLAS: 1994 Amendments, IMO Sales No. IMO-190E (1995); 1994 *IMO News*, No. 3, at 1–4.

[45] In one of them, MARPOL 73/78, three of the annexes are optional in the sense that a party may declare that it does not accept any one or all of them. Apart from that, the MARPOL annexes are binding. MARPOL 73/78, note 43 above, art. 14.

[46] This procedure has been modified for amendments to annexes to the Convention on the Prevention of Marine Pollution by Dumping of Wastes and Other Matter, Dec. 29, 1972 (hereinafter the London Ocean Dumping Convention), 26 UST 2403, TIAS No. 8165, 1046 UNTS 120. IMO acts as the Secretariat for parties to the Convention, but implied-consent/ opt-out amendments to annexes are approved by meetings of the parties, not by IMO committees: London Ocean Dumping Convention, art. XV(2). For a convenient guide, including the text of the Convention and Annexes as amended through 1989, see IMO, The London Dumping Convention: The First Decade and Beyond (1991).

standards, regulations, procedures, and/or practices) would encompass many of the IMO standards and procedures of the sort discussed here. The 1982 Convention binds its parties to "generally accepted" IMO regulations on marine safety and pollution, including amendments adopted under these procedures, insofar as it uses mandatory language when it refers to them.[47] In some instances the 1982 Convention simply requires its parties to take account of these norms, but that too is a duty, and it would not be limited to IMO member states.

The World Health Organization, acting through its Health Assembly, has express authority – acting by simple majority – to adopt regulations binding on all members except those that notify the Director-General of rejection or reservations within a designated time.[48] The authority has been used sparingly. The Assembly has in fact adopted only two sets of regulations, and of these, only the International Health Regulations[49] are of major importance. The Health Regulations try to preclude the international spread of such diseases as cholera, the plague, and yellow fever, without unduly interfering with international trade and travel.

Because the Health Regulations have the effect of a rather elaborate treaty for member states that do not manifest their rejection of them, the Health Assembly struggled with the question whether or not to allow reservations. The issue was essentially whether to strive for universality by permitting a wide range of reservations, or to strive for uniformity of application by strictly limiting them. A solution was reached that tends toward the uniformity goal.[50] A reservation is not valid unless it is accepted by the Health Assembly. The Regulations do not enter into force for a state that maintains a reservation, if the Assembly objects to it on the ground that it substantially detracts from the character and purpose of the Regulations.[51] In effect, the Assembly has the power to determine that a reservation is "incompatible with the object and purpose" of the treaty-like Regulations.[52] The Assembly has rejected several reservations on these grounds.[53] It may do this by a simple majority of members present and voting.[54]

---

[47] See pp. 78–79 below.

[48] WHO Basic Documents 1, 7 (39th ed., 1992). The regulations have the force of treaties, and are published in the United States Treaties (UST) series.

[49] July 25, 1969, WHO Doc. WHA22.46 (1969), reprinted in 21 UST 3003, and in 764 UNTS 3. See WHO, International Health Regulations (3d ann. ed., 1992).

[50] See C.-H. Vignes, "Le Réglement Sanitaire International," 11 Ann. Français de Droit Int'l 649, 659–64 (1965), discussing the forerunner Sanitary Regulations.

[51] International Health Regulations, note 49 above, art. 101.

[52] See Vienna Convention on the Law of Treaties, May 23, 1969, art. 19(c), 1155 UNTS 331.

[53] See WHO Doc. A27/B/6 and Corr.1 (1974), reprinted in WHO OR No. 217, 27th World Health Assembly, pt. I: Resolutions and Decisions, Annexes, at 75, 76–77 (Annex 9, 1974); Res. WHA27.47 (1974), reprinted in Handbook of Resolutions and Decisions of the World Health Assembly and the Executive Board 1973–1984, II, at 58 (1985); Alexandrowicz, note 35 above, at 52–53.   [54] WHO Const., note 48 above, art. 60(b).

The Health Assembly's legislative authority regarding the Health Regulations is thus extraordinary. It has adopted binding regulations that have replaced, among states subject to them, twelve previously existing conventions.[55] The escape hatch for dissenting members closed relatively soon after the Assembly acted, and it maintained a veto power over reservations, exercisable by simple majority vote.

The WHO experience illustrates both the potential strengths and weaknesses of strong international legislation: in an important area of international concern – preventing the spread of communicable diseases – states have been willing to grant legislative power to the relevant organization, but they have not been willing to do so often and not without an escape hatch. More disturbingly, they have not fully cooperated to make the legislative scheme effective. They have not always notified WHO of an outbreak of a communicable disease, nor have they always limited themselves to the border controls permitted by the Health Regulations. WHO usually acts by nonbinding recommendations rather than by binding regulations. The unambiguously binding character of regulations has made them politically unpopular.

Agencies that have not developed a tacit-consent/opt-out procedure have been known to experience frustration at the often-cumbersome, slow process of concluding or amending treaties within their purview.[56] The fact that several specialized agencies do use some form of the streamlined procedure testifies to its utility when treaty-making delays would be harmful.[57] It is a virtue, rather than a vice, of the tacit-consent/opt-out procedure that it may be left indeterminate whether the rules are formally binding upon states that do not opt out. This encourages states to refrain from formal objection unless they have significant objections, and operates in practice roughly as would a regime of formally binding nontreaty rules. Sterile arguments about violations of essentially technical rules are minimized. In the current stage of development of international organizations' rule-making powers, such a process is likely to be the closest many organizations can come to true legislation.

Nevertheless, there are some limitations. For one thing, even this process, with its escape hatch, may be too cumbersome and too legislative to be practical for all rule-making activities of an organization. For another, governments have been loath to apply the process to treaty norms other than rather technical standards usually found in annexes or appendixes to the treaty.

---

55 See Skubiszewski, note 35 above, at 217.
56 See, e.g., *Review of the Multilateral Treaty-Making Process*, UN Doc. ST/LEG/SER.B/21, at 384, 390–92 (1985), discussing the Food and Agriculture Organization.
57 In addition to the agencies mentioned above, the Universal Postal Union has adopted streamlined procedures for some purposes.

The time allotted for states to opt out must be neither so short that governments are hard pressed to make informed decisions nor so long as to cause the process to lose momentum and thus to delay needed reform unnecessarily. If the allotted time is relatively short, inattentive governments may find themselves committed before they realize it.[58] Even an attentive government may have difficulties, if – for example – technical instruments need to be translated into its language before it can act.[59] The problems inherent in allotting a relatively long time may be alleviated by making the new rules provisionally applicable during the allotted time.

Yet another problem relates to the obligation to notify the relevant organ when a state wishes to opt out. It is a difficult obligation to enforce. As practice in such agencies as ICAO indicates, some member states have found it impracticable to apply some rules, but have not given the required notification that they are opting out. If it is truly impracticable for some members to comply, the organization cannot very well take the position that all nonnotifying members are equally subject to all rules adopted under this process. The result is a quasi-legislative system with inherent uncertainties as to which states are fully participating in it and as to whether nonparticipation actually stems from impracticability.

The best available solution to the dilemma just mentioned is often the provision of technical assistance to members in need of it. With technical assistance, what may have been impracticable has at least some chance of becoming practicable. This, of course, requires effective communication between organizations and their members, as well as adequate budgets to support technical assistance programs.

D. Other norm-creation by formal acts

1. Formally binding legislation

With a few notable exceptions, specialized agencies do not possess formal powers to legislate by nontreaty methods, unless the powers are linked with a tacit-consent/opt-out process. The primary exceptions relate to certain activities in international air and marine spaces. The affected areas are *res communis*, as in the case of the high seas and the air above them, or are particularly important to the international community from a political, safety, or environmental viewpoint, as in the case of navigation through international straits.[60]

---

[58] See R. Kbaier, L'Elaboration des conventions sous les auspices de l'Organisation Maritime Internationale 199–200 (thesis, University of Rennes I, 1987).

[59] See, e.g., 1989 ITU Plenipotentiary Conference, ITU Doc. PP89/372-E, at 3 (1989) (remarks of the delegate of Japan).

[60] A special case is the IAEA's authority under UN SC Res. 687, paras. 12 & 13 (1991), to develop a plan, binding on Iraq, for the monitoring and verification of the neutralization of

If binding international legislation is to be found anywhere, it is not surprising that it would be found in these areas. It is also not surprising that the formal legislative authority is tied to painstaking preparatory processes, involving abundant opportunity for member governments to influence the content of the legislation.

The ICAO possesses formal legislative authority for civil aviation over the high seas, except for state (noncommercial) aircraft. The Chicago Convention authorizes the ICAO Council to adopt international standards and recommended practices concerning, *inter alia,* the rules of the air.[61] The Council has adopted Rules of the Air in the form of international standards, without any recommended practices.[62] These include Rules of the Air over the high seas, pursuant to Article 12 of the Chicago Convention. It provides in part: "Over the high seas, the rules in force shall be those established under this Convention."

It is arguable that all ICAO international standards are formally binding on member states, except to the extent that a member has opted out under a procedure set forth in the Convention.[63] However that may be for most international standards, those in force over ocean areas recognized as the high seas or their equivalents for navigational purposes are formally binding by virtue of Article 12. Moreover, ICAO does not acknowledge any right to opt out of any standards that apply over free navigation ocean areas.[64]

These standards are binding even under the system created by the 1982 Convention on the Law of the Sea,[65] which includes exclusive economic zones, international straits regimes, and archipelagic sea lanes encompassing navigational rights equivalent to those on the remaining high seas. Chicago Convention Article 12 makes ICAO standards binding wherever the 1982 Convention recognizes freedoms of navigation and overflight, even as to some waters within international straits and archipelagos that formerly were not part of the high seas.[66]

Iraq's nuclear weapons capability. In this case, the IAEA is the vehicle for the Security Council's authority under Chapter VII of the UN Charter.

[61] Chicago Convention, note 20 above, arts. 37(c) & 54(l).   [62] See *ibid.,* Annex 2.

[63] See text at note 61 above.

[64] See Annex 2, note 62 above, Foreword. See also ICAO Secretariat, "Study on United Nations Convention on the Law of the Sea – Implications, if any, for the Application of the Chicago Convention, Its Annexes and Other International Air Law Instruments," ICAO Doc. LC/26-WP/51 (1987) (hereinafter ICAO Secretariat Study), reprinted in 3, *International Organizations and the Law of the Sea: Documentary Yearbook,* 1987, at 243, 252 (hereinafter *Documentary Yearbook* 1987); M. Milde, "Interception of Civil Aircraft vs. Misuse of Civil Aviation," 11 *Annals of Air & Space L.* 105, 106 (1986).   [65] Note 18 above.

[66] See ICAO Secretariat Study, note 125 above, in *Documentary Yearbook* 1987, note 64 above, at 251–56; *Oceans Policy News,* June 1989, at 2 (remarks of de Mestral). As to international straits and exclusive economic zones, see M. Milde, "United Nations Convention on the Law of the Sea – Possible Implications for International Air Law," 8 *Annals of Air & Space L.* 167, 184–86, 192–94 (1983).

Member states seem to have acknowledged the safety and efficiency imperatives supporting the delegation of authority to ICAO. Thus, for nonstate aircraft over the high seas, binding rules are made by two-thirds majority vote in a representative ICAO body. That is an extraordinary, but eminently sensible, delegation of legislative authority to an international organization.

The legislative authority of the International Maritime Organization, unlike that of the ICAO, stems only in the most general terms from the Organization's constituent instrument. For the most part, it derives from related treaties, such as those discussed on pp. 72–74 above. In many instances, the IMO's rule-making authority is exercised by means of formally recommendatory instruments. They come with a variety of names — codes, guidelines, regulations, recommendations, etc.[67] These are considered on pp. 84–88 below.

In several instances relating to maritime safety and environmental protection, IMO codes and other nontreaty instruments have become binding on parties to the IMO-related treaties that cover the same subjects. To take just one safety-related example, Rule 10 of the Regulations attached to the Convention on the International Regulations for Preventing Collisions at Sea, 1972 (COLREG),[68] requires vessels using a route for which there is a traffic separation scheme adopted by the IMO Maritime Safety Committee to comply with the scheme. A vessel using a traffic separation scheme must proceed in the appropriate lane and keep clear of the line or zone separating traffic headed in opposite directions. All IMO member states are entitled to participate in the work of the Committee.[69] Each state party to COLREG is under a duty to give effect to each of these traffic separation schemes,[70] even though it may have voted against the scheme in the Committee (and even if it is not a member of IMO). A member of IMO that is not a party to COLREG does not appear to be bound by treaty to give effect to such schemes, since COLREG – not the IMO Convention – makes them binding.[71]

Under the 1982 UN Convention on the Law of the Sea,[72] sea lanes and traffic separation schemes in international straits and archipelagic waters

---

[67] See C. Henry, *The Carriage of Dangerous Goods by Sea* 73 (1985).

[68] Note 43 above, 28 UST at 3475, 1050 UNTS at 25–26, reprinted in *International Maritime Law Conventions*, I, note 37 above, at 18.

[69] Convention on the International Maritime Organization, art. 27, in 1 IMO Basic Documents 11 (1986).

[70] See COLREG, art. 1, note 43 above, 28 UST at 3461, 1050 UNTS at 19, reprinted in *International Maritime Law Conventions*, I, note 37 above, at 18; S. Mankabady, *The Law of Collision at Sea* 187–92 (1987).

[71] Within territorial waters, the coastal state presumably could make its traffic separation scheme binding on vessels of all states, so long as it does not interfere with the right of innocent passage. Cf. Mankabady, note 70 above, at 188.   [72] Note 18 above, arts. 41(4) & 53(9).

are to be adopted by "the competent international organization," which IMO construes to mean itself,[73] in agreement with the strait or archipelagic state. That state is not at liberty to deviate from the IMO-adopted scheme. In all other contexts, the 1982 Convention says that a coastal state may establish sea lanes and traffic separation schemes in its territorial sea, merely taking into account the recommendations of "the competent international organization."[74]

In several other respects, the Convention on the Law of the Sea incorporates by reference "generally accepted" international norms ("rules, standards, regulations, procedures and/or practices"), in contexts that point to those adopted by IMO organs and widely respected in practice.[75] These have to do with such things as pollution-control regulations to be obeyed by vessels passing through international straits and archipelagos,[76] minimum standards for flag states' pollution-control regulations for their own vessels,[77] standards for coastal states' control of pollution from vessels in their exclusive economic zones,[78] and measures for removal of installations and structures to ensure safety of navigation.[79] Many of these standards are adopted by the tacit-consent/opt-out procedure discussed in the previous section. In each of these contexts a state that has not explicitly consented to be bound by an IMO standard – even a state that is not a member of IMO – could be bound. This could occur as a matter of treaty law for parties to the Convention on the Law of the Sea, or even as a matter of customary law emerging from the general recognition of IMO's standard-setting authority in these areas.

Some agencies have treaty-based authority to make conclusive findings of legislative facts in discrete fields, without having full regulatory authority over the activities to which their findings relate. For example, the World Health Organization has this limited, but decisive, authority concerning scientific assessment of psychotropic substances for purposes of interna-

---

[73] See IMO Secretariat Study, "Implications of the United Nations Convention on the Law of the Sea, 1982, for the International Maritime Organization," IMO Doc. LEG/MISC/1, reprinted in *Documentary Yearbook* 1987, note 64 above, at 340.

[74] UN Convention on the Law of the Sea, note 18 above, art. 22.

[75] See B. Oxman, "The Duty to Respect Generally Accepted International Standards," 24 *NYU J. Int'l L. & Pol.* 109, 149–58 (1991).

[76] UN Convention on the Law of the Sea, note 18 above, arts. 39(2) & 54.

[77] *Ibid.*, art. 211(1) & (2).

[78] *Ibid.*, art. 211(5) & (6). In environmentally sensitive areas of an exclusive economic zone, art. 211(6) gives a coastal state limited authority to deviate from the international rules and standards, if "the organization" – presumably the IMO – agrees.

[79] *Ibid.*, art. 60(3). See V. Andrianov, "The Role of the International Maritime Organization in Implementing the 1982 UNCLOS," 14 *Marine Policy* 120 (1990). The IMO Assembly has adopted guidelines and standards for the removal of offshore installations and structures. See IMO Assembly Res. A.672(16), reprinted in IMO Assembly Resolutions and Other Decisions, 16th Sess., 1989, at 293 (1990).

tional control. WHO does not, however, have regulatory authority over the substances.

WHO's authority emanates from the Convention on Psychotropic Substances.[80] The Convention deals with about forty listed substances divided among four schedules denoting different degrees of control.[81] Under the Convention, if WHO finds that a psychotropic substance has the capacity to produce dependence and is likely to be abused, it communicates to the UN Commission on Narcotic Drugs its assessment of the substance and its societal effects, along with recommendations on control measures. The assessments are "determinative as to medical and scientific matters."[82] These determinative assessments include not only factual findings regarding such things as the chemical characteristics of a substance, but also scientific opinions regarding its effects.[83] The UN Commission may add the substance to, or delete it from, one of the schedules, or may transfer it from one schedule to another. But in doing so, it must treat WHO's medical and scientific assessments as legislative facts.

A WHO assessment even has preclusive legislative effect when it finds that a substance does not have the dangerous properties the Convention contemplates. The official commentary to the Convention asserts that the Commission could not properly place such a substance under control. To do so "would be incompatible with the provision that the WHO assessment should be 'determinative as to medical and scientific matters.'"[84] In such a case, WHO has decided conclusively that the substance should not be restricted for public health purposes.

The Single Convention on Narcotic Drugs,[85] which controls about 110 narcotic substances,[86] does not expressly make WHO assessments "determinative." But it does give WHO recommendations on control of narcotics a limiting character not found in most recommendations. The UN Commission's only choice is between adopting the WHO recommendation or eschewing any action at all. It may not place a narcotic substance under control, change its level of control, or remove controls on it except "in accordance with the recommendation of the World Health Organiz-

---

[80] Feb. 21, 1971, 32 UST 543, TIAS No. 9725, 1019 UNTS 175.

[81] See B. Rexed, K. Edmondson, I. Khan, & R. Samson, *Guidelines for the Control of Narcotic and Psychotropic Substances* 34, 36–37 (1984).

[82] Convention on Psychotropic Substances, note 80 above, art. 2(5).

[83] See Commentary on the Convention on Psychotropic Substances, UN Doc. E/CN.7/589, at 69 (1976).   [84] *Ibid.*, at 71.

[85] Mar. 30, 1961, 18 UST 1407, TIAS No. 6298, 520 UNTS 204, with Protocol of Mar. 25, 1972, 26 UST 1439, TIAS No. 8118, 976 UNTS 3.

[86] See Rexed et al., note 81 above, at 34.

ation."[87] The Convention on Psychotropic Substances does not limit the Commission in this way.

The examples in this section illustrate both the constructive role that specialized agencies may play as true rule-makers and the reluctance of states to endow the agencies with broad, formal legislative powers. Nonterritorial ocean and air spaces beckon formal international regulation if chaos and severe environmental harm are to be avoided. International drug control does too. Regulation through treaty-making would be far too cumbersome, so a more streamlined method has been found. Of course, there is an intermediate method, examined in the previous section, that could have been chosen: treaty-making, with a tacit-consent/opt-out procedure for new standards or amendments to standards, to keep pace with changing conditions. There is also a soft law method that could have been chosen: resolutions formally amounting only to recommendations. That method will be examined below. The streamlined legislative techniques discussed in this section have been adopted because of (a) their limited scope; (b) the need for effective regulation in those limited areas, (c) the assurances; provided by procedures that ensure careful preparation of the standards with significant input from governments; and (d) the relatively slight risks that the rules will impose significant disadvantages on governments or their important constituents vis-à-vis their foreign rivals, or will substantially impair other important interests sought to be protected by governments.

At the present stage of world political development, governments are unlikely to yield significant, formal legislative authority to UN agencies in new areas, at least in the absence of an opt-out mechanism. This is a matter not just of governments' proclivity to retain as much power as possible, but also of democratic principle – since UN agencies wielding binding legislative authority are not directly answerable to the people in their member states.[88] But the use of UN agencies to establish legislative facts may be promising beyond the relatively discrete models provided so far by such agencies as WHO. Preservation of the global environment would be a strong candidate for further development of this technique.[89]

---

[87] Single Convention on Narcotic Drugs, note 85 above, art. 3; Commentary on the Single Convention on Narcotic Drugs, UN Sales No. E.73.XI.1, at 90, 95–96 (1973).

[88] Cf. K. Kaiser, "Transnational Relations as a Threat to the Democratic Process," 25 *Int'l Org.* 706, 713–15 (1971).

[89] The Montreal Protocol to the 1985 Vienna Convention for the Protection of the Ozone Layer, Sept. 16, 1987, art. 2(9), 26 ILM 1550 (1987), already contains a limited legislative authorization for parties' adjustments to reductions of production or consumption of substances controlled by the Protocol. See D. Caron, "Protection of the Stratospheric Ozone Layer and the Structure of International Environmental Lawmaking," 14 *Hastings Int'l & Comp. L. Rev.* 755, 766–67 (1991).

2. Agencies' recommendations to members

Typically, the plenary body and the smaller executive body of a specialized agency have the express authority to adopt nonbinding recommendations addressed to its membership. Unanimity is rarely required, though serious attempts are often made to achieve consensus (defined as the absence of formal objection). Insofar as votes are taken, recommendations are normally adopted by a simple majority or by two-thirds. Thus, to the extent that resolutions in the form of recommendations actually channel members' conduct, they have legislative characteristics within the meaning given at the beginning of this chapter.

As in the case of treaty-making, the ILO has the most sophisticated system among specialized agencies for promulgating and overseeing recommendations. Like conventions, ILO recommendations are adopted by two-thirds of the votes cast in the tripartite International Labour Conference. Members must bring adopted recommendations before the competent domestic authorities for the enactment of legislation or other action. They must inform the ILO Director-General of the measures taken, and they must report periodically on the extent to which they have given effect to the recommendations and on any modifications found necessary in adopting or applying them.[90]

As noted earlier, many ILO recommendations complement labor conventions, supplying details and acting almost as protocols. The overwhelming majority of ILO recommendations in recent years have been of this nature.[91] Others stand alone, often testing the waters to see if governments are ready for regulation in a new area of labor relations. If it transpires that they are, one or more conventions may follow. Still others stand alone for another reason: circumstances in member countries may be so different that a convention could not meaningfully regulate them, even with flexibility clauses.[92]

The ILO supervisory system concentrates primarily on members' application of ratified conventions. To the extent that recommendations serve as aids to the interpretation of conventions, the supervisory bodies take them into account. The supervision of recommendations, as such, focuses largely on members' duty to submit them to the competent

---

[90] ILO Const., note 5 above, art. 19(6).

[91] From 1971 through 1988, thirty-one of thirty-four recommendations supplemented a convention. See ILO, *International Labour Standards: A Workers' Education Manual* 38 (3d rev. ed., 1990).

[92] See V.-Y. Ghebali, *The International Labour Organisation: A Case Study on the Evolution of UN Specialized Agencies* 210 (1989); N. Valticos, "The International Labour Organization," in Schwebel ed., note 31 above, at 135.

domestic authorities.[93] In addition, members are asked periodically to report on their law and practice regarding a few recommendations at a time.

Since so many recommendations are tied to conventions, it is difficult to assess their independent impact on members. Nevertheless, there is one interesting study of a free-standing recommendation. The study dealt with the Termination of Employment Recommendation, 1963.[94] It noted that between 1963 and 1976, over forty countries had adopted measures reflecting the recommendation's central principle – that a worker's employment should not be terminated without a valid reason. The study was able to show a direct relationship between the new measures and the recommendation in some of those countries.[95]

Under the WHO constitution, each member is required to report annually on the action it has taken on recommendations adopted by the Health Assembly.[96] Since WHO relies heavily on recommendations to establish norms for its members even though it has formal authority to adopt conventions and binding regulations, the reporting requirement is significant. WHO recommendations have had the intended effect of channeling members' conduct.[97] Many of them are in the form of codes or guidelines, discussed below.

ICAO recommendations come in the form of recommended practices adopted by the Council. Although they are by definition somewhere below ICAO international standards on the spectrum running from legal obligation to nonobligation, in ICAO practice they are often lumped together with standards. The package is collectively known as SARPs (standards and recommended practices). A former ICAO Senior Legal Officer has said that there is "a certain expectation of compliance" with recommended practices.[98]

It is even more difficult to evaluate the impact of ICAO recommended practices on members than it is to evaluate the impact of ILO recommenda-

---

[93] See, e.g., Report of the Committee of Experts on the Application of Conventions and Recommendations, Int'l Labour Conf., 76th Sess., Report III, Part 4A, at 496–509 (1989).

[94] Recommendation No. 119, in Int'l Labour Conventions and Recommendations 1919–1981, at 138 (1982).

[95] E. Yemin, "Job Security: Influence of ILO Standards and Recent Trends," 113 *Int'l Lab. Rev.* 17, 19–23 (1976). This recommendation was one that led eventually to a convention. In 1982 the ILO adopted the Termination of Employment Convention (No. 158), 65 *ILO Official Bull.*, Ser. A, No. 2, at 72 (1982). At the same time the ILO adopted a new Termination of Employment Recommendation (No. 166), *ibid.*, at 78, superseding the 1963 recommendation. That the 1963 recommendation led to a convention is some evidence of its positive impact on members.

[96] WHO Const., art. 62, reprinted in Kapteyn et al. eds., note 22 above, and in WHO Basic Documents 1 (37th ed., 1988).

[97] C.-H. Vignes, Role of WHO in International Health Legislation 57 (unpublished manuscript, undated).   [98] Fitzgerald, note 31 above, at 190.

tions, because they are so closely tied to international standards. Together, ICAO SARPs clearly have had a substantial impact, reflecting the care with which they are formulated, the input of the governments that are to be subject to them, and the recognized importance of international norms for the safety and efficiency of civil aviation.

Several specialized agencies have adopted "codes" or "guidelines," setting forth standards that are not linked to binding instruments. Many of these codes or guidelines are quite comprehensive in their fields. They are adopted by representative bodies within the agencies, such as committees in which all agency members are entitled to participate. Formally, they amount to recommendations and thus are not binding on those to whom they are addressed. For the most part, however, they are quite effective in channeling conduct. They could well be called "super-recommendations."

The IMO's IMDG Code is an excellent example. It was adopted by the IMO Assembly in 1965 to harmonize the practices of states carrying dangerous goods by sea.[99] The IMO has amended it several times, for safety and for environmental protection purposes. Although it complements the International Convention for the Safety of Life at Sea (SOLAS) and is mentioned in two footnotes in the annex to SOLAS, neither the Convention nor any other treaty makes it mandatory for parties. Nevertheless, it has been widely incorporated into the domestic legislation of IMO member states. Arguably, states that have implemented it have effectively shielded their vessels from liability for damage from the carriage of dangerous goods in accordance with it.[100]

The IMDG Code may be analogized to some ILO recommendations, in that it complements a convention adopted under the auspices of the organization. Some other IMO codes and guidelines are related to conventions, and some – such as some ILO recommendations – have been the forerunners of conventional obligations. Occasionally, conventions – or amendments to conventions – have transformed previously nonbinding codes or guidelines into regulations binding upon parties to the conventions.[101] In these instances, the regulations are kept current by using the tacit-consent/opt-out amendment procedures in the conventions.

---

[99] See IMO, International Maritime Dangerous Goods Code, vol. I, Foreword (Consol. ed., 1994) (hereinafter IMDG Code).

[100] See Henry, note 67 above, at 109; IMDG Code, note 99 above.

[101] This is the case, for example, with the International Code for the Construction and Equipment of Ships Carrying Dangerous Chemicals in Bulk (IBC Code), IMO Res. MSC.4(48) (1983), and the International Code for the Construction and Equipment of Ships Carrying Liquefied Gases in Bulk (IGC Code), IMO Res. MSC.5(48) (1983). These were made mandatory by amendment to SOLAS 1974, in IMO Res. MSC.6(48) (1983). See IMO, SOLAS (Consol. ed. 1992). See also Henry, note 67 above, at 80, 90 n. 97.

IMO practice exemplifies another way in which agency recommendations may have law-making significance. In 1990, Australia obtained the Marine Environmental Protection Committee's nonbinding designation of the Great Barrier Reef as a "particularly sensitive area" in which the coastal state could apply special protective measures. The concept of "particularly sensitive" maritime areas does not appear explicitly in the Convention on the Law of the Sea, nor had it theretofore been established in customary international law. In making its proposal to the IMO, Australia recognized that approval might well influence the development of custom and the interpretation of conventional international law.[102] Indeed, this is one way in which new normative concepts may become recognized, even for nonmembers of an organization, if general acquiescence in the new concept is forthcoming.

Both WHO and FAO have promulgated codes and guidelines in their fields. The most comprehensive of these codes is a joint FAO/WHO project, the Codex Alimentarius. It is a collection of food standards adopted by the Codex Alimentarius Commission, a body of more than 130 states that are members or associate members of FAO and WHO.[103] It was established in 1962 to implement the FAO/WHO Food Standards Programme. The objective is to protect health and to facilitate international trade in food products. The Commission has adopted about 200 standards for individual foods relating to such things as food hygiene and additives, plus several general standards dealing with such matters as labeling of packaged foods and of food additives. It has also adopted maximum limits for pesticide residues in foods. These measures are developed through an elaborate committee procedure that provides for input by experts and by governments.[104]

The Codex standards and pesticide residue limits are submitted to governments for their acceptance, and do not obligate a government unless

---

102 See IMO Doc. MEPC 30/19/3, at 10 (1990); MEPC Doc. 30/24, Annexes 16 & 17 (1991). After the MEPC had approved the proposal, Australia announced that it would extend its territorial seas to include all marine areas within 12 nautical miles of its baselines, bringing all of the Great Barrier Reef within its jurisdiction. *Oceans Policy News*, Dec. 1990/Jan. 1991, at 8.

103 See Codex Alimentarius Comm'n Procedural Manual 1, 23 (7th ed., 1989); Report by the WHO Director-General, The Codex Alimentarius Comm'n, reprinted in WHO Exec. Bd., 79th Sess., Resolutions and Decisions, Annex 12, WHO Doc. EB79/1987/ REC/1 (1987).

104 See J. Dobbert, "Some Aspects of the Law and Practice of FAO," in *The Effectiveness of International Decisions*, note 31 above, at 206, 240; D. Leive, *International Regulatory Regimes* 389–92, 435–59, 601–5, II (1976). Most of vol. II of Leive's book is devoted to the Codex. See also Alexandrowicz, note 35 above, at 75–82; J. Dobbert, "Le Codex Alimentarius: Vers une nouvelle méthode de réglementation internationale," 15 *Ann. Français de Droit Int'l* 677 (1969).

and until accepted.[105] Governments are permitted to withdraw or amend their acceptances simply by informing the Commission's secretariat. They "should" give reasons, if possible, and should give as much advance notice as possible.[106]

Knowledgeable participants and observers have treated fully accepted Codex standards as obligatory for accepting governments.[107] On the other hand, one might argue that the ease with which an acceptance may be withdrawn or amended renders any such "obligation" illusory. It is not crucial for most purposes to determine whether or not accepted Codex standards are formally binding. States fully accepting Codex standards may be expected to comply with them virtually as they would comply with treaty obligations, unless and until they withdraw their acceptances.

The Commission has had some difficulty in obtaining acceptances. Consequently, for a number of states, many of the standards are not formally binding under any interpretation. In such cases, the standards amount only to recommendations.[108] Nevertheless, Codex standards and other Codex measures are widely used by governments and by the international food trade.[109] The number of acceptances thus is not a reliable guide to the channeling effect of the standards. In other words, their normative impact does not depend entirely on the extent to which states are arguably bound by them. This, of course, does not mean that formal commitment is unimportant. In particular, acceptance gives other states assurance that a standard will have the intended impact in the accepting state. Consequently, the Commission does what it can to obtain acceptances.[110]

Several other examples could be given. We shall consider examples from just one more agency. The International Atomic Energy Agency's Statute gives it the authority to adopt safety standards for the peaceful use of atomic energy.[111] These standards are mandatory in respect of activities carried out by the IAEA itself or with its assistance. Otherwise, they are only recommendatory.[112] Under this authority, IAEA has adopted safety

---

[105] In addition to standards and pesticide residue limits, the Codex includes codes, guidelines, and recommendations that are not treated as standards and thus are not subject to the acceptance procedure. Of particular significance is the Code of Ethics for International Trade in Food, FAO/WHO Doc. CAC/RCP 201979. It provides some safeguards for developing countries that might not have adequate infrastructures to protect consumers against health hazards in food and against fraud. *Ibid.* at iii.

[106] Codex Alimentarius Comm'n Procedural Manual, note 103 above, at 30.

[107] See Alexandrowicz, note 35 above, at 79; Dobbert, note 104 above, at 108; Leive, note 104 above, at 464.   [108] See Alexandrowicz, note 35 above, at 78.

[109] Codex Alimentarius Comm'n, Rep. of 17th Sess., FAO Doc. ALINORM 87/39, at 20.

[110] See *ibid.* at 4, 97.

[111] For discussion of the promulgation process and of the effect of IAEA safety standards, see P. Szasz, *The Law and Practice of the International Atomic Energy Agency* 659–701 (1970).

[112] IAEA Stat., note 22 above, arts. III(A)(6), XI(F), XII(B).

standards such as the Regulations for the Safe Transport of Radioactive Material,[113] Guidelines for the Physical Protection of Nuclear Material,[114] five codes of practice for nuclear power plants,[115] and a Code of Practice on the International Transboundary Movement of Radioactive Waste designed to forestall radioactive waste transfer to a country without its informed consent.[116]

The Director of the IAEA Legal Division has said that it is not important whether the radioactive waste transfer code is technically binding or not, so long as its rules satisfy common concerns.[117] This is consistent with experience under most of the other IAEA codes and standards, and under other agencies' codes.

Codes – relatively comprehensive sets of formally nonbinding norms promulgated by representative bodies – perform an important channeling function in several agencies. They have the great advantage of flexibility, precisely because they are nonbinding. Governments have shown themselves to be more willing to accept amendments to codes to keep up with changing times than if they were formally bound either to comply or to declare their decision to opt out. Moreover, codes are more likely to be adopted in the first place if they are nonbinding than if they are formally obligatory – at least if the subject being regulated is complex and requires implementation by governments within their own territories.

There is little evidence that the degree of compliance with these codes is any less satisfactory than it would be if they were binding, at least if the political sensitivity level of the endeavor being regulated is relatively low. On the other hand, the aftermath of the Chernobyl nuclear reactor disaster shows that codes and guidelines may need to be hardened into treaty law when political sensitivities are likely to inhibit compliance. After that accident, IAEA guidelines on responses to nuclear accidents were promptly revised and transformed through negotiations into two conventions, in an effort to tighten the norms and to give greater assurance of compliance.[118]

The keys to effective norm-promulgation by codes and guidelines are the

---

[113] IAEA Safety Series, No. 6 (1985 ed.).   [114] IAEA Doc. INFCIRC/225/Rev.1 (1977).

[115] See IAEA Safety Series No. 50-SG-06 (1982).

[116] See IAEA Res. GC(XXXIV)/RES/530 (1990), reprinted in 30 ILM 557 (1991); and IAEA Doc. GC(XXXIV)920 (1990), reprinted in 30 *ILM* 558 (1991).

[117] Mohammed el-Baradei (interview), 12 *UN Observer & Int'l Rep.*, No. 6, at 3 (1990). See also O. Jankowitsch, "A Code of Practice on the International Transboundary Movement of Radioactive Waste," 32 *IAEA Bull.*, No. 4, at 28 (1990).

[118] The conventions are the Convention on Early Notification of a Nuclear Accident, Sept. 26, 1986, IAEA Doc. INFCIRC/335, reprinted in 25 *ILM* 1370 (1986), and the Convention on Assistance in the Case of a Nuclear Accident or Radiological Emergency, Sept. 26, 1986, IAEA Doc. INFCIRC/336, reprinted in 25 ILM 1377 (1986). See L. van Gorkom, "Nuclear Accidents: Two Conventions through Effective IAEA Action after Chernobyl," in *Effective Negotiation: Case Studies in Conference Diplomacy* 149 (J. Kaufmann ed., 1989).

care with which they are prepared, including the opportunity for input from governments and other entities that will be subject to them,[119] and the fact that government representatives and others whose job it is to carry them out often have had a significant hand in preparing them. These factors, plus the fact that codes and guidelines are often more technical and less political than other normative acts of a UN agency, set them apart as instruments with an impact often bordering on, and in some cases virtually equal to, that of treaty obligations.

III. *AD HOC* NORM-CREATION

Some UN-related agencies have adopted rules and principles essentially by common law methods. This has happened, for example, when an organization has a dispute-settlement or treaty-interpretation mechanism that acts with some degree of formality and with some attention to precedent.

The ILO Governing Body's Committee on Freedom of Association has evolved since 1951 from a body screening complaints of alleged violations of trade union rights to a quasi-adjudicative body making findings of fact and conclusions of law.[120] In the process of interpreting the ILO's freedom of association conventions, it has established some new trade union rights. For example, it has established the right to strike as a basic rule of international labor law, although no such right is spelled out in any of the freedom of association conventions or recommendations.[121] This carries with it the duty upon governments to refrain from measures precluding or significantly restricting the right to strike, except in the case of truly essential public services.[122] Similarly, the Committee has developed rights of trade unionists to basic civil liberties, including such things as freedom from arbitrary arrest and detention, in decisions that go well beyond the provisions of formal ILO conventions or recommendations.[123]

---

[119] See, e.g., B. Okere, "The Technique of International Maritime Legislation," 30 *Int'l & Comp. L. Q.* 513, 530–32 (1981).

[120] See G. von Potobsky, "Protection of Trade Union Rights: Twenty Years' Work by the Committee on Freedom of Association," 105 *Int'l Lab. Rev.* 69, 70 (1972).

[121] See J. Hodges-Aeberhard & A. Odero de Dios, "Principles of the Committee on Freedom of Association Concerning Strikes," 126 *Int'l Lab. Rev.* 543 (1987); A. Pouyat, "The ILO's Freedom of Association Standards and Machinery: A Summing Up," 121 *Int'l Lab. Rev.* 287, 297 (1982).

[122] The ILO Committee of Experts has come to the same conclusions as has the Committee on Freedom of Association regarding the right to strike and the corresponding governmental duties. See General Survey by the Committee of Experts on the Application of Conventions and Recommendations, Freedom of Association and Collective Bargaining, Int'l Labour Conf., 69th Sess. 62–66 (1983).

[123] See Pouyat, note 121 above, at 298–300; see also UN Doc. A/43/739, at 49 (1988). Decisions on civil liberties draw in part on the ILO General Conference's Resolution Concerning Trade Union Rights and Their Relation to Civil Liberties, in Int'l Labour Conf., 54th Sess., Record of Proc. at 733 (1970).

Ad hoc rule-making can emerge from formal interpretations of existing rules by such bodies as the Executive Board of the IMF[124] and the main committees of the IMO.[125] For example, in 1949 the IMF Executive Board issued an interpretation of the Fund Agreement that – if applied faithfully by domestic courts in member states – has the effect of superseding any inconsistent domestic choice-of-law rule in certain cases involving members' exchange control regulations.[126]

Ad hoc rule-making also occurs when agency secretariats interpret existing rules. Sometimes this is done relatively formally, as in the ILO, where the International Labour Office issues interpretations of labor conventions unless a request relates to an active dispute between members,[127] and in the Universal Postal Union, where the International Bureau interprets the Union's acts even when there is an active dispute (if all directly concerned postal administrations join in the request).[128]

Informal interpretations, often shaping standards of conduct not explicitly found in formal instruments, take place in the daily routine of agency affairs. These occur during person-to-person contacts with representatives of member governments in such contexts as meetings to steer governments toward compliance with existing norms, or in connection with technical assistance.

IV. CONCLUSION

UN-related agencies have been given, or have devised, an impressive variety of ways to promulgate norms to channel the conduct of their members.

---

[124] Fund Agreement, note 24 above, art. XXIX.

[125] According to arts. 69 and 70 of the IMO Convention, questions of interpretation are to be referred to the IMO Assembly, though interpretation by other organs is contemplated when questions arise during the exercise of their functions; an ICJ advisory opinion is the last resort. Convention on the International Maritime Organization, *International Organization and Integration*, note 22 above, pt. I.B.1.10.a, and in 1 IMO Basic Documents 11 (1986). In practice, IMO committees do most of the interpreting, and they do it with great care. Members have treated these interpretations as authoritative. Interview with Dr. Thomas A. Mensah, Assistant Secretary-General, IMO, July 22, 1988.

[126] See Unenforceability of Exchange Contracts, Dec. 446–4 (1949), in Selected Decisions and Selected Documents of the International Monetary Fund 325 (19th issue, 1994) (interpretation of Fund Agreement, art. VIII(2)(b)). See also the thorough discussions in J. Gold, *The Fund Agreement in the Courts* (4 vols., 1962, 1982, 1986 & 1989).

[127] See International Labour Office, The International Labour Code, I, 1951, Preface, at cviii–cix (1952); J. McMahon, "The Legislative Techniques of the International Labour Organization," 41 *Brit. Y. B. Int'l L.* 1, 90–91 (1965–66).

[128] See UPU Gen. Regs. art. 113(2) and annotation 2 thereto, reprinted in Annotated Code of the Universal Postal Union, 75, 117 (1991). See also M. Menon, "Universal Postal Union," *Int'l Conciliation* No. 552, at 41, 46 (1965). The Bureau's interpretations have been known to fill gaps in the Postal Convention and Regulations, pending their formal revision. See, e.g., the opinion on allocation among postal administrations of costs incurred in handling containerized mail, 1987 Report on the Work of the Union 88–91.

They go far beyond the traditional sources of international law – principally custom and treaties that are subject to orthodox ratification procedures – to include such normative instruments as "super-treaties" (treaties with strings attached such as a duty to submit them to a ratification process and a duty to report periodically to the promulgating agency on compliance); provisional application of some treaties before they formally enter into force; treaty-implementing standards that enter into force upon tacit consent, subject to a limited opt-out privilege; formally binding regulations, sometimes linked to an opt-out privilege; authoritative findings of legislative facts, to be implemented by regulatory regimes within or outside the agency; recommendations, often in the form of codes or guidelines, that clearly have more than hortatory design and effect; pronouncements developing a "common law" for members, including formal pronouncements as part of dispute-settlement proceedings or as reasoned interpretations by agency organs; and informal interpretations during contacts with individual members.

Despite the clear difference in theory between formally binding and nonbinding instruments, the demarcation between a UN-related agency's binding instruments and its normative, carefully articulated, nonbinding instruments is often much less clear when it comes to effectiveness in channeling conduct.[129] It is true that formal treaty obligations may be more susceptible to close supervision by the agency than are nonbinding standards, and that supervision should help to channel members' conduct. The ILO is a case in point. But in some organizations, even nonbinding norms may be effectively supervised, while formally binding ones may not be.[130]

The various types of instrument may be visualized as occupying bands, sometimes overlapping, on a continuum of legal obligation ranging from nonlaw to true law.[131] Informal exhortation would be at the low end of the continuum; formal treaty commitment is at the high end. Recommendations adopted by plenary organs fall between the extremes, and not all recommendations would occupy the same band. For example, recommendations serving virtually as protocols to treaties in force would occupy higher bands than would *ad hoc* resolutions. So would meticulously

---

[129] See, e.g., C. Schreuer, "Recommendations and the Traditional Sources of International Law," 20 *German Y. B. Int'l L.* 103, 105 (1977).

[130] See, e.g., G. van Hoof & K. de Vey Mestdagh, "Mechanisms of International Supervision in Supervisory Mechanisms," in *International Economic Organisations* 1, 30–31 (P. van Dijk ed., 1984).

[131] For an insightful analysis of the relativity of international normative obligation, stressing the degree of legitimacy of any given rule and of the process by which it has been promulgated, see T. Franck, *The Power of Legitimacy Among Nations* (1990). Professor Franck refers to international "rules" rather than to international "law."

prepared codes of conduct in relatively apolitical spheres where, for virtually all states, the benefits of cooperation clearly outweigh the costs.[132] WHO codes demonstrate the point. WHO has the authority to adopt binding standards, but finds for the most part that nonbinding codes serve the purpose as well. They are easier to adopt and to amend, without sacrificing much in terms of compliance.

Of course, there is a clear demarcation between the effect on a member that has accepted a rule or standard (expressly or tacitly) and a member that has effectively exercised a right to opt out of it.[133] There are also reasons to favor one type of normative instrument over another, depending on factors such as those discussed below. The point being made here is simply that, for members subject to whatever norm is being created, the expectation of compliance (the legal or quasi-legal effect) does not sharply diminish, as a matter of course, simply because a normative instrument is formally nonbinding.[134] A nonbinding instrument may be quite effective, provided that (a) it deals with subject areas in which some form of international order is widely regarded as important; (b) it has been promulgated in a procedural framework that gives members a meaningful opportunity to participate; and (c) it is sufficiently flexible to take account of any significant differences in the circumstances of member states – such as materially different stages of technological development if the standards in the instrument depend on technology for their application.

In some cases, significant recommendations have paved the way for subsequent treaty obligations. There may be a desire to formalize the obligation in order to strengthen the level of political commitment to the norms in question, or to subject members to a treaty supervisory system administered by the organization, or to enhance the likelihood that the regulatory standards will be incorporated into domestic law in member states. In such cases, practice under a recommendation may well demonstrate that a more formal obligation would be acceptable to governments and, once adopted, would be obeyed. ILO practice is in this vein.

Certain situations seem to call for regulation by formal treaty, even when

---

[132] See, e.g., H. Schermers, "The International Organizations," in *International Law: Achievements and Prospects* 67, 69, 71 (M. Bedjaoui ed., 1991).

[133] This does not necessarily depend on the opting-out member's compliance with its duty to notify the organization. The duty to notify may be a pure promise, rather than a condition precedent to the exercise of the right to opt out. It has been treated as such in connection with ICAO international standards.

[134] The Director-General of the IAEA has said it is not a matter for concern that many states have accepted nonbinding IAEA nuclear safety standards, but are not yet ready to convert them into binding obligations. "It may seem paradoxical but, while we find that legal commitments are not always fulfilled, it is not infrequent that non-binding commitments are faithfully complied with." H. Blix, "The Role of the IAEA in the Development of International Law," 58 *Nordic J. Int'l L.* 231, 238 (1989).

there have been no antecedent recommendations. This is so particularly when some governments are reluctant to commit substantial resources to comply with regulatory standards, or it is perceived that a high level of political commitment is needed, or governments are concerned about competitive disadvantage unless other governments – or perhaps only selected other governments – are formally committed to the same standards. Some IMO conventions fill in the latter scenario.

If the field to be regulated by treaty is such that relatively frequent revisions may be needed, as would be the case with respect to technical standards, the usual technique is to place detailed regulations in annexes that are subject to revision by a tacit-consent/opt-out procedure.[135] Such a procedure occupies a middle ground between the often difficult process of treaty modification by orthodox means and the easier process of setting and revising standards by pure recommendation. Organs of international organizations provide useful fora for consideration and initial approval of tacit-consent/opt-out revisions. ICAO and IMO have used this technique to advantage.

The use of UN-related agencies to establish legislative facts is a little-known and probably underused device. Agencies with technical expertise – WHO, FAO, WMO, IAEA, and others – are able to make scientific determinations that could form the basis for regulation, either by the same agency or by a separate organization. WHO's role in narcotics regulation is an example.

Another underrecognized phenomenon is the formulation of "common law" rules by organs asked to interpret treaty norms. The ILO's Committee on Freedom of Association, acting on a case-by-case basis, has played a pathbreaking role in formulating a body of trade union law to fill gaps in the conventions on freedom of association.

Few knowledgeable observers contend that the international community is yet ready for a true world legislature. Neither the United Nations nor its related agencies act as such. But they do find ways to channel members' conduct in discrete areas, and they often do it without the express consent of each member to each norm they promulgate. This ability to promulgate norms that are reasonably effective even as to passive participants in the system is a major contribution to the international legal process. It is significant theoretically, as a movement away from strict legal positivism and toward a flexible concept of international legal obligation.[136] Of course, it also has great practical importance, in a world where political, economic, technological, and cultural diversities tend to impede effective

---

[135] See, for example, the discussion of this technique in the context of technical standards, in ITU Doc. 328-E, at 3–4 (1989). Essentially the same point is made in IMO Doc. OPPR/PM/15, at 8 (1990).   [136] Cf. Skubiszewski, note 35 above, at 273.

norm-promulgation if no government has any degree of obligation without its explicit consent to the obligating norm. Departure from that positivist system enables organizations to circumvent such phenomena as "the bottom line rule" (multilateral treaties will reflect only the norms acceptable to the least enthusiastic party) and "the slowest boat rule" (multilateral treaties will enter into force only when the most dilatory of the group of required ratifiers gets around to signifying formal acceptance).[137]

It is quite possible to argue that this development is undemocratic in the sense that decisions essentially legislative in character are made without the participation of popularly elected parliaments.[138] But most of the norms promulgated without the explicit consent of all governments affected by them (and thus without even the indirect consent of persons within member states) are somewhere below the "true law" top of the legal continuum. Moreover, the normative system often gives governments an opportunity to opt out, thus giving peoples' representatives a role (albeit a negative one) in the decision-making process, to the extent that any given government is itself the product of a democratic domestic system. In the relatively few instances where an agency's promulgation regime is binding and offers no opportunity to opt out – as in the case of ICAO Rules of the Air over certain sea areas – the norms tend to be technical, with low political impact. Nevertheless, further attention needs to be given to developing new mechanisms to enable the public, or the public's elected representatives, to participate in international tacit-consent processes by which norms are promulgated. The need increases as the norms become policy driven, rather than purely technical.

Explicit consent by all affected nations has never been required for the development of customary norms, within or outside international organizations. Those norms are generated by the familiar process of assertion and acquiescence. Much the same process is involved when an organization adopts a new set of standards, or amends an existing set. The process goes on within the adopting body, and in the case of tacit-consent/opt-out regimes, it continues during the allotted time for objection. It allows international organizations to promulgate norms more efficiently and with greater precision than could be done by traditional custom-generating processes, without all the disadvantages of orthodox treaty-making. Their norm-promulgating techniques, and the legal regimes that emerge from the use of those techniques, are indispensable to the conduct of modern international relations throughout the spectrum of human endeavors embraced by UN-related agencies.

---

[137] See Sand, note 35 above, at 6, 14–15.   [138] Cf. Kaiser, note 88 above, at 713–15.

SELECTED BIBLIOGRAPHY

Alexandrowicz, C., *The Law-making Functions of the Specialised Agencies of the United Nations* (Angus & Robertson, 1973)

Ameri, H., *Politics and Process in the Specialized Agencies of the United Nations* (Gower, 1982)

Bowett, D., *The Law of International Institutions* (Stevens & Sons, 4th ed., 1982)

The Effectiveness of International Decisions (S. Schwebel ed.; Oceana, 1971)

A Handbook on International Organizations (R.-J. Dupuy ed.; Nijhoff, 1988)

International Organization and Integration (P. Kapteyn, P. Kooijmans, R. Lauwaars, & H. Schermers eds.; Nijhoff, 2d rev. ed., 1981)

Jacobson, H., *Networks of Interdependence: International Organizations and the Global Political System* (Knopf, 2d ed., 1984)

Kirgis, F., *International Organizations in Their Legal Setting* (West, 2d ed., 1993)

Leive, D., *International Regulatory Regimes*, II (Lexington Books, 1976)

Luard, E., *International Agencies: The Emerging Framework of Interdependence* (Oceana, 1977)

Morgenstern, F., *Legal Problems of International Organizations* (Grotius, 1986)

Schermers, H., *International Institutional Law* (Sijthoff & Noordhoff, 1980)

Yemin, E., *Legislative Powers in the United Nations and Specialized Agencies* (Sijthoff, 1969)

PART II

SUBSTANTIVE LAW

CHAPTER FOUR

FORCE AND ARMS

John F. Murphy

I. INTRODUCTION

The "law" on the use of force that has developed through the United Nations is substantial indeed. As Article 1, paragraphs 1 and 2 of the UN Charter suggest, the primary purposes of the United Nations are: "(1) To maintain international peace and security, and to that end: to take effective collective measures for the prevention and removal of threats to the peace, and for the suppression of acts of aggression or other breaches of the peace, and to bring about by peaceful means, and in conformity with the principles of justice and international law, adjustment or settlement of international disputes or situations which might lead to a breach of the peace"; and "(2) To develop friendly relations among nations based on respect for the principle of equal rights and self-determination of peoples, and to take other appropriate measures to strengthen universal peace."

The United Nations Charter contains a host of provisions relevant to the use of force. For example, several General Assembly resolutions, adopted without dissent or with near unanimity, have restated, amplified, and clarified the meaning of these Charter provisions. Perhaps the most authoritative is the 1970 Declaration on Principles of International Law Concerning Friendly Relations and Co-operation Among States in Accordance with the Charter of the United Nations (Friendly Relations Declaration).[1] Although some dispute exists in regard to the precise legal status of the Declaration, it is generally regarded as an authoritative interpretation of broad principles of international law expressed in the Charter.[2] Another, and more controversial, example is the General Assembly's "Definition of Aggression" resolution.[3]

---

[1] GA Res. 2625, UN GAOR, 26th Sess., Supp. No. 28, at 121, UN Doc. A/8028 (1971).
[2] See R. Rosenstock, "The Declaration of Principles of International Law Concerning Friendly Relations: A Survey," 65 *AJIL* 713, 714 (1971).
[3] GA Res. 3314, UN GAOR, 29th Sess., Supp. No. 31, at 142, UN Doc. A/0631 (1975).

The UN Charter does not speak to intervention by states; rather, under Article 2(7) it precludes the Organization itself from intervening "in matters which are essentially within the domestic jurisdiction of any state." Hence the General Assembly's Declaration on the Inadmissibility of Intervention in the Domestic Affairs of States and the Protection of Their Independence and Sovereignty,[4] adopted in 1965 by a vote of 109 to none with one abstention (the United Kingdom),[5] takes on special legal significance. The Declaration, *inter alia,* provides that: "No State has the right to intervene, directly or indirectly, for any reason whatever, in the internal or external affairs of any other State. Consequently, armed intervention and all other forms of interference or attempted threats against the personality of the State or against its political, economic and cultural elements are condemned."[6] The Declaration also provides that "no State shall organize, assist, foment, finance, incite or tolerate subversive, terrorist or armed activities directed towards the violent overthrow of the regime of another State, or interfere in civil strife in another State."[7]

The Security Council and the General Assembly are the primary organs of the United Nations that have responsibility under the Charter to regulate the use of force. Sharp debate has arisen over the precise allocation of authority in this area between the Council and the Assembly, and a focal point of this debate has been the Assembly's "Uniting for Peace" resolution,[8] whereby the Assembly claims the authority to recommend collective measures in situations where the Council is unable to deal with a breach of the peace or act of aggression due to a veto. The International Court of Justice's advisory opinion in the Certain Expenses case,[9] while not directly addressing the legality of the Uniting for Peace resolution, contains dictum relevant to this issue and generally constitutes an authoritative discussion of the Charter's allocation of powers between the Council and the Assembly. Similarly, the Court's advisory opinion in the Namibia case[10] has much to say about the scope of decision-making authority in both organs. Even when Council and Assembly decisions are not regarded as binding, they may be considered as interpretations of the Charter entitled to some weight.

The "case law" of the United Nations on the use of force consists

---

[4] GA Res. 2131, UN GAOR, 20th Sess., Supp. No. 14, at 11, UN Doc. A/6014 (1966).

[5] UN GAOR, 20th Sess., First Comm., at 430–31, UN Doc. A/C.1/SR 1422 (Dec. 20, 1965).

[6] Declaration on the Inadmissibility of Intervention in the Domestic Affairs of States and the Protection of Their Independence and Sovereignty, note 4 above, art. 1.

[7] *Ibid.*, art. 2.

[8] GA Res/337A, UN GAOR, 5th Sess., Supp. No. 20, at 10, UN Doc. A/1775 (1951).

[9] Certain Expenses of the United Nations, 1962 ICJ 151 (Advisory Opinion).

[10] Advisory Opinion on the Continued Presence of South Africa in Namibia (South West Africa), 1971 ICJ 16.

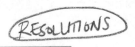 *RESOLUTIONS*

primarily of Security Council resolutions. In such cases as Korea, Rhodesia, South Africa, and Iraq, among others, Security Council resolutions have developed the law of the Charter.

Certain interpretations or legal opinions by the Secretary-General on the use of force also may carry some weight. As the chief administrative officer of the United Nations,[11] the Secretary-General is obliged to carry out functions assigned him by the principal organs of the Organization, including the General Assembly and the Security Council.[12] He has no independent law-making authority. His responsibility is rather to implement resolutions of the deliberate organs pursuant to their terms, which, however, may at times be cast in the most general language. In such cases the Secretary-General must interpret the resolution himself. Secretary-General Dag Hammarskjöld, for example, in implementing Security Council resolutions that authorized him to provide the government of the Congo with military assistance, created considerable controversy with his interpretations of the authority conferred upon him by these resolutions.

ICJ DECISIONS

Several decisions and advisory opinions of the International Court of Justice bear on the use of force. Although the doctrine of *stare decisis* does not apply to ICJ decisions, and such decisions do not create law in the common law sense, they nonetheless constitute an authoritative statement of the law and are a crucially important part of the international legal process.

A significant factor in the development of United Nations law on the use of force is the practice of states within and outside the Organization. This state practice consists of the conclusion of treaties (the North Atlantic Treaty Organization [NATO] Treaty and several non-aggression pacts, for example) and claims and counter-claims in diplomatic intercourse regarding the content of applicable norms. Some contend that votes in United Nations organs constitute state practice, although this proposition is controversial. At a minimum these votes may constitute evidence of *opinio juris*; that is, that states are engaging in the practice under a sense of legal obligation.

PRACTICE & AGREE-MENTS

Finally, UN law may be developed through the writings of eminent jurists. Such writings may include reports of the International Law Commission, a subsidiary organ of the General Assembly that has addressed use-of-force issues.

JURISTS

This chapter begins with a discussion of the United Nations system for regulation of the use of force, both the paradigm set forth in the United Nations Charter and its implementation in practice. The discussion focuses first on Charter limitations on the use of force by states and then on the

---

[11] See UN Charter, art. 97. [12] *Ibid.*, art. 98.

authority of the United Nations to regulate the use of force through the peaceful settlement of disputes, collective security, peacekeeping, and regional arrangements. As to each of these areas, the United Nations system in practice will be examined. Here we will see that practice often deviates from the paradigm as the Organization has striven to adapt to a rapidly changing international environment.

II. THE UNITED NATIONS SYSTEM: PARADIGM AND PRACTICE

A. Limitations on the use of force by states

In the wake of the carnage of World War II participants at the Dumbarton Oaks and San Francisco conferences determined that, unlike the Covenant of the League,[13] the United Nations Charter should outlaw war.[14] To this end they agreed that states should accept the obligations to settle all disputes peaceably and to refrain from the use of force in their international relations. A substantial amount of scholarly attention has been directed to the second of these obligations. Relatively less consideration has been given to the first, and it is to this obligation that we now turn.

1. The obligation to settle disputes peaceably

The Charter requires that "all Members shall settle their international disputes by peaceful means in such a manner that international peace and security, and justice, are not endangered."[15] Later the Charter is more specific about the "peaceful means" that should be employed, noting that "The parties to any dispute, the continuance of which is likely to endanger the maintenance of international peace and security, shall, first of all, seek a solution by negotiation, enquiry, mediation, conciliation, arbitration, judicial settlement, resort to regional agencies or arrangements or other peaceful means of their own choice."[16] The obligation is to settle such disputes peaceably. The choice of means is up to the parties. The Charter further obligates parties to such a dispute, if they fail to settle the matter by the means specified, to refer it to the Security Council.[17]

---

[13] The Covenant of the League of Nations prohibited member states from resorting to war in some circumstances, but not all; in particular, members were permitted to resort to war in cases where specified means of peaceful settlement had failed.

[14] See O. Schachter, "The Right of States to Use Armed Force," 82 *Mich. L. Rev.* 1620 (1984).

[15] UN Charter, art. 2, para. 3.   [16] *Ibid.*, art. 33, para. 1.   [17] *Ibid.*, art. 37, para. 1.

2. Articles 2(4) and 51

The drafters of the UN Charter sought to outlaw "war"; however, because the terms "aggression" and "war" – emphasized in the Covenant of the League of Nations – had caused problems of interpretation for the League in practice, the drafters of the United Nations Charter decided on a different approach. Article 2, paragraph 4 of the Charter provides that:

All Members shall refrain in their international relations from the threat or use of force against the territorial integrity or political independence of any state, or in any other manner inconsistent with the Purposes of the United Nations.

But this approach was not uniformly followed elsewhere in drafting the Charter, and this has raised questions as to the proper interpretation and application of Article 2(4). For example, Article 1 proclaims the first purpose to be the maintenance of international peace and security by taking effective collective measures to prevent or remove "threats to the peace" and to suppress "acts of aggression or other breaches of the peace." It does not use the words "force" or "threat of force." The application of the qualifying words "in conformity with the principles of justice and international law" to the Organization's first purpose, moreover, has led some to claim that, as long as law and justice are served, recourse to force may be justified. Similarly, the principle of self-determination in Article 1(2) has been cited to support the contention that force can be used on behalf of "wars of national liberation." Also, as discussed later, the Security Council is directed "to determine the existence of any threat to the peace, breach of the peace, or act of aggression" and to make recommendations or decide on measures to restore international peace and security. This means that there is "no necessary identity between what is legally prohibited by Article 2(4) and what the Council seeks to control in the discharge of its responsibilities."[18]

Those who favor limited constraints on the right of states to use armed force have relied on textual analysis to interpret Article 2(4) as authorizing a number of exceptions to that article's prohibition against the "threat or use of force." Some have claimed that these words greatly qualify the prohibition against force. The qualifying language, for example, would allow the use of force solely to vindicate or secure a legal right, i.e., an exercise in self-help. As Oscar Schachter has observed, this argument has enjoyed little governmental or scholarly support.

Similar textual arguments have been made to support the use of force by states to take territory they consider rightfully theirs (e.g., Argentina and

---

[18] L. M. Goodrich, E. Hambro, & A. Simons, *Charter of the United Nations* 46 (1969).

the Malvinas/Falkland Islands, Iraq and Kuwait), or a right of "humanitarian intervention," and the right to self-determination (including, in its most recent manifestation, a claim of right to overthrow a repressive or tyrannical government, as well as to achieve freedom from foreign domination). Schachter examined each of these arguments in detail in recent writings[19] and has concluded:

Many governments attach importance to the principle that any forcible incursion into the territory of another state is a derogation of that state's territorial sovereignty and political independence, irrespective of the motive for such intervention or its long-term consequences. Accordingly, they tend to hold to the sweeping article 2(4) prohibition against the use or threat of force, except where self-defense or Security Council enforcement action is involved.[20]

In addition to these textual arguments, commentators have argued that recent developments in international relations have significantly altered the conditions on which the restrictive rules were based.[21] The recent developments most often cited are widespread violations of Article 2(4)[22] and the failure of the United Nations system of collective security.[23] Widespread violations of Article 2(4), some contend, constitute state practice that has superseded the Charter provision and its customary law analog. This argument has several flaws. First, there are relatively few blatant violations of Article 2(4). Moreover, almost every clearly illegal use of armed force has been condemned by large numbers of states and by the political organs of the United Nations. Most important, this argument has not been accepted by states. On the contrary, many states, including the United States, have taken the legal position that Article 2(4) is a peremptory norm (*jus cogens*). The argument also was expressly rejected by the International Court of Justice in *Nicaragua* v. *United States*.[24]

As to the failure of the United Nations collective security system, the legislative history of Article 2(4) lends no support to the thesis that the effective functioning of a system of collective security is regarded as a condition of the continuing validity of the article's severe constraints on the

[19] See Schachter, note 14 above; O. Schachter, "In Defense of International Rules on the Use of Force," 53 *U. Chi. L. Rev.* 113 (1986) (hereinafter Schachter, "Use of Force"); O. Schachter, "Self-Defense and the Rule of Law," 83 *AJIL* 259 (1989).
[20] Schachter, note 14 above, at 1632.
[21] As reported in Schachter, "Use of Force," note 19 above at 113, 124–25.
[22] See T. Franck, "Who Killed Article 2(4)? or: Changing Norms Governing the Use of Force by States," 64 *AJIL* 809 (1970); E. Rostow, "The Legality of the International Use of Force by and from States," 10 *Yale J. Int'l L.* 286 (1985).
[23] A. V. Thomas & A. J. Thomas, Jr., *Non-Intervention* 209 (1956).
[24] Military and Paramilitary Activities in and against Nicaragua (*Nicar.* v. *US*), 1986 ICJ 14, 98 (Judgment of June 27).

use of force.[25] Moreover, recent developments may have given new life to the Charter's concept of collective security.

A variant of this changed circumstances argument relies on the concept of reciprocity – widespread violations of law by some states should release others from the obligation to comply, an argument by analogy to the right of one treaty party to suspend the treaty between it and a violator for a violation especially affecting that party.[26] Several problems are inherent in this argument. First, as we have seen, Article 2(4), in addition to being a treaty provision, is widely regarded as an archetypical peremptory norm from which no derogation is permitted. Second, and significantly, the reciprocity thesis finds no support in state practice; no state has cited another state's violation of Article 2(4) as a basis to suspend that provision's obligations in relations between it and the violator. Third, the Charter permits a variety of responses to a breach of Article 2(4): the right to self-defense in the event of an armed attack; recourse to the Security Council or the General Assembly; and, if a jurisdictional basis is available under its statute, to the International Court of Justice.[27]

The justification for recourse to armed force most often cited by states is, of course, the right to self-defense. Article 51 provides:

Nothing in the present Charter shall impair the inherent right of individual or collective self-defense if an armed attack occurs against a Member of the United Nations, until the Security Council has taken measures necessary to maintain international peace and security. Measures taken by Members in the exercise of this right of self-defense shall be immediately reported to the Security Council and shall not in any way affect the authority and responsibility of the Security Council under the present chapter to take at any time such action as it deems necessary in order to maintain or restore international peace and security.

The issues that have arisen with respect to interpretation and application of Article 51 are at least as numerous and as hotly debated as those that have arisen with respect to Article 2(4). Some of the more prominent of these issues include: (a) whether Article 51 simply preserves the right of self-defense as it existed under customary international law prior to adoption of the Charter or places further limits on that right; (b) the relationship between self-defense and the requirement that states settle

[25] See, e.g., D. Noncic, *The Problem of Sovereignty in the Charter and in the Practice of the United Nations* 72, 76–77 (1970) (guarantees of territorial integrity in art. 2(4) were not intended to limit the article's broad prohibition of self-help measures), cited in Schachter, "Use of Force," note 19 above, at 125–26 n. 56.

[26] See Address by Ambassador Jeane Kirkpatrick, "Law and Reciprocity," reprinted in Proc. of the 78th Ann. Meeting of the Am. Soc'y of Int'l L. 59, 67 (1984).

[27] See Schachter, "Use of Force," note 19 above, at 129–30.

disputes through peaceful measures; (c) the meaning of proportionality and its relationship to the doctrine of necessity; (d) the content of the right to collective self-defense; (e) the circumstances in which, if any, self-defense can serve as a justification for intervention by armed force in internal conflicts; and (f) the extent to which, if at all, Article 51 of the Charter precludes the use of force in self-defense once the Security Council has acted.

B. UN regulation of the use of force

The drafters of the Charter envisaged that severe limitations on the use of force by states would be offset by the United Nations playing an active role in the maintenance of international peace and security, including, where necessary, the use of armed force against an aggressor state. With rare exceptions, the United Nations has not been able to play the role envisaged by the drafters of the Charter. Some commentators have claimed that the United Nations' failure to fulfill its responsibilities has released member states from the constraints on the use of force imposed by Article 2(4). This claim has not been accepted by most scholars or reflected in state practice. Moreover, although the United Nations has not functioned according to the paradigm, it has taken steps in practice to adapt law and the legal process to the realities of the post-World War II environment, and its record in maintaining international peace and security is better than some of its critics give it credit for. We turn now to a consideration of the basic Charter paradigm, the extent to which UN practice has deviated from that paradigm, and the legal implications of this deviation.

1. Peaceful settlement of disputes: the UN's authority

As noted previously, the Charter enjoins states to settle their disputes peacefully. To what extent does the United Nations have the authority to enforce, or at least to facilitate the fulfillment of, these obligations?

Under the Charter the United Nations has substantial authority to become involved in any dispute that may threaten international peace and security. For its part the Security Council is given "primary responsibility" under the Charter for the maintenance of international peace and security.[28] The Council *may* "investigate any dispute, or any situation which might lead to international friction or give rise to a dispute, in order to determine whether the continuance of the dispute or situation is likely to endanger the maintenance of international peace and security."[29] The

---

[28] UN Charter, art. 24, para. 1.   [29] *Ibid.*, art. 34.

Council is required, "when it deems necessary," to call on the parties to a dispute likely to endanger the maintenance of international peace and security to settle it by peaceful means.[30] The Council is also authorized by the Charter to recommend appropriate procedures for settling such disputes[31] – while bearing in mind that "legal disputes should as a general rule be referred by the parties to the International Court of Justice."[32] The Council's authority to recommend terms of settlement is normally limited to situations where it is satisfied that the parties' efforts to settle peaceably have failed and that the continuance of the dispute is likely to endanger the maintenance of international peace and security.[33] If all parties to any dispute so request, however, the Council may make recommendations regarding a peaceful settlement to the dispute.[34]

A recent exercise of the Council's residuary authority under Article 24 would seem to be the provisions in the Council's landmark Resolution 687,[35] the cease-fire resolution in the Iraq–Kuwait conflict, which demand (a) that Iraq and Kuwait respect the inviolability of the international boundary and allocation of islands between them set forth in a 1963 agreement; (b) call upon the Secretary-General to lend his assistance to help Iraq and Kuwait demarcate the boundary between them; and (c) decide to guarantee the inviolability of this boundary. As pointed out by the British government,[36] these provisions were not determining the boundary between Iraq and Kuwait (that had been done by the 1963 agreement); instead, these provisions were requiring the demarcation of the boundary, as well as monitoring of it, and guaranteeing the inviolability of the boundary against future violations. The dispute between Iraq and Kuwait over the boundary threatened international peace and security, and the Council had the authority under Article 24 to adopt these provisions in order to meet this threat.

By the terms of the Charter, the General Assembly is assigned a relatively subsidiary role in the maintenance of international peace and security. It is to serve as a forum for public discussion and multilateral diplomacy designed to achieve the peaceful adjustment of unsatisfactory situations and the acceptance of the principles of cooperation.[37]

Although it can discuss any question relating to the maintenance of international peace and security brought before it by a member state,[38] the Assembly is prohibited from making recommendations while the Security

---

[30] *Ibid.*, art. 33, para. 2.   [31] *Ibid.*, art. 36, para. 1.   [32] *Ibid.*, art. 36 para. 3.
[33] *Ibid.*, art. 37, para. 2.   [34] *Ibid.*, art. 38.
[35] SC Res. 687 (April 3, 1991), reprinted in 30 *ILM* 847 (1991).
[36] See S/PV 2981, at 112–15, reported in A. Lowe & C. Warbrick, "Current Developments: Public International Law," 40 *Int'l & Comp. L. Q.* 965, 969 (1991).
[37] See generally, UN Charter, arts. 10, 11, 12, & 14.   [38] *Ibid.*, art. 11, para. 2.

Council is dealing with the issue.[39] In cases where "action" is required, the Assembly must refer the issue to the Security Council.[40] The ICJ has given a narrow interpretation to the word "action," however, limiting it to coercive measures of enforcement, and an expansive interpretation to the "measures" that the General Assembly may recommend for the peaceful adjustment of any situation "which it deems likely to impair the general welfare or friendly relations among nations."[41] Hence, in practice the Assembly has assumed, at least until recently, a greater role in the maintenance of international peace and security than a strict reading of the Charter would indicate. With the recent rapprochement between the Soviet Union (now Russia) and the United States in the Security Council, the General Assembly has returned to the more modest role envisioned for it in the Charter.

Under the Charter, the Secretary-General becomes the chief administrative officer of the United Nations.[42] An issue that has arisen regarding the Secretary-General, and one that has created tension in the Organization in the context of the pacific settlement of disputes, is the extent to which he can also be regarded as an international executive with some measure of autonomy – both from member states and from the representative organs of the Organization itself. As also noted elsewhere in this study, some measure of support for such a role is found in the terms of the Charter. Therein, the Secretary-General is specifically directed not to seek or receive instructions from any government. He and his staff are to act as international officials responsible only to the Organization.[43] The Secretary-General's authority to bring to the Security Council any matter he believes may threaten the maintenance of international peace and security[44] has been interpreted to include the right to conduct independent inquiries and to engage in informal diplomacy regarding potentially dangerous situations.

The political organs of the United Nations normally refrain from attempting to enforce the obligation of states to settle their disputes peacefully and attempt instead to facilitate such settlement. In this respect the political organs may serve as mediators or conciliators.

In the wake of its decision in *Nicaragua* v. *United States*, and termination by the United States of its acceptance of the compulsory jurisdiction of the International Court of Justice, considerable attention has been directed toward the role of the Court in the peaceful resolution of disputes.[45] The expectations of the founders of the Court were that "the judicial process

---

[39] *Ibid.*, art. 12.   [40] *Ibid.*, art. 11, para. 2.
[41] Certain Expenses of the United Nations, 1962 ICJ 151 (Advisory Opinion).
[42] UN Charter, art. 97.   [43] *Ibid.*, art. 100, para. 1.   [44] *Ibid.*, art. 99.
[45] See *The International Court of Justice at a Crossroads* (L. Damrosch ed., 1987).

will have a central place in the plans of the United Nations for the settlement of international disputes by peaceful means."[46] With the benefit of hindsight, one can say that the expectations of the founders were perhaps overly ambitious. States recently have begun to make greater use of the Court. At this writing the Court has eleven cases pending. Moreover, in light of the current movement toward a less confrontational world order, one may be guardedly optimistic that the Court may be able to play a still more meaningful role in the control of international violence.

2. Collective security: the UN's authority

Before considering the collective security approach of the United Nations, it is useful to examine the salient aspects of a collective security system. The theoretical model of collective security requires guarantees that an attack by any member state of the system will be resisted by all the other states whose contribution to the common defense may be required.

Under the collective security approach neutrality is theoretically impermissible since by definition neutrality requires that a state refuse to distinguish between an aggressor and its victim. In practice, however, because many post-World War II conflicts have been civil wars, with states intervening from outside, it has often been difficult to determine who was the aggressor and who was the victim. Also, a collective security system assumes that the world is so interdependent that a breach of order anywhere threatens the security interests of all states, even those geographically remote from the breach.

Perhaps the most important feature of the collective security approach is "its theoretical promise to make any victim of aggressive attack conspicuously stronger than its attacker."[47] That is, a potential victim state should be able to call upon the combined military might of the community if it becomes the victim of aggression. Conversely, a potential aggressor should be deterred by the realization that its aggression will be met by a massive collective response.

The United Nations Charter gives "primary responsibility" and considerable discretion for maintaining international peace and security to the Security Council.[48] The Council is authorized under Chapter VII of the Charter to determine the existence of any threat to the peace, breach of the peace, or act of aggression, and to make recommendations and decisions as to whether economic or military sanctions should be employed.[49] Any such

---

[46] I. Claude, *Swords into Plowshares* 245 (1971).

[47] I. Claude, "Theoretical Approaches to National Security and World Order," in *National Security Law* 38 (J. Moore, F. Tipson, & R. Turner eds., 1990).

[48] UN Charter, arts. 27, 39.   [49] *Ibid.*, arts. 39, 41, & 42.

decision of the Council is binding upon member states under Articles 25 and 48 of the Charter. At the same time the five permanent members of the Council – the United States, Great Britain, Russia, China, and France – are able through the veto power to prevent any enforcement action of which they disapprove.

Until Iraq invaded Kuwait, the Security Council made relatively little use of its authority under Chapter VII. Indeed, in only one case, Korea, did the Council take action to meet an aggression, and it was able to act in this case only because of the fortuitous circumstance that the Soviet delegate had previously walked out in protest at the Council's decision to seat the Nationalist Chinese as the lawful representative of China. Rather than taking a decision to use armed force pursuant to Articles 42 and 43 of the Charter,[50] the Council merely issued in June 1950 a recommendation that members of the United Nations repel the armed attack by providing military or other assistance to a unified command under the United States, requested the United States to designate the commander of these forces, and authorized the unified command at its discretion to use the UN flag concurrently with the flags of the various participating countries.[51] On August 1, 1950, the Soviet delegate returned to the Council and blocked it from taking any further action.

In response, and at the initiative of the United States of America, the General Assembly adopted the so-called "Uniting for Peace" resolution.[52] The resolution provided that the General Assembly would meet to recommend collective measures in situations where the Council was unable to deal with a breach of the peace or act of aggression because of a veto. In

---

[50] Article 42 of the UN Charter provides:

Should the Security Council consider that measures provided for in Article 41 would be inadequate or have proven to be inadequate, it may take such action by air, sea, or land forces as may be necessary to maintain or restore international peace and security. Such action may include demonstrations, blockade, and other operations by air, sea, or land forces of Members of the United Nations.

Article 43 of the Charter provides:

1. All Members of the United Nations, in order to contribute to the maintenance of international peace and security, undertake to make available to the Security Council, on its call and in accordance with a special agreement or agreements, armed forces, assistance, and facilities, including rights of passage, necessary for the purpose of maintaining international peace and security.

2. Such agreement or agreements shall govern the numbers and types of forces, their degree of readiness and general location, and the nature of the facilities and assistance to be provided.

3. The agreement or agreements shall be negotiated as soon as possible on the initiative of the Security Council. They shall be concluded between the Security Council and Members and between the Security Council and groups of Members and shall be subject to ratification by the signatory states in accordance with their respective constitutional processes.

[51] For further discussion, see J. Murphy, *The United Nations and the Control of International Violence* 29–33 (1982).   [52] GA Res. 377A (Nov. 3, 1950).

such a case a special emergency Assembly session could be convened within twenty-four hours, by a procedural vote not subject to veto, of any seven (now nine) Council members. On February 1, 1951, in response to China's armed intervention in Korea and with the Council unable to act, the Assembly, acting under Uniting for Peace procedures, passed a resolution condemning the Chinese action as aggression, calling upon them to withdraw their forces from Korea, and recommending that all states lend every assistance to the United Nations action in Korea.[53]

In light of the International Court of Justice's advisory opinion in the Certain Expenses case, it is questionable whether the General Assembly has the authority it claims in the Uniting for Peace resolution to recommend the establishment of an armed force under its auspices to enforce the peace against an aggressor state.[54] The question is largely academic now, however, because with the loss of their control of voting patterns in the General Assembly, the permanent members have tacitly agreed to the Soviet position expressed in the Certain Expenses case – that only the Security Council should authorize the use of armed force.

Prior to the Iraq–Kuwait crisis the Security Council twice employed its authority under Article 41 of the Charter[55] to apply mandatory economic sanctions – against Rhodesia during the 1960s[56] and South Africa in 1977.[57] In the case of Rhodesia it is worth noting that the Council also authorized Great Britain, pursuant to its request, to use military force against a specific oil tanker heading for the port of Beira, Mozambique, with a full cargo of oil destined for Rhodesia.[58] In contrast to its actions concerning Korea, the Council explicitly authorized the use of military force by decisions rather than by recommendation. Although the Council determined under Chapter VII that the situation in Rhodesia constituted a threat to the peace, it failed to specify any particular articles of Chapter VII as the basis for its authorizing Great Britain to employ armed force. There would seem to be three possible bases under the Charter for the Council's action: Article 40, Article 42, or the Council's general power under Chapter VII. Each of these will be discussed in turn.

Article 40 authorizes the Security Council to "prevent an aggravation of

---

[53] GA Res. 498 (Feb. 1, 1951).
[54] For discussion, see Murphy, note 51 above, at 81–82.
[55] Article 41 provides:

> The Security Council may decide what measures not involving the use of armed force are to be employed to give effect to its decisions, and it may call upon the Members of the United Nations to apply such measures. These may include complete or partial interruption of economic relations and of rail, sea, air, postal, telegraphic, radio, and other means of communication, and the severance of diplomatic relations.

[56] See Murphy, note 51 above, at 139–46.   [57] *Ibid.*, at 146.
[58] SC Res. 217 (Nov. 12, 1965).

the situation" and, before making recommendations or deciding upon Article 41 or 42 measures, to "call upon the parties concerned to comply with such measures as it deems necessary or desirable." Secretary-General Dag Hammarskjöld characterized UN military operations undertaken in the Congo, pursuant to a Security Council resolution,[59] to prevent civil war as "provisional measures" under Article 40.[60] In authorizing Great Britain to use armed force to intercept the tanker, the Council could be viewed as taking preventive action to avoid an aggravation of the situation that could have led to a recommendation or decision to use armed force against the illegal regime in Rhodesia.[61]

The use of Article 42 as a possible basis for Security Council action is complicated by the article's uncertain relationship with Article 43. There seems little doubt that, absent the conclusion of the kinds of agreements envisaged under Article 43, the Council has no authority to command member states to commit their armed forces to a UN military enforcement action. This would not necessarily preclude the Council, however, from authorizing a member state or states to use armed force to maintain or restore international peace and security.

Finally, the Security Council may have had the authority to authorize Great Britain to use force simply on the basis of its general authority to maintain international peace and security under Chapter VII. As demonstrated recently by the Council's actions during the Iraq–Kuwait crisis, the Security Council often does not refer to specific articles when acting under Chapter VII. Moreover, according to the ICJ's advisory opinion on Namibia, the "members of the United Nations have conferred upon the Security Council powers commensurate with its responsibility for the maintenance of international peace and security. The only limitations are the fundamental principles and purposes found in Chapter I of the Charter."[62] Although this proposition is debatable, if correct it would afford the Council maximum flexibility in dealing with threats to the peace and enable it to pass resolutions in such cases without a fixed basis in any particular article of the Charter.

(a) The Iraq–Kuwait crisis
Surely the most extraordinary example of UN exercises in collective security is the Organization's response to Iraq's invasion of Kuwait on August 2, 1990. The Security Council adopted numerous resolutions[63]

---

[59] UN Doc. S/4741 (Feb. 21, 1961).
[60] For discussion, see Murphy, note 51 above, at 154.   [61] See *ibid.*, at 139–46.
[62] Note 10 above.
[63] The UN Security Council resolutions have the following numbers (in order of their adoption): 660, 661, 662, 664, 665, 666, 667, 669, 670, 674, 677, 678, 686, 687, 688, 689, 692, 699, 700, 705, 706, 707, 712, 715.

and took a variety of other measures to meet the aggression and to ameliorate its effects. The situation continues to develop, and the final outcome has yet to be determined. Still, the crisis provides a textbook example of the prospects for and the problems raised by the collective security approach to maintaining international peace and security. Because of length constraints, this chapter does not attempt an exhaustive analysis of the situation in the Gulf. Rather, it attempts to highlight the most significant legal developments whose importance transcends this particular crisis.

In immediate response to the invasion the Security Council passed Resolution 660[64] on August 2, 1990. Expressly acting under Articles 39 and 40 of the Charter, the Council, *inter alia*, determined that the invasion constituted a breach of international peace and security, demanded that Iraq withdraw immediately and unconditionally from Kuwait, and called upon Iraq and Kuwait to begin "intensive negotiations" for the resolution of their differences. With one exception, this was the last time the Council referred to a specific article in Chapter VII. In its later resolutions the Council either referred generally to Chapter VII as the basis for its action or made no reference to specific provisions of the Charter.

By adopting Resolution 660, the Security Council rejected Iraq's contention that Kuwait was part of its territory and affirmed the proposition that territorial claims do not justify the use of armed force. Similar claims were made by Iraq when it began its war against Iran, by Argentina when it invaded the Falkland/Malvinas Islands, and by India when it moved its troops into Goa. The Security Council's reactions to these incidents had left a record "not free from ambiguity," although on balance there appeared to be "no significant support among states for so far-reaching an exception to Article 2(4)."[65]

On August 6, 1990, referring to Chapter VII, the Council adopted Resolution 661[66] which imposed a trade and financial embargo against Iraq and occupied Kuwait; established a sanctions committee, which consists of all Security Council members, to monitor implementation of the sanctions; and forbade the recognition of any regime established in Kuwait by Iraq. The preamble of the resolution contains a paragraph that affirmed "the inherent right of individual or collective self-defence, in response to the armed attack by Iraq against Kuwait." Although no specific Charter provision was cited, the sanctions were the type envisaged by the terms of Article 41.

In response to Iraq's declaration of a "comprehensive and internal

[64] SC Res. 660 (Aug. 2, 1990), reprinted in 29 *ILM* 1325 (1990).
[65] Schachter, note 14 above, at 1627–28.
[66] SC Res. 661 (Aug. 6, 1990), reprinted in 29 *ILM* 1325 (1990).

merger" with Kuwait, on August 9 the Council adopted a resolution[67] by which it decided that annexation of Kuwait by Iraq has no legal validity and is considered null and void, called on states and international organizations not to recognize the annexation, and demanded that Iraq rescind its annexation. Rosalyn Higgins has suggested that "the Security Council may make authoritative and binding interpretations of Members' legal obligations under the Charter, even if such legal obligations as such are not covered by the Charter."[68] This may be *a fortiori* the case where the dispute involves the maintenance of international peace and security for which the Council has "primary responsibility." Higgins has further suggested that "Article 2(4) makes it clear, by implication at least, that an aggressor should not be allowed to retain the fruits of its aggression."[69] Similarly, the General Assembly's resolution defining aggression provides: "No territorial acquisition or special advantage resulting from aggression is or shall be recognized as lawful."[70] The Council's deciding that Iraq's annexation of Kuwait was legally invalid and null and void would accordingly seem to be well within its competence.

On August 12, US Secretary of State James Baker announced that the United States had decided to employ an "interdiction" of Iraqi commerce at sea.[71] It made this decision without consulting its allies or other UN member states. As legal justification, Secretary Baker cited a request from the Kuwaiti government as the basis for individual or collective self-defense under Article 51 of the Charter. Other member states of the Security Council,[72] as well as the Secretary-General,[73] reportedly argued that such a "blockade" could only be authorized by the Security Council under Article 42 after determining that the sanctions were not being enforced.

The US reliance on Article 51 as justification for its "interdiction" at sea of Iraqi commerce raises the issue of the relationship between self-defense and collective security. Article 51 preserves the inherent right to self-defense "until the Security Council has taken measures necessary to maintain international peace and security." Some commentators have interpreted this language as precluding the use of force in self-defense once the Security Council has acted.[74] In their view the right to self-defense is inextricably intertwined with collective security, and in effect is superseded once the Security Council has taken collective security measures.

By contrast others have claimed that the right to self-defense may be

---

[67] SC Res. 662 (Aug. 9, 1990), reprinted in 29 *ILM* at 1327.
[68] R. Higgins, "The Place of International Law in the Settlement of Disputes by the Security Council," 64 *AJIL* 1, 6 (1970). [69] *Ibid.*, at 7–8.
[70] Resolution on the Definition of Aggression, note 3 above, art. 5, para. 3.
[71] *NY Times*, Aug. 18, 1990, at A1, col. 1. [72] *Ibid.* [73] *Ibid.*, at A12, col. 1.
[74] A. Chayes, "The Use of Force in the Persian Gulf," in *Law and Force in the New International Order* 3 (L. F. Damrosch & D. J. Scheffer eds., 1991).

totally independent of collective security and that the Charter cannot and does not place any limits on a state's exercise of its right to self-defense.[75] Still others have taken a middle ground and suggested that Article 51 does constitute a limitation on a state's right to use force in self-defense but only to the extent that the Council has taken measures necessary to maintain international peace and security.[76] Under this view the key question would seem to be: Who decides whether the Council's measures have met the test of necessity, or, in other words, are sufficient to maintain the peace?

On September 25, the Council adopted a resolution[77] that further tightened the embargo against Iraq by extending the sanctions to cover all means of transport, including aircraft. Interestingly, the resolution also reaffirms that the Geneva Convention on Protection of Civilian Persons in Time of War applied to Kuwait, and that Iraq was liable for "the grave breaches committed by it, as are individuals who commit or order the commission of grave breaches." Under this provision Saddam Hussein, at least in theory, could be held criminally and civilly liable for his orders to Iraqi troops in Kuwait.

None of these resolutions had any discernible effect on Iraq's determination to remain in occupation of Kuwait. Partly as a consequence, on November 29, by a 12–2 (Yemen, Cuba)–1 (China) vote, the Council adopted Resolution 678,[78] which authorized member states to use armed force against Iraq if it failed to comply fully with its resolutions and "decides, while maintaining all its decisions, to allow Iraq one final opportunity, as a pause of good will, to do so." Unless Iraq did so, "on or before January 15, 1991," member states were authorized, in cooperation with Kuwait, "to use all necessary means to uphold and implement [the previous Council resolutions] and to restore international peace and security in the area."

As noted, Resolution 678 refers only to Chapter VII of the Charter and does not otherwise specify the provisions of the Charter that authorize its issuance. There have been discussions in various other fora about possible Charter bases for this resolution.[79] Articles 42 and 51 have been most often suggested as authority for the resolution. As Oscar Schachter has noted, this resolution could be regarded as both an authorization of collective self-defense under Article 51 and UN action under Article 42.

One issue raised in public debates on the Gulf crisis was whether it would be compatible with the principles and purposes of the United Nations for

---

75 M. Reisman, "Allocating Competences to Use Coercion in the Post-Cold War World: Practices, Conditions, and Prospects," in Damrosch & Scheffer eds., note 74 above, at 26.

76 O. Schachter, "Authorized Uses of Force by the United Nations and Regional Organizations," in *ibid.*, note 74 above, at 65.

77 SC Res. 665 (Sept. 25, 1990), reprinted in 29 *ILM* 1329 (1990).

78 SC Res. 678 (Nov. 29, 1990), reprinted in 29 *ILM*, at 1565.

79 See, e.g., several articles in the July 1991 issue of the *AJIL*.

the coalition forces to eliminate the military capability of Iraq and remove its leadership.[80] In any event the political decision of the coalition forces was to stop the attack in Iraq well short of an invasion of Baghdad. On January 16, 1991, the multinational force began an aerial bombardment of Iraq, and this was later extended to military targets in Kuwait. The aerial bombardment, along with abortive diplomatic efforts to end the conflict, continued until February 27, when President George Bush went on television to announce his intention to suspend offensive combat operations at midnight and set forth the procedures for reaching a formal cease-fire. Iraq accepted this offer to suspend combat and said it was willing to abide by all UN resolutions.

On April 3, 1991, again acting under Chapter VII of the Charter, the Security Council adopted Resolution 687,[81] which represents one of the most ambitious projects the Council has ever undertaken. Among Resolution 687's many landmark provisions is one whereby the Council demanded that Iraq and Kuwait respect the inviolability of the international boundary and allocation of islands between Iraq and Kuwait set forth in a 1963 agreement between them, an agreement whose validity had been a matter of dispute between the two countries. The resolution called on the Secretary-General to make arrangements with Iraq and Kuwait to demarcate the boundary between them.

Resolution 687 decided that Iraq must unconditionally accept the destruction, under international supervision, of all its chemical and biological weapons and all its ballistic missiles with a range greater than 150 kilometers; and must unconditionally agree not to acquire or develop nuclear weapons or nuclear-weapons-usable material and to place all such materials under the exclusive control, for custody and removal, of the International Atomic Energy Agency (IAEA). Resolution 687 would create a fund to compensate for any such loss or damage and to establish a commission to administer the fund.

On April 5, 1991, "Recalling Article 2, paragraph 7, of the Charter of the United Nations," the Council adopted Resolution 688,[82] which condemned Iraq's repression of its civilian population and noted that this repression led to "a massive flow of refugees towards and across international frontiers and to cross-border incursions, which threaten international peace and security in the region." Resolution 688 further demanded that Iraq, "as a contribution to removing the threat to international peace and security in the region," immediately cease this repression, insisted that Iraq allow immediate access by international humanitarian organizations

---

[80] See, e.g., O. Schachter, "United Nations Law in the Gulf Conflict," 85 *AJIL* 468 (1991).
[81] SC Res. 687 (Apr. 3, 1991), reprinted in 30 *ILM* 847 (1991).
[82] SC Res. 688 (Apr. 5, 1991), reprinted in 30 *ILM*, at 858.

to all those in need of assistance in all parts of Iraq, requested the Secretary-General to pursue his humanitarian efforts in Iraq and to use all the resources at his disposal to address the critical needs of the refugees, and appealed to all member states and to all humanitarian organizations to contribute to these humanitarian relief efforts. The United States, Great Britain, and France cited this resolution as support for the establishment by armed force of refugee camps in northern Iraq, but the Secretary-General disagreed and suggested the need for Iraq's consent and further Security Council action.

Surely the Secretary-General is right on this issue. As a preliminary matter one should note that Resolution 688 does *not* invoke Chapter VII of the Charter; rather, it recalls Article 2(7), which precludes the United Nations from intervening in matters that are "essentially within the domestic jurisdiction of any state," unless the "application of enforcement measures under Chapter VII" is involved. By adopting Resolution 688, the Council thus decided that Iraq's repression of its civilian population was not a matter essentially within its domestic jurisdiction. But it does not follow that the resolution therefore authorized the use of armed force to prevent that repression by setting up enclaves in northern Iraq.

As is well known, the Charter system of collective security collapsed with the advent of the Cold War. Indeed, it is worth noting that forces under the UN flag in Korea engaged in battle directly with one permanent member of the Council (China) and indirectly with another (the Soviet Union). Because of dramatic improvement in relations between the noncommunist permanent members of the Council, on the one hand, and the communist permanent members of the Council, on the other, the Council was able to authorize the use of force against Iraq. If this improvement in relations continues, it may be possible to return to the task of concluding Article 43 agreements, although some have argued that this is unnecessary, or even undesirable, because the Gulf crisis has demonstrated that the United Nations can counter aggression effectively without Article 43 agreements in place.

At this writing the latter view has prevailed. There has been no effort to conclude Article 43 agreements, and the peacekeeping force established to implement the peace agreement for Bosnia and Herzegovina signed on December 14, 1995 in Paris operates under NATO auspices. By resolution the Security Council authorized the NATO peacekeeping force to replace UN peacekeepers in Bosnia and to take 'such enforcement action . . . as may be necessary to ensure implementation' of the peace agreement.[83]

[83] SC Res. 1031 (Dec. 15, 1995).

3. Peacekeeping

As seen in the previous section, until recently the United Nations has been unable to take measures to enforce the peace. Faced with this inability, the Organization has in practice employed other methods to maintain international peace and security. Perhaps the most important of these has come to be known as *peacekeeping*. Interestingly, the word "peacekeeping" does not appear in the UN Charter. Moreover, the constitutional basis for it has been hotly debated.

As defined by a former Legal Counsel of the United Nations, peacekeeping operations are "actions involving the use of military personnel on the basis of the consent of all parties concerned and without resorting to armed force except in cases of self-defense."[84] The term "peacekeeping" was first applied in a UN context to the UN Emergency Force (UNEF) established by the General Assembly during the 1956 Suez war to oversee the withdrawal of Anglo-French and Israeli forces from Egyptian territory.

Usually UN peacekeeping forces are introduced after the fighting has stopped in an effort to avoid a new outbreak of violence. One might also note that recent peacekeeping operations – such as those in Namibia and Nicaragua – have expanded their functions to include the monitoring of free elections, and operations such as those in Cambodia are more expansive still, including the United Nations running the government of the country as an interim measure.

There now appears to be general agreement that UN peacekeeping has played a highly constructive role in maintaining international peace and security, evidenced most dramatically by the award in 1988 of the Nobel Peace Prize to UN peacekeeping forces. The creation and operation of these forces, nonetheless, has raised some crucial and controversial legal issues.

Few doubt that the Security Council has the authority to establish peacekeeping operations, although some disagreement exists as to the specific Charter basis for the Council's authority. Some have argued that the only Charter basis – and the only one that is needed – is the general basic purpose of maintaining international peace and security. Others have classified peacekeeping forces as "provisional measures" authorized by Article 40. Still others, stressing peace*keeping* as a part of peace*making*, point to Chapter VI as the appropriate Charter basis. Under Article 36, for example, the Council may, at any stage of a dispute or dangerous situation, recommend appropriate procedures or methods of adjustment.[85]

The fundamental disagreement has been over the allocation of authority under the Charter for peacekeeping among the Security Council, the

---

[84] Suy, "Peace-Keeping Operations," in *A Handbook on International Organizations* (R. Dupuy ed., 1988).   [85] See Suy, note 84 above, at 383.

General Assembly, and the Secretariat, represented by the Secretary-General.

In the Certain Expenses case a majority of the International Court of Justice was of the opinion that, contrary to the arguments of the Soviet Union and France, the General Assembly has residual authority, under Articles 11 and 14 of the Charter, to establish peacekeeping operations except where enforcement action is required. As to the division of authority between the Council and the Secretary-General, the majority of the Court confirmed the Council's prerogatives but advised that, in the case of the Congo, the Council had either authorized or ratified the Secretary-General's actions.

The primary goal of UN peacekeeping has been the avoidance of armed conflict, and UN peacekeeping forces have been instructed to limit their use of armed force to self-defense situations. In the Congo, however, the UN force, at a late stage of its activities, was authorized by the Security Council to resort to armed force in order to be able to fulfill its mandate. Also, the United Nations Interim Force for Southern Lebanon (UNIFIL) has as part of its mandate the goal of "restoring international peace and security and assisting the Government of Lebanon in ensuring the return of its effective authority in the area."[86] In theory, at least, fulfillment of this mandate could involve the use of offensive force, although no step in this direction has been or is likely to be taken. As noted above, the Security Council has expressly authorized the peacekeeping force for Bosnia and Herzegovina established under NATO auspices to take "enforcement action" to implement the peace agreement.

(a) Article 2(7) limits on peacekeeping
Article 2(7) of the United Nations Charter imposes the primary limitations on the Organization's regulation of internal conflicts. It provides that nothing in the Charter "shall authorize the United Nations to intervene in matters which are essentially within the domestic jurisdiction of any state," subject to the exception that this principle shall not prejudice the application of enforcement measures under Chapter VII. By definition peacekeeping measures are not enforcement measures. As noted by the International Court of Justice in the Certain Expenses case, this was true even in the Congo, since the UN force was in the country with the consent and at the invitation of the Congolese government and the armed forces that were used in the Congo did not take action against any state, only against the province of Katanga.[87]

Nonetheless, in practice Article 2(7) has not been a barrier to UN

---

[86] SC Res. 425, para. 3 (March 19, 1978). For further discussion of this topic, see Suy, note 84 above, at 390. [87] For discussion, see Murphy, note 51 above, at 148–61.

peacekeeping for several reasons. For Article 2(7) to apply, the UN action must constitute intervention, the substantive matter must be "essentially within the domestic jurisdiction" of a state, and the application of enforcement measures must not be involved. Since peacekeeping requires the consent of the government in whose territory the UN force is stationed, there normally would be no "intervention" by the United Nations, except arguably in a civil war situation where there is some question as to who the legitimate government in the country is. In any event usually the internal conflicts that have resulted in UN peacekeeping were not essentially domestic. On the contrary, they have involved the threat of or actual intervention by outside states; the danger of or the actual spread of violence beyond the territorial borders of the state in which the internal conflict is taking place; wars of national liberation against colonial powers; or the violation of treaty or customary international law during the conflict – all matters not essentially within the domestic jurisdiction of states. The Security Council's willingness to establish a peacekeeping force in the former Yugoslavia is a recent rejection of the argument that a civil war is necessarily "essentially within the domestic jurisdiction" of states.

4. The role of regional arrangements

The UN Charter in its Chapter VIII imposes primary responsibility for maintaining international peace and security on the Security Council. Article 52, however, expressly recognizes the right of member states to establish regional arrangements or agencies for dealing with matters relating to the maintenance of international peace and security, subject to the limitations that the matters dealt with must be "appropriate for regional action," and that the arrangements and agencies and their activities must be "consistent with the Purposes and Principles of the United Nations." At the same time the article imposes an obligation on member states to make every effort to settle "local disputes" through such means before referring them to the Security Council, as well as on the Council to encourage the use of regional arrangements and agencies for the settlement of local disputes. But paragraph 4 of the article expressly preserves the authority of the Council under Article 34 to investigate disputes and situations to determine whether their continuance is likely to endanger the maintenance of international peace and security, as well as the right of any member state of the United Nations, under Article 35, to bring Article 34-type disputes to the attention of the Security Council or of the General Assembly.

The authority of regional arrangements and agencies under Chapter VIII is limited to the peaceful settlement of local disputes. Under Article

53, with the exception of measures against the enemy states of World War II, "no enforcement action shall be taken under regional arrangements or by regional agencies without the authorization of the Security Council." Under Article 54 the Security Council is to be kept fully informed of any regional activities for the maintenance of international peace and security.

The United Nations has declined to define what constitutes regional arrangements and agencies. A proposal to have such a definition in the Charter was rejected, and neither the General Assembly nor the Security Council has sought to develop such a definition, although the issue has been raised in both organs.[88]

A paradigm case is the Cuban missile crisis of 1962. The United States sought to justify the "quarantine" of Cuba as an action taken by a regional organization under Chapter VIII of the Charter. As Leonard Meeker, then Deputy Legal Adviser to the US Department of State, averred:

The quarantine was based on a collective judgment and recommendation of the American Republics made under the Rio Treaty. It was considered not to contravene Article 2, paragraph 4, because it was a measure adopted by a regional organization in conformity with the provisions of Chapter VIII of the Charter. The purposes of the Organization and its activities were considered to be consistent with purposes and principles of the United Nations as provided in Article 52. This being the case, the quarantine would no more violate Article 2, paragraph 4, than measures voted by the Council under Chapter VII, by the General Assembly under Articles 10 and 11, or taken by United Nations Members in conformity with Article 51.[89]

With respect to the issue of whether the Cuban quarantine conformed with Article 53 of the Charter, Meeker argued first that the quarantine did not constitute enforcement action because this concept does not cover action of a regional organization that is recommendatory rather than obligatory to the members of the organization. He cited the majority opinion in the Certain Expenses case in support of this proposition.[90] In any event, he added, the authorization required by Article 53 need not be prior authorization and it need not be express. Therefore the Security Council's failure to adopt a draft Soviet resolution that would have condemned the quarantine constituted an implicit endorsement by the Council of the OAS action.[91]

Others have challenged the Meeker arguments.[92] Similar debates have arisen with respect to the 1983 invasion of Grenada by the United States

---

[88] Goodrich, Hambro, & Simons, note 18 above, at 356–57.
[89] L. Meeker, "Defensive Quarantine and the Law," 57 *AJIL* 515, 523–24 (1963).
[90] *Ibid.*, at 521.   [91] *Ibid.*, at 522.
[92] See, e.g., L. Henkin, *How Nations Behave* 291–92 (2d ed., 1979).

and several Caribbean states[93] and to the 1965 OAS establishment of a peace force in the Dominican Republic.[94]

Despite arguments that were raised concerning these and other incidents, neither the political organs of the United Nations nor the International Court of Justice has issued authoritative statements regarding the scope of the authority of regional organizations or agencies to threaten or to use armed force to maintain international peace and security. The issue is likely once again to occupy a prominent place on the world community's agenda because of the security problems posed by new developments in Eastern Europe and by the dissolution of the Soviet Union. The Soviet Union's disengagement from Eastern Europe has allowed nationalism, ethnic unrest, and border disputes to reemerge as security threats to Eastern European states. The horrendously complex situation in Bosnia–Herzegovina clearly exemplifies the tragic gravity of the situation.

III. ARMS CONTROL, DISARMAMENT, NONPROLIFERATION, AND SAFEGUARDS

Arms control, disarmament, nonproliferation, and its safeguards are closely related to regulation of the use of force. The Iraq–Kuwait crisis produced developments that have involved the United Nations in an unprecedented effort to force a member state of the Organization unilaterally to disarm with respect to weapons of mass destruction. Moreover, partly as a result of developments in the Gulf, the United Nations is playing a more active role in the field of arms control and disarmament than it has previously, and the nonproliferation and safeguards regime may be substantially strengthened.

A. Arms control and disarmament

Although the maintenance of international peace and security is a primary purpose of the United Nations, the Charter places little emphasis on arms control and disarmament. Article 1 of the Charter, which sets forth the purposes of the United Nations, does not explicitly refer to disarmament.

---

[93] Compare J. N. Moore, "Grenada and the International Double Standard," 78 *AJIL* 145, 154–59 (1984) (supporting the US position) with C. Joyner, "Reflections on the Lawfulness of Invasion," 78 *AJIL* 131, 135–37, 142 (1984) (opposing the US position).

[94] For the US position, see J. Stevenson, "Principles of UN–OAS Relationship in the Dominican Republic," 52 *Dep't St. Bull.* 975, 976–77 (1965). For a contrary view, see V. Nanda, "The United States Action in the 1965 Dominican Crisis: Impact on World Order – Part I," 43 *Denv. L. J.* 439 (1966); V. Nanda, "The United States Action in the 1965 Dominican Crisis: Impact on World Order – Part II," 44 *Denv. L. J.* 225 (1967).

Rather, Article 11(1) provides simply that the General Assembly "may consider the general principles of cooperation in the maintenance of international peace and security, including the principles governing disarmament and the regulation of armaments," and may make recommendations concerning such principles to member states or to the Security Council. Similarly, under Article 47, the Military Staff Committee, established to assist the Security Council in its efforts to maintain international peace and security, may advise on "the regulation of armaments, and possible disarmament." Also, under Article 26, the Security Council is assigned the responsibility "for formulating, with the assistance of the Military Staff Committee referred to in Article 47, plans to be submitted to the Members of the United Nations for the establishment of a system for the regulation of armaments."

Hiroshima and Nagasaki highlighted the inadequacies of the Charter regarding arms control and disarmament,[95] and resulted in a flurry of activity. The initial step was the creation by the General Assembly of the United Nations Atomic Energy Commission. In creating the Commission, the Assembly's resolution called on it to develop, "with the utmost dispatch," a plan to provide for: (a) the exchange of knowledge for peaceful purposes; (b) the control of atomic energy to limit its use to peaceful purposes; (c) the elimination of atomic and other weapons of mass destruction; and (d) the establishment of an inspection and enforcement system to safeguard against evasions.[96]

The General Assembly has created a variety of fora for the discussion of arms control and disarmament issues,[97] among the most prominent of which are the Conference on Disarmament, the First (Political and Security) Committee of the General Assembly, and the Disarmament Commission. Although most actual negotiations on arms control and disarmament have occurred outside the United Nations – often as bilateral negotiations between the United States and the former Soviet Union – there has been some movement recently toward allowing the United Nations, especially the Conference on Disarmament, to play a more meaningful role.

In addition to serving occasionally as fora for negotiation, United Nations organs as well as several UN specialized agencies[98] have performed such other functions as allowing key issues to be aired, bringing pressure on the superpowers to make more progress in their bilateral negotiations,

---

[95] L. Goodrich, *The United Nations* 219 (1959).

[96] For discussion, see R. Riggs & J. Plano, *The United Nations: International Organization and World Politics* 162–63 (1994).   [97] *Ibid.*, at 156–57.

[98] For discussion, see Goldblat, "The Role of the United Nations in Arms Control: An Assessment," in United Nations Institute for Training and Research, *The United Nations and the Maintenance of International Peace and Security* 369, 379–80 (1987).

commissioning scholarly studies on technical questions, passing resolutions that contain recommendations to the General Assembly and through it to various negotiating bodies, calling for the establishment of nuclear-free zones, such as in Africa and the Middle East, and inducing countries not previously involved in the arms control and disarmament process, such as the People's Republic of China, to participate. Similarly, special sessions on disarmament called by the General Assembly have served to focus the attention of world leaders on the dangers of the arms race and have stimulated widespread disarmament movements among large segments of the general public.

The United Nations and its negotiating conferences and committees also have been the negotiating forum for some important arms control agreements, with perhaps the most significant being the Nonproliferation Treaty, discussed in the next section of this chapter. Another noteworthy recent accomplishment was the conclusion, after years of effort, in 1993 of the Convention on the Prohibition of the Development, Production, Stockpiling and Use of Chemical Weapons.[99] The Convention is scheduled to come into force 180 days after sixty-five countries have ratified it. As of mid-1996, at least twenty-seven states are parties to the Convention.

B. Nonproliferation of nuclear weapons and safeguards

One facet of the arms control and disarmament field where the United Nations has played the lead role is the nonproliferation of nuclear weapons and safeguards to ensure that peaceful uses of nuclear materials are not diverted to military ends. Both the United Nations and the International Atomic Energy Agency have been primary actors in this field.

In 1954, President Dwight Eisenhower, speaking before the United Nations, introduced his "Atoms for Peace" program.[100] Under this plan President Eisenhower called for the creation of an International Atomic Energy Agency (IAEA) that would promote the peaceful use of atomic power so as "to provide abundant electrical energy in the power-starved areas of the world."[101] President Eisenhower's proposal came to fruition when, in 1957, the IAEA was established with the twin goals of promoting the peaceful and safe development of atomic energy and ensuring that the assistance provided by the Agency was not used for any covert activity. The latter goal is the focus of Article XII of the Statute of the IAEA, which

---

[99] Text reprinted in 37 *ILM* 800 (1993). For a summary, see "Chemical Weapons Convention," 88 *AJIL* 323 (1994). The Chemical Weapons Convention was signed by 144 states.

[100] President Dwight David Eisenhower, Address before the United Nations General Assembly (Dec. 8, 1953), reprinted in Cong. Res. Service, 96th Cong., 2d Sess., *Nuclear Proliferation Factbook* 24 (Joint Comm. Print, 1980).   [101] *Ibid.*, at 29.

defines the Agency's safeguards and inspection system designed to prevent the diversion of fissionable materials used in nuclear power reactors for clandestine manufacture of nuclear weapons. To improve the effectiveness of the safeguards system, the IAEA has promulgated a series of safeguards documents.[102]

Until 1968 the IAEA played a relatively minor role. With the adoption in that year upon recommendation by the General Assembly of the Treaty on the Nonproliferation of Nuclear Weapons (NPT),[103] the IAEA was transformed into an agency with a key role to play in arms control and disarmament.

The NPT resulted from years of negotiations in various UN fora. Although the United States and the Soviet Union took the lead in these negotiations, many other states contributed to the final product. As of this writing the NPT has more than one hundred and fifty states parties.

The first two articles of the NPT allocate responsibilities between nuclear weapons and nonnuclear weapons states. Article I requires the nuclear weapons states not to transfer nuclear weapons or devices, or control over them, and not to assist nonnuclear weapons states in acquiring nuclear weapons. Article II reciprocally obligates nonnuclear weapons states not to manufacture or acquire nuclear weapons. The key provision of the NPT is Article III, which requires bilateral "full scope safeguards" agreements with IAEA on all nuclear facilities of nonnuclear weapons states that are NPT parties, and IAEA safeguards in nuclear exports by any of its parties. Articles IV and V assure nonnuclear weapons states full access to nuclear power technology and to any benefits from peaceful nuclear explosions. Under Article VI the nuclear weapons states agree to seek an early end to the nuclear arms race and to pursue nuclear disarmament as well as general and complete disarmament "under strict and effective international control."

The safeguards system of the NPT and the IAEA is the keystone of the nonproliferation regime, and Article III of the NPT is the linchpin of the safeguards system. It is worth quoting in full:

1. Each non-nuclear-weapon State Party to the Treaty undertakes to accept safeguards, as set forth in an agreement to be negotiated and concluded with the International Atomic Energy Agency in accordance with the Statute of the International Atomic Energy Agency and the Agency's safeguards system, for the exclusive purpose of verification of the fulfillment of its obligations assumed under this Treaty with a view

---

[102] For discussion, see Poulose, "The United Nations and Arms Control," in United Nations Institute for Training and Research, note 98 above, at 387, 388–89.

[103] Treaty on the Nonproliferation of Nuclear Weapons, July 1, 1968, 21 UST 483, TIAS No. 6839, 729 UNTS 161 (hereinafter NPT).

to preventing diversion of nuclear energy from peaceful uses to nuclear weapons or other nuclear explosive devices. Procedures for the safeguards required by this article shall be followed with respect to source or special fissionable material whether it is being produced, processed or used in any principal nuclear facility or is outside any such facility. The safeguards required by this article shall be applied on all source or special fissionable material in all peaceful nuclear activities within the territory of such State, under its jurisdiction, or carried out under its control anywhere.

2. Each State Party to the Treaty undertakes not to provide: (a) source or special fissionable material, or (b) equipment or material especially designed or prepared for the processing, use or production of special fissionable material, to any non-nuclear weapon State for peaceful purposes, unless the source or special fissionable material shall be subject to the safeguards required by this article.

3. The safeguards required by this article shall be implemented in a manner designed to comply with article IV of this Treaty, and to avoid hampering the economic or technological development of the Parties or international cooperation in the field of peaceful nuclear activities, including the international exchange of nuclear material and equipment for the processing, use or production of nuclear material for peaceful purposes in accordance with the provisions of this article and the principle of safeguarding set forth in the Preamble of the Treaty.

4. Non-nuclear-weapon States Party to the Treaty shall conclude agreements with the International Atomic Energy Agency to meet the requirements of this article either individually or together with other States in accordance with the Statute of the International Atomic Energy Agency. Negotiation of such agreements shall commence within 180 days from the original entry into force of this Treaty. For States depositing their instruments of ratification or accession after the 180-day period, negotiation of such agreements shall commence not later than the date of such deposit. Such agreements shall enter into force not later than eighteen months after the date of initiation of negotiations.

As Article III indicates, the safeguards system applies unequally to nuclear weapons and nonnuclear weapons states parties to the NPT, and only indirectly, if at all, to states not party to the NPT. Under paragraph 1 of Article III, each nonnuclear weapons state party to the Treaty undertakes to accept safeguards "for the exclusive purpose of verification of the fulfillment of its obligations assumed under this Treaty with a view to preventing diversion of nuclear energy from peaceful uses to nuclear weapons or other nuclear explosive devices." Paragraph 1 goes on to require that all source or special fissionable material in all the peaceful nuclear activities of nonnuclear weapons states parties to the NPT be placed under IAEA safeguards in order to verify that such material is not diverted to nuclear weapons or other nuclear explosive devices. Similarly, paragraphs 1 and 2 of the IAEA's model agreement on NPT safeguards[104] also require such "full scope" safeguards, and paragraph 28 of the model agreement defines the goal of NPT safeguards as follows:

The Agreement should provide that the objective of safeguards is the timely detection of diversion of significant quantities of nuclear materials from peaceful nuclear activities to the manufacture of nuclear weapons or of other nuclear explosive devices or for purposes unknown, and deterrence of such diversion by the risk of early detection.

By contrast, nuclear weapons states parties to the NPT are not under an obligation to submit the peaceful nuclear activities within their territories or under their jurisdiction to the safeguards required by Article III. They are required, however, by paragraph 2 of Article III, not to provide source or special fissionable material or equipment or material especially designed or prepared for the processing, use, or production of special fissionable material to any nonnuclear weapons state unless it agrees to the application of IAEA safeguards. Moreover, the United States and the United Kingdom have submitted their peaceful nuclear activities to safeguards, although they are under no obligation under Article III to do so, and each of the five nuclear weapons states has accepted IAEA safeguards on some of its civilian nuclear reactors to reduce the appearance of discrimination and encourage nonnuclear weapons parties to accept safeguards.

Nonnuclear weapons states that are not parties to the NPT nonetheless have to accept safeguards if they are to receive nuclear assistance from parties to the NPT, because of the obligation under paragraph 2 of Article III on states parties to require the application of safeguards by their transferees. One purpose of this provision is to insure that nonnuclear weapons states not parties to the Treaty would not enjoy a privileged position in international peaceful nuclear transactions compared to the nonnuclear weapons states parties to the NPT. Only nonnuclear weapons states that are parties to the NPT, however, are required to accept the application of safeguards to all their peaceful nuclear activities, i.e., the "full scope" safeguards. This gap in the law has been filled, at least to some extent, by the decision of most state exporters of nuclear material to require recipient states to agree to full-scope IAEA safeguards. Still, several

[104] IAEA Doc. INFCIRC/153.

nonnuclear weapons states not parties to the NPT have successfully resisted the application of full-scope safeguards.

Under paragraph 4 of Article III nonnuclear weapons states parties to the NPT are required to conclude safeguards agreements with the IAEA, and it is the terms of these individual safeguards agreements that define the precise obligations of these states. However, these agreements are to be in accord with these states' obligations under the NPT and with the IAEA's Statute. Moreover, the model agreement prepared by the IAEA serves as a further guide for these safeguards agreements and to ensure consistency of obligation. The safeguards system applied by the IAEA prior to the NPT remains operational for states not parties to the NPT.

Under Article VIII of the NPT review conferences have been held at five-year intervals, the first being held in 1975, the second in 1980, the third in 1985, and the fourth in 1990. In 1995 parties decided to extend the term of the NPT indefinitely. The NPT parties at the same time decided that "decisions adopted by the [IAEA's] Board of Governors aimed at further strengthening the effectiveness of Agency safeguards should be supported and implemented and the Agency's capability to detect undeclared nuclear activities should be increased."[105]

In 1968 the United States, the United Kingdom, and the Soviet Union gave, in a letter to the President of the Security Council,[106] security assurances to nonnuclear weapons states that each would seek immediate Security Council action to assist any nonnuclear weapons state party to the NPT that was the target of nuclear aggression or threats.

The regime established by the NPT has come under sharp criticism. Several nonnuclear weapons states that have the capacity to become nuclear weapons states have rejected the NPT on the ground that states would receive adequate security guarantees only in the event of nuclear disarmament and that, contrary to their obligations under Article VI of the NPT, the nuclear weapons states have been expanding their nuclear weapons capacity. States that pose the greatest proliferation risks – India, Pakistan, and Israel – have refused to sign the NPT.

Critics of the regime also have alleged that IAEA safeguards are not adequate for the task. They have alleged, among other things, that the IAEA is underfunded, understaffed, and that it has been weakened by political questions not relevant to nonproliferation. Moreover, these critics contend,

[105] See Recommendation and Report of the American Bar Association, Section of International Law and Practice on the International Atomic Energy Agency, approved by the ABA House of Delegates in August 1995, at 6–7.
[106] See Letter from the US, USSR, and UK to the President of the Security Council (June 12, 1968), 23 UN SCOR Supp. (Apr.–June 1968) at 216, UN Doc. S/8630 (1968). See also Res. 255 Pertaining to Treaty on Nonproliferation of Nuclear Weapons, 23 UN SCOR, Res. Decis. (Apr.–June 1968), reprinted in 13 UN Doc. S/8631 (1968).

the IAEA "full scope" safeguards stipulated in Article III of the NPT are designed only to detect a diversion of nuclear material to military uses and do not prevent a clandestine nuclear program.[107]

Critics of the IAEA safeguards system have especially pressed their arguments since the discovery by a UN and IAEA inspection team in the summer of 1991 of a secret Iraqi nuclear arms program in violation of Iraq's safeguard agreements with IAEA. In response on December 6, 1991, Hans Blix, Director-General of the International Atomic Energy Agency, formally proposed strengthening the Agency's system of safeguarding nuclear material.[108] At a meeting of the IAEA's Board of Governors, Mr. Blix requested the board to back special inspections on sites where the Agency suspects that safeguards agreements are being violated. Such special inspections, which would be possible only in the eighty-eight countries that have full safeguards agreements with the Agency, would be aimed at sites that a country had not declared to the Agency, such as the dozen secret nuclear installations discovered in Iraq. On February 24–25, 1992, the IAEA Board approved most of Mr. Blix's recommendations.[109]

Although the IAEA apparently already has the authority to undertake special inspections, it had never made them on undeclared sites before the Iraqi case. The purpose of Blix's proposal was to alert countries with which the IAEA has safeguards agreements that no site is off limits for inspectors. If a country refuses to permit a special inspection, the Director-General could take the matter to the UN Security Council, which then would have to decide whether the country posed a threat to international peace and security.

More recently the issue came to the fore in the case of North Korea,[110] which concluded a safeguards agreement with the IAEA in January 1992. North Korea accepted six IAEA inspection visits before refusing access to two facilities near its Yongbyon nuclear reactor complex, on the ground that these were conventional military facilities. IAEA experts, however, suspected that North Korea may have used more nuclear fuel, and may have been able to separate more plutonium for possible weapons use, than it had declared. As a consequence, on April 1, 1993, the IAEA's Board of Governors ruled that North Korea had violated its safeguards agreement, and referred the issue to the UN Security Council. For its part North Korea gave formal notice of its intention to withdraw from the Nonproliferation

---

[107] See, e.g., Report of the Nuclear Energy Policy Study Group: Nuclear Power Issues and Choices (1977). [108] *NY Times*, Dec. 7, 1991, at A3, col. 1.

[109] *Financial Times*, Feb. 27, 1992, at 2, col. 8.

[110] See R. Smith, "Move Against North Korea Seen as Turning Point in Arms Control," *Wash. Post*, April 7, 1993, at A23, col. 1; R. Smith, "N. Korea and the Bomb: High-Tech Hide-and-Seek," *Wash. Post*, April 27, 1993, at A1, col. 1; *Financial Times* (London), April 2, 1992, at 3, col. 5.

Treaty. Induced by economic and technical assistance from the United States, negotiations were successfully concluded in 1995 that persuaded North Korea to remain a member of the NPT and to submit to the requested inspections.

There is a fundamental tension in the NPT between the promise in Article IV of enhanced cooperation with NPT parties in the peaceful uses of nuclear energy and concern about the most sensitive nuclear materials, facilities, and technology. In an effort to abort some impending international transfers of sensitive facilities, the United States in the late 1970s organized the Nuclear Suppliers Group and persuaded other major supplier countries to exercise restraint regarding the export of sensitive materials. The United States also enacted legislation designed to use US leverage to help ensure such restraint. The nonnuclear weapons states parties to the NPT reacted sharply to these steps, contending that they were inconsistent with Article IV of the NPT.

Article VII of the NPT preserves the "right of any group of States to conclude regional treaties in order to assure the total absence of nuclear weapons in their respective territories." The Treaty of Tiateloloco, or the Treaty for the Prohibition of Nuclear Weapons in Latin America,[111] was concluded in 1967 and therefore predates the NPT. It nonetheless is an example of the kind of regional agreement envisaged by Article VII of the NPT. Protocol I to the Treaty of Tiateloloco applies to non-Latin countries that have possessions in Latin America. Protocol II applies to nuclear weapons states. The United States has ratified both Protocols, and all five nuclear weapons states have ratified Protocol II.

By contrast some significant states in the region have not become parties. Cuba has refused to sign the Treaty, and Argentina has signed but not ratified it. Although Brazil and Chile have technically ratified, the Treaty is not in force for either of them, since they did not waive the entry-into-force requirement that all eligible states ratify. On the other hand, in 1992 Argentina and Brazil concluded a bilateral agreement in which they agreed not to acquire nuclear weapons as well as a full-scope safeguards agreement with the IAEA. There are also reports that Chile may now waive the Tiateloloco Treaty's entry-into-force provisions. If so, this would leave only Cuba outside the nonproliferation regime in Latin America.

Perhaps Hans Blix has most aptly summarized the current status of the nonproliferation regime:

The greatest challenge to the non-proliferation effort is the achievement of universality of acceptance. To achieve this a non-nuclear-weapon status must be

---

[111] Treaty of Tiateloloco or Treaty for the Prohibition of Nuclear Weapons in Latin America, Feb. 14, 1967, 22 UST 762, TIAS No. 7137, 634 UNTS 281.

made attractive to those few, but important, States that remain outside its scope, if these States are to join. Such commitment would not necessarily have to be NPT membership. It could also be done through the Tiateloloco or other future regional treaties, through mutual declarations or acceptance of full-scope safeguards. A major set-back is any military attack on a peaceful nuclear installation under safeguards. The whole idea of a non-proliferation regime is to give one's neighbors and potential adversaries assurances of the peaceful nature of installations. If any doubt were to persist in this regard, the international legal framework to investigate it should be pursued.

The world has been remarkably successful so far in preventing a spread of nuclear weapons to further countries. There is a high degree of international goodwill as regards co-operation in the peaceful uses of nuclear energy and China's taking up membership in the IAEA is indicative of the practical usefulness which that country attaches to peaceful nuclear co-operation. What remains is for the nuclear-weapon-States to take advantage of this relatively stable situation and negotiate real reductions in the world's nuclear arsenals. The risk of horizontal proliferation represents a potential threat. The some 50,000 existing nuclear warheads subject us all to an actual threat of extinction.[112]

IV. CONCLUSION

Since World War II, the United Nations and its affiliated agencies have contributed significantly to creating international law expressly designed to curb and prohibit the use of force between states. These efforts extend from the UN Charter itself which imposes particular limits on the use of force, to numerous binding resolutions adopted by the Security Council dealing with bilateral dispute situations, to the designation of various peacekeeping operations, to the broader international issues of arms control and disarmament. Attention by the United Nations most recently focused on a convention to ban chemical weapons and extension of the Nonproliferation Treaty in the post-Cold War era. If the past is prologue, the United Nations will continue to play a vital role in developing the international legal order to restrain the use of force among its member states.

SELECTED BIBLIOGRAPHY

Arend, A. and R. Beck, *International Law and the Use of Force* (Routledge, 1993)

Claude, I., "Theoretical Approaches to National Security and World Order," in *National Security Law* 31 (J. Moore, F. Tipson, & R. Turner eds.; Carolina Academic, 1990)

---

[112] H. Blix, "The Role of the IAEA and the Existing NPT Regime," in *Nuclear War, Nuclear Proliferation, and their Consequences* 62 (S.A. Khan ed., 1986).

Dinstein, Y., *War, Aggression and Self Defence* (Grotius, 1988)

Law and Force in the New World Order (L. Damrosch and D. J. Scheffer eds.; Westview, 1991)

Murphy, J., *The United Nations and the Control of International Violence* (Allanheld, Osmun, 1982)

Nuclear War, Nuclear Proliferation, and Their Consequences (S. A. Khan ed.; Oxford University Press, 1986)

Riggs, R. and J. Plano, *The United Nations: International Organization and World Politics* (2d ed., Wadsworth, 1994)

Schachter, O., "The Right of States to Use Armed Force," 82 *Mich. L. Rev.* 1620 (1984)

"In Defense of International Rules on the Use of Force," 53 *U. Chi. L. Rev.* 113 (1986)

"Self Defense and the Rule of Law," 83 *AJIL* 259 (1989)

United Nations Institute for Training and Research, *The United Nations and the Maintenance of International Peace and Security* (Martinus Nijhoff, 1987)

CHAPTER FIVE

HUMAN RIGHTS

Hurst Hannum

I. INTRODUCTION

In perhaps no other area has the United Nations been so prolific or, some would argue, so successful as it has been in the adoption of new international norms for the protection of human rights. A recent UN compilation of human rights instruments lists sixty-seven conventions, declarations, and other documents adopted under UN auspices, and even this number is surely incomplete.[1] These instruments range from narrowly focused recommendations, such as the UN Standard Minimum Rules for the Administration of Juvenile Justice,[2] to such basic human rights texts as the two International Covenants on human rights.[3]

Without duplicating the general discussion of UN law-making in part I, one should nevertheless observe that human rights instruments have been adopted by the United Nations through nearly every possible means.[4] They have been initiated by states, UN organs, nongovernmental organizations, and individual experts appointed by the United Nations.[5] Most declar-

---

[1] UN Centre for Human Rights, A Compilation of International Instruments (1988) (hereinafter UN *Compilation*). The compilation includes two conventions adopted prior to 1945 and only a very short selection of instruments adopted by specialized agencies such as the International Labour Organization and UNESCO. Among the most significant post-1988 instruments are the Convention on the Rights of the Child, GA Res. 44/25 (Nov. 20, 1989), and the International Convention on the Protection of the Rights of All Migrant Workers and Members of Their Families, GA Res. 45/158 (Dec. 18, 1990).

[2] GA Res. 40/33 (Nov. 29, 1985).

[3] International Covenant on Economic, Social and Cultural Rights, Dec. 16, 1966, 999 UNTS 3 (1966) (*entered into force* Jan. 3, 1976) (hereinafter ESC Covenant); International Covenant on Civil and Political Rights, Dec. 16, 1966, 999 UNTS 171 (1966) (*entered into force* Mar. 23, 1976) (hereinafter CPR Covenant).

[4] A survey of the United Nation's treaty-making concludes laconically that "no general pattern emerges" from an examination of the legislative procedures used in over a dozen human rights instruments. United Nations, *Review of the Multilateral Treatymaking Process* 19 (1985); cf. *ibid.*, at 177–216.   [5] Cf. *ibid.*, at 204–6.

131

ations have been adopted by the General Assembly upon the recommendation of one of its main committees, with varying degrees of prior substantive discussion.[6] Some important standards have been adopted by subsidiary or related bodies, such as the Economic and Social Council,[7] the UN Congresses on the Prevention of Crime and the Treatment of Offenders,[8] or the specialized agencies.

Conventions have been adopted based on texts elaborated by open-ended working groups of the General Assembly,[9] after earlier consideration and adoption of nonbinding declarations on the same topic,[10] and after years of consideration by subsidiary bodies such as the Commission on Human Rights.[11] Agreement on the text of new human rights treaties is normally reached at the level of the Commission on Human Rights or a working group, but substantive changes (particularly regarding implementation measures) may be made at plenary discussions of the General Assembly's Third or Sixth Committee or the Assembly itself.[12] Conventions drafted by UN human rights organs may be adopted and opened for ratification by the General Assembly or by special conferences.[13]

It would be impossible to address the substantive law of human rights within the confines of the present chapter, and many more detailed works are available.[14] Nevertheless, the only way to present an accurate picture of

[6] E.g., Universal Declaration of Human Rights, GA Res. 217A (III) (Dec. 10, 1948); Declaration on the Rights of the Child, GA Res. 1386 (XIV) (Nov. 20, 1959); Declaration on the Rights of Disabled Persons, GA Res. 3447 (XXX) (Dec. 9, 1975).

[7] E.g., Standard Minimum Rules for the Treatment of Prisoners, *adopted* in ESC Res. 663C, UN ESCOR, 24th Sess., Supp. No. 1, at 11, UN Doc. E/3048 (1957), *extended,* ESC Res. 2976 (LXIII), UN ESCOR, 62d Sess., Supp. No. 1, at 35 (1977).

[8] E.g., Basic Principles on the Independence of the Judiciary, *adopted* at the Seventh UN Congress in 1985, reprinted in UN *Compilation*, note 1 above, at 265.

[9] E.g., International Convention on Migrant Workers, note 1 above.

[10] E.g., Convention on the Rights of the Child, note 1 above.

[11] The Covenant on Economic, Social and Cultural Rights and the Covenant on Civil and Political Rights, note 3 above, were considered by the Commission on Human Rights from 1948 through 1954; following the extensive debates in the Commission and subsequently in the General Assembly's Third Committee, the Covenants were adopted by the General Assembly only in 1966. See generally M. Bossuyt, *Guide to the* Travaux Préparatoires *of the International Covenant on Civil and Political Rights* (1987).

[12] Cf. *Review of the Multilateral Treatymaking Process*, note 4 above, at 209–13.

[13] An example of the latter is the Supplementary Convention on the Abolition of Slavery, the Slave Trade, and Institutions and Practices Similar to Slavery, Sept. 7, 1956, 266 UNTS 3 (*entered into force* Apr. 30, 1957), which was adopted by an conference convened by the UN Economic and Social Council.

[14] See selected bibliography at the end of this chapter and particularly, J. Carey, *UN Protection of Civil and Political Rights* (1970); *Human Rights in International Law* (T. Meron ed., 1984); *The International Bill of Rights, the Covenant on Civil and Political Rights* (L. Henkin ed., 1981); *The International Bill of Rights, the Covenant on Economic, Social And Cultural Rights* (L. Sohn ed., forthcoming); *The International Dimensions of Human Rights* (K. Vasak & P. Alston eds., 1982); *US Ratification of the International Covenants on Human Rights* (H. Hannum & D. Fischer eds., 1992); T. Meron, *Human Rights Law-making in the United*

the contribution made by the United Nations to the substantive international law of human rights is at least to survey the United Nations' record in adopting and implementing the major human rights instruments.[15] This survey will be preceded by a brief discussion of the United Nations' changing approach to human rights since 1945. It will be followed by an analysis of the current status of human rights in customary international law, which may be viewed as having been derived, in part, from the normative role played by the United Nations.

II. HUMAN RIGHTS, THE CHARTER, AND INSTITUTIONAL DEVELOPMENTS

One of the purposes of the United Nations is "to achieve international co-operation . . . in promoting and encouraging respect for human rights and for fundamental freedoms for all without distinction as to race, sex, language, or religion."[16] Each UN member state pledges "to take joint and separate action in co-operation with the Organization for the achievement of . . . universal respect for, and observance of, human rights."[17] Other Charter references reaffirm this commitment to human rights and, whatever the full legal import of these obligations, there can be no doubt that human rights was a concern of the United Nations from its inception.[18] Early General Assembly resolutions directly addressed alleged

Nations (1986); F. Newman & D. Weissbrodt, *International Human Rights* (1990); P. Sieghart, *The International Law of Human Rights* (1983); United Nations, *United Nations Action in the Field of Human Rights* (1988). See also H. Hannum, *Materials on International Human Rights and US Constitutional Law* (1985); H. Hannum, *Materials on International Human Rights and US Criminal Law and Procedure* (1989); R. Lillich, *International Human Rights* (2nd ed., 1991).

15 While no two observers might agree on which instruments are the most important, the present chapter will use the following conventions and declarations (listed in chronological order) as illustrative: Universal Declaration of Human Rights, note 6 above; International Convention on the Elimination of All Forms of Racial Discrimination, Dec. 21, 1965, 660 UNTS 195 (*entered into force* Jan. 4, 1969); International Covenant on Economic, Social and Cultural Rights, note 3 above; International Covenant on Civil and Political Rights, note 3 above; Convention on the Suppression and Punishment of the Crime of Apartheid, GA Res. 3068 (XXVIII) (Nov. 30, 1973) (*entered into force* July 18, 1976); Convention against Torture and Other Cruel, Inhuman or Degrading Treatment or Punishment, GA Res. 39/46 (Dec. 10, 1984), 39 UN GAOR, Supp. (No. 51) at 197 (1984) (*entered into force* June 28, 1987); Convention on the Rights of the Child, note 1 above; International Convention on the Rights of Migrant Workers, note 1 above. The Convention on the Elimination of All Forms of Discrimination against Women, GA Res. 34/180 (Dec. 18, 1979), 34 UN GAOR, Supp. (No. 46) 193 (1979) (*entered into force* Sept. 3, 1981) is discussed below, ch. 7.

16 UN Charter, art. 1(3).   17 *Ibid.*, arts. 56, 55(c).

18 See generally Carey, note 14 above; L. Sohn & T. Buergenthal, *International Protection of Human Rights* 505–856 (1973).

133

violations of human rights in several Eastern European countries,[19] despite the prohibition against UN intervention "in matters which are essentially within the domestic jurisdiction of any state" contained in Article 2(7) of the Charter. Among the earliest acts of the Economic and Social Council was to create commissions on human rights and on the status of women and to approve the establishment of subcommissions on the prevention of discrimination and protection of minorities and on freedom of information and the press.[20]

The work of the United Nations in the field of human rights has evolved in several different phases. The first phase, which began immediately after creation of the United Nations in 1945, was primarily concerned with standard-setting; this work has continued to the present, as evidenced by the recent adoption of conventions on children's and migrants' rights and the drafting of formal declarations on the rights of minorities and indigenous peoples.

The second phase consisted in public discussion of alleged violations of human rights in specific countries. While early General Assembly resolutions criticized the human rights situation in a few specific countries,[21] public discussion of specific violations soon became limited (apart from questions of decolonization) to condemnation of apartheid in South Africa and Israeli practices in the territories it occupied after the 1967 Arab–Israeli war. Following adoption of Resolution 1235 by the Economic and Social Council in 1967, which authorized the ECOSOC's subsidiary bodies to discuss the violation of human rights in any country, and the overthrow of President Allende in Chile in 1973, human rights debates in the United Nations became increasingly frequent and direct.

The third stage consisted of creating mechanisms to implement accepted norms more effectively. These included creation of a procedure under which individual communications concerning a consistent pattern of gross violations of human rights could be considered[22] and the appointment of rapporteurs and working groups to investigate human rights violations in specific countries or to report on particular types of human rights violations (e.g., torture or "disappearances").

While most of this chapter will be concerned with standard-setting, i.e., law-making, an appreciation of the contemporaneous development of

---

[19] See, e.g., GA Res. 272 (III) (Apr. 30, 1949); 285 (III) (Apr. 25, 1949); 294 (IV) (Oct. 22, 1949).

[20] The Subcommission on Freedom of Information and the Press was discontinued in 1952.

[21] See GA Res. 44 (I) (Dec. 8, 1946) (Indians in South Africa); 285 (III) (Apr. 25, 1949) (Soviet Union); 272 (III) (Apr. 30, 1949) (Bulgaria and Hungary).

[22] See discussion of ESC Res. 1503 (XLVIII) (May 27, 1970), notes 33–36 below and accompanying text.

procedures to promote and protect human rights also is essential to an understanding of the UN's law-making role.

For its first two decades, the United Nations limited its human rights activities (apart from standard-setting and protection of refugees) to occasional political debates, the preparation of studies, and achieving progress in the process of decolonization. The notable exception to this purely rhetorical concern was South Africa, and the General Assembly established a Special Committee on Apartheid in 1962. The Special Committee reports annually to the General Assembly, sponsors international conferences, and encourages opposition to apartheid through various means.[23] In 1967, the Commission on Human Rights created an *ad hoc* Working Group of Experts on Human Rights in Southern Africa, which has since become permanent. Eventually, the Security Council imposed mandatory economic sanctions against the regimes in Southern Rhodesia[24] and South Africa,[25] sanctions designed essentially to implement the basic human right of equality. More recently, respect for human rights and/or humanitarian law has been linked to the maintenance of international peace and security in the cases of the Kurds in Iraq,[26] Somalia,[27] Cambodia,[28] El Salvador,[29] Bosnia–Herzegovina,[30] and Haiti.[31]

The second country-specific concern of the United Nations was the territories occupied by Israel after the 1967 Arab–Israeli war. In 1968, the General Assembly again created a "Special Committee," this time to Investigate Israeli Practices Affecting the Human Rights of the Population of the Occupied Territories. The Special Committee has, *inter alia*, held hearings of witnesses who have testified on matters within its mandate, although it has not been granted permission by Israel to conduct an on-site investigation in the territories.[32]

While selected country-specific situations were thus subject to United Nations scrutiny during the first two decades, attempts by individuals to raise human rights violations before UN bodies during this period were rebuffed. The Economic and Social Council approved a statement by the Commission on Human Rights that "it [the Commission] has no power to take any action in regard to any complaints concerning human rights."[33] Eventually, it was decided that two lists would be prepared for distribution

---

[23] A brief description of the Special committee's work may be found in *United Nations Action in the Field of Human Rights*, note 14 above, at 10–11.
[24] SC Res. 232 (Dec. 16, 1966); 253 (May 29, 1968); 333 (May 22, 1973); 338 (Apr. 6, 1976).
[25] SC Res. 418 (Nov. 4, 1977).   [26] SC Res. 688 (Apr. 5, 1991).
[27] See, e.g., SC Res. 794 (Dec. 3, 1992).   [28] See, e.g., SC Res. 745 (Feb. 28, 1992).
[29] See, e.g., SC Res. 693 (May 20, 1991).
[30] See, e.g., SC Res. 771 (Aug. 13, 1992) and 827 (May 25, 1993).
[31] See, e.g., GA Res. 47/20 B (Apr. 20, 1993); SC Res. 940 (July 31, 1994).
[32] See *United Nations Action in the Field of Human Rights*, note 14 above, at 12.
[33] ESC Res. 75 (V) (Aug. 5, 1947).

to Commission members: a nonconfidential list would summarize communications dealing with "principles" of human rights, while a confidential list would contain "a brief indication of the substance of other communications concerning human rights."[34] It was not until 1970 that the Commission and Subcommission were authorized to consider, in confidential sessions, communications "which appear to reveal a consistent pattern of gross and reliably attested violations of human rights and fundamental freedoms."[35]

In 1967, the Economic and Social Council approved a request from the Commission that the Commission and Subcommission be allowed to consider "the violation of human rights . . . in all countries" and, ultimately, "make a thorough study of situations which reveal a consistent pattern of violations of human rights."[36] Particularly after the military coup in Chile in 1973, which overthrew the leftist government of Salvador Allende, public debates in the Commission and Subcommission became increasingly direct regarding human rights violations in specific countries; by the 1980s, appeals by states that such discussions violated the proscription against interference with "domestic jurisdiction" were widely viewed as anachronistic.

As human rights became more acceptable politically, new procedures – based only on the inherent authority of the Commission on Human Rights and its parent body, the ECOSOC – were developed to move UN action from mere discussion to monitoring and supervision. While the Commission and Subcommission had long undertaken scholarly studies of human rights issues (such as the right to leave and return or the issue of arbitrary detention), the 1980s saw a greater focus on highlighting serious violations. A Working Group on Enforced or Involuntary Disappearances was created in 1980 and was soon followed by the appointment of special rapporteurs on summary or arbitrary executions (1982), torture (1985), and religious intolerance and discrimination (1986).[37] These "thematic" bodies receive specific allegations of violations, attempt to respond effectively in order to prevent imminent violations, and submit a country-specific annual report to the Commission.[38]

[34] ESC Res. 728F (XXVIII) (July 30, 1959), para. 2; cf. Sohn & Buergenthal, note 18 above, at 746–72.
[35] ESC Res. 1503, note 22 above, para. 1. The merits of "Resolution 1503" have been widely debated; see, e.g., I. Guest, *Behind the Disappearances, Argentina's Dirty War against Human Rights and the United Nations* (1990); Lillich, note 14 above, at 374–441; Newman & Weissbrodt, note 14 above, at 118–30, 140–41; H. Tolley, Jr., *The UN Commission on Human Rights* 70–82, 124–33, 205–11 (1987). [36] ESC Res. 1235 (XLII) (June 6, 1967).
[37] A special rapporteur on mercenaries was appointed in 1987, with a somewhat more restricted mandate.
[38] See Newman & Weissbrodt, note 14 above, at 145–90; Tolley, note 35 above, at 104–11; D. Weissbrodt, "The Three 'Theme' Special Rapporteurs of the UN Commission on Human Rights," 80 *AJIL* 685 (1986).

Perhaps the strongest action that can be taken by the Commission is adoption of a public resolution expressing concern over or condemning a specific country for human rights violations. This may be accompanied by the appointment of a rapporteur to collect additional information on allegations, whose report is then discussed the following year. While the mere adoption of a resolution may seem to be a minimal sanction, the efforts exerted by states to prevent such actions testify to the power of diplomatic embarrassment and isolation.[39]

The United Nations' contribution to law-making in the field of human rights should be understood in the context of these institutional attempts to protect human rights, which generally have followed the creation or clarification of new human rights norms.

III. HUMAN RIGHTS LAW-MAKING IN THE UNITED NATIONS

The mere recitation of the human rights treaties, declarations, resolutions, and studies adopted by the United Nations would exhaust the space available for this chapter. The brief discussion that follows is therefore highly selective and is designed to illustrate the various approaches to law-making that the United Nations has adopted in the human rights field. The focus is on multilateral conventions adopted under the direct auspices of the United Nations, to which there are now well over 1,500 states parties,[40] as opposed to those adopted by the specialized agencies.[41]

A. Conventions

1. The international bill of rights

At its first session in 1946, the General Assembly approved an ECOSOC proposal for the Commission on Human Rights to formulate "an international bill of rights."[42] While the Universal Declaration of Human Rights adopted two years later was intended to be an aspirational, nonbinding "common standard of achievement for all peoples and all nations,"[43] it was only the beginning of a process designed to culminate in

---

[39] See, e.g., Guest, note 35 above; Tolley, note 35 above, at 111–24.

[40] United Nations, Human Rights, Status of International Instruments (1987; *updated* Dec. 31, 1990) at nn. 1, 691 (ratifications of twenty-four UN treaties or protocols concerned with human rights).

[41] The specialized agencies are discussed at notes 103–10 below and accompanying text. See pp. 148–49.   [42] GA Res. 43 (I) (Dec. 11, 1946).

[43] See note 6 above, Pmbl. As noted explicitly by Eleanor Roosevelt, then Chairman of the UN Commission on Human Rights, in a statement to the General Assembly just prior to adoption of the Declaration: "It is not a treaty; it is not an international agreement. It is not and does not purport to be a statement of law or of legal obligation." Quoted in M. Whiteman, 1 *Digest of International Law* 55 (1963).

Univ. Declaration the adoption of legally binding human rights norms. While not "law" in the traditional sense, the Universal Declaration set forth the basic principles upon which subsequent conventions would be based. At least some of the principles proclaimed in the Universal Declaration have ripened into customary international law, binding on all states.[44]

The Commission on Human Rights was instructed by the General Assembly, in a separate part of the same resolution that proclaimed the Universal Declaration of Human Rights, to prepare a draft covenant on human rights and measures of implementation. After disagreements arose within the Commission over the appropriate implementation measures for civil and political rights, on one hand, and economic, social, and cultural rights, on the other hand, the Assembly in 1952 authorized the drafting of two covenants, which would deal with the two sets of rights separately.

The Commission completed its work on the draft covenants in 1954. The General Assembly's Third Committee then proceeded to an exhaustive article-by-article consideration of the covenants, which were finally adopted and opened for signature and ratification in December 1966.[45] As of December 31, 1994, there were 131 parties to the Covenant on Economic, Social and Cultural Rights and 128 parties to the Covenant on Civil and Political Rights.

It is far beyond the scope of this chapter to consider the substantive rights set forth in the covenants in detail, but they remain the most comprehensive statements of conventional human rights law yet adopted. Each begins with a common article that sets forth the right of "all peoples" to self-determination, defines certain general obligations of the states parties, details the specific rights guaranteed, and creates a supervisory mechanism to oversee implementation of the covenant.

The Covenant on Economic, Social and Cultural Rights also establishes immediate legal obligations, but these are limited in most instances to obligations "to take steps . . . with a view to achieving progressively the full

[44] See discussion at notes 111–20 below and section V, the Declaration of Teheran, adopted by a UN-sponsored governmental conference on human rights, UN Doc. A/CONF.32/41 (1968) (the Universal Declaration "states a common understanding of the peoples of the world . . . and constitutes an obligation for the members of the international community"); the nongovernmental Montreal Statement of the Assembly for Human Rights, reprinted in 9 *J. Int'l Comm. Jurists* 94 (June 1968) (the Declaration "constitutes an authoritative interpretation of the Charter of the highest order, and has over the years become a part of customary international law"). For a contemporary view of the customary international law of human rights, see American Law Institute, *Restatement (Third) of The Foreign Relations Law of the United States*, II, 702, at 161 (1987) (hereinafter *Restatement*).

[45] The best general description of the process that led to adoption of the two covenants is probably found in the relevant United Nations Yearbooks; a short summary with specific references to the debates may be found in *Review of the Multilateral Treatymaking Process*, note 4 above, at 183–85. Cf. Bossuyt, note 11 above; V. Pechota, "The Development of the Covenant on Civil and Political Rights," in Henkin ed., note 14 above, at 32–71.

realization of the rights recognized" in the covenant.[46] These rights include the right to work and to have the opportunity to choose work freely; the right to just and favorable conditions of work, including fair remuneration, equal pay for equal work, safe and healthy working conditions, and equality of opportunity; the right to form and join trade unions, including the right to strike; the right to receive social security; the right to special protection and assistance for the family, particularly mothers and children; the right to an adequate standard of living, including adequate food, clothing, and housing; the right to the highest attainable standard of physical and mental health; the right to education; and the right to participate in cultural life and enjoy scientific freedom.

Some US commentators have criticized the concept of economic, social, and cultural rights as "myths" which do not deserve the appellation of "rights."[47] Nevertheless, there can be no doubt that the admittedly aspirational rights set forth in the Covenant on Economic, Social and Cultural Rights represent values shared around the world, including in the United States. Indeed, it is significant that no state to date has ratified the Covenant on Civil and Political Rights without also ratifying the Covenant on Economic, Social and Cultural Rights (although Greece, Guatemala, the Solomon Islands, and Uganda have ratified only the latter). While the right to education or to social security, for example, may not enjoy the status of constitutionally guaranteed rights in the United States, they are fundamental obligations of government both in the United States and the rest of the world.

The Covenant on Civil and Political Rights contains guarantees much more familiar to Americans, and each party undertakes "to respect and to ensure to all individuals within its territory and subject to its jurisdiction" all the rights recognized in the covenant.[48] These rights include, *inter alia*, the right to life and to protection against the arbitrary deprivation of life (excluding any reference to the issue of abortion); freedom from torture or cruel, inhuman, or degrading treatment or punishment; freedom from slavery; the right to liberty and security of person; the prohibition of arbitrary arrest or detention; the right to a fair and public trial; the right of detainees to be treated with dignity; the prohibition of imprisonment for debt; freedom of movement and residence, including the right to leave any

---

[46] Note 3, art. 2(1) (hereinafter ESC Covenant); cf. P. Alston and G. Quinn, "The Nature and Scope of States Parties' Obligations under the International Covenant on Economic, Social and Cultural Rights," 9 *Hum. Rts. Q.* 156 (1987).

[47] This view was particularly widespread among officials in the Reagan Administration. See, e.g., P. Dobriansky, "US Human Rights Policy: An Overview," US Dept. of State, Bureau of Public Affairs, Current Policy No. 1091 (1988). For a sampling of different views on this issue, see Newman & Weissbrodt, note 14 above, at 359–410.

[48] Note 3 above, art. 2(1).

country; protection for aliens lawfully within a state's territory against arbitrary expulsion; the prohibition of retroactive punishment; the right to recognition as a person before the law and to equality before the law; protection against arbitrary interference with privacy, family, home, and correspondence; freedom of thought, conscience, religion, opinion, expression, association, and peaceful assembly; protection for the family and children; the right to participate in public affairs; the prohibition of discrimination; and the right of minorities to enjoy their own cultures, practice their religions, and use their own languages.

Neither covenant creates an international body capable of delivering binding or authoritative judgments on the rights included therein. However, both oblige parties to submit periodic reports on the measures they have adopted to achieve or guarantee the relevant rights.[49] The Covenant on Economic, Social and Cultural Rights provides only that these reports will be considered by the Economic and Social Council, which, after two unsuccessful attempts, created an expert committee in 1986 to review the reports.[50] This committee has begun to prepare "general comments" on the substance of the rights guaranteed under the Covenant. Although these observations do not by themselves have the status of authoritative interpretations, they may be significant as reflections of state practice or expert opinion which, in turn, can contribute to the formation of customary law.[51]

The Covenant on Civil and Political Rights does create a special body of independent experts to oversee its implementation, the Human Rights Committee. The eighteen-member Committee is elected by the states parties and examines the reports submitted to it by states under Article 40 of the Covenant. Its annual reports to the General Assembly include a summary of the discussions of the reports among Committee members and state representatives, and the Committee also has adopted a number of interpretive "general comments" on various provisions of the covenant.[52]

Fifty-one states have accepted the Optional Protocol to the Covenant on Civil and Political Rights, under which the Human Rights Committee is

---

[49] ESC Covenant, note 3 above, art. 16; CPR Covenant, note 3 above, art. 40.

[50] See P. Alston, "Out of the Abyss: The Challenges Confronting the New UN Committee on Economic, Social and Cultural Rights," 9 *Hum. Rts. Q.* 332 (1987).

[51] The methods of work of the committee are described in Committee on Economic, Social and Cultural Rights, Report on the Fourth Session, 1990 ESCOR, Supp. No. 3, at 6–11 (1990), UN Doc. E/1990/23.

[52] See generally D. Fischer, "Reporting under the Covenant on Civil and Political Rights: The First Five Years of the Human Rights Committee," 76 *AJIL* 142 (1982). The general comments adopted by the Committee up to April 1989 may be found in UN Doc. CCPR/C/21/Rev.1 (1989). The response of states to the Committee's comments is analyzed in C. Cohn, "The Early Harvest: Domestic Legal Changes Related to the Human Rights Committee and the Covenant on Civil and Political Rights," 13 *Hum. Rts. Q.* 295 (1991).

granted competence to consider communications from individual victims alleging violations of the Covenant. Although the Committee is not a court with the power to issue judgments and may only "forward its views" to the state and individual concerned, its consideration of hundreds of communications under the Optional Protocol has enabled it to interpret the covenant in a wide variety of specific-fact situations. While the body of jurisprudence that the Committee is developing does not constitute binding precedent, the Committee's opinions certainly contribute to defining the international norms of the covenant.[53] The general acceptance of the Committee's "views" by states further contributes to the evidentiary value of the Committee's opinions.[54]

2. Convention on the Elimination of All Forms of Racial Discrimination[55]

The Convention on the Elimination of All Forms of Racial Discrimination (CERD) was adopted by the General Assembly in 1965, one year before the covenants and only two years after the Assembly adopted a declaration on the same subject.[56] Perhaps because of its more limited focus, as well as more general agreement on its contents, the CERD was drafted much more quickly than the covenants. It is one of the most widely ratified human rights conventions (excluding the 1949 Geneva Conventions on the laws of war) with at least 141 parties as of 1995.

The relatively short Convention commits states, *inter alia*, "to pursue by all appropriate means and without delay a policy of eliminating racial discrimination in all its forms and promoting understanding among all races."[57] States agree to guarantee equality before the law with respect to a wide range of civil, political, economic, social, and cultural rights and to prohibit the dissemination of propaganda based on ideas of racial superiority or that incite racial hatred. The term "racial discrimination" includes distinctions based on "race, colour, descent, or national or ethnic origin," although temporary affirmative action programs are specifically excluded from this definition.[58]

The implementation procedures of the CERD are similar to those created under the CPR Covenant. Under Article 9, states must submit periodic reports to the Committee. Only nineteen states have made the

---

[53] The Committee's decisions are published in its annual reports to the General Assembly. Two compilations of Selected Decisions under the Optional Protocol also have appeared: see UN Doc. No. CCPR/C/OP/1 (1985); UN Doc. No. CCPR/C/OP/2 (1990).

[54] See, e.g., the responses of Canada, Mauritius, and Finland to the Committee's views in particular cases, reprinted in Selected Decisions (1990), note 53 above, at 224–26.

[55] Note 15 above.

[56] Declaration on the Elimination of All Forms of Racial Discrimination, GA Res. 1904 (XVIII) (Nov. 20, 1963).   [57] *Ibid.*, art. 2(1).   [58] *Ibid.*, arts. 1(1) & 1(4).

optional declaration under Article 14 that permits the Committee to consider individual complaints, and no party has availed itself of the right provided in Articles 11–13 to file a complaint against another state party.

An analysis of the comments made by the Committee on specific periodic reports may permit one to discern the opinions of Committee members as to the compatibility of various acts with the CERD, but it is difficult to conclude that the Committee exercises any law-making functions. While, like the Human Rights Committee, its interpretations may eventually acquire a certain persuasive status, the positive law of the Convention is now defined only by the text itself.

3. Convention against Torture and Other Cruel, Inhuman or Degrading Treatment or Punishment [59]

Like the CERD and the covenants, the Convention against Torture was preceded by a General Assembly declaration on the same matter.[60] The initiative for both the declaration and subsequent Convention came from a nongovernmental organization, Amnesty International, supported in particular by Denmark, Sweden, and the Netherlands. The General Assembly first addressed the specific issue of torture in 1973,[61] and the following year it requested the Fifth UN Congress on the Prevention of Crime and Treatment of Offenders (which was meeting in 1975) to consider the problem. The declaration finally adopted was based on a draft prepared by the Congress.

In 1977, the General Assembly requested the Commission on Human Rights to prepare a draft convention against torture, which the Commission did over the next several years. Agreement on the Convention's implementation mechanisms was reached at the 1984 session of the General Assembly, and the Convention was adopted; by 1995 there were eighty-five parties.

The prohibition against torture undoubtedly formed part of customary international law by the time the Convention was adopted in 1984,[62] and

---

[59] Note 15 above.

[60] Declaration on the Protection of All Persons from Being Subjected to Torture and Other Cruel, Inhuman or Degrading Treatment or Punishment, GA Res. 3452 (Dec. 9, 1975). For a history of the declaration and Convention, see N. Rodley, *The Treatment of Prisoners under International Law* 17–48, 125–32 (1987).

[61] See GA Res. 3059 (XXVIII) (Nov. 2, 1973).

[62] See, e.g., *Restatement*, note 44 above, § 702 cmnt. g, at 164, and reporters' note 5, at 169–71; *Filartiga v. Peña-Irala*, 630 F.2d 875 (2d Cir. 1980). More than a hundred states are bound by the absolute prohibition against torture in the Covenant on Civil and Political Rights and/or the European, American, or African human rights conventions, and regional conventions against torture have been adopted by the Council of Europe and the OAS.

the unanimous approval by the General Assembly of the declaration and Convention is best interpreted as confirming the existence of such a customary international law norm. The Convention does set forth a detailed definition of torture (although not of "cruel, inhuman or degrading treatment or punishment"), which would certainly be relevant in determining whether or not a particular act fell within the customary law prohibition. Procedural obligations on parties to the Convention are similar to those under the CPR Covenant.

4. Convention on the Rights of the Child[63]

Thirty years after its adoption of a Declaration on the Rights of the Child,[64] the General Assembly adopted a corresponding convention. Based on the decade-long work of an open-ended working group of the Commission on Human Rights, led by Poland, the Convention addresses a wide range of rights. As is the case for the Convention on Migrant Workers, many of these provisions simply reiterate rights guaranteed to everyone by other conventions,[65] although others do address issues of specific concern to children.[66]

The Convention on the Rights of the Child creates a treaty-monitoring body of experts, the Committee on the Rights of the Child, which is to review periodic reports submitted to it by states parties. However, the Committee may only "make suggestions and general recommendations" based on information in the reports;[67] there is no provision for even an optional complaint mechanism. The Convention does encourage the participation of the UN specialized agencies (such as UNICEF) in the Committee's work, as appropriate. By early 1995, the Convention had been ratified by at least 174 states and its provisions have thus become binding legal obligations for most states.

5. Convention on the Protection of the Rights of All Migrant Workers and Members of Their Families[68]

Rather unusually, the Convention on Migrant Workers was drafted by an open-ended working group of the General Assembly itself, established in 1979, in which all UN member states could participate.[69] Perhaps because

---

[63] Note 1 above.   [64] GA Res. 1386 (XIV) (Nov. 20, 1959).

[65] See, e.g., arts. 13 (freedom of expression), 14 (freedom of conscience), 15 (freedom of association), & 16 (right to privacy).

[66] E.g., arts. 3 (best interests of the child to guide social welfare institutions), 20 (obligation to protect children without families), & 34 (protection from sexual exploitation).

[67] Art. 45(d).   [68] Note 1 above.   [69] GA Res. 34/172 (Dec. 17, 1979).

of this broad participation (and also due to substantive disagreements as to the scope and purpose of the convention), it took ten years for agreement to be reached on a text that was eventually adopted without a vote by the Assembly in 1990.

Another complicating factor was the subject matter, which clearly fell within the competence of the International Labour Organization. In fact, the Preamble to the Convention refers to the "principles and standards" set forth in relevant ILO instruments, noting in particular the Conventions concerning Forced Labor (No. 29) (1930), Migration for Employment (Revised) (No. 97) (1949), Abolition of Forced Labor (No. 105) (1957), and Migrations in Abusive Conditions and the Promotion of Equality of Opportunity and Treatment of Migrant Workers (No. 143) (1975).

The lengthy Convention guarantees basic human rights, essentially tracking the International Bill of Human Rights, to all migrant workers, whether they and their families are in the country of residence legally ("documented") or illegally ("non-documented"). Additional rights are granted to documented workers and their families. The very broad scope of the Convention, as well as the sensitive nature of its subject matter (which many states perceive as being essentially of domestic concern), may explain the fact that it had received only six ratifications as of December 31, 1995.

6. Convention on the Suppression and Punishment of the Crime of Apartheid[70]

Unlike most of the treaties discussed thus far, the Convention against Apartheid had a relatively quick passage from proposal to adoption. A draft was first submitted to the General Assembly in 1971; following revisions and comments over the next two years by governments, the Commission on Human Rights, the Assembly's Special Committee on Apartheid, and the Third Committee, the Convention was approved and opened for ratification only two years later.[71]

In view of the refusal of most Western states to ratify the Convention, its provisions should be considered to be legally binding only on the states parties. However, the fact that apartheid has been designated as an international crime by the ninety-nine states that have ratified the Convention does underscore the customary international law prohibition of the practice of systematic racial discrimination (excluding the issue of individual criminal liability).[72]

---

[70] Note 15 above.
[71] See *Review of the Multilateral Treatymaking Process*, note 4 above, at 187–88.
[72] Cf. *Restatement*, note 44 above, § 702(f) reporters, note 7, at 172.

7. *Convention and Protocol on the Status of Refugees*[73]

The office of UN High Commissioner for Refugees was created by the General Assembly in 1950,[74] primarily to respond to the great numbers of refugees caused by World War II and its aftermath. The UNHCR's mandate, originally limited to those fleeing individual persecution in Europe, has been gradually expanded to include various categories of internationally displaced persons,[75] and UNHCR is today probably one of the best-known UN agencies; it has twice been awarded the Nobel Prize for Peace.

The basic obligation of the more than one hundred parties to the Convention and/or Protocol is not to return a refugee to a country in which "his life or freedom would be threatened on account of his race, religion, nationality, membership of a particular social group or political opinion."[76] The activities of the UNHCR are governed by the General Assembly, in much the same manner as any UN agency is subject to the Assembly's ultimate authority. Thus, in addition to the obligations binding on parties to the treaties, all UN member states are bound by the institutional decisions that have gradually expanded the UNHCR's role.

B. Declarations, resolutions, and principles

As noted in part I above, adoption by the UN General Assembly and other bodies of formally nonbinding declarations, statements of principles, and ordinary resolutions can have an impact on the creation of international law. As noted in 1962 by the UN Office of Legal Affairs,

> in view of the solemnity and significance of a "declaration," it may be considered to impart, on behalf of the organ adopting it, a strong expectation that members of the international community will abide by it. Consequently, in so far as the expectation is gradually justified by State practice, a declaration may by custom become recognized as laying down rules binding upon States.[77]

In the field of human rights, UN resolutions may be usefully placed in one of three categories. The first, mentioned above, includes those resolutions that are adopted by consensus, provide additional content or more specific definition to already accepted rights, and are widely seen as constituting a step in a process which will lead to the adoption of a binding convention on

---

[73] Convention Relating to the Status of Refugees, July 28, 1951, 189 UNTS 137 (*entered into force* Apr. 22, 1954); Protocol Relating to the Status of Refugees, *opened for signature* Jan. 31, 1967, 606 UNTS 267 (*entered into force* Oct. 4, 1967).

[74] GA Res. 428 (V) (Dec. 14, 1950).

[75] See G. Goodwin-Gill, *The Refugee in International Law* 6–13 (1983).

[76] Refugee Convention, note 73 above, art. 33.

[77] Quoted in *United Nations Action in the Field of Human Rights*, note 14 above, at 309.

the topic. Examples of such resolutions are the Universal Declaration of Human Rights,[78] Declaration on the Rights of the Child,[79] Declaration on the Elimination of Discrimination against Women,[80] the Declaration against Torture,[81] the Declaration on the Elimination of All Forms of Intolerance and of Discrimination Based on Religion or Belief,[82] and the Declaration on the Rights of Persons belonging to National or Ethnic, Religious or Linguistic Minorities.[83] Adoption of such declarations by the General Assembly at the very least legitimizes continuing interest by the United Nations in the subject and identifies areas in which new law is likely to be developed.

Resolutions in the second category set forth nonbinding guidelines or principles on fairly specific subjects.[84] Because of their specificity or the diverse practice of states, there is no intention for their provisions to become immediately or universally binding, and they are not generally perceived as appropriate for development into conventions. Many of these resolutions are within the area of the administration of criminal justice and the treatment of detainees,[85] such as the Standard Minimum Rules for the Treatment of Prisoners,[86] Code of Conduct for Law Enforcement Officials,[87] Principles of Medical Ethics Relevant to the Protection of Prisoners and Detainees,[88] Safeguards Guaranteeing Protection of the Rights of Those Facing the Death Penalty,[89] Standard Minimum Rules for the Administration of Juvenile Justice,[90] Declaration of Basic Principles of Justice for Victims of Crime and Abuse of Power,[91] Basic Principles on the Independence of the Judiciary,[92] Standard Minimum Rules for Non-

---

[78] Note 6 above.   [79] *Ibid.*   [80] GA Res. 2263 (XXII) (Nov. 7, 1967).

[81] Note 61 above.

[82] GA Res. 36/55 (Nov. 25, 1981). As of the end of 1990, there were no plans to draft a convention on the subject matter of the declaration, perhaps reflecting the sensitivity of most governments to the issue. The Subcommission on Prevention of Discrimination and Protection of Minorities appointed a rapporteur to study factors that should be considered before a binding instrument is adopted, which it determined "should be considered in the light of the complexity of the subject matter which requires careful preparatory work, sound research and analysis," Subcommission Res. 1989/23 (Aug. 31, 1989). The Commission on Human Rights appointed a special rapporteur to report annually on implementation of the declaration, CHR Res. 1986/20 (Mar. 10, 1986).   [83] GA Res. 47/135 (18 Dec. 1992).

[84] See generally J. Toman, "Quasi-Legal Standards and Guidelines for Protecting Human Rights," in *Guide to International Human Rights Practice* (H. Hannum ed., 2d ed., 1992).

[85] See generally Rodley, note 60 above and R. Clark, *The United Nations Crime Prevention and Criminal Justice Program* (1994).

[86] ESC Res. 663C (XXIV) (July 31, 1957), *extended,* ESC Res. 2076 (LXIII) (May 13, 1977).

[87] GA Res. 34/169 (Dec. 17, 1979).   [88] GA Res. 37/194 (Dec. 18, 1982).

[89] ESC Res. 1984/50 (May 25, 1984).

[90] GA Res. 40/33 (Nov. 29, 1985) (known as the "Beijing Rules").

[91] GA Res. 40/34 (Nov. 29, 1985).

[92] *Adopted* by the Seventh UN Congress on the Prevention of Crime and the Treatment of Offenders and *endorsed* by GA Res. No. 40/32 (Nov. 29, 1985) and GA Res. No. 40/146 (Dec. 13, 1985).

Custodial Measures,[93] and Guidelines for the Prevention of Juvenile Delinquency.[94]

The third category comprises resolutions that proclaim human rights standards in new and more controversial areas.[95] Many of these resolutions concern economic and social rights, and they have often been adopted with dissenting or abstaining votes (or, at least, qualifying statements by governments which disagree with the principles being adopted but choose not to force a vote). Within this category would be the Declaration on Social Progress and Development,[96] Declaration on the Right of Peoples to Peace,[97] Declaration on the Right to Development,[98] Declaration on Race and Racial Prejudice,[99] and Declaration on Fundamental Principles Concerning the Contribution of the Mass Media to Strengthening Peace and International Understanding, to the Promotion of Human Rights and to Countering Racialism, Apartheid and Incitement to War.[100]

The degree of "law-making" significance of the UN declarations discussed in this section and similar resolutions or recommendations varies considerably. In the human rights area, however, the political impact is likely to be as significant as the purely legal effect. For example, minorities and indigenous peoples have cited draft declarations being considered in UN forums as a "standard of achievement" (to borrow a phrase from the Universal Declaration of Human Rights) in their discussions with governments.[101]

At the time of their adoption, most UN resolutions on human rights are promotional rather than restatements or reaffirmations of legal norms. However, to suggest that they do not contribute to law-making is to underestimate the impact of "merely" moral or political statements in the area of human rights.

C. Studies and reports

Some UN studies and reports have had a significant influence in developing the content of international human rights norms, although such studies

---

93 GA Res. 45/110 (Dec. 14, 1990).

94 GA Res. 45/112 (Dec. 14, 1990) (known as the "Riyadh Guidelines").

95 When they were adopted, some of the resolutions on self-determination might be considered to have fallen within this category, although the decolonization norms they expressed were subsequently accepted by states.   96 GA Res. 2542 (XXIV) (Dec. 11, 1969).

97 GA Res. 39/11 (Nov. 12, 1984).   98 GA Res. 41/128 (Dec. 4, 1986).

99 UNESCO Res. of Nov. 27, 1978.   100 UNESCO Res. of Nov. 28, 1978.

101 Cf. H. Hannum, "Contemporary Developments in the International Protection of the Rights of Minorities," 66 *Notre Dame L. Rev.* 1431 (1991); H. Hannum, "New Developments in Indigenous Rights," 28 *Va. J. Int'l L.* 649 (1988). The Commission on Human Rights began considering a draft declaration on indigenous rights in 1995, following its adoption by the Subcommission.

studies & reports

enjoy no legal standing and do not purport to be authoritative interpretations of customary or conventional law. Most have been undertaken under the auspices of the UN Subcommission on Prevention of Discrimination and Protection of Minorities, and they are often based primarily on information compiled by the UN Secretariat from government submissions.[102]

The attention accorded to any particular study depends as much on the reputation of the author as on the thoroughness of the work. In most instances, studies undertaken by rapporteurs appointed by the Subcommission identify gaps in either normative standards or implementation; their conclusions may become the basis for future consideration of formal declarations or conventions. Studies are not normally "approved" by UN bodies, and they remain the opinions of the authors rather than formal statements of the United Nations.

IV. LAW-MAKING BY THE UN'S SPECIALIZED AGENCIES

The law-making role of the General Assembly in adopting treaties pales when compared to that of many of the specialized agencies. The International Labour Organization had adopted 175 conventions as of 1996, which had received a total of over 6,000 ratifications. Most of the ILO conventions can be considered to concern human rights, and among the most important are the conventions on forced labor,[103] freedom of association and the right to organize,[104] collective bargaining,[105] indigenous peoples,[106] and discrimination in employment.[107]

The UN Educational, Scientific and Cultural Organization (UNESCO) also has adopted a number of conventions, the most important of which is the Convention against Discrimination in Education.[108] Treaties and binding regulations adopted by organizations such as the World Health Organization, International Telecommunications Union, and other "technical" organizations under the United Nations umbrella may have significant indirect effects on human rights, such as freedom of information and access to communication.

In addition, the specialized agencies may address recommendations to states either by means of general resolutions or through the provision of technical assistance, advisory services, and other informal or country-

---

[102] A list of the major studies undertaken through 1988 may be found in *United Nations Action in the Field of Human Rights*, note 14 above , at 337–40.

[103] Nos. 29 (1930) & 105 (1957).   [104] No. 87 (1948).   [105] No. 98 (1949).

[106] Nos. 107 (1957) & 169 (1989).   [107] No. 111 (1958).

[108] Dec. 14, 1960, 429 UNTS 93 (*entered into force* May 22, 1962).

148

specific means. It has become common practice for the ILO to adopt detailed recommendations in conjunction with newly adopted conventions, and UNESCO also has adopted a wide range of declarations and recommendations.

The ILO has a very well-developed system for supervising the implementation of ILO conventions and recommendations, which includes discussion by both individual experts and state representatives of alleged instances of the nonfulfillment of conventional obligations.[109] The ILO also has developed mechanisms for considering complaints of violations of the right of freedom of association.[110] While such procedures do not lead to legally binding judgments being issued by courts (although many human rights treaties do include provisions that would allow the International Court of Justice to decide disputes between parties as to the interpretation of the convention), they do gradually develop what might be termed "common practice" as opposed to "common law."

V. CUSTOMARY INTERNATIONAL LAW OF HUMAN RIGHTS

All of the above-mentioned acts by the United Nations – the adoption of conventions and resolutions, the opinions of international monitoring bodies, studies and reports, statements made in the United Nations by government representatives – may contribute to creating customary international law. Given the extent of UN activities in the field of human rights, the United Nations' contribution to the customary international law of human rights may be greater than its contribution in any other field.[111]

A "juristic debate has taken place for some years on whether human rights in whole or in part has become part of general customary international law."[112] Several distinguished commentators have taken the position that the entire Universal Declaration of Human Rights now

---

109 The ILO's Committee of Experts on the Application of Conventions and Recommendations submits a detailed public report, which includes criticisms of the actions of named countries with respect to specific conventions, to each session of the International Labour Conference.

110 See L. Swepston, "Human Rights Complaint Procedures of the International Labor Organization," in Hannum ed., note 84 above.

111 Of course, regional organizations, such as those established under the European Convention on Human Rights, American Convention on Human Rights, and African Charter on Human and Peoples' Rights, also play a role in developing customary law.

112 O. Schachter, *International Law in Theory and Practice* 335 (1991). Schachter suggests that the issue of whether human rights obligations have become customary law "cannot readily be answered on the basis of the usual process of customary law formation" and, after surveying various arguments, concludes that "a number of human rights are now part of customary law." *Ibid.* at 336, 342. A survey of state practice regarding the Universal Declaration may be found in H. Hannum, "The Status of the Universal Declaration of Human Rights in National and International Law," 25 *Ga. J. Int'l & Comp. L.* 287 (1995/96).

represents customary international law,[113] although such expansive claims are probably not supported by a majority of international legal scholars.

A more restrained and undoubtedly more widely accepted view is presented in the *Restatement (Third) of The Foreign Relations Law of the United States,* which identifies the following acts as violations of international law, if practiced, encouraged, or condoned as a matter of state policy: (a) genocide; (b) slavery or slave trade; (c) the murder or causing the disappearance of individuals; (d) torture or other cruel, inhuman, or degrading treatment or punishment; (e) prolonged arbitrary detention; (f) systematic racial discrimination; and (g) a consistent pattern of gross violations of internationally recognized human rights.[114]

The United Nations has made a substantial contribution to identifying and defining each of these norms.

Genocide is largely defined by the Convention on the Prevention and Punishment of the Crime of Genocide,[115] which was adopted in 1948 by the UN General Assembly. Slavery was outlawed well before the establishment of the United Nations, but the most widely ratified convention was adopted by a conference convened by the Economic and Social Council.[116] Pursuant to these treaties, each of which has been ratified by more than a hundred states, countries agree to punish genocide and slavery as crimes under their domestic laws.

"Disappearances" came to the attention of the world (and the United Nations) in the 1970s, primarily in response to use of the practice of unacknowledged detention (and often torture and murder) in Chile and Argentina. The UN Commission on Human Rights created a working group on disappearances in 1980 and, along with the Inter-American Commission of Human Rights, was largely responsible for identifying and condemning this new form of human rights violation.[117]

As noted above, the United Nations General Assembly adopted a Declaration against Torture in 1975 and the widely ratified Convention

---

[113] See, e.g., M. McDougal, H. Lasswell, & L. Chen, *Human Rights and World Public Order* 274, 325, 338 (1980); J. Humphrey, "The International Bill of Rights: Scope and Implementation," 17 *Wm. & Mary L. Rev.* 527, 529 (1976); L. Sohn, "The Human Rights Law of the Charter," 12 *Tex. Int'l L.J.* 129, 133 (1977); H. Waldock, "Human Rights in Contemporary International Law and the Significance of the European Convention," in *The European Convention of Human Rights* 1, 15 (Brit. Inst. Int'l & Comp. L. Ser. No. 5, 1965).

[114] *Restatement,* note 44 above, § 702.

[115] Genocide is defined as a number of acts, such as killing, "committed with intent to destroy, in whole or in part, a national ethnical, racial or religious group, as such." Convention on the Prevention and Punishment of the Crime of Genocide, *opened for signature* Dec. 9, 1948, 78 UNTS 277, art. 2 (*entered into force* Jan. 12, 1951; *entered into force for US* Feb. 23, 1989).

[116] Supplementary Convention on the Abolition of Slavery, the Slave Trade, and Institutions and Practices Similar to Slavery, Sept. 7, 1956, 266 UNTS 3 (*entered into force* Apr. 30, 1957); cf. ESC Res. 608 (XXI) (Apr. 30, 1956).

[117] See Rodley, note 60 above, at 191–218.

against Torture in 1984. Similar prohibitions are contained in regional human rights instruments.

Prolonged arbitrary detention has been recognized by US courts as violating customary international law,[118] and the International Bill of Rights and other UN activities have complemented longstanding domestic prohibitions against arbitrary arrest and imprisonment. Systematic racial discrimination, as exemplified by the practice of apartheid, has long been condemned vociferously by the United Nations.

The catch-all prohibition against "a consistent pattern of gross violations of human rights" is drawn directly from Economic and Social Council Resolution 1503, which uses this language as the standard for determining whether the United Nations will consider allegations of human rights.[119] This language also has been used by the US Congress in placing restrictions on the provision of military and economic assistance to countries that violate human rights.[120]

Thus, the UN contribution to the formation of customary international law in the area of human rights has been formidable. While the United Nations itself may not be able to "create" law, its growing concern with human rights has led states to recognize their legal obligation to promote and protect a growing number of fundamental human rights.

VI. CONCLUSION

Criticisms of the United Nations' role in human rights law-making are similar to those directed to its law-making activities in general.[121] Responding in part to such criticisms, the General Assembly adopted in 1986 a resolution on "Setting international standards in the field of human rights."[122] Recognizing that "standard setting should proceed with adequate preparation,"[123] the resolution offers guidelines for the development of additional international human rights instruments, which should:

(i) be consistent with the existing body of international human rights law;

(ii) be of fundamental character and derive from the inherent dignity and worth of the human person;

[118] *Rodriguez-Fernandez* v. *Wilkinson*, 505 F.Supp. 787 (D. Kan. 1980), *aff'd on other grounds*, 654 F.2d 1382 (10th Cir. 1981). [119] See discussion above, at notes 33–36.
[120] See, e.g., §§ 116 & 502B of the Foreign Assistance Act.
[121] See, e.g., Meron (1986), note 14 above; P. Alston, "Conjuring up New Human Rights: A Proposal for Quality Control," 78 *AJIL* 607 (1984).
[122] GA Res. 41/120 (Dec. 4, 1986). [123] *Ibid.*, Preamble.

(iii) be sufficiently precise to give rise to identifiable and practicable rights and obligations;

(iv) provide, where appropriate, realistic and effective implementation machinery, including reporting systems; [and]

(v) attract broad international support.[124]

No one has yet drafted the perfect treaty, and the two major human rights conventions adopted since 1986 – the Convention on the Rights of the Child and the Convention on Migrant Workers – are not without their problems. Both set forth the rights guaranteed in exhaustive detail, perhaps in order to conform to the first injunction noted above. Certainly children and migrant workers deserve special protection, and there was broad international support for addressing the rights of these groups (despite substantial differences on specific provisions). The provisions of the two conventions do leave quite a bit of room for interpretation, and there may be some question as to whether they are "sufficiently precise to give rise to identifiable and practicable rights and obligations."[125] Nevertheless, the standards are far from illusory, and all treaties (whether in the human rights or any other field) rely primarily on the good faith of governments for their implementation.

The mandate for "realistic and effective implementation" is particularly difficult for a human rights convention to meet. What is "realistic" may be, in many instances, an extremely weak supervisory system, while the opposite may be needed to ensure "effective" implementation. Neither the children's nor the migrant workers' convention provides for a mandatory complaint mechanism, although the latter does include optional provisions for individual and interstate complaints. Yet the review of obligatory periodic reports does at least require states to justify their compliance before an independent international body; it also provides a focus for the more important domestic constituencies that may be expected to follow implementation of each convention closely.[126]

Substantive criticism of the United Nations' human rights law-making has focused on the fringes, not on the broadly accepted core of human rights instruments. There is a vast body of human rights law upon which there is broad agreement, most of which was identified and defined by the United Nations, its human rights organs, or its specialized agencies.

---

[124] *Ibid.*, para. 4.

[125] All of the rights in the Convention on the Rights of the Child, for example, are subject to the general provision in art. 6 that "States Parties shall respect the responsibilities, rights, and duties of parents . . . to provide . . . appropriate direction and guidance in the exercise by the child of the rights recognized in the present Convention."

[126] This might be compared to the 1948 Genocide Convention, note 115 above, which contains no provision whatsoever for its implementation or supervision.

Without the international standards developed by the United Nations, the linkage of foreign policy to human rights conditions in other countries would be open to devastating charges of "cultural imperialism" or interference in "domestic affairs." Agreement on international norms also has made possible the increasingly frequent linkage by the UN Security Council of respect for human rights with the maintenance of international peace and security, in situations such those in Bosnia–Herzegovina and Haiti.

Without minimizing the contribution to human rights made by regional organizations and many states, international human rights law is largely a creation of the United Nations. And, without ignoring the substantial problems of implementation, it is a creation that ranks as one of the United Nations' great accomplishments.

SELECTED BIBLIOGRAPHY

Carey, J., *UN Protection of Civil and Political Rights* (Syracuse, 1970)

Center for the Study of Human Rights, *Human Rights: A Topical Bibliography* (Westview, 1983)

Hannum, H., *Guide to International Human Rights Practice* (2d ed., University of Pennsylvania Press, 1992)

Human Rights in International Law (T. Meron ed.; Clarendon Press, 1984)

The International Bill of Rights, the Covenant on Civil And Political Rights (L. Henkin ed.; Columbia University Press, 1981)

The International Dimensions of Human Rights (K. Vasak and P. Alston eds.; Greenwood, 1982)

Lawson, E., *Encyclopedia of Human Rights* (Taylor & Francis, 1991)

Lillich, R. and Hannum, H., *International Human Rights* (3d ed.; Little Brown, 1995)

Meron, T., *Human Rights Lawmaking in the United Nations* (Oxford University Press, 1986)

Newman, F. and D. Weissbrodt, *International Human Rights* (Anderson, 1990)

Sieghart, P., *The International Law of Human Rights* (Clarendon Press, 1983)

Sohn, L. and T. Buergenthal, *International Protection of Human Rights* (Bobbs-Merrill, 1973)

The United Nations and Human Rights (P. Alston ed., 1992)

United Nations, *United Nations Action in the Field of Human Rights* (1988)

United Nations, *A Compilation of International Instruments* (1988)

US Ratification of the International Covenants on Human Rights (H. Hannum and D. Fischer eds.; Transnational, 1992)

Vincent-Daviss, D., "Human Rights Law: A Research Guide to the Literature – Part I: International Law and the United Nations," 14 *NYU J. Int'l L. & Pol.* 209 (1981); "Part II: International Protection of Refugees and Humanitarian

Law," 14 *NYU J. Int'l L. & Pol.* 487 (1982); "Part III: The International Labor Organization and Human Rights," 15 *NYU J. Int'l L. & Pol..* 211 (1982)

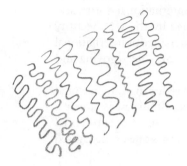

CHAPTER SIX

REFUGEES AND MIGRATION

David A. Martin

I. INTRODUCTION

The field of human migration may seem an unlikely setting for exploring the impact of international law. Ordinarily national governments are jealously protective of their sovereign right to control the entry and sojourn of foreigners. Leading courts have issued broad pronouncements ratifying unconstrained political discretion over choices in this domain and holding squarely that international law blesses this sovereign prerogative.[1] And executive branch authorities, not surprisingly, are fond of intoning the sounds of sovereignty in meetings on these subjects.

In most respects, international law at the global level has made only limited inroads in this realm. (Regional initiatives are another matter altogether. For example, common markets, most prominently the European Community, typically include free-movement arrangements that cede a substantial portion of the usual national control over migration.)[2] In one particular migration subfield, however, UN-generated international law plays a powerful role, a role of growing significance in the 1990s as migration pressures increase. That subfield is refugee law. Hundreds, perhaps thousands, of administrative and judicial decisions each day interpret and apply the international legal standards as the crucial test determining whether individuals will be permitted to remain within a haven state's territory. These decisions rely centrally on two UN treaties, the Convention and Protocol relating to the Status of Refugees,[3] to which over a hundred states are parties.

---

[1] See, e.g., *Nishimura Ekiu* v. *United States*, 142 US 651 (1892); *Musgrove* v. *Chun Teeong Toy*, 1891 AC 272.

[2] See generally R. Plender, *International Migration Law* 193–215, 273–88 (rev. 2d ed., 1988); G. Goodwin-Gill, *International Law and the Movement of Persons between States* (1978).

[3] Convention Relating to the Status of Refugees, *opened for signature* July 28, 1951, 189 UNTS 137 (hereinafter Convention); Protocol Relating to the Status of Refugees, *opened for signature* Jan. 31, 1967, 19 UST 6223, TIAS No. 6577, 606 UNTS 267 (hereinafter Protocol).

Even in states that have not signed these instruments, UN refugee law has an important effect, often framing the terms of national and regional responses to refugee flows. The 1989 Comprehensive Plan of Action to deal with the ongoing flow of asylum seekers from Indochina affords a recent and significant example. There the states of the region, most of whom are not parties to the treaties, agreed to institute a screening procedure based firmly on the UN Convention.[4] State practice of this sort also fortifies claims that at least some of the provisions of the Convention and Protocol now reflect customary international law.[5] Moreover, in virtually every refugee crisis, the office of the UN High Commissioner for Refugees (UNHCR), created by General Assembly resolution in 1950, plays a central role. Today the office works to enhance the legal protection of refugees – originally planned as its principal, if not sole, function – but also manages an annual budget of roughly half a billion US dollars for assistance to refugees.

II. THE UNHCR

A. The Statute

On December 14, 1950, the General Assembly adopted the Statute of the Office of the United Nations High Commissioner for Refugees, the initial statement of legislative authority for the new UN organ.[6] The Statute provided for a temporary organization, to be reconsidered by the General Assembly in late 1953 for a decision whether the Office should be continued.[7] (Its mandate was of course renewed, and certainly will continue to be renewed for the foreseeable future.) The General Assembly elects the High Commissioner, on the nomination of the Secretary-General, and the Office is based in Geneva.[8] High Commissioners' stated terms have varied in length between three years and five years, depending on the governing resolution at the time of election, and High Commissioners may be reelected. Reflecting the Office's status as a subsidiary organ of the General Assembly under Article 22 of the Charter, the Statute provides that UNHCR administrative expenditures are part of the mandatory UN budget, while any other outlays – including any for assistance to refugees – must derive from voluntary contributions. Prominent UN members were concerned in 1950, however, not to replicate the operational International Refugee Organization (IRO), a specialized agency that had taken the lead role in the UN's response to Europe's lingering refugee issues from 1947 to

---

[4] The text of the Comprehensive Plan of Action is published in 1 *Int'l J. Refugee L.* 574 (1989).
[5] See, e.g., Plender, note 2 above, at 425–33 (summarizing and evaluating claims as to the customary law status of certain refugee protections embodied in treaties).
[6] GA Res. 428 (V) (Annex) (Dec. 14, 1950).   [7] *Ibid.*, para. 5.   [8] *Ibid.*, paras. 13, 19.

1950. Therefore the Statute forbids the UNHCR to solicit voluntary contributions without prior approval of the General Assembly.[9]

Under the Statute, the High Commissioner's authority is thus essentially limited to the function of "providing international protection" for refugees within his mandate, and paragraph 8 sets forth a somewhat restricted list of ways in which that function is to be carried out.[10] That paragraph places primary emphasis on UNHCR's role in encouraging the voluntary action of states to extend rights to refugees, but it also speaks of promoting the conclusion of international treaties to these ends, and it envisions occasional UNHCR action in concert with private voluntary agencies. In the words of the leading historian on the Office, the UNHCR was not to be a "kind of government for refugees," as some had wished, but instead was to function, in the General Assembly's concept, as merely "an instrument for collaboration with the national authorities," who would ordinarily play the most important role in assisting and protecting refugees.[11] Paragraph 2 of the Statute furthers this message in providing that the "work of the High Commissioner shall be of an entirely non-political character; it shall be humanitarian and social and shall relate, as a rule, to groups and categories of refugees."

B. Expansion

Many of these provisions proved unrealistic in practice. UNHCR has found room for growth and flexibility within its original authorities, and it has also managed through the years to secure from the General Assembly expanded competence in many areas.[12]

[9] *Ibid.*, paras. 10, 20.
[10] Professor Holborn describes UNHCR's protection function as "an international substitute for the diplomatic and consular protection of a state which refugees by definition lack[; its purpose] is to give refugees a recognized legal status analogous to that of other nationals living abroad." L. Holborn, *Refugees: A Problem of Our Time: The Work of the United Nations High Commissioner for Refugees, 1951–1972*, I, 87 (1975). More recent usage explicitly incorporates another task for protection, one not described so candidly in earlier times because it seemed a more direct challenge to national sovereignty: "promotion of favourable conditions of admission of refugees and for the grant of asylum." J. Sztucki, "The Conclusions on the International Protection of Refugees Adopted by the Executive Committee of the High Commissioner's Programme," 1 *Int'l J. Refugee L.* 285, 291 (1989).
[11] Holborn, note 10 above, at 106. For a recent example of this state-focused perspective, see J. Kelley, "Refugee Protection: Whose Responsibility Is It Anyway?," *Int'l J. Refugee L.* 277 (Special Issue, Sept. 1990).
[12] It is important to bear in mind that the Statute is not a full statement of the legislative authority of the Office. Later General Assembly resolutions are of equal stature in setting the bounds of its mission and competence. The Office has compiled these legislative authorities (and similar statements from the ECOSOC, through which UNHCR reports to the General Assembly) in a looseleaf collection, frequently updated: United Nations Resolutions and Decisions Relating to the Office of the United Nations High Commissioner for Refugees, UN Doc. HCR/INF.49 (Geneva, 1989).

1. Political or humanitarian?

To begin with, the nonpolitical character of the Office is fictional; in a world of sovereign states, no High Commissioner could secure effective protection for refugees without a high degree of political skill. Nevertheless, the directive of paragraph 2 is honored in a limited but important sense of the word "political": the Office avoids assigning blame for the generation of refugee flows. The fiction thus remains useful, for states often find it possible to cooperate with the strictly "humanitarian" UNHCR in situations where more overtly political bodies would not be welcome. The Office thus can ameliorate the condition of refugees while resisting pressure to choose sides in the underlying conflict that caused their uprooting.

2. Protection versus assistance

The Statute's ostensible decision to confine the Office to protection functions, greatly downplaying any role in assistance, soon proved unworkable, for protection often is closely linked with the provision of material aid. As early as 1952, after vigorous debate, the General Assembly therefore granted limited permission to the Office to solicit contributions for an Emergency Fund to be used for assistance to needy refugees.[13] Over time, permission of this sort became routine, and by now the portion of the budget funded by voluntary contributions dwarfs the mandatory administrative budget by a factor of over thirty to one. In 1989, UNHCR spent over $570 million in voluntary funds. By 1992, the total exceeded $1 billion.[14] As a result, fundraising has become a major preoccupation of the High Commissioner in recent times, to provide care and maintenance for refugees increasingly turning up in developing countries unable to muster adequate financial resources on their own. The efforts of the donor countries, however, have often failed to keep pace with the needs, and in the late 1980s the UNHCR began facing a chronic funding crisis that has caused painful reassessment of priorities.[15]

During the first year of the Office, the ECOSOC exercised the optional authority granted by paragraph 4 of the Statute and created an advisory committee of state representatives to assist the High Commissioner. In 1954, this advisory committee was replaced by the UN Refugee Emergency Fund Executive Committee with directory authority over material assistance, which, as indicated, was becoming a more significant component of

---

[13] GA Res. 538B (VI) para. 1 (Feb. 2, 1952). See Holborn, note 10 above, at 135–39.

[14] Report of the UN High Comm'r for Refugees (1990), UN GAOR, Supp. 12, at 8, 38, UN Doc. A/45/12 (1990); ibid. (prelim. ed., 1993), UN Doc. E/1993/20, at 12 (1993).

[15] An instructive account appears in N. Morris, "Refugees: Facing Crisis in the 1990s – A Personal View from within UNHCR," Int'l J. Refugee L. 38 (Special Issue, Sept. 1990).

UNHCR activities. In 1958, this structure was in turn replaced by a body with similar authority that has continued with little modification to this day: the Executive Committee of the High Commissioner's Programme (Ex Comm). Now composed of forty-four members, the Ex Comm adopts the budget and oversees the operations of the office.[16] It also has assumed an important advisory role in adopting "Conclusions" on international protection, of which more later. The Ex Comm meets annually in Geneva in October, and occasionally gathers for other special meetings.[17]

Even as UNHCR has moved wholeheartedly into the assistance business, however, it has respected much of the original concern that it not become operational. Unlike the IRO, UNHCR owns no fleet. It ordinarily implements assistance projects not through its own extensive staff or inventory, but rather through contractual arrangements with private voluntary agencies, other UN bodies such as the Food and Agriculture Organization, and sometimes governments. The agencies are thus the operational partners, although UNHCR of course must maintain a sizeable staff of its own to oversee implementation, coordinate efforts of various players, and monitor the results.

3. Groups versus individuals: from "good offices" to an expanded mandate

Finally, the directive in paragraph 2 of the Statute, that the work of the Office would relate, as a rule, to groups and categories of refugees, coexisted uneasily with the sections of the Statute defining "refugee." Under the League of Nations, such a problem could not have arisen. Nansen and his successors could indeed concentrate on groups, for the instruments giving them authority defined refugees in categorical terms, referring for example to uprooted Russians or Armenians or Assyrians. The Statute of the UNHCR, in contrast, is a milestone on a long path away from time-limited and group-based designations toward a more neutral and abstract refugee definition.

In essence, the Statute defines a refugee as a person outside his or her own country, unwilling to claim its protection (or to return to its territory) because of a "well-founded fear of persecution for reasons of race, religion, nationality, or political opinion."[18] In some circumstances, of course, this

---

[16] GA Res. 45/138 (Dec. 14, 1990) increased the size of the ExComm to forty-four members.
[17] GA Res. 1166 (XII) (Nov. 26, 1957); ECOSOC Res. 672 (XXV) (Apr. 30, 1958). See Holborn, note 10 above, at 92; Sztucki, note 10 above, at 288–95.
[18] Statute, note 6 above , para. 6B. Para. 6B renders moot the limitations on the definition appearing in para. 6A, which was drafted to parallel the definition appearing in the then-current drafts of the UN Refugee Convention. Those limitations, primarily in the form of a dateline applying the definition only to those uprooted "as a result of events occurring before 1 January 1951," is described below at note 50 and accompanying text, p. 171.

definition might lend itself to group-based application – in exactly those circumstances where governments relentlessly persecute whole groups, as with Nazi Germany's treatment of Jews. But in most circumstances, one could not know whether an individual claiming to be a refugee met the definition without a highly individualized inquiry into his or her personal situation.[19]

Beyond this tension with paragraph 2 of the Statute, the definition often generated political sensitivities that hampered effective action by the Office. To treat a collection of displaced persons as refugees under the Statute's original mandate is to make a finding that the source state persecutes. Such an implicit insult posed a more limited problem during the early days, for refugee issues tended to reflect the East–West split, and the East was estranged from the Office and its work anyway. But when new situations arose outside the European context, new legal doctrines proved necessary.

A key precipitating event was the flight of Chinese from the mainland into Hong Kong, particularly in the mid-1950s. The United Kingdom, which governed Hong Kong, had recognized the communist government in Beijing and was unwilling to allow the nationalist government on Taiwan to assume the normal functions of diplomatic protection or assistance to nationals. Nevertheless Hong Kong was severely burdened by the influx and hoped to find a way to enlist UNHCR in helping to collect and channel needed material assistance. The nationalist government held China's seat at the UN, however, and the Statute's definition plainly did not cover the refugees if the Taiwan-based authorities were considered the relevant national government.

The legal breakthrough came when the General Assembly passed Resolution 1167 in 1957. Without any reference to the Statute, it declared the Hong Kong situation to be "of concern to the international community," and it explicitly authorized the High Commissioner "to use his *good offices* to encourage arrangements for contributions."[20] Employing a different verbal formulation, but still avoiding any reference to the Statute, the next year the General Assembly blessed the Office's involvement in providing assistance to refugees from Algeria who had fled to Morocco and Tunisia.[21] It thereby avoided a potentially delicate confrontation with France, another permanent member of the Security Council, which had been fighting to hold on to Algeria and would hardly have tolerated any suggestion that the Statute applied. A 1959 General Assembly resolution then firmly implanted the "good offices" concept, when in general terms it

---

[19] See generally D. Martin, "Reforming Asylum Adjudication: On Navigating the Coast of Bohemia," 138 *U. Pa. L. Rev.* 1247, 1270–87 (1990).

[20] GA Res. 1167 (XII) (Nov. 26, 1957) (emphasis added).

[21] GA Res. 1286 (XIII) (Dec. 5, 1958).

authorized the High Commissioner "in respect of refugees who do not come within the competence of the United Nations, to use his good offices in the transmission of contributions designed to provide assistance to these refugees."[22]

Gradually the Office's involvement with such groups expanded to include not only assistance but also classical protection functions as well. Often such an expansion was explained on the ground of a prima facie eligibility determination covering whole groups. Such an approach is considered justifiable – perhaps unavoidable – when refugees arrive in large numbers, thereby precluding fine-grained judgments about whether the threats facing specific individuals meet the persecution criteria of the Statute.[23]

In the early years General Assembly resolutions and UNHCR pronouncements maintained a fairly sharp distinction between mandate refugees and those for whom the High Commissioner simply extended good offices, thereby more scrupulously noting that the latter did not meet the criteria of the Statute. Since approximately 1965, however, General Assembly resolutions have tended to speak more broadly, referring simply to refugees within the High Commissioner's "competence" or "concern," without further subdivision of categories. By 1975, the General Assembly went still further, beginning what has now become a common reference to "refugees and displaced persons," who are considered proper subjects for UNHCR action.[24]

Practice now often includes among "displaced persons" both those who cross a national boundary for reasons distinct from those recognized in the Statute – principally fleeing war or civil strife, which is not necessarily linked to persecution per se – and those who have been driven from their homes but never crossed an international frontier. It remains a matter of greater delicacy to justify UNHCR involvement with the latter group,[25] but the world community seems increasingly willing to turn to the High Commissioner's Office as the key player in providing assistance in such circumstances. The recent crises in Iraq and the former Yugoslavia afford

22 GA Res. 1388 (XIV) (Nov. 20, 1959).
23 See Holborn, note 10 above, at 441–47; Office of the UN High Comm'r for Refugees, *Handbook on Procedures and Criteria for Determining Refugee Status*, para. 44 (1979).
24 See, e.g., GA Res. 3454, 3455 (XXX) (Dec. 9, 1975); GA Res. 31/35 para. 2 (Nov. 30, 1976); GA Res. 41/124 para. 9 (Dec. 4, 1986); GA Res. 44/137 (Dec. 15, 1989).
25 UNHCR first became involved with the internally displaced in the course of assisted return programs, beginning with Sudan in 1972. Because the international community was providing assistance to those crossing a frontier to return to their homelands, after the initial threat had ceased, it seemed pointless to exclude those equally uprooted but who had for whatever reason failed to cross a national boundary in the course of flight. See Sadruddin Aga Khan (then High Commissioner), "Legal Problems Relating to Refugees and Displaced Persons," 1976 [I] *RCADI* 287, 342.

notable examples. Concurrently, the UN system is beginning to devote more systematic attention to the international community's role in assisting the internally displaced.[26] Today one occasionally still finds attempts to draw distinctions between refugees in the sense of the original Statute and "good offices" refugees. But more commonly one finds the terminology treating all the above categories as within the UNHCR's "mandate."[27]

This evolution has made it far easier for the High Commissioner to avoid the political sensitivities implicated when the Statute's definition provided the only available conceptual framework. It also helps the Office to target most of its activities today on groups and categories, as paragraph 2 originally envisioned. For these and other reasons, the trend is to be welcomed. The international community should indeed be able to call upon the High Commissioner, with all the skills and technical expertise the Office has accumulated, whenever large groups of people are uprooted by politics or war – without bogging down in technical arguments about the exact nature of their flight. But this is a separate question from whether similar expansion is appropriate for purposes of determining the strict legal obligations of states under treaties to be considered in the next section.

III. THE UN CONVENTION AND PROTOCOL

A. Background

While the United Nations labored in 1949–50 to create a new institution, which eventually became UNHCR, it also worked toward the adoption of a new treaty to deal with the problem of the uprooted. Early stages of the deliberations tended to refer to these questions generically under the rubric of statelessness.[28] As the deliberations progressed, however, the debates

---

[26] In 1991, the new High Commissioner, Mme. Sadako Ogata, highlighted the needs of the internally displaced in her address to the Ex Comm. Report of the 42d Session of the Executive Committee of the High Commissioner's Programme, UN Doc. A/AC.96/783, at 24. The 1992 Note on International Protection, prepared by UNHCR, discussed a variety of innovative approaches, reflecting in part the Office's experiences in the former Yugoslavia. UN Doc. A/AC.96/799. It expressed the view that the UNHCR mandate is "resilient enough" to include "prevention and in-country protection." Ibid., at 5. On the consideration of these questions in other UN fora, see generally Analytical Report of the Secretary-General on Internally Displaced Persons, UN Doc. E/CN.4/1992/23 (1992) (prepared in response to ECOSOC Res. 1990/78 (July 27, 1990)); Report on Refugees, Displaced Persons and Returnees, Prepared by Mr. Jacques Cuénod, Consultant, UN Doc. E/1991/109/Add.1 (1991).

[27] See, e.g., Aga Khan, note 25 above, at 338–43; J. Hathaway, The Law of Refugee Status 13 (1991).

[28] The influential early report by the Secretary-General took this approach, A Study on Statelessness, UN Doc. E/1112 & Add. 1 (1949), and much of the early drafting work on both the UNHCR Statute and the Convention took place in an ad hoc Committee on Statelessness, created by the ECOSOC in 1949. ECOSOC Res. 248 (IX) (B) (Aug. 8, 1949). The

began to differentiate more sharply the *de jure* stateless from the category of refugees (recognizing, of course, that some persons may belong to both groups). By the time final work began on the treaties, the two topics had been firmly separated. The international community proceeded first on a refugee treaty, and not until 1954 was a treaty on the status of stateless persons concluded. A Convention on the Reduction of Statelessness followed in 1961. The statelessness treaties are not widely accepted, however, and neither has had anything approaching the practical impact of the refugee treaties.[29]

B. The provisions of the 1951 convention relating to the status of refugees

1. Generally

The refugee treaty that resulted from the UN deliberations in 1949–51 focuses on what its title advertises: the status of refugees, rather than admission or asylum. It details the treatment required in a variety of social, legal, and economic realms, usually by reference to the comparable treatment under domestic law of nationals or of aliens generally, or by use of a most-favored-nation standard.[30] For example, with regard to access to the courts, or when rationing is necessary, refugees must receive the same treatment as nationals (Articles 16, 20). In the domain of property rights, refugees must be treated no less favorably than aliens generally under the laws of the haven state (Article 13). And with regard to employment, contracting states must accord to refugees lawfully staying in the territory most-favored-nation treatment. That is, their access to the labor market must be equivalent to the access available to nationals of that foreign country most favorably treated under domestic law (Article 17). Although some of the treaty protections apply to all refugees physically present in the territory of a contracting state, an important qualification limits the reach of many of the Convention's substantive articles. In these cases, the protections apply only to refugees "lawfully in" or "lawfully staying in" the territory of the state party.

Certain provisions deserve more detailed attention, for they have provided core protections for refugees.

Committee's reports appeared as UN Doc. E/1618, E/AC.32/5 (1950) and UN Doc. E/1850, E/AC.32/8 (1950).

[29] Convention Relating to the Status of Stateless Persons, Sept. 28, 1954, 360 UNTS 117 (*entered into force* June 6, 1960); Convention on the Reduction of Statelessness, Aug. 30, 1961, UN Doc. A/CONF.9/15 (1961) (*entered into force* Dec. 13, 1975). As of December 31, 1991, the former treaty had thirty-six parties, the latter only sixteen. See Human Rights: Status of International Instruments, UN Doc. ST/HR/5 (1987) (Supp., Dec. 31, 1991).

[30] Convention, note 3 above. A comprehensive description and explanation of the provisions may be found in P. Weis, "The International Protection of Refugees," 48 *AJIL* 193 (1954).

2. Travel Documents

Travel documents for refugees have been a special concern since the time of the League of Nations. Article 28 of the Convention, augmented by an accompanying Schedule and Specimen Travel Document, sets forth highly detailed requirements for the papers to be issued to refugees lawfully staying in the territory of the contracting state. Unlike the League's arrangements, the 1951 Convention specifically requires that the issuing state guarantee readmittance of the bearer at any time during the period of validity of the document. That period will ordinarily be two years, but may be reduced in exceptional cases to no less than three months.[31]

The readmittance guarantee can be vitally important if a refugee is to travel, for states are often quite resistant to admission of aliens, even on a temporary basis, unless they are sure that they will have a place to send the individuals whenever it might be deemed necessary to enforce their removal. In the usual circumstances, of course, the country of nationality is obligated under international law to receive its nationals,[32] but for refugees that link is broken. The Convention Travel Document provides tangible evidence to the admitting state that there remains, nevertheless, another nation under a duty to readmit the refugee when his stay is ended.

3. The role of UNHCR

The parties to the Convention agree to cooperate with the Office of the UNHCR "and shall in particular facilitate its duty of supervising the application of the provisions of this Convention" (Article 35). To this end, they are required to provide certain information concerning refugees and their condition, as well as information on laws and regulations that implement the Convention. Some states see these provisions as requiring only general cooperation with the Office, leaving most of the authority and responsibility with national officials, while others have at times gone to the other extreme, delegating significant decision-making authority to UNHCR.[33]

---

[31] Convention, note 3 above, Sched., paras. 5, 13. For US regulations implementing art. 28, see 8 CFR § 223a (1991).

[32] See G. Goodwin-Gill, *International Law and the Movement of Persons between States* 8 (1978).

[33] For example, a UNHCR official sits as one of three voting members on every panel of the *Commission des recours*, France's appeals commission. See F. Tiberghien, *La Protection des Réfugiés en France* 3–41 (2d ed., 1988). In Belgium, until 1988 all decisions on the refugee status claims filed by asylum seekers were made by UNHCR, without any role for national officials. See C. Johnson, "Refugee Law Reform in Europe: The Belgian Example," 27 *Colum. J. Transnat'l L.* 589 (1989). For a wide-ranging account of national systems implementing the Convention, see G. Goodwin-Gill, *The Refugee in International Law* 165–207 (1983).

4. Removal

Refugees lawfully in the territory of a state that is a party to the 1951 Convention are sheltered by Article 32 against expulsion "save on grounds of national security or public order." Even then, paragraph 2 specifically requires "a decision reached in accordance with due process of law." If a refugee is not "lawfully in" the territory, however, he cannot claim the protection of Article 32, but he is still shielded by the *non-refoulement* guarantee of Article 33.

This latter guarantee is probably the single most important provision of international refugee law; its centrality is underscored by the Convention's ban on reservations to the *non-refoulement* provision (Article 42). Article 33 provides in paragraph 1:

No Contracting State shall expel or return (*"refouler"*) a refugee in any manner whatsoever to the frontiers of territories where his life or freedom would be threatened on account of his race, religion, nationality, membership of a particular social group or political opinion.

Paragraph 2 then permits limited exceptions, when there are "reasonable grounds for regarding [the refugee] as a danger to the security of the country" or when the individual, "having been convicted of a particularly serious crime, constitutes a danger to the community of that country."

Although the language of paragraph 1, especially the phrase "in any manner whatsoever," would seem to preclude repulse of asylum seekers at the border, at least if they are coming directly from a state where they were prima facie threatened, the *travaux préparatoires* paint a different picture. The participants in the conference took pains to record the understanding that the guarantee would apply only to those who had gained admission to the territory, even if illegally.[34] Nevertheless, in light of state practice since 1951, a strong case can be made that *non-refoulement* now includes nonrejection at the frontiers, and, further, that *non-refoulement* of refugees has crystallized as a rule of customary international law binding on all states.[35] The current debate tends to focus on who is protected by this rule –

[34] See *ibid.*, at 74.
[35] See *ibid.*, at 97–100; Plender, note 2 above, at 425–33. The US government's interdiction on the high seas of Haitian boats containing asylum seekers, beginning in 1981, has led to considerable litigation over whether the *non-refoulement* guarantee applies outside the territory of a state party. See, e.g., *Haitian Refugee Center, Inc.* v. *Gracey*, 809 F.2d 794 (D.C.Cir. 1987); *Haitian Refugee Center, Inc.* v. *Baker*, 949 F.2d 1109 (11th Cir. 1991) (*per curiam*); *Haitian Refugee Center, Inc.* v. *Baker*, 953 F.2d 1498 (11th Cir.) (*per curiam*), cert. den., 112 S.Ct. 1245 (1992) (rejecting legal challenges to the interdiction program). During earlier phases, the program included some kind of interview (aboard ship or later at the US naval base at Guantanamo Bay, Cuba) to determine whether the individuals involved had plausible claims to refugee status; if so, they were supposed to be brought on to the United

that is, whether or in what circumstances it extends beyond refugees as defined in the UN Convention and Protocol.[36]

Article 33 is more limited than Article 32. It does not require that the refugee be permitted to stay in the country of refuge, nor that his status be regularized there (so that he would thenceforth be "lawfully staying"). It requires only that he be not returned to a country that threatens persecution. In theory, he could be sent to any other country. In practice, however, states wishing to confine their offer of refuge to a temporary period often find it quite difficult to persuade another country to accept admission in these circumstances.

5. Illegal entry or presence

Article 31 recognizes that refugees may be in the country illegally. It therefore precludes the imposition of penalties on "refugees who, coming directly from a territory where their life or freedom was threatened in the sense of Article 1, enter or are present in their territory without authorization, provided they present themselves without delay to the authorities and show good cause for their illegal entry or presence." Those refugees who fail to meet the requirements of the proviso can be penalized, but expulsion to the home country is not among the valid penalties. Article 33, the *non-refoulement* provision, still shields such persons.

C. Asylum

In the traditional understanding of international law, the right of asylum is not an individual right; it is instead a right of states.[37] States, in their discretion, may provide asylum to those they choose to shelter; they do not thereby commit a wrong against any other state.[38] Article 14 of the

States for full consideration of the claim. In May 1992, however, faced with a great increase in the boat flow, President Bush ordered immediate return of all boat passengers to Port-au-Prince, without any screening, presenting the *non-refoulement* question in its sharpest form. A court of appeals ruled that this new policy violated applicable law, but the Supreme Court stayed the lower court injunction pending further review, and eventually reversed, finding that the Treaty does not apply outside the territory of a state party. *Sale* v. *Haitian Centers Council,* Inc., 113 S.Ct. (June 21, 1993), rev'g. *Haitian Centers Council, Inc.* v. *McNary,* 969 F.2d 1350 (2d Cir. 1992).

[36] See, e.g., J. Hartman, "The Principle and Practice of Temporary Refuge: A Customary Norm Protecting Civilians Fleeing Internal Armed Conflict," in *The New Asylum Seekers: Refugee Law in the 1980s* 87 (D. Martin ed., 1988); G. Goodwin-Gill, "Nonrefoulement and the New Asylum Seekers," *ibid.* at 103; K. Hailbronner, "Nonrefoulement and 'Humanitarian' Refugees: Customary International Law or Wishful Legal Thinking?," *ibid.* at 123.

[37] See Goodwin-Gill, note 33 above, at 121; A. Grahl-Madsen, *The Status of Refugees in International Law,* II, 6 (1972).

[38] See Plender, note 2 above, at 393–99 (noting some evolution toward an individual right of asylum); Grahl-Madsen, note 37 above, at 7–77.

Universal Declaration of Human Rights was carefully worded so as to avoid disturbing that doctrine or the notion of the sovereign right of control over the entry of aliens that it reflects.[39]

1. The limited effect of the 1951 convention

Similarly, the drafters of the 1951 Convention Relating to the Status of Refugees were careful to make sure that their work could not be read as creating a right of asylum.[40] The treaty deals with *status* for populations already in place and accepted. It does not create obligations for admission,[41] nor for granting full residence rights to those who may be within the territory and are able to establish that they are refugees. This feature is sometimes missed by those who canvass the text of the Convention and are impressed by the detail and range of its coverage. When they find precise guarantees dealing with education, public assistance, social security, property ownership, rights to employment and self-employment, and even artistic rights, they may be moved to ask what more "asylum" could entail.

To be sure, any person enjoying the full range of rights described in the Convention would undoubtedly be said to have found asylum. But the key point is that full Convention rights are not automatic for those who simply establish physical presence on the territory of a state party and prove that they meet the refugee definition. As previously noted, most of the more demanding obligations imposed on states are qualified, including, for example, those articles announcing refugees' rights to employment, housing, public assistance, and freedom of movement. These rights attach only to refugees "lawfully in" or "lawfully staying in" the haven state.[42]

---

[39] The original draft set forth a right "to seek and to be granted" asylum from persecution. Because of concerns that this language might give rise to a claim against receiving states in derogation of their territorial sovereignty, the text was changed to declare a right "to seek and to enjoy" asylum. GA Res. 217A (III), art. 14 (Dec. 10, 1948). See H. Lauterpacht, "The Universal Declaration of Human Rights," 25 *Brit. Y. B. Int'l L.* 354, 374 (1948).

[40] The drafters compensated in a modest way for the failure of the Convention to deal with asylum as such, when they included Recommendation D in the Final Act of the Conference of Plenipotentiaries. It recommends "that Governments continue to receive refugees in their territories and that they act in concert in a true spirit of international co-operation in order that these refugees may find asylum and the possibility of resettlement." Reprinted in Goodwin-Gill, note 33 above, at 251.

[41] Early in the process the drafters decided to drop a proposed chapter on admission, and at several points in the *travaux préparatoires*, delegates were careful to place on record that the Convention did not deal with admission or the right of asylum. Some even went further to stress that Article 33 did not cover cases of mass migration. See N. Robinson, *Convention Relating to the Status of Refugees: Its History, Contents, and Interpretation: A Commentary* 163 & n. 275 (1953); P. Weis, "Legal Aspects of the Convention of 28 July 1951 relating to the Status of Refugees," 30 *Brit. Y. B. Int'l L.* 478, 482 (1953).

[42] Arts. 17–19 (relating to employment), 21 (housing), 23 (public relief), & 26 (freedom of movement).

And the *travaux préparatoires* make it clear that decisions about regularizing status remain within the discretion – the sovereignty – of states. Merely proving that one is a refugee in accordance with the Convention definition does not mean that one is lawfully in the state of refuge; lawful status ordinarily awaits a further exercise of the state's sovereign discretion.[43]

It is useful to remember that the focus of the drafters of the 1951 Convention was the contemporary situation in Europe. A large group of expatriates was already living in haven states that were generally prepared to accept their continuing presence as lawful – subject to ongoing efforts to resettle as many as wished to do so in the traditional immigration countries such as Canada or the United States. The major questions confronting the drafters related not to obligations of admission but to details of the treatment of these persons whose presence was not greatly controversial. (Even this focus sometimes seems a puzzle to American readers, but only because they are accustomed to a national legal system little affected by the doctrine of legislative reciprocity, a system wherein admitted aliens, whatever their nationality or precise status, easily are accorded treatment almost on a par with US nationals.)

2. Efforts to create a secure right of asylum

The failure of the 1951 Convention to deal with asylum has spurred ongoing efforts to remedy this situation. In 1967, these efforts resulted in the General Assembly's adoption of a Declaration on Territorial Asylum, after several years of preparatory work in the Commission on Human Rights and the Third and Sixth Committees. Even though such declarations do not as such create obligations for states, care was taken in the final drafting stages to remove any implication that an individual right to asylum was suggested.[44] The word "right" was deleted from the Declaration's title, and the first operative paragraph reads: "Asylum granted by a State in the exercise of its sovereignty . . . shall be respected by all other States." The Declaration explicitly includes nonrejection at the frontier within its *non-refoulement* article – a clear sign of progressive development when compared with the stance in 1951. But it then announces exceptions to the

---

[43] As explained in the Report of the *ad hoc* Committee on Statelessness and Related Problems, UN Doc. E/1618, E/AC.32/5, at 47 (Mar. 2, 1950):

The expression "lawfully within their territory" throughout this draft convention would exclude a refugee who while lawfully admitted has over-stayed the period for which he was admitted or was authorized to stay or who has violated any other condition attached to his admission or stay.

[44] See Goodwin-Gill, note 33 above, at 105; P. Weis, "Draft United Nations Convention on Territorial Asylum," 50 *Brit. Y. B. Int'l L.* 151, 151–52 (1980).

nonreturn and nonrejection guarantee of potentially wider reach than the exceptions to Article 33 of the Convention. "Exception may be made . . . only for overriding reasons of national security or in order to safeguard the population, as in the case of a mass influx of persons."[45]

In 1970, new efforts for a treaty on the subject were launched. After successive drafts by groups of experts and rounds of comment by governments, the General Assembly provided for the call of a conference of plenipotentiaries to consider a convention on territorial asylum, to be held in Geneva in January 1977. By the time of this meeting, however, increased migration in the mid-1970s, including the first round of the exodus from Vietnam, coupled with wider participation from all parts of the globe (a natural consequence of decolonization), brought impulses toward caution once again to the fore. At the conference, progressive provisions included in the experts' drafts were watered down to the point that the treaty threatened to undermine even some of the key protections guaranteed more securely under the 1951 Convention. The conference closed after dealing with only three proposed articles, and the effort to create a global asylum treaty has in essence been abandoned.[46]

3. Evaluation

Thus at the global level it remains the case that no treaty guarantees asylum; no individual right of asylum exists.[47] But laments over this state of affairs are often exaggerated. Practice and domestic legislation have created in many states, particularly the Western democracies, a *de facto* individual right of asylum for those who establish physical presence and demonstrate that they meet the applicable refugee definition – even though states are often reluctant to describe their practices in these terms. It has come to pass

---

[45] GA Res. 2312 (XXII) (Dec. 14, 1967).   [46] See Weis, note 44 above.

[47] According to one expert, the only treaty concluded under the auspices of the United Nations obligating states to grant asylum (within limited and carefully defined circumstances) is the Agreement Relating to Refugee Seamen, Nov. 23, 1957, 506 UNTS 125 (*entered into force* Dec. 27, 1961). See esp. arts. 2, 3, 11. Only nineteen states are parties, however. G. Jaeger, "Les Nations Unies et les Réfugiés," 1989/1 *RBDI* 18, 93.

Regional treaties in Africa and Latin America do contain provisions bearing on a right of asylum. The OAU Convention Governing the Specific Aspects of Refugee Problems in Africa, 1001 UNTS 45 (*entered into force* June 20, 1974), provides in Article II(1) that member states "shall use their best endeavors consistent with their respective legislations to receive refugees and to secure [their] settlement." Paragraph 4 provides a mechanism for assistance, "in the spirit of African solidarity and international cooperation," to help lighten the burden of states harboring large numbers of refugees. The American Convention on Human Rights, Nov. 22, 1969, OAS Treaty Series No. 36, at 1, OAS Off. Rec. OEA/Ser.L/V/II.23 doc. 21, rev. 6, 9 *ILM* 99 (1970) (*entered into force* July 18, 1978), provides in Article 22(7): "Every person has the right to seek and be granted asylum in a foreign territory, in accordance with the legislation of the state and international conventions, in the event he is being pursued for political offenses or related common crimes."

that most states with elaborate refugee-status adjudication systems quite readily extend the full rights we would associate with the concept of asylum, including indefinite residence rights, work authorization, and family reunification, once the individual is adjudged a refugee according to the Convention definition.

This *de facto* right of asylum is a direct and laudable result of the UN treaty regime, even though it was certainly not required by the precise terms of those treaties. In most of the Western countries, it has become politically unthinkable to deny (save in isolated cases, usually involving criminal behavior) full residence rights to persons judged to fit the applicable definition of "refugee." Today's controversies focus instead on who meets this standard, not what follows for those who prove they do. Usually taken for granted in the debates, even by most of the restrictionist hard-liners, is the routine whereby those who are adjudged refugees gain a full and secure status, despite the irregularities of their initial entry.

It is therefore appropriate to turn to what has become the central question for much of refugee law today, the question of refugee definition.

D. The refugee definition

1. The 1951 Convention

In the drafting of the 1951 Convention, it was generally agreed to move beyond the purely categorical approach common in the League of Nations era (usually designating covered refugees by national group), and so to accept something like the more abstract concept of "refugee" employed in the UNHCR Statute adopted a year earlier. The central language of the Convention definition mirrors that of the Statute: a refugee is someone outside his home country, having a "well-founded fear of being persecuted for reasons of race, religion, nationality, membership of a particular social group or political opinion" if he were to return or otherwise claim that country's protection.[48] But a major concern of the drafters of the 1951 Convention was to avoid issuing a "blank cheque"[49] that might make states parties vulnerable to far-reaching and immeasurable obligations into the unforeseeable future. As a result, the Convention definition applies by its

---

[48] Convention, note 3 above, art. 1(A)(2). This language is virtually identical to the equivalent portion of the definition in the UNHCR Statute, except that, at Sweden's initiative, the Convention adds to the "reasons" catalog the language regarding "membership of a particular social group." See Robinson, note 41 above, at 53; Grahl-Madsen, I, note 37 above, at 219; Hathaway, note 27 above, at 157.

[49] The phrase appears, *inter alia*, in the statement of Mr. van Heuven Goedhart, High Commissioner, UN Conference of Plenipotentiaries on the Status of Refugees and Stateless Persons, Summary Record of the 21st Meeting, at 12, UN Doc. A/CONF.2/SR.21 (1951).

terms only to persons who are outside their home country "as a result of events occurring before 1 January 1951."[50]

In principle, then, the Convention – in contrast to the UNHCR Statute – protected only a finite group of persecuted individuals, and any nation's exposure was ostensibly circumscribed by this dateline. For states even more concerned about unlimited exposure, the Convention offered a further possibility for limiting its obligations. Each state party could declare at the time of adherence that the definition would be understood to apply only to events occurring *in Europe* before the dateline.[51]

Predictably, a definition thus limited grew increasingly obsolete as 1951 faded further into the past. Creative interpretation sometimes overcame the problem, as when tens of thousands fled the Soviet tanks that crushed the Hungarian uprising in 1956. Host states, with the agreement of an Ex Comm working group, eventually decided that this displacement resulted from events occurring before 1951; the results were simply felt at a later date.[52] Hence the Convention applied. But such interpretive acrobatics grew increasingly difficult as time wore on.

2. The 1967 Protocol

By the mid-1960s, persons concerned about the plight of refugees were actively seeking ways to extend the reach of the Treaty. After considering many options, the High Commissioner ultimately proposed an ambitious step: a protocol that would eliminate the dateline altogether from the Convention definition. Though proponents had feared state resistance to such a proposal, the idea was taken up with surprising speed. The ease of adoption perhaps reflects some luck of timing. The early 1960s had been a time of comparative quiet on refugee matters, at least for the European states that had traditionally taken the lead on these issues. Refugee flows appeared relatively small and manageable, thus dampening concerns about "blank cheques" and bringing humanitarian considerations to the fore.

The High Commissioner circulated a draft text to states for comment in 1965. The UNHCR Executive Committee then approved its version in October 1966 and sent it to the General Assembly. Instead of convening a new conference of plenipotentiaries, the General Assembly, in an unusual procedure, adopted a resolution in December 1966 that simply "takes note" of the Protocol text received from UNHCR and asks the Secretary-General to transmit it to states, "with a view to enabling them to accede to the Protocol."[53] Thus the Ex Comm's approved draft was presented

---

[50] Convention, note 3 above, art. 1(A)(2).   [51] *Ibid.*, art. 1(B).
[52] Aga Khan, note 25 above, at 298; Holborn, note 10 above, at 178.
[53] GA Res. 2198 (XXI) (Dec. 16, 1966).

without change to governments. By October 1967 it had the necessary accessions to enter into force.[54] Many states used the occasion of their acceptance of the Protocol to eliminate their former declarations limiting coverage to Europe, and by 1992 111 states were parties to these fundamental refugee treaties.[55]

3. The current treaty definition

As modified by the 1967 Protocol, the governing treaty definition now provides that a refugee is any person who:

owing to a well-founded fear of being persecuted for reasons of race, religion, nationality, membership of a particular social group or political opinion, is outside the country of his nationality and is unable or, owing to such fear, is unwilling to avail himself of the protection of that country; or who, not having a nationality and being outside the country of his former habitual residence, is unable or, owing to such fear, is unwilling to return to it.[56]

The balance of Article 1, the definitional provision, consists primarily of cessation and exclusion clauses. Paragraph C provides that the Convention shall cease to apply to an individual, for example, if he voluntarily reavails himself of the protection of his country of nationality, if he acquires a new nationality and enjoys protection from the new country, or if "the circumstances in connexion with which he has been recognized as a refugee have ceased to exist" in the home country.[57]

---

[54] Protocol, note 3 above. See generally Holborn, note 10 above, at 177–82.

[55] As of December 31, 1991, 104 states were parties to both the Convention, and Protocol. another three were parties only to the Convention, and four, including the United States, parties only to the Protocol. Human Rights: Status of International Instruments, note 29 above.

Most treaties labeled "protocols" cannot stand alone; they are wholly ancillary to the underlying treaty. The Protocol Relating to the Status of Refugees, however, is deliberately constructed so that it sets forth a complete treaty regime in its own right (besides working some modifications for those states that happen to be parties as well to the Convention). Art. I, para. 1, incorporates all the substantive provisions (arts. 2–34) of the 1951 Convention, and para. 2 adopts the Convention's definition of refugee (art. 1), except that it removes the dateline. The remaining articles provide for various administrative matters, most of them paralleling the final clauses of the Convention. This unusual structure apparently eased the way for US accession, which occurred in November 1968. 19 UST 6223, TIAS No. 6577. Owing primarily to domestic politics in the 1950s, the United States had never become a party to the Convention. But this omission makes no practical difference. Through the Protocol the United States is derivatively bound to all the operative Convention articles.

[56] Convention, note 3 above, art. 1(A)(2), as modified by the 1967 Protocol, note 3 above, art. I(2). Article 1(A)(1) of the Convention, a kind of grandfather clause, includes within the definition anyone who had been considered a refugee under various instruments adopted during the League of Nations period or under the constitution of the IRO. For obvious reasons, this paragraph is of little practical significance today.

[57] This final cessation ground will not apply to certain pre1951 refugees if "compelling reasons arising out of previous persecution" justify a refusal to return to the protection or territory of the original country. This limited proviso, drafted with the victims of Nazism in mind,

Paragraph F excludes from Convention coverage, *inter alia* , those who have committed war crimes or crimes against humanity, and those who have "committed a serious non-political crime outside the country of refuge prior to [their] admission to that country as a refugee." Paragraph D excludes "persons who are at present receiving from organs or agencies of the United Nations other than [UNHCR] protection or assistance." This rather cryptic language means that most Palestinians do not come within the coverage of the Convention and Protocol, owing to the ongoing role of UNRWA, the UN Relief and Works Agency, which has provided assistance to Palestinians since its creation in 1949. Under many domestic legal systems, however, Palestinian asylum seekers may still claim analogous protections.

E. Continuing points of controversy regarding the definition

Despite the wide acceptance of the Convention definition, as modified by the Protocol, there remains considerable room for disagreement over its application.

1. Factual difficulties

In part, controversy derives from the difficult factual determinations that must be made when an individual applies for recognition as a refugee (and hence for asylum under many domestic systems). There are usually no available witnesses, other than the applicant, to the events that he describes as the basis for his claim that he justifiably fears persecution in the home country. Credibility judgments are therefore inescapable. These are always difficult, but they are rendered even more so by the cross-cultural communication barriers that often hamper effective testimony and impede valid adjudication. Several authorities prescribe, in recognition of these problems, that refugees should be given the benefit of the doubt,[58] but such an approach does not eliminate the factual difficulties present in the cases. Moreover, as the numbers of asylum claimants have risen in the past decade or so, adjudicators have in practice been less likely to resolve uncertainties in this way, for fear of creating an overly large opening for fraudulent or marginal claimants.[59]

Moreover, refugee adjudicators must also make judgments concerning conditions in distant foreign countries (such as the prevalence of prison

---

acknowledges that at least the most abused of persecution victims may find it psychologically difficult or impossible to return, even after political changes that eliminate the objective threat. Though the Convention proviso covers only an extremely limited class of refugees, some states allow for similar treatment in a wider range of circumstances. See, e.g., Matter of Chen, Interim Dec. No. 3104 (Bd. Immig. App. 1989); 8 CFR § 208.13(b)(1) (1991).

[58] See UNHCR *Handbook*, note 23 above, paras. 203–4.
[59] See Martin, note 19 above, at 1280–87.

abuses or the availability of domestic remedies),[60] about which information may be sketchy at best. Inescapably, judgments about the severity of such threats are colored by the observer's preconceptions,[61] and for many years those preconceptions followed Cold War precepts. After the fall of the Berlin Wall, those generalizations no longer come so easily, but the attitudes of officials and publics have adjusted unevenly. Some of the more bitter recent battles, including over the question of forced repatriation to Vietnam of persons adjudged not to be Convention refugees, derive from such discontinuities.

2. Doctrinal issues

Beyond these factual and attitudinal difficulties, the definition presents several thorny legal problems, owing to the somewhat indefinite language in which it is couched.[62]

The central concept in the Convention definition is a "well founded fear of persecution." But when is a fear well-founded? Anyone who flees a country where persecution has been known to occur has a rational foundation for the claimed fear; the fear is not fanciful. Yet most contemporary interpreters are united in holding that the Treaty does not bless large-scale relocation whenever some such persecution takes place in a country of origin. In consequence, administrative and judicial decisions have wrestled with the question of just how much the persecution must be targeted on the claimant, or persons similarly situated, before the Convention applies. Some authorities require a showing that the individual is likely to be "singled out" for persecution, but others believe this formulation too severe.[63] The most helpful rephrasing may be that which requires a showing that persecution is a "reasonable possibility" if the person were to return[64] – but obviously this concept still leaves much to case-by-case application.

[60] The UNHCR *Handbook*, note 23 above, para. 42, seems to suggest that authorities need not pass judgment on the conditions in the country of origin, but state practice is to the contrary.
[61] See Martin, note 19 above, at 1273–75.
[62] An excellent exploration of the whole range of legal questions presented by the Convention's refugee definition may be found in Hathaway, note 27 above.
[63] For a useful summary and critique, see C. P. Blum, "The Ninth Circuit and the Protection of Asylum Seekers since the Passage of the Refugee Act of 1980," 23 *San Diego L. Rev.* 327, 343 (1986).
[64] This formulation is employed in *INS* v. *Cardoza-Fonseca*, 480 US 421, 440 (1987), and it is repeated in the crucial language in recently revised US asylum regulations. See 8 CFR § 208.13(b)(2). See also Report of the *ad hoc* Comm. on Statelessness, note 43 above, at 39 (the expression "well-founded fear of being persecuted" is meant to signify that "a person has either been actually a victim of persecution or can show good reason why he fears persecution"). For a summary and critique of the subtly different formulation used by the US Board of Immigration Appeals, see T. A. Aleinikoff & D. Martin, *Immigration: Process and Policy* 759–63 (2d ed., 1991).

Second, what is persecution? The term is undefined in the Convention. Some guidance may be drawn from Article 33, which speaks of threats to life or freedom. But controversy persists over the extent to which other kinds of serious impositions may amount to persecution. Particularly difficult cases arise where the individual is likely to be punished under duly enacted and generally applicable criminal statutes, but where the underlying policy of the law is considered objectionable in the haven state. Application of the home country's conscription laws to conscientious objectors, of exit control laws, or of nationwide family-planning policies to persons who prefer to have more children have raised these issues in particularly poignant fashion.[65]

Finally, as national authorities have become more concerned in recent years about rising numbers of asylum seekers, increasing attention is being paid to the language of the definition referring to a well-founded fear of persecution "*for reasons of* race, religion, nationality, membership of a particular social group, or political opinion." Some opinions have been excessively narrow in denying refugee status even though the proof of likely persecution is strong, because of the adjudicator's finding that the mistreatment would not be for reason of one of the five listed factors.[66]

3. Beyond the convention definition?

Recent years have seen massive uprooting of people the mass media call refugees, some 17 million in one oft-cited reckoning. Yet the majority of these people do not meet the Convention definition, for they have been uprooted by war, invasion, or civil strife, rather than the kind of targeted persecution that brings the definition into play. Consequently calls are increasingly heard in political forums and scholarly literature for applying more "realistic" definitions and so affording firmer protection to a larger proportion of the displaced. Some commentators even argue that customary international law has already evolved a wider definition, requiring at least *non-refoulement* for the expanded categories. In this connection they can point to certain regional instruments, notably the OAU Convention,[67] which contain a broader refugee definition specifically embracing those who flee war or civil strife. Some also point to the expanded mandate of the

---

[65] See *ibid.* at 804–25.

[66] See, e.g., *Campos-Guardado* v. *INS*, 809 F.2d 285 (5th Cir. 1987); Matter of Maldonado-Cruz, 19 Immig. & Nationality Dec. 504 (Bd. Immig. App. 1988). A recent US Supreme Court decision, *INS* v. *Elias-Zacarias*, 112 S.Ct. 812 (1992), appears to give support to this restrictive trend, although it is subject to other readings. For a cogent critique of the trend, see T. A. Aleinikoff, "The Meaning of 'Persecution' in US Asylum Law," in *Refugee Policy: Canada and the United States* 292 (H. Adelman ed., 1991).

[67] OAU Convention, note 47 above, art. I(2).

UNHCR, discussed earlier, which now is generally understood to embrace both refugees and displaced persons.[68]

Such claims carry an unmistakable humanitarian appeal, but deserve close examination. To the extent that they assert that state practice and *opinio juris* already recognize the wider obligations, they almost surely overread the existing evidence.[69] Beyond this, by opening up a prospect of extensive new legal obligations, such claims risk undermining the political support – already threatened in a time when Western nations are receiving unprecedented numbers of direct asylum applications – that is essential if even Treaty commitments are to retain vitality.[70] Moreover, to assert that an expanded UNHCR mandate entails an expansion in the direct legal obligations of states is to create incentives for shrinking the mandate.

4. Harmonizing interpretation

The Convention and Protocol contain dispute-resolution clauses permitting final determination by the International Court of Justice.[71] But states have few incentives to invoke this remedy against other contracting parties, and it has never been used. In practice, interpretive disputes such as those canvassed above must be resolved in domestic forums, administrative or judicial. Obviously this leaves room for divergences in interpretation – the more so as occasions for interpretation have increased in recent years because of the rapid growth in asylum claims. Efforts to collect and systematize these decisions, and sometimes to share them across national boundaries, have also expanded over the last decade.[72]

Some guidance on questions of interpretation and implementation of international refugee law comes from the Conclusions on International Protection adopted by the Executive Committee of the High Commissioner's Programme. Although purely "soft law" – the Ex Comm has no formal competence to issue authoritative interpretations of the Convention and Protocol – these instruments have often been useful in pulling together

---

[68] See, e.g., Hartman, note 36 above; Goodwin-Gill, note 36 above.

[69] See Hailbronner, note 36 above.

[70] See D. Martin, "The New Asylum Seekers," in Martin ed., note 36 above, at 12; D. Martin, "Effects of International Law on Migration Policy and Practice: The Uses of Hypocrisy," 23 *Int'l Migration Rev.* 547, 564–68 (1989).

[71] Convention, note 3 above, art. 38; Protocol, note 3 above, art. IV.

[72] See generally P. Rudge and M. Kjaerum, "The Information Aspects of Refugee Work – Time for a Full-scale Information Strategy," *Refugee Abstracts*, Dec. 1988, at 1. A new quarterly, *The International Journal of Refugee Law*, launched with UNHCR support in 1989, has stimulated useful scholarly studies on these subjects and pulled them together in one readily accessible location. The journal also devotes a section of each issue to reports on important case law in domestic courts of many countries, and another to reproducing important documents such as Ex Comm Conclusions.

international thinking on various subjects of pressing importance to refugees and to national governments. The Conclusions have discussed, for example, guidelines for minimum procedures in national adjudication systems, protection of asylum seekers in situations of large-scale influx, manifestly unfounded asylum applications, voluntary repatriation, and detention of asylum seekers and refugees.[73]

Early examples of the Conclusions often contained highly progressive doctrine. Over time, and particularly as many states found themselves in the midst of what they considered to be an asylum crisis brought on by mushrooming caseloads, government officials began to find that measures taken in response to these new problems came into conflict with some of the language of earlier Conclusions. Although the Conclusions are not hard law, local activists were not shy about invoking them in domestic political debates. Governments that had voted for a Conclusion (or at least acquiesced in the Ex Comm's consensus) could not convincingly justify their departure from it simply by pointing out the technicality that Conclusions are not binding.

More recently, chastened by this real-world law-making impact of the Conclusions, states have become far more careful about the texts for which they vote. Some proposed Conclusions were therefore delayed for many years, including one on armed attacks on refugee camps and settlements and a later one concerning irregular movements of asylum seekers.[74] In 1988, the Executive Committee decided to permit the recording of "reservations" or "interpretative declarations" by states not fully in agreement with an adopted Conclusion. Two states took advantage of that option that year,[75] and the number grew to ten the following year.[76] This practice reflects the greater seriousness with which states now approach the Conclusion-drafting process, but it may also portend a fragmentation of consensus that might deprive the Conclusions of much of their influence in the future.[77]

[73] The Conclusions are published as part of the annual report of the UNHCR ExComm, which is usually Supp. 12A to the annual UN GAOR. UNHCR also publishes a looseleaf collection, affixing the sequential numbering commonly employed: Conclusions on the International Protection of Refugees adopted by the Executive Committee of the UNHCR Program (1980 and annual supps.) (hereinafter cited as UNHCR Conclusions). The Conclusions mentioned in the text appear in that volume as Conclusions No. 8, 22, 30, 40, and 44.

[74] These were eventually agreed to as Conclusion No. 48, Military and Armed Attacks on Refugee Camps and Settlements, reprinted in UNHCR Conclusions, note 73 above, at 109 (1987), and Conclusion No. 58, The Problem of Refugees and Asylum-Seekers Who Move in an Irregular Manner from a Country in which they had already found Protection, UNHCR Ex Comm, UN GAOR, 40th Sess., Supp. No. 12A, para. 25, UN Doc. A/44/12/Add.1 (1989).

[75] Report of the UNHCR Ex Comm, 39th Sess., UN GAOR Supp. No. 12A, para. 36, UN Doc. A/43/12/Add.1 (1988).   [76] Report of the 40th Sess., note 74 above, para. 36.

[77] A most useful canvass of these issues appears in Sztucki, note 10 above.

One other product of the UN process has probably been even more influential in national adjudications of claims to refugee status or asylum. In 1977, the Ex Comm asked the High Commissioner to consider "issuing – for the guidance of Governments – a handbook relating to procedures and criteria for determining refugee status."[78] Drafted by a committee of experts, this book appeared in 1979, and was eagerly put to use by national officials.[79] *Handbook* provisions of course remain subject to displacement by authoritative domestic rulings, but with surprising frequency, domestic courts look to the *Handbook* for guidance in drafting their own controlling doctrine. On occasion courts have overturned rulings of domestic immigration or aliens authorities when they considered that the administrators' doctrine diverged from the *Handbook*.[80]

IV. LOOKING TO THE FUTURE

Each of the international instruments examined here, to varying degrees, has been adopted in an atmosphere of caution and government concern about the prerogatives of sovereignty. Nevertheless, creative and persistent interpretation and implementation, coupled with important domestic support for the cause of refugees, have brought significant humanitarian achievement, quite beyond the scope of what was originally envisioned. The UN refugee treaties and the definition they contain have become the centerpiece for virtually all national and regional systems, while some such systems also go further in extending protection to other categories as well. Through the beneficent influence of these instruments, supplemented by the efforts of UNHCR, millions of uprooted people have found refuge and assistance. A high proportion of them have also been able to resettle permanently in other countries. One must not lose sight of the needs that have gone unmet, but by any measure, the UN system's role in refugee affairs should be seen as a significant success story.

Nevertheless, the large-scale movements of the 1980s and 1990s have posed enormous challenges. By and large they have not brought a direct undermining of the protections for refugees built on the Convention and Protocol. Instead, their effects are more subtle. In some circumstances, the earlier policy of accepting for resettlement or asylum broad groups of the

---

[78] Conclusion No. 8, Determination of Refugee Status, UNHCR Conclusions, note 73 above, at 16–18.   [79] UNHCR *Handbook*, note 23 above.

[80] See, e.g., *INS v. Cardoza-Fonseca*, note 64 above at 439; *Canas-Segovia v. INS*, 902 F.2d 717, 724 (9th Cir. 1990), *vacated and remanded on other grounds*, 112 S.Ct. 1152 (1992); *Dwomoh v. Sava*, 696 F. Supp. 970 (S.D.N.Y. 1988). Of course, the administrative authorities make use of the UNHCR Handbook as well. See, e.g., "Matter of Vigil," 19 *Immig. & Nationality* Dec. 572, 579 (Bd. Immig. App. 1988).

displaced has been supplanted by policies opening such opportunities only to those who meet the narrower UN treaty definition. Clearly this has happened in Southeast Asia, under the Comprehensive Plan of Action adopted in June 1989 to deal with future migration from Indochina.[81] What had been essentially a promise of resettlement to all who escaped Vietnam was transformed, under the pressure of compassion fatigue (after fifteen years of migration), into a limited promise covering only those who are Convention refugees. Those not meeting this standard are supposed to repatriate. Many European countries are also acting to end acceptance of wider categories of humanitarian or *de facto* refugees, henceforth extending asylum almost exclusively to Convention refugees.[82] At the same time, increasingly restrictive interpretation of the Convention definition is also evident in the practice of some national authorities.[83] Finally, recognizing that Convention refugees who manage to gain physical presence on their territory will in fact receive asylum, more states have adopted policies making it difficult for asylum seekers to establish such presence – through use of maritime interdiction, for example, or more broadly applicable visa regimes that make it harder for certain nationalities to join the ranks of the "jet people."[84]

These developments make it hard to muster optimism for further progressive developments in the 1990s and beyond. Efforts to expand legal rights in this field may even be counterproductive. A better focus for creative thinking and advocacy may be selective efforts to discourage the more troubling of the restrictive practices with which states are now experimenting. Success in that endeavor will probably require recognition of states' legitimate need to find ways to restrict some of their perceived exposure, so as to counter domestic backlash. Cooperation in devising new methods to reduce debilitating delays in the adjudication of claims to refugees' status or asylum is also sorely needed.[85]

Increased attention to root causes, coupled with more direct action (ranging from vigorous human rights diplomacy all the way to possible humanitarian intervention) to protect abused or threatened individuals within their home countries, also holds some promise. In addition, the shift

---

[81] See note 4 above.

[82] In 1966, the Interior Ministers (*Land* and federal) of the Federal Republic of Germany adopted a policy whereby virtually all East-Bloc asylum seekers would be allowed to remain in Germany, no matter what the decision on their refugee claims. In April 1989, they revoked this policy. 75 Documentation-Réfugiés 3 (25 mai/3 juin 1989). In December 1989, Sweden announced that it would severely restrict its earlier policy of acceptance of *de facto* refugees who did not meet the Convention definition. P. Nobel, "What Happened with Sweden's Refugee Policies?" 2 *Int'l J. Refugee L.* 265, 271 (1990).

[83] See, e.g., 1990 Report of the UNHCR, note 14 above, at 5–7.

[84] The phrase is from W. Smyser, *Refugees: Extended Exile* 92 (1987).

[85] See Martin, "The New Asylum Seekers," note 70 above, at 14–15.

in focus from cure to prevention of refugee crises may encourage more states to become strong supporters of human rights and development initiatives. Such a trend would be welcome. But the basic task remains daunting, because the removal of the root causes of refugee flows requires nothing less than the prevention of war, deterrence or rectification of human rights violations, and the amelioration of poverty. These may be the highest objectives of international diplomacy and politics, but their attainment is aided only slightly now that the world more readily notices their linkage to refugee flows. A strong UN refugee protection system will still be necessary for as long as political conflict produces violence and persecution.

SELECTED BIBLIOGRAPHY

Aga Khan, S., "Legal Problems Relating to Refugees and Displaced Persons," 1976 [I], *RCADI* 287 (1976)

Aleinikoff, T. A. and D. Martin, *Immigration: Process and Policy* (3d ed., West Pub., 1995)

Goodwin-Gill, G., *International Law and the Movement of Persons between States* (Clarendon Press, 1978)

The Refugee in International Law (Oxford University Press, 1983)

Hannum, H., *The Right to Leave and Return in International Law* (Martinus Nijhoff, 1987)

Hathaway, J., *The Law of Refugee Status* (Butterworths, 1991)

Holborn, L., *Refugees: A Problem of Our Time: The Work of the United Nations High Commissioner for Refugees, 1951–1972* (Scarecrow, 1975)

Martin, D., "Effects of International Law on Migration Policy and Practice: The Uses of Hypocrisy," 23 *Int'l Migration Rev.* 547 (1989)

The Movement of Persons Across Borders (L. Sohn and T. Buerganthal eds.; American Society of International Law, 1992)

The New Asylum Seekers: Refugee Law in the 1980s (D. Martin ed.; Martinus Nijhoff, 1988)

Office of the UN High Commissioner for Refugees, *Handbook on Procedures and Criteria for Determining Refugee Status* (1979)

Plender, R., *International Migration Law* (rev. 2d edn, Sijthoff, 1988)

CHAPTER SEVEN

WOMEN

Rebecca J. Cook

I. INTRODUCTION

The United Nations system of protection of human rights recognized the need for nondiscrimination on grounds of sex in its founding instrument, the UN Charter of 1945.[1] The existing pattern of UN instruments and institutions for the protection and promotion of human rights may be regarded as offering women not so much the security that their rights are safeguarded as the opportunity for recognition that the wrongs done to them are violations of their rights. That is, women cannot regard the UN system as guaranteeing their rights, but only as offering the prospect that women will have access to the means to expose violations of their rights and to pursue prospects of redress.

The UN, a product of its time, is an institution created at a point in a long continuum of male-centered conceptualization. Classical international law is the law of nations, and advancement of the interests of nations was considered the work of men. The development of the laws of peace to curb and eventually supersede the laws of war were similarly the goals of men who had the vision to seek to contain the military instincts of men toward territorial expansion. The modern laws and practices of diplomacy that lubricated the interactions of nations, and created international institutions designed to secure enduring peace, saw military aggression as the principal danger to peace and military containment as the ultimate instrument of pacification. The underlying concepts of conflict and its resolution were perceived in terms of adversarial combat that were essentially dominated by male imagery. The modern development of international human rights law was similarly moved by perceptions of the cruelty and injustice done by man to man; the injustices suffered by women

---

[1] The United Nations, *The United Nations and the Advancement of Women, 1945–1995* (United Nations, 1995).

were perceived, more by intuition than intellect, to be derived from the injustices done to husbands, fathers, and sons. The "feminization" of human rights[2] is designed not to mask or disguise the extent of violations of the rights of men, but to buttress the claim that violations of women's human rights are also an affront to human dignity even though their liability to suffer violations of human rights may differ from that of men.

The present challenge to prevent and redress international human rights violations against women is both pragmatic and theoretical. The pragmatic challenge is to identify, expose, and remedy the violations of human rights that affect women. Fact-finding reports[3] and empirical studies, including those developed by the UN and its specialized agencies,[4] demonstrate how all societies neglect women's well-being.

A powerful development in the formulation of rights has been the emergence of feminist legal theories.[5] These theories have developed beyond elaborating a monolithic feminist jurisprudence to recognizing pluralism and disagreement in feminist understanding of law and of legal institutions.[6] Feminist theories and methods, particularly those that are evolving from Third-World contexts,[7] provide important foundations on which to build increasingly stronger strategies to provide redress for the violation of women's rights. The challenge is to apply evolving feminist theories of jurisprudence to international law in general,[8] and to international human rights law in particular,[9] in order to improve the situation of women.

---

[2] See generally R. Cook & V. Oosterveld, "A Select Bibliography on Women's Human Rights," 44 *Amer. U. L. Rev.* 1429 (1995).

[3] Amnesty International, *Women in the Front Line: Human Rights Violations against Women* (1991); Human Rights Watch, *The Human Rights Watch Global Report on Women's Human Rights* (1995).

[4] United Nations, *Violence against Women in the Family*, (Centre for Social Development and Humanitarian Affairs, 1989); United Nations, *The World's Women 1995: Trends and Statistics* (1995); C. AbouZahr & E. Royston, *Maternal Mortality: A Global Factbook*, World Health Organization (1991).

[5] See generally R. West, "Jurisprudence and Gender," 55 *U. Chi. L. Rev.* 1 (1988); C. MacKinnon, *Toward a Feminist Theory of the State* (1989).

[6] See generally N. Duclos, "Lessons of Difference: Feminist Theory on Cultural Diversity," 38 *Buff. L. Rev.* 325 (1990).

[7] See generally, *Faith and Freedom: Women's Human Rights in the Muslim World* (M. Afkhami ed., 1995); R. Coomarswamy, "To Bellow Like a Cow: Women, Ethnicity, and the Discourse of Rights," in *Human Rights of Women: National and International Perspectives* (R. Cook ed., 1994); I. Plata and M. Yanusova, *Los Derechos Humanos y La Convención Sobre la Eliminación de Todas las Formas de Discriminacion Contra la Mujer 1979* (Human Rights and the 1979 Convention on the Elimination of All Forms of Discrimination against Women) (1988).

[8] See generally H. Charlesworth, C. Chinkin, & S. Wright, "Feminist Approaches to International Law," 85 *AJIL* 613 (1991).

[9] See generally C. Bunch, "Women's Rights as Human Rights: Toward a Re-vision of Human Rights," 12 *Hum. Rts. Q.* 486 (1990); A. Byrnes, "Women, Feminism and International Human Rights Law – Methodological Myopia, Fundamental Flaws or Meaningful Marginalization," 12 *Austl. Y. B. Int'l L.* 205 (1992).

Feminist legal theorists generally take as their starting point the fact of women's subordination and oppression, and they evaluate law in terms of its actual and potential contribution to dismantling such oppression.[10] Varying methodologies all attempt to translate women's experiences of oppression and exclusion into legal analysis, and to enrich legal understanding from the female frame of reference.[11] One feminist legal method starts by "asking the woman question."

In law, asking the woman question means examining how the law fails to take into account the experiences and values that seem more typical of women than of men, for whatever reason, or how existing legal standards and concepts might disadvantage women. The question assumes that some features of the law may be not only non-neutral in a general sense, but also male in a specific sense. The purpose of the woman question is to expose those features and how they operate, and to suggest how they might be corrected.[12]

In asking this question, one is challenging the assumption of the law's gender neutrality:

Without the woman question, differences associated with women are taken for granted and, unexamined, may serve as a justification for laws that disadvantage women. . . . In exposing the hidden effect of laws that do not explicitly discriminate on the basis of sex, the woman question helps to demonstrate how social structures embody norms that implicitly render women different and thereby subordinate.[13]

The application of such feminist methods will improve the application of international human rights law to ensure respect for women's dignity and rights.

Human rights can be divided into individual rights and relative rights. Individual rights, such as the right to liberty and security of the person and the right to be free from inhuman or degrading treatment, are rights individuals possess without regard to such features as their sex, race, or, for instance, religion. Observance of relative rights is assessed by reference to how an individual is treated in comparison or contrast to how relevant others are treated, and amount to rights of nondiscrimination on such grounds as sex, race, or religion. Both individual and relative human rights need to be invoked more vigorously to protect women's interests.

Nondiscrimination rights will appear more obviously to affect women, because of recognized practices of disfavoring and disentitling women, but violations of individual rights can also disproportionately affect women. International human rights law has not generally been applied to women's particular grievances. This is apparent in the historic failure to recognize the

---

[10] N. Lacey, "Legislation against Sex Discrimination: Questions from a Feminist Perspective," 14 *J. L. & Soc'y* 411 (1987).
[11] See generally K. Barlett, "Feminist Legal Methods," 103 *Harv. L. Rev.* 829 (1990).
[12] *Ibid.* at 837.   [13] *Ibid.* at 843.

systemic, pervasive, and egregious nature of violence against women as violating women's rights to be free from cruel, inhuman, or degrading treatment.[14]

II. DEVELOPMENT OF INTERNATIONAL HUMAN RIGHTS LAW RELATING TO WOMEN

A. General international human rights law

The foundation of the UN was a reaction not simply to the institutional failure of the League of Nations, but to the failure of states to respect the human rights of individuals, including their own citizens. The UN Charter[15] provides a legal foundation for international cooperation among its members for respect for human rights, including the elimination of discrimination on grounds of sex. This goal is to be pursued through the UN, its specialized agencies, and specialized bodies established under UN conventions that promote and enforce human rights. The Preamble to the UN Charter places human rights before the rights of nations, and affirms "the equal rights of men and women." Article 1(3) of the Charter establishes the purposes of the UN, which include "promoting and encouraging respect for human rights and for fundamental freedoms for all without distinction as to race, sex, language, or religion", and repeats this sequence in subsequent articles.[16]

In December 1948, the General Assembly of the UN adopted the Universal Declaration of Human Rights.[17] The emphasis that the Declaration gives to entitlement to all of its rights and freedoms "without distinction of any kind, such as race, colour, sex . . . or other status"[18] finds an explicit basis in the articles of the UN Charter. The Declaration is not legally binding in itself, but it is widely treated as the international community's authoritative guide to the meaning of human rights.[19]

Legal force was given to the Declaration through two covenants of a

---

[14] T. Randall, "The Montreal Massacre of 14 Women: Men Cannot Know the Feelings of Fear," *The Globe and Mail (Toronto)*, Dec. 12, 1989, at A7 & A8; J. Perlez, "Kenyans Do Some Soul-Searching After Rape of 71 Schoolgirls," *NY Times*, July 29, 1991, at A1 & A7.

[15] 1976 *Y. B. UN* 1043.

[16] See art. 8 (no restrictions on eligibility of women to participate in any capacity in UN affairs); art. 13(1) (the General Assembly shall initiate studies to promote international economic and social co-operation without distinction as to . . . sex); arts. 55(c) & 56 (the UN and its members shall promote respect for international economic and social co-operation without distinction as to . . . sex); art. 62(2) (the Economic and Social Council shall promote respect for human rights and fundamental freedoms for all); and art. 76(c) (the UN Trusteeship system shall encourage respect for human rights and fundamental freedoms for all without distinction as to . . . sex). [17] GA Res. 217A (III), UN Doc. A/810 (1948).

[18] *Ibid.*, art. 2. [19] See generally H. Hannum's chapter on human rights in this book (ch. 5).

general character, namely the International Covenant on Civil and Political Rights (the Political Covenant)[20] and the International Covenant on Economic, Social and Cultural Rights (the Economic Covenant).[21] Each state party to one or both of the covenants undertakes to respect individuals' rights recognized in each covenant "without distinction of any kind, such as race, colour, sex . . . or other status."[22] Nondiscrimination on grounds, among others of sex, appears at several points in each of the two general covenants, in particular in Article 26 of the Political Covenant requiring equality before the law and equal protection of the law.[23]

The nondiscrimination conventions, such as the International Convention on the Elimination of All Forms of Racial Discrimination (the Race Convention)[24] and the Convention on the Elimination of All Forms of Discrimination against Women (the Women's Convention)[25] amplify the legal content to the general prohibition of discrimination. Sex discrimination is also prohibited in the regional human rights conventions such as the European Convention for the Protection of Human Rights and Fundamental Freedoms (the European Convention),[26] the American Convention on Human Rights (the American Convention),[27] and the African Charter on Human and Peoples' Rights (the African Charter).[28]

Both the two general covenants and such specialized conventions as the Convention against Torture and Other Forms of Cruel, Inhuman and Degrading Treatment or Punishment,[29] the international conventions

[20] GA Res. 2200 (XXI), UN GAOR, 21st Sess., Supp. No. 16, at 52, UN Doc. A/6316 (1966), reprinted in 999 UNTS 171 and in 6 *ILM* 368 (1967) (*entered into force* Mar. 23, 1976) (hereinafter ICCPR).

[21] GA Res. 2200 (XXI), UN GAOR, 21st Sess., Supp. No. 16, at 52, UN Doc. A/6316 (1966), reprinted in 993 UNTS 3 and in 6 *ILM* 360 (1967) (*entered into force* Jan. 3, 1976) (hereinafter ICESCR). [22] ICCPR, 2(1); ICESCR, art. 2(2).

[23] For specific prohibitions of discrimination, see ICCPR, note 20 above, art. 3 (equal rights of men and women with respect to the rights set forth in the Covenant); art. 4 (measures derogating from the obligations cannot involve discrimination on grounds of . . . sex); art. 14 (equality before the law); art. 23 (equality of rights and responsibilities of spouses as to marriage, during marriage and at its dissolution); art. 24 (equal protection of the child irrespective of . . . sex); and art. 25 (equal rights of citizens without distinction on grounds of . . . sex with respect to voting, public service and public representation). See also ICESCR, note 21 above, art. 3 (equal rights of men and women with respect to the rights set forth in the Covenant) & art. 7 (equal pay for work of equal value).

[24] International Convention on the Elimination of All Forms of Racial Discrimination, 660 UNTS 195 (1965), reprinted in 5 *ILM* 352 (1966).

[25] Convention on the Elimination of All Forms of Discrimination against Women, Dec. 18, 1979, UN GAOR, 34th Sess., Supp. No.21, at 193, UN Doc. A/Res/34/180 (*entered into force* Sept. 3, 1981), reprinted in 19 *ILM* 33 (1980) (hereinafter CEDAW).

[26] 213 UNTS 221 (1955).

[27] OASTS 1 (1969), reprinted in 9 *ILM* 99 (1970) and in 65 *AJIL* 679 (1971).

[28] OAU Doc. CAB/LEG67/3/Rev. 5 (1981), reprinted in 21 *ILM* 58 (1982).

[29] GA Res 39/46, Annex, A/39/51 (1984), reprinted in United Nations, *Human Rights: A Compilation of International Instruments* 212 (1988), UN Sales No. E.88, XIV.1 (*entered into force* June 26, 1987).

dealing with refugees,[30] and the Convention on the Rights of the Child[31] primarily address individual human rights requiring observance of minimum standards of treatment of persons. In contrast, the Race Convention and the Women's Convention impose obligations of nondiscrimination.

The greatest accomplishments of the UN system regarding human rights law relating to women have been to define discrimination against women, to identify normative standards for the elimination of discrimination against women that states parties to the Women's Convention must pursue in both the public and private sectors of their national life, and to provide mechanisms by which discriminatory practices may be identified and remedied. However, enforcement of such standards and achievement of remedies for their violation have not been adequate.

The UN has not been widely successful in advancing recognition that many violations of individual human rights, such as the right to be free from inhuman or degrading treatment, significantly affect women. That is, while the UN is concerned in principle with such general violations of human rights protected by the mainstream human rights conventions whose treaty bodies are based in Geneva or the regional human rights systems, it pays insufficient attention to the application of these mainstream conventions to violations that affect women.[32]

B. Treaties addressing specific indignities and discriminations against women

The General Assembly has adopted a number of major conventions, most developed by the UN Commission on the Status of Women (the Women's Commission), that specifically identify and serve the human rights of women. These include the Convention for the Suppression of the Traffic in Persons and of the Exploitation of the Prostitution of Others,[33] the Convention on the Political Rights of Women,[34] the Convention on the Nationality of Married Women,[35] and the Convention on Consent to Marriage, Minimum Age for Marriage and Registration of Marriages.[36] These conventions remain in effect among ratifying states, but their purpose of protecting women's legal rights equally with those of men is incorporated into the Women's Convention.

The Convention for the Suppression of the Traffic in Persons and of the Exploitation of the Prostitution of Others refers equally to men and

---

[30] 1951 Convention Relating to the Status of Refugees, 189 UNTS 137 (No. 2545); 1967 Protocol Relating to the Status of Refugees, 606 UNTS 267 (No. 8791).
[31] A/Res./44/25 (Nov. 20, 1989).   [32] Byrnes, note 9 above.
[33] 96 UNTS 272 (1950).   [34] 193 UNTS 135 (1953).
[35] 309 UNTS 65 (1957).   [36] 521 UNTS 231 (1962).

women, but in practice applies mainly to women because they are the overwhelming majority of victims of such traffic and exploitation. Similarly, the Supplementary Convention on the Abolition of Slavery, the Slave Trade and Institutions and Practices Similar to Slavery[37] is applicable *de jure* to both sexes, but particularly relevant to the protection of women.

UNESCO promulgated the Convention against Discrimination in Education.[38] The ILO has a history long predating the UN of setting standards for the specific protection of women in the workforce, concerning such matters as maternity protection (1919), night work (1919), employment in underground mines (1935), and the Convention Concerning Equal Remuneration for Men and Women Workers for Work of Equal Value.[39] In the last-mentioned convention, the ILO pioneered the principle of women's entitlement to equal pay for work of equal value to that performed by men. As a specialized agency of the UN, the ILO continues to be concerned with setting standards to address the problems of female workers.

The Women's Commission was concerned about the inability of these conventions to improve the actual status of women and as a result commissioned a working paper.[40] The working paper noted that the 1967 Declaration on the Elimination of Discrimination against Women (the Women's Declaration)[41] was not legally binding on states even though it had moral force, and found that existing instruments that could be legally binding were not yet widely ratified.[42] In addition, the working paper stated that, despite these instruments, "inequality of the sexes is, in fact, still 'part of the idealized heritage of a large part of public opinion which sees in this nothing that is odious or persecutory' while discrimination based on other differences such as race and religion is not considered permissible."[43]

C. The Women's Convention

1. The significance of the Convention

The Women's Convention is the definitive international legal instrument requiring respect for and observance of the human rights of women; it is

37 International Convention for the Abolition of Slavery and the Slave Trade, 60 UNTS 253 (1927); Supplementary Slavery Convention, 266 UNTS 3 (1957).
38 429 UNTS 93 (1960).
39 ILO Convention, No. 100, reprinted in 165 UNTS 303 (1951). See generally V. Leary, chapter on ILO in this book (ch. 8).
40 UN ESCOR, 54th Sess., Supp. No. 5, para. 2, UN Doc. E/CN.6/573 (1973).
41 GA Res. 2263, UN GAOR, 22d Sess., Supp. No. 16, at 35, UN Doc. A/6716 (1967).
42 UN ESCOR, 54th Sess., Supp. No. 5, note 40 above, paras. 9–11. At that time the Convention on the Political Rights of Women had been ratified by only half of the states members of the UN.   43 *Ibid.*, para. 16.

universal in reach, comprehensive in scope, and legally binding in character. It was adopted unanimously by the UN General Assembly on December 18, 1979[44] and came into force in September 1981 after ratification by the twentieth state party.

The Convention characterizes the problem of women's inferior status and their oppression not just as a problem of inequality between men and women, but rather as a function of discrimination against women as such. The Convention is intended to be effective to liberate women to maximize their individual and collective potentialities, and not merely to allow women to be brought to the same level of protection of rights that men enjoy. It goes beyond the goal of equal treatment of women with men, as required by the UN Charter, the Universal Declaration, and its two implementing covenants, to address specifically the disadvantaged positions of women. In contrast to previous human rights treaties, the Women's Convention frames the legal norm as the prohibition of all forms of discrimination against women as distinct from sexual nondiscrimination. That is, it develops the legal norm from a sex-neutral norm that requires equal treatment of men and women, usually measured by how men are treated, to recognize the fact that the particular nature of discrimination against women and their distinctive characteristics is worthy of a legal response. The Convention is thereby able to address the particular nature of women's disadvantages.

The special significance of the Women's Convention is its underlying recognition that women have historically been subjected not simply to specific areas of disadvantage, but to systemic discrimination and oppression founded on hostile stereotypes and presumptions rooted in cultures and often reinforced by political and religious convictions. Accordingly, the goals of the Women's Convention are not only to redress specific inequities, but also to change negative stereotyping and presumptions about women's capacities and special functions that result in systemic denial of women's human rights and fundamental freedoms.

The Preamble to the Women's Convention notes the roles of the UN Charter, the Universal Declaration, the Women's Declaration, the two international covenants, and UN and specialized agencies' resolutions, declarations, and recommendations promoting equality of rights of men and women. The Preamble also expresses concern, however, "that despite these various instruments extensive discrimination against women continues to exist."[45] The Preamble concludes with an expression of determination "to adopt the measures required for the elimination of such

---

[44] CEDAW, note 25 above. See generally L. Rehof, *Guide to the Travaux Préparatoires of the United Nations Convention on the Elimination of All Forms of Discrimination against Women* (1993). [45] CEDAW, note 25 above, para. 6.

discrimination in all its forms and manifestations."[46] The Women's Convention is a unifying instrument through which states parties demonstrate a positive commitment to the comprehensive prohibition of discrimination against women.

The Fourth World Conference on Women, which took place in Beijing in 1995, finalized the Declaration and Platform for Action.[47] The 187 governments that adopted the Beijing Declaration and Platform for Action urge universal ratification of the Women's Convention by the year 2000.[48]

2. What constitutes discrimination against women?

For the purposes of the Women's Convention, a legal definition of "discrimination against women" was required. Discussion leading to the development of the Women's Declaration into the Women's Convention showed an intention to define discrimination against women for purposes of legal application and enforcement.[49] The definition in Article 1 of the Women's Convention reads:

The term "discrimination against women" shall mean any distinction, exclusion, or restriction made on the basis of sex which has the effect or purpose of impairing or nullifying the recognition, enjoyment or exercise by women, irrespective of their marital status, on a basis of equality of men and women, of human rights and fundamental freedoms in the political, economic, social, cultural, civil or any other field.

In determining whether laws, policies, practices, or other measures constitute "discrimination against women," two questions must be asked:

1. Do the laws, policies, practices, or other measures at issue make "any distinction, exclusion, or restriction" on the basis of sex?
2. If they do make such a distinction, exclusion, or restriction, do they have "the effect or purpose of impairing or nullifying the recognition, enjoyment or exercise by women, irrespective of their marital status, on a basis of equality of men and women, of human rights and fundamental freedoms?"

Where a law does make a distinction that has the effect or purpose of impairing in any way women's rights, then it constitutes discrimination under this definition, violates the Convention, and must accordingly be changed by the state party.

Not all laws or practices that place women at a disadvantage constitute

---

[46] *Ibid.*, para. 15.
[47] The United Nations, Report of the Fourth World Conference on Women, A/Conf.177/20, 17 Oct. 1995.   [48] *Ibid.*, at para. 320 (b).
[49] UN Doc. 54, UN ESCOR, Supp. No.5, paras. 9 & 23.

"discrimination against women" within the meaning of Article 1. A law that makes no express distinction on the basis of sex in its language cannot be impugned under this definition despite its having a discriminatory effect. For example, rules for bank loans that require collateral security in the form of land holdings will be unavailable to many women where legal systems prohibit or obstruct succession to land by widows and daughters.[50] Such rules on bank loans do not expressly discriminate against women, but their effect is discriminatory in countries where women cannot hold or inherit land.

Subtle forms of exploitation are correlated to cultural, religious, and family conditions that have constrained the advancement of women and intensified their marginalization and oppression. Employment and apprenticeship programs that are neutral on the surface often have discriminatory effects because girls cannot meet educational eligibility standards. Family conditions may require that school-age girls remain in the home, for instance to care for siblings while their mothers work outside the home. Admission criteria for apprenticeship programs may not offend Article 1 of the Women's Convention, because they do not discriminate in their terms, but they may violate Article 3, which echoes the Preamble in requiring states parties "to ensure the full development and advancement of women, for the purpose of guaranteeing them the exercise and enjoyment of human rights and fundamental freedoms on a basis of equality with men." In addition to impugning laws and practices that are detrimental in their effect but neutral on the surface, Article 3 prohibits practices that are detrimental to women as such, including for instance nonprovision of obstetric services. This article, therefore, catches those discriminatory practices that do not come within the scope of the Article 1 definition.

The goal of Article 3 is reinforced by Article 4, which specifies that "temporary special measures aimed at accelerating *de facto* equality between men and women shall not be considered discrimination as defined by the Convention." This allows for the possibility of determinate, concrete practices to secure "equality of opportunity and treatment."

The goals of eliminating discrimination against women and ensuring the full development and advancement of women are also enhanced by Article 5 of the Women's Convention. By this article, states parties are obligated to take all appropriate measures to modify social and cultural patterns of conduct based on "the idea of the inferiority or the superiority of either of the sexes or on stereotyped roles for men and women," and to ensure that family education will contribute to parents and children

---

[50] See generally F. Butegua, "Using the African Charter on Human & Peoples' Rights to Secure Women's Access to Land in Africa," in *The Human Rights of Women: National and International Perspectives* 495–514 (R. Cook ed., 1994).

gaining proper understanding of equality of the sexes within the family.

The elimination of marital-status discrimination is a goal in addition to and separate from that of securing equal developmental opportunities for women and men. This objective is shown in the provision in the definition that offensive conduct is that which distinguishes on the basis of sex, and which has the effect or purpose of denying women "irrespective of their marital status" their human rights and fundamental freedoms in the "civil or any other field." For example, a practice of health clinics to require wives, but not unmarried women, to secure the authorization of their husbands in order to receive health care constitutes marital status discrimination that violates the Convention and would accordingly have to be changed.[51]

The Article 1 definition, read in the context of the entire Women's Convention, now represents an international consensus on what constitutes "discrimination against women," even though the definition is contained in a particular convention. The Human Rights Committee, established by the Political Covenant, has referred to the Women's Convention in its General Comments on the norm of nondiscrimination and formulated the Covenant's prohibition of discrimination against women in similar terms.[52]

3. Scope: "all forms of discrimination"

The inclusion in the title of the Women's Convention of the phrase "all forms"[53] emphasizes the determination to adopt a treaty to eliminate "such discrimination in all its forms and manifestations" described in paragraph 15 of its Preamble. The Preamble[54] makes clear that the Convention is designed to amplify the general framework of international human rights conventions that prohibits discrimination on several grounds including sex, and to extend beyond the series of conventions designed to eliminate specific forms of discrimination against women.

The Women's Convention, in addressing all forms of discrimination, is intended to be comprehensive and to recognize that women are not only subject to specific indignities and inequalities but that they are also subject to pervasive forms of discrimination that are woven into the political, cultural, and religious fabric of societies. The Convention progresses beyond the earlier specialized conventions[55] by addressing the pervasive

---

[51] See generally R. Cook, "International Protection of Women's Reproductive Rights," 24 *NYU J. Int'l L. & Pol.* 645, 682–83 (1992).

[52] General Cmnt. 18(37), CCPR/C/21/Rev.1/Add.1 (1989), paras. 6–7.

[53] The title of the Women's Declaration does not contain these words. See note 41 above and accompanying text, p. 187.   [54] CEDAW, note 25 above, paras. 1–4.

[55] See notes 33–39 above.

and systemic nature of discrimination against women, and develops the modern general conventions on human rights by identifying the need to confront the social causes of women's inequality by addressing "all forms" of discrimination that women suffer.[56]

In contrast to the Race Convention, the Women's Convention is not confined to governmental obligations regarding public life; rather, it imposes obligations in the private or "civil" field since the Convention obligates states to address social as well as political wrongs against women. The strongest emphasis on the need to combat private discrimination came from UNESCO, which was constantly vigilant lest states might have lost sight of the need to commit themselves to influence the private and family sectors of national life.[57]

More specifically, Article 15(2) requires that states parties "shall accord to women, in civil matters, a legal capacity identical to that of men . . . In particular they shall give women equal rights to conclude contracts and to administer property." Article 15(3) provides that "States Parties agree that all contracts and all other private instruments of any kind with a legal effect which is directed at restricting the legal capacity of women shall be deemed null and void." This article shows a forceful intention to intervene in private contractual, property, and other interactions with a view to eliminating discrimination against women. For instance, rules of intestate succession, even if they are embedded in customary or tribal law, cannot exclude women from being successors to estates nor from undertaking their administration. Indeed, the provision may even threaten the execution of wills "directed at restricting the legal capacity of women," for instance by requiring legislation to the effect that unjustified exclusions of women from succession or fair entitlement shall be corrected or held void or voidable.

Article 16 affects matters relating to marriage and family relations. It addresses private matters by requiring states parties to ensure the same rights for men and women to enter marriage, the same rights and responsibilities during marriage, the same rights and responsibilities with respect to children and at dissolution of marriage. Ample evidence exists, therefore, of an intention in the Convention that states parties eliminate discrimination in private and family matters.

The framers were concerned "that in situations of poverty women have the least access to food, health, education, training and opportunities for employment and other needs."[58] As a result, the Convention entitles

---

[56] UNESCO, Report of the Meeting of Experts on the Social and Cultural Factors that Impede the Promotion of Equality and the Application of the Convention on the Elimination of All Forms of Discrimination against Women, UN Doc. SHS87/Conf.805/11, para. 13 (1987).

[57] UN Doc. A/32/218, at para. 14 (1977).

[58] CEDAW, note 25 above, Preamble & para. 8.

women to equal enjoyment with men not only of civil and political rights but also of the economic, social, and cultural rights. Article 10 advances the pursuit of equality in the field of education by requiring states parties to ensure, among other things, access for women to educational establishments that have the same academic standards, qualifications of staff, and school premises and equipment as are available to men. Article 11(1) addresses state responsibilities toward women in employment including, *inter alia,* rights to equal remuneration, promotion opportunities, and job security. Article 12 requires states parties to take all appropriate measures to eliminate discrimination in matters of health care and ensure that women have "appropriate services in connexion with pregnancy, confinement and the post-natal period." Article 13 concerns elimination of discrimination in areas of economic and social life, including equal rights to family benefits, to financial services such as bank loans, and to recreational activities.

The obligation that states parties to the Women's Convention accept to eliminate discrimination that occurs in private relationships does not directly bind individuals or organizations in their private conduct. Private individuals and organizations are not subjects of international law, and are not legally accountable for nonconformity with conventions ratified by their countries. It is the responsibility of states parties themselves, however, to take appropriate measures to eliminate private discrimination in order to ensure the states' compliance with the Convention. States must employ their legal powers to prevent or remedy private discrimination in order to escape state responsibility. States parties cannot invoke legal incapacity under their domestic constitutions or laws as a defense to failure to discharge the responsibility they have assumed through ratification of the Convention.

States parties to the Women's Convention undertake:

to take all appropriate measures to eliminate discrimination against women by any person, organization or enterprise;[59]

and

to take all appropriate measures, including legislation, to modify or abolish existing laws, regulations, customs and practices which constitute discrimination against women.[60]

Private discrimination would accordingly render a state party internationally accountable, unless the state had acted appropriately to prevent or provide a remedy for such breach of its duty under the Convention. A difficulty that many states face is that discriminatory conduct may result

[59] *Ibid.,* art. 2(e).   [60] *Ibid.,* art. 2(f).

not simply from long-accepted customs and practices, but from conduct of religious organizations that invoke divine inspiration, revelation, and mandate for such practices, for instance, as the exclusion of women from certain religious offices and entitlements. States parties must resolve the conflict within their states between claims to freedom of religious organizations and women's equality, and women must resolve conflicts between their rights to equality and their voluntary participation in religious organizations that practice discrimination against them.[61]

A state party may deny inequality on the ground that women accept limitation of their roles in religious organizations to which they voluntarily adhere, and the organizations themselves may claim that female members enjoy rights that are separate but equal. Where private discrimination is found, the legal issue under the Women's Convention is whether the responsibility of states is to achieve the elimination of that form of discrimination against women, or only to employ means in good faith toward this objective.

4. Obligations to eliminate discrimination

Upon becoming parties to the Women's Convention, states undertake obligations to establish the means to eliminate discrimination against women as well as actually to achieve that result. Article 2 provides that states parties "agree to pursue, by all appropriate means and without delay, a policy of eliminating discrimination against women" by undertaking constitutional, legislative, administrative, and other measures. It emphasizes the duty to embody principles of equality in national constitutions and legislation,[62] to adopt "appropriate legislative and other measures, including sanctions" prohibiting all discrimination against women,[63] and to repeal national penal provisions that discriminate against women.[64]

In order to extend beyond existing conventions that are aimed at specific forms of discrimination, the Convention was designed to prohibit discrimination that occurs in fact as well as by any express provision of law. In order to eliminate *de facto* discrimination, states parties agree to "refrain from any act or practice of discrimination."[65] It has been seen that they also undertake to prohibit discrimination against women by private individuals and organizations.[66]

Article 3 reinforces Article 2 by requiring states parties to ensure the full development and advancement of women. Article 24 underscores Articles 2 and 3 by requiring states parties "to adopt all necessary measures at the

---

[61] See generally D. Sullivan, "Gender Equality and Religious Freedom: Toward a Framework for Conflict Resolution," 24 *NYU J. Int'l L. & Pol.* 795 (1992).
[62] CEDAW, note 25 above, art. 2(a).   [63] *Ibid.*, art. 2(b).
[64] *Ibid.*, art. 2(g).   [65] *Ibid.*, art. 2(d).   [66] *Ibid.*, art. 2(e), (f).

national level aimed at achieving the full realization of the rights recognized in the present Convention." Articles 2, 3, and 24 accordingly impose obligations of means to be pursued "without delay" toward the ultimate result.

5. Reservations to the Women's Convention

At least 151 countries have now joined the Women's Convention by ratification or accession. Twenty-one of these countries, however, have filed over a total of eighty substantive reservations to the terms of the Convention by which they limit their obligations. In contrast, 146 countries have joined the International Convention on the Elimination of All Forms of Racial Discrimination and only two countries have reserved certain of their obligations to eliminate racial discrimination. Had the statistics been reversed, there understandably would have been an international outcry, but sadly such an outcry has not been heard against reservations to the Women's Convention.

Reservations have been made where practices that can be questioned on grounds of sexual discrimination are part of:

(i) religious or customary laws that generally limit inheritance and property rights;
(ii) nationality laws that do not grant women equal rights with men to acquire, change, or retain their nationality upon marriage or convey their nationality to their children;
(iii) laws that limit women's economic opportunities, access to land and financial credit, freedom of movement, and choice of residence;
(iv) laws affecting marriage and family relations.

The pattern of reservations is stark testimony to the fact that states do not readily agree on what constitutes discrimination against women. Some hold that societal roles assigned to women on religious or cultural grounds do not fall within the ambit of such discrimination. Others disagree. They would argue that these reservations reflect a patriarchal model of society that preserves sex-role stereotyping and systemic discrimination against women, which is contrary to the object and purpose of the Women's Convention.

The reservations indicate that some states parties are not ready in their domestic institutions, legislatures, and courts to recognize or create equality for women. To date, very few states parties have withdrawn or even narrowed their reservations despite pleas by the Committee on the Elimination of Discrimination against Women.[67] Moreover, biennial

---

[67] CEDAW General Recommendation 4 (on Reservations), Report of the Committee on the Elimination of Discrimination against Women (Sixth Session) A/42/38 (1987).

meetings of states parties to the Women's Convention, the Commission on the Status of Women or the Subcommission on the Prevention of Discrimination and Protection of Minorities have failed to take measures to protect the integrity of the Women's Convention. These bodies could, for example, request the Economic and Social Council (ECOSOC) to seek an advisory opinion of the International Court of Justice on the compatibility of the substantive reservations with the object and purpose of the Women's Convention.[68] Seeking an advisory opinion, with the possible consequence that some reserving states parties might be found not to be party to the Convention, raises the issue in international human rights conventions of either promoting their universality or protecting their integrity. Universality may be so desirable that less than complete commitment is tolerable, but integrity of observance of human rights may be more important than feigned allegiance of states not committed to the rights the conventions serve.[69]

III. PROTECTION OF WOMEN'S INTERNATIONAL HUMAN RIGHTS

Methods of protection of international human rights at the international and national levels depend for their effectiveness on the will of states. At the national level, systems for implementation and enforcement are far more advanced than at the international level. International protection of human rights functions in the context of the law of nations, traditionally the law of reciprocal acceptance of customs and of agreements that depend on mutuality of benefit and enlightened self-interest for effectiveness. It is international moral consensus and the potential for international embarrassment, however, rather than mutuality of benefit, that propel the application of international human rights law.

Methods of international protection of women's human rights range from recourse to limited international judicial or quasi-judicial processes to the application of broader means of furthering states parties' accountability, such as through reporting requirements.[70] The application of human rights norms to national laws and practices that are alleged to violate women's rights has to be approached in a variety of direct and indirect

---

[68] See generally Advisory Opinion on Reservations to the Genocide Convention, 1951 ICJ 15 (Advisory Opinion of May 28); Applicability of Article VI, Section 22, of the Convention on the Privileges and Immunities of the United Nations (the Mazilu case), 1989 ICJ 177.

[69] See generally R. Cook, "Reservations to the Convention on the Elimination of All Forms of Discrimination against Women," 30 *Va. J. Int'l L.* 643 (1990).

[70] See A. Byrnes, "Towards More Effective Enforcement of Women's Human Rights through the Use of International Human Rights Law and Procedures," in Cook ed., note 7 above, at 189–227.

ways, because any one method is fragile and inadequate. Ways include use of preventive, injunctive, restorative, compensatory, and punitive methods. Available approaches will be examined below from the perspective of different protective bodies that derive their authority from separate human rights treaties or from the UN Charter.

Methods of national protection of women's human rights will in the long run be more effective than international protection. National protection of international human rights derives its legal force from incorporation of international human rights treaties into domestic law through national legislation and through judicial application of treaties ratified by the state or adopted into legislation.

The application at both the international and domestic levels of international human rights norms to women's experiences and victimization helps to develop a much-needed common legal perspective and to crystallize the content of women's international human rights.

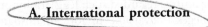

A. International protection

1. Treaty-based bodies

(a) The Human Rights Committee

Over fifty states parties to the Political Covenant have accepted its Optional Protocol, under which individuals who claim to be victims of violations of their rights protected by the Covenant may complain against such states to the Human Rights Committee. The Human Rights Committee, established under the Covenant, is beginning to develop valuable jurisprudence on women's rights and sexual nondiscrimination.[71] The primary activity of the Human Rights Committee under the Optional Protocol with respect to women has been to condemn sexual discrimination that was deliberately enacted in states parties' legislation.

Applications for remedies against violations of women's human rights have been meager. Only five complaints against states parties regarding women's rights have been lodged successfully with the Human Rights Committee. The limited number and nature of the challenges remains despite the fact that the Human Rights Committee has extended its jurisdiction to include cases where discrimination in observance of rights protected by the Economic Covenant and the Women's Convention has been alleged.[72]

---

[71] See generally R. Cook, "International Human Rights Law Concerning Women: Case Notes and Comments," 23 *Vand. J. Transnat'l L.* 779 (1990).

[72] *Broeks* v. *The Netherlands*, Communication No. 172/1984, UN GAOR, 42d Sess., Supp. No. 40, at 139, UN Doc. A/42/40 (1987); *Zwaan-de Vries* v. *The Netherlands*, Communication No. 182/1984, UN GAOR, 42d Sess., Supp. No. 40, at 160, UN Doc. A/42/40 (1987).

The first case to come before the Human Rights Committee involving a violation of a woman's rights was *Lovelace* v. *Canada*.[73] Canadian legislation, which gave effect to treaties by which Canada was bound, provided that a native Indian man who married a non-Indian woman retained his Indian status, but that an Indian woman lost her status and rights when she married a non-Indian husband, and that she did not reacquire her status and rights, including to return to her tribal lands, upon divorce. The Human Rights Committee concluded nevertheless that the refusal to recognize her as a member of her Indian tribe was an unjustifiable denial of her right to enjoy her own culture, recognized by Article 27 of the Covenant,[74] and Canada has accordingly changed its legislation.

In the Aumeeruddy-Cziffra case,[75] Mauritius was found in violation of the Political Covenant's provisions against sex discrimination because of its legislation that limited the rights of foreign husbands of Mauritian women to attain residence status in Mauritius, but that permitted Mauritian men to obtain residence status for their foreign wives. The Human Rights Committee regarded such legislation not as affording such foreign wives privileges unavailable to foreign husbands, but rather as discriminating against the Mauritian women who petitioned the Human Rights Committee. The Committee determined that the legislation promoted unlawful sex discrimination against Mauritian women, and as a result, Mauritius has changed its legislation to bring it into conformity with the Covenant.

A further condemnation of legislation containing explicit discrimination between the sexes occurred in the case of *Ato del Avellanal* v. *Peru*.[76] The Peruvian Civil Code provided that matrimonial property could be represented before the courts only by husbands. The complainant, a married woman, was accordingly denied the right to sue in her own name to recover unpaid rent from tenants of buildings she had acquired that were included in her matrimonial property. After exhausting local remedies when the Supreme Court of Peru upheld the legality of the Civil Code provision, she complained to the Human Rights Committee. The Committee upheld the complaint, concluding that the provision of the national Civil Code violated Article 3 of the Political Covenant, which requires nondiscrimination in the enjoyment of rights, Article 14(1), which requires equality before the courts, and Article 26, which mandates equality before the law and equal protection of the law. It remains unclear whether

---

[73] Commun. No. R.6/24, UN Doc a/36/40, reprinted in 2 *HRLJ* 158 (1981).

[74] *Ibid.*, para. 13.2.

[75] *Aumeeruddy-Cziffra et al.* v. *Mauritius*, Communication No. 35/1978, A/36/40 (1981), reprinted in 2 *HRLJ* 139 (1981).

[76] *Avellanal* v. *Peru*, Communication No. 202/1986, A/44/40 (1989) reprinted in 9 *HRLJ* 262 (1988).

Peru has changed the relevant provisions of its Civil Code to bring it into conformity with the Covenant.

Perhaps the most significant decisions of the Human Rights Committee for equal access of women to economic and social rights are in the cases of *Broeks* v. *The Netherlands*[77] and *Zwaan-de Vries* v. *The Netherlands*.[78] These cases both involved legislation providing that, in order to receive certain unemployment benefits, a married woman had to prove that she was a "breadwinner," while a married man received such benefits automatically without having to prove such a role in his family. After the complaints were filed, The Netherlands changed its legislation to remove the sexually discriminatory provision, but the Committee continued to hear the cases in full. It concluded that the earlier differentiation was not reasonable and constituted a violation of Article 26 of the Political Covenant.

The particular significance of the *Broeks* and *Zwaan-de Vries* judgments arises from the fact that the Committee accepted the complaint on the ground of an alleged violation not only of Article 26 of the Political Covenant, but also of Article 9 of the Economic Covenant, which recognizes the right to social security including unemployment payments. The Committee explained that Article 26 of the Political Covenant requires that, once a state adopts social security legislation, it must provide the benefits equally between the sexes. The Committee showed its willingness to condemn discrimination, even when such discrimination was covered by provisions of the Economic Covenant or, indeed, other conventions. The Committee expressly declared that discrimination provisions of the Political Covenant "would still apply even if a particular subject-matter is referred to or covered in other international instruments, for example . . . the Convention on the Elimination of All Forms of Discrimination Against Women."[79]

The willingness of the Human Rights Committee to scrutinize discrimination practices with respect to rights protected in other conventions enables women in those eighty-seven countries that have accepted the Optional Protocol to bring complaints about violations of their rights of equal access and equal entitlements to rights protected by the Economic Covenant and, for example, the Women's Convention, provided that those countries are parties to the latter-mentioned conventions.

(b) The Committee on the Elimination of Discrimination against Women
The Women's Convention establishes through Article 17 the Committee

---

[77] *Broeks*, note 72 above.   [78] *Zwaan-de Vries*, note 72 above.
[79] *Broeks*, note 72 above, para. 12.1; see also General Cmnt. 18 (37), CCPR/C/21/ Rev.1/Add.1 (1989), para. 12.1.

199

on the Elimination of Discrimination against Women (CEDAW),[80] whose task is to monitor states parties' behavior and performance. CEDAW is composed of twenty-three experts who, though nominated by states parties and elected on a rotating basis at the biennial meetings of states parties, serve for a term of four years in their expert personal capacity.

The primary responsibility of CEDAW is to examine reports submitted to it by states parties on the steps they have taken to implement the Convention. States parties are obligated under Article 18 of the Convention to report within one year of ratification or accession, and subsequently every four years, on measures that they have taken to eliminate discrimination against women and to indicate factors and difficulties they have encountered in fulfilling their treaty obligations. CEDAW examines the governmental reports in public meetings at which governmental representatives are present to answer questions put by CEDAW members.

Consideration of these reports provides significant opportunities to address practices that constitute discrimination against women and to identify what states parties have done to eliminate such practices. For example, biological differences between men and women are often considered justification for setting legal ages of marriage lower for women than for men. Committee members often query representatives of reporting states with lower ages of marriage for women than for men as to why they have not raised these lower ages to be equal with those for men. Members often explain that a lower age of marriage for women stereotypes them into childbearing and service roles, and that denying women the extra years of education, preparation, and experience to be "breadwinners"[81] made available to men is unjustified. Of all households, those headed by women range from 13 percent in Southern Asia to 20 percent in Sub-Sahara Africa, to 35 percent in the Caribbean.[82]

The work of CEDAW in considering governmental reports is far more effective when CEDAW members have recourse to sources of information in addition to that contained in reports of states parties. Accordingly, CEDAW has requested the Division for the Advancement of Women at the UN Secretariat to compile statistics garnered from official UN sources relevant to members' reports,[83] and also requested UN specialized agencies to submit information relevant to CEDAW's agenda.[84]

---

[80] See generally A. Byrnes, "The 'Other' Human Rights Treaty Body: The Work of the Committee on the Elimination of Discrimination against Women," 14 *Yale J. Int'l L.* 1 (1989); A. Byrnes, "CEDAW #10: Building on a Decade of Achievement," International Women's Rights Action Watch Working Paper Series (March, 1991) (hereinafter "CEDAW #10").

[81] Initial Report of the Socialist Republic of Vietnam, CEDAW/C/5/Add.25, at 4 (Oct. 4, 1985).   [82] *The World's Women*, note 4 above, at 5–6.

[83] UN Doc. E/1987/28, para. 320 (1987).

[84] Decision 2, UN Doc. A/42/38, at para. 580 (1987).

CEDAW members have emphasized the importance of nongovernmental organizations (NGOs) providing them with information about the position of women in their countries when they are reviewing countries' reports.[85] CEDAW has encouraged NGOs to send them information through the Division for the Advancement of Women particularly on major problems and priorities facing women. CEDAW, through Article 21, has the power to formulate suggestions and General Recommendations, and reports annually to the United Nations General Assembly, through ECOSOC, on these Recommendations and its overall activities. A noted commentator on the work of CEDAW has explained that:

CEDAW's power to adopt general recommendations is potentially a powerful tool for promoting the implementation of the Convention. For government officials charged with the implementation of the Convention or for non-governmental organizations who wish to use it as a standard for assessing laws and government policies, general recommendations which give detailed guidance as to the content of particular articles and the type of steps which should be taken to give effect to those obligations can be particularly valuable. As the considered collective pronouncements of [CEDAW], general recommendations should have considerable authority, even if formally they do not constitute a binding interpretation of the Convention.[86]

The General Recommendations adopted to date have ranged from procedural issues, such as general guidelines on the form and content of periodic reports and reservations to the Convention, to substantive issues such as measures to eliminate stereotyping of women, the use of temporary special measures, violence against women, equal remuneration for work of equal value, female circumcision, and, for example, unremunerated domestic activities of women.[87]

Some of the Recommendations show how certain forms of discrimination against women are covered by several articles of the Convention. For example, the 1992 General Recommendation on violence against women explained how gender-based violence could be addressed under such articles as those dealing with the prohibition of private discrimination,[88] stereotyped attitudes that diminish women,[89] exploitation of prostitution and trafficking in women,[90] sexual harassment in public workplaces,[91] the perpetuation of violence against women in the healthcare system whether it be by lack of contraceptives, coerced sterilization, or abortion and the condoning of female circumcision,[92] and, for example, family violence.[93]

---

[85] Byrnes, "CEDAW #10", note 80 above, at iii.   [86] *Ibid.*, at 16.
[87] For a listing of the General Recommendations through 1991, see *ibid.*, at 28; for the actual Recommendations see CEDAW annual reports.   [88] CEDAW, note 25 above, art. 2(e).
[89] *Ibid.*, art. 5.   [90] *Ibid.*, art. 6.   [91] *Ibid.*, art. 11.   [92] *Ibid.*, art. 12.   [93] *Ibid.*, art. 16.

(c) Other treaty-based bodies

Other treaty-based bodies, such as the Committee on the Elimination of All Forms of Racial Discrimination (the Race Committee) and the Committee against Torture (the Torture Committee) have individual complaint procedures that can be used in cases involving women for denial of their rights to racial nondiscrimination and their rights to be free from torture. Still other treaty-based bodies, such as the Committee on Economic, Social and Cultural Rights (the Economic Committee), can underscore the importance of the application of economic, social, and cultural rights to women.

In the case of *Yilmaz-Dogan* v. *The Netherlands,*[94] Ms. Yilmaz-Dogan, a Turkish national residing in The Netherlands, petitioned the Race Committee claiming that her dismissal from her job in a textile factory was racially motivated. The Race Committee decided that Ms. Yilmaz-Dogan's right to work had not been adequately protected and recommended that the Dutch government investigate whether Ms. Yilmaz-Dogan now had adequate employment and, if not, to assist her in securing employment or provide her with appropriate relief. No information is available on whether there has been any follow-up by the state party on the Committee's opinion.

The Economic Committee, the monitoring body for the Economic Covenant, has developed some innovative working methods to enhance its normative functions. They include such methods as formally receiving written submissions from nongovernmental organizations, holding annual "general discussions" on certain rights contained in the Economic Covenant and involving "recognized experts" to provide oral testimony during these discussions.[95] These methods provide significant opportunities to develop a feminist content to economic, social, and cultural rights.

Important research showing how economic development has exacerbated women's marginalization has led to programmatic initiatives to integrate women into development in order to maximize their chances of benefiting from development programs.[96] The Economic Committee might invite those researchers as "recognized experts" during the annual "general discussions" to explain why some of these programs have not been successful in improving women's actual status,[97] and what implications

---

[94] Commun. No. 1/1984, CERD/C36/D/1/1984 (Aug. 15, 1988).

[95] S. Leckie, "An Overview and an Appraisal of the Fifth Session of the UN Committee on Economic, Social and Cultural Rights," 13 *Hum. Rts. Q.* 545, 546 (1991).

[96] See generally *Persistent Inequalities: Women and World Development* (I. Tinker ed., 1990).

[97] A. M. Goetz, "Feminism and the Claim to Know: Contradictions in Feminist Approaches to Women and Development," in *Gender and International Relations* 133–57 (R. Grant & K. Newland eds., 1991); E. Rathgeber, "WID, WAD, GAD: Trends in Research and Practice," 24 *J. Developing Areas* 489 (1990).

these insights might have for the effective application of economic, social, and cultural rights. Such discussions with these experts might result in the formulation of a General Comment on how states parties might more effectively ensure that women enjoy these rights.

2. Charter-based bodies

(a) The UN Commission on the Status of Women

The Women's Commission, established by the ECOSOC in 1946, is the primary UN body responsible for advancing the status of women throughout the world.[98] The Commission consists of representatives of states who reflect the geographical distribution of UN membership. The Women's Commission meets annually in Vienna and receives staff support from the Division for the Advancement of Women of the UN Centre for Social Development and Humanitarian Affairs.

Historically, the most prominent achievements of the Women's Commission in promoting the rights of women were the development and drafting of the specialized conventions dealing with women[99] culminating in 1979 when the General Assembly adopted the Women's Convention.

Currently, the overall functions of the Commission are to make recommendations and reports to the ECOSOC on the promotion of the rights of women in political, economic, civil, social, and educational fields; to make recommendations to the ECOSOC on urgent problems requiring immediate attention in the field of women's rights with the object of implementing the principle that men and women shall have equal rights; and to develop proposals to give effect to such recommendations.[100] Additional functions of the Commission include promoting equality, development, and peace, monitoring the implementation of measures for the advancement of women, and reviewing progress made at the national, sub-regional, regional, sectoral, and global levels. Further functions of the Commission are to make recommendations through the ECOSOC to the UN Secretary-General and UN bodies to promote participation of women within the UN system, and implementation and coordination of UN programs to advance women's rights.

The Beijing Platform for Action calls for government support for the

---

[98] See generally M. Galey, "Promoting Non-Discrimination against Women: The UN Commission on the Status of Women," 23 *Int'l Stud. Q.* 273 (1979); M. Galey, "International Enforcement of Women's Rights," 6 *Hum. Rts. Q.* 463, 469–71 (1984); S. Coliver, "United Nations Machineries on Women's Rights: How They Better Help Women Whose Rights Are Being Violated," in *New Directions in Human Rights* 25–49 (E. L. Lutz, H. Hannum, & K. J. Burke eds., 1989); L. Reanda, "The Commission on the Status of Women," in *The United Nations and Human Rights: A Critical Appraisal* 265 (P. Alston ed., 1992).

[99] Notes 33–42 above.

[100] ECOSOC Res. 11 (II), June 21, 1946, *as amended by* ECOSOC Res. 48 (IV), Mar. 29, 1947.

Work of the Commission on the Status of Women to draft an Optional Protocol to the Women's Convention.[101] An Optional Protocol would provide for a complaint procedure to the Committee on the Elimination of Discrimination against Women, similar to the Optional Protocol to the International Covenant on Civil and Political Rights enabling complaints to the Human Rights Committee.[102]

(b) The UN Subcommission on the Prevention of Discrimination and Protection of Minorities

The Subcommission on the Prevention of Discrimination and Protection of Minorities has used several procedures to address human rights violations where women are particularly vulnerable. These procedures include the Working Group on Contemporary Forms of Slavery, which has developed a Plan of Action for governments on child prostitution and child pornography and a Plan for the Prevention of the Traffic in Persons and the Exploitation of the Prostitution of Others,[103] and a Special Rapporteur on Traditional Practices Affecting the Health of Women and Children.[104] The Subcommission, in considering the role and equal participation of women in development as a subissue of the New International Economic Order and the promotion of human rights, and the prevention of discrimination and protection of women as a subissue of the Promotion, Protection and Restoration of Human Rights at National, Regional and International Levels, has the advantage of the Reports of CEDAW and the Women's Commission.[105]

B. Domestic protection

Domestic protection of women's human rights is in many ways the first line of defense for women. A general rule exists in international law that domestic remedies (where they exist) have to be exhausted before international tribunals will take up a case. Moreover, international human rights mechanisms for redress of violations are too limited in number and scope to deal with the magnitude and complexity of violations.

As the examples below show, domestic protection can be considerably strengthened by the application of international human rights principles

---

[101] Note 47 above, at 230 (k).   [102] See notes 71–82 above.

[103] See generally Report of the Working Group on Contemporary Forms of Slavery, 15th Sess., UN Doc. E/CN.4/Sub.2/1990/44, Aug. 23, 1990.

[104] See generally Report of the Special Rapporteur on Traditional Practices Affecting the Health of Women and Children, UN Doc. E/CN.4/Sub.2/1991/6.

[105] See generally UN Sec'y-Gen., Annotations to the Provisional Agenda of the Forty-Third Session of the Sub-Commission on Prevention of Discrimination and Protection of Minorities, UN Doc. E/CN.4/Sub.2/1991/1/Add.1, May 17, 1991.

contained in human rights treaties that a state has ratified or incorporated directly into domestic law through legislation or presidential decrees.[106] Once human rights treaties are directly incorporated into internal law, they may be invoked before and enforced by the courts and administrative authorities.[107]

In *Attorney General* v. *Unity Dow*,[108] the Court of Appeal of Botswana affirmed the lower court's decision holding unconstitutional the provision of the Botswana Citizenship Act of 1984, whereby a female citizen of Botswana who is married to a foreigner cannot convey citizenship to her children born in wedlock in Botswana, while a male citizen married to a foreigner can convey citizenship. Specifically, the Court of Appeal decided that this provision of the Citizenship Act infringes Unity Dow's fundamental rights and freedoms, her liberty of movement, and her rights to nondiscrimination. The chief judge, noting the obligations of Botswana as signatories to the Universal Declaration of Human Rights and the Declaration on the Elimination of Discrimination against Women and as a state party to the African Charter on Human and Peoples' Rights, said that

Botswana is a member of the community of civilised States which has undertaken to abide by certain standards of conduct, and, unless it is impossible to do otherwise, it would be wrong for its Courts to interpret its legislation in a manner which conflicts with the international obligations that Botswana has undertaken.[109]

In view of the fact that women's disabilities with regard to citizenship are a problem in many countries, as underscored by the fact that Article 9 on nationality is one the most highly reserved articles of the Women's Convention,[110] this decision could have important persuasive authority for cases that are currently pending in other countries, or cases that might be brought on behalf of similarly situated women and their families.

IV. CONCLUSION

The nature and extent of violations of women's international human rights continue to be cruel and pervasive. In many countries, violations remain

---

[106] See, e.g., The Colombian Presidential Decree No. 1398, July 3, 1990; Law for the Promotion of Equality for Women, No. 7142, Mar. 2, 1990.

[107] Information on domestic legislation enacted pursuant to the Women's Convention and other human rights conventions can be found in the reports of states parties submitted to the human rights treaty bodies.

[108] Court of Appeal of Botswana, Civil Appeal No. 4/91 (unreported, 1992).

[109] *Ibid.* at 54, reprinted in V. Dow, *The Citizenship Case* (1995).

[110] See the section on Reservations to Women's Convention, pp. 195–96 above.

not simply unremedied, but unnoticed as discriminatory or as an affront to the dignity of women. This widespread failure to honor international obligations erodes the accomplishments to date in the international protection of women's human rights and human rights generally.

States parties to human rights treaties are obligated to change their laws and practices to ensure respect for women's rights and to provide redress for violations of such rights. States do not need to wait for laws and practices to be challenged by members of human rights committees, such as CEDAW, or for international human rights tribunals to consider alleged violations of rights before moving to protect women. They can begin by changing their laws and practices that are similar to those of other countries that have been successfully challenged before international human rights tribunals.[111]

The UN must broaden its general work devoted to securing human rights to include solutions to the violations of women's human rights. The UN system of human rights protection must respond to the challenge of protecting women's rights with more adequate leadership and resources and reinforce the institutions it has created to ensure respect for women's rights and dignity.

If international human rights are to be taken seriously as a necessary part of the international legal order, the rights of half of humanity have to be respected and protected more vigorously. It would be ironic for the United Nations, which has been so instrumental in proclaiming the need for the protection of human rights, to ignore or discount the interests of women when the extent of violation of women's human rights is so apparent. This poses a challenge to the credibility of the UN and the universality and justice of international law.

SELECTED BIBLIOGRAPHY

Burrows, N., "The 1979 Convention on the Elimination of All Forms of Discrimination against Women," 32 *Neth. Int'l L. Rev.* 419–60 (1985)

Byrnes, A., "The 'Other' Human Rights Treaty Body: The Work of the Committee on the Elimination of Discrimination against Women," *Yale J. Int'l L.* 1–67 (1989)

"Women, Feminism and International Human Rights Law," 12 *Austl. Y. B. Int'l L.* 205–40 (1992)

Charlesworth, H., C. Chinkin, and S. Wright, "Feminist Approaches to International Law," 85 *AJIL* 613–45 (1991)

Coliver, S., "United Nations Machineries on Women's Rights: How They Better Help Women Whose Rights are Being Violated," in *New Directions in*

---

[111] Notes 71–79 above.

Human Rights 25–49 (E. L. Lutz, H. Hannum and K. J. Burke eds.; University of Pennsylvania Press, 1989)

Cook, R., "Reservations to the Convention on the Elimination of All Forms of Discrimination against Women," 30 *Va. J. Int'l L.* 643–709 (1990)

"Women's International Human Rights: A Bibliography," 24 *NYU J. Int'l L. & Pol.* 857–88 (1992)

Fraser, A., *UN Decade for Women: Documents and Dialogue* (Westview Press, 1987)

McDougal, M., H. Lasswell and I. Chen, "Human Rights for Women and World Public Order: The Outlawing of Sex-Based Discrimination," 9 *AJIL* 497–533 (1975), revised and republished in *Human Rights and World Public Order* 612–50 (M. McDougal ed.; Yale University Press, 1980)

Pietila, H. and J. Vickers, *Making Women Matter: The Role of the United Nations* (Zed Books Ltd., 1990)

United Nations, *Compendium of International Conventions Concerning the Status of Women*, ST/CSDHA/3, Sales No.: E.88.IV.3 (1988)

CHAPTER EIGHT

LABOR

Virginia A. Leary

I. INTRODUCTION

The body of norms on labor adopted within the United Nations constitutes a most complete and detailed international system of rules governing a field traditionally of domestic concern. In few other fields has there been such extensive and continuing legislative-type activity by UN-related organizations or such effective monitoring of adopted standards.

Although international regulation of labor did not begin with the establishment of the United Nations, such regulation proliferated in the post-World War II period, largely – although not exclusively – through the work of the International Labour Organization (ILO), a specialized agency of the United Nations. Under ILO auspices 174 international labor conventions have been adopted (as of January 1995) establishing standards of conduct for states on freedom of association, discrimination in employment, forced labor, occupational safety and health, labor inspection, social security, industrial relations, work of women and children, and conditions of work. The list of international labor standards is extensive, ranging from general norms to numerous detailed regulations on, for example, hours of work in road transport, seafarers' identity documents, and safety in the use of asbestos. Supervisory organs of the ILO have interpreted the meaning and scope of this extensive body of standards.

Section II (pp. 209–23), the major part of this chapter, focuses on these international labor standards: their historical development; the role of the ILO in the establishment of standards; and the scope, content, and monitoring of the standards. In view of its centrality in the field, the concept of freedom of association for trade unions is given special attention.

"International labour standards" (or "internationally recognised workers' rights" as the standards are sometimes called) have become important recently in the context of issues of international trade. Countries whose labor legislation and practices fail to provide minimum international labor standards or to accord internationally recognized worker rights, it is alleged, have an unfair competitive advantage warranting retaliatory trade actions by countries that abide by such standards.

Attempts have been made – unsuccessfully in the Uruguay Round of GATT and successfully in the US Congress – to introduce the concept of internationally recognized worker rights, or minimum international labor standards, into trade negotiations and agreements. Section III discusses the extent to which recourse has been made to international labor standards developed within the UN system to provide clarification of the concepts of "internationally recognised workers' rights" or "minimal international labour standards" – terms included in national legislation and in international trade agreements.

Although the ILO is the main UN agency concerned with labor issues, it does not have a monopoly within the UN system. UNESCO shares with the ILO concerns relating to the employment of teachers and the World Health Organization (WHO) has collaborated with the ILO on standards relating to nursing personnel. Human rights conventions adopted by the General Assembly, including the International Covenants on Civil and Political Rights, and on Economic, Social and Cultural Rights, as well as the Convention on the Rights of the Child, contain provisions relating to labor. The Working Group on Slavery of the Human Rights Subcommission on Prevention of Discrimination and Protection of Minorities concerns itself, *inter alia*, with bonded labor and child labor.

The adoption by the General Assembly in 1990 of a major convention on migrant labor was the first time a comprehensive convention on labor matters had been adopted by a UN body other than the International Labour Organization. The Migrant Labor Convention is significant because of its subject matter, and the fact that it is not subject to the highly developed supervisory system of the ILO since it was adopted outside the ILO. It is also noteworthy as it represents a departure from the minimum standards approach to labor in the United Nations, as it adopts a more general human rights approach. The Convention and its significance is treated in section IV.

II. INTERNATIONAL LABOR STANDARDS

A. Historical development

The need to establish uniform international labor standards can be traced to social conditions in nineteenth-century Europe. Efforts to improve unhealthy working conditions resulting from the Industrial Revolution were often stymied by fears of economic competition, since some countries were reluctant to limit child labor and long working hours, or to raise wages, out of fear that others that did not do so would gain trade advantages. A corollary of this concern exists today, as mentioned earlier.

Intermittent efforts were made through nongovernmental and inter-governmental arrangements in the late nineteenth and early twentieth centuries to develop labor standards. The Swiss government led efforts to convene international conferences in 1905 and 1906 that adopted the first two international labor conventions. No monitoring provisions were adopted for the application of these conventions, however, and no procedure or institution was established for systematic consideration of new standards. An intergovernmental institution that could draft new standards on a regular basis and provide monitoring of those standards seemed in order. The basis for the future ILO was laid by these earlier efforts to develop international labor standards.[1]

B. Role of the International Labour Organization

1. Structure and functions

The International Labour Organization was founded in 1919 at the Paris Peace Conference to abolish the "injustice, hardship and privation" suffered by workers and to guarantee "fair and humane conditions of labor." The immediate call for a post-war labor charter had come from the American Federation of Labor (AFL) in 1914 and Samuel Gompers, president of the AFL, presided at the Commission of the Peace Conference where part XIII of the Treaty of Versailles establishing the ILO was drafted.[2] One of the fundamental principles of the ILO, incorporated in its basic documents, that "labour should not be regarded merely as a commodity or article of commerce" originated from an AFL proposal.[3] Concern regarding international competitiveness and labor standards was evidenced by another principle proposed for international adoption by the American labor organization: "No article or commodity shall be shipped or delivered in international commerce in the production of which children under the age of sixteen years have been employed or permitted to work."[4]

An additional impetus for founding the ILO in 1919 stemmed from the fear of Western European countries that the 1917 Russian Bolshevik

---

[1] For a discussion of the historical development of labor standards and the establishment of the ILO, see N. Valticos, *International Labour Law* 17–18 (1989); see also J. T. Shotwell, *The Origins of the International Labour Organisation* I & II (1934).

[2] Shotwell, I, note 1 above, at 17, 128.

[3] Proposals of the American Federation of Labor to the Inter-Allied Labour and Socialist Conference, September, 1918, Concerning the Peace Conference, Shotwell, II, note 1 above, at 75.   [4] *Ibid.*, at 76.

Revolution might lead to worker revolt in their countries. The victors of World War I at the Paris Peace Conference foresaw labor unrest as an obstacle to a future peace, and included in the Treaty of Versailles a plan for the establishment of the ILO, an organization to set uniform labor standards. Despite the important participation of Gompers and the AFL in the founding of the ILO, the United States did not become a member of the organization until 1934.

An unusual aspect of the ILO is its provision for full participation of nongovernmental employer and worker organizations in all its activities, including standard-setting and monitoring. The role of worker representatives in ILO activities has been particularly notable. They have frequently provided the impetus for improved labor standards and for better monitoring of standards. Regretfully, in view of the positive ILO experience, no other UN-related organization includes NGO representatives as full participating members.

The ILO functioned effectively from 1920 to 1940, and a skeleton staff kept the organization in existence in Montreal throughout World War II. After the war, it became a specialized agency, part of the newly created United Nations, and in 1944 the original aims of the ILO were restated in the Declaration of Philadelphia. The adoption and monitoring of international labor standards, mainly laid down in international labor conventions, has always been the core activity of the ILO, although technical assistance and research now form a substantial, perhaps even a major, part of its work.

The ILO's system for the adoption of conventions is systematic, regular, and unusually expeditious as compared with other UN bodies. It resembles more closely the activity of national legislatures than the *ad hoc* method employed by other UN organs. The Governing Body, the executive organ of the ILO, is composed of government, employer, and worker representatives and sets the agenda of annual ILO conferences that adopt new conventions and recommendations, thus establishing priorities in standard-setting.

2. Scope and content of ILO standards

ILO standards established through the adoption of codes, guidelines, and declarations, as well as conventions and recommendations, cover an extraordinarily wide scope and are referred to collectively as The International Labour Code.[5] Indication of the scope of the code is evidenced by the

---

[5] The complete text of ILO conventions and recommendations adopted prior to 1981 are published in ILO International Labour Conventions and Recommendations 1919–1981. Conventions and recommendations adopted since 1981, as well as the earlier conventions and recommendations, are available from the ILO as separate texts.

following categories used by the ILO to classify conventions and recommendations:

  (i) basic human rights (freedom of association, forced labor, discrimination in employment, equal pay);
 (ii) employment;
(iii) conditions of work and social policy;
(iv) social security;
 (v) industrial relations;
(vi) employment of women;
(vii) employment of children and young persons;
(viii) special categories of workers (seafarers, dockworkers, plantation workers, tenants and sharecroppers, indigenous and tribal populations, workers in nonmetropolitan territories, migrant workers, nursing personnel);
(ix) labor administration; and
 (x) tripartite consultation.

ILO conventions have received varying numbers of ratifications. As of 1995, eight conventions (mainly the basic human rights conventions) had received more than one hundred ratifications; some thirty-five conventions had received fifty to one hundred ratifications; and ninety-two had received the ratifications of ten to fifty member states.[6] Newer conventions are, of course, not yet widely ratified, but some older conventions have also received few ratifications and may be considered to have fallen into desuetude.[7]

No reservations are permitted to ILO conventions, but since they are intended to be applied in countries with varying degrees of economic and social development, "flexibility devices" have been included in some. General terms such as "reasonable," "appropriate," "practicable," and "suitable" are used in a number of conventions to provide flexibility in application. In others, exceptions from the rules or prescriptions are permitted in particular circumstances. Some conventions permit a ratifying state to exclude certain parts of a convention when accepting it.[8]

(a) Basic human rights standards
The ten ILO basic human rights conventions establish standards on freedom of association, forced labor, and nondiscrimination in employ-

---

[6] The ILO regularly publishes an up-to-date ratification chart of its conventions.
[7] No ratifications have been registered for Conventions on Reduction of Hours of Work (Public Works), 1926 (No. 51); Reduction of Hours of Work (Textiles), 1927 (No. 61); and Migration for Employment, 1929 (No. 66).
[8] But see references by Frederic L. Kirgis in ch. 3, above, at n. 15, suggesting that the ILO "has not yet fully resolved the problem of providing sufficient flexibility to accommodate conditions in countries at different stages of development."

ment, and are also laid down in human rights conventions adopted by the General Assembly and by regional organizations.[9] Since World War II, the ILO has stressed the importance of these conventions and has made particular efforts to obtain their ratification by member states. Each of the major human rights conventions has received more than one hundred ratifications. The United States has ratified only one of the human rights conventions, Convention No. 105 on the Abolition of Forced Labor (ratified September 25, 1991).

(b) Multinational enterprises
The ILO (as well as the United Nations, the Organization for Economic Cooperation and Development [OECD], and the European Economic Community [EEC]) has established standards relating to multinational or transnational enterprises. In 1977, the ILO Governing Body approved the ILO Tripartite Declaration of Principles concerning Multinational Enterprises and Social Policy[10] and established a follow-up procedure on implementation of the Declaration. The text of the Declaration has had an influence within Europe where it was used on one occasion to interpret the application of the OECD Guidelines on Multinational Enterprises.[11]

(c) Indigenous populations
ILO standard-setting on issues relating to indigenous and tribal populations has been considered by some as an anomaly (and criticized as such), since the ILO convention and revised convention on indigenous and tribal populations contain standards not limited to labor issues. Convention No.

---

[9] The ILO publishes the *Classified Guide to International Labour Standards*. It lists the following ten conventions as "basic human rights" conventions:

 (1) Freedom of Association and Protection of the Right to Organise Convention, 1948 (No. 87);
 (2) Right to Organise and Collective Bargaining Convention, 1949 (No. 98);
 (3) Workers' Representatives Convention, 1971 (No. 135);
 (4) Rural Workers' Organisations Convention, 1975 (No. 141);
 (5) Labour Relations (Public Service) Convention, 1978 (No. 151);
 (6) Right of Association (Agriculture) Convention, 1921 (No. 11);
 (7) Right of Association (Non-Metropolitan Territories) Convention, 1947 (No. 84);
 (8) Forced Labour Convention, 1930 (No. 29);
 (9) Abolition of Forced Labour Convention, 1957 (No. 105); and
 (10) Discrimination (Employment and Occupational) Convention, 1958 (No. 111).

[10] The ILO Tripartite Declaration is published in 27 *ILM* 423–30 (1978).
[11] In the late 1970s, the OECD Committee responsible for the supervision of OECD Guidelines for Multinational Enterprises used a provision of the ILO Tripartite Declaration to interpret the Guidelines. A Danish branch of the Hertz Company had attempted to break a local strike by importing labor from other EEC countries. The Guidelines had no express prohibition of such a practice but the ILO Tripartite Declaration expressly condemned the move. "In the OECD Committee, there was consensus that the 'gap' in the . . . Guidelines was to be filled by 'reference to' the appropriate provision of the ILO Declaration." H. Baade, "The Legal Effects of Codes of Conduct for Multinational Enterprises," 22 *German Y. B. Int'l L.* 45 (1979).

107 on Indigenous and Tribal Populations was adopted by the conference in 1957 and contained not only provisions on recruiting and employment conditions, but also provisions on citizenship rights, cultural and religious values, customs and institutions, land ownership, health, social control, and criminal penalties. The Convention was criticized for its assimilationist orientation and for including matters beyond the mandate of the ILO. A new convention, No. 169, was adopted in 1990, revising Convention No. 107 and eliminating the assimilation emphasis.

(d) Protectionist standards: night work for women

ILO conventions are often revised as a result of changed circumstances. A recent example is the 1990 revision of the Night Work for Women Convention (adopted in 1948) which itself had been a revision of an earlier convention prohibiting night work for women. In recent years, it has been increasingly argued that protective legislation for women is discriminatory and prevents them from accepting available employment. The situation of women in developed countries in particular was perceived as no longer requiring protective legislation. ILO conventions prohibiting night work for women were criticized, and a new convention and recommendation on Night Work and a Protocol to the Night Work for Women Convention of 1948 were adopted in 1990. The new Convention and Recommendation no longer apply solely to women, but lay down certain limitations and requirements for night work in general – for both men and women, although certain limitations on the employment of pregnant women are preserved. The discussions within the ILO evidenced a general conviction that shift work and night work were not advisable for *any* workers, but should be permitted, if necessary, with limitations and restrictions.[12]

(e) Promotional conventions: employment policy

In recent years, the ILO has adopted several conventions referred to as "promotional conventions" which, rather than laying down precise standards, set objectives of a more general character. For example, ILO Convention No. 122 concerning Employment Policy states: "Each Member shall declare and pursue, as a major goal, an active policy designed to promote full, productive and freely chosen employment." Nicolas Valticos, former Assistant Director-General of the ILO and Adviser for International Labour Standards, in recognizing the limitations of standard-setting in this area, has written:

---

[12] For a discussion of ILO standards on women, see L. Compa, "International Labor Standards and Instruments of Recourse for Working Women," 17 *Yale J. Int'l L.* 151 (1992).

The adoption of international labour standards cannot, of course, bring by itself a solution to the problem (of unemployment). Employment raises broad questions of economic, financial and monetary policy which go well beyond labour problems in the strict sense and it finally calls for action of a practical character. International standards can, however, establish principles which might promote systematic and coordinated national and international action.[13]

Perceiving the need for a practical program of action in addition to standard-setting in the employment field, the ILO launched the World Employment Programme in 1969. David M. Trubek has pointed out that, with the development of the World Employment Programme,

the ILO proposed a new approach to development. It would incorporate the lessons of the employment-oriented approach to development, but would include other elements as well . . . The creation of more and better jobs is not enough; employment issues are intimately connected to the wider issues of poverty and inequality. Therefore, the ILO proposed that development planning include as an explicit goal and high priority the satisfaction of an absolute minimum level of basic needs.[14]

Under the World Employment Programme a number of studies and reports on employment issues have been prepared and missions sent to assist the development of employment strategies in Colombia, Sri Lanka, Iran, Kenya, the Philippines, the Dominican Republic, and the Sudan.[15]

3. Freedom of association: the basic ILO labor standard

Freedom of association for occupational organizations, and particularly trade unions, is the linchpin of workers' rights and labor standards. From its earliest beginning, the ILO recognized that freedom of association for both employers and workers was an important principle of social justice. Freedom of association is mentioned in the 1919 constitution, reaffirmed in the 1944 Declaration of Philadelphia, and translated into binding standards for ratifying states by the adoption in 1948 of the Freedom of Association and Protection of the Right to Organize Convention (No. 87), and in 1949 of the Right to Organize and Collective Bargaining Convention (No. 98). Membership in the ILO implies a commitment to freedom of association, as defined by ILO organs, regardless of whether the relevant conventions on freedom of association have been ratified. According to Valticos, former Assistant Director-General of the ILO, "the ILO Constitution, which the States Members of the Organisation have

---

[13] Valticos, note 1 above, at 114.
[14] D. M. Trubek, "Economic, Social and Cultural Rights in the Third World," in *Human Rights in International Law: Legal and Policy Issues* 237–38 (T. Meron ed., 1984).
[15] *Ibid.*, at 118.

accepted, lays down the principle of freedom of association; it has therefore been held that this principle should be observed by all States Members by virtue of their membership of the Organization alone."[16]

It is evident, however, from the ILO's own criticisms of the legislation and practice of member states, that the commitment to freedom of association is regularly, and often massively, violated by ILO members.

Nevertheless, an impressive effort is continually made within the ILO to promote freedom of association by defining its scope and implications; by developing machinery permitting allegations of violations to be brought before ILO monitoring organs expeditiously, and condemned (if found substantiated); and by assisting states in observing freedom of association.

Seven ILO conventions have been adopted on freedom of association, but the two most important are Conventions Nos. 87 and 98. Both recognize freedom of association for occupational associations – employer and worker organizations. As of January 1995, 112 states had ratified Convention No. 87, and 124 had ratified No. 98.

Freedom of association is enshrined as a right not only within ILO conventions but also in the Universal Declaration of Human Rights (UDHR) and all the major human rights conventions. The UDHR provides, in Article 20, that "everyone has the right to freedom of peaceful assembly and association," but also provides that "no one may be compelled to belong to an association"; this clause, however, does not appear in either of the two major human rights treaties, the International Covenant on Civil and Political Rights or the International Covenant on Economic, Social and Cultural Rights. Article 23(4) of the Declaration provides that "everyone has the right to form and to join trade unions for the protection of his interests."

Article 22 of the International Covenant on Civil and Political Rights is almost identical to the provisions in the UDHR and provides that "everyone shall have the right to freedom of association with others, including the right to form and join trade unions for the protection of his interests." Article 22(2) contains the usual restriction clause permitting limitations on the right to freedom of association, if "prescribed by law" and "necessary in a democratic society in the interests of national security or public safety, public order (*ordre public*), the protection of public health or morals or the protection of the rights and freedoms of others."

Article 8 of the International Covenant on Economic, Social and

---

[16] Valticos, note 1 above, at 248. See also Resolution on Freedom of Association and Industrial Relations in Europe, *unanimously adopted by* the Second European Regional Conference of the ILO in January 1974, cited in G. Caire, *Freedom of Association and Economic Development* 29 (1977).

Cultural Rights is more lengthy. It includes most of the provisions of ILO Convention No. 87 on Freedom of Association, with the exception that, unlike the ILO conventions, which do not explicitly refer to the right to strike, it affirms in paragraph 1(d) that states parties undertake to ensure "the right to strike, provided that it is exercised in conformity with the laws of the particular country."

(a) Right to strike

Neither Convention No. 87 nor No. 98 expressly refers to the right to strike, but ILO supervisory organs have frequently held that "the right to strike is one of the essential means available to workers and their organisations for the promotion and protection of their economic and social interests."[17] The right to strike is interpreted to include "other forms of industrial action such as picketing, selective work-bans, go-slow, etc." The right to strike implicit in the ILO interpretation of freedom of association is, however, subject to some important qualifications:

1. The exercise of the right must be peaceful.

2. It may be made subject to preconditions such as giving of notice, cooling-off periods, or recourse to conciliation, as long as the conditions are reasonable and not an outright ban.

3. It may be denied to public servants and workers engaged in "essential services," interpreted narrowly as those "whose interruption would endanger the life, personal safety, or health or the whole or part of the population."

4. The right may be denied or curtailed in circumstances where it is necessary to do so by reason of, or in order to avert, an acute national emergency.

(b) Union security clauses; closed shop arrangements

Convention No. 87 on Freedom of Association and the Right to Organize provides that "workers and employers without distinction whatsoever, shall have the right to establish and, subject only to the rules of the organisation concerned, to join organisations without previous authorisation" (Art. 2), but there is no correlative right, recognized in the

---

[17] General Survey on Freedom of Association by the Committee of Experts on the Application of Conventions and Recommendations, Int'l Lab. Conf., 69th Session, para. 200 (1983) (hereinafter General Survey). See also J. Hodges-Aeberhard & A. Odero de Dios, "Principles of the Committee on Freedom of Association Concerning Strikes," 126 Int'l Lab. Rev. 543 (1987).

Convention, not to join an association. The Convention, therefore, leaves to each state decisions regarding union security clauses. Nevertheless, the ILO Committee of Experts (see discussion of this Committee under section on inducing compliance, pp. 220–21) has specified that union security clauses imposed by law, as contrasted with those agreed upon between unions and employers, are incompatible with Article 2.[18] The European Court of Human Rights has interpreted the provisions on freedom of association in the European Convention on Human Rights to mean imposing limitations on union security or closed shop arrangements.[19]

(c) The United States and the freedom of association conventions

The United States has not ratified any of the ILO conventions on freedom of association. However, since the United States is a member of the ILO it is committed by virtue of that membership to the obligation of freedom of association for occupational associations. The United States recently ratified the International Covenant on Civil and Political Rights and is thus also committed to freedom of association by virtue of Article 22 of the Covenant. During consideration by the Senate of the ratification of the Covenant, Senator Moynihan asked whether Article 22 would alter or amend existing legal requirements under the National Labor Relations Act. The answer provided by the administration stated that it would not, since Article 22 "only provides for a general right of freedom of association," nor was Article 22 to be construed as conforming precisely to obligations that might arise under ILO Freedom of Association Convention No. 87, if ratified.[20] It was pointed out that "the two agreements [the Covenant on Civil and Political Rights and ILO Convention No. 87] are different in the scope of the rights and obligations they provide." The reply noted that Article 22 did not refer to the right to strike and that ratification of the Covenant did not entail any obligation to ratify ILO Convention 87.

A recent panel report of the Economic Policy Council of the United Nations Association of the United States has strongly urged ratification of ILO freedom of association conventions, stating: "The EPC panel believes that the freedom of association and the rights to organize and bargain collectively are cornerstones of democratic society and that the US must

---

[18] General Survey, note 17 above, para. 145; Freedom of Association, Digest of Decisions and Principles of the Freedom of Association Committee of the Governing Body of the ILO, para. 248 (3d ed., 1985).

[19] See A. Young et al., Eur. Ct. H.R. (ser. A) No. 44, para. 52 (Aug. 13, 1981), especially the concurring opinions of seven judges in relation to freedom of association under the European Convention on Human Rights.   [20] 31 *ILM* 661 (1992).

find a way to ratify the conventions that assert them . . . US law substantially goes beyond ILO Conventions 87 and 98."[21]

(d) Freedom of association supervisory machinery[22]

A Committee on Freedom of Association composed of nine members of the Governing Body, including employer, worker, and government representatives, has become the major ILO organ for examining allegations of infringements of freedom of association. As of July 1991, the Committee (founded in 1951) had examined almost 1,600 cases of alleged governmental violations of freedom of association. Although allegations may be brought by worker or employer organizations or governments (but not individuals), the overwhelming majority of complaints has been brought by workers' organizations. The consent of the state involved is not necessary for the allegation to be investigated. It is primarily the work of the Committee on Freedom of Association, in examining violations of such, that has refined and developed the extent and content of the concept of freedom of association.

The Committee functions in a quasi-judicial manner, although its members are not independent experts but members of a political organ, the ILO Governing Body. It does not itself make on-spot investigations; rather, it conducts examinations on the basis of written statements by complainants and governments and, on occasion, may invite oral presentations. It has developed a special procedure for dealing with urgent cases "involving human life or personal freedom, or new or changing conditions affecting the freedom of action of a trade union movement as a whole, and cases arising out of a continuing state of emergency and cases involving the dissolution of an organization."[23]

4. Inducing compliance with ILO labor standards

In addition to the freedom of association supervisory system, the ILO has developed an impressive array of methods to induce compliance with all

---

[21] The International Labour Organisation and the Global Economy, Econ. Pol'y Council of the UN Ass'n USA 43 (1991). But see E. Potter, *Freedom of Association and the Right to Organize and Collective Bargaining, the Impact on US Law and Practice of Ratification of ILO Conventions, No. 87 and No. 98* (1984) (urging nonratification).

[22] For a description of the ILO Freedom of Association supervisory system, see M. Servais, "ILO Standards on Freedom of Association and Their Implementation," 123 *Int'l Lab. Rev.* 765 (1985); A. Pouyat, "The ILO's Freedom of Association Standards and Machinery: A Summing Up," 121 *Int'l Lab. Rev.* 287 (1982); V. Leary, "Learning from the Experience of the ILO," in *The United Nations and Human Rights* (P. Alston ed., 1992).

[23] Outline of the existing procedures for the examination of complaints alleging infringement of trade union rights ILO, GB/LS May 1982.

ILO standards.[24] Over a period of seventy years it has developed a cohesive system, unique to the United Nations, for the supervision and implementation of conventions and recommendations. Its sophisticated supervisory system is often praised and used as a model for other conventions – particularly the increasing number of human rights conventions.

The main elements of the ILO supervisory machinery are: (a) the so-called "regular system of supervision" (a reporting system whereby states that have ratified conventions must provide regular reports on their implementation, which are then examined by the International Labour Office [the ILO Secretariat] and by ILO committees); (b) special constitutional procedures for the filing of complaints against states for failing to implement ratified conventions; and (c) the ILO's procedures on freedom of association, explained previously. Unlike the systems established by many of the human rights conventions, there is no provision for filing complaints by individual victims. The formal ILO systems have been supplemented by a number of other means, such as "direct contacts" by ILO officials, regional international labor advisers, and technical assistance.

The ILO reporting system, which is referred to as the "regular system of supervision," consists of a two-tier examination of reports on ILO conventions: first, by the Committee of Experts on the Application of Conventions and Recommendations, a twenty-member quasi-judicial body; and, second, by a much larger committee at the Annual Conference composed of governments, employers and workers – often numbering around two hundred persons. States must file an initial report immediately on ratification of a convention and must file regular reports on ratified conventions at two- or four-year intervals.

The Committee of Experts is composed of prominent judges, professors, and labor law experts from different geographic areas appointed in their individual capacities.[25] Experts are appointed by the ILO Governing Body on the nomination of the Director-General – a system to minimize political influence in the appointment of the experts. Established in 1927, the Committee has an acquired reputation for objectivity, competence, and integrity that has been a major contribution to the accolades often bestowed on the ILO supervisory system.

The Committee examines an extraordinary number of reports in each annual two-week session. At the 1991 meeting, for example, the twenty Committee members examined 1,409 reports.[26] Such a volume is possible

---

[24] For information on the ILO supervisory system, see Valticos, note 1 above, at 239–57; Leary, note 22 above.

[25] The late Chief Justice Earl Warren of the US Supreme Court and Frank McCulloch, former Chairman of the Nat'l Lab. Rel. Bd., have been members.

[26] ILO, Report of the Committee of Experts on the Application of Conventions and Recommendations, 78th Sess., rep. III, pt. 4A, para. 79 (1991).

only because of the extensive preliminary examination of the reports by ILO officials of the International Labour Standards Department, each of whom is specialized in a particular group of conventions.

The committee formulates "observations," or "direct requests," which it addresses to governments if discrepancies are noted between the terms of the convention and the law and practice of the ratifying states. Criticism of the Committee by those states subjected to repeated comments by the Committee has not been lacking, and efforts were made in the past, before the ending of the Cold War, to curtail the work of the Committee.

At each annual conference, the large tripartite Committee on Application of Conventions and Recommendations discusses the more serious cases examined previously by the Committee of Experts. Unlike the latter, the former's examination is conducted in public, and government representatives are invited to present their cases concerning discrepancies noted by the Committee of Experts. The Conference Committee prepares a report calling attention to particularly significant cases of discrepancies between the law and practice of particular states and conventions they have ratified. Especially persistent and egregious violations are noted in a special paragraph.

Under Articles 24–26 of the ILO constitution, complaints on the failure of states to implement conventions they have ratified may be made by member states, by industrial associations of employers or workers, or by Conference delegates. The Governing Body has the authority to appoint commissions of inquiry if it feels such action is necessary to investigate these complaints (termed "representations" when made by occupational organizations). Few such commissions have been appointed, but of those that have several have been particularly important. Commissions of inquiry are normally composed of three respected jurists who carry out on-the-spot investigations (but only with the consent of the government concerned) and hear witnesses under formal procedures. In recent years, commissions have examined situations in the Dominican Republic, the Federal Republic of Germany, Nicaragua, and Romania.

A particularly important commission was named in 1982 to investigate the failure of the government of Poland to observe freedom of association conventions that had been ratified. The government refused to cooperate, and the commission was unable to carry out its investigation within Poland. Instead, it held hearings outside the country. The Governing Body informed Poland that the competence of the commission was beyond doubt in international law under Article 26 of the ILO constitution and that the noncooperation of the government was a breach of international obligation. The commission concluded that Poland was not in conformity with the conventions in several regards; Poland subsequently announced its intention to withdraw from the ILO, but eventually did not do so. It gave effect to freedom of association after the communist regime disappeared.

The ILO attempts to link its standard-setting activities and its technical-assistance activities. Consultants and officials being sent to a developing country to assist with vocational training or employment projects are routinely apprised of the situation concerning the adoption and application of ILO conventions and recommendations in that country.

How effective is this highly developed ILO system? Cause and effect in the field of labor standards is difficult to prove, as in many others. The most complete analysis of the efficacy of the system was published some years ago by Ernest Landy, a former ILO official.[27] Studies are regularly published by the ILO on the influence of its conventions on national legislation. There is clearly evidence in Landy and other studies of the adoption of new legislation in many countries, particularly developing countries, due to the influence of ILO standards and supervision. Whether the legislation remains a "law on the books" rather than "law in practice" is not always clear.

Workers' representatives in the ILO frequently have argued for more radical measures to be adopted to enforce ILO standards. During discussions concerning the work of the Governing Body Committee on Freedom of Association, worker members suggested that severe measures should be adopted for governments that persistently refuse to carry out Committee recommendations. Such measures could include the withholding of technical assistance, a refusal to hold meetings in the country, or the closure of ILO field offices in countries where there were serious violations of human rights. The Committee as a whole (composed of two-thirds government and employer representatives) expressed serious doubts about the proposals, and they were not adopted.[28]

5. Interpretation of ILO standards

Questions or disputes concerning the interpretation of the ILO constitution or of its conventions are the responsibility of the International Court of Justice (Permanent Court of International Justice prior to 1945), according to Article 37 of the ILO constitution. In the early years of the ILO, three cases were referred to the Permanent Court for advisory opinions on the interpretation of the constitution,[29] and only one case, in 1930, was referred to the Court relating to the interpretation of a

---

[27] E. Landy, *The Effectiveness of International Supervision, Thirty Years of ILO Experience* (1966).
[28] 193d Report of the Freedom of Association Committee, Law and Practices, 209th Sess., Feb.–Mar. 1979, at 60, paras. 33–37, UN Doc. GB.209/619 (1990).
[29] See 1922 PCIJ (ser. B) Nos. 2 & 3, at 9 (conditions of labor of persons employed in agriculture); 1922 PCIJ (ser. B) Nos. 2 & 3, at 49 (conditions in agricultural production); 1926 PCIJ (ser. B) No. 13, at 6 (personal work of employers).

convention – the Night Work (Women) Convention, 1919 (No. 4).[30]

Article 37 of the constitution also provides, as a result of an amendment in 1946, for the possibility of appointing a tribunal for the expeditious determination of any dispute or question relating to the interpretation of a convention. No recourse has ever been made to such a tribunal, but discussion has taken place at recent international labor conferences about the possibility of setting up a tribunal to resolve questions concerning the interpretation of the Freedom of Association and Protection of the Right to Organize Convention. In practice, the Office interprets conventions for ILO member states on many occasions. Requests for interpretation are answered, but they routinely contain the proviso that the interpretation is unofficial and that the International Court of Justice is the only organ with authority to provide an official interpretation. In addition to the Office, interpretations of ILO conventions are also made by commissions of inquiry set up by the ILO, as discussed earlier.

The interpretation of conventions by the Committee of Experts on the Application of Conventions and Recommendations, in their regular monitoring activities, has recently created controversy at the annual conference. Employer members of the Conference Committee have questioned some interpretations of conventions by the Committee of Experts. The Committee responded by claiming its right of interpretation in the absence of a definitive interpretation by the International Court of Justice. Rarely has a UN monitoring body so clearly asserted its right to interpret a treaty. The 1991 annual report of the Committee contained the following comment:

[The Committee] considers that the proper functioning of the standard-setting system of the International Labour Organisation requires that a State should not contest the views expressed by the Committee of Experts on the application of a provision of a Convention that it has ratified and at the same time refrain from making use of the established procedure for obtaining a definitive interpretation of the Convention in question.

. . . It is essential for the ILO system that the views that the Committee is called upon to express in carrying out its functions . . . should be considered as valid and generally recognised, subject to any decisions of the International Court of Justice which is the only body empowered to give definitive interpretations of Conventions.[31]

III. INTERNATIONAL TRADE AND LABOR STANDARDS

Current interest in international labor standards adopted within the United Nations has been stimulated by the perceived link between

---

[30] 1932 PCIJ (ser. A/B) No. 50, at 365.   [31] Note 26 above.

competitive advantages in trade and low labor standards. Long hours of work, low wages, child labor, and poor working conditions are said to be a type of "social dumping" or "unfair subsidy" that permits developing countries or newly industrializing countries (NICs) to market goods at a low price on the international market.

The response to these allegations of social dumping has come as national legislation linking trade benefits and labor standards, the incorporation of "social clauses" in international trade agreements, discussions within the GATT and, most recently, discussions regarding cheap labor as an unfair subsidy in relation to the North American Free Trade Agreement are under way.[32] In these endeavors, the labor standards adopted at the international level have served as reference points for determination of adequate national standards.

Many factors other than labor costs are important in the international competitiveness of products, including the cost of raw materials, educated workers and availability of capital, but emphasis on labor conditions has been a major focus in recent discussions on trade issues. Developing and newly industrializing countries with lower labor standards have become important economic competitors of the United States and other Western countries. The US trade deficit is worrisome. Firms are moving to countries that lack independent labor unions and thus provide low wages and working conditions.

During earlier sessions of the Uruguay Round, the United States called – unsuccessfully – for a working group on international trade and labor standards. Its call was met by strong opposition, particularly from developing countries. The effort to include "social clauses" in international trade agreements specifying that trading partners must conform to minimum international labor standards, or to label low labor standards an unfair subsidy, is considered by many to be an excuse for protectionism. In addition, such measures may be considered an interference in domestic affairs, or the imposition of rich countries' values on poorer countries just entering the competitive international trade arena.

It is also argued that economic development is hindered by trade union rights and that stressing economic development first will lead eventually to

---

[32] P. Alston, "Labour Rights Provisions in US Trade Law: 'Aggressive Unilateralism'?", paper presented at symposium on Human Rights and Labor Rights in the Global Economy, Schell Center for International Human Rights, Yale Law School (Mar. 1992); N. Brown et al., "Making Trade Fair," *World Pol'y J.* 309 (Spring 1992); Stanford, *Going South: Cheap Labour as an Unfair Subsidy in North American Free Trade*, Canadian Centre for Policy Alternatives (1991). See also S. Charnovitz, "The Influences of International Labour Standards on the World Trading Regime: An Historical Overview," 126 *Int'l Lab. Rev.* 565 (1987); I. Ballon, "The Implication of Making the Denial of Internationally Recognized Worker Rights Actionable under Section 301 of the Trade Act of 1974," 28 *Va. J. Int'l L.* 73 (1987).

better working conditions and worker rights. On the other hand, it is contended that social progress should keep pace with economic progress and that the West should avoid collaborating with the exploitation of workers.

In most discussions involving issues of trade and labor rights, the terms "internationally recognized labor standards" or "minimum international labor standards" are employed, but in the United States four pieces of legislation refer to "internationally recognized worker rights." The Generalized System of Preferences (GSP) Renewal Act of 1984 provides that the president may not designate as a GSP beneficiary any country that "has not taken or is not taking steps to afford internationally recognized worker rights."[33] Under the Caribbean Basin Initiative, the president, in determining whether to grant duty-free treatment to a country, may take into account the extent to which workers enjoy "reasonable workplace conditions and enjoy the right to organize and bargain collectively."[34] The Overseas Private Investment Corporation (OPIC) legislation provides that OPIC may only ensure US investment in countries that are "taking steps to adopt and implement laws that extend internationally recognized worker rights" to its workers.[35]

The most important US legislation on the subject is contained in the Omnibus Trade and Competitiveness Act of 1988, which provides that the systematic denial of internationally recognized worker rights constitutes an unreasonable trade practice, thereby permitting sanctions to be imposed by the Executive Branch if there arises a burden or restriction on US commerce.[36]

But just what are the "internationally recognized worker rights" referred to in the US legislation? And what are the "minimum international labor standards" referred to in much of the trade literature? Which of the many ILO standards should be singled out as constituting the essential core of international labor standards? In 1984, a report was prepared by the Netherlands National Advisory Council for Development Cooperation which, in a thoughtful and thorough manner, attempted to arrive at a clearer perception of the identification and definition of "minimum international labor standards."[37]

---

[33] *Enacted as* Title V of the Trade and Tariff Act of 1984, § 502(b)(7), Pub. L. No. 98–573, 98 Stat. 3020, 19 USCA 2462 (West Supp. 1988).

[34] Caribbean Basin Economic Recovery Act, 19 USC § 2702(9(c)(8) (Supp. IV, 1986).

[35] Overseas Private Investment Corporation Amendment Acts of 1985, Pub. L. No. 99–204, 99 Stat. 1669 (1985), 22 USCA § 2191a(a) (West Supp. 1988).

[36] Trade Act of 1974, Pub. L. No. 93–618, 88 Stat. 2066 (1975); 19 USCA § 2462(b)(1)–(6) (1980), *amended by* Omnibus Trade and Competitiveness Act of 1988, Pub. L. No. 100–418, 102 Stat. 1107, 1301 (1988), 19 USCA § 2411(a).

[37] Recommendation on Minimum Labour Standards, National Advisory Council for Development Cooperation, The Netherlands, Nov. 1984, Ministry of Foreign Affairs, The Hague.

The report was prepared in response to a request from the Dutch Minister for Development Cooperation regarding the desirability of inserting into international economic and trade agreements clauses concerned with minimum labor standards. The report suggests that minimum labor standards can be determined by reference to three criteria: (a) a social criterion; (b) a political/and legal criterion; and (c) an economic criterion. The international labor standards established by the ILO play an important role in the first two criteria.

The authors of the report found that twelve ILO conventions, relating to standards also included in the major human rights covenants, were of such fundamental importance that they met the social criterion; that is, they were not concerned with administrative or technical matters and particular occupations, but related to basic human needs and human rights. The second criterion, the political and legal criterion, concerned the degree of international acceptance of the standard. The authors of the report considered that minimum labor standards should normally include only conventions having broad international support as demonstrated by the extent of ratification – including by states with varying degrees of international development. The economic criterion was applied to ensure that the conventions would not impose any economic hardship or impair further development.

Applying these three criteria, the authors considered that only eight ILO conventions constituted the minimum package of international labor standards: six basic human rights standards relating to (a) forced labor (two conventions); (b) freedom of association (four conventions); (c) discrimination in employment; (d) equal remuneration; (e) employment policy; and (f) minimum age for employment.[38]

The Dutch report relied to a considerable extent on the international labor standards adopted within the UN system – either by ILO conventions or in human rights treaties. No such extensive and careful analyses of UN-established international labor standards has been employed by any US agency to determine what is included in the concept of "internationally recognized worker rights" contained in US legislation.

Professor Philip Alston has criticized US legislation for its failure to refer sufficiently to international labor standards adopted by the ILO, for the imposition on trading partners of standards they have not ratified and which have not yet become customary international law, and for the failure of the United States to ratify the major ILO basic human rights

---

[38] See note 9 above for the list of conventions on forced labor, freedom of association and discrimination in employment. Equal Remuneration Convention, 1951 (No. 100); Employment Policy Convention, 1964 (No. 122); Minimum Age Convention, 1973 (No. 138).

conventions.[39] The authors of the Dutch report concluded that labor standards provisions should be included in international agreements only if certain conditions are met, namely: (a) the agreement itself must first contribute to the conditions needed to facilitate the observance of minimum international labor standards; (b) it must provide for a satisfactory procedure for the settlement of disputes by an independent body; and (c) the enforcement of minimum international labor standards must be based on reciprocity (must not be used by countries that have not themselves accepted the standards – presumably by ratification of the relevant ILO standards).

IV. HUMAN RIGHTS APPROACH TO LABOR ISSUES: THE NEW CONVENTION ON MIGRANT LABOR

Labor matters within the UN system, as we have seen, have traditionally been primarily the province of the ILO, but the recent drafting and adoption of the International Convention on the Protection of the Rights of All Migrant Workers and Members of Their Families by the UN General Assembly,[40] bypassing the ILO, represents a substantial inroad on the latter's jurisdiction. But more important, the Convention represents a change in orientation in the regulation of labor matters within the United Nations from a "labor standards" approach to a "human rights" approach. Under the "labor standards" approach, minimum standards are adopted for various categories of workers or workers in a particular situation or occupation. The "human rights" approach adopts an equal treatment emphasis: in the case of migrant workers, the emphasis is on prohibiting discrimination on the basis of nationality; migrant workers and native workers are to be treated equally.[41] The human rights approach is especially significant for the protection it provides for undocumented workers or workers in an irregular situation within a country. The Convention does not, however, simply adopt a national treatment approach. It includes some provisions relating specifically to the special problems of migrant workers, such as family reunion issues and issues of cultural adaptation.

International regulation of migrant labor has proved particularly difficult in view of the highly charged political nature of the subject. The

---

[39] Alston, note 32 above.
[40] Adopted at the 45th Sess. of the UNGA on Dec. 18, 1990, UN Doc. A/UNDOC/45/ 158. For an extensive discussion of the convention, see articles in 25 *Int'l Migration Rev.* (special issue on the Migrant Labor Convention, 1991) (hereinafter *IMR*, Special Issue).
[41] J. Lonnroth, "The International Convention on the Rights of All Migrant Workers and Members of Their Families in the Context of International Migration Policies: An Analysis of Ten Years of Negotiation," *IMR*, Special Issue 711, 726.

ILO has adopted three major conventions on migrant labor; the extent of their acceptance, or lack of acceptance, demonstrates the difficulty of international legislation on this subject. The first convention (No. 66), adopted in 1939, has not received a single ratification; the second (No. 97), which revised the 1939 Convention, and was adopted in 1949, has been ratified, as of 1995, by forty states; and the third (No. 143), adopted in 1975, has received only seventeen ratifications as of 1995.

International concern over problems of migrant labor intensified during the late 1970s. Increasingly large numbers of migrant workers were entering Western Europe and the United States – some legally and some illegally. Illegal trafficking of migrant workers grew, resulting in serious problems. Undocumented workers were often deprived of the most fundamental rights. A desire to improve the lot of workers was voiced at the ILO and the United Nations, but a concern was also voiced, particularly by developing countries, that labor migration might be curtailed, depriving their countries of substantial economic benefits.

When international conditions led to a call for a new convention regulating migrant labor, the question remained why the drafting was not entrusted to the ILO and why a human rights approach was adopted rather than a minimum labor standards approach. On the one hand, it has been remarked that "the UN General Assembly being the world's political conscience, the issue would get more attention in the international community" if adopted by the General Assembly rather than by a specialized agency. Moreover, it was important "to give the human rights aspects, as well as problems other than mere labor rights, more weight in drafting. Such reasoning clearly favored the General Assembly."[42]

A participant in the negotiations of the UN Migrant Labor Convention has also referred to the fear expressed that, if the ILO were strongly involved, nongovernmental interests from nonratifying states might participate in the drafting of the convention.[43] This is presumably a reference to the possible participation of US labor and employer groups (who participate in the drafting of all ILO conventions), since the United States has ratified few ILO conventions and was considered unlikely to ratify a new convention on migrant labor. Another concern was that if employer representatives participated in the drafting, as is done in drafting ILO conventions, it might be difficult to adopt sanctions against illegal trafficking of migrant labor. On the other hand, political reluctance to accept more stringent standards and supervision by the ILO on such a sensitive subject has also been alleged as a reason for turning away from the ILO.[44]

---

[42] *Ibid.*, at 726–27.   [43] *Ibid.*, at 727.

[44] R. Bohning, "The ILO and the New UN Convention on Migrant Workers: The Past and Future," *IMR*, Special Issue, at 698.

228

The Migrant Labour Convention permits reservations to substantive articles; reservations are not permitted to ILO conventions. A new and untried supervisory system is created under the Migrant Labour Convention; ILO conventions are subject to the highly sophisticated and long-developed effective ILO supervisory system. Developing countries, particularly Morocco and Mexico, were particularly favorable to drafting the new treaty in the United Nations rather than through the ILO. They felt that they had more influence in the General Assembly than in ILO bodies. An ILO official opined that they were also more favorable to the United Nations because "the ILO was a symbol of trade unions that were independent of governments, a system not in fashion in many African countries and Mexico, for example."[45]

The drafting of the Migrant Labour Convention continued over an eleven-year period from 1979 to 1990. Drafting of ILO conventions is much more expeditious, usually taking not more than three to four years, including discussion at only two consecutive sessions of the ILO Conference. Nevertheless, the lengthy period of drafting the General Assembly convention may have had a positive outcome, resulting in a substantial consensus among interested states, according to one participant in the convention negotiations.[46]

Twenty-nine articles of the Migrant Labour Convention restate human rights provisions contained in other human rights instruments and apply them to all migrant workers – whether documented or undocumented. Since the human rights provisions of other instruments apply to *all persons*, it seems unnecessary to adopt a treaty reiterating rights, but that specifically relates them to migrant workers.[47] Given the frequent failure, however, to accord rights to undocumented workers in particular, an instrument that refers specifically to the rights of migrant workers is useful, especially because such workers are defined in the instrument as including undocumented workers. Still the Convention continues to distinguish between the rights of documented/undocumented workers. In addition to the twenty-nine articles referring to rights of both documented and undocumented workers, an additional twenty-one articles refer to the human rights of documented workers only.

Many important problems facing migrant workers are covered by the Convention. States parties are urged to facilitate family reunion of documented workers, for instance. And the Convention goes beyond other instruments in extending compensation to migrant workers for expropriated property, and provides important safeguards concerning expulsion.

[45] *Ibid.*, at 700.   [46] Lonnroth, note 41 above, at 721–25.
[47] See J. Nafziger & B. Bartel, "The Migrant Workers Convention: Its Place in Human Rights Law," *IMR*, Special Issue, at 771.

The Migrant Labour Convention has been criticized for its inadequacies *vis-à-vis* ILO conventions, its duplication of provisions in human rights conventions and some ILO conventions, and its limitations regarding rights of undocumented workers. Yet it has also been praised as a "major achievement" and as the most ambitious document to date to deal with the rights of undocumented workers.[48] Even so, it has received only three ratifications as of 1995, and the United States has indicated that it will not ratify it. Its future as a binding international legal instrument thus remains somewhat uncertain.

V. THE FUTURE

International labor standards and worker rights have not been the focus of much attention by scholars and activists, despite their importance. The very competence of the ILO in setting standards and its general nonpolitical approach may be, in part, responsible, as well as the fact that activities of the specialized agencies draw less attention than activities of the United Nations itself. Also, labor matters tend to be regarded more as technical issues of interest to a limited audience than as human rights issues.

This relative lack of interest may well be changing. The adoption of the Convention on Migrant Workers by the General Assembly, whatever its motivation, has again highlighted labor issues as an important human rights issue. The linking of worker rights to trade issues has focused attention on the extensive international standards already developed in this field. The United States has recently ratified the International Covenant on Civil and Political Rights and the ILO Convention on Abolition of Forced Labor. The Senate is seeming to overcome its long aversion to giving advice and consent to the ratification of some human rights covenants and ILO conventions.

Given the current concern and interest in international labor issues, it appears likely that the United Nations and UN-related bodies will continue to actively promote and establish international legal rules in labor matters.

SELECTED BIBLIOGRAPHY

Compra, L., "International Labor Standards and Instruments of Recourse for Working Women," 17 *Yale J. Int'l L.* 151 (1992)

Economic Policy Council of the UNA/USA, *The International Labour Organisation and the Global Economy* (1991)

---

[48] Lonnroth, note 41 above, at 724.

International Labour Organization, *Classified Guide to International Labour Standards*
International Labour Conventions and Recommendations, 1919–1981 (ILO, 1982)

Landy, E., *The Effectiveness of International Supervision, Thirty Years of ILO Experience* (Oceana, 1966)

Pouyat, A., "The ILO's Freedom of Association Standards and Machinery: A Summing Up," 121 *Int'l Labor Rev.* 287 (1982)

"Special Issue on the Migrant Labor Convention," 25 *Int'l Migration Rev.* (1991)

The United Nations and Human Rights (P. Alston, ed.; Oxford University Press,1992)

Valticos, N., *International Labour Law* (Kluwer, 1979)

CHAPTER NINE

ECONOMIC RELATIONS AND DEVELOPMENT

Stephen Zamora

I. INTRODUCTION

Economic organizations in the United Nations system fulfill two separate roles that affect the international economy: as *operational entities*, they carry out activities – making loans, providing technical assistance, organizing donor consortia, organizing negotiations between nations, disseminating information – that directly affect economic affairs; as *rule-creating and rule-enforcing entities*, they have been responsible for establishing regimes to regulate economic behavior within the scope of their jurisdictions. While many international economic organizations exemplify both roles, it is common for one or the other role to predominate. Thus, the General Agreement on Tariffs and Trade (GATT)[1] predominates as a rule-creating agency, while also carrying out operational activities (providing an important forum for trade negotiations). The World Bank is an example of an operational agency through its lending and technical assistance programs, but it has also established subsidiaries to formulate and administer (ICSID) formal rules dealing with investment disputes and investment guarantees (MIGA).

This study focuses on the ways in which UN agencies carry out rule-creating roles, while recognizing that rule-creating and operational

---

[1] For example, the General Agreement on Tariffs and Trade (hereinafter GATT), which is treated as a specialized agency in this chapter, see note 13 below, prescribes rules for the establishment of customs unions and free trade areas. See GATT, art. XXIV. Regional organizations such as the European Economic Community have had to observe these rules, in addition to observing the more general rules of international trade. See F. Abbott, "GATT and the European Community: A Formula for Peaceful Coexistence," 12 *Mich. J. Int'l L.* 1, 13–18 (1990); *The European Community and GATT* (M. Hilf, F. Jacobs, & E. Petersmann eds., 1986).

roles are not entirely distinct. Indeed, operational functions themselves generate norms of behavior, if not formal rules, of international economic law.[2]

If legal regimes of the specialized and related agencies are included, the UN system has generated more rules of an economic law nature, with broader application, than any other category of UN activity. There are several reasons for this. The subject matter itself – international economic relations – is extremely broad, due to the steadily increasing volume and diversity of economic activities carried out between states. Furthermore, the United Nations has followed the general historical trend in international law to encompass within its scope of concern ever-widening fields of economic activity.[3] The broad scope of international economic law encompasses both public and private actors, as the United Nations increasingly becomes involved with the adoption of international economic rules applicable to private parties – as shown, for example, by the adoption of the UNCITRAL-sponsored Convention on Contracts for the International Sale of Goods or by the promotion of the ECOSOC-sponsored draft Code of Conduct on Transnational Corporations.

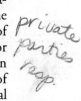

II. THE UN STRUCTURE FOR DEALING WITH INTERNATIONAL ECONOMIC RELATIONS

The high priority given by the United Nations to economic matters reflects the post-World War II governmental policies of its most powerful member states. The United States, in particular, favored the establishment within the UN system of an array of functional agencies that would bring order to specific spheres of activity. Experts in international relations adopted a theory – functionalism – to explain this method of enhancing international cooperation through the creation of separate, narrowly defined functional

---

[2] See below text accompanying notes 107–10, pp. 266–67.

[3] P. VerLoren Van Themaat lists the following areas of international economic policy addressed by governments on a multilateral basis: international trade, international monetary relations, economic development issues, supply of energy and raw materials, population, environment, food supply, ocean regime, control of multinational enterprises, and coordination of economic policies in general. P. VerLoren Van Themaat, *The Changing Structure of International Economic Law* 200 (1981). See also P. Kohona, *The Regulation of International Economic Relations through Law* 4 (1985); W. Friedman, *The Changing Structure of International Law* 69 (1964) ("The most serious challenge to the conception and in particular to the teaching of international law arises from the increasing diversity of the subject-matter regulated in hundreds of international conventions.").

agencies.[4] According to proponents of functionalism, public welfare (and international relations) would be better served if specialized international organizations replaced nation-states as the principal providers of noncontroversial welfare activities. Functionalism would lead to

a devaluation of the state, whose organization traditionally governed specific territorial entities and, in some cases, specific ethnic groupings, in favor of organized activities tailored to perform observable and specific functions necessary to the well-being of the members of the political community. The scope of these functions is limited internally by the specificity of their various objectives and externally or instrumentally by their contribution to the overriding end of political communities.[5]

In short, international agencies operating in well-defined technical fields would develop policies and carry out operations free of the narrow political interference of national governments. The United States, which would carry a heavy budgetary burden in applying this approach to the United Nations, expected the functional agencies to promote economic and political doctrines consonant with American foreign policy – an increasingly important goal as the Cold War developed. According to the model established in the UN Charter itself, the United Nations was meant to promote economic cooperation on two levels. On one level, the central organs of the United Nations – the General Assembly and the Economic and Social Council – would set policies and would coordinate the activities of functional agencies. At a second level, the functional agencies would carry out operations within their spheres of competence.

Experience indicates that this model has only worked on the operational level – the level that will be the principal focus of this chapter. The United Nations Organization has not fulfilled the central policy-making and coordination function. This failure is not surprising, however, if one

---

[4] R. Cox, "Problems of Global Management," in *The US, the UN and the Management of Global Change* 64, 69 (T. Gati ed., 1983).

As explained by Evan Luard, former UK delegate to the UN General Assembly:

Many people hoped that these non-political activities [of the United Nations] would be one of the most important features of the new organisation. Some subscribed to the notion of "functionalism": the idea, that is, that cooperation among nations in various functional fields would encourage and promote cooperation in the more difficult political area. Eventually the process might lead to a more peaceful world generally. Responsibility for organising cooperation of this kind should be shared between the specialized agencies, each confronting particular areas – labour affairs, civil aviation, health, education, meteorology, and so on – and subordinate bodies of the UN itself.

E. Luard, *The United Nations: How It Works and What It Does* 56 (1979).

[5] J. Eastby, *Functionalism and Interdependence* 4 (1985). On functionalism generally, see *Functionalism: Theory and Practice in International Relations* (A. Groom & P. Taylor eds., 1975); J. Sewell, *Functionalism and World Politics: A Study Based on United Nations Programs Financing Economic Development* (1966).

resistance to centrality

subscribes to the underlying theory of functionalism. It is much easier to address specific economic problems through the gradual development of rules and operations by technically oriented agencies than it is to attack problems in a coordinated fashion. Over time, technical agencies are able to gain experience and the respect of their constituents. At the same time, diversity of interests and a more even distribution of economic power among states have caused the international economy to resist attempts at central coordination, as the experience with the declarations on a New International Economic Order demonstrates.[6]

A. The ECOSOC and its subordinate committees and commissions

Article 55 of the UN Charter avers that the United Nations shall promote "higher standards of living, full employment, and conditions of economic and social progress and development . . . [and] (b) solutions of international economic . . . problems." Responsibility for this function was given to the Economic and Social Council (ECOSOC) (Article 60), which was to establish specialized commissions for this purpose (Article 68). The principal commissions and committees of economic interest here are the regional economic commissions[7] and the Commission on Transnational Corporations, which was established as a standing committee in 1974.

The ECOSOC was also assigned the task of coordinating the activities of the specialized agencies (Articles 58, 63). The specialized agencies themselves were brought into relationship with the United Nations through agreements made with the ECOSOC and approved by the General Assembly (Article 63).

Despite the central position given to it in the UN Charter, the global policy-making importance of the ECOSOC in economic affairs has never been realized. As the number and importance of the developing countries increased, these countries felt underrepresented in the ECOSOC.[8] Responding to developing-country pressure, the UN General Assembly established other policy-making organs that were perceived by developing nations as more amenable to their needs than the ECOSOC: the United Nations Conference on Trade and Development (UNCTAD), created in 1964; the United Nations Industrial Development Organization

ECOSOC replaced

---

[6] See below text accompanying notes 52–3, 91–9, pp. 254, 263–65.

[7] Economic Commission for Africa, Economic and Social Commission for Asia and the Pacific, Economic Commission for Europe, Economic Commission for Latin America, and Economic Commission for Western Asia. The regional economic commissions have been important in the development of economic policies, but have been peripherally involved in the development of international economic law.

[8] As originally established, the ECOSOC had eighteen members. This number was later increased to twenty-seven, and presently to fifty-four members.

(UNIDO), also created in 1964; the United Nations Development Programme (UNDP), established in 1965; and the World Food Council (WFC), created in 1974.[9] These organs have proved to be more important fora for debates over international economic policy than has the ECOSOC. UNCTAD, in particular, has largely taken over the task of coordinating policy options concerning trade and development. In this regard, it has also been indirectly responsible for generating rules of international economic law.[10]

The ECOSOC has also failed to fulfill its role in coordinating the activities – including rule-making activities – of the specialized agencies. Whatever coordination that does exist between specialized agencies is undertaken jointly by the specialized agencies themselves.[11]

B. Specialized agencies

The specialized agencies are responsible for generating most international economic law developed by the UN system. These agencies are also responsible for carrying out economic operations that, if not rule-creating per se, arguably may give rise over time to the development of international economic norms of behavior.

There are sixteen specialized agencies of the United Nations, a majority of which include economic matters as important elements on their agendas.[12] This chapter focuses on those agencies and organs that create legal norms in international trade (the GATT/WTO,[13] UNCTAD),

[9] J. Kaufmann, *United Nations Decision Making* 55–56 (1980); Van Themaat, note 3 above, at 139.
[10] See below text accompanying notes 29–31, pp. 243–44.
[11] On coordination between specialized agencies themselves, see Van Themaat, note 3 above, at 208–10.
[12] The specialized agencies are: (a) those dealing with matters of economic importance: FAO, IFAD, IBRD, IDA, IFC, ICAO, ITU, IMO, IMF, ILO, UNIDO, WIPO, WTO; and (b) those dealing with matters of indirect importance to the world economy: UNESCO, UPU, WHO, WMO. Concerning the status of the GATT as a specialized agency, see note 13 below.
[13] The status of the GATT/WTO in the UN system requires some explanation. In 1947, the principal industrialized nations attempted to establish an International Trade Organization (ITO), to administer a regime to liberalize international trade in goods. The United States withdrew its support of the ITO, over issues of institutional control, thereby leaving a substantive set of trade rules – the General Agreement on Tariffs and Trade, or GATT – without a formal agency to administer them. The United States and most other countries eventually adhered to the GATT rules through a Protocol of Provisional Application, and the GATT, with offices in Geneva, began to function as if it were part of the UN system, albeit lacking the formality of a duly constituted international organization. See John Jackson, *The World Trading System* 30–37, 45 (1989). The GATT has sometimes been referred to as a *de facto* specialized agency of the UN, although it did not submit annual reports to the ECOSOC, as do other specialized agencies. Kaufmann, note 9 above, at 63.
The irregular nature of the GATT in the UN system carried over after the Uruguay Round Agreements and led to creation of the GATT/WTO. The Uruguay Round Final Act,

international monetary relations (the IMF), international finance and development (the IBRD, IFC, IDA, and IFAD), and international transfer of technology (the World Intellectual Property Organisation, or WIPO).

UN specialized agencies are distinguished by four main characteristics:

1. They are free-standing intergovernmental organizations established by intergovernmental agreement, rather than by resolution of a UN organ; they are therefore not part of the United Nations *per se*.[14]

2. They have global (rather than regional) responsibilities.

3. They are budgetarily separate from the United Nations Organization.[15]

4. They are brought into a relationship with the United Nations by virtue of an agreement concluded with the ECOSOC and approved by the General Assembly.[16]

As autonomous organs, the specialized economic agencies are largely independent of any control or coordination imposed from the center of the United Nations Organization.[17] The specialized agencies – especially the financial agencies – enjoy a great deal of policy independence, due to the failure of both the ECOSOC and the General Assembly to carry out their powers to coordinate international economic policy decisions of UN

comprised of a set of agreements negotiated between 1987 and 1994, resulted in the creation of a new international organization, the World Trade Organization (WTO), with legal personality, formal membership, and traditional voting rules. The Uruguay Round Agreements preserved the substantive rules of the GATT – now referred to as GATT 1994 – but excised the Protocol of Provisional Application. The Uruguay Round Agreements also include a number of additional trade agreements, such as the General Agreement on Trade in Services, a Dispute Settlement Understanding, revised multilateral agreements (or 'MTN codes') that had been appended to the GATT over the years, and certain other agreements.

Despite having created a formal organization, the members of the WTO have not attempted to conclude a specialized agency agreement with the United Nations. Thus, the GATT/WTO continues to assume the status of an agency allied informally to the UN system.

In this chapter, the term "GATT" refers to the pre-WTO trade entity; "GATT 1947" refers to the substantive GATT rules prior to the Uruguay Round; "GATT 1994" refers to the post-Uruguay Round rules; and "GATT/WTO" refers to the international trade organization that has resulted from the adoption of the WTO character. On the creation of the WTO, see Thomas J. Dillon, "The World Trade Organization: A New Legal Order for World Trade?," 16 *Mich. J. Int'l L.* 349 (1995); Raymond Vernon, "The World Trade Organization: A New State in International Trade and Development," 36 *Harv. Int'l L. J.* 329 (1995).

[14] Although not established by UN vote, certain specialized agencies, such as the International Finance Corporation, have benefited from positive votes of UN organs that have favored their creation. J. Sewell, *Functionalism and World Politics* 108–9 (1966).

[15] Under Article 17(3) of the UN Charter, the General Assembly theoretically has the power to examine budgetary arrangements and administrative budgets of the specialized agencies. However, the General Assembly has not really exercised this authority. R. Asher et al., *The United Nations and the Promotion of General Welfare* 75 (1957); Van Themaat, note 3 above at 208.   [16] Asher et al., note 15 above, at 61–77.

[17] Van Themaat, note 3 above, at 78–79.

agencies. The budgetary independence of the specialized agencies is even more important. With sizable capital bases,[18] the IMF and the World Bank are assured of a continuing impact on their members (especially the developing-country members) without being overly sensitive to sudden shifts in policy, either from individual member states or from the less specialized organs of the United Nations. Even those specialized agencies that must constantly approach their memberships for budgetary contributions can do so on narrow, functional terms, which allows them to develop their own constituencies and to respond to particularized budgetary constraints, without getting caught in the budgetary morass of the United Nations generally. The relative independence of the specialized agencies helps to explain why they have had an important impact on international economic relations.

C. Other bodies

Other organs established by the UN General Assembly have had indirect effects in generating international economic law. The most important among these, the United Nations Conference on Trade and Development (UNCTAD), was established in 1964 as a result of developing-country pressures for change in the international economic system.[19] While UNCTAD has seldom directly created rules of international economic law, it has occasionally influenced the creation of international economic rules by other organizations, including the specialized agencies.[20]

The United Nations Development Programme (UNDP), established by the General Assembly in 1965, and the World Food Council (WFC), created by the General Assembly in 1974, are primarily involved in technical and policy assistance to developing countries on issues relating to economic development and agricultural production. Although lacking their own funding sources, both agencies work with the development banks, including the World Bank, to identify operational projects. Neither agency has been important in the generation of rules of international

---

[18] The funds that allow the IMF and the World Bank Group to carry out their operations are derived from the capital subscriptions of member governments, which have periodically increased. In July 1990, the Executive Directors of the IMF approved an increase in the quotas of subscribed capital to SDR 135,214.7 million, a figure that is equal to approximately US$183.9 billion. *IMF Annual Report*, 1990, at 47. The World Bank also has a capital base provided by members' subscriptions, but acquires most of the funds that it lends on international capital markets. As of June 30, 1990, the World Bank's total subscribed capital was $125.26 billion, of which about $8.9 billion was paid in. This capital supported a lending program for 1990 of $138.26 billion for the World Bank alone. *World Bank Annual Report*, 1990, at 189, 197.   [19] M. Van Meerhaeghe, *Int'l Economic Inst.* 140 (1987).

[20] See, e.g., the text accompanying notes 29–31 below, pp. 243–44. See generally Walters, "UNCTAD: Intervener between Poor and Rich States," 7 *J. World Trade L.* 527 (1973).

economic law. Finally, the International Law Commission (ILC), established in 1947 to fulfill the General Assembly's goal of "encouraging the progressive development of international law and its codification" (UN Charter, Article 13(1)), has chosen not to address directly issues of international economic law, although some ILC projects deal indirectly with issues of international economic concern.[21]

III. THE UNITED NATIONS AS A SOURCE OF INTERNATIONAL ECONOMIC LAW

The United Nations system, through the specialized agencies and other organs, has been responsible for generating rules of international economic law through four different processes:[22]

(i) the treaty-making and treaty-amending process;
(ii) the promotion of codes of conduct that amount to quasi-legal regimes;
(iii) the generation of rules of customary international law; and
(iv) the development of administrative rules that contribute to the development of international economic regimes.

A. Creating international economic law by treaty

1. The Bretton Woods system

At the center of the international economic regime overseen by the United Nations is the Bretton Woods system of international economic organizations, named after the site of the 1944 conference establishing the World Bank and the IMF. The IMF and the World Bank were founded on the basic notion that liberal rules of free trade, free payments, monetary stability, and capital mobility would best promote international economic welfare. Consequently, international agencies created after Bretton Woods

WB
IMF

---

[21] See generally I. Sinclair, *The International Law Commission* 21–32 (1987). The ILC topic most directly relevant to international economic law is the project dealing with the most-favored-nation (MFN) clause, which was taken up by the ILC in 1967. The ILC produced a set of draft articles on the MFN clause in the mid-1970s, but wide disagreement on the draft has prevented the conclusion of even an agreed text. *Ibid.*, at 79–82.

The ILC continues to address other subjects that are related to international economic law, including jurisdictional immunities of states and their properties; the law of treaties; law of the sea; state responsibility; and nonnavigational uses of international watercourses. United Nations, *The Work of the International Law Commission* (4th ed., 1988).

[22] For a detailed analysis of the various law-making functions of the specialized agencies generally, see C. Alexandrowicz, *The Law-Making Functions of the Specialised Agencies of the United Nations* 11, 85–87 (1973).

– the GATT, the regional development banks, and other specialized agencies of the United Nations – that adopt the same liberal philosophy have been encompassed by the term "Bretton Woods system."

The United Nations cannot take credit for the creation of the Bretton Woods system. The three main pillars of Bretton Woods – the IMF, the World Bank, and the GATT – were all established outside the UN framework.[23] These organizations have been brought into the UN fold as specialized agencies, and the ECOSOC in theory serves a coordinating role with respect to them. However, it is important to recognize that the treaty-based rules of the Bretton Woods system emanate from the specialized agencies, which act according to their own legislative and operational agendas.

The United Nations General Assembly or the ECOSOC will occasionally press for treaty reforms on economic subjects, but in general these centralized institutions focus attention on general problems that should be taken up by the specialized agencies themselves. The most obvious example of this indirect influence on treaty-making by specialized agencies consists of the campaign, generated within the framework of UNCTAD, for a New International Economic Order (NIEO). The Bretton Woods system, then, is a treaty-based system, with the bulk of its treaty-based law originating in the specialized agencies. Among the most important areas of economic activity that have been the subject of treaty-based rules are international trade, international monetary relations, international finance for development, and protection of intellectual property. Certain other areas – such as technology transfer and foreign investment – have not yet given rise to extensive, treaty-based regimes, but have been the subject of certain law-making efforts.

2. The international trade regime – the GATT/WTO and UNCTAD

(a) The GATT/WTO

Prior to the adoption of the GATT Agreement, problems of international trade between states were resolved primarily through bilateral agreements (an exception being several international commodity agreements of a quasi-governmental nature). With the creation of the GATT, the major trading nations committed themselves for the first time to broadly multilateral solutions to problems caused by international trade competition.

---

[23] The 1944 Bretton Woods agreements preceded the adoption of the UN Charter. The ECOSOC was instrumental in calling for a conference to draft a charter for an International Trade Organization (ITO). Jackson, note 13 above, at 32. However, the resulting Geneva conference, which led to adoption of the GATT Agreement in 1947, was held outside the UN framework. The ITO itself never came into existence.

There is insufficient space here to provide details of the many idiosyncrasies that characterize the GATT and its system of rules, but some explanations are necessary in order to understand the GATT's role in fostering an international trade regime. The GATT was originally intended as a multilateral agreement to be administered by the International Trade Organization (ITO), but that organization was never established, largely because the United States withdrew its support.[24] The GATT Agreement itself was adopted, however, and was made effective through a protocol of "provisional" application. The organizational features of the GATT, therefore, were rudimentary, and as a consequence the GATT has traditionally functioned less as a decision-making organization than as a forum for negotiation.[25] Nor does the GATT have as sizable a secretariat as one would expect for an organization dealing with global trade issues.

In 1993, the GATT contracting parties took a major step toward strengthening the international trading system by concluding a round of trade negotiations – the Uruguay Round – that culminated in the establishment of a World Trade Organization, or WTO. The Uruguay Round Agreements strengthened the trade dispute mechanisms of the GATT/WTO, broadened the organization's jurisdiction, and also formalized the international organizational status of the agency.

The institutional oddities of the GATT help explain why the principal agency dealing with international trade has traditionally functioned less as an organization than as a meeting ground. The GATT/WTO is a meeting ground in two senses. First, the substantive rules (most-favored-nation, national treatment, prohibition of quantitative restrictions, non-discrimination, etc.) that are written into the GATT Agreement constitute a common position on the basic rules that should govern international trade. Second, the GATT/WTO has provided a highly structured forum in which groups of countries can negotiate solutions to international trade problems. Thus, the GATT has succeeded in bringing about the reduction of tariff and nontariff barriers through specific negotiations (or trade negotiation

---

[24] K. Dam, *The GATT: Law and International Economic Organization* 10–14 (1970); Jackson, note 13 above, at 33–34.

[25] Under Article XXV(1) of the GATT Agreement, the contracting parties are empowered to meet from time to time to take joint action. Although the decision-making scope is potentially broad, few issues were actually put to formal decisions in the GATT. The decision-making process itself underscores the perception of the GATT as a meeting ground for subgroups of individual members rather than as a decision-making organization with quasi-legislative powers. Thus, under the original GATT Agreement, any decision jointly taken was designated as a decision of the CONTRACTING PARTIES (denoted by capital letters) rather than as a decision of the GATT *qua* organization. Jackson, note 13 above, at 48. The WTO agreement replaces this odd apparatus with a more recognizable process – the WTO as an agency makes decisions on the basis of one nation, one vote.

"Rounds") among the contracting states. The tariff reductions ("bindings") that result from GATT negotiations are one way in which the GATT creates international economic law. Another way involves the GATT's success as a negotiating forum that has generated a number of secondary international agreements that go beyond the original rules written into the GATT Agreement. This point deserves some elaboration.

By the end of the Kennedy Round of trade negotiations that concluded in 1967, it became apparent that the principal barriers to free trade were not tariffs, but rather nontariff barriers and other distortionary practices of governments. Rather than amend the GATT Agreement to deal with these issues, during the Tokyo Round (1974–79) the GATT sponsored the conclusion of seven side treaties, or codes (referred to as the MTN Codes), which were submitted as international agreements to the individual contracting states for their adherence. None of the contracting parties was obligated to adhere to the MTN Codes, and while all of the Codes have become effective, many GATT members refused to adopt at least some of them. In 1994, as a result of the Uruguay Round Agreements, these MTN Codes, in revised form, were assumed into the body of GATT/WTO rules that comprise the multilateral trade regime, and they are obligatory on all members.

This piecemeal approach ("Balkanization," in the words of Professor John Jackson)[26] to the generation of international trade law can be criticized as detracting from the effort to create a single, workable system of rules applicable to all countries. The MTN Code experience exemplifies how the GATT operates, however. The GATT has been a pragmatic agency committed to accomplishing specific improvements even at the expense of overall uniformity or consistency.

In addition to the Balkanization of the GATT regime through MTN Codes, other phenomena complicate the monolithic effectiveness of the GATT trade regime. First, there exists the tendency of states to settle bilateral trade issues outside the GATT framework, through the conclusion of voluntary restraint agreements (VRAs) or other *ad hoc* measures covering trade in specific products.[27] A more important centrifugal force consists of the creation of customs unions and free trade areas, which are permissible under Article XXIV of the GATT Agreement. While customs unions and free trade agreements do not necessarily defeat the objectives of the GATT/WTO regime (the question whether customs unions or free trade areas are trade diverting or trade creating is unsettled), they divert attention

---

[26] *Ibid.*, at 56.
[27] See below the discussion of enforcement of GATT rules at text accompanying notes 140–43, pp. 276–77.

away from a single, international trade regime and towards multiple sets of regimes based on regional groupings.[28]

(b) The United Nations Conference on Trade and Development (UNCTAD)

Created in 1964 as a subsidiary organ of the UN General Assembly, UNCTAD has earned a reputation as the principal forum for the study and discussion of international economic issues of importance to developing countries. The chief accomplishments of UNCTAD lie in its *indirect* influence on the creation and amendment of treaties dealing with international economic law, although UNCTAD has also had some limited success in generating treaties on subjects – most notably in the fields of shipping and trade in commodities – that are of prime concern to developing countries.[29]

In the area of international trade law, the greatest treaty-making accomplishment of UNCTAD is also indirect. UNCTAD has been instrumental in forcing changes in the GATT to recognize that the GATT rules should reflect the needs of developing countries, even to the extent of "violating" the most-favored-nation principle by allowing preferential treatment for developing-country trade. Even before its establishment as a permanent organ of the General Assembly (in 1964), UNCTAD was inducing the GATT to respond to developing-country demands through an amendment designed to deal with special issues of developing-country trade.[30] UNCTAD also brought about a major deviation in GATT rules

---

[28] For a discussion of the economic effects, see Abbott, note 1 above, at 6–8; A. Swan & J. Murphy, *Cases and Materials on the Regulation of International Business and Economic Relations* 277–83 (1991). Professor Abbott's article, note 1 above, analyzes the deleterious effects of regional trading agreements in the GATT system.

[29] UNCTAD has sponsored several treaties dealing with ocean shipping: Convention on the Code of Conduct for Liner Conferences; Convention on Transit Trade of Land-locked Countries; Convention on International Multimodal Transport of Goods; Convention on Registration of Ships. Only the first two of these treaties have become effective, and neither of them has had an important impact due to the lack of ratification by states with important interests in the subject.

On UNCTAD's contributions in drafting and promoting international commodity agreements, see the text following note 31 below, p. 244. See generally Paul D. Reynolds, *International Commodity Agreements and the Common Fund: A Legal and Financial Analysis* (1978); A. D. Law, *International Commodity Agreements: Setting, Performance and Prospects* (1975).

On the accomplishments of UNCTAD generally, see Krishnamurti, "UNCTAD as a Negotiating Institution," 15 *J. World Trade L.* 3 (1981); Walters, note 20 above.

[30] There can be little doubt that this step [the 1964 amendment adding Part IV of the GATT Agreement] was a reaction to the preparations, already in progress, for the 1964 United Nations Conference on Trade and Development and the increasing grandeur of the format during the year and one-half of drafting was a reaction to the growth of the UNCTAD from an isolated United Nations conference to a permanent body commanding the allegiance of the entire less-developed world.   Dam, note 24 above, at 237

through the promotion of a generalized system of preferences (or "GSP") for developing country exports. This informal "system" amounts to the acceptance of a policy under which individual states are permitted, due to a blanket waiver accepted by the CONTRACTING PARTIES, to deviate from the most-favored-nation rule of GATT Article I by giving preferential treatment to imports from developing countries.[31] This indirect creation of international trade law has been among UNCTAD's most important achievements in creating international law.

3. International monetary relations

Even with the disruptions of the international monetary system during the past twenty-five years – the abandonment of the fixed-exchange-rate system, the subsequent volatility in exchange rates, and the third world debt crisis – the International Monetary Fund (IMF) stands as a successful experiment in the management of international economic relations through law. That the IMF should be so unfortunate as to oversee an impossibly complex and conflicting set of institutions and policies should not detract from its accomplishments.

As already noted, the IMF and the World Bank predated the United Nations, but were brought into the UN system by virtue of achieving specialized agency status. However, both the IMF and the World Bank were careful to negotiate specialized agency agreements that protected their budgetary independence, insulated them from full supervision by the ECOSOC, protected confidential information, and provided for complete independence in lending operations.[32]

The IMF virtually "created" international monetary law.[33] As with the GATT, it represented the first concerted multilateral effort to deal with the subjects assigned to it. The IMF was created to serve five principal functions: (a) to oversee exchange rate practices of members; (b) to provide funds to member governments that encounter balance of payments difficulties; (c) to promote a liberal regime of international payments; (d) to provide information and financial statistics; and (e) to provide a forum for consultation on international monetary relations.

The first three of these functions have involved the creation and application of rules of international monetary law. Some of these rules were incorporated into the original IMF Agreement, while others have been added, either by amendment or by other forms of administrative rule-

---

[31] R. Hudec, *The Developing Countries and the GATT* (1987); Jackson, note 13 above, at 278.

[32] E. Mason and R. Asher, *The World Bank since Bretton Woods* 56–59 (1973).

[33] S. Zamora, "Sir Joseph Gold and the Development of International Monetary Law," 23 *J. Int'l L.* 1009, 1010–14 (1989).

making. For the most part, however, the IMF – unlike its sister agency, the World Bank – has not generated a significant number of secondary treaties that add to the corpus of international economic law.[34] Furthermore, the IMF Articles of Agreement have not been easily augmented or amended in order to create a more effective international monetary regime.

(a) Exchange-rate stabilization
Article IV of the original IMF Agreement established relatively rigid and well-monitored rules to insure that member states would maintain exchange rates within a narrow band of 1 percent on each side of the parity between two currencies, based on par values established for each currency.[35] By the early 1970s, this regime had begun to break down, due in part to a weakening of the US dollar, the linchpin of the IMF regime. In August 1971, facing severe balance of payments pressures, the United States – the most powerful member of the IMF – unilaterally declared a devaluation of its currency and refused to maintain gold convertibility of the dollar. As a result, other IMF members refused to abide by the full strictures of Article IV. After a period of considerable uncertainty and negotiation, the Second Amendment of the IMF Agreement (adopted in 1976, and made effective in 1978) significantly altered Article IV.[36] The fixed-exchange-rate system was abandoned in favor of a highly flexible regime allowing members the freedom to adopt whatever exchange arrangements they prefer, subject only to very general policy guidelines.[37] While constituting a new "creation" of treaty-based law, the amendment of Article IV could hardly be said to constitute an advancement of the IMF's rules. Instead, the amended Article IV represents a relaxation of the international monetary regime. Some experts question whether it constitutes a legal regime at all.[38]

(b) Balance of payments assistance
Article V establishes very broad outlines of the regime for providing balance of payments assistance to members from the general resources of the IMF. These resources come from contributions of members to the IMF's general resources account, payable in the form of quotas that vary with the size and economic importance of the member state. Additional law-making by

---

34 The IMF Agreement has served as a model for later, regional, agreements, such as the European Monetary System and the European Monetary Cooperation Fund.
35 See generally J. Gold, *Exchange Rates in International Law and Organization* (1988); R. Edwards, *International Monetary Collaboration* ch. 11 (1985).
36 For a discussion of the events leading up to the Second Amendment and the negotiation of the amendment itself, see generally K. Dam, *The Rules of the Game: Reform and Evolution in the International Monetary System* (1982).   37 See Edwards, note 35 above, at 507–68.
38 See F. A. Mann, *The Legal Aspect of Money* 515 (4th ed., 1982).

treaty in this area has been insignificant,[39] although the IMF has served as a model for other funds, such as the European Monetary Cooperation Fund established by the European Community. However, much of the treaty-based regime has been supplemented by the IMF's administrative practice and by Executive Board declarations. An additional form of potential balance of payments assistance was created by the First Amendment to the IMF Agreement in 1969. The First Amendment created the Special Drawing Right (SDR) (Articles XV to XXI), a creative and important addition to international monetary law. The SDR is both a unit of account and an international reserve asset.[40] In the latter capacity, allocations of SDRs are made to member governments in proportion to their quotas in the IMF, and these newly created assets can be used for international payments purposes between governments.

The greatest importance of the First Amendment in advancing international monetary law, however, may have been in the creation of the SDR as a new unit of account to be used in international monetary and financial transactions. The SDR derives its value from the relative values of a basket of currencies (at present, five currencies determine the value of the SDR: the US dollar, the Deutsche Mark, the French franc, the Japanese yen, and the UK pound sterling). As fixed exchange rates gave way to floating rates, the SDR provided a more stable unit of value than any individual currency. The idea of a "basket currency" was sufficiently attractive to influence the European Community to establish a similar currency, the European Currency Unit (ECU), which derives its value from the currencies of its members.

The creation of the SDR has not proved to be as significant a development as some early proponents might have wished, however, since the total value of SDR allocations represents only a small percentage of central bank reserve assets.[41]

(c) The international payments regime

The third set of rules established by the IMF Articles of Agreement consists of those provisions designed to promote a system of international payments

---

[39] In a development related to the Fund's balance of payments assistance, on June 28, 1990, the Board of Governors approved a Third Amendment of the IMF Agreement, to become effective when accepted by three-fifths of the members exercising 85 percent of the voting power. This amendment to the Articles of Agreement will permit the Executive Board, by a 70 percent majority vote, to suspend the voting rights of a member that "fails to fulfill any of its obligations under this Agreement." The purpose of the amendment is to put additional pressure on Fund members to eliminate repayments arrears.

[40] On the SDR generally, see Edwards, note 35 above, at 167–221; IMF, The Role of the SDR in the International Monetary System (IMF Occasional Paper No. 51, March 1987).

[41] In March 1990, IMF members held total reserve assets of 856 billion SDRs. Allocations of SDRs constituted only 2.3 percent (20.4 billion) of the total. *IMF Annual Report*, 1990, at 66.

that would be secure, nondiscriminatory, and free from undue govern-mental restrictions. In the decade of economic depression and world war leading up to Bretton Woods, governments had increasingly restricted the freedom with which parties, either public or private, could make payments in international commerce. This was especially true, of course, during World War II.

The IMF Agreement struck a compromise between total freedom of international payments and governmental restriction of them. In effect, the Agreement allows governments to restrict *capital movements* (Article VI, section 3), but imposes a requirement of IMF approval of any restriction on the making of payments and transfers for *current international transactions* (which includes exports and imports of goods and services) (Article VIII, section 2(a)). "Transitional arrangements" under Article XIV – which many countries have availed themselves of for decades – permit the maintenance of exchange restrictions in force when a member adhered to the IMF Agreement.[42] Finally, Article VIII, section 2(b) directs the judicial and administrative authorities of IMF members to refrain from enforcing a contract that is contrary to the exchange-control regulations of another IMF member – a form of limited international recognition of the temperate use of exchange controls.

The IMF payments regime represented a significant advance in interna-tional monetary law. Prior to Bretton Woods, the payments system was a patchwork quilt of ephemeral bilateral accords. While establishing only general rules concerning international payments (rules which have often been deviated from), the IMF Agreement nevertheless plugged a poten-tially significant hole that could have frustrated the overall goals of international monetary stability and cooperation.

(d) The IMF regime evaluated

Measured against the statement of purposes listed in its Articles of Agreement, success of the IMF regime must be viewed as mixed. During the 1970s, the IMF had great difficulty in dealing effectively with exchange-rate disruptions, and eventually had to abandon the discipline of the fixed-exchange-rate system. During the 1980s, the IMF was unable to confront effectively the debt crises and balance of payments disequilibria that afflicted many developing countries. As a result, patchwork "sol-utions" to the debt crises (many of which still persist) were devised outside the IMF system. Excuses can be offered for the inadequacies of the IMF regime during 1970s and 1980s: the unrealistic use of a single currency, the US dollar, as the linchpin of the exchange-rate system; the lack of IMF

[42] S. Zamora, "Articles of Agreement of the International Monetary Fund," in *Basic Documents of International Economic Law* I, 316 (S. Zamora & R. Brand eds., 1990).

jurisdiction over private lending by commercial banks. Rather than indictments of the regime, however, these inadequacies might be viewed as indications of the difficulty of the task facing the IMF.

4. International finance and development assistance

The United Nations has been actively involved in promoting development assistance – financial, technical, and otherwise – to developing countries. As the number of developing nations proliferated, the United Nations' concern for more equitable distribution of economic benefits grew as well. Much of this concern is not law-generating, however, but more operational.

(a) The World Bank Group

The IMF's sister organization, the International Bank for Reconstruction and Development (IBRD, better known as the World Bank), was created to promote the economic development of its member countries by providing loans and technical assistance for specific projects and for programs of economic reform in developing countries. Since its creation in 1944, the World Bank has approved loans aggregating over 155 billion US dollars,[43] using funds from borrowings in international capital markets. In the field of development finance from public sources, the World Bank has become the predominant institution in the world, and its lending policies have affected economic development trends throughout the world. In short, the operational importance of the World Bank is easily recognized.

What may not be so obvious is the Bank's importance for the development of international economic law. Although not directly responsible for their creation, the Bank served as an important model for the treaties establishing the regional development banks – the Inter-American Development Bank (created in 1959), the African Development Bank (created in 1964), the Asian Development Bank (created in 1966),[44] and, most recently, the European Bank for Reconstruction and Development (created in 1990). (The regional development banks are formally outside the UN system, since they lack specialized agency status.)

---

[43] K. Hudes, "Articles of Agreement of the International Bank for Reconstruction and Development," in Zamora & Brand eds., note 42 above, at 421.

[44] See Mason and Asher, note 32 above, at 578–86. The establishment of regional development banks "is at once a tribute and a rebuke to the World Bank: a tribute in the sense that it could not have happened without the example previously set by the World Bank of probity, technical and economic competence, and ability to raise funds in capital markets and put them to productive use in low-income countries; a rebuke in the sense that, had the World Bank been as popular in those countries as it thought it was, their desire for regional banks would have been weaker." *Ibid.*, at 578.

248

In addition, the World Bank has been directly responsible for creating *treaties* subsequent treaties of importance not only for development finance, but also for private investment in developing countries. Thus, the Bank has spawned other operational agencies: the International Finance Corporation (IFC) to encourage private investment in member countries; the *IFC* International Development Association (IDA) for the purpose of making *IDA* highly concessional loans to the least-developed nations; the Convention on the Settlement of Investment Disputes between States and Nationals of Other States (the ICSID Convention), which established the International Centre for Settlement of Investment Disputes; and the Multilateral Investment Guarantee Agency (MIGA), to encourage foreign investment in member countries by issuing guarantees to investors. All these agencies, which constitute the "World Bank Group," were established by international treaty, and each of them received its impetus from World Bank study and sponsorship.

(b) Other programs for development assistance
The World Bank is the most highly visible UN agency actively involved in development assistance, but it is joined by other UN agencies as well. Of them, the most important are the United Nations Development Programme (UNDP), established in 1965 by the General Assembly; and the United Nations Industrial Development Organization (UNIDO), established in 1967 (it became a specialized agency in 1986). The UNDP is the world's most important source of technical assistance to developing countries. Such assistance is mostly nonmonetary, consisting of the provision of experts' services, equipment, and fellowships. The UNDP cooperates with the World Bank to identify and help design economic development projects. UNIDO also provides technical assistance to developing countries concerning industrial development policies and projects. Unlike the World Bank, these agencies have not been responsible for generating treaty-based international economic law. Whether the development programs of these and other UN bodies generate non-treaty-based law is couched in customary international law, which will be discussed below.

5. Protection of intellectual property rights

Conventions for the protection of intellectual property rights long preceded the creation of the United Nations. The earliest such convention, the Paris Convention for the Protection of Industrial Property, was adopted in 1883 and was quickly followed by the Berne Convention for the Protection of Literary and Artistic Works (1886). Despite being a relative latecomer, the United Nations system has become engaged in efforts both to create international legal regimes that govern intellectual property, and to administer existing regimes, primarily through the World Intellectual Property Organization (WIPO).[45] WIPO was created in 1967 to promote the protection of intellectual property rights throughout the world and to provide administrative cooperation among the various intellectual property treaties or unions that are within its jurisdiction. WIPO became a specialized agency of the United Nations in 1974.

The most important treaties entrusted to WIPO are the Paris and Berne Conventions. The Paris Convention facilitates patent and trademark protection, by providing for rules of national treatment that attempt to create uniformity of industrial property protection. The Paris Convention also establishes rules concerning the determination of rights of priority granted to inventors. The Berne Convention provides uniform rules for the protection of authors of literary and artistic works, based on national treatment and automatic protection.

While WIPO is "responsible" for about two dozen treaties altogether, it has been involved in the actual drafting and negotiation of only a small number of them – most notably, the International Patent Cooperation Treaty of June 19, 1970. WIPO's most recent effort has been to promote the adoption of an international convention on patent harmonization.

WIPO currently faces a jurisdictional challenge from the GATT. The United States and the European Community attempted to press for an international agreement on "trade-related intellectual property rights" (TRIPS) during the Uruguay Round of multilateral trade negotiations. The developing countries objected to this effort to bring into the sphere of GATT rule-making a subject that is perceived as coming under the clear jurisdiction of other agencies, such as WIPO, UNCTAD, and UNESCO, in which they feel that their interests are more effectively represented.[46] While a TRIPS agreement was concluded, it did not comprise a comprehensive regime to enforce intellectual property rights.

In addition to jurisdictional conflicts and enforcement issues, WIPO faces other challenges. First, the established regimes of intellectual property protection may not be adequate to deal with new technologies, such as

---

[45] UNESCO is responsible for the conclusion of the Universal Copyright Convention, which entered into force in 1955. UNESCO administers this agreement, which provides protection to a wide range of literary, scientific, and artistic works.

[46] F. Abbott, "Protecting First World Assets in the Third World: Intellectual Property Negotiations in the GATT Multilateral Framework," 22 *Vand. J. Transnat'l L.* 689, 713 (1989).

Developing countries' perceptions about their lack of decision-making power in the GATT are due to the character of the GATT, described earlier, as a negotiating forum in which the power to influence rule-making depends on the economic power that a country brings to the negotiations, rather than on voting power in a one-nation, one-vote system.

genetic engineering or computer programming, that redefine our notions of intellectual property.

Second, basic notions of protection of intellectual property have been challenged by developing countries as incompatible with an equitable international economic order. The owners of intellectual property are primarily located in developed countries, while the developing countries are largely consumers. Strict enforcement of rules to protect the rights of an intellectual property owner can be used to extract monopolistic rents from users, it is argued, to the clear disadvantage of economic development in the less technologically advanced countries.

Third, the intellectual property regime consists of a haphazard collection of agreements administered by various agencies – WIPO, UNESCO, and the European Patent Organization (not affiliated with the United Nations).[47] The existing conventions serve to coordinate matters such as the filing of applications for protection under national patent systems, searches to determine originality, and harmonization of certain standards. However, the determination of actual property rights, as well as their enforcement, depends on national patent laws that are not uniform. There is no system for the registration of an "international patent" or an "international trademark," nor is there an agreed regime of substantive rules.[48] In a world in which products, services, and manufacturing processes are distributed throughout the world, it becomes increasingly illogical to depend on the conflicting norms of national laws.

6. Foreign investment and transfer of technology

Under the rubric of the Bretton Woods system, specialized agencies affiliated with the United Nations have adopted regimes covering the major categories of international economic relations. An important gap exists in the Bretton Woods system, though: no multilateral treaty, either UN sponsored or otherwise, sets forth a regime for foreign investment.[49]

[47] The European Patent Organization administers the Convention on the Grant of European Patents, *adopted* 1973, *entered into force* 1977, which establishes a centralized search and examination system for the grant of patents under participating state laws that conform to certain standard rules.

[48] The closest thing to such an international regime, both for patent registration and for establishment of substantive rules, is the Convention for the European Patent for the Common Market (Community Patent Convention) of 1975, 15 *ILM* 5 (1975), which is open to ratification by member states of the European Community. However, the Community Patent Convention has not come into force after fifteen years, and the prospects for it are uncertain.

[49] P. Christy, "Negotiating Investment in the GATT: A Call for Functionalism," 12 *Mich. J. Int'l L.* 743, 753, 763–64 (1991). See also D. Carreau, P. Juillard, & T. Flory, *Droit International Economique* 374, 391 (1978); D. Wallace, *International Regulation of Multinational Corporations* 6 (1976).

Foreign investment covers a number of different subjects. The term is used here to include both foreign direct investment (controlling interests in productive enterprises) and portfolio investment (purchase of securities, bank deposits, etc., that do not carry majority control of an enterprise). Foreign investment may also be defined broadly to include licensing agreements for the transfer of technology, since such agreements may contain controls over the production of goods or services produced by the licensee.

There is no multilateral treaty dealing with the subjects of foreign investment or transfer of technology, although there have been UN-sponsored efforts to draft nonbinding codes of conduct that may eventually have legal effects. The reason for absence of a multilateral investment treaty in the Bretton Woods system is no mystery – it is due to the inability to bring together the widely divergent views of rich and poor countries. On the one hand, multinational corporations are quick to pursue profitable enterprises in any corner of the globe, and they feel justified in demanding assurances of the property and contractual rights that they acquire in this pursuit – a position fully supported by their governments. On the other hand, developing countries, responding in part to a legacy of economic domination during the age of colonialism, see the spread of powerful multinational corporations as a neo-colonialist incursion that endangers their economic sovereignty and their long-range welfare.

Among the important legal subjects for which there are no multilaterally agreed rules, the following topics stand out:

(i)   rules regarding the expropriation of foreign-owned property;
(ii) guarantees of and limitations on repatriation of investments;
(iii) remedies, if any, for breaches of investment agreements;
(iv) operations of multinational corporations, and the liability of parent corporations for acts of subsidiaries;
(v)   rules governing the licensing of technology, including limitations imposed by licensors on licensees.

To say that there are no multilaterally agreed rules on these subjects is not to conclude that there is no international treaty law relating to them, however. On a bilateral basis, outside the UN system, over three hundred bilateral investment treaties, or "BITs," have been concluded between capital-exporting states and developing nations. The former have promoted BITs as a means of insuring protection for foreign investors, since BITs generally set forth rules of fair treatment. Developing nations have accepted BITs with the hope that they will result in increased levels of foreign investment in their economies. BITs do not represent, however, a comprehensive scheme for regulating investor–host country relations.

252

While UN agencies have not developed treaty-based rules on these subjects, they have not ignored them. Certain UN agencies – in particular the ECOSOC and its affiliate, the UN Commission on Transnational Corporations – have drafted codes of conduct setting forth voluntary rules for some of these subjects. Furthermore, despite an inability to build consensus on substantive rules, UN agencies have increasingly emphasized the development of dispute-settlement arrangements and guarantee schemes that will bring at least some element of legal order to the field of foreign investment. Thus, the World Bank has been responsible for promoting treaties that are related to foreign investment issues: the ICSID Convention that establishes a framework for settling investment disputes, although the Convention does not establish rules to apply in deciding them; and the MIGA Convention, which not only provides for guarantees of foreign investments but could eventually give rise to side agreements dealing with these subjects.

7. Preliminary evaluation and criticism of the treaty-based Bretton Woods regime

Since the end of World War II, organs and specialized agencies of the United Nations have created a considerable body of treaty-based international economic law. In most areas studied, the establishment of a specialized agency – the GATT for international trade, the IMF for monetary affairs, the World Bank for development finance – represented the first attempt to deal with that particular subject matter on a multilateral basis, rather than on a bilateral or unilateral basis. Multilateralism represented an important advance in the development of a viable international economic legal order. The agreements establishing the GATT, the IMF, and the World Bank and its affiliates not only created substantive rules, however; equally important, they established agencies to administer and enforce those rules, agencies that have since been staffed with secretariats that have earned positive reputations. The administration and enforcement of these regimes have been imperfect, suggesting that pragmatic solutions to legal problems have prevailed over formalistic ones. Even with these imperfections, the creation of an international economic regime from the composite activities of specialized agencies constitutes a major accomplishment of the United Nations.

(a) Developing-country criticism of the Bretton Woods system

Beginning in the 1960s, the Bretton Woods regime came under increasing criticism for its inability to confront the special problems of developing countries. In the critical view of these countries, the post-war international economic regime had been designed by only one segment of the UN membership – the developed, industrialized countries. By the 1970s, it had also become apparent that the gap between rich and poor countries was widening, rather than contracting, and that the benefits of the Bretton Woods regime were being unequally distributed. Thus, while the GATT could take partial credit for the increase in the volume of world trade due to trade liberalization, developing countries could validly complain about a GATT legal system that permitted protectionism in agricultural goods,[50] which the developing countries produced. Not surprisingly, the developing-country share of total world trade fell from 32 percent in the early 1950s to 17 percent in 1972, and when oil-exporting countries were excluded, the share amounted to only 10 percent.[51]

The developing countries reacted to this disappointing performance with a campaign to create a new, significantly altered international economic regime that would better reflect their interests and would give the developing countries greater decision-making and negotiating powers. This campaign, initiated in the early 1970s within UNCTAD, culminated in the adoption in 1974 of UN General Assembly resolutions calling for the establishment of a New International Economic Order (NIEO)[52] and adopting a Charter of Economic Rights and Duties of States.[53]

Extremely broad in scope and general in their provisions, the NIEO resolutions more strongly resemble a social cause than a detailed plan for realistic changes in the Bretton Woods legal regime. As a consequence, the NIEO has been more important for its expressions of dissatisfaction with the Bretton Woods regime than for the legal effects, direct or indirect, that it has generated.

(b) *Difficulty of amending* the basic economic treaties: the "Balkanization" of the Bretton Woods regime

The Bretton Woods system created separate legal regimes for trade, monetary affairs, and development finance. In each case, an administering agency, backed by a professional secretariat, was supposed to promote the rule of law by adapting the regime to new circumstances. The basic regimes of the GATT, IMF, and World Bank performed well for almost twenty-five years, but once they began to break down, under political and economic pressures in the 1970s, the proponents of multilateral legal solutions

---

[50] See, e.g., GATT art. XI, sec. 2(c), permitting import restrictions to be used to complement domestic price-support programs.
[51] K. Hossain, *Legal Aspects of the New International Economic Order* 2 (K. Hossain ed., 1980).
[52] GA Res. 3201 (S–VI) (May 4, 1974), UN Doc. A/9559.
[53] GA Res. 3281 (XXIX) (Dec. 12, 1974).

encountered extreme difficulties in amending the basic Bretton Woods agreements.

The experience of the IMF shows the difficulty in strengthening the Bretton Woods regime through amendment. In the early 1970s, the IMF's fixed-exchange-rate system – a linchpin of the entire Bretton Woods system – came under attack. In the early 1980s, the IMF faced another test – the third-world debt crisis – which placed the international economic system under severe strain.

Changes in the IMF regime could have helped to resolve these problems, but the political consensus to amend the IMF Agreement was difficult or impossible to come by.[54] In fact, the IMF Agreement has undergone only two significant alterations[55] during its forty-five years of existence: the First Amendment, in 1969, which created the SDR; and the Second Amendment, in 1976, which abandoned the fixed-exchange-rate system, in recognition of the widespread *de facto* abandonment of that system by its members. The Second Amendment, in particular, involved protracted negotiations and much compromise.[56] The resulting amendment of Article IV of the IMF Agreement, far from bolstering the IMF legal regime, represented a further softening of that regime. In the words of one expert, the amended Article IV "reads somewhat more like a press communiqué than a formal statement of legal obligations."[57]

There are several reasons why the IMF has been able to function, despite profound changes in the international monetary system, without making major changes in its charter. First, the IMF is more important as an operational entity than it is as a rule-enforcing agency; in the former capacity, significant changes have occurred in lending practices which have precluded the need to amend the basic IMF charter. Second, the few IMF rules that do proscribe certain conduct of members are sufficiently general that the IMF is able to apply them flexibly.[58]

Inadequacies of the amendment process are even more pronounced in regard to the GATT. The basic GATT Agreement has only been amended twice, in 1957 and in 1966 (the latter to add part IV). In the words of Professor John Jackson, "amending the GATT is almost impossible."[59]

---

[54] Under IMF art. XXVIII, amendment of the Articles of Agreement requires majority approval of three-fifths of the members exercising 85 percent of the voting power. The United States alone, with approximately 19 percent of the voting power, can effectively veto any amendment.

[55] There has been a recent, more minor, amendment of the IMF Agreement. On June 28, 1990, the IMF Board of Governors approved a Third Amendment, to allow for the suspension of voting and related rights of members that do not fulfill their obligations (especially repayment obligations) to the IMF. *IMF Annual Report* 1990, at 105–9.

[56] See generally Dam, note 36 above.   [57] Edwards, note 35 above, at 506.

[58] This point is developed further in Zamora, note 42 above, at 1014–17.

[59] Jackson, note 13 above, at 303.

Instead of amendment, the GATT contracting parties, spurred on by the industrialized countries, have adopted a collection of side agreements, including seven "MTN codes," that are open to adherence by any GATT contracting party, but are not obligatory.[60]

The recent conclusion of the Uruguay Round Agreements, and the establishment of the WTO, have not changed this. While expanding the jurisdiction of the GATT/WTO to include services, intellectual property, and other subjects, the Uruguay Round did not alter the basic GATT rules, and left many lingering areas of concern.[61]

One upshot of the inability to amend the Bretton Woods regime has been the tendency for governments to slip outside that regime to undertake more informal arrangements and to find solutions to economic problems that are not dictated by the Bretton Woods frameworks. In international monetary relations, this phenomenon can be seen in the periodic meetings of Group of Seven countries (the principal industrialized nations) to coordinate their monetary policies (exchange-rate intervention, coordination of interest rates, etc.).[62] In international trade, importing nations, especially the United States, have forced exporting countries to agree to "voluntary restraint agreements" (VRAs) that reduce the level of exports, despite the fact that the GATT regime makes no specific provision for VRAs.[63] The developing countries especially have criticized the more economically powerful states for their refusal to stay within the bounds of the formal international regimes in dealing with major economic problems.

(c) Overlapping jurisdiction and lack of coordination of international economic agencies

The most enthusiastic proponents of the Bretton Woods legal order envisaged a single regime for trade, administered by the ITO; a single regime for monetary affairs, administered by the IMF; a single regime for development finance, under World Bank supervision. More than fifty years later, the simplicity of such a plan seems naive. We now recognize that the world economy does not consist of independent fields; rather, it is the sum of many interrelated parts. Few international economic problems can be placed neatly in one category, to be resolved only by reference to a single

---

[60] See above, p. 242 text preceding note 26. Greater effort has been made to secure broad agreement to the Uruguay Round Agreements discussed therein.

[61] Rules governing unfair trade practices, lack of free trade in agriculture, problems of subsidization in international trade, and other important issues continue to pose problems under the loose regime of the GATT. For a critical evaluation of the Uruguay Round Agreements in general, see the articles cited at the end of note 13 above.

[62] See generally Y. Funabashi, *Managing the Dollar: From the Plaza to the Louvre* (2nd ed., 1989). For a more legal analysis, see J. Gold, *Legal Effects of Fluctuating Exchange Rates* 400–6 (1990); Gold, note 35 above, at 447–59.

[63] J. Jackson & W. Davey, *Legal Problems of International Economic Relations* 614 (2nd ed., 1986).

256

regime. Thus, international trade and monetary issues are often inter-twined; policies of economic development affect both trade and monetary affairs; and intellectual property rights affect the growth of foreign investment.

The complexity of international economic issues helps to explain why, as the number of international economic agencies has increased, so has the opportunity for overlapping jurisdiction, and even conflict, when these agencies administer their "separate" regimes.[64] Even where specialized agencies already occupy a field, pressures for regional control of economic activities have led to the creation of overlapping regional agencies. International economic agencies have also tended to spin off related agencies and regimes, further complicating the institutional picture.

The fragmentation of rules of international economic law, administered by agencies with overlapping jurisdictions, has been severely criticized by some observers, who believe that the international economic system is ill served by a UN system in which a multiplicity of agencies operate in uncoordinated fashion to deal separately with economic issues that are interrelated. As a result, global economic problems are ineffectively confronted by UN agencies.[65] The UN General Assembly, through the ECOSOC, was supposed to coordinate the economic policies of UN agencies, including the specialized agencies; such coordination has not come about, however. In the mid-1970s, a movement to confront the lack of coordination of UN economic agencies resulted in the establishment, within the United Nations Organization, of a Director-General for Development and International Economic Policy. However, this institutional change did not have any appreciable effect, since the Director-General was given neither a budget nor any real authority over UN agencies.[66]

(d) The "soft law" nature of international economic law

The legal regimes produced by the Bretton Woods system have not escaped characterization as "soft law" — a term often used to describe the imprecision and lack of enforcement of rules of international law in general.[67] A legal regime can be "soft" in terms of its substantive rules,

---

[64] Van Themaat, note 3 above, at 204.

[65] See, e.g., D. B. Steele, "The Case for Global Economic Management and UN System Reform," 39 Int'l Org. 561 (1985) (calling for the establishment of a "higher-level guiding body with an element of discretionary power, which would establish the major lines of short- and medium-term global economic management." Ibid., at 561). See also Van Themaat, note 3 above, at 204, 211; Kaufmann, note 9 above, at 66.

[66] R. Meltzer, "UN Structural Reform: Institutional Development in International Economic and Social Affairs," in The US, the UN, and the Management of Global Change 238, 251 (T. Gati ed., 1983).

[67] See generally P. Weil, "Towards Relative Normativity in International Law?," 77 AJIL 413 (1983); panel discussion, "A Hard Look at Soft Law," 1988 Am. Soc'y Int'l L. Proc. 371–95.

which may be drafted in vague language, or where important exceptions allow for deviations. Alternatively, rules may be precisely drafted, but enforcement of the rules may be left flexible, subject to waiver, or administered haphazardly (or subjected to political pressures). The Bretton Woods regime has elements of softness both in its substantive rules and in its mechanisms of enforcement. For example, the Second Amendment of the IMF Articles of Agreement replaced the relative hardness of the fixed-exchange-rate rules of Article IV with an extremely loose set of "rules" that do not appreciably circumscribe the behavior of member states.[68] In the GATT/WTO regime, on the other hand, relatively "hard" rules, such as interdictions against export subsidies or against the use of quantitative restrictions, are vitiated by a system of enforcement that is "soft." (The subject of enforcement will be addressed below.)

Some international economic "soft law" exists in the form of international instruments that are not intended to be binding, such as codes of conduct, declarations, resolutions, and other nonbinding texts. Though not binding on states, the principles set forth in such instruments do influence the economic practice of states; they may also become enforceable rules when adopted by national legislation. One example of this phenomenon can be found in the adoption of UN resolutions on permanent sovereignty over natural resources. These resolutions have influenced national laws, treaties, and judicial case law.

B. Creating international economic law through nontreaty processes

International treaties are not the only instruments by which UN agencies have attempted to influence international economic relations. Several international organizations, including UN agencies, have explored nontreaty alternatives for resolving international economic conflicts, and the instruments and practices that have resulted from these efforts have added to the substance of international law.

1. Resolutions of the UN General Assembly

Resolutions of the UN General Assembly are not a formal source of international law, since the General Assembly does not have a law-making function *per se* (other than to establish its own internal rules). Nevertheless,

---

[68] J. Gold, "Strengthening the Soft International Law of Exchange Arrangements," 77 *AJIL* 443 (1983); Zamora, note 42 above, at 1024–26.

"few would deny that General Assembly resolutions have had a formative influence in the development of international law in matters of considerable importance to member states."[69]

In the area of international economic law, the most important General Assembly resolutions (in terms of their influence on the generation of rules and practices that influence the behavior of states) are those dealing with the New International Economic Order (NIEO) and those concerning state sovereignty over natural resources and foreign-owned business activities. The NIEO resolutions are discussed below, in connection with customary international economic law. The resolutions on natural resources deserve mention here, since they have been instrumental in establishing generally recognized principles dealing with economic sovereignty and the treatment of foreign investors.

The most important of these resolutions is the 1962 Declaration on Permanent Sovereignty over Natural Resources.[70] Resolution 1803, adopted by the General Assembly by a vote of eighty-seven to two (with twelve abstentions), declared certain basic principles that should be recognized under national and international law, including the following:

4. Nationalization, expropriation or requisitioning shall be based on grounds or reasons of public utility, security or the national interest which are recognized as overriding purely individual or private interests, both domestic and foreign. In such cases the owner shall be paid appropriate compensation, in accordance with the rules in force in the State taking such measures in the exercise of its sovereignty and in accordance with international law.

In recognizing a right of expropriation for public purposes, Resolution 1803 established a principle that has been relied upon by international and national judicial tribunals, as well as in subsequent enactments by the General Assembly and by other organizations; the crucial issue of the level of compensation for expropriation remains unsettled, however.[71]

---

[69] O. Schachter, "International Law in Theory and Practice," 178 *RCADI* 111 (1982–V). See also I. Brownlie, *Principles of Public International Law* 14–15 (3d ed., 1979; reprint, 1984), and the discussion at notes 88–94 below, pp. 263–64.

[70] UNGA Res. 1803 (XVII), 17 UN GAOR Supp. (No. 17) 15), reprinted in 2 *ILM* 223 (1963).

[71] Several important arbitral tribunals have cited Resolution 1803. See, e.g., Arbitration between Kuwait and the American Indep. Oil Co. (AMINOIL), 21 *ILM* 976, 1032–34 (1982); *Texas Overseas Petroleum Co.* v. *Libyan Arab Rep.*, 17 *ILM* 1, 30 (1978) ("Resolution 1803 (XVII) seems to this Tribunal to reflect the state of customary law existing in this field.").
   Concerning the issue of compensation for expropriations of foreign-owned property, see *Restatement (Third) of Foreign Relations Law of the United States*, Sec. 712, reporters' notes 1 & 2; O. Schachter, "Compensation for Expropriation," 78 *AJIL* 121 (1984).

2. Codes of Conduct

A second means of creating international economic law has involved the adoption of quasi-legal instruments known as codes of conduct.[72] Like treaties, codes of conduct are contractual in nature (being adopted by voluntary agreement of participating states). Unlike treaties, however, codes of conduct do not create binding rules of international law. Instead, they establish voluntary guidelines that are intended to influence the behavior of both governments and private enterprises. Codes of conduct, as discussed here, do not provide for international enforcement mechanisms, but rely instead on governments to adopt national laws that would reflect the policies of the codes. No provisions are made for penalizing governments that do not act in this regard.

Within international economic law, the motivation for adopting codes of conduct was the recognition that the Bretton Woods system contained a major gap in coverage; it included no regime defining the rights and obligations of foreign investors, nor any organization with clear jurisdiction to create such a regime. Furthermore, the Bretton Woods regimes did not single out, either for study or for regulation, the activities of multinational corporations (MNCs). Nevertheless, MNC activities became increasingly dominant in the international economy, so that by the 1970s the international community began to focus more sharply on these issues.[73] Since then, the gap has been filled, albeit to a limited extent, by the activities of organizations other than UN specialized agencies – in particular, by organizations that are dominated by developing countries and that have broad jurisdiction to address international economic law issues, but possess little enforcement power and lack sophisticated institutional mechanisms. This helps to explain why codes of conduct have been developed as quasi-legal means for addressing this important area of economic activity.

Various international organizations – including the International Labour Organization (ILO),[74] the ECOSOC (through the UN Commission on Transnational Corporations) and UNCTAD,[75] and the World Health

---

[72] See generally P. Reynolds, "Clouds of Codes: The New International Economic Order Through Codes of Conduct: A Survey," 75 *Law Library J.* 315 (1982).

[73] See generally J. Kline, *International Codes and Multinational Business* 9–28 (1985); S. Dell, *The United Nations and International Business* 55ff. (1990).

[74] See the ILO-sponsored Tripartite Declaration of Principles Concerning Multinational Enterprises and Social Policy, reprinted in 17 *ILM* 422 (1978). The Tripartite Declaration addresses MNC issues that are of particular importance to labor, such as collective bargaining, working conditions, training, and freedom of association. The Declaration was later incorporated into the ECOSOC Draft Code of Conduct on Transnational Corporations, discussed below. See ECOSOC Code, para. 46.

[75] See, e.g., the UNCTAD-sponsored UN Code on Restrictive Business Practices, UN Doc. TD/RBP/CONF/10(1980), reprinted in 19 *ILM* 813 (1980). The Code on Restrictive Business Practices, which addresses the regulation of monopolistic and other restrictive

Organization (WHO)[76] – have promoted the adoption of codes of conduct to deal with the activities of MNCs. Non-UN agencies, such as the Organization for Economic Cooperation and Development (OECD)[77] and the International Chamber of Commerce (ICC),[78] have also promoted codes of conduct or voluntary guidelines.

Most important thus far has been the ECOSOC-sponsored Code of Conduct on Transnational Corporations (TNCs).[79] Negotiations for the adoption of such a code began in the 1970s, and have been carried out under the auspices of the UN Commission on Transnational Corporations, created in 1975 by the ECOSOC. The ECOSOC Code remains in a draft form; the language of its provisions is still under negotiation, and it is unclear whether a large number of countries, especially industrialized countries, will eventually support the Code. If sufficient support does materialize, it is expected that the ECOSOC Code will be submitted to the UN General Assembly for adoption as a nonbinding set of principles.

The nonbinding nature of codes of conduct has made it easier for governments to adopt them, but this also raises the question about what purpose they should serve. To say that codes of conduct are not legally binding is not to say that they do not influence international economic relations, nor does it mean that they produce no legal effects whatsoever.[80] Codes of conduct permit at least limited agreement among governments on the broad outlines of policies in areas where more specific agreement is not yet possible. In this way, codes of conduct can provide important indications, both to governments and to private parties, of the future direction of both national and international economic regulation. Codes may be forerunners of binding legal obligations, both nationally (if governments adopt laws that reflect the codes) and internationally (should an international organization eventually adopt a binding set of obligations). Consequently, codes of conduct are seen by private business as a guide to voluntary standards of behavior that, if followed, will prevent

practices of business enterprises, has been incorporated into the draft ECOSOC Code of Conduct on Transnational Corporations, discussed below. See ECOSOC Code, para. 35. See generally Dell, note 73 above, at 22–36.

[76] International Code of Marketing of Breast Milk Substitutes, WHO Doc. WHA34.22 (1981), reprinted in 20 *ILM* 1004 (1981).

[77] See the OECD-sponsored Declaration by the Governments of OECD Member Countries and Decisions of the OECD Council on International Investment and Multinational Enterprises of 21 June 1976.

[78] See the ICC-sponsored Guidelines for International Investment, ICC Doc. No. 272 (1972). [79] See generally Dell, note 73 above, at 73–90.

[80] On the legal effects of codes of conduct, see Kline, note 73 above, at 71–76; A. Fatouros, "On the Implementation of International Codes of Conduct," 30 *Amer. U. L. Rev.* 941 (1981); H. Baade, "The Legal Effects of Codes of Conduct for Multinational Enterprises," 22 *German Y. B. Int'l L.* 11 (1979); C. Chance, "Codes of Conduct for Multinational Corporations," 33 *Bus. Law.* 1799 (1978).

conflict with host governments and will forestall more severe regulation.[81] They may also be cited in litigation and can provide important starting points for the negotiation of future treaties.

3. Customary international economic law

Most international economic law that has arisen from UN activities has been established by treaty, either directly (through the adoption of UN-sponsored multilateral or bilateral agreements) or indirectly (as, for example, when a specialized agency creates rules through quasi-legislative acts – a subject addressed below).[82] *Customary* international law – rules emanating from the practices of states that are followed out of a sense of legal obligation (*opinio juris*) – could also develop out of the economic activities of UN agencies. There is no doctrinal reason why the practices followed by states in their undertakings with UN agencies could not give rise to rules of customary international law. Some authors have asserted that specialized agencies have indeed sown the seeds of customary international law.[83] Nevertheless, in the field of international economic relations, there has been scant identification of rules of customary international economic law, whether or not emanating from the practice of UN agencies.[84] The International Law Commission, which is charged with the codification and progressive development of international law, including the transform-ation of customary law into treaty obligations, has largely ignored the subject of international economic law.[85] To some extent, UNCITRAL has filled this breach.

(a) The New International Economic Order and the generation of international economic law

During the 1970s, the United Nations General Assembly adopted two resolutions on the New International Economic Order (NIEO) – the Declaration on the Establishment of a New International Economic

---

[81] Kline, note 73 above, at 5–7, 71–76, 156.
[82] Jackson & Davey, note 63 above, at 261; G. Schwarzenberger, "The Principles and Standards of International Economic Law," 117 *RCADI* 7, 12 (1966).
[83] See, e.g., Alexandrowicz, note 22 above, at 11, 98–117. The author cites the Universal Postal Union, the International Telecommunications Union, the International Civil Aviation Organization, and the Inter-Governmental Maritime Consultative Organisation as giving rise to customary international law, although he is vague about what the precise rules are.
[84] See Jackson, note 13 above, at 22: "In economic affairs, . . . there are very few recognized norms of customary international law." See generally S. Zamora, "Is There Customary International Economic Law?," 32 *German Y. B. Int'l L.* 9 (1989).
[85] Zamora, note 84 above, at 22.

Order[86] and the Charter of Economic Rights and Duties of States.[87] These resolutions, as UN General Assembly resolutions in general,[88] do not create binding rules of international economic law, despite the contrary protestations of some developing-country supporters.[89] Nevertheless, it is possible for the NIEO resolutions to promote the development of new rules of international law indirectly. First, UN resolutions such as the NIEO may help bring about the development of new rules of customary international law,[90] either by moving states into patterns of uniform state practice or by providing evidence of *opinio juris*. However, considerable resistance has arisen, especially in the United States, to the notion that the NIEO resolutions have generated customary international law. Critics point to the polemical nature of many NIEO provisions and the opposition of important members of the world economy, in particular the United States government.[91]

Second, the NIEO resolutions may influence other organizations, including the specialized agencies, to develop new rules of international economic law to coincide with the principles espoused in the resolutions. Some evidence suggests that the NIEO resolutions have produced legal effects in this regard. The NIEO Declaration and the Charter of Economic Rights and Duties of States are extremely broad in their coverage.[92] Proponents of the Charter conceived it as a set of fundamental principles covering many spheres of economic and political activities, including international trade, multinational corporations, expropriation, international economic cooperation, development of natural resources, industrialization, transfer of technology, and exploitation of the seabed.[93] Conse-

---

[86] UNGA Res. 3201 (S–VI) (May 4, 1974), UN Doc. A/9559.

[87] UNGA Res. 3281 (XXIX) (Dec. 12, 1974).

[88] M. Mendelson, "The Legal Character of General Assembly Resolutions: Some Considerations of Principle," in Hossain, note 51 above, at 95; Van Themaat, note 3 above, at 43–44.

[89] See M. Bulajic, "Legal Aspects of a New International Economic Order," in Hossain ed. note 51 above, at 45, 60; Chowdhury, "Legal Status of the Charter of Economic Rights and Duties of States," in *ibid.*, at 79, 82.

[90] J. Davidow & L. Chiles, "The United States and the Issue of the Binding or Voluntary Nature of International Codes of Conduct Regarding Restrictive Business Practices," 72 *AJIL* 247, 255 (1978). Compare L. Sohn, "The Shaping of International Law," 8 *Ga. J. Int'l & Comp. L.* 1, 21–22 (1978); O. Schachter, *Sharing the World's Resources* 3–4 (1977).

[91] J. Gamble & M. Frankowska, "International Law's Response to the New International Order: An Overview," 9 *B. C. Int'l & Comp. L. Rev.* 257, 286 (1986). See also M. E. Ellis, "Comment, The New International Economic Order and General Assembly Resolutions: The Debate over the Legal Effects of General Assembly Resolutions Revisited," 15 *Cal. W. Int'l L. J.* 647 (1985).

[92] One commentator has characterized the Charter as an example of the "cornucopia approach to legal drafting: when in doubt, put everything in and leave it to subsequent historians to work out why." E. McWhinney, *United Nations Law Making: Cultural and Ideological Relativism and International Law Making for an Era of Transition* 181 (1984).

[93] Hossain ed., note 51 above, at 5.

quently, the Charter extends to subjects covered by all UN specialized economic agencies. In each subject area, NIEO objectives have sought to increase developing countries' control over their economic destinies, to accelerate these countries' economic growth, to promote industrial development in developing countries, and to narrow the gap in *per capita* income levels between rich and poor countries.[94]

In general, attempts to make the principles espoused by the NIEO operational through specific measures adopted by functional UN agencies have yielded only a few concrete results.[95] The NIEO-inspired principles of nonreciprocity and preferential treatment for developing countries helped solidify support for preferential treatment to favor developing-country trade within the framework of the GATT. The NIEO emphasis on a need for long-term commodity agreements also provided fuel for the adoption of the UNCTAD-inspired Integrated Program for Commodities.[96] The NIEO also helped to inspire the adoption of the draft codes of conduct for multinational corporations, as discussed earlier.

In sum, the NIEO has been more important as a political instrument, focusing developing-country support and chastising developed-country intransigence, than it has as a generator of specific rules of international economic law.

(b) International law and development assistance

Scholars of international law have long addressed the question whether the international legal system has generated rules of customary international law surrounding the provision of development assistance to developing countries. Analysis has focused on both the repeated patterns of development assistance that stem from formal arrangements (bilateral and multilateral arrangements through treaties or international contracts), and pronouncements of international agencies (UN resolutions, including the NIEO resolutions).[97] These aid patterns and resolutions may arguably constitute evidence of the state practice or *opinio juris* required to support an emerging norm of customary international law.

Different characterizations of customary norms have been proposed, although each of these relates to a general notion of an emerging international obligation to provide development aid:

---

[94] Gamble & Frankowska, note 91 above, at 259.
[95] McWhinney, note 92 above, at 180–86. Compare M. Bulajic, *Principles of International Development Law* 59–66, 154–80 (1986).   [96] Carreau et al., note 49 above, at 88–90.
[97] See O. Schachter, "The Evolving International Law of Development," 15 *Colum. J. Transnat'l L.* 1, 2–5 (1976).

(i) "capability, an obligation to contribute to development;"[98]
(ii) "international entitlement to aid;"[99]
(iii) "the right to development;"[100] and
(iv) "the emergence of a norm of customary law which makes it obligatory for the affluent countries to assist the poor nations in their development is not only sensible, but is also inevitable."[101]

 possible norms

Going beyond a general obligation to contribute to development assistance to needy countries, some commentators have alluded to a specific quantitative target amount of development assistance – 0.7 percent of gross national product – as an indicator of compliance with the general obligation to contribute to needy countries, if not an enforceable rule of law.[102]

fulfillment of obligation

It is debatable that an obligation of development assistance has gradually arisen under customary international law. Most donor countries reject the notion. As Professor Oscar Schachter has observed, in the view of donor countries, "they have full discretion to determine in what circumstances, to what extent and in what way they would render assistance. Their continued and even predictable behavior in extending aid does not, as they see it, give rise to an obligation of a legal character since it is clearly understood by all that their actions are voluntary."[103]

4. Creation of international economic law through the dissemination of general principles of law

International law can also be based on general principles of law that are recognized by states. Unlike customary international law, the binding character of general principles of law stems not from the practice of states *inter se* but instead from the simultaneous existence of such principles in the municipal legal systems of states. To rise to the level of international law, such principles should be universally and uniformly followed.[104]

---

[98] H. Lasswell, "The Relevance of International Law to the Development Process," *Proceedings of the American Society of International Law*, Sixtieth Annual Meeting, at 1, 4 (1966).

[99] Schachter, note 97 above, at 9.

[100] K. de Vey Mestagh, "The Right to Development," 28 *Neth. Int'l L. J.* 30, 33 (1981). Mestagh speaks of the right to development as a general principle of law, rather than customary international law, but his analysis is similar to that employed for customary law. *Ibid.*, at 38ff.

[101] I. Haq, "From Charity to Obligation: A Third World Perspective on Concessional Resource Transfers," 14 *Tex. Int'l L. J.* 389, 420 (1979).

[102] *Ibid.*, at 397. See also K. Tomasevski, *Development Aid and Human Rights* 4 (1989).

[103] O. Schachter, "Principles of International Social Justice," in *Essays in Tribute to Wolfgang Friedmann* 249, 251 (G. Wilner ed., 1979).

[104] Statute of the International Court of Justice, art. 38. On general principles of law as a source of international law, see B. Cheng, *General Principles of Law as Applied by International Courts and Tribunals* (1987).

Specialized agencies have generated general principles of law by influencing developments in the municipal law of member states. Through recommendations, conventions, and operational practices, the specialized agencies have exerted pressures that have led to uniform municipal law-making.[105] Since few experts have addressed this subject, the creation of general principles of law through the activities of specialized agencies may be granted in theory, but examples in practice are rare. Thus, freedom of trade union association, long espoused by the International Labour Organization (ILO), may arguably be considered a general principle of law due to its wide acceptance in municipal law.[106]

5. Generation of international economic norms through the operations of specialized agencies

If the specialized economic agencies of the United Nations have not been responsible for generating a large body of customary international law, they have nevertheless given rise to the generation of numerous practices, sometimes referred to as "usages," that mold international economic behavior.[107] In these instances, the practices of states in conformity with the operations of specialized agencies are not intended to create binding rules, since they are not carried out under a sense of legal obligation; such usages may nevertheless place important constraints on states' behavior.

The importance of operational rules or usages has not been emphasized by international lawyers. Writing in 1964, Wolfgang Friedmann pointed out that specialized agencies such as the IMF and the World Bank, though operationally important, do not make decisions that directly restrict the legislative, executive, or judicial prerogatives of member states.[108] This observation, though still correct in a doctrinal sense, underplays the normative effects produced by the operations of specialized economic agencies. For instance, under IMF balance of payments assistance, member states must conform to well-defined usages (conditionality of access to Fund resources, observance of performance criteria under stand-by arrangements) even though such assistance is not embodied in a binding, legal agreement.[109] Since commercial banks often require IMF financing to precede a restructuring of external debt, the IMF's decision not to enter into a stand-by arrangement can doom a private restructuring agreement

---

[105] Alexandrowicz, note 22 above, at 88–97.   [106] *Ibid.*, at 90.   [107] *Ibid.*, at 159.

[108] W. Friedmann, *The Changing Structure of International Law* 286 (1964).

[109] Alexandrowicz, note 22 above, at 123ff. On IMF balance of payments assistance generally, see Edwards, note 35 above, at 222–98; J. Gold, "Balance of Payments Transactions of the International Monetary Fund," in *International Financial Law*, II, 65–82 (R. Rendell ed., 2d ed., 1983).

sought by a developing-country borrower.[110] In such cases, it is small comfort to the borrowing country that its legislative or executive power had not been formally infringed upon.

The normative effects generated by the operations of specialized agencies are precisely the results that proponents of functionalism applaud. Whether or not such norms rise to the level of formal rules of international law is of less consequence from the functionalist point of view. What matters is that an organization is able to promote international cooperation through its operational activities.

funct.

6. International economic law and the International Court of Justice

unimportant

According to Article 38 of the Statute of the International Court of Justice (ICJ), decisions of national and international tribunals may provide evidence of international law. In theory, therefore, decisions of the ICJ could be important in creating international economic law (through the issuance of advisory opinions), and in defining international economic law (through the identification of rules of customary international law, or through the interpretation of international economic treaties). This has not been the case, however. The ICJ has occasionally confronted issues of international economic law, particularly in relation to the rights of foreign investors under national laws; for the most part, however, the Court has not played an important role in generating rules of international economic law.[111] Furthermore, the Court has never been asked to issue an advisory opinion on an issue of international economic law.

Not the case

In short, the interpretation of international economic law has largely been left to national courts and to the organizations themselves. This may change, however, as an increasing number of bilateral accords (e.g., treaties of friendship, navigation and commerce) and multilateral agreements make reference to the ICJ as a last resort for the settlement of disputes.

---

[110] On the connection between IMF financing and commercial bank lending, see B. Tew, *The Evolution of the International Monetary System, 1945–88* 238–44 (4th ed., 1988); M. Garritson de Vries, *The IMF in a Changing World 1945–85* 186–89 (1986); A. Lowenfield, *The International Monetary System* 390ff. (2d ed., 1984).

[111] Schwarzenberger, note 82 above, at 16. Cases in which the Court has addressed issues of foreign investment and property ownership include: Anglo-Iranian Oil Company case, 1952 ICJ 93; USA (Rights of Nationals of) in Morocco case, 1952 ICJ 176; Nottebohm case, 1955 ICJ 4; Interhandel case, 1959 ICJ 6; Barcelona Traction case, 1970 ICJ 4; Elettronica Sicula S.p.A (ELSI) case, 1989 ICJ 15. On the ELSI case, see International Decisions, Elettronica Sicula S.p.A (ELSI), 84 *AJIL* 249 (1990); F. A. Mann, "Foreign Investment in the International Court of Justice: The ELSI Case," 86 *AJIL* 92 (1992).

IV. AUTHORITATIVE INTERPRETATION AND ENFORCEMENT OF INTERNATIONAL ECONOMIC LAW

Given the generality of rules within the Bretton Woods regime, it becomes clear that the effectiveness of the UN-based international economic regime depends on interpretation of these rules and on the mechanisms of enforcement adopted by the specialized agencies that oversee these regimes. In domestic legal systems, interpretation and enforcement are usually combined in one entity, the judicial system; the same court that interprets a legal provision issues a judgment or order enforcing the application of the provision to the litigants. In the Bretton Woods regime, however, the tasks of authoritative interpretation and enforcement are sometimes assigned to separate entities. For reasons of analysis, therefore, the subjects of authoritative interpretation (i.e., the adoption of interpretations that are intended to bind subsequent cases that arise under the regime) and enforcement will be dealt with separately.

A. Authoritative interpretation

Since international economic law is primarily treaty based, the task of authoritative interpretation is occupied almost exclusively with finding the meaning of rules set forth in the multilateral agreements that comprise the Bretton Woods regime and in related agreements. There are several possible fora for such interpretation: *international tribunals*, especially the International Court of Justice; the *specialized agencies* themselves; *national courts*, which are occasionally called upon to adjudicate cases in which the applicable specialized agency has not issued an authoritative interpretation of one of its rules; and *international arbitral panels*.

Before discussing these fora, it should be noted that under accepted principles of international law, the decisions of tribunals – whether the ICJ national tribunals, or international arbitral panels – do not create binding precedent.[112] Nevertheless, Article 38 (1)(d) of the Statute of the International Court of Justice recognizes that judicial decisions of national and international tribunals are subsidiary means of identifying and interpreting rules of international law. International arbitral decisions serve a similar purpose, even though they are not, strictly speaking, judicial decisions. Thus, decisions of the ICJ and of other tribunals often refer to prior judicial and arbitral decisions as persuasive expressions of rules of international law.[113]

---

[112] Statute of the ICJ, art. 59 ("The decision of the Court has no binding force except between the parties and in respect of that particular case."). See generally I. Brownlie, *Principles of Public International Law* 20–25 (3d ed., 1979).

[113] L. Henkin, R. Pugh, O. Schachter, & H. Smit, *International Law: Cases and Materials* 107–11 (1987); Brownlie, note 112 above, at 20.

268

1. Interpretation by international tribunals

The International Court of Justice, highest judicial body within the United Nations, has had very few occasions to address issues of international economic law. This is true even though the ICJ has occasionally been designated in an agreement as the appropriate body for issuing authoritative interpretations. For instance, the relationship agreement granting UN specialized agency status authorizes certain organizations, such as the IMF, to seek advisory opinions of the ICJ; however, no such opinion has ever been sought.[114] Similarly, the Paris Convention for the Protection of Intellectual Property (Article 28), the Berne Convention for the Protection of Literary and Artistic Works (Article 33), the Universal Copyright Convention (Article XV), and the Patent Cooperation Treaty of June 19, 1970 (Article 59) all state that disputes concerning interpretation of the convention may be brought before the ICJ, but the Court has never been asked to render a judgment involving one of these conventions.[115] Nor has any case involving the GATT ever been brought before the ICJ.[116]

There are several possible reasons for the reluctance to refer international economic law questions to the Court. First, economic conflicts are particularly adaptable to compromise solutions through negotiation, and networks for international negotiations over conflicting policies have long existed in the economic field. Some networks are formal, as in the GATT-sponsored rounds of international trade negotiations, and some are informal or *ad hoc*. Second, the specialized agencies themselves have established enforcement mechanisms that, even if not exclusive, are considered more appropriate than the ICJ for enforcing the agencies' regimes. Finally, some states, especially those whose interests are well represented in the Bretton Woods regime, fear that political considerations may spill over into the adjudication of economic issues before the ICJ. For these states, the politicization of the economic regime would be undesirable. They prefer to seek solutions that allow them to bring economic influence to bear on the outcome.

2. Interpretation by specialized agencies

Most specialized agencies are empowered to interpret their constitutional instruments, as well as to interpret quasi-legislative acts and subsequent agreements that arise out of such instruments. The specialized agencies lack separate adjudicatory bodies for this purpose, and the principal decision-making organ of the agency therefore acts as the interpretive organ.

[114] Edwards, note 35 above, at 38 n. 169.
[115] S. Ricketson, *The Berne Convention for the Protection of Literary and Artistic Works* 137, 832 (1987) (stating that there have been no applications to the ICJ for interpretations under the Berne Convention).   [116] Jackson, note 13 above, at 91.

In the case of the World Bank and the IMF, the Articles of Agreement explicitly grant to the Executive Directors (Executive Board of the IMF) the power to interpret their own Articles.[117] Any member may ask that an interpretation by the executive organ be referred to the respective Board of Governors, whose decision is final. Such formal interpretive decisions of the IMF and World Bank are generally considered binding on national courts and on executive organs of member states.[118] At first glance this appears to grant considerable power to the Executive Boards of these agencies. This theory of authoritative interpretive power is not deemed to apply to all decisions of the executive body, however. It applies only to those that are formally designated as binding interpretations under Article IX (World Bank) or Article XXIX (IMF). In fact, only a few of the many Executive Board decisions of the Fund have been characterized by the Board as formal interpretations under Article XXIX.[119] This point has not always been recognized by courts, however, which tend to give authoritative recognition to Executive Board decisions, and even to pronouncements of the Fund's staff, whether or not the full authority of Article XXIX is employed.[120] In the case of the World Bank, the executive directors have given a number of interpretations under Article IX, none of them, however, arising in connection with a dispute; rather, the interpretations have served as operational guidelines.[121]

Formal, authoritative interpretations of the GATT Agreement's provisions are similarly infrequent. The original GATT Agreement did include an annex of agreed interpretations that is still considered authoritative, but these should be seen as original treaty provisions rather than later interpretations. Unlike the IMF and World Bank Agreements, however, the GATT Agreement does not explicitly grant to the GATT governing body, the CONTRACTING PARTIES, the power to issue interpretations that are binding in future cases.[122]

---

[117] IMF Articles of Agreement, art. XXIX; World Bank Articles of Agreement, art. IX. See generally Edwards, note 35 above, at 37ff. Similarly, the Convention Establishing the Multilateral Investment Guarantee Agency (MIGA) provides for exclusive interpretation of the provisions of the MIGA Convention by the Board of Directors, with appeal to MIGA's Council of Governors. MIGA Convention, art. 56.

[118] Edwards, note 35 above, at 37 n. 165, and authorities cited therein.

[119] *Ibid.*, at 38. Decisions of the IMF Executive Board are published in Selected Decisions of the International Monetary Fund and Selected Documents (15th Issue, April 30, 1990). One of the few instances of a formal Article XXIX interpretation involved the Executive Board's decision in June 1949, concerning the interpretation of Article VIII, section 2(b). Unenforceability of Exchange Contracts, Exec. Bd. Dec. No. 446–4, June 10, 1949, reprinted in Selected Decisions, at 318.

[120] See e.g., generally, *Callejo* v. *Bancomer,* 764 F.2d 1101, 1120 (5th Cir. 1985), discussed in J. Gold, *The Fund Agreement in the Courts,* III, 656–58 (1986).

[121] Broches, "The World Bank," in Rendell ed., note 109 above, at 90.

[122] Article XXV does authorize "joint action . . . with a view to facilitating the operation and furthering the objectives" of the GATT Agreement, but it is not clear that such a general statement provides sufficient basis for concluding that CONTRACTING PARTIES can

GATT/WTO panel reports that are issued in individual cases of dispute settlement might be seen as establishing authoritative interpretations, especially if a common pattern of decisions should become evident. Formally speaking, though, GATT/WTO panel reports are only binding on parties to the dispute; one must construct an argument based on the law of treaty interpretation to hold that panel reports may give rise to authoritative interpretations.[123] The Uruguay Round revisions of the procedures just described strengthen the potential of the GATT/WTO in interpretation of GATT rules. One of the Uruguay Round Agreements, a Dispute Settlement Understanding, creates an Appellate Body, composed of recognized experts who will review the interpretation of GATT/WTO agreements that are made by WTO panels.[124]

In the area of intellectual property, the agreements administered by WIPO and by other international agencies tend to be procedural in nature (filing of applications, rights of priority, etc.) and leave the substantive rules of intellectual property rights to domestic law. Consequently, there has been little occasion for international agencies to issue authoritative interpretations of substantive rules of international intellectual property protection. WIPO itself does not serve a role in providing binding interpretations even of the conventions for which it is the administering authority;[125] as previously mentioned, this role is assigned by the conventions to the ICJ.

3. Interpretation by national courts

Lacking authoritative interpretation by the International Court of Justice or by the specialized agencies, it is apparent that whenever a rule of international economic law comes before a domestic court of law, the court will itself be compelled to interpret the rule as best it can, in accordance with the rules of international law.[126] Of course, since it is concerned primarily with intergovernmental economic relations, much of the Bretton Woods regime is beyond the competence of domestic courts. Nevertheless,

issue authoritative interpretations that bind either members or the organization itself. Jackson, note 13 above, at 90–91.

[123] Jackson, note 13 above, at 90, raises the possibility that panel reports may constitute evidence of "practice in the application of the treaty which establishes the agreement of the parties regarding its interpretation." See Vienna Convention on the Law of Treaties, art. XXXI(3), especially where panel reports are adopted by a consensus vote of the CONTRACTING PARTIES. See also W. Davey, "Dispute Settlement in GATT," 11 *Fordham Int'l L. J.* 51, 89 (1987) (no general acceptance that a panel decision constitutes a binding precedent to be followed in future cases); J. Waincymer, "GATT Dispute Settlement: An Agenda for Evaluation and Reform," 14 *NC J. Int'l L. & Com. Reg.* 81 (1989) (panel reports are not strictly binding in subsequent cases, but GATT practice shows a pattern of reliance on approaches taken by earlier panels).   [124] See Dillon, note 13 above, at 385–87.

[125] *Accord,* Ricketson, note 115 above, at 138, 140.

[126] Vienna Convention on the Law of Treaties, arts. 31 & 32.

there are occasions on which a rule of international economic law established by treaty does require application before a national court.[127] The best example of this is Article VIII, section 2(b) of the IMF Agreement.

The experience of Article VIII, section 2(b) reveals the drawbacks of interpretation by national courts. Interpretations by the courts of one state do not create binding precedents beyond their jurisdiction. Consequently, conflicting interpretations in different states are bound to occur.[128] This has been evident in cases involving Article VIII, section 2(b): German courts have taken an expansive interpretation of the scope of application of this provision, while courts in the United States and the United Kingdom have interpreted it narrowly.[129] Despite these conflicts, the IMF Executive Board has not issued an authoritative interpretation that would clarify ambiguities.

Conflicting interpretations by national courts may frustrate the goal of uniformity that international economic law attempts to procure.[130] Nevertheless, lacking authoritative interpretations of international economic law either by international tribunals or by the specialized agencies themselves, there is little remedy for this.

4. Interpretation by international arbitrators

International arbitration, the final forum for interpreting the UN international economic law regime, suffers a defect similar to that which affects interpretation by national courts, since the decisions of international arbitrators are not considered sources of binding interpretations. Despite this fact, arbitral decisions are often cited by courts and by commentators in support of international legal principles.[131] To the extent that an arbitration proceeding is impartial and conducted according to accepted rules, international arbitral decisions may have more persuasive interpretive power than the decisions of national courts.

---

[127] In addition to the example of IMF art. VIII, sec. (2)(b), there exists the possibility under US law for a private citizen to bring a "Section 301 action," to petition the US Trade Representative for redress of an action by a foreign nation that violates a trade agreement to which the United States is a party. Trade Act of 1974, *as amended,* §§ 301–6; 19 U.S.C. §§ 2411–16. If the citizen is not satisfied with the Trade Representative's response, recourse can be made to the federal courts, which might then be called upon to determine if a rule of the GATT, or one of the MTN codes, had been violated.

[128] Edwards, note 35 above, at 479–489; Gold, note 120 above, chs. 17, 23, and 24.

[129] W. Ebke, "Article VIII, Section 2(b), International Monetary Cooperation, and the Courts," 23 *Int'l Law.*, 677, 687ff (1989).

[130] Compare A. Rosett, "Critical Reflections on the United Nations Convention on Contracts for the International Sale of Goods," 45 *Ohio St. L. J.* 265 (1984) (questioning the uniformity to be achieved by the Vienna Convention on Contracts for the International Sale of Goods, since the Convention will be interpreted by national courts).

[131] Brownlie, note 112 above, at 20.

International arbitration has become an increasingly important means of resolving international economic disputes between private parties, or between private parties and states. For this reason, the decisions of arbitrators can be expected to generate persuasive, if not binding, interpretations of international economic law. For example, the opinion of a single arbitrator, René-Jean Dupuy, in the *Texaco Overseas Petroleum Company* v. *Libyan Arab Republic* arbitration, has received considerable attention for its interpretation that customary international law establishes a right of "appropriate" compensation for expropriation of property of foreign investors, as well as for its evaluation of the NIEO resolutions.[132]

The United Nations has long promoted international commercial arbitration as a method of resolving private disputes.[133] In addition, UN agencies have devised specialized arbitration schemes for resolving foreign investment disputes between states and private parties. The best-known example of the latter was the adoption in 1965 of the World Bank-sponsored Convention on the Settlement of Investment Disputes between States and Nationals of Other States (ICSID Convention).[134] In addition to providing a set of rules to govern arbitration of investment disputes, the Convention established the International Centre for the Settlement of Investment Disputes (ICSID). While ICSID does not itself arbitrate, it maintains panels of arbitrators that may be selected by the parties to an investment dispute. From 1966 to 1988, twenty-two disputes were submitted to ICSID for arbitration and two cases for conciliation; almost half of these cases were settled or discontinued.[135] Most of the disputes brought before ICSID to date have involved interpretation of national laws and of particular contract provisions, rather than interpretation of rules of international economic law. Nevertheless, if the United Nations, through the GATT or otherwise, should arrive at an agreed set of rules governing the rights and obligations of foreign investors (including multinational corporations), ICSID would probably become an important forum for interpreting such rules.

Another potential source of interpretation of international economic law

---

132 *Texas Overseas Petroleum Co./California Asiatic Oil Co.* v. *Government of the Libyan Arab Rep.*, reprinted in 17 *ILM* 1, 30 (1978).

133 See, e.g., United Nations Convention on the Recognition and Enforcement of Foreign Arbitral Awards, 21 UST 2517, TIAS No. 6997, 330 UNTS 38; UNCITRAL Model Law on International Commercial Arbitration, UN Doc. A/40/17 (1985), reprinted in 24 *ILM* 1302 (1985).

134 17 UST 1270, TIAS No. 6090, 575 UNTS 159, reprinted in 4 *ILM* 532 (1965). See generally I. Shihata, "The Settlement of Disputes Regarding Foreign Investment: The Role of the World Bank, with Particular Reference to ICSID and MIGA," 1 *Am. U. J. Int'l L. & Pol'y* 97 (1986).

135 3(2) News and Notes from the Institute for Transnational Arbitration (Southwestern Legal Foundation) 4 (April 1988).

might be found in the Iran–United States Claims Tribunal, established in The Hague in 1981 as a product of the Algiers Accords that ended the Iranian hostage crisis. While the Tribunal was not established under the auspices of the United Nations *per se*, its proceedings have been conducted in accordance with UNCITRAL Arbitration Rules.[136] Since the Tribunal deals with important subjects of international economic law, from expropriation to the effects of exchange control, it could be a source of interpretation of international economic law. Nevertheless, the precedential value of Tribunal awards appears to be open to question, due to allegations of politicization of the arbitration proceedings.[137]

V. SPECIALIZED AGENCIES AND THE ADMINISTRATION OF DISCRETE LEGAL REGIMES

In the field under consideration here – international economic law – the subject of administration of discrete regimes represents such a vast subject of inquiry that it is only possible to give a bare outline of the activities of the UN specialized agencies. Indeed, the strength of the specialized agencies lies more in their operational or functional effects than in their generation of binding rules, especially when one considers the criticism of the "soft law" nature of those rules.

For instance, the IMF and the World Bank have profoundly affected international economic relations by their financial operations in member countries. The World Bank, in more than forty years of operations, has granted loans aggregating over $155 billion to member countries for economic development projects.[138] In addition to this financial assistance, the World Bank's sizable staff of experts gives considerable technical assistance to borrowing countries. Through its affiliate organizations, ICSID and MIGA, the Bank carries out activities to promote foreign investment in developing countries.

The financial operations of the IMF are equally important. In 1989–90, the Fund committed SDR 11.3 billion in balance of payments assistance to member countries.[139] Such assistance from the Fund occurs only after extensive consultations with borrowing countries, through which the Fund provides considerable technical assistance to help correct the payments imbalance. The Fund's ongoing surveillance of the exchange arrangements

---

[136] D. Caron, "The Nature of the Iran–United States Claims Tribunal and the Evolving Structure of International Dispute Resolution," 84 *AJIL* 104 (1990).

[137] *Ibid.*, at 105 n. 4.

[138] K. Hudes, "Introduction: Articles of Agreement of the International Bank for Reconstruction and Development," in *Basic Documents of International Economic Law*, I, 421, 422 (S. Zamora & R. Brand eds., 1990).   [139] *IMF Annual Report*, 1990, at 33.

of its members, through regular consultations between Fund staff and government officials of the members, are an important source of technical assistance to members. The IMF carries out extensive informational activities, gathering and publishing financial statistics that are essential to decision-making in public and private sectors.

Compared with the IMF and the World Bank, the WTO is not an important operational agency; it does not have a large secretariat, and it does not conduct extensive operations in contracting states. Even so, if one includes the WTO's role in fostering periodic multilateral trade negotiations (or "rounds") as an operational activity, it is apparent that the WTO successfully administers an operational regime. There have been nine international trade rounds to date, through which the WTO has accomplished major reductions in trade barriers.

not WTO

In addition to promoting the adoption of treaties covering intellectual property rights, WIPO carries out numerous complementary activities, including technical assistance to developing countries. For instance, WIPO's International Patent Documentation Centre in Vienna maintains an extensive computer database of bibliographic information relating to patent documents, and provides access to that data by patent offices, industry, and research and development institutions.

These few examples, which have counterparts in every international economic agency attached to the United Nations, demonstrate the continued vitality of functionalism. The combined operations of these agencies, each working in a specialized field, form an extensive web of activities in numerous regions, and contribute significantly to economic growth and to the reduction of the potential for economic conflict between states.

VI. ENFORCING INTERNATIONAL ECONOMIC REGIMES: DISPUTE RESOLUTION

The institutions of the Bretton Woods system, by enforcing rules of international economic law, have substantially reduced the potential hold that raw economic power has over international relations. This is not to say that economic power is unimportant, or that the Bretton Woods regime is enforced with unbending regularity and efficiency. Economically powerful states still wield considerable influence over the conduct of economic relations and may still dictate the resolution of conflicts in many cases. Nevertheless, in the gradual evolution from economic power to rule orientation, the Bretton Woods regime has represented an important advance. Even though imperfectly enforced, it has had the effect of controlling and channeling the economic power of states to conform with rules that benefit the world economy as a whole.

In contrast with domestic economic regulation, the enforcement of international economic law is characterized by an aversion to the imposition of sanctions following formal judicial proceedings. This is due to the reluctance of states to transfer economic sovereignty to international institutions. Instead, international economic organizations have established enforcement mechanisms that rely on negotiation and other amicable means of settlement. Rarely does one find the enforcement of a rule of international economic law by the imposition of a clear sanction levied by an international organization or tribunal.[140]

There are three basic models for enforcing international economic law: direct enforcement by an international organization; enforcement by states, using dispute-settlement mechanisms devised by the international organization administering the regime; and *ad hoc* procedures, including reliance on national courts for enforcement.

A. Direct enforcement by international economic organizations

Some specialized economic agencies – especially those that carry out financial operations with their member states – take direct responsibility for enforcement of their regimes. The potential "police power" of such an enforcement method is reduced, however, by several approaches common to these agencies. First, they use extensive consultations to achieve consensus, thus avoiding clear conflict with members that oppose the application of a rule. Second, they use a "carrot" rather than a "stick" approach: instead of levying sanctions against members, these agencies can influence a member to act in accordance with rules by withholding benefits from those who do not comply.

The IMF and the World Bank Group follow this model of enforcement. The IMF operates through rules and procedures that minimize the likelihood of formal violations, in the following way:

1. The IMF's Articles of Agreement are sufficiently flexible on matters, such as exchange rates, that the Fund can issue "guidelines" to be monitored flexibly rather than legislating precise obligations. In order to avoid serious confrontations, the Fund maintains continuing consultations with members for the purpose of commenting on members' policies.

2. The balance of payments operations of the Fund, through stand-by arrangements that are not legally enforceable, are a perfect example of

[140] Kohona, note 3 above, at 227; Carreau et al., note 49 above, at 20–22.

the "carrot" approach – if a member does not comply with performance *earning loans* criteria, it simply doesn't receive any more money.

3. Whenever a legally binding decision is made, the Fund makes an effort to insure broad consensus, and to achieve a position acceptable to the affected member.

4. The Articles of Agreement, in numerous instances, give the Fund the authority to grant waivers or to suspend the application of provisions of the Articles. This is particularly evident in regard to the Fund's rules governing governmental restrictions on international payments.[141]

5. The Fund almost never levies sanctions against members. There has been only one instance in which the Fund declared a member ineligible to use the Fund's financial resources, and only one time that the Fund has ordered compulsory withdrawal of a member: both actions involved Czechoslovakia, in 1953 and 1954.[142]

6. Finally, in pragmatic fashion, the Fund has been willing to overlook *consensus* even wholesale departures from its rules when consensus supporting those rules clearly has broken down. Thus the Fund failed to take action after numerous countries refused to abide by the fixed-exchange-rate obligations of Article IV, during the period from 1971 until the Second Amendment revised the rule in 1976.

The World Bank may be characterized more as an operational than a normative organization. The Bank does not administer a formal code of conduct.[143] The enforcement of rules governing its lending practices and the use of loan proceeds are enforced primarily through its operations – by withholding future loans from members that seriously deviate from the economic policies favored by the Bank. The Bank's power, under Article VI, section 2 of its Articles of Agreement, to suspend a member for failing to fulfill its obligations to the Bank has rarely been used.[144] The General Conditions Applicable to Loan and Guarantee Agreements (Article VII, section 7.01) permit the Bank to accelerate the maturity of a loan, or to cancel or suspend disbursements. Acceleration of maturity has never been used, but on some occasions loans have been canceled; suspension of disbursements has been more common as a means of insuring that the borrower is fulfilling the obligations of the loan agreement.[145] Disputes arising out of the Bank's loan agreements are subject to arbitration (General

---

141 Edwards, note 35 above, at 39.   142 *Ibid.*, at 40–41.

143 It could be argued that the Bank's lending practices do have normative effects. The Bank does influence its members to adopt both microeconomic and macroeconomic policies that are favored by the Bank; if they do not, the Bank merely refuses to fund a project.

144 Czechoslovakia (in 1954) is the only Bank member to have suffered suspension of membership and expulsion.   145 Mason & Asher, note 32 above, at 435.

suspension rarely used

Conditions, Article X, section 10.04). It is a mark of the Bank's success in working with borrowers to achieve compliance that no such arbitration has ever taken place.

B. Enforcement by states through dispute-settlement procedures administered by the rule-creating agency

A second method of rule enforcement depends on member states to police the observance of rules by other states, using dispute-settlement mechanisms administered by the agency responsible for creating the rules. The most prominent example of this occurs in the GATT/WTO.

During much of its history, the GATT lacked the formal attributes of international organization status and administered a system of rule enforcement that was imperfect at best. A contracting party could institute a GATT dispute-settlement proceeding by complaining to the GATT that an obligation of the GATT had been violated by a trading partner; or that a benefit secured to it by the GATT had been 'nullified or impaired' under Article XXIII, even if there had been no violation of a GATT obligation. The matter then would be referred to a panel of three to five experts appointed by the GATT. The panel would receive evidence and eventually secure a report. Even if the report were referred to the CONTRACTING PARTIES (the quasi-institutional formulation of the GATT membership as a decision-making body), the GATT had no authority to require a party to remove the offending practice. Instead, the principal remedy consisted of authorizing the wronged party to take self-help retaliatory measures ("compensatory countermeasures") by suspending the application of concessions made to the offending party (e.g., by raising tariffs, imposing quotas, etc.).

From 1947 to 1986, there were 233 disputes submitted to the GATT, of which 73 resulted in panel or working-party reports that were forwarded to the CONTRACTING PARTIES. Most of the reports were "adopted," but in only one case – involving a dispute between the United States and the Netherlands over import restraints on dairy products – did the CONTRACTING PARTIES formally authorize the suspension of concessions in accordance with Article XXIII.[146] In most instances, the panel's report resulted in changes in the offending party's practices, removal of the offending action, or some other type of compensation.

The original GATT dispute-settlement mechanism was the subject of much criticism. Panel reports did not result in closely reasoned legal opinions, but were seen more as expressions of conciliation or compromise.

---

[146] Jackson, note 13 above, at 96–99.

The dispute-settlement procedures, the subject of much criticism,[147] were among the principal subjects of negotiation in the Uruguay Round. The Uruguay Round Final Act included a Dispute Settlement Understanding that was intended to correct numerous deficiencies, including delay, lack of conformity in interpretation, non-compliance, etc. The new understanding attempts to remedy those deficiencies by increasing the scope of coverage of the dispute-settlement process, facilitating establishment of GATT/WTO panels, and establishing an Appellate Body to review panels' decisions. It is too early to tell how successful the new regime will be.[148]

C. Other enforcement mechanisms

If enforcement mechanisms are not provided for by the specialized agency or other organization responsible for administering a regime, then resort must be made to international judicial or arbitral tribunals, or sometimes to enforcement by national courts (in the case of those rules that are self-executing or have otherwise become incorporated into municipal law). International arbitration has been the predominant method by which rules of international economic law have been enforced.

Increasingly, too, states individually and in concert are using economic sanctions to achieve the enforcement of rules and decisions in the political or public law spheres. In the words of one group of experts, "economic power is a prime factor in the assessment of the capacity of a state, a group of states, or an international organization to be effective in the achievement of its objectives and values. Where military force is illegal or inadvisable, economic strength is now the principal source of a state's authority in the international system."[149] Thus, for instance, the actions undertaken by both the United States and the United Nations to the Iraqi invasion of Kuwait in 1990 included comprehensive trade and financial sanctions against Iraq.[150]

[147] See, e.g., *ibid.*, at 97, 109–13; R. Hudec, "GATT Dispute Settlement after the Tokyo Round, An Unfinished Business," 13 *Cornell Int'l L. J.* 145 (1980); J. Jackson, "The Jurisprudence of International Trade: The DISC Case in GATT," 72 *AJIL* 747 (1978).

[148] On GATT/WTO dispute settlement, see Michael Young, "Dispute Resolution in the Uruguay Round: Lawyers Triumph over Diplomats," 29 *Int'l Law.* 389 (1995); David Schwarz, "WTO Dispute Resolution Panels: Failing to Protect against Conflicts of Interest," 10 *Am. U. J. Int'l L. & Pol'y* 955 (1995); and articles cited in note 13 above.

[149] J. Sweeney, C. Oliver, & N. Leech, *Cases and Materials on the International Legal System* 1132 (3d ed., 1988).

[150] The US and UN boycotts are discussed in B. Carter & P. Trimble, *International Law* 1305–21 (1991), and C. Joyner, "Sanctions, Compliance and International Law: Reflections on the United Nations' Experience against Iraq," 32 *Va. J. Int'l L.* 1 (1991). On economic sanctions generally, see M. Malloy, *Economic Sanctions and US Trade* ch. 10 (1990); G. Hufbauer, J. Schott, & K. Elliott, *Economic Sanctions Reconsidered: History and Current Policy* (2d. ed., 1990); B. Carter, *International Economic Sanctions: Improving the Haphazard US Legal Regime* (1988).

International economic law has not addressed this increasingly import-ant subject in a systematic way, although some of the specialized agencies do address the subject both in practice and in their charters.[151] If economic sanctions (whether unilateral or multilateral) should become more preva-lent, the international community may wish to consider the adoption of general rules to limit the abuses and disruptions that are certain to accompany such measures.

we need rules guarding sanction-use

VII. INTERNATIONAL ECONOMIC REGULATION AND THE UNITED NATIONS – AN EVALUATION

The United Nations and its related agencies have sought to improve international economic relations by developing legal and quasi-legal processes to help resolve conflicts and promote world economic growth. The institutions that have been created for this purpose, and the regimes that they administer, must constantly adapt to an economic system that is constantly changing and hopelessly complex. Given the double challenge of change and complexity, it is no wonder that the achievements of the United Nations system are regarded as imperfect by some, and denigrated by others.

A third factor – international economic interdependence – further complicates the desire to create functional economic regimes. The term "interdependence" is often used to describe the linking up of economic sectors in different national economies, thus creating conditions under which economic forces that originate in one country may have reper-cussions far beyond that country's borders. Interdependence thus increases the stakes of UN involvement, since international economic forces, and the UN's attempts to deal with them, reach ever more deeply into domestic economies.

The accomplishments of the United Nations system in generating and administering international economic law must be measured against these imposing obstacles: constant change, increasing complexity, and heightened interdependence.

A. Accomplishments of the United Nations system in establishing an international economic legal order

To appreciate the importance of United Nations agencies in the world economy, one might follow a simple exercise. Consider, for a moment, a

[151] See, e.g., GATT art. XXI (Security Exceptions), discussed in Jackson, note 13 above, at 203–6.

280

world monetary system without the International Monetary Fund; the global trading system without the GATT; the financing of economic development in developing countries without the World Bank or any of its related agencies, or the regional development banks that have sprung up. *better than nothing* Imagine how effective the developing countries would be in influencing international economic measures without having the forum of UNCTAD available to them. Think of how well intellectual property rights would be protected without WIPO and UNESCO. Consider as well how the world would operate without other economically oriented agencies such as UNCITRAL, IMO, ICAO, or FAO.

Lacking the global institutions of the United Nations, international economic relations would be conducted largely through bilateral agreements and regional groupings. Not only would the operational activities of the UN agencies be missed, but also the rudimentary regulatory backstop that these agencies provide for the international economic system. Without this backstop, corporations and individuals would face a more complex array of *ad hoc* and particularized regulations. Since international law has not generated a large body of customary rules of economic law, it is likely that overarching rules now taken for granted – principles of fair treatment in international trade, international monetary affairs, protection of property rights, etc. – would be sorely lacking.

Even with its imperfections, the UN-sponsored Bretton Woods system represents an important beginning in multilateral cooperation for the furtherance of international economic relations. Since the early 1970s, however, the Bretton Woods system has been undergoing an extended mid-life crisis. The original rules of the IMF, the GATT, and other agencies have been undergoing reexamination. In concluding, it is appropriate to consider some of the important problems that the United Nations must face as it adjusts the international economic regime to new conditions, as well as the prospects for their solution.

B. The international economic regime – problems and prospects

In developing international economic regimes well suited to world economic conditions, the United Nations and its agencies confront a number of imposing challenges.

1. The challenge of global markets

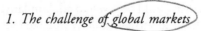

Technological advances in transportation and communications have changed the ways in which goods and services are produced and sold throughout much of the world. Most manufactured goods are made from combinations of raw materials and manufactured components that are produced in many different countries. On the demand side, governments, companies, and individuals have a truly global market from which to purchase goods and services, from which to borrow money, or in which to place their investments.

Despite the increasing globalization of markets, the United Nations continues to depend on national systems of regulation to confront economic problems. These national systems are supposed to conform to economic regimes that bind governments; many deviations exist, however, not to mention gaps in regulation and enforcement both at the national and international levels.

It is questionable whether effective economic regulation of global markets can take place if such regulation is not itself global, but must instead rely entirely on national regulators. To take one example, protection of intellectual property rights depends on national enforcement of domestic laws, but there is great unevenness in the vehemence of enforcement from country to country, as well as in the substantive rights conferred on property owners. Manufacturers of goods and services have good cause to complain when they assert that the protection of their rights in global markets is haphazard.

Another example of discrepancy between global markets and national regulation exists in international securities trading, an area in which there is a growing amount of national regulation but as yet very little international coordination, let alone regulation. Global trading mechanisms, using computer and telecommunication links, are opening the way for nonstop trading in financial instruments throughout the world. National regulators are trying to develop rules to govern this activity, but the international community – including the United Nations – has not begun to address the increasingly apparent need for international regulation.

2. The liberal economic regime versus managed trade: "Balkanization" of the Bretton Woods regime

In the halcyon days of Bretton Woods, proponents of multilateralism envisaged a liberal regime of free trade and free payments, a regime that would be applicable to all countries. The bedrock of this regime was the most-favored-nation principle of Article I of the GATT: concessions given to one trading partner would be given to all. Similarly, the rule of the IMF would be applied to all countries similarly situated (with a certain flexibility built in, however).

The GATT regime, as well as that for the IMF and other institutions, has since succumbed to a fracturing of the "single, liberal rule for all" concept.

Even after the creation of the WTO, the GATT/WTO regime continues to comprise a complex web of side agreements and exceptions that belie the "one rule for all" principle. We can expect increasing conflicts to arise over the uncertainties generated by overlapping regimes for regional and multilateral trade.

More worrisome, however, is the tendency of major trading countries simply to construct *ad hoc*, specialized arrangements to deal with difficult economic problems, without reference to the formal rules of the game. This occurs, for instance, in the voluntary restraint agreements (VRAs) that limit exports to important importing countries and in arrangements made among the Group of Seven countries to manage international monetary affairs outside the formal IMF arrangement.

The tendency of the Bretton Woods regime to become "Balkanized," and the propensity for *ad hoc*, bilateral solutions to international economic problems – rather than the application of an agreed set of multilateral rules – represent serious threats to the construction of a viable regime of international economic law administered by the United Nations and its agencies. Proponents of multilateralism must work harder to devise workable regimes that respond to differences in economic conditions of countries, while still maintaining a single set of rules for all nations.

3. Regionalism versus a global regime

One variant of managed trade exists in the increasing trend toward the establishment of regional trading blocs – customs unions and free trade areas. These arrangements, permissible exceptions to the GATT most-favored-nation principle, allow countries to grant trading preferences to certain trading partners and not others. Most of these arrangements are regional in nature (the European Communities, the European Free Trade Area, the North American Free Trade Agreement), and can thus be viewed as necessary steps toward regional harmony. Other free trade arrangements (e.g., the US–Israel Free Trade Agreement and the Lome Conventions between the European Union countries and their former colonies) have scant regional connection.

Regional economic integration is probably desirable. The United Nations has long promoted such movements; for example, the Economic Commission for Latin America and the Caribbean has supported free trade and investment agreements among Latin American countries. Nevertheless, as such agreements proliferate, they may undermine the effectiveness and the vitality of the multilateral trading regime of the GATT. The Bretton Woods system has not yet developed an adequate response to the centripetal forces represented in free trade agreements and customs unions.

4. Developing-country criticisms

The harshest criticism of the Bretton Woods system may well come, justifiably, from developing countries. In many parts of the world – especially in sub-Saharan Africa – the economic lives of people have not been improved after decades of UN-sponsored development activities. Poverty remains endemic to much of the third world. After a decade of external debt crises, many developing countries face worse economic conditions today than they did in the early 1980s.

The liberal economic regimes devised in the aftermath of Bretton Woods appear to work well for countries that are economically and politically powerful enough to play by these rules. Many developing countries do not fare so well, however – even with changes in the rules to permit some preferential treatment for them.

It may be that the international system should not be expected to bestow economic growth and stability on developing nations from the outside. In a system of nation-states, the responsibility for achieving these goals must lie with national governments themselves. Nevertheless, the United Nations must work harder to help provide the necessary external conditions that will foster internal growth and stability, through the adoption of beneficial international arrangements. The United Nations must also work with creditor countries to provide more effective financial assistance for developing countries.

5. Overlapping jurisdiction of international economic agencies: lack of coordination

One premise of the Bretton Woods system was assignment of specific areas of economic problem solving to separate agencies with narrow, well-defined jurisdictions over subject matters. It has become increasingly apparent that international economic problems do not fall into such neat categories. Issues surrounding international trade in goods spill over into international monetary affairs; protection of intellectual property rights affects international trade in goods; development assistance influences the capacity for international trade, and so on.

The interdependence of economic problems complicates the task of UN agencies that possess limited jurisdiction over discrete subject matters. Certain agencies have responded by enlarging their jurisdictions. Thus, the GATT/WTO has begun to concern itself with international trade in services, with protection of intellectual property, and even with environmental issues. Similarly, the World Bank has abandoned its earlier reluctance to grant loans for structural adjustment purposes, a lending

abundance of overlapping & lack of cooperation

activity formerly deemed the sole responsibility of the IMF. These are individual institutional efforts, however. As yet, cooperative approaches among UN agencies toward economic problem solving are still the exception. Jurisdictional conflicts sometimes arise, and no agency, UN or otherwise, has assumed an overall responsibility for coordinating individual agencies' approaches to economic problems.

There have been some tentative steps by UN agencies to establish cooperative efforts across jurisdictional lines. For instance, the World Bank, the United Nations Development Programme (UNDP), and the United Nations Environment Programme (UNEP) are on the verge of concluding an interagency agreement that will administer a global environment financing facility (the Global Environment Facility, or GEF). The GEF will establish

a pilot program under which grants or concessional loans will be provided to developing countries to help them implement programs that protect the global environment . . . Since no single international agency commands all the skills and experience needed to carry out these functions, participants have agreed that the program of activities to be financed under the GEF should be implemented through a tripartite arrangement by the UNEP, UNDP and the World Bank.[152]

There are also problems associated with interagency coordination. UN agencies, like any association of individuals, have a tendency to guard their boundaries against loss of jurisdictional authority, and may be threatened by cooperative efforts that tend to break down boundaries. Furthermore, governments that comprise the membership of UN agencies may not be willing to accede to the accumulation of supranational economic power that an alliance of UN agencies might wield.

Finally, the muddying of jurisdictional waters goes against the notion of functionalism[153] that was important to the design of the Bretton Woods system. Perhaps it is time to adapt the functionalism of Bretton Woods into a more cooperative model, by maintaining the jurisdictional boundaries *Prescriptive* necessary to preserve and strengthen the specific expertise of each agency, while pushing the agencies towards more cooperative and coordinated solutions to international economic problems.

SELECTED BIBLIOGRAPHY

Basic Documents of International Economic Law (S. Zamora & R. Brand eds.; CCH International, 1990)

[152] The World Bank, Establishment of the Global Environment Facility 1, 4 (unpublished manuscript, Apr. 11, 1991).   [153] See text accompanying notes 4–5 above, pp. 234–35.

Carreau, D., P. Juillard, & T. Flory, *Droit International Economique* (Librairie générale de droit et de jurisprudence, 1978)

Dam, K., *The Rules of the Game: Reform and Evolution in the International Monetary System* (University of Chicago Press, 1982)

Dell, S., *The United Nations and International Business* (Duke, 1990)

Edwards, R., *International Monetary Collaboration* (Transnational, 1985)

Gold, J., *Exchange Rates in International Law and Organization* (American Bar Association, 1988)

Legal Effects of Fluctuating Exchange Rates (IMF, 1990)

Hudec, R., *The Developing Countries in the GATT Legal System* (Gower, 1987)

Jackson, J., *The World Trading System* (MIT, 1989)

Kohona, P., *The Regulation of International Economic Relations through Law* (Martinus Nijhoff, 1985)

Ricketson, S., *The Berne Convention for the Protection of Literary and Artistic Works* (Kluwer, 1987)

Schachter, O., *Sharing the World's Resources* (Columbia University Press, 1977)

Tew, B., *The Evolution of the International Monetary System* (4th ed., Hutchinson Education, 1988)

Van Meerhaeghe, M. *International Economic Institutions* (Kluwer, 1992)

VerLoren Van Themaat, P., *The Changing Structure of International Economic Law* (Martinus Nijhoff, 1981)

CHAPTER TEN

ENVIRONMENT

Ved P. Nanda

I. INTRODUCTION

The United Nations Conference on Environment and Development (UNCED), held in Rio de Janeiro June 3–14, 1992, was a milestone as it brought together more than a hundred heads of state and representatives from 175 countries – the largest ever such gathering – to address the interlocking global economic and environmental challenges.[1] A culmination of two years of negotiations,[2] UNCED marked the twentieth anniversary of the first major United Nations effort to discuss environmental issues, the Stockholm Conference on the Human Environment.[3]

During this short span of twenty years, from 1972 to 1992, international environmental issues have reached the forefront of the global political agenda. International action, spurred by mounting concern over the fragility of the global environment and the increasing environmental damage occurring both within national boundaries and transcending those boundaries, has included negotiations on a large number of international

---

[1] See Brazilian President Proud of UNCED, 15 *Int'l Envt. Rep.* (*BNA*), Curr. Rep. 395 (June 17, 1992).

[2] The UNCED Preparatory Committee (Prep Comm) began work on the agenda and negotiating procedures in Nairobi in August 1990. A later meeting in Geneva in March 1991 reviewed reports and laid more groundwork. Negotiations actually began in Geneva in August 1991. The final negotiating session lasted five weeks, ending in New York on April 4, 1992. For an overview of the process leading up to UNCED, see "Highlights: Overview of the UNCED Process," *Greenwire*, June 1, 1992. For the work of the Prep Comm in elaborating principles of international environmental law, see A. Adede, International Environmental Law from Stockholm 1972 to Rio de Janeiro 1992: An Overview of Past Lessons and Future Challenges paras. 40–72 (Background Paper presented at the inaugural seminar on international environmental law, at the Moi University, Eldoret, Kenya, Jan. 31, 1992); P. Sand, International Law on the Agenda of the United Nations Conference on Environment and Development (unpublished manuscript, Aug. 2, 1991).

[3] See Report of the United Nations Conference on the Human Environment, UN Doc. A/CONF. 48/14 and Corr. 1 (1972) (hereinafter Stockholm Report).

environmental conventions with binding legal obligations for states parties, many of which are now in force.[4] Equally important is the development of general guidelines and principles (soft law) embodied in nonlegally binding instruments. In addition, international organizations, publicists' writings, and judicial and arbitral decisions have contributed to the emergence of general legal principles.[5]

These activities have resulted in the development of a growing body of national and international environmental laws which are designed to protect the environment. Although impressive in its reach, international environmental law, which is the focus of this chapter, has developed in a piecemeal fashion and still remains imperfect. The work highlighted here is primarily that of the United Nations Environment Programme (UNEP), the leading UN organ established to address environmental challenges. The work of other UN agencies active in the environmental field will also be referenced, where appropriate.

Preceding the discussion of such contributions, a brief discussion of the historical context is provided which outlines the law-making activities in the pre-Stockholm period, and the events that led to the Stockholm Conference and the establishment of UNEP. This is followed by a discussion of the activities of UNEP during the first ten years of its existence, as well as UNEP's current activities and plans. These discussions provide the context for an appraisal of international environmental law-making at the UN, especially by UNEP. The next section outlines the UNCED and its accomplishments. The concluding section appraises emerging trends and offers recommendations for the future.

II. LAW-MAKING IN THE PRE-STOCKHOLM PERIOD, EVENTS LEADING TO THE STOCKHOLM CONFERENCE, AND THE ESTABLISHMENT OF UNEP

In the history of international environmental law, the 1972 UN Conference on the Human Environment is a watershed for the emergence of concerted international activity. Prior to that conference, international efforts toward management of environment issues were sporadic and ineffectual.

Although serious concern for the global environment is of relatively recent origin, humankind's concern for the environment is reflected in very

---

[4] See note 55 below.
[5] See generally O. Schachter, "The Emergence of International Environmental Law," 44 *J. Int'l Aff.* 457 (1991) (hereinafter Schachter).

early history.[6] In modern times, it has been generally recognized that environmental degradation respects no political boundaries. However, given the horizontal structure of the world community, the concept of "global management" has developed painfully slowly, notwithstanding the clear need for international cooperation.

Of the modern efforts to codify this concern, the earliest of note was the 1909 Boundary Waters Treaty[7] between the United States and Great Britain, on Canada's behalf. Other pre-World War II treaties comprised an array of international conservation treaties on birds and migratory wildlife,[8] as well as the unsuccessful League of Nations' efforts during the 1920s and 1930s.[9] Similarly, a limited number of judicial and arbitral decisions also characterize this period.[10] Of these, the 1935 Trail Smelter Arbitration[11] is noteworthy for strengthening and solidifying the principle of state responsibility for transnational environmental damage:

Under the principles of international law, as well as of the law of the United States, no State has the right to use or permit the use of its territory in such a manner as to cause injury by fumes in or to the territory of another or the properties or persons therein, when the case is of serious consequence and the injury is established by clear and convincing evidence.[12]

After World War II, the International Court of Justice strongly reaffirmed this *sic utere* principle, i.e., states' obligations not to cause damage to neighboring territories, in the 1949 Corfu Channel case.[13] This principle subsequently found expression in a number of diplomatic cases addressing international environmental issues. The principle was also reiterated in the 1973 decision of the ICJ in the Nuclear Tests case (France's responsibility for nuclear testing in the South Pacific).[14]

---

[6] For example, as early as 1273, a statute against air pollution was enacted in England. This was followed by a 1307 Royal Proclamation banning the use of coal in village furnaces. See UNEP, Environmental Law: An In-Depth Review 5 (*UNEP Rep. No. 2*, 1981) (hereinafter *UNEP Rep. No. 2*).

[7] Treaty with Great Britain Relating to Boundary Waters between the United States and Canada, Jan. 11, 1909, 36 Stat. 1448, T.S. No. 548. See generally V. Nanda, "The Establishment of International Standards for Transnational Environmental Injury," 60 *Iowa L. Rev.* 1089, 1106–8 (1979), and the authorities cited there for a discussion of the United States–Canada experience regarding the utilization of the Treaty and of the regulatory machinery created under the Treaty for environmental purposes.

[8] *UNEP Rep. No. 2*, note 6 above, at 5.

[9] See *ibid.* For a listing of conventions, see *Register of International Conventions and Other Agreements in the Field of the Environment*, UNEP/GC.15/Inf. 2 (1989) (hereinafter *UNEP Register*).   [10] See, e.g., *UNEP Rep. No. 2*, note 6 above, at 5.

[11] See 3 *R. Int'l Arb. Awards* 1911 (1938).   [12] *Ibid.*, at 1965 (1941).

[13] The Corfu Channel case (*Alb.* v. *UK*), 1949 ICJ 4 (Apr. 9, 1949).

[14] See 1973 ICJ 99, 135 (June 22, 1973); 1974 ICJ 252, 257 (Dec. 20, 1974). Note, however, that the Court declared the question moot without reaching a decision on the merits, since France had halted nuclear tests.

By the late 1960s, concern with accelerated environmental decay catalyzed a proliferation of bilateral, regional, and multilateral conventions on many diverse issues.[15] Despite these advances, it was clear by the early 1970s that environmental efforts were scattered, overlapping, and inadequate to meet the global environmental challenge.

In 1972 the Club of Rome published its controversial study, *The Limits to Growth*,[16] which painted a bleak picture of humankind's future as a consequence of resource and environmental degradation. The following year, the United Nations responded to the need for coordination by convening the UN Conference on the Human Environment in Stockholm.[17] It adopted the Stockholm Declaration, which represented the first time that the world community had collectively agreed upon the nature and scope of the environmental challenges facing humankind, and produced an Action Plan containing 109 recommendations for environmental management, as well as establishing the United Nations Environment Programme (UNEP).

In the post-Stockholm period, mounting concern with the environment led to increasing awareness of, and attention to, environmental issues. At the national level, within a decade after the Stockholm Conference, over eighty nations had established environmental agencies, compared with only a few in 1972.[18] Moreover, many developing states increasingly began to accept the linkage between development and environmental protection.[19] The UNEP Governing Council's Session of a Special Character in May 1982[20] illustrated this development.

---

[15] See *UNEP Rep. No. 2*, note 6 above, at 5. For a listing of conventions, see *UNEP Register*, note 9 above. See also *Developments in the Field of Natural Resources – Water, Energy and Minerals – Technical Aspects of International River Basin Development*, UN Doc. E/C. 7/35, at 13 (1972); T. Mensah, "International Environmental Law: International Conventions Concerning Oil Pollution at Sea," 8 *Case W. Res. J. Int'l L.* 110 (1976).

[16] D. Meadows et al., *The Limits to Growth* (Report to the Club of Rome, 1972).

[17] See generally *Stockholm Report*, note 3 above.

[18] See, e.g., Donahue, "Earthwatch," 46 *America* 453 (1982).

[19] See, e.g., then Prime Minister of India Indira Gandhi's comment at the 1981 UN Conference on New and Renewable Sources of Energy: "We do not attach priority to the environment. We have to make our people more alive to the fact that conservation is not something extra, but is essential in the counting of costs – social costs and even basic economic costs." "Interview: Mrs. Gandhi," 6 *UNITERRA*, No. 5, at 5 (1981).

In contrast, at the Stockholm Conference, while advocating the position of developing states, she had said:

The rich countries may look upon development as the cause of environmental destruction, but to us it is one of the primary means of improving the environment of living . . . How can we speak to those who live in villages and in slums about keeping the oceans, rivers and air clean when their own lives are contaminated at the source?

Quoted in *NY Times*, June 15, 1972, at 12, col. 3.

[20] See Report of the Governing Council at Its Session of a Special Character, UN Doc. UNEP/GC (SSC) 4 (June 28, 1982).

At the international level, UN specialized agencies and UN organs began to include, as far as relevant, environmental considerations in their policies and programs.

It was not, however, until the occurrence of the environmental disasters in Bhopal, Chernobyl, and Basel in the mid-1980s,[21] and the 1987 discovery of the ozone hole over the Antarctic,[22] that the world community was literally brought face to face with global environmental challenges. Mostafa K. Tolba, Executive Director of UNEP, identified 1988 as the year when the environment became "a top item on the world's political agenda."[23]

Two important documents on the global environment appeared in 1987, both of which contributed toward enhancing environmental awareness. The first, *Environmental Perspective to the Year 2000 and Beyond,* cautioned that "despite noteworthy developments . . . environmental degradation has continued unabated, threatening human well-being and, in some instances, the very survival of life on our planet."[24] The second was the seminal report of the World Commission on Environment and Development (WCED), entitled *Our Common Future.*[25] In its report, the WCED, based upon three years of hearings and study, outlined a series of imperatives that were necessary for the world community to be able to achieve environmental protection and sustainable development. The UNEP Governing Council accepted the WCED's report "as a guideline for the future work of UNEP."[26]

In December 1988, the UN General Assembly resolved that a UN Conference on Environment and Development be convened in 1992.[27] Maurice Strong, Secretary-General of the Conference, proposed that the Conference agree on an "Earth Charter," a set of principles for the conduct of peoples and nations toward each other and the earth, and a prioritized agenda to implement it, to be known as "Agenda 21."[28] The Conference, popularly known as the Earth Summit, has linked issues of environment

---

[21] See generally V. Nanda & B. Bailey, "Export of Hazardous Waste and Hazardous Technology: Challenge for International Environmental Law," 17 *Denv. J. Int'l L. & Pol'y* 155 (1988).

[22] See R. Watson et al., *Present State of Knowledge of the Upper Atmosphere 1988: An Assessment Report* 18 (NASA Ref. Pub. 1208, Aug. 1988).

[23] See UNEP, 1988 Annual Report of the Executive Director, at 1, UN Doc. UNEP/GC. 15/4 (1989) (hereinafter 1988 Annual Report).

[24] UN GAOR, 42d Sess., Supp. No. 25, Annex II, para. 1, UN Doc. A/42/25 (1987).

[25] World Commission on Environment and Development, *Our Common Future* (OUP ed., 1987) (hereinafter *Our Common Future*).

[26] Per decision 1/14, see UN Doc. UNEP/GC. 14/26, Annex 1, at 39 (1987).

[27] See GA Res. 196 (Dec. 20, 1988), UN GAOR, 43d Sess., UN Doc. a/43/915/Add. 7 (1988); GA Res. 53, UN GAOR, 43d Sess., UN Doc. A/43/905 (1988).

[28] See "Foundation Laid for 1992 Conference on Environment and Development," 27 *UN Chronicle*, No. 4, at 63 (Dec. 1990).

and development by placing sustainable development at the center of international decision-making worldwide.

As a consequence of these events and reports, a clearer recognition has emerged that, in order adequately to address environmental threats such as depletion of the ozone layer,[29] global warming,[30] biodiversity, deforestation, and desertification, concerted global efforts are needed; unilateral, bilateral, even regional efforts would not suffice. This realization has reinforced an enhanced role for international organizations, especially UNEP, to undertake more fully the task of addressing and managing international environmental problems and threats.

III. UNEP ACTIVITIES AND PLANS

At its establishment, UNEP was envisioned as a vehicle for coordinating the goals of global environmental assessment and environmental management.[31] The Action Plan adopted at Stockholm outlined a three-part functional framework consisting of environmental assessment, environmental management, and supporting measures.[32] As the body responsible for supervising the Action Plan, UNEP assumed responsibility for all these activities.

A. Environmental assessment

To highlight the global perspective that was emphasized at Stockholm, in 1977 UNEP established an environmental assessment arm, Earthwatch, whose program included evaluation and review, research, monitoring, and information exchange.[33]

The major components of Earthwatch during the first decade of UNEP included: (a) the Global Environmental Monitoring System (GEMS);[34]

---

[29] See generally V. Nanda, "Stratosphere Ozone Depletion: A Challenge for International Law and Policy," 10 *Mich. J. Int'l L.* 482 (1989).

[30] See V. Nanda, "Global Warming and International Environmental Law: A Preliminary Inquiry," 30 *Harv. Int'l L. J.* 375 (1989).

[31] See GA Res. 2997, UN GAOR, 27th Sess., Supp. No. 30, at 43, UN Doc. A/8730 (1972).

[32] See Stockholm Report, note 3 above, at 59.

[33] UNEP, *The Environment Programme: Medium-Term Plan 1982–1983*, UNEP/GC.9/ 6, at 11 (Mar. 1981) (hereinafter *1982–83 Plan*). In the following discussion in this section, I have relied on my earlier work, V. Nanda & P. Moore, "Global Management of the Environment: Regional and Multilateral Initiatives," in *World Climate Change* 93, 98–103 (V. Nanda ed., 1983).

[34] GEMS encourages and coordinates the acquisition, analysis, storage, and dissemination of environmental data by governments and international organizations. See UNEP, *Report of the Governing Council of the United Nations Environment Programme on the Work of Its Ninth Session, Nairobi, 13–26 May 1981*, UNEP/GC. 9/15 (5 June 1981), at 48–49; *Environment*

(b) the International Referral System for Sources of Environmental Information (INFOTERRA);[35] and (c) the International Register of Potentially Toxic Chemicals (IRPTC).[36]

B. Environmental management

1. Overview

During its first decade, UNEP's activities related to environmental management included the development of frameworks for the preparation of environmental impact assessments and for the application of cost-benefit analysis to environmental protection measures.[37]

2. Environmental law

UNEP was given the primary responsibility for implementing the principles incorporated in the Stockholm Declaration of the Human Environment, including the obligation to formulate environmental law rules. In the decade following the Stockholm Conference, UNEP's activities in this area included establishment of a working group of experts to prepare draft principles for the guidance of states in the conservation and harmonious exploitation of natural resources which they share in common.[38] A set of draft principles was presented by the experts group in 1978, principles which the General Assembly requested all states to use as guidelines in the formulation of bilateral or multilateral conventions regarding natural resources shared by two or more states.[39]

Subsequently, a team of experts in environmental law which met in the latter part of 1981 concluded that UNEP should give priority to three areas in developing guidelines, principles, or agreements: marine pollution from land-based sources; protection of the stratospheric ozone layer; and transport, handling, and disposal of toxic and dangerous wastes.[40]

The experts also recommended that periodic review of environmental law be undertaken by UNEP,[41] and that in the process of the "codification, progressive development, and implementation of environmental law,"

Programme: *Programme Performance Report – Report of the Executive Director*, UNEP/GC. 9/5 (Feb. 25, 1981), at 812 (hereinafter *Performance Report*).
[35] INFOTERRA provides a referral network for the exchange of available environmental information.   [36] See 1982–83 Plan, note 33 above, at 11–54.
[37] See UNEP, *Environmental Management – An Overview* 12–16 (*UNEP Rep. No. 3*, 1981).
[38] See *UNEP Rep. No. 2*, note 6 above, at 28; see also GA Res. 3129, UN GAOR, 28th Sess., Supp. No. 30, at 49, UN Doc. A/9030 (1973).
[39] See *UNEP Rep. No. 2*, note 6 above, at 28.
[40] See UNEP, *Programme Performance Report – Addendum*, UNEP/GC. 10/5 Add. 2 (Dec. 7, 1981), at 2.   [41] See *ibid.*, at 4.

special attention be given to the developing countries' need for technical cooperation and other assistance in the field of "institution building, education, training and information regarding environmental law."[42] UNEP adopted specific goals and strategies to address this issue in a four-pronged approach: (a) the promotion of national environmental law; (b) the stimulation of environmental law education and research; (c) promotion of wider acceptance and implementation of international environmental agreements; and (d) technical cooperation among developing countries to develop environmental legislation.

C. Supporting measures

These measures included environmental education and training; communication of environmental information to decision-makers and to the public at large; and technical assistance.[43]

D. Current UNEP activities and plans

The United Nations System-Wide Medium-Term Environment Programme – 1990–1995 (1990–1995 Program),[44] which UNEP unveiled in 1988, comprises all the environment-related activities of the United Nations system planned for that period. The Program acknowledges the close relationship between environmental issues and developmental policies and practices and the need to undertake anticipatory and preventive policies.[45]

1. Substantive environmental issues

The Program identifies a comprehensive set of twenty-six substantive environmental issues which the world community currently faces.[46] These are divided into ten major headings: atmosphere; water; terrestrial ecosystems; coastal and inland systems; oceans; lithosphere; human settlements and the environment; human health and welfare; energy, industry, and transportation; and peace, security, and the environment. On each issue, specific problems are noted, and general and specific objectives are identified. Also, a system-wide strategy to address the problems is prescribed and, to implement the strategy, the activities of the UN system through UNEP, in coordination with other UN bodies, are detailed.

The Program recognizes that maintenance and protection of habitat, as well as control of land utilization, are essential for the preservation of biological diversity.

---

[42] *Ibid.*   [43] See *Performance Report*, note 34 above, at 68.
[44] UNEP/GCSS. 1/7/Add. 1 (Nairobi, 1988) (hereinafter *UNEP 1990–95 Program*).
[45] See *ibid.*, at 3, para. 5.   [46] See *ibid.*, at 17–82, paras. 45–326.

UNEP's efforts have included provisions for the secretariat of the Convention on International Trade in Endangered Species of Wild Fauna and Flora (CITES).[47] Another recent UNEP effort assisted in increased geographical protection for wildlife under the Convention on the Conservation of Migratory Species of Wild Animals (CMS).[48]

2. Environmental assessment

The general objective under which the entire UN scientific and technical information system is currently operating is "to accumulate and improve reliable and comparable scientific and technical information about environmental issues and to develop and apply means of collecting, storing, retrieving and processing such information that will make it readily available to decision makers and specialists."[49]

A second set of objectives arising from the recommendations of the WCED report[50] focuses on the relationship between environment and development. Within this context, the general objective of the UN monitoring and environmental data systems is "to promote comprehensive assessments of environmental issues on the basis of socio-economic data and data on the major components and processes of the global and regional environments, [and] to monitor, in an appropriate way, the transition toward sustainable development."[51]

3. Environmental management

Environmental management activities of UNEP now comprise the following areas: oceans and coastal areas, including the global marine environment and the regional seas program; water resources; terrestrial ecosystems, including renewable resources; desertification control; environmental health, including agricultural chemicals; peace, security, and the environment; and technology and environment, including energy, industry, and transportation, human settlements and natural disasters.[52]

4. Supporting measures

In 1988, UNEP published the International Strategy for Action in the Field of Environmental Education and Training for the 1990s.[53] Under

---

[47] Per art. 12, para. 2, 27 UST 1087, TIAS No. 8249, reprinted in 12 *ILM* 1085 (1973) (*entered into force* July 12, 1975). On the role of CITES in saving the elephant, see M. Glennon, "Has International Law Failed the Elephant?," 84 *AJIL* 1 (1990).

[48] Reprinted in 14 *ILM* 15 (1980) (*entered into force* Nov. 1, 1983).

[49] *UNEP 1990–95 Program*, note 44 above, at 84.

[50] See *Our Common Future*, note 25 above and accompanying text, p. 291.

[51] *UNEP 1990–95 Program*, note 44 above, at 87.

[52] See 1988 Annual Report, note 23 above, at 39–58. [53] See *ibid.*, at 49.

this strategy, there are nine major areas of action: access to environmental information; research and experimentation; development of programs and teaching materials; training of personnel; incorporation of an environmental dimension into technical and vocational education; its incorporation into general university education; educating and informing the public; provision of specialist environmental training; and development of international and regional cooperation.[54]

IV. INTERNATIONAL ENVIRONMENTAL LAWMAKING AT THE UNITED NATIONS

A. Overview

The United Nations system, comprising an array of specialized agencies in addition to the UN organs, is actively engaged in the development of international environmental law. At the inception of UNEP, several of these agencies already were engaged in activities with substantial environmental dimensions, and they continue to perform their environmental functions, often in conjunction with UNEP. These include the Food and Agriculture Organization of the United Nations (FAO), the International Maritime Organization (IMO), UNESCO, the World Health Organization (WHO), the World Meteorological Organization (WMO), the International Atomic Energy Agency (IAEA), and the World Bank, among others. A discussion of their specific contributions is beyond the scope of this chapter and, therefore, little more will be said here concerning their involvement in environmental law-making.

This section highlights two conventions adopted under UNEP's auspices.[55] It then notes UNEP's regional seas program,[56] which has been a successful model in initiating a two-step process toward the creation of binding international obligations. In addition, it discusses UNEP's

---

[54] *Ibid.*, at 68.

[55] UNEP has overseen the adoption of several binding multilateral conventions and protocols. See Environmental Law in UNEP (*UNEP Envt'l. L.* No. 1, 1991); International Conventions and Protocols in the Field of the Environment, UN Doc. A/C. 2/46/3 (1991); UNEP/GC.16/ Inf. 4 (Nairobi, 1991); UNEP, *International Legal Instruments in the Field of the Environment*, Decision 15/31 of the Governing Council of the United Nations Environment Programme (May 25, 1989), reprinted in UNEP, *Report of the Governing Council on the Work of Its Fifteenth Session*, UN GAOR, 44th Sess., Supp. No. 25, Annex I, at 158, UN Doc. A/44/25 (hereinafter *GC Fifteenth Session Rep.*). See also Decision 15/33 of the Governing Council of UNEP, reprinted in *GC Fifteenth Session Rep.*, at 160, noting the adoption of the Basel Convention on the Control of Transboundary Movements of Hazardous Wastes and Their Disposal, *opened for signature* Mar. 22, 1989, reprinted in 28 *ILM* 649 (1989) (*entered into force* May 5, 1992) (hereinafter Basel Convention).   [56] See note 71 below.

contribution in the adoption of several nonbinding guidelines and principles of international environmental law.

This is followed by a consideration of the contributions of the International Law Commission, which is the UN body responsible for codification and progressive development of international law. Next, the international environmental law implications of UNCLOS will be discussed.

B. Conventional international environmental law

It is worth noting that UNEP is responsible for twenty-three of the thirty-plus environmental accords on major marine regions.[57] The process by which UNEP has operated begins with the accumulation and analysis of pertinent scientific data, in conjunction with the scientific community. This is followed by the preparation of a draft convention/protocol, which sets the stage for UNEP to convene an *ad hoc* working group of experts, both legal and technical, to review the draft and to make the necessary revisions.[58]

UNEP then consults with those parties considered critical for political acceptance and eventual adoption of a proposed convention. These include governments, especially those of developing countries, to which it pays special attention;[59] industrial and special interest groups; and nongovernmental organizations. Once it has built a consensus on the basic issues, UNEP convenes a diplomatic conference to consider the draft convention.[60] If no binding legal instrument is contemplated, the revised draft guidelines or principles are presented to the Governing Council for its adoption. This process has been used successfully by UNEP both for reaching agreement on specific conventions and in the regional seas program.

1. Conventions

UNEP's serious attention to stratospheric ozone depletion dates back to 1980, when its Governing Council decided that the agency should take

[57] See P. Sand, *Marine Environmental Law in the United Nations Environment Programme* ix (1988).
[58] See, e.g., Rules and Procedures of the Governing Council of the United Nations Environment Programme, UN Doc. UNEP/GC/3/Rev. 3 (Jan. 1, 1988).
[59] Per GA Res. 2997, pt. 1, para. 2(f), note 31 above.
[60] See generally C. Petsonk, "The Role of the United Nations Environment Programme (UNEP) in the Development of International Environmental Law," 5 *Am. U. J. Int'l L. & Pol'y* 351 (1990).

measures for such protection.[61] The next year, the Governing Council specifically opted for a convention,[62] reiterating in 1982 its call that UNEP develop a convention to limit, reduce, and prevent activities that may have adverse effects on stratospheric ozone[63] by building scientific, economic, and political consensus over a number of years. UNEP accomplished its goal partially in 1985, with the adoption of the framework Vienna Convention for the Protection of the Ozone Layer (Vienna Convention),[64] before moving nearer to its goal in 1987 with the adoption of the Montreal Protocol on Substances that Deplete the Ozone Layer (Montreal Protocol),[65] and the 1990 London Amendments.[66]

UNEP was also responsible for the negotiation and adoption of the Basel Convention on the Control of Transboundary Movements of Hazardous Wastes and Their Disposal (Basel Convention).[67] UNEP's preparatory work for this Convention included its issuing of the 1985 Cairo Guidelines and Pri)nciples for the Environmentally Sound Management of Hazardous Wastes[68] and its initial 1987 Draft Convention on the Transboundary Shipment of Hazardous Waste.[69] As with the ozone convention, after an *ad hoc* working group of experts convened by UNEP prepared recommendations for the project, the final draft of the Basel Convention was presented.[70]

[61] See UNEP, *Report of the Governing Council on the Work of Its Eighth Session*, UN GAOR, 35th Sess., Supp. No. 25, Annex I, at 118, UN Doc. A/35/25 (1980) (hereinafter UNEP, *GC Eighth Session Rep.*).

[62] See UNEP, *Report of the Governing Council on the Work of Its Ninth Session*, UN GAOR, 36th Sess., Supp. No. 25, at 118, UN Doc. A/26/25 (1981).

[63] See UNEP Montevideo Programme for the Development and Periodic Review of Environmental Law, in *Environmental Law Programme, Environmental Law Unit, Montevideo Programme* (1982), at II. A1.b.

[64] Reprinted in 26 *ILM* 1516 (1987).

[65] Reprinted in 52 Fed. Reg. 47,515 (Dec. 14, 1987), and in 26 *ILM* 1541 (1987) (hereinafter Montreal Protocol). See generally T. Doolittle, "Underestimating Ozone Depletion: The Meandering Road to the Montreal Protocol and Beyond," 16 *Ecology L. Q.* 407 (1989).

[66] See Report of the Second Meeting of the Parties to the Montreal Protocol on Substances that Deplete the Ozone Layer, UN Doc. UNEP/Ozl.Pro.2/3 (June 29, 1990). For a commentary, see J. Patlis, "The Multilateral Fund of the Montreal Protocol: A Prototype For Financial Mechanisms in Protecting the Global Environment," 25 *Cornell Int'l L. J.* 181 (1992).

[67] For the text, see 28 *ILM* 657 (1989).

[68] See UNEP, *Ad hoc Working Group of Legal and Technical Experts with a Mandate to Prepare a Global Convention on the Control of Transboundary Movements of Hazardous Wastes*, UN Doc. UNEP/WG 11/1. 1/Add. 3/Rev. 1 (1985).

[69] Draft Convention on the Control of Transboundary Movements in Hazardous Wastes and Their Disposal, UN Doc. UNEP/1G.80/1.4/Add. 1–5 (1989).

[70] See UNEP, *Ad hoc Working Group of Legal and Technical Experts with a Mandate to Prepare a Global Convention on the Control of Transboundary Movements of Hazardous Wastes*, UNEP/WG.191/5, 5th Sess., at 1 (Mar. 13, 1989); "Waste Shipment Incidents Spur Interest in UNEP Agreement to Deal with Problem," 11 *Int'l Envt. Rep.* (BNA), Curr. Rep. 471 (Dec. 1988).

2. Regional Seas Program

During the mid-1970s, UNEP initiated a series of systems, known as the "Regional Seas Program." It succeeded in drafting, negotiating, and obtaining the adoption of several conventions and protocols designed to protect the marine environment of several regional seas. These efforts began in 1976 with the signing at Barcelona of the Convention for the Protection of the Mediterranean Sea against Pollution, together with several protocols, which since have been supplemented by further protocols.[71]

The Regional Seas Program has encompassed the negotiation of conventions for many regions, including the Persian Gulf, West and Central Africa, the South East Pacific region, the Red Sea and the Gulf of Aden, the Caribbean, East Africa, the South Pacific, and the Zambezi River Basin. UNEP serves as the secretariat for these conventions. It is anticipated that in the near future, framework conventions obligating states to cooperate in the protection of marine environments of their regional seas will be extended to several other areas.

C. Soft law – nonbinding principles and guidelines

While conventional international law creates legal obligations for states, nonbinding legal regimes in the form of principles and guidelines arguably create community expectations which influence state behavior, thus paving the way for concordant state practice. This state practice can then give rise to a customary norm of international law or to the eventual adoption of a convention on the subject.

In this vein, UNEP has developed several sets of nonbinding principles and guidelines. These include the 1978 principles on the conservation and

---

[71] Convention for the Protection of the Mediterranean Sea against Pollution, Feb. 16, 1976, reprinted in 15 *ILM* 290 (1976) (*entered into force* Feb. 12, 1978); Protocol for the Prevention of Pollution of the Mediterranean Sea by Dumping from Ships and Aircraft, Feb. 16, 1976, reprinted in 15 *ILM* 300 (1976) (*entered into force* Feb. 12, 1978); Protocol Concerning Co-operation in Combating Pollution of the Mediterranean Sea by Oil and Other Harmful Substances in Cases of Emergency, Feb. 16, 1976, reprinted in 15 *ILM* 306 (1976) (*entered into force* Feb. 12, 1978); Protocol for the Protection of the Mediterranean Sea against Pollution from Land-Based Sources, May 17, 1980, reprinted in 19 *ILM* 869 (1980) (*entered into force* June 17, 1983); Protocol Concerning Mediterranean Specially Protected Areas, Apr. 3, 1982, reprinted in Sand, note 57 above, at 37 (*entered into force* Mar. 23, 1986). See generally S. Kuwabara, *The Legal Regime of the Protection of the Mediterranean against Pollution from Land-Based Sources* (1984) (discussing various agreements relating to the Mediterranean). A draft Protocol Concerning the Protection of the Mediterranean Sea against Pollution Resulting from Exploration and Exploitation of the Continental Shelf and the Sea-Bed and Its Sub-soil is under consideration.

harmonious use of shared natural resources.[72] In 1980, the UN General Assembly adopted a resolution requesting states to use these principles in the formulation of conventions, both bilateral and multilateral, on shared resources.[73]

During the 1980s, UNEP developed many of these principles and guidelines on a variety of subjects, such as weather modification,[74] marine pollution prevention,[75] hazardous wastes,[76] environmental impact assessment (EIA),[77] and shipment of banned and severely restricted chemicals.[78]

D. International Law Commission's role

The thirty-four-member International Law Commission (ILC) was created by the UN General Assembly to work on codification and progressive development of international law.[79] Of interest in the context of international environmental law was the ILC's inclusion of Article 19 in its 1976 Draft Articles on State Responsibility.[80] This article characterizes the serious breach of an international obligation of essential importance for

[72] See UNEP, Report of the Fifth Session of the Intergovernmental Working Group of Experts on Natural Resources Shared by Two or More States, UN Doc. UNEP/GC.6/ 17 (1978), reprinted in 17 *ILM* 1091 (1978), which contains Draft Principles of Conduct in the Field of the Environment for the Guidance of States in the Conservation and Harmonious Utilization of Natural Resources Shared by Two or More States. The Governing Council approved of these draft principles, see UNEP, *Report of the Governing Council on the Work of Its Sixth Session*, UN GAOR, 33d Sess., Supp. No. 25, Annex 1, at 154, 120 UN Doc. A/33/25 (1978).

[73] See GA Res. 186, UN GAOR, 34th Sess., Supp. No. 46, at 128, UN Doc. A/34/46 (1980).

[74] See Decision 8/7A of UNEP Governing Council, reprinted in UNEP, *GC Eighth Session Rep.*, note 61 above, at 117.

[75] See Montreal Guidelines, reprinted in Final Report of the ad hoc Working Group of Experts on the Protection of the Marine Environment against Pollution from Land-Based Sources, UN Doc. UNEP/WG. 120/3 (1985). See also Decision 13/8 (II) of the UNEP Governing Council, encouraging states' consideration of these guidelines, reprinted in UNEP, *Report of the Governing Council on the Work of Its Thirteenth Session*, UN GAOR, 40th Sess., Supp. No. 25, Annex I, at 53, UN Doc. A/40/25 (1985).

[76] See UNEP, Ad hoc Working Group of Legal and Technical Experts with a Mandate to Prepare a Global Convention on the Control of Transboundary Movements of Hazardous Wastes, UN Doc. UNEP/WG. 122/L.1/Add.3/Rev. 1 (1985).

[77] See UNEP, Goals and Principles of Environmental Impact Assessment, UN Doc. UNEP/ GC.14/17, Annex III (1987); Decision 14/25 of the UNEP Governing Council, Adopting the Goals and Principles of the EIA, reprinted in UNEP, *Report of the Governing Council on the Work of Its Fourteenth Session*, UN GAOR, 42d Sess., Supp. No. 25, Annex I, at 77, UN Doc. A/42/25 (1987).

[78] See Amended London Guidelines for the Exchange of Information on Chemicals in International Trade, UN Doc. UNEP/GC.15/9/Add.2/Supp. 3 (1989); Environmentally Safe Management of Chemicals, in Particular Those That Are Banned and Severely Restricted in International Trade, Decision 15/3 of the Governing Council (May 25, 1989), reprinted in *GC Fifteenth Session Rep.*, note 55 above, at 156 (adopting the Amended London Guidelines).

[79] See UN Doc. A/CN. 4/4/Rev. 2 (1982).

[80] See UN GAOR, 31st Sess., Supp. No. 10, at 170, UN Doc. A/31/10 (1976), reprinted in (1976) 2 *Y. B. Int'l L. Comm.* 73, UN Doc. A/CN.4/Ser.A/1976/Add.1.

safeguarding and preserving the human environment as an international crime.[81] Activities causing massive pollution of the atmosphere or the seas would fall into this category.

The ILC has recently studied two other topics especially pertinent to international environmental law: "International Liability for Injurious Consequences Arising Out of Acts Not Prohibited by International Law,"[82] and "The Law of the Non-Navigational Uses of International Watercourses."[83] The ILC work has thus far resulted in the provisional approval of several articles addressing a state's obligation "when the physical consequences of . . . activities [within its territory or under its jurisdiction or control] cause, or create a risk of causing, transboundary harm throughout the process."[84] States of origin are obligated to "take appropriate measures to prevent or minimize the risk of transboundary harm or, where necessary, to contain or minimize the harmful transboundary effects of such activities. To that end they shall, in so far as they are able, use the best practicable, available means."[85]

The 1990 report also addressed the question of liability for harm to the environment in areas beyond national jurisdiction, the "global commons."[86] The Special Rapporteur noted a difficulty in addressing the issue of harm to the environment *per se* in the areas beyond the national jurisdiction, for "currently in general international law there was no liability to the environment of the global commons which did not affect persons or property."[87] He identified another difficulty in applying the concept of liability for harm to the global commons, namely the identification of affected states which would be harmed.[88]

As to the law of nonnavigational uses of watercourses, the ILC includes provisions for the protection and preservation of the ecosystem of international watercourses.[89] Other articles call for the prevention of the introduction of new species, protection of estuaries, mitigation of environmental harm, and provisions for notifying neighboring states of emergencies.[90] The articles also follow the formulae utilized in Article 194 of the

---

[81] *Ibid.*, art. 19(3)(d).

[82] See *Report of the International Law Commission*, UN GAOR, 42d Sess., Supp. No. 10, at 242 (1990) (hereinafter *42d Session Report*). For an excellent analysis, see generally Schachter, note 5 above, at 461–93.   [83] See *42d Session Report*, note 82 above, at 113.

[84] *Ibid.*, at 251 n. 305 (art. 1).   [85] *Ibid.*, at 257 n. 307 (art. 8).

[86] See *ibid.*, at 282. For international liability to attach, acts not prohibited under international law would need to have physical consequences. See *ibid.*, at 251 (art. 1).

[87] See *ibid.*, at 284.   [88] See *ibid.*

[89] See *ibid.*, at 145 (art. 22). For a commentary on the protection and preservation of the ecosystems of international watercourses, see V. Nanda, *International Environmental Law and Policy*, at ch. 12 (1995) (hereinafter Nanda, *Law & Policy*). See also V. Nanda, "Protection and Preservation of Ecosystems, Harmful Conditions and Emergency Situations, and Protection of Water Installations," 3 *Colo. J. Int'l L. & Pol'y* 175 (1992).

[90] See *42d Session Report*, note 82 above, at 145–46 (arts. 23–27).

1982 UNCLOS with regard to the prevention, reduction, and control of marine pollution.[91]

E. The UN Convention on the Law of the Sea (UNCLOS) and the world environment[92]

The 1982 UN Convention on the Law of the Sea represents an important step forward in international environmental law, for it raises to binding treaty status the ideals of Principle 21 of the Stockholm Declaration,[93] and strives to balance environmental protection and resource management with the requirements of free navigation.

The Convention sets forth a contracting party's general obligation "to protect and preserve the marine environment,"[94] and the right of states to exploit their natural resources pursuant to their policies is stated in terms of a recognized "duty" toward the marine environment.[95] Parties are obligated to take necessary steps "to prevent, reduce and control pollution of the marine environment from any source, using for this purpose the best practical means at their disposal and in accordance with their capabilities."[96]

Developing states are given special status in recognition of their "obvious limitations . . . and the special duties of those who have the technology and the economic means to protect the oceans."[97] Among other provisions, Article 207(4) calls for taking into account "the economic capacity of developing states and their need for economic development" in setting standards regarding pollution from land-based sources; Article 202 provides for scientific and technical assistance to developing states from industrialized countries; and Article 203 requires preferential treatment of the developing countries by international financial organizations.

[91] United Nations Convention on the Law of the Sea, Dec. 10, 1982, UN Doc. A/ CONF.62/121, reprinted in 21 *ILM* 1261 (1982) (hereinafter UNCLOS).
[92] See *ibid.*, at pt. XII. See also Nanda, *Law & Policy*, note 89 above, at ch. 11.
[93] See note 3 above.
[94] UNCLOS, note 91 above, art. 192.
[95] See *ibid.*, art. 193. See generally M. Belsky, "The Ecosystem Model Mandate for a Comprehensive United States Ocean Policy and Law of the Sea," 26 *San Diego L. Rev.* 417 (1989), discussing the underlying theory of comprehensive ecosystem management and, at 461–81, UNCLOS's role in such policy. For the nature of the problem, see, as an illustration, C. Joyner & S. Frew, "Plastic Pollution in the Marine Environment," 22 *Ocean Dev. & Int'l L.* 33 (1991).
[96] UNCLOS, note 91 above, art. 194.
[97] J. Vallarta, "Protection and Preservation of the Marine Environment and Marine Scientific Research at the Third United Nations Conference on the Law of the Sea," *Law & Contemp. Probs.*, Spring 1983, at 147, 148, quoting the Mexican chairman of the informal consultation group on the protection and preservation of the marine environment at the Conference.

V. THE UNITED NATIONS CONFERENCE ON ENVIRONMENT AND DEVELOPMENT (UNCED)

At UNCED in Rio de Janeiro in June 1992 the participants signed the Rio Declaration,[98] a statement of basic principles designed to guide nations toward sustainable development and environmental protection. The delegates, from 155 nations, including the European Community, also signed the Climate Change Convention.[99] Similarly, over one hundred and fifty states signed the Biological Diversity Treaty.[100]

Among other highlights of UNCED: delegates affirmed a proposal offered by African states to call for a treaty to halt the spread of deserts;[101] environmental ministers adopted nonbinding global forestry principles, but failed to agree on a specific call from UNCED for a forestry treaty;[102] an agreement was signed on a comprehensive plan of action, the massive 600-page Agenda 21,[103] a blueprint for fighting pollution and poverty, moving toward better use of the earth's resources into the twenty-first century and charting a new course of global partnership for sustainable development; and an agreement was reached to establish a Sustainable Development Commission to monitor the progress of governments toward implementing the UNCED agreements.[104]

A. The Rio Declaration

The Rio Declaration affirms and updates Principle 21 of the Stockholm Declaration, which provides a delicate balance of recognizing the sovereign rights of all states to exploit their own resources pursuant to their own environmental and development policies, but at the same time proclaiming their "responsibility to ensure that activities within their jurisdiction and control do not cause damage to the environment of other States or of areas beyond the limits of national jurisdiction."[105] It builds on the Stockholm Declaration by recognizing the principle of intergenerational equity and yet proclaiming "common but differentiated responsibilities" of states, thereby acknowledging the special responsibility of the developed countries "in the international pursuit of sustainable development in view of the

---

[98] This was originally intended to be an Earth Charter, but due in part to North/South conflicts it was downgraded to a declaration. For the text of the twenty-seven principles constituting the Declaration, see 21 *ILM* 876 (1992). See also United Nations, *The Global Partnership for Environment and Development: A Guide to Agenda* 21, at 1–4 (1992) (hereinafter *Global Partnership*).   [99] See 15 *Int'l Envt. Rep.* (BNA), Curr. Rep. 421 (June 17, 1992).

[100] See *ibid.*, at 414.   [101] See *ibid.*, at 416.   [102] See *ibid.*, at 415.

[103] See *Global Partnership*, note 98 above; 29 *UN Chronicle*, June 1992, at 44.

[104] See 15 *Int'l Envt. Rep.* (BNA), Curr. Rep. 419 (June 17, 1992).

[105] Principle 2 of the Rio Declaration, reprinted in 21 *ILM* 876 (1992).

pressures their societies place on the global environment and of the technologies and financial resources they command."[106]

The Rio Declaration calls for a wider application of the "precautionary approach by States according to their capabilities,"[107] and the application of the polluter-pays principle.[108] It also calls for the right to development to be fulfilled,[109] obliges states to undertake environmental impact assessment,[110] and especially recognizes the vital role of the participation of women[111] and of indigenous people and their communities[112] in the achievement of sustainable development.

B. The Framework Convention on Climate Change

The Framework Convention on Climate Change[113] was opened for signature at the UNCED Conference. The Convention had been adopted at the New York session (from April 30 to May 9, 1991) of the Intergovernmental Negotiating Committee, a body established by the UN General Assembly. The Convention sets guidelines to achieve the objective of "stabilization of greenhouse gas concentrations in the atmosphere at a level that would prevent dangerous anthropogenic interference with the climate system."[114]

The Convention aims at returning emissions of carbon dioxide and other greenhouse gases not controlled by the Montreal Protocol to their 1990 levels by the year 2000.[115] Thus, the parties undertake to maintain national inventories of emissions by sources and removal by "sinks" of greenhouse gases,[116] and to report on the implementing measures.[117] The developed countries and countries that are undergoing the process of transition to market economy[118] also undertake the commitment to reduce their emissions of greenhouse gases and enhance their greenhouse gas "sinks and reservoirs."[119]

The Convention envisages a continuing review and monitoring process and future negotiations,[120] which should keep pressure on the parties to meet their commitments. It is important to note that under the Convention the developed countries are obliged to provide "new and additional financial resources"[121] and environmentally sound technologies and

---

[106] Principle 7 in *ibid.*, at 877. See also Principle 8 in *ibid.*
[107] Principle 15 in *ibid.*, at 879.   [108] Principle 16 in *ibid.*, at 879.
[109] Principle 3 in *ibid.*, at 877.   [110] Principle 17 in *ibid.*, at 879.
[111] Principle 20 in *ibid.*, at 879.   [112] Principle 22 in *ibid.*, at 880.
[113] For the text, see 31 *ILM* 849 (1992) (hereinafter Convention). See also Nanda, *Law & Policy*, note 89 above, at ch. 10.   [114] See Convention, note 113 above, art. 2.
[115] *Ibid.*, art. 4(2)(a) & (b).   [116] *Ibid.*, art. 4(1)(a).   [117] *Ibid.*, art. 4(1)(b).
[118] *Ibid.*, art. 4(2)(a). See also 4(2)(g), under which other parties may also accept this commitment.   [119] *Ibid.*, art. 4(2)(a).   [120] *Ibid.*, arts. 4(d), (e), (f); 7; 12.
[121] *Ibid.*, arts. 4(3); 12(1).

know-how[122] to developing countries to help them in complying with their obligations and implementing the Convention's provisions. The Convention establishes a subsidiary body to provide "timely information and advice on scientific and technological matters relating to the Convention."[123]

Although the Convention can be faulted for only making stabilization of the emissions voluntary, thus falling short of mandating firm targets and timetables, it should be noted that the problem is so complex that the usual international legal remedies enshrined in any treaty are bound to be only a small step toward addressing the problem.[124] In light of such complexities, this Framework Convention is certainly an important step forward. In a striking recent development, the Intergovernmental Panel on Climate Change (IPCC) under the Convention issued its "Second Assessment Report," in which it provided scientific data proving that human activities do contribute to global warming.[125]

C. The Convention on Biological Diversity

The Convention on Biological Diversity,[126] adopted on May 22, 1992, was opened for signature at the UNCED Conference. The Convention provides for: national identification and monitoring of biological diversity;[127] in-situ[128] and ex-situ[129] conservation measures; "environmental impact assessment of [a party's] proposed projects that are likely to have a significant adverse effect on biological diversity"[130] and an obligation to take appropriate measures to minimize such adverse impacts;[131] participation by developing countries in technology research activities[132] and sharing of "the results and benefits arising from biotechnologies based upon genetic resources provided by"[133] developing countries; access to and transfer of technology to developing countries;[134] and undertaking by the developed countries to provide "new and additional financial resources" to developing countries to meet their obligations under the Convention.[135]

The Convention envisages the establishment of an institutional structure for carrying out operations of a financial mechanism to provide financial resources on a grant or concessional basis to developing countries.[136] The

---

[122] *Ibid.*, art. 4(5).   [123] *Ibid.*, art. 9.

[124] See generally C. D. Stone, "Beyond Rio: 'Insuring' against Global Warming," 86 *AJIL* 445 (1992).

[125] See "Climate Panel Takes up Final Revisions to Second Assessment of Global Warming," *Int'l Env. Daily* (BNA), Dec. 12, 1995.

[126] For the text, see 31 *ILM* 818 (1992) (hereinafter Convention).

[127] Convention, note 126 above, art. 7.   [128] *Ibid.*, art 8.   [129] *Ibid.*, art. 9.

[130] *Ibid.*, art. 14(a).   [131] *Ibid.*, art. 14(b)–(e).   [132] *Ibid.*, art. 19(1).

[133] *Ibid.*, art. 19(2).   [134] *Ibid.*, art. 16.   [135] *Ibid.*, art 20.   [136] *Ibid.*, art. 21.

Global Environment Facility (GEF) of the United Nations Development Programme, UNEP, and the World Bank is to act as such an institution on an interim basis until the parties meet to decide otherwise.[137] In a recent conference of the parties to discuss implementation, UNEP released a report warning that up to 25 percent of all rain-forest species are faced with extinction by loss of degradation of habitats.[138]

D. The Commission on Sustainable Development

The delegates approved the establishment of the CSD, a high-level institution to watch over the performance of governments in the implementation of the ambitious and complex agreements contained in Agenda 21.[139] The CSD reports to the General Assembly through the UN Economic and Social Council and has already convened to effect monitoring of the Rio agreements.[140]

E. The financing mechanism

The delegates agreed on how environmental and development programs should be financed and how the funds for Agenda 21 projects are to be used.[141] Developed countries are urged to meet a target "as soon as possible" for providing 0.7 percent of their gross national product as aid to developing nations. The Global Environment Facility is to funnel foreign aid to developing nations.

VI. ASSESSMENT

Despite a growing interest in the environment and some encouraging developments since the 1972 Stockholm Conference, the UNEP Executive Director reported in 1990 that the overall picture was bleak.[142] However, but for the various national, bilateral, regional, and international efforts, the situation would be still worse.

---

[137] *Ibid.*, art. 39.

[138] See 18 *Int'l Env. Rep.* (BNA), Curr. Rep. (Nov. 15, 1995). See also "WMO Reports Worst Ozone Depletion on Record for 1995 Antarctic Winter," *Int'l Env. Daily* (BNA), Dec. 1, 1995.   [139] See Nanda, *Law & Policy*, note 89 above, at 299–300.

[140] See J. Gaunt, "Earth Summit to Produce UN Watchdog," *Reuter Lib. Rep.*, June 8, 1992.

[141] See 15 *Int'l Envt. Rep.* (BNA), Curr. Rep. 395 (June 17, 1992).

[142] See UNEP, Second Special Session of the Governing Council: Priority Involving Environmental Issues – Report of the Executive Director, UN Doc. UNEP/GCSS. II/2, at 3 (May 28, 1990). The Executive Director called for "action rather than rhetoric, deeds rather than words, commitments rather than communiques." *Ibid.*

International environmental law – both as conventional law and as guidelines, principles, and standards – continues to grow at a rapid rate. The approach, however, remains piecemeal and sector by sector. UNCED recognized the need to review the existing international environmental law and to seek further development and strengthening of the law so that it can address environmental challenges of the twenty-first century. The need is to build on the accomplishments at UNCED.

While states have generally accepted international environmental law principles imposing an obligation to inform, assess, and consult in case of impending environmental harm or significant risk of such harm to others,[143] international environmental law in such areas as liability and compensation,[144] states' obligation to prevent and minimize harm and appreciable risk,[145] and enforcement and remedies[146] remains inadequate and ineffective. Also, emerging new concepts such as intergenerational and intragenerational equity and responsibility, sustainable development, shared and differentiated responsibilities, resource transfer, and environmental security need to be further defined with precision and developed so that some of these principles might graduate from their status as soft law to inclusion in legally binding instruments.

The law-making function is presently undertaken by many UN and non-UN bodies which keep proliferating globally. The need has been widely recognized to reform the UN institutions in the field of environment and development.

It is essential that the UN body responsible for coordinating environmental programs in the UN system has adequate resources to function effectively. This is not the case today. Additionally it is imperative that that body also effectively coordinates the law-making functions of other regional intergovernmental bodies, such as the OECD, the European Community, the Nordic Council, OAS, and OAU.

For law-making to be effective, three prerequisites have to be met. First, there must be full integration of environmental and development concerns and policies in all guidelines and regulatory mechanisms incorporated into conventions, declarations, etc. Second, reviewing and monitoring mechanisms should become part of every regulatory and control process. The Montreal Protocol Scheme, which allows parties to modify their control measures in light of the monitoring process, is a useful model for future conventions.

Third, it is essential that developing states' needs for external finances and environmentally sound technology are adequately addressed. The

---

[143] For an insightful analysis, see Schachter, note 5 above, at 475–79.
[144] See *ibid.*, at 479–89.   [145] See *ibid.*, at 468–75.   [146] See *ibid.*, at 489–93.

Global Environmental Facility's function is to help poor countries develop "in a manner which protects the global environment."[147] The Montreal Protocol provisions and the decision of the signatories of the Protocol at their 1990 meeting in London to create a special fund to assist the developing countries[148] reflect this concern. With UNCED highlighting this concern it is hoped that concerted international efforts will follow to provide such assistance.

Implementation of the decisions taken at UNCED should expedite the process of international environmental law-making.

SELECTED BIBLIOGRAPHY

Adede, A., *International Environmental Law from Stockholm 1972 to Rio de Janeiro 1992: An Overview of Past Lessons and Future Challenges* (1992)

Kaufman, J. and N. Schrijver, *Changing Global Needs: Expanding Roles for the United Nations System* (ACUNS, 1990)

Nanda, V., "Global Warming and International Environmental Law: A Preliminary Enquiry," 30 *Harvard Int'l L. J.* 375 (1989)

International Environmental Law and Policy (Transnational, 1995)

Petsonk, C., "The Role of the United Nations Environmental Programme (UNEP) in the Development of International Environmental Law," 5 *Am. U. J. Int'l L. & Pol'y* 351 (1990)

Schachter, O., "The Emergence of International Environmental Law," 44 *J. Int'l Aff.* 457 (1991)

Stone, C. D., "Beyond Rio: Insuring against Global Warming," 86 *AJIL* 445 (1992)

Tharpes, Y., "International Environmental Law: Turning the Tide in Marine Pollution," 20 *U. Miami Inter-American L. Rev.* 579 (1989)

United Nations, Report of the United Nations Conference on the Human Environment, UN Doc. A/CONF.48/14 and Corr.1 (1972)

The Global Partnership for Environment and Development: A Guide to Agenda 21 (UNCED, 1992)

United Nations Environmental Programme, *Annual Report of the Executive Director*

Environmental Law in UNEP (1991)

---

[147] See *UN Chronicle*, Dec. 1990, at 63.
[148] See 13 *Int'l Envt. Rep.* (BNA), Curr. Rep. 275 (July 1990).

CHAPTER ELEVEN

LAW OF THE SEA

Bernard H. Oxman

I. INTRODUCTION

The sea covers most of the planet. The activities and interests addressed by the law of the sea are so varied that they are likely to be relevant from time to time to the work of virtually any United Nations organ or undertaking. Since its founding,[1] there is no significant period in which the United Nations has not dealt with the law of the sea in some way.

Much of this activity has taken place in the General Assembly and its committees, in the International Law Commission, at conferences convened by the General Assembly, and in specialized agencies of the United Nations. The International Court of Justice[2] has made a significant contribution not only to the resolution of disputes involving law of the sea issues, but to the development of the law of the sea itself. Arms-control measures sponsored or encouraged by the United Nations have had a significant impact on military uses of the sea.[3]

The Security Council has not attempted to resolve the substantive issues of the law of the sea as such. Its efforts to assist in conflict resolution have nevertheless involved it in conflicts regarding rights under the law of the sea.[4] The exercise of its powers to maintain and restore international peace

---

[1] The UN Charter was *signed* on June 26, 1945 and *entered into force* on October 24, 1945.

[2] The Court is the principal judicial organ of the United Nations. UN Charter, art. 92.

[3] Notable examples of multilateral efforts are the Nuclear Test Ban Treaty and the Seabed Arms Control Treaty. Treaty Banning Nuclear Weapon Tests in the Atmosphere, in Outer Space and under Water, *done* at Moscow Aug. 5, 1963, 14 UST 1313, TIAS No. 5433, 480 UNTS 43 (*entered into force* Oct. 10, 1963); Treaty on the Prohibition of the Emplacement of Nuclear Weapons and Other Weapons of Mass Destruction on the Seabed and the Ocean Floor and in the Subsoil thereof, *done* at Washington, London, and Moscow Feb. 11, 1971, 23 UST 701, TIAS No. 7337, 955 UNTS 115 (*entered into force* May 18, 1972) (hereinafter Seabed Arms Control Treaty).

[4] An example is the dispute between Egypt and Israel concerning navigation in the Strait of Tiran and the Gulf of Aqaba. The dispute was ultimately addressed in the peace treaty between the parties.

and security have entailed decisions affecting activities at sea that impose embargoes on trade, approve the use of force, and deal with the consequences of military action.[5]

It is difficult and potentially misleading to separate the law of the sea from the corpus of international law as a whole. Changes in the law of the sea and in other branches of international law do not occur in isolation. Both often occur in response to the same forces. For example, the explosion of public interest in environmental protection during the relatively short period between the negotiation of the 1958 Geneva Conventions on the law of the sea[6] and the 1982 United Nations Convention on the Law of the Sea[7] is evident in the extensive treatment of environmental matters in the 1982 Convention as compared with relatively sparse references in the earlier conventions.[8] In important respects, the 1982 Convention was the first practical attempt to establish a general global treaty regime implementing and elaborating upon the general environmental principles enunciated in the seminal Stockholm Declaration on the global environment.[9]

Even if no mention is made of the sea as such, virtually any resolution of a United Nations organ, treaty negotiated under its auspices, or decision of the International Court of Justice dealing with the general rights and duties of states may well affect their rights and duties at sea in some way.

The law of the sea nevertheless has been regarded as a distinct if not unique branch of international law. Grotius, sometimes called the father of modern international law, is often best remembered for his work devoted to the law of the sea.[10] The *raison d'être* for the distinction may well be found in the historical fact that the Grotian conception of the freedom of the seas

[5] An example is the response to the Iraqi invasion of Kuwait.

[6] Convention on the Territorial Sea and the Contiguous Zone, Apr. 29, 1958, 15 UST 1606, TIAS No. 5639, 516 UNTS 205 (hereinafter Territorial Sea Convention); Convention on the High Seas, Apr. 29, 1958, 13 UST 2312, TIAS No. 5200, 450 UNTS 82 (hereinafter High Seas Convention); Convention on Fishing and Conservation of the Living Resources of the High Seas, Apr. 29, 1958, 17 UST 138, TIAS No. 5969, 559 UNTS 285 (hereinafter Fishing and Conservation Convention); Convention on the Continental Shelf, Apr. 29, 1958, 15 UST 471, TIAS No. 5578, 499 UNTS 311 (hereinafter Continental Shelf Convention).

[7] United Nations Convention on the Law of the Sea., Dec. 10, 1982, UN Pub. Sales No. E.83.V.5, reprinted in 21 *ILM* 1261 (1982) (hereinafter Law of the Sea Convention).

[8] Even with respect to conservation of fisheries, it is not clear that the primary concern addressed by the conservation rules in the 1958 Fisheries and Conservation Convention was environmental rather than economic. The focus was on the maintenance over time of a sustainable yield of commercially exploited stocks. Fishing and Conservation Convention, note 6 above, art. 2. The 1982 Convention expands the focus on living resources to include matters such as habitat and ecosystem protection, rare or endangered species, coordinated stock management across jurisdictional lines, associated or dependent species, introduction of alien species, pollution control, and special protection of marine mammals. Law of the Sea Convention, note 7 above, arts. 61, 63–67, 119–20, 123, 192–96, 206, 297(3).

[9] Declaration of the United Nations Conference on the Human Environment, UN Doc. A/CONF.48/14 (1972), 11 *ILM* 1416 (1972).

[10] H. Grotius, *Mare Liberum* (R. Magoffin trans., 1916).

prevailed for a long time, and therefore that the system of territorial sovereignty that forms the foundation for allocation of competence among states on land did not apply at all, or at least in the same way, to much if not all of the sea.[11]

The traditional focus of the law of the sea has been allocation of competence among states specifically related to activities at sea and to limitations on those activities. The basic question addressed by Grotius, and still at the heart of the subject, concerns the rights of all states and their nationals to use the seas free of foreign control, and their duties to respect the interests of others and the community as a whole in exercising those rights. The same question may be posed conversely as one that addresses the rights of individual states, particularly coastal states, to exclude or regulate the use of the seas by all in specific areas, and their duties to respect the interests of others and the community as a whole in exercising those rights. A relatively new aspect of the underlying question concerns the competence, and even the duty, of states acting collectively through international organizations to impose limitations on the exercise of rights to use the sea and rights to regulate uses by others.

II. THE SPECIALIZED AGENCIES AND OTHER ORGANIZATIONS

A conception of the law of the sea that focuses on the allocation of competence and duties peculiar to the sea, which are understood to operate in conjunction with other generally applicable rules of international law,[12] permits us to narrow the focus of the present inquiry to a considerable degree.

With rare exceptions, the International Maritime Organization, other specialized agencies of the United Nations, and other global organizations have not attempted to resolve basic questions of the law of the sea regarding allocation of competence among states. By and large, they have directed their work to elaborating specific rules of conduct for states without addressing the extent of their competence, occasionally including cross-references to international law in general or law of the sea conventions on the competence question.

An interesting exception is the Chicago Convention on International

---

[11] One notes in this regard that the basic criminal law component of the law of the sea, namely the law of piracy, was applied to *terra nullius* on land. High Seas Convention, note 6 above, art. 15, para. 1(b); Law of the Sea Convention, note 7 above, art. 101(a)(2).

[12] The Preamble of the Law of the Sea Convention "affirm[s] that matters not regulated by this Convention continue to be governed by the rules and principles of general international law." Law of the Sea Convention, note 7 above, Preamble.

Civil Aviation.[13] The Chicago Convention makes a distinction between overflight of the high seas and overflight of the territorial sea. The latter is assimilated to overflight of the land territory of a state.[14] On the high seas, the coastal state does not have competence to alter the international regulations established under the Convention.[15] The Convention thus explicitly applies to airspace the *summa divisio* between the territorial sea and the high seas in the traditional international law of the sea.

Having accepted the *summa divisio* without qualification, the Convention nevertheless does not address the question of the boundary between the territorial sea and the high seas, that is, the maximum permissible breadth of the territorial sea at least for purposes of that Convention.

Avoiding the question of precise limits is not necessarily inevitable. Whatever their rights in general on the continental shelf or the seabed beyond, states parties to the Seabed Arms Control Treaty[16] are precluded from emplacing nuclear weapons and other weapons of mass destruction in the seabed beyond 12 miles,[17] and must respect verification efforts consistent with the Treaty.[18]

Avoidance of the question of precise limits is nevertheless common. One of the more interesting examples, undertaken in the context of negotiations outside the UN system, is found in the Antarctic Treaty.[19] That treaty, while expressly applying up to 60° south latitude and expressly including ice shelves, provides that "nothing in the present Treaty shall prejudice or in any way affect the rights, or the exercise of rights, of any State under international law with regard to the high seas within that area."[20] No attempt is made to define the limits of the high seas. Although completed soon after the 1958 conventions on the law of the sea, the Treaty also ignores the question of competence in derogation of high seas freedoms beyond the territorial sea. The approach taken was doubtless related in part to the fact that territorial claims in Antarctica, and thus the very existence of a coastal state, were contested in principle.[21]

---

[13] Convention on International Civil Aviation, Dec. 7, 1944, 61 Stat. 1180, TIAS No. 1591, 3 Bev. 944, 15 UNTS 295 (*entered into force* Apr. 4, 1947).   [14] *Ibid.*, arts. 1–2.

[15] *Ibid.*, art. 12.   [16] Seabed Arms Control Treaty, note 3 above.

[17] The prohibitions also apply within 12 miles "except that . . . they shall not apply either to the coastal State or to the seabed beneath its territorial waters." *Ibid.*, art. 1.

[18] *Ibid.*, art. 3.

[19] Antarctic Treaty, Dec. 1, 1959, 12 UST 794, TIAS No. 4780, 402 UNTS 71 (*entered into force* June 23, 1961).   [20] *Ibid.*, art. 6.

[21] The practical difficulties occasioned by the high seas exclusion were remedied in part by special treaties on seals and on conservation of living resources. Convention for the Conservation of Antarctic Seals, Jun. 1, 1972, 29 UST 441, TIAS No. 8826 (*entered into force* Mar. 11, 1978); Convention on the Conservation of Antarctic Marine Living Resources, May 20, 1980, 33 UST 3476, TIAS No. 10240 (*entered into force* Apr. 7, 1982). Whaling is separately regulated. Convention for the Regulation of Whaling, Sep. 24, 1931, 49 Stat. 3079, T.S. 880, 3 Bev. 26, 155 LNTS 349 (*entered into force* Jan. 16, 1935), and Protocol to the Convention, Nov. 19, 1956, 10 UST 952, TIAS No. 4228, 338 UNTS 366 (*entered into force* May 4, 1959).

In the period between the Second and Third UN Conferences on the Law of the Sea, an unsuccessful attempt was made in the Intergovernmental Oceanographic Commission (IOC) of UNESCO to address some of the problems posed by the coastal state right to require consent for marine scientific research, particularly on the continental shelf.[22]

But some things were learned at IOC. Developing coastal states seemed more prepared to be flexible about the operation of the consent regime when the scientific research was being conducted not only with their participation but under the auspices of an international organization in which they had participated in formulating the project. Until it was watered down at the instigation of France, the texts before the Third UN Conference on the Law of the Sea contained a relatively strong provision alleviating the effects of the consent regime on oceanographic projects of international organizations.[23]

In sum, while the role of the specialized agencies and other organizations is important, one must look elsewhere for most efforts to resolve the basic issues of the law of the sea.

III. THE LAW OF THE SEA CONFERENCES

The most ambitious efforts of the United Nations to promote the codification and progressive development of international law are associated with the three conferences on the law of the sea convened by the General Assembly in 1958, 1960, and 1973–82. I, II, III

Work on the articles submitted to the First Conference was begun by the International Law Commission in 1950.[24] The Second Conference, essentially a continuation of the first, was called in a renewed attempt to resolve the question of the maximum permissible breadth of the territorial sea.

Preparations for the Third Conference in effect commenced with the establishment in 1967 of the *ad hoc* Committee on the Seabed and the Ocean Floor beyond the Limits of National Jurisdiction.[25] At the end of

[22] See A. H. A. Soons, *Marine Scientific Research and the Law of the Sea*, 89–92 (1982).
[23] The author discussed this change in B. Oxman, "The Third United Nations Conference on the Law of the Sea: The Ninth Session (1980)," 75 *AJIL* 211, 236 (1981).
[24] At its first meeting, the International Law Commission placed the regime of the high seas and the regime of the territorial sea on its provisional list of topics for consideration, and placed the regime of the high seas on a short list of items to which it would give priority. *1949 Y. B. Int'l. L. Comm.* 281. Substantive consideration began the next year. *1950 Y. B. Int'l L. Comm.*, 1 at 178–239; 2, at 36–113, 383–85.
[25] GA Res. 2340 (XXII) (Dec. 18, 1967). The next year the *ad hoc* committee was converted to a standing committee with somewhat enlarged membership of 42. GA Res. 2467 A (XXIII) (Dec. 21, 1968). In 1970, the General Assembly decided to convene a new comprehensive conference on the law of the sea in 1973, more than doubled the membership of the Seabed Committee to 96, and entrusted the Committee with preparations for the conference. GA Res. 2750 C (Dec. 17, 1970).

the Third Conference, a preparatory commission convened by the General Assembly began work on seabed mining regulations and other matters in preparation for entry into force of the United Nations Convention on the Law of the Sea.[26]

A. The International Law Commission

The First Conference represented the culmination of the original, and classic, procedure for the codification and progressive development of international law.

Responsibility for preparing draft articles was assumed by the International Law Commission (ILC), an independent body of experts in international law elected by the General Assembly.[27]

The Commission proceeded in methodical fashion to receive reports and studies from special rapporteurs as well as experts engaged by the UN Secretariat. On the basis of these reports, articles were drafted on particular subjects. These were submitted to governments for comment between sessions. Articles were voted upon separately.

B. The 1958 Geneva Conventions

The General Assembly decided to convene a conference of plenipotentiaries on the law of the sea,[28] which met in 1958.

Over eighty states attended. The Conference organized itself into committees concerned with the high seas, the territorial sea, the continental shelf, and fishing[29] and the ILC's Articles served as the basis of negotiation, with states submitting amendments to the basic text. Amendments and texts were then approved on an article-by-article basis in committee and in plenary. Most of the Commission's text was approved without substantial change.

It is difficult to determine whether the decision of the Conference to divide the Commission's Articles into four separate conventions was primarily a response to substantive and political concerns or mainly a result of the organization of the Conference.[30] The question is not unlike that

---

[26] Resolution I of Third United Nations Conference on the Law of the Sea, Annex I to the Final Act of the Conference, UN Pub. Sales No. E.83.V.5 158, 175 (1983).

[27] The Commission was established by GA Res. 174 (II) (Nov. 21, 1947).

[28] GA Res. 1105 (XI) (Feb. 21, 1957).

[29] With the exception of the few dealing expressly with marine pollution and marine scientific research, all of the substantive articles that emerged from these committees would be within the purview of one committee (the Second) at the Third UN Conference on the Law of the Sea.

[30] The General Assembly authorized the Conference "to embody the results of its work in one or more international conventions or such other instruments as it may deem appropriate," but

posed by the issue of reservations: there is a tension between the goal of comprehensive substantive uniformity of obligation and the goal of widespread ratification.[31] The Grotian model for the law of the sea was confirmed and refined in some respects and modified in others. The Convention on the High Seas elaborates a comprehensive system of rights and duties based on the underlying principle of the freedom of the seas articulated by Grotius.

The Convention on the Territorial Sea and the Contiguous Zone establishes precise rules for establishing baselines enclosing internal waters and a regime for a territorial sea under the sovereignty of the coastal state that notably includes a right of innocent passage for ships of all states. While the Convention provides that the contiguous zone immediately seaward of the territorial sea may not extend beyond 12 miles from the baseline from which the breadth of the territorial sea is measured, and thus may reflect the view that a territorial sea beyond 12 miles would be unlawful, no agreement could be reached on the maximum permissible limit of the territorial sea within the ranges of 3, 6, and 12 miles that had significant support. Thus a key issue in the Grotian model, namely the precise geographic extent of the free high seas, was not as such resolved.

At the same time, there were important breaks with the traditional model. The most significant is the Convention on the Continental Shelf, which confirmed and refined the trend in state practice begun by the United States with the Truman Proclamation in 1945 claiming coastal state control over seabed resources of the continental shelf beyond the territorial sea. Once again the issue of precise limits could not be resolved, and the Conference confirmed the Commission's recommendation of a minimum seaward limit of the 200-meter isobath, which might be expanded as technology permitted seabed exploitation at greater depths.[32]

The Convention on Fishing and Conservation of the Living Resources of the High Seas articulates a clear, and then arguably new, duty of conservation as a limitation on freedom of fishing. While some attempts were made to accommodate coastal state concerns regarding conservation,

also noted in the Preamble the view "that the various sections of the law of the sea hold together, and are so closely interdependent that it would be extremely difficult to deal with one part and leave the others aside." GA Res. 1105 (XI) (Feb. 21, 1957). The Assembly had previously recommended that the Commission study simultaneously the regime of the high seas and the regime of the territorial sea, and then decided not to deal with any aspect of those regimes until all the interrelated problems of the law of the sea had been reported on by the Commission. GA Res. 798 (VIII) (Dec. 7, 1953).

[31] Thus, for example, the decision to deal with settlement of disputes in a separate instrument reflected a desire to protect the substantive provisions from the opposition of some states to compulsory arbitration or adjudication.

[32] The author analyzed the history of this provision in B. Oxman, "The Preparation of Article 1 of the Convention on the Continental Shelf," 3 *J. Mar. L. & Comm.* 245, 445, 683 (1972).

the question of fisheries allocation was not addressed and coastal state rights even with respect to prescription or enforcement of nondiscriminatory conservation measures were extremely limited. Whether one regards a duty of conservation as a logical concomitant of the freedom of the seas or a limitation on its exercise, apart from this duty the Grotian model was applied in essentially pure form to fisheries.

The Convention on the Territorial Sea and the Contiguous Zone contains two interesting examples of the influence of decisions of the International Court of Justice on the codification process. One concerns baselines, and the other straits.

In the Anglo-Norwegian Fisheries case,[33] the Court rejected Great Britain's challenge to the system of straight baselines that Norway had established along the fjords and islands of its highly irregular coastline. The Convention articulates a general rule regarding straight baselines drawn in most significant respects from the Court's opinion, including the Court's refusal to articulate precise mileage limits for individual segments and closing lines.[34] At the same time, the Convention resolves an important issue that was not squarely before the Court, namely whether there is a right of innocent passage in waters enclosed by straight baselines.[35]

In the Corfu Channel case,[36] Great Britain successfully maintained that Albania had unlawfully mined the channel, thereby damaging British warships exercising a right to navigate through the channel. The Convention reflects the opinion of the Court in its rule that there must be notice of dangers or obstructions to navigation,[37] that innocent passage may not be suspended in straits, and that the important question in this regard is whether the strait is "used" (and not necessarily essential or customarily used) for international navigation.[38] The interpretation of the nonsuspension rule by the International Law Commission expressly confirms its application to warships in light of the Court's decision.[39]

---

[33] Fisheries case (*United Kingdom* v. *Norway*), 1951 ICJ 116.

[34] Territorial Sea Convention, note 6 above, art. 4, repeated with some refinements in Law of the Sea Convention, note 7 above, art. 7.

[35] Territorial Sea Convention, note 6 above, art. 5, para. 2, repeated in substance in Law of the Sea Convention, note 7 above, art. 8, para. 2, applied to straits in *ibid.*, art. 35(a), and applied to archipelagic waters in *ibid.*, arts. 52–53.

[36] Corfu Channel case (*United Kingdom* v. *Albania*), 1949 ICJ 4.

[37] Territorial Sea Convention, note 6 above, art. 15, para. 2, repeated in substance in Law of the Sea Convention, note 7 above, art. 24, para. 2.

[38] Territorial Sea Convention, note 6 above, art. 16, para. 4, repeated in substance with respect to both transit passage and innocent passage in straits in Law of the Sea Convention, note 7 above, arts. 37, 44, 45.

[39] Report of the International Law Commission, *1956 Y. B. Int'l L. Comm.*, 2, at 253, 277 (paras. 3 & 4 of commentary on article 24). This conclusion is particularly interesting in light of the Commission's proposed Article 24 permitting the coastal state to impose requirements of prior authorization for the innocent passage of warships generally. That article was not accepted by the Conference.

316

On the other hand, the High Seas Convention, the only one of the four whose preamble declares it to be a codification of international law, in effect is inconsistent with what might be regarded by common law-trained lawyers as the narrow "holding" of the Permanent Court of International Justice in the *Lotus* case.[40] In that case, France unsuccessfully challenged Turkey's right to prosecute an officer of a French ship for causing a collision with a Turkish ship on the high seas. The High Seas Convention provides that in collision cases only the flag state and the state of nationality of the accused may institute penal proceedings against the master or any other person in the service of the ship.[41]

The four 1958 conventions on the law of the sea were a substantial achievement. Nothing approaching that level of widespread agreement on the substance and articulation of the rules of the law of the sea, or for that matter most other rules of international law, had ever been accomplished. The importance of the contribution is sometimes overlooked precisely because so much of what was done in the conventions is accepted as authoritative as a matter of course and was repeated without significant alteration in the United Nations Convention on the Law of the Sea.

C. The Second Conference

The Second Conference on the Law of the Sea was convened by the General Assembly primarily to resolve the outstanding question of the maximum permissible breadth of the territorial sea.[42] While bearing a conceptual resemblance to the contiguous zone and even the continental shelf, the approach taken probably represented the first widely supported attempt to try to resolve the question of the breadth of the territorial sea by linking it to accommodation of coastal state interests beyond the territorial sea in a zone of more limited competence. A proposal to establish a 6-mile maximum limit for the territorial sea with an additional 6-mile fisheries zone failed by one vote to achieve the requisite two-thirds majority.[43]

One result was that, in the ensuing years, a significant number of states claiming less than a 12-mile territorial sea established fisheries zones extending up to that limit.

D. Unsolved problems, new issues, and new players

Although accepted by principal maritime states, the 1958 Geneva Conventions never achieved the widespread ratification for which many had

---

[40] *SS Lotus case* (*France* v. *Turkey*), PCIJ Ser. A No. 10 (1927).

[41] High Seas Convention, note 6 above, art. 11, para. 1, repeated with minor editorial changes in Law of the Sea Convention, note 7 above, art. 97, para. 1.

[42] Its purpose was not to review or reconsider the work of the 1958 Conference but, in essence, to complete that work.   [43] See M. Whiteman, 4 *Digest of International Law* 91–137 (1965).

hoped.[44] This is not an unusual problem with "law-making" conventions. In many cases, their impact on state practice is far greater than would be suggested by ratification alone. Although this proved true of the Geneva Conventions in many respects, the fundamental questions regarding allocation of competence, including the maximum permissible breadth of the territorial sea, became increasingly contentious.

The dispute was no longer a seemingly narrow one between 3-mile and 12-mile limits, with the West on one side and the Soviet Union on the other. The claims of some Latin American states to 200-mile territorial seas or maritime zones, all but ignored by the International Law Commission and the 1958 and 1960 Conferences, increasingly proliferated in Latin America and elsewhere. The claim of a 100-mile zone in the Arctic in which Canada proposed to regulate navigation for environmental purposes was a special shock, given Canada's geographic, political, and economic position in the world.[45]

The effect of these claims was to reopen the basic debate between Grotius and Selden[46] at the dawn of modern international law regarding the question of whether, in a literal sense, the major seas of the world were *mare liberum* or *mare clausum*.[47] Moreover, with advancing technology, it was possible to imagine a partition of all of the world's seabeds by coastal states arguably supported by, rather than in overt defiance of, the text of the "depth of exploitability" test of the 1958 Convention on the Continental Shelf, notwithstanding the intent of the Convention and the context in which that language was used.

The process of decolonization was only partially complete at the time of the 1958 Conference, but greatly accelerated soon thereafter. Newly independent countries did not feel any particular commitment to efforts to

[44] As of January 1, 1996, the US Department of State publication "Treaties in Force" lists sixty-two parties to the High Seas Convention, fifty-one parties to the Territorial Sea Convention, fifty-seven parties to the Continental Shelf Convention, and thirty-seven parties to the Fishing and Conservation Convention.

[45] See R. B. Bilder, "Canadian Arctic Waters Pollution Prevention Act: New Stresses on the Law of the Sea," 69 *Mich. L. Rev.* 1 (1970); L. Henkin, "Arctic Anti-Pollution: Does Canada Make – or Break – International Law?," 65 *AJIL* 131 (1971); L. H. J. Legault, "Freedom of the Seas: A License to Pollute?," 21 *U. Toronto L. J.* 211 (1971).

[46] J. Selden, *Of the Dominion or Ownership of the Sea* (1652). Ambassador J. Alan Beesley, Canada's Representative to the Third UN Conference on the Law of the Sea and Chairman of its Drafting Committee, was fond of the quip, "I come to bury Grotius, not to praise him."

[47] A limit of 200 miles would in itself embrace most if not all of the most important "seas" in the world, including the Arabian Sea, Baltic Sea, Bering Sea, Black Sea, Caribbean Sea, East China Sea, Mediterranean Sea, Gulf of Mexico, North Sea, Persian Gulf, Red Sea, and South China Sea, as well as those in which the Bahamian, Indonesian, Philippine, and other archipelagos are situated. Moreover, the legal justification of such extensive claims implied that there was no effective limit to coastal state claims. It might be noted in this regard that the seminal Santiago Declaration of 1952 issued by Chile, Ecuador, and Peru refers to 200 miles as a minimum, not a maximum, limit.

articulate customary or conventional international law undertaken without their participation. Many associated existing rules of international law, particularly the freedom of the seas, with colonial expansionism. Some Latin American states, with which newly independent states were associated in the developing country caucus in the United Nations (the so-called Group of 77), exploited these sentiments in an attempt to undermine the legitimacy of the law of the sea as traditionally understood and as articulated in the 1958 Conventions.

There were two important responses to these developments, one initially outside the United Nations and one inside. In 1967, the Soviet Union circulated diplomatic communications to a number of capitals suggesting the possibility of a new diplomatic conference to fix the breadth of the territorial sea at 12 miles. With its emergence as a major maritime power, the Soviet Union's preoccupation had shifted from achieving agreement on the widest potentially negotiable limit of the territorial sea in 1958, namely 12 miles, to achieving agreement on the narrowest potentially negotiable limit of the territorial sea in 1967, namely 12 miles. Discussions between the United States and the Soviet Union ensued, from which three articles emerged as a basis for consultations with other states. One fixed the maximum breadth of the territorial sea at 12 miles. Another provided for freedom of navigation and overflight through straits. A third provided for limited coastal state rights over fisheries seaward of the territorial sea.[48]

Almost simultaneously, following remarks to similar effect one year earlier by James Roosevelt of the United States, Ambassador Arvid Pardo of Malta raised the question of the seabeds in the UN General Assembly. His concern was to establish an international regime for the seabeds beyond the "present" limits of national jurisdiction.[49] In effect, Ambassador Pardo was suggesting a new system entailing the exercise of substantial competence by an international organization as an alternative to both existing options for the allocation of competence among states, namely coastal state jurisdiction and freedom of the seas. The UN General Assembly established an *ad hoc* committee to study the question raised by Ambassador Pardo.[50] Studies and research were commissioned, in part as delaying tactics.

Both of these efforts originally focused on matters left unresolved by the Geneva Conventions. Neither necessarily entailed a comprehensive review of the law of the sea. In at least political terms, the US–Soviet approach represented a threat to 200-mile claims because it sought an accommoda-

---

[48] See B. Oxman, *From Cooperation to Conflict: The Soviet Union and the United States at the Third United Nations Conference on the Law of the Sea* at 4–9 (1984). The United States introduced revised versions of the three articles in the Second Subcommittee of the Seabed Committee in 1971. UN Doc. A/AC.138/SC.II/L.4 (Jul. 30, 1971.)

[49] The deletion of the word "present" in relevant General Assembly resolutions would prove highly prophetic.   [50] GA Res. 2340 (XXII) (Dec. 18, 1967).

tion of underlying fisheries interests within the framework of the high seas regime in the context of a 12-mile territorial sea. The Pardo initiative, with its broad internationalist appeal, potentially posed an even greater threat of stimulating interest in many developing countries in maximizing the area subject to international regulation, and therefore minimizing the area of coastal state control.

The response to these challenges by some Latin American states was to redirect attention to the complaint that the entire corpus of the law of the sea had been developed without regard to the interests of developing and newly independent countries, and therefore needed to be examined as a whole or not at all.

E. Preparations for the Third Conference

Having decided to prepare for a new conference on the law of the sea, the General Assembly took the relatively expedient step of expanding the mandate of the Seabed Committee to include preparations for the Conference and expanding the membership of the Committee.[51] It is instructive that not only was the law of the sea not referred to the International Law Commission, but it was overseen by the First Committee of the General Assembly, whose mandate is political matters, rather than the Sixth Committee, whose mandate is legal matters.

Apart from identification of major issues, and positions with respect to those issues, the Seabed Committee made little progress in preparing for the Conference. The problems were too diverse and the Committee was too large either to function well by consensus or to permit voting on issues where a minority of participants had important interests that required accommodation. Many delegations were controlled by personnel from permanent missions to the UN who were more interested in having a free hand to deal with the matter and to exercise their skills in ideological and coalition politics than in stimulating careful interministerial analysis of national interests in their capitals.[52]

---

[51] *Ibid.*

[52] It is interesting to note that while US delegations at the time were encouraged to favor UN headquarters in New York as the venue for UN-sponsored negotiations, that policy did not apply to the law of the sea negotiations. The US preferred to distance the negotiations from the permanent delegations in New York in the hope of stimulating other countries to send instructions or officials from capitals primarily responsive to their governments' substantive interests and priorities. Indeed, one of the less obvious purposes of the very extensive bilateral consultations undertaken by the United States between negotiating sessions was to stimulate foreign governments, in anticipation of a visit by US officials, to focus on their own interests and formulate coordinated governmental views at a reasonably high level, and thereafter to issue substantive instructions to their delegations, whether or not consistent with US substantive preferences.

It became apparent that the issue was whether to convene the Conference without a basic text before it or to delay the Conference indefinitely. The former decision was taken.[53]

F. The Third Conference

Approximately twice as many states attended the Third UN Conference on the Law of the Sea as had attended the First Conference in 1958.[54] Essentially all the additional states were developing countries associated with the Group of 77. The Conference was thus faced with the same problem that had come to plague the General Assembly and other global conferences, namely the capacity of one self-identified interest group of developing countries to control the outcome of votes requiring a simple majority and, in many cases, votes requiring the traditional two-thirds majority necessary for matters of substance such as approval of treaty articles.

The solution in the Conference Rules of Procedure had two important elements. One was confirmation of the "Gentlemen's Agreement" reached earlier that no voting would occur until all efforts at reaching consensus had been exhausted.[55] Another was that the two-thirds majority of delegates present and voting required for approval of texts if voting occurred must include a majority of delegations participating in that session of the Conference.[56]

It is extraordinary to consider that the Conference – which met for several months each year for almost ten years, which had no basic text before it when it convened, and which conducted almost all of its substantive deliberations in "informal" meetings of committees and groups open to all delegations – never resorted to a vote on matters of substance apart from a few relatively minor amendments at the end and, of course, the vote on the Convention as a whole requested by the United States.[57] The

---

53 GA Res. 3067 (XXVIII) (Nov. 16, 1973).

54 Delegations from 164 states went to the Third Conference; 142 states signed the Final Act of the Third Conference; 159 states and other competent entities signed the 1982 UN Convention.

55 Rules of Procedures, Third United Nations Conference on the Law of the Sea, Appendix, UN Doc. A/CONF.62/30/Rev.3, UN Pub. Sales No. E.81.I.5 (1981).

56 *Ibid.*, Rules 37–40. Thus, for example, a vote of seventy in favor, thirty against, with fifty abstentions would not suffice.

57 There is a certain irony in the fact that the United States had consistently opposed resort to voting, but that the only significant substantive decision taken by the Conference by a formal vote, that on the Convention as a whole, was the result of a demand for a vote by the United States. There is reason to believe that the three other states that voted against the Convention or those that abstained would not themselves have requested a vote.

key was a procedure sometimes described as consensus, but more accurately described as an iterative process emphasizing informal negotiation.

In 1975, the Conference authorized the chairmen of its main committees and the president of the Conference to issue a single negotiating text. These texts were typically issued at the end of a session, and revised in light of negotiations between sessions and at subsequent sessions.

In the Second Committee, whose mandate included virtually all of the matters addressed by the four Geneva Conventions, including the basic issues of coastal state competence, the Chair relied heavily on the results of informal negotiations among interested delegations, which in many instances yielded the 1958 Geneva Convention texts verbatim or with useful refinements, and in others revolutionary changes. The process was so successful that the Committee ultimately adopted a "rule of silence" pursuant to which failure to comment on a particular provision in the article-by-article review of the negotiating text was deemed to indicate no objection. A delegate once described the virtues of the process as follows: Don't ask me to say "yes" and I won't say "no."

The Committee resolved the basic question of allocation of competence by a "package" that establishes a 12-mile maximum limit for the territorial sea, within that limit establishes a liberal transit regime for navigation and overflight in straits, and beyond that limit establishes substantial coastal state competence (including control of fisheries and seabed resources) in an exclusive economic zone that may extend up to 200 miles from the baseline. It resolved the question of whether the "straight baseline" system adopted from the Anglo-Norwegian Fisheries case may be applied by mid-ocean archipelagic states such as Indonesia and the Philippines by establishing a new regime of archipelagic waters, subject to transit rights substantially the same as those applicable in straits. It resolved the question of the seaward limit of the continental shelf by defining a precise limit of the continental shelf that extends to the edge of the continental margin or to 200 miles from the baseline, whichever is further seaward. The text requires coastal states to make international contributions of designated percentages of the value of production from the continental margin seaward of 200 miles.

In the First Committee, whose mandate was the regime for the seabeds beyond the limits of national jurisdiction (determined in the Second Committee), the process did not produce widespread agreement. One of the reasons was the sharp ideological split between developing countries and industrialized states. It is important in this regard to consider that ideology was an obstacle to agreement with respect to an activity (mining for hard minerals seaward of 200 miles and the continental margin) that did not yet exist, and that did not engage anything approaching the

322

magnitude of social, economic, and security interests affected by the widely accepted Second Committee text. Control over virtually all of the seabed hydrocarbons and marine fisheries of the world was allocated by the Second Committee with barely a hint of ideological conflict over demands for a New International Economic Order or otherwise.

The Third Committee produced a new and remarkably powerful environmental protection regime affecting all uses of the sea. From that Committee came one of the few new sweeping duties enunciated by the Convention: "States have the obligation to protect and preserve the marine environment."[58] From that Committee came one of the rare enunciations of human rights obligations in a treaty devoted to other subjects: "recognized rights of the accused" must be observed in trials for environmental violations committed by a foreign vessel.[59]

States are required to adopt pollution-control regulations that are no less effective than relevant international standards with respect to virtually all activities at sea.[60] They also have a duty to ensure that such standards are developed.[61] The difficult problem of accommodating environmental and navigation interests is resolved by elaborate provisions, including those requiring enforcement of generally accepted international standards by the flag state[62] and permitting enforcement of such standards by port states[63] and by coastal states in the territorial sea and the exclusive economic zone.[64]

The work of the Third Committee reflected the desire of the overwhelming majority of coastal states for substantial control over scientific research in the exclusive economic zone and on the continental shelf. The text nevertheless contains some standards and criteria that may promote regularity in coastal-state procedures and protect marine scientists from mere inaction or wholly political failures to grant consent to conduct research. Although subject to the rights of coastal states, a universal right to conduct marine scientific research is enunciated in the first article of the relevant chapter.

One of the most extraordinary features of the Convention is the decision by the Plenary to provide for compulsory arbitration or adjudication of disputes.[65] Compromissory clauses of this sort are not common in general

---

[58] Law of the Sea Convention, note 7 above, art. 192.   [59] *Ibid.*, art. 230, para. 3.

[60] *Ibid.*, arts. 21(4), 39(2), 54, 94, 208(3), 210(6), 211(2). Warships are excluded as such from the environmental provisions of the Convention, but are required to comply to the extent reasonable and practicable. *Ibid.*, art. 236

[61] *Ibid.*, arts. 145, 197, 207(4), 208(5), 209(1), 210(4), 211(1), 212(3).

[62] See note 60 above.

[63] Law of the Sea Convention, note 7 above, arts. 218, 220(1).

[64] *Ibid.*, art. 220. The coastal state also has certain prescriptive competence with respect to pollution from ships in innocent passage in the territorial sea and from ships navigating in ice-covered areas in the territorial sea and exclusive economic zone. *Ibid.*, arts. 21, 211(4), 234.   [65] *Ibid.*, art. 286.

multilateral conventions of the scope of the Law of the Sea Convention. The fact that alternative procedures,[66] a new standing tribunal,[67] and substantial exceptions[68] were necessary parts of a generally acceptable dispute-settlement text should not obscure the significance of the basic agreement to require states to arbitrate or adjudicate unresolved law of the sea disputes.

In contrast to the decisions taken in Geneva in 1958, the Plenary decided to incorporate all substantive and dispute-settlement provisions in a single Convention that does not permit reservations.[69] The underlying conception is one of a "package deal" in which substantive and political relationships, priorities, and accommodations are too complex and intertwined to be separated.[70] To some degree, the decision was also a reaction to an intervening opinion of the International Court of Justice in the North Sea Continental Shelf cases observing that the fact that a provision is subject to reservations may suggest that it was not intended to be declaratory of international law.[71]

The decision of the International Court of Justice in the North Sea Continental Shelf cases also had more direct effects on the Convention. In the course of its opinion, the Court emphasized the nature of the continental shelf as the natural prolongation of the land territory of the coastal state.[72] This language is reflected in the Convention's definition of the continental shelf.[73]

But the rule of the North Sea cases regarding delimitation of the continental shelf between neighboring coastal states was not repeated. By deciding that delimitation of the exclusive economic zone and continental shelf between neighboring coastal states should be effected "by agreement on the basis of international law in order to achieve an equitable solution,"[74] the Conference in effect left the task of articulating the details of the law in this field to the International Court of Justice and other tribunals to which states were submitting the issue with increasing frequency. While one cannot reasonably conclude that all participants thereby expressed satisfaction with the developing jurisprudence, one can

---

[66] *Ibid.*, arts. 282, 287.   [67] *Ibid.*, Annex VI.   [68] *Ibid.*, arts. 297–99.

[69] *Ibid.*, art. 309. Declarations are provided for in connection with specified optional exceptions to the obligation to arbitrate or adjudicate disputes. *Ibid.*, art. 298.

[70] See H. Caminos & M. Molitor, "Progressive Development of International Law and the Package Deal," 79 *AJIL* 871 (1985); R. Y. Jennings, "Law Making and the Package Deal," in *Mélanges offerts à Paul Reuter, Le droit international: unité et diversité*, 347–55 (1981).

[71] North Sea Continental Shelf cases (*Fed. Rep. Germany* v. *Denmark, Fed. Rep. Germany* v. *Netherlands*), 1969 ICJ 4, paras. 63–64.

[72] *Ibid.*, paras. 43, 101. The preamble of the 1945 Truman Proclamation states that "the continental shelf may be regarded as an extension of the land-mass of the coastal nations." Presidential Proclamation 2667, Sept. 28, 1945, 10 Fed. Reg. 12303 (1945).

[73] Law of the Sea Convention, note 7 above, art. 76, para. 1.   [74] *Ibid.*, arts. 74 & 83.

conclude that no more specific directives commanded sufficiently wide-spread support.[75]

The decision of the International Court of Justice in the UK–Iceland Fisheries Jurisdiction case[76] had little direct impact on the negotiations. Nevertheless, the practical difficulties faced by the United Kingdom and others in dealing with the Icelandic claims both before and after the Court's decision may have helped persuade governments that resistance to extended fisheries jurisdiction was too costly.[77] The fact that the case was brought also may have helped persuade some coastal states to oppose compulsory arbitration or adjudication of disputes regarding fisheries in the exclusive economic zone.[78]

G. Historical evaluation

Taken as a whole, the United Nations Convention on the Law of the Sea represents both a substantial affirmation of and a substantial departure from the historical Grotian model.

[75] One might conclude that at least some Conference participants may have been surprised by the fact that the Court, in the Libya–Malta Continental Shelf case, extracted important delimitation implications from the use of the distance of 200 miles as the limit of the exclusive economic zone and as an alternative limit of the continental shelf. The Court concluded that there was essentially no role for the natural prolongation concept, in a physical sense, in delimitations of overlapping 200-mile zones where distance constituted the basis of title. Case Concerning the Continental Shelf (*Libyan Arab Jamahiriya* v. *Malta*), 1985 ICJ 4, paras. 34, 39–40.

While there were many reasons for the strong refusal to subsume the continental shelf regime within the new exclusive economic zone regime at the Law of the Sea Conference, almost all reflected a desire to preserve the continental shelf regime as a whole. The continental shelf regime contains a more detailed elaboration of rights and duties with respect to the seabed than does the exclusive economic zone regime. The regime for living resources of the exclusive economic zone is expressly subordinated to that of the continental shelf with respect to sedentary species.

The question of possible delimitation implications being drawn from the nature of the seaward limits of coastal state jurisdiction was in fact addressed at the Conference. The argument as to whether the definition of the continental shelf should refer first to natural prolongation and the continental margin, or first to the 200-mile limit (if at all), was resolved both by referring to natural prolongation and the continental margin first and by adding a specific paragraph stating that the provisions establishing the seaward limits of the continental shelf "are without prejudice to the question of delimitation of the continental shelf between States with opposite or adjacent coasts." Art. 76, paras. 1 & 10.

Albeit not entirely ignored, it is not clear that these factors had any impact on the Court's willingness either to emphasize the seaward limits as indicative of the basis of title or to select distance as the effective basis of title over the continental shelf landward of 200 miles.

[76] Fisheries Jurisdiction case (*United Kingdom* v. *Iceland*), 1974 ICJ 3.

[77] The late Guy Ladreit de Lacharrière, who represented France at the Third Law of the Sea Conference and was subsequently elected to the International Court of Justice, remarked with respect to the so-called "cod war" between Iceland and the United Kingdom that at the cost of maintaining even a small warship off the Icelandic coast to protect British fishermen, the price of cod would soon exceed the price of smoked salmon.

[78] See Law of the Sea Convention, note 7 above, art. 297, para. 3.

From the perspective of navigation,[79] overflight, and related uses, the dominant regime remains freedom of the seas beyond a 12-mile territorial sea and, for purposes of transit, in straits and archipelagic sea lanes. This is, however, qualified by significant coastal state rights regarding pollution from ships in the exclusive economic zone:[80] to enforce generally accepted international standards;[81] to prescribe and enforce certain standards in special areas with the approval of the competent international organization;[82] and to prescribe and enforce standards in ice-covered areas.[83]

From the perspective of seabed activities, on the other hand, not much is left of the Grotian model. Indeed, at least as of the middle of the twentieth century, some may question whether the freedom of the seas was ever in fact exercised by a state other than the coastal state with respect to commercial extraction of hydrocarbons or minerals from the seabed.[84] To be sure, the Grotian model continues to apply to activities related to navigation (such as anchoring). It also applies to other communications uses such as the laying and maintenance of submarine cables and, in qualified form, pipelines. But in many other respects, the situation is quite different.

The 1945 Truman Proclamation effectively excluded exploitation of the natural resources of the continental shelf from the Grotian model. The 1958 Convention on the Continental Shelf confirmed and refined the exclusion and at least potentially extended its geographic scope. The 1982 Convention expanded the substantive scope of coastal state jurisdiction to include all drilling and virtually all installations and structures, and expanded the geographic scope of coastal state jurisdiction to include the continental margin as well as all other seabed areas within 200 miles of the coast. As a result, from the perspective of the right to exploit most known seabed hydrocarbon deposits and most significant seabed living resources, the Grotian model does not apply at all.

The question of whether the freedom of the seas applies as such to the exploitation of the mineral resources of the seabed beyond the continental shelf is contested.[85] Notwithstanding this fact, the basic principle of

---

[79] Grotius's primary concern.

[80] While differently articulated, generally similar rights exist with respect to ships transiting straits and archipelagic sea lanes. See Law of the Sea Convention, note 7 above, arts. 41–42, 53–54, 233. In this regard it should be borne in mind that a ship in transit will normally have to navigate through the exclusive economic zone before entering and after leaving archipelagic waters or the internal waters and territorial sea of a strait.

[81] *Ibid.*, art. 211, para. 5, art. 220, paras. 1, 3–7.

[82] *Ibid.*, art. 211, para. 6, art. 220, para. 8.   [83] *Ibid.*, art. 234.

[84] One may assume for this purpose that the harvesting of pearls is regarded as exploitation of living resources. In any event pearl fisheries tend to be conducted by coastal populations.

[85] The issue is whether those resources may be exploited apart from or in the absence of a generally agreed international regime. In connection with its decision to convene a new law of the sea conference, the General Assembly, by a vote of sixty-two to twenty-eight with twenty-eight abstentions, declared a moratorium on exploitation (but not exploration) of deep

universal access associated with the freedom of the seas is also articulated by the Convention,[86] albeit subject to significant regulatory conditions for mining. An international system for regulation of mining open to all, administered in important respects by the state of nationality,[87] is certainly more consistent with the Grotian model than it is with coastal state jurisdiction or other forms of national appropriation.[88] Apart from the question of regulation of exploitation of mineral resources, the application of the principles and rules of high seas law to the seabed beyond the continental shelf is not a subject of serious dispute.[89]

The 200-mile exclusive economic zone is the Convention's most significant departure from the Grotian model. It applies to the waters of the sea as such. Freedom of fishing is eliminated for most commercially exploited fisheries of the world. There are coastal state rights to exclude or regulate other important activities. While the high seas freedoms of navigation, overflight, and related uses are preserved in the zone, navigation is nevertheless subject to certain environmental rights of the coastal state already noted.

The exclusive economic zone represents a dramatic shift from a geographical allocation of competence between areas of territorial sovereignty and areas of the free high seas to a functional allocation of competence in the same area based on the nature of the activity being conducted.[90] Some activities are expressly subject to varying degrees of coastal state competence.[91] Others are expressly free of coastal state competence to varying degrees.[92] The question of residual competence that is not expressly allocated by the Convention is not resolved in principle one way or the other; its resolution depends on the specific activity and interests

seabed resources pending the establishment of an international regime. GA Res. 2574 D (XXIV) (Dec. 15, 1969). Major industrial states rejected the moratorium and, in ensuing years, enacted legislation authorizing deep seabed mining in accordance with high seas principles and entered into agreements with each other to avoid conflicting allocations of mine sites. Article 137 of the Law of the Sea Convention prohibits the parties from recognizing any claim, acquisition, or exercise of rights with respect to minerals recovered from the deep seabed except in accordance with the Convention. The Conference adopted a resolution expressly providing a procedure for protection of so-called pioneer investments in exploration of particular areas pending entry into force of the Convention. Resolution II, Final Act of the Third United Nations Conference on the Law of the Sea, Annex 1, UN Pub. Sales No. E.83.V.5, at 158, 177 (1983).   [86] Law of the Sea Convention, note 7 above, art. 141.

[87] The "sponsoring State" under the Convention. See *ibid.*, art. 139; art. 153, paras. 2,4; art. 190; ann. 3, art. 4, paras. 1, 3–4.

[88] The author has elaborated his views on this question elsewhere. See B. Oxman, "The High Seas and the International Seabed Area," 10 *Mich. J. Int'l L.* 526 (1989).   [89] *Ibid.*

[90] While this shift may have been presaged by the emergence of the continental shelf doctrine, its application to a vast area of the sea itself is more significant for historical, conceptual, and practical reasons.

[91] Law of the Sea Convention, note 7 above, arts. 56, 60, 61–73, 77, 81, 208, 210, 214, 216, 246–55.   [92] *Ibid.*, arts. 58, 79, 211, 220, 221, 234.

involved.[93] If the question is posed as to whether the exclusive economic zone is *mare liberum* or *mare clausum*, the typical answer may be "neither" but the more accurate answer may be "both."

The Convention takes a significantly new approach to resolving the basic dispute over competence that began at the dawn of modern international law. In some respects, it is conservative in the sense that it draws on and directly accommodates the options conceptually identified by Grotius and Selden, albeit in new ways. In other respects, however, it represents a new departure from traditional thinking with respect to the law of the sea.

Some may regard its controversial attempt to endow an international organization with direct regulatory competence over deep seabed mining as its most radical departure. In theory they may be right. But deep seabed mining is not a traditional, or even a current, use. In many if not most respects, the debate about the deep seabed mining regime is a debate about political and economic abstractions.

The more significant departure in the Convention in practice may well be found in its other attempts to provide for international mechanisms to deal with the functional problems of the law of the sea in the future and to adapt to changed circumstances and unanticipated needs. There are three interrelated elements:

(i) some shift in emphasis from the allocation of rights (be it coastal-state jurisdiction or flag-state freedoms) to the elaboration of duties in the exercise of rights;[94]

(ii) a link between those duties and detailed standards emanating from the competent international organizations; and

(iii) compulsory arbitration or adjudication of many types of disputes.

The most significant illustration of this new approach is in the field of environmental protection. The Convention recognizes that while allocation of competence may sometimes help achieve underlying environmental goals, neither a flag state nor a coastal state may have sufficient expertise or interest to ensure adequate environmental control of activities subject to its jurisdiction. Thus it is not only the flag-state freedoms, but the coastal-state rights as well, that are subjected to strong environmental duties including,

---

[93] *Ibid.*, arts. 55, 59. This should be contrasted both with the territorial sea where, apart from the right of innocent passage, all uses are generally subject to coastal state sovereignty, and with the classic high seas where, apart from specific coastal state rights, all uses generally may be conducted by all states without coastal state regulation.

[94] The terms "rights" and "duties" are not used here in the Hohfeldian sense that a right of one person entails a corresponding duty of another. The distinction suggested is rather one between a right of self-help (e.g., flag-state freedom to take the fish, coastal-state jurisdiction to exclude foreign fishermen) and a right to demand that a foreign state comply with a duty (e.g., flag-state duty to ensure that its ships' crews are instructed in navigation safety, coastal-state duty to ensure that continental shelf oil drilling is environmentally safe).

in particular, a duty to comply with certain international standards elaborated by the competent international organization. Failure to respect these standards is subject to compulsory arbitration or adjudication.

Another manifestation of the new emphasis on international organizations is the establishment of combined national and international competence. The coastal state is empowered to enforce generally accepted international environmental standards, promulgated by the competent international organization, against foreign ships navigating in the exclusive economic zone. The coastal state shares with the competent international organization the power to prescribe sea lanes and traffic separation schemes in straits and archipelagos[95] and the power to prescribe special anti-pollution measures for ships in special areas within the exclusive economic zone.[96] The coastal-state determination of the precise seaward limits of its continental shelf beyond 200 miles is final and binding if consistent with the recommendations of an international commission of experts in geology, geophysics, and hydrography to which the coastal state submits proposed limits and supporting data.[97]

Such provisions are too new and incomplete to suggest that we are moving beyond *mare liberum* and *mare clausum* to *mare communum*. But they do suggest that the complaint that the Convention is insufficiently internationalist in perspective may prove to be premature. There may not be a world oceans organization as such, but there would be a tribunal on the law of the sea, and there are established and respected international organizations within the United Nations system capable of assuming the new roles provided for in the Convention. The 1995 UN convention on fishing, which elaborates on the Law of the Sea Convention's provisions regarding straddling stocks and highly migratory species, conditions freedom of fishing on cooperation with regional fisheries organizations and compliance with their regulations.

Perhaps most importantly, it is impossible to read the environmental provisions of the Convention without concluding that, at least in this respect, the community interest is given priority, and the community is given new tools to work its will in universally binding form subject to compulsory arbitration or adjudication. It may be some time before other treaties do so much to give practical institutional effect to the community interest in the environment, particularly if this effort is left to founder.

---

[95] Law of the Sea Convention, note 7 above, arts. 41, 53. Even before the Convention was completed, the shared competence was interpreted broadly to include under-keel clearance regulations in the Straits of Malacca proposed by the straits states and approved by the International Maritime Organization.   [96] *Ibid.*, art. 211, para. 6.

[97] *Ibid.*, art. 76, para. 8 and ann. 2.

IV. CUSTOMARY INTERNATIONAL LAW

There can be no doubt that the First, Second, and Third UN Conferences on the Law of the Sea, and especially the resultant conventions, had a significant impact on both the practice of states and their perception of their legal obligations. This is of course the stuff of customary international law.[98]

The work of the United Nations on the law of the sea has stimulated extraordinary scholarship and analysis on the influence of so-called "law-making" conferences and treaties on the rights and duties of nonparties under customary international law. Indeed, the most extensive commentary on that question by the International Court of Justice arose with respect to the 1958 Convention on the Continental Shelf.[99]

This impact on customary international law is frequently cited to demonstrate the "success" of the law-making effort. The argument is simple enough. The negotiation of a treaty is a means to achieving a larger end, namely widespread acceptance of the same legal rules. If that end is achieved through the operation of customary international law without widespread ratification, then it may be argued that the negotiation achieved its ultimate objective.

Since the impact of law-making treaties on the rights and obligations of nonparties is traditionally regarded as issue specific, the fact that one concedes the success of the endeavor as a whole in terms of its impact on customary international law may not significantly prejudice one's ability to challenge the customary international law impact of a particular provision. In the common remark that a particular convention is generally declaratory of international law, much work is being done by the word "generally."

Those with an agenda are under very considerable pressure to articulate their preferences regarding what should be the law as statements of what the customary law is. But few of us are comfortable with the idea of lying about the law. Thus, there is an inexorable tendency to relax the meta-law, that is to expand the number and authority of sources of customary international law so as to enhance the plausibility of assertions regarding its content, or at least ease the conscience of the speaker.

In the latter half of the twentieth century this tendency has been fed by at least two substantive and two structural objectives. The two substantive objectives are the promotion of human rights and the protection of the environment. The two structural objectives are stabilizing international law in general, and the law of the sea in particular, and strengthening global institutions.

---

[98] See Statute of the International Court of Justice, art. 38, para. 1 (b).
[99] North Sea Continental Shelf cases, note 71 above.

The particular significance of discussing the impact of the 1982 Convention on the Law of the Sea on customary international law is that it represents a confluence of both structural objectives. The only plausible basis for achieving stability in the law of the sea for the foreseeable future is respect for the rules set forth in the Convention. The Convention itself is the result of the most ambitious global institutional law-making effort ever undertaken. Its introduction of global compulsory arbitration, its conferral of quasi-legislative authority on a host of "competent international organizations" in the environmental and safety fields, and its establishment of an international organization to regulate deep seabed mining are widely regarded as significant steps in strengthening global institutions in and of themselves, and as precedents.

It seems reasonably clear that stability in the law of the sea is best served (albeit not guaranteed) by widespread ratification of the Convention. Even opponents of the Convention tend to refrain from challenging this proposition as such. At least two major institutional contributions of the Convention itself – compulsory dispute settlement and a deep seabed organization – are legally dependent upon entry into force of the Convention and politically dependent upon more widespread ratification to achieve the underlying institutional goals.

On issues where alternative positions are plausible, this would suggest to many commentators on the subject a position regarding the relationship between the Convention and customary law most likely to enhance widespread ratification. But what precisely is that? It is in this broader context that one must consider the relevance of the customary law question to the underlying issue of the contributions of the United Nations to international law. For those who believe that the purpose of the Law of the Sea Convention was to effect a peaceful change in the law that would force distant water fishermen to purchase their way into vast areas off foreign coasts and refrain from competing with coastal operators, there can be no doubt that the Convention succeeded even before it was completed. The same may well be true for a fair number of other changes in the law, especially provisions expanding the powers of the coastal state.[100]

But for those concerned with protection of a rational and efficient international communications regime, for those hoping to strengthen international environmental controls, and for those interested in promoting the stability of international law and the authority of international negotiating processes, institutions, and tribunals, it is at best a misleading and self-deceptive half-truth to proclaim the effort a success on the grounds

---

[100] There is, unfortunately, insufficient indication that the coastal states are approaching concomitant duties, such as the duty to conserve fisheries in the 200-mile zone, with the same enthusiasm.

of its absorption into customary law. Whatever the theory, the extent of that absorption in practice is unclear today. It is likely to be even less clear tomorrow as more evidence of state practice accumulates. And even if it were clear, these objectives cannot be realized fully if at all by customary law alone.

V. THE FUTURE

The Law of the Sea Convention entered into force on November 16, 1994. Almost all of the first sixty states to ratify the Convention were developing countries. At the same time, the efforts of the Secretary-General of the United Nations, commenced in 1990, bore fruit. Negotiations under his auspices produced a new agreement in the summer of 1994 regarding the implementation of part XI of the Convention.[101] The new agreement accommodates important objections of the industrialized states to the deep seabed mining regime, incorporates more market-oriented approaches to resource management, and is designed to facilitate widespread ratification of the Convention. It is in force provisionally for almost all states, including the major industrial states, many of which have become or are about to become parties to the Convention and the Implementing Agreement. The number of parties to the Convention is increasing rapidly – in late 1996 they number at least 108 – but it remains unclear whether and if so when universal ratification will be achieved.

In less than fifty years, the United Nations has moved from the codification and progressive development of the law of the sea to the drafting of what has been called "a constitution for the oceans."[102] The question now is whether the United Nations Convention on the Law of the Sea will in fact be that constitution.

There is no doubt that the Convention may be "implemented" by states without ratification, and may be regarded as "generally" declaratory of international law for the moment. Coastal states raced to assert the new jurisdictions permitted by the Convention well before the ink was dry. But one may question whether anything properly regarded as a constitution may exist in the absence of both written text that has legal force as such and authoritative institutions (including but not limited to courts) to ascertain and develop a constitution's meaning.

[101] Resolution and Agreement Relating to the Implementation of Part XI of the 1982 United Nations Convention on the Law of the Sea (July 29, 1994).

[102] Title of remarks by Tommy T. B. Koh, President of the Third United Nations Conference on the Law of the Sea, published by the United Nations with the text of the Convention and the Final Act of the Conference, UN Pub. Sales No. E.83.V.5, at xxxiii (1983).

Some societies may have sufficient cultural homogeneity and institutional strength and stability to dispense with the need for text at least in some respects. Some may have powerful enough courts or other authoritative institutions to graft an "unwritten" constitution onto a written one or even create a constitution over time. There is little if anything in existing international life to suggest a parallel development in the international law of the sea. Experience in the twentieth century would suggest the contrary.

The reality is that the Convention supplies both the text and the institutional strength. The latter may well be more important than the former, particularly over time. The question is not whether custom and practice are the ultimate arbiters of a constitutional order. The question is rather how to guide, restrain, and influence that practice.

Without a universally ratified Convention, arbitration or adjudication is possible, but generally not compulsory for nonparties. Fewer cases may be brought, and those that are brought are less likely to be decided with conscious attention to the development and adaptation of the Convention. Sooner or later, a respected international tribunal will refuse to regard some provision of the Convention as declaratory of customary international law, and the symbolic legitimacy (and therefore the restraining force) of the Convention as a whole may well be impaired.

Without a universally ratified Convention, universal respect for international environmental and other standards promulgated by international organizations is possible, but not mandatory in any meaningful sense.[103] Specialized agencies and other organizations will continue to depend almost entirely on ratification of specialized treaties and voluntary compliance with standards not otherwise binding.

The importance of the Convention for the international system, and thus for the United Nations, is found not only in what it says the law is but also in what it symbolizes and in how it provides for the law's development and adaptation. If it is to be a true constitution, then it needs more than formal (and inevitably cumbersome) amendment procedures in order to respond to changing needs and circumstances. But if the adaptations are to be consistent with the underlying notion of a constitutional order, then there ultimately must be authoritative arbiters of the continuing struggles

---

[103] It would be difficult to convince a state that it is bound by customary law to ensure that its nationals obey a technical regulation of an international organization that the state has not agreed to respect. One need only imagine trying to persuade the United States Congress of such a proposition. Provisions to this effect in the new Restatement may be laudable, and their exclusion would have been inconsistent with the Restatement's sound approach to the Convention in general, but they are essentially untested' and, in any event, are not automatically subject to arbitration or adjudication for most states. See *Restatement (Third) of the Foreign Relations Law of the United States*, secs. 502, 601, 603. The author addresses this matter in B. Oxman, "The Duty to Respect Generally Accepted International Standards," 24 *NYU J. Int'l L. & Pol'y* 109 (1991).

about change and accommodation. These are more readily available if the Convention is universally ratified.

No body of law stands still. The question is whether we wish to continue to lurch from one law of the sea conference to another because law of the sea conferences are the only available collective institution with sufficient legitimacy to restrain conflicting state practice and accommodate conflicting interests even temporarily. Perhaps so. Many of us could imagine a better convention. The difficulty is that we may disagree about what "better" means.

For many of those involved, the Convention represents a repudiation of the idea that what has been called "the struggle for law" is appropriately resolved without reference to community institutions representing all, be they conferences, courts, or organizations. Many, although by no means all, developing countries believed that their interest in having a fair degree of influence over the course of the law of the sea was best protected by the development of conventional rather than customary law because adoption of conventions requires numerical majorities. Many, although by no means all, industrialized maritime states believed that their interest in having a fair degree of influence over the claims and practices of a large number of developing countries was best protected by the development of conventional rather than customary law because conventions, and changes to conventions, require the affirmative consent of the parties.

These were not romantic notions. Countries in the former group wondered whether they could win a lonely, direct struggle with a richer or more powerful state. Countries in the latter group were concerned about their ability to sustain the costs of (and reasonably consistent platform of principle for) a direct and continuing struggle with different states in different parts of the world. Both groups imagined that a universally ratified convention, although not wholly satisfactory to anyone, could be a better alternative than no convention at all.

If they were wrong, then perhaps the world can do well enough without either a universal ratification of the current Convention or calling a new conference on the law of the sea. But if they were right, then prudence suggests that efforts be intensified to promote universal ratification.

The challenge is a daunting one. So long as it appears that the Convention has stabilized state practice, the relative advantages of a universally ratified convention are less apparent. The Convention could well be the victim of its own success.

The problem is that the window of opportunity may not remain open. Once newly articulated divergences from the Convention proliferate in national legislation and state practice on issues other than deep seabed mining, it will be more difficult to achieve universal ratification without in effect, if not form, a new open-ended conference or series of conferences on the law of the sea. There is reason to doubt whether many governments would view such a prospect with equanimity.

SELECTED BIBLIOGRAPHY

Clingan, T. A., Jr., "An Overview of Second Committee Negotiations in the Law of the Sea," 63 *Oregon L. Rev.* 52 (1984)

Dean, A. H., "The Geneva Conference on the Law of the Sea: What Was Accomplished," 52 *AJIL* 607 (1958)

Dupuy, R.-J. and D. Vignes, *Traité du Nouveau Droit de la Mer* (1985); *A Handbook on the New Law of the Sea* (English version, Martinus Nijhoff, 1991)

The Exclusive Economic Zone, A Latin American Perspective (F. Orrego Vicuña ed.; Westview, 1984)

International Maritime Boundaries (J. I. Charney & L. M. Alexander eds.; American Society of International Law, 1993)

Jessup, P. C., "The Geneva Conference on the Law of the Sea: A Study in International Law-Making," 52 *AJIL* 730 (1958)

O'Connell, D. P., *The International Law of the Sea* (I. Shearer ed., 1982, 1994)

Panel on the Law of Ocean Uses, *International Ocean Law and US Oceans Policy* (ASIL, 1988)

Oxman, B. H., "The Preparations for the Law of the Sea Conference," 68 *AJIL* 1 (1974) (with J. R. Stevenson)

"The 1974 Caracas Session," 69 *AJIL* 1 (1975) (with J. R. Stevenson)

"The 1975 Geneva Session," 69 AJIL 763 (1975) (with J. R. Stevenson)

"The 1976 New York Session," 71 *AJIL* 247 (1977) (with J. R. Stevenson)

"The 1977 New York Session," 72 *AJIL* 57 (1978) (with J. R. Stevenson)

"The Seventh Session (1978)," 73 *AJIL* 1 (1979) (with J. R. Stevenson)

"The Eighth Session (1979)," 74 *AJIL* 1 (1980) (with J. R. Stevenson)

"The Ninth Session (1980)," 75 *AJIL* 211 (1981) (with J. R. Stevenson)

"The Tenth Session (1981)," 76 *AJIL* 1 (1982) (with J. R. Stevenson)

Sohn, L. B. & K. Gustafson, *The Law of the Sea in a Nut Shell* (West, 1984)

Treves, T., "Codification du Droit International et Pratique des Etats dans le Droit de la Mer," 223 *RCADI* (1990–IV)

CHAPTER TWELVE

OUTER SPACE

Ralph G. Steinhardt

I. INTRODUCTION

At its threshold, any account of international space law must confront a fundamental ambiguity. From one perspective, there exists a relatively well-articulated legal regime governing the activities of state and private actors in outer space. That regime consists in the five space treaties adopted since 1967,[1] and in general international law, which has long been assumed to apply in space.[2] In this view, the United Nations – operating largely by consensus – has been the dominant actor, providing an effective framework for the conscious, harmonious response to rapid technological and

---

[1] The basic space treaties are:

1. *The Outer Space Treaty.* The Treaty on Principles Governing the Activities of States in the Exploration and Use of Outer Space, Including the Moon and Other Celestial Bodies, Dec. 19, 1966, 18 UST 2410, TIAS No. 6347, 610 UNTS 205 (*adopted* by the General Assembly in GA Res. 2222 (XXI)) (*entered into force* October 10, 1967).
2. *The Rescue and Return Agreement.* The Agreement on the Rescue of Astronauts, the Return of Astronauts, and the Return of Objects Launched into Outer Space, Dec. 19, 1967, 19 UST 7570, TIAS No. 6599, 672 UNTS 119 (*adopted* by the General Assembly in GA Res. 2345 (XXII)) (*entered into force* Dec. 3, 1968).
3. *The Liability Convention.* The Convention on International Liability for Damage Caused by Space Objects, *opened for signature*, Mar. 29, 1972, 24 UST 2389, TIAS No. 7762, 961 UNTS 187 (*adopted* by the General Assembly in GA Res. 2777 (XXVI) (Nov. 29, 1971));
4. *The Registration Convention.* The Convention on the Registration of Objects Launched into Outer Space, Nov. 12, 1974, 28 UST 695, TIAS No. 8480, UN GAOR, 29th Sess., Supp. (No. 31), A/9631 (*adopted* by the General Assembly in GA Res. 3235 (XXIX)) (*entered into force* September 15, 1976).
5. *The Moon Agreement.* The Agreement Governing the Activities of States on the Moon and Other Celestial Bodies, 18 *ILM* 1434, GA Res. 34/68, GAOR, 34th Sess., Supp. No. 46, at 77 (*entered into force* July 12, 1984).

Other treaties explicitly apply in part to activities in space but are not limited to such activities, e.g., Multilateral Treaty Banning Nuclear Weapon Tests in the Atmosphere, in Outer Space, and Under Water, Aug. 5, 1963, 14 UST 1313, TIAS No. 5433, 480 UNTS 43.

[2] GA Res. 1721 (XVI) (Dec. 29, 1961).

diplomatic changes. We may also observe the proliferation of normative "types," i.e., the adoption by states of nonbinding principles and guidelines, rather than treaties, as legitimate and authoritative statements of their mutual expectations.

But the legal historian must also confront a more skeptical perspective of these events, a view of the norms governing conduct in space as *sui generis* at best, dominated by the rhetoric of globalism and the reality of bipolar power politics, regulating a unique and inaccessible place, and now in any event in a state of stagnation after two initial decades of activity. With the exploration and exploitation of space historically confined to a handful of states, these principles may be thought largely irrelevant and untested by state practice. As a consequence in this view, the body of space law remains aspirational rather than recognizably law-like: the space treaties themselves are not universally accepted, and some of the most interested or affected states have declined to become parties.

The issue that distinguishes these competing visions of contemporary history is whether the specialized norms developed within the United Nations and purporting specifically to govern activities in outer space are meaningful. Have the prodigious efforts of the United Nations actually produced a definable space law, *lex spatialis*, above and beyond the obligations of general international law?

The answer to this question inevitably turns on prior jurisprudential issues about how such law might be defined or proved, questions that are beyond the scope of this study. But the raw data for interpretation – the intergovernmental assertions of legal claims and understandings about activities in space – remain strikingly constant and fall into repeated patterns. Indeed, the history of space law reveals clusters of asserted legal principles, not always coherently conceived or expressed, which seem to recur. Some of these principles are better established or more concrete than others, but any assessment of the meaning and the success of international space law must account for them.

These clusters of persistent principles may be summarized under four headings or regimes:

(i) a regime of *cooperation*, under which states are obliged to defer to the international community's interests in space as the "province of mankind," and comprising such principles as the nonappropriability of space and celestial bodies, the obligation to use space exclusively for peaceful purposes, and the obligation to share the benefits of space exploration;

(ii) a regime of *responsibility*, under which states are obliged to minimize the unique hazards posed by their space activities and to compensate those who may be injured by them. Within this regime are the complex liability principles adopted in the Liability Convention of 1972, the requirement that states retain jurisdiction and control over their space objects, and the emerging norms of environmental protection in space;

(iii) a regime of *freedoms,* subject to the limitations of the other regimes, under which states are presumptively free to use outer space, for such purposes as exploration, research, communication, or remote sensing from satellites; and

(iv) a regime of *relative normativity,* by which states acknowledge a range of principles or regulations that are nonbinding but that are nonetheless viewed as relevant and authoritative expressions of emerging norms of space law. In part, this phenomenon is attributable to the workings of multiple, sometimes overlapping, agencies within the United Nations and the incremental process by which international law evolves within that organization.

In combination, these four regimes of principle give structure to international space law and allow us to test its effectiveness.

II. THE STRUCTURE OF INTERNATIONAL SPACE LAW-MAKING

A. Law-making within the United Nations

Space issues became a pressing concern in the United Nations within days after the launch of Sputnik in October 1957. In the following month, the General Assembly resolved "to ensure that the sending of objects through outer space shall be exclusively for peaceful and scientific purposes."[3] At its next session, the General Assembly established an *ad hoc* Committee on the Peaceful Uses of Outer Space and required the Committee *inter alia* to identify issues of law and policy that might arise from state activities in outer space.[4] The *ad hoc* Committee produced a substantive – even prescient – report,[5] but its usefulness was diminished by a perceived pro-US bias in the composition of the Committee. Once the two superpowers agreed on an expanded membership, the General Assembly created a permanent Committee on the Peaceful Uses of Outer Space (COPUOS).[6] The United States and the Soviet Union continued to dominate these proceedings, but the Committee itself has been expanded

[3] GA Res. 1148 (XII) (Nov. 14, 1957).
[4] GA Res. 1348 (XIII) (Dec. 13, 1958). P. Jessup & H. Taubenfeld, The "*Ad Hoc* Committee on the Peaceful Uses of Outer Space," 53 *AJIL* 877 (1959).   [5] UN Doc. A/4141 (1959).
[6] GA Res. 1472A (XIV) (Dec. 12, 1959).

repeatedly until today, when roughly one-third of the nations of the world are members.

Administrative and technical support for COPUOS is provided by the Outer Space Affairs Division of the Department of Political and Security Council Affairs within the UN Secretariat. At least a dozen specialized UN agencies and programs are concerned with issues of space law or space applications,[7] but most of these rely on space technologies to fulfill their mandates (or treat the dissemination and development of such technologies as part of their mandates).[8] Their role in the creation of space law *per se* has been modest.

1. COPUOS

By contrast, the Committee on the Peaceful Uses of Outer Space has become the premier institution in the articulation of international space law, even though it has neither law-making nor adjudicative powers. Through its two subcommittees[9] and multiple working groups,[10] and with the assistance of other specialized agencies and offices within the United Nations Organization,[11] COPUOS has provided a permanent forum for the discussion of legal and technical issues. It has also drafted each of the major space treaties and, on occasion, proposed draft principles or guidelines when the prospects for treaty-making seemed remote.

Typically, COPUOS has drafted these treaties or guidelines in a working group or subcommittee, with subsequent consideration by the committee as a whole, followed by review in a main committee of the General

---

[7] The considerable responsibility of coordinating these efforts falls to a Subcommittee on Outer Space Activities within the Administrative Committee on Coordination (ACC).

[8] For example, various satellites are employed by the World Meteorological Organization (WMO); the World Health Organization (WHO); the World Intellectual Property Organization (WIPO); the Food and Agriculture Organization (FAO); the International Maritime Organization (IMO); the International Maritime Satellite Consortium (INMARSAT); and the High Commissioner for Refugees (UNHCR).

Other specialized programs within the United Nations have either used space to gather and disseminate information or assisted states in developing the capacity to use space in their own interest: the United Nations Programme on Space Applications; the United Nations Development Programme (UNDP); the United Nations Environment Programme (UNEP); the Natural Resources and Energy Division (NRED); the United Nations Disaster Relief Coordinator (UNDRO); the International Bank for Reconstruction and Development (IBRD); and the various regional commissions (ECA, ECLA, ESCAP, ECWA).

[9] COPUOS has a Legal Subcommittee and a Scientific and Technical Subcommittee. The Legal Subcommittee – with a membership frequently including high-profile international lawyers from many states – has been unusually dominant in the activities of COPUOS, especially in the negotiation and drafting of the major space treaties and declarations.

[10] COPUOS working groups have been established to address issues arising out of the use of navigational satellites, broadcasting satellites, remote sensing, and nuclear power sources in space.   [11] See note 8 above.

Assembly (e.g., the Special Political Committee), and finally by the General Assembly itself, which adopts a resolution containing the agreed text of the treaty or declaration and recommending it for the approval of states. Using this procedure, the United Nations has produced five international agreements: (a) the Outer Space Treaty of 1967, which states in general terms the freedoms of outer space and their limits; (b) the Rescue and Return Agreement of 1968, which provides an international mechanism for humanitarian assistance to astronauts and the return of space objects that fall to earth; (c) The Liability Convention of 1972, which lays out the general contours of a launching state's liability for damage caused by its space objects; (d) the Registration Convention of 1976, which requires a party to furnish to the UN Secretary-General information on the general function of its space objects; and (e) the Moon Agreement of 1979, which, without the participation of the space powers to date, purports to regulate the exploration and exploitation of celestial bodies, including the moon.

Each of these treaties evolved after COPUOS had identified some recurring issue and had articulated principles for the resolution of that issue. Although the pace of treaty-making has slowed significantly in the last decade, the process of identifying authoritative principles continues. For example, COPUOS has produced principles governing the use of nuclear power sources in space,[12] remote sensing of the earth,[13] and direct television broadcasting from satellites.[14] Plainly, the process of articulating normative guidelines short of treaties has become a characteristic mode of operation within the United Nations.

COPUOS has usually drafted, negotiated, and adopted these treaties and principles by consensus, meaning "general agreement without vote, but not necessarily unanimity."[15] Under the consensus rule, the text of a proposed treaty or set of principles is revised and negotiated until all parties consent to it. Abstentions and unilateral interpretations of a provision do not qualify as dissent in this process, and consent during the deliberations does not obligate a state to become a party to the treaty. In practice, the consensus process has had the advantages of promoting compromise and ultimately of encouraging states to ratify and respect the treaties.[16]

---

[12] UN Doc. A/AC.105/C.2/L.154/Rev. 5, reprinted in Annex III.A.3 of the Report of the Legal Subcommittee of COPUOS on the Work of its Twenty-Eighth Session (A/AC.105/ 430). See generally M. Benko, W. De Graaff, & G. C. M. Reijnen, *Space Law in the United Nations* 49–119 (1985).   [13] GA Res. 41/65 (Dec. 3, 1986).

[14] Principles Governing the Use by States of Artificial Earth Satellites for International Direct Television Broadcasting, GA Res. 37/92 (Dec. 10, 1982).

[15] *UN Jurid. Y. B.* 164 (1974).

[16] N. Jasentuliyana, "Treaty Law and Outer Space: Can the United Nations Play an Effective Role?," 11 *Annals Air & Space L.* 219, 223 (1986). See also N. Hosenball, "The United Nations Committee on the Peaceful Uses of Outer Space: Past Accomplishments and Future Challenges," 7 *J. Space L.* 95, 97 (1979).

But the consensus rule has also been criticized on the grounds that it has prolonged negotiations and diluted the resulting legal product into a catalog of platitudes. With the steady expansion in COPUOS membership, consensus has also seemed increasingly unworkable: in contrast to the early phases of the space age, the uses of space are more readily apparent today, making self-interests both easier to perceive and harder to accommodate on a group basis. But the most serious political objection to the consensus rule has been that it frustrates the will of the majority, primarily the less developed countries, by giving the relatively few space powers inordinate influence. As a consequence, the General Assembly has on occasion circumvented the consensus rule altogether, voting for example by majority rule to adopt the principles governing direct television broadcasting. The United States and several other states voted against the principles, and it is unlikely that any particular space law regime asserted by resolution but rejected by the space powers will be viable.

This conflict between majoritarianism and pragmatism has become more pronounced in the law-making process of the last decade, and it now seems likely that COPUOS will depart from its traditional commitment to consensus and proceed through a rule of qualified consensus, under which "voting is resorted to as a last resort in cases where the dissenters from consensus are considered to constitute an unreasonable and isolated or unimportant minority."[17] Whether such a rule will produce norms actually respected by the space powers remains to be seen of course, though the threat of fragmentation in the law of outer space cannot be discounted. The Committee may well yield to other UN bodies, and multiple bilateral and regional institutions outside the UN altogether, as the dominant creative force in international space law.

2. Specialized and associated agencies

As noted above, the bulk of the space activities within the United Nations has been the use and dissemination of space technology applications. But in these efforts, three UN organizations have made especially notable contributions to the law and its development by addressing recurrent issues of distributive justice and the overall coherence between space law and correlative international regimes.

The International Telecommunications Union (ITU), for example, operating under the 1973 International Telecommunications Convention, has dealt with two limited natural resources critical to space telecommunications: the geostationary orbit and the radio frequency spectrum. The

---

[17] Jasentuliyana, note 16 above, at 224.

ITU, which had been responsible for bringing order to terrestrial radio services, was the natural vehicle for bringing order to space telecommunications as well.[18]

Through its Administrative and Radio Regulations, the ITU has attempted to rationalize the use of the radio spectrum and the geostationary orbit, supervise frequency assignment notifications and registration, and related matters. But even in this technical milieu of rationalizing services, the ITU has confronted the recurring tension between a communitarian principle of equal access and an entrepreneurial principle of "first-come-first-served" – a broad theme in the evolution of international space law generally, as shown below.

The United Nations Educational, Scientific and Cultural Organization (UNESCO) has confronted similar issues of distributional equity but has more freely adopted the perspective of the nonspace powers. For example, in its declaration of principles governing satellite broadcasting,[19] UNESCO tended toward the adoption of a prior consent rule for such broadcasts, a rule largely advocated by the less developed countries, empowering them against the dissemination of unwanted information and images. The General Assembly subsequently adopted similar guidelines, and, although these provisions were not adopted by consensus (and were indeed opposed by the United States and other states), they are evidence of some institutional commitment to resource equity. As suggested below, the possibility of further legal developments along these lines cannot be ruled out.

By contrast, the International Civil Aviation Organization (ICAO) has not regularly addressed North–South issues of fairness, being primarily interested in the operational applications of space technology to civil aviation (especially communications and navigation). But ICAO has monitored the evolution of space law and space applications within the United Nations, bringing to that forum the constraints imposed by the related but distinct international legal regime governing airspace and

[18] Closely affiliated with the ITU and telecommunications generally are "common user organizations," which are organizations "of two or more ITU Administrations that jointly own and operate a satellite system for their international and/or domestic requirements." W. Dizard, *Space WARC and the Role of International Satellite Networks* 15 (1984). These include the International Telecommunications Satellite Organization (INTELSAT) and various regional systems. M. L. Smith, *International Regulation of Satellite Communication* 33 (1990). Although these organizations are themselves the product of innovative legal arrangements, see, e.g., S. Doyle, "INMARSAT: The International Maritime Satellite Organization – Origins and Structures," 5 *J. Space L.* 45 (1977), their legislative contribution is more properly considered in connection with international telecommunications law rather than space law *per se*. See generally F. Lyall, *Law and Space Telecommunications* (1989).

[19] Declaration of Guiding Principles on the Use of Satellite Broadcasting for the Free Flow of Information, the Spread of Education and Greater Cultural Exchange, UN Doc. A/AC.105/109 Corr. 1 (Feb. 16, 1973).

aviation. In consequence, ICAO has considered such issues as the definition and delimitation of outer space, the potential hazards posed to international aviation by space activities and space debris, and the regime necessary to regulate aerospace vehicles.[20]

B. International law-making outside the UNO

The United Nations and its specialized and associated agencies have played a dominant but not an exclusive role in the articulation of international space law. Other international institutions – organized by region or by specialized function – have contributed to the overall development of norms by adopting them in their constitutive agreements or by respecting them in institutional practices. This is especially true of the various telecommunications organizations,[21] but general purpose[22] and *ad hoc* arrangements[23] have also proliferated.

Equally importantly, states have reached hundreds of bilateral, generally technical agreements dealing *inter alia* with the distribution of information from space or the cooperative use of facilities necessary for the successful completion of space missions. The United States and the Soviet Union have also signed bilateral agreements on cooperation and arms control in space. Taken together, these arrangements contribute to a minimalist common law of peace in space and thereby reaffirm outside the United Nations the peaceful uses principle first articulated within it.

The domestic space agencies of various countries have also made a "legislative" contribution in the form of state practice combined at least occasionally with articulations of *opinio juris*. For example, the United States[24] and the members of the European Space Agency have relatively extensive domestic laws pertaining to space, and many of these provisions – in the form of statutes, regulations, and policies – implement international obligations spelled out first in the United Nations. Indeed, these domestic regimes are a measure of the success of the United Nations in producing an

---

[20] For further details of the space-related work of ICAO, see Background Paper, Second United Nations Conference on the Exploration and Peaceful Uses of Outer Space, UN Doc. A/CONF.101/BP/IGO/1 (1982).   [21] See note 18 above.

[22] The European Space Agency (ESA) is the most developed multilateral organization outside the UN system, established "to provide for and to promote, for exclusively peaceful purposes, cooperation among European states in space research and technology and their space applications." Convention for the Establishment of a European Space Agency art. II, 1297 UNTS 161 (1983), reprinted in 14 *ILM* 864 (1975) (*entered into force* October 30, 1980).

[23] See, e.g., Agreement among the Government of the United States of America, Governments of the Member States of the European Space Agency, the Government of Japan, and the Government of Canada in the Detailed Design, Development, Operation, and Utilization of the Permanently Manned Civil Space Agency, Sept. 29, 1988, reprinted in S. Comm. on Commerce, Sci. & Transp., *Space Law and Related Documents* 151 (3d ed., 1990).

[24] *United States Space Law: National & International Regulation* (S. Gorove ed., 1990).

effective international law of space: the nexus between domestic law and international law is strong in such regulatory areas as telecommunications, liability, and the registration of space objects. In other areas (such as environmental protection and national security), the role of international law is considerably less pronounced, a reality that simply reflects the uneven and incremental development of norms at the international plane. It is to that phenomenon that we now turn.

III. THE FOUR REGIMES OF INTERNATIONAL SPACE LAW

Communal int.

A. The regime of cooperation

The regime of cooperation in international space law refers to that cluster of principles that reserve space as *res communis*, the province of humankind, the property of the community of nations. These are principles in other words that require space-faring states to acknowledge and accommodate communal interests, though, as will be seen, these seemingly modest norms are regularly recruited in the international politics of redistribution and military competition.

1. Nonappropriability

The dominant norm of cooperation is the nonappropriability of outer space and celestial bodies. Article II of the Outer Space Treaty of 1967 expressly blocks territorial claims in space: "Outer space, including the moon and other celestial bodies, is not subject to national appropriation by claim of sovereignty, by means of use or occupation, or by any other means." This provision reflected an understanding that had achieved near-universal support from the first days of the space age.[25] By Resolution 1721, for example, the General Assembly had approved a program of multilateral cooperation in space and offered, as one of the foundational principles for the guidance of states, that "outer space and celestial bodies are free for exploration and use by all States in conformity with international law and are not subject to national appropriation."[26] The history of this provision – like its analog in the Antarctic Treaty of 1959[27] –

---

[25] See, e.g., GA Res. 1348 (XIII) (Dec. 13, 1958); GA Res. 1721 (XVI) (Dec. 29, 1961); GA Res. 1962 (XVIII) (Dec. 13, 1963). See generally I. A. Csabafi, *The Concept Of State Jurisdiction in International Space Law* (1971). The prohibition on sovereign claims in space has been repeated in the Moon Agreement of 1979, note 1 above.

[26] GA Res. 1721 (XVI) (Dec. 20, 1961), at ¶1(b).

[27] Article 4(2) of the Antarctic Treaty, 12 UST 794, TIAS No. 4780, 402 UNTS 71 (*entered into force* June 23, 1961), provides in part:

shows that nonappropriability served common and urgent values, namely that space be used for exclusively peaceful purposes and that states enjoy equitable and free use of the space environment. Formulated in this way, the principle may claim customary status.

The norm of nonappropriability though universally approved, was not self-defining, however, and questions about its meaning have arisen. It is clear, for example, that the preclusion of claims in space places an upper limit on the presumption that a state enjoys plenary sovereignty in the airspace above its territory.[28] The traditional sovereignty in airspace obviously must stop where space begins, but there is no definition in the Outer Space Treaty (or related resolutions) of where physically the regimes change. States have avoided an explicit definition, perhaps on the assumption that it would provoke more disputes than it would resolve, and state practice suggests that disputes can be settled without recourse to definition.[29]

space ends airspace begins

But the failure to reach explicit agreement on the issue of where space begins has proved to be significant. In 1976, eight equatorial nations adopted the Bogotá Declaration, stating that the corridor of geostationary orbits above their respective territories was a scarce natural resource over which they proclaimed sovereignty.[30] This was consistent with the Charter on Economic Rights and Duties of States[31] and other elements of the New International Economic Order, but it could not readily be squared with the norm of nonappropriability codified in the Outer Space Treaty of 1967. The Bogotá declarants questioned the applicability of that norm to the geosynchronous orbit, on the ground that outer space, never having been delimited, did not necessarily include that orbit: "There is no valid or satisfactory definition of outer space which may be advanced to support the argument that the geostationary orbit is included in the outer space."[32] Uncertain perhaps that any claim excluding an orbit from "outer space" was legally or factually tenable, they also argued that the seemingly neutral

No acts or activities taking place while the present Treaty is in force shall constitute a basis for asserting, supporting, or denying a claim to territorial sovereignty in Antarctica or create any rights of sovereignty in Antarctica.

[28] See, e.g., Convention on International Civil Aviation, Dec. 7, 1944, art. 1, 61 Stat. 1180, TIAS No. 1591, 15 UNTS 295: "The contracting States recognize that every State has complete and exclusive sovereignty over the airspace above its territory."

[29] There is considerable controversy about the altitude and other physical parameters of the lowest sustainable earth orbit. G. Reynolds & R. Merges, *Outer Space: Problems of Law and Policy* 11–12 (1989).

[30] A copy of the Bogotá Declaration appears in C. Christol, *The Modern International Law of Outer Space* 891–96 (1982). See generally J. Marchan, *Derecho Internacional del Espacio: Teoria y Politica* 797–907 (1987).

[31] GA Res. 3281 (XXIX) (Dec. 12, 1974), at art. 2(1).

[32] Christol, note 30 above, at 894.

norm of nonappropriability actually perpetuated the space powers' unfair advantage in space: "Under the name of a so-called non-national appropriation, what was actually developed was a technological partition of the orbit, which is simply a national appropriation, and this must be denounced by the equatorial countries."[33] From this perspective, the free access principle serves only the interests of the space powers and renders their advantage in space permanent. The norm of nonappropriability and free access is thus perceived to have distinct distributional assumptions.[34]

2. Peaceful uses and purposes

The obligation to use space for exclusively peaceful purposes is another constituent principle in the regime of cooperation. In resolution after resolution,[35] the General Assembly has attempted to prohibit acts of aggression in space, and the Outer Space Treaty contains multiple references to peaceful uses. Under Article III, for example, "the exploration and use of outer space must be carried out in accordance with international law, including the UN Charter, in the interest of maintaining international peace and security." And, under Article IX, consultations are required before any activity or experiment is undertaken which may "cause potentially harmful interference with activities of other states Parties in the peaceful exploration and use of outer space."

But the most pointed provisions for securing the peace appear in the two paragraphs of Article IV. Under paragraph 1, the parties pledge not to place in orbit any objects carrying nuclear weapons or any other weapons of mass destruction. Nor may they install such weapons on celestial bodies or station them in outer space. Paragraph 2 preserves the moon and other celestial bodies exclusively for peaceful purposes. Weapons may not be tested and military maneuvers generally may not be undertaken, though military personnel may be employed to conduct research and for other peaceful purposes.

The twin restrictions in Article IV are fundamental and reflect the drafters' limited commitment to demilitarization: paragraph 1, while applicable to the whole of the space environment, is limited functionally and prohibits only nuclear weapons and weapons of mass destruction.

---

[33] *Ibid.*, at 894–95.

[34] The Bogotá Declaration, though largely disregarded by the space powers as a legal claim, has not fallen into desuetude. The Legal Subcommittee of COPUOS continues to debate its underlying premises. See Report of the Legal Subcommittee of COPUOS on the Work of its Thirty-First Session (A/AC.105/514) at 8–12. The ITU's concern with equity in the distribution of the orbit-spectrum resource is at least partly attributable to the concerns of the equatorial and less developed states as expressed in the Declaration.

[35] See, e.g., GA Res. 1721 (XVI) (Dec. 20, 1961); GA Res. 1884 (XVIII) (Oct. 17, 1963); GA Res. 1962 (XVIII) (Dec. 13, 1963); GA Res. 43/70 (Dec. 7, 1988); GA Res. 44/112 (Dec. 15, 1989).

Paragraph 2, while apparently more comprehensive in requiring peaceful purposes, is limited spatially and excludes outer space from the scope of that requirement; indeed, the failure to include outer space in the peaceful uses paragraph of Article IV was apparently intentional. By contrast, the peaceful purposes provision of the Antarctica Treaty is comprehensive, prohibiting all measures of a military nature, such as the establishment of military bases and fortifications, the carrying out of military maneuvers, and the testing of any type of weapons. The drafters of the space treaty plainly had the model of an authentic ban before them and chose something else.

Inevitably perhaps, the United Nations continues to grapple with the norm of peaceful uses, even after the demise of the Soviet Union and the end of the Cold War. The Second UN Conference on the Exploration and Peaceful Uses of Outer Space (UNISPACE 82) explored various approaches to controlling the incipient arms race in outer space.[36] Since that time, states have considered a draft treaty banning all weapons from outer space. Negotiating an effective and verifiable agreement prohibiting anti-satellite weaponry assumed a high priority on the agenda of the United Nations in the late 1980s, and the majority of states has supported the complete demilitarization of outer space. But these efforts implicitly suggest the limits of the peaceful purposes principle in its current state: demilitarization initiatives would obviously be unnecessary if military activities were already illegal under the peaceful uses principle.

Broad issues do persist beyond the limited core of agreement captured in the peaceful purposes principle. For example, does the limited interpretation of peaceful purposes espoused by the United States and the former Soviet Union prevail juridically over the predominant view of the rest of the international community that military uses of any sort – other than surveillance from space – are inconsistent with the UN Charter or customary international law? Is it plausible to suggest that the demilitarization of space qualifies for regulation by general principles of international law rather than by tightly tailored arms agreements as to which consent may be easier to obtain and discern? And more generally, have the forms of aggression changed so fundamentally in the nuclear age as to trivialize the nonaggressive gloss on the peaceful uses principle?[37] But these questions,

---

[36] See 1981 Report of COPUOS, 36th Sess., Supp. No. 20, Doc. A/36/20, ¶68; Report of the Second United Nations Conference on the Exploration and Peaceful Uses of Outer Space, Doc. A/Conf.101/10, ¶¶520–24 (1982).

[37] It seems obvious that, in the age when mutual assured destruction was the dominant strategic goal, the development of a high technology defense in the laboratories of the Silicon Valley would potentially be as threatening and as destabilizing as a division of Panzers crossing the Vistula River was in an earlier age. In the modern era, force need not be physically projected across a border for other nations to perceive aggression. In these circumstances, the nonaggressive gloss on the peaceful purposes principle may address the problem that does not exist and ignore the problem that does.

real as they may be, should not obscure the genuine accomplishment represented by the peaceful uses principle, a limited rule that could not have been predicted in the earliest tense moments of the space age.

3. Sharing

A third constitutive element of the regime of cooperation in space is the principle that the benefits of space exploration and exploitation must be shared with the community at large. In this view, the resources of space, like space itself, fall within "the province of mankind" and therefore may not be appropriated by any single state. The treaties, principles, and resolutions that make up the body of international space law resist entrepreneurialism, declaring in various contexts that all states should enjoy the benefits of space "irrespective of the stage of their economic or scientific development."[38] In its ideal, the norm of sharing is related to but distinct from the common heritage principle, which attempts to give financial and regulatory bite to the abstract interest of all states in territories beyond national jurisdiction, such as the deep seabed and the moon.

But sharing – perhaps because it is less elaborate – has arguably been more successful than the common heritage principle. In its deliberations on geosynchronous orbital slots for communications satellites, for example, the International Telecommunications Union has been guided by the recognition that "radio frequencies and the geostationary satellite orbit are limited natural resources, that they must be used efficiently and economically so that countries or groups of countries may have equitable access to both in conformity with the provisions of the Radio Regulations according to their needs and the technical facilities at their disposal."[39]

The interests of the less developed countries (LDCs) in preserving these limited natural resources and sharing in them have been accommodated if not fully respected. After the World Administrative Conference in 1971, a "first come, first served" rule prevailed in the distribution of radio frequencies, but new provisions on coordination, notification, and registration provided even those states without space technology some opportunity to use the orbit-frequency spectrum for their own purposes. There could be for example no permanent priority for any individual country or group of countries, and the goal of "efficiency" was interpreted to include the seemingly counter-Pareto assumption that every state should be able to

---

[38] See, e.g., Article I of the Outer Space Treaty, note 1 above, which provides in part: "The exploration and use of outer space, including the moon and other celestial bodies, shall be carried out for the benefit and in the interests of all countries, irrespective of their degree of economic or scientific development, and shall be the province of all mankind."

[39] International Telecommunications Convention of 1973, Oct. 25, 1973, art. 33(2), 128 UST 2495, TIAS No. 8572, 1209 UNTS 32 (*entered into force* Jan. 1, 1975).

develop its own telecommunications system. The "arc allotment plan" finally adopted in 1988 respects these principles and assures every state at least one orbital slot.[40] The hard business of negotiating orbital slots and frequencies continues of course, and there is little doubt that the field is tilted in favor of the existing space powers. But the fact that negotiations take place at all – that the LDCs are empowered even modestly as a matter of law – suggests that the principle of sharing cannot be dismissed as wholly rhetorical or precatory. Indeed, the humanitarian instinct behind the norm of sharing extends to all states' presumptive obligations to rescue astronauts in peril and return fallen space objects,[41] to consult with other nations that may be adversely affected by space activities,[42] and to cooperate in the dissemination of information gathered from space.[43]

B. The regime of responsibility

The regime of responsibility refers to that cluster of principles under which states are liable for their activities in space. Beginning with resolutions early in the space age, continuing through the Outer Space Treaty of 1967 and the Liability Convention of 1972, and reinforced by subsequent state practice, the United Nations has developed an international tort law governing a state's liability for its activities in space, including damage on the earth, in air space, and in outer space. Although preexisting international norms might have sufficed to establish a state's general liability for damages caused by its space activities, the members of COPUOS perceived the need for a special liability regime that was responsive to the unique risks posed by the exploration and exploitation of space, and the details of that regime took several years to work out. In fact, particularly contentious liability issues remain on the law-making agenda of COPUOS.

1. State liability generally

Article VII of the Outer Space Treaty explicitly established, without spatial limitation, a state's liability in money damages for harms caused by its space activities, including harms in space, on earth, and in airspace. In this respect, the Treaty replicated a consensus that had been reached several years earlier.[44] Equally important, state liability would attach to the activities of private actors; indeed, the Outer Space Treaty made it clear that

---

[40] S. Doyle, "Space Law and the Geostationary Orbit: The ITU's WARC-ORB '85–'88 Concluded," 17 *J. Space L.* 13, 18 (1989).

[41] The Rescue and Return Agreement, note 1 above, arts. 1, 2, & 5.

[42] The Outer Space Treaty, note 1 above, art. IX.

[43] See text accompanying notes 68–73, pp. 355–56 below.

[44] See GA Res. 1962 (XVIII) (Dec. 13, 1963), at ¶8:

extension to individuals in space [handwritten margin note]

the state liability regime could admit no distinction between public and private actors.[45] Under Article VI, the launching state is responsible for the activities of its nationals in space, even if those nationals are acting in a seemingly private capacity, and under Article VIII, the very notion of "private capacity" is itself strictly limited, since the state of registry must retain "jurisdiction and control over [its space] object, and over any personnel thereof, while in outer space or on a celestial body."

These initial provisions, significant as their absence would have been, did not create a full regime for determining liability. There was no definition of the scope of liability, including whether it would be absolute or fault based, nor was there any indication of whether liability could be limited, no specification of the kinds of damage considered compensable, no articulation of a claims procedure, no algorithm for selecting the governing law in determining compensation, and so forth. At the time that COPUOS agreed to the liability provisions of the Outer Space Treaty, each member understood that those provisions were not exhaustive and that a more detailed and expansive regime would follow.

What followed was the Liability Convention of 1972, which established broad principles of responsibility, including *inter alia*,[46]

(i) *a dual system of liability*, under which a state's obligation to compensate for damages turns on where the damages occur: absolute or strict liability under Article II for damages[47] on the surface of the earth (or to aircraft in flight);[48] and fault-based liability under Article

---

[45] The Outer Space Treaty, note 1 above, art. VI:

> States parties to the treaty shall bear international responsibility for national activities in outer space, including the moon and other celestial bodies, whether such activities are carried on by governmental agencies or by non-governmental entities . . . The activities of non-governmental entities in outer space, including the moon and other celestial bodies, shall require authorization and continuing supervision by the [state concerned].

[46] See generally C. Christol, "International Liability for Damage Caused by Space Objects," 74 *AJIL* 346 (1980).

[47] The Liability Convention, note 1 above, art. I, defines compensable damages as "loss of life, personal injury or other impairment of health or loss of or damage to property of states or of persons . . . or of international intergovernmental organizations." Article 12 states that the amount of compensation "shall be determined in accordance with international law and the principles of justice and equity, in order to provide such reparation . . . as will restore the [claimant] to the condition which would have existed if the damage had not occurred," a restitution standard descending from the decision of the Permanent Court of International Justice in The Chorzow Factory case (*Ger. v. Pol.*), PCIJ Ser. A No. 17 (1928).

[48] Under the absolute standard, the victim need not prove fault or negligence on the part of the launching state in order to establish liability under the Treaty. It is sufficient merely to establish a causal connection between the space object and the damage. Such a standard received near-unanimous approval on the grounds that the evidence of fault in such cases would be hard to find and possibly classified, that space activities were abnormally dangerous or ultra-hazardous, and that there was a basic inequality as between launching and victim states in wealth and in the ability to control risk or take precautions.

III for damages which occur "elsewhere than on the surface of the earth" to a space object (or to persons or property on board a space object) belonging to another launching state;[49]

(ii) *limited principles of exoneration*: under Article VI, the launching state can avoid liability only by showing that the damage resulted wholly or partially from gross negligence or from an act or omission done with intent to cause damage on the part of the claimant state or the persons it represents. There can be no exoneration whatever if the launching state's activities are themselves in violation of international law;

(iii) *a broad definition of the "launching state"*: a state need not have been a participant in the launch to be liable: the space object need only have been launched from its territory for it to be considered a "launching state" for purposes of the Treaty, even if it had no control in fact over the launch or the object that caused harm.[50] States jointly engaged in launching a space object are jointly and severally liable for damages that may result,[51] and intergovernmental organizations that conduct activities in space may also be subject to the liability regime;[52] and

(iv) *a relatively well-defined claims procedure*: under Articles VIII through XIII, the Liability Convention provides for the presentation and resolution of claims, and, under Articles XIV through XX, the convening of a claims commission in the event that the parties in dispute are unable to settle the claim through diplomatic negotiations. The exhaustion of local remedies is expressly waived as a precondition for asserting the claim.[53]

(v) To these principles might be added *a duty under the Registration Convention of 1976 to provide information* "to the greatest extent feasible" in the event that a space object causes damage to a state or becomes "of a hazardous or deleterious nature."[54]

Isolated but pertinent state practice attests the normative status of this regime. In 1978, a Soviet satellite, Cosmos 954, fell from orbit and crashed, scattering radioactive debris over remote portions of Canada. Invoking both the Liability Convention and international law generally, Canada submitted a claim seeking $6 million in partial compensation for total expenditures assertedly in excess of $14 million. Without explicitly

---

[49] If Article III applies, liability depends on the fault of the launching state or the persons for whom that state was responsible. The grounds for the fault standard as between space states included assumption of risk, the relative equality in bargaining power, and avoiding the absurd result that, under an absolute liability standard, space powers would have to pay each other's damages.

[50] Liability Convention, note 1 above, art. I(c)(ii). As a consequence, private launch services – where they are available – are generally strictly controlled through licensing procedures.

[51] *Ibid.*, arts. IV & V.   [52] *Ibid.*, art. XXII.   [53] *Ibid.*, art. XI.

[54] The Registration Convention, note 1 above, art. VI.

acknowledging any obligation under the Convention or international law, the Soviet Union eventually paid $3 million which Canada accepted in full satisfaction of its claim.[55]

The Cosmos 954 incident is only partial evidence that the liability regime of the Outer Space Treaty and the Liability Convention can work. Canada's claim was submitted not solely on the basis of these treaties but "jointly and separately [on the basis of] (a) . . . relevant international agreements . . . *and* (b) general principles of international law."[56] Second, the strategic reluctance of the parties to assign specific dollar amounts to the discrete elements of the claim or the settlement leaves uncertain whether some types of damage (e.g., moral or dignitary damages and mitigation costs) are compensable. As a result, it remains unclear, for example whether states are liable for damages under the restitution standard of Article XII of the Liability Convention in the absence of damages as defined in Article I of that treaty. Nor finally does the incident or its resolution establish "rules of the road" for traffic in space, as to which proof of fault under Article III of the Liability Convention is likely to be profoundly more difficult. Of course, a regime need not be seamless to be effective, and the general outlines of an international tort law in space are clear, at least when death or personal injury or property damage occurs.

2. Emerging norms of environmental protection

The liability regime is somewhat less successful in the absence of such damages and in particular in the protection of the space environment itself. Building on the promise of the Limited Nuclear Test Ban Treaty, the Outer Space Treaty suggests that states bear international responsibility for contaminating the environment of outer space, that pollution of any sort in space is subject to the general liability provisions of Article VII which govern "damage . . . on the Earth, in air space, or in outer space, including the moon and other celestial bodies." Indeed, Article IX of the Treaty provides explicitly that "States Parties to the Treaty shall pursue studies of outer space, including the moon and other celestial bodies, and conduct exploration of them so as to avoid harmful contamination and also adverse changes in the environment of the Earth resulting from the introduction of extraterrestrial matter."[57] Thus, for example, putting aside all issues of

[55] See generally B. Schwartz & M. Berlin, "After the Fall: An Analysis of Canadian Legal Claims for Damage Caused by Cosmos 954," 27 *Revue de Droit de McGill* 676 (1982).
[56] Statement of Claim against the USSR, Note No. FLA268 (Jan. 23, 1979), ¶14, reprinted in 18 *ILM* 899, 905 (1979) (emphasis supplied).
[57] The Outer Space Treaty, note 1 above, art. IX. Taken together, Articles VII and IX of the Outer Space Treaty exemplify Principle 21 of the 1972 Stockholm Declaration on the Human Environment, under which states are responsible for "ensur[ing] that activities within their jurisdiction and control do not cause damage to the environment of other states or of *areas*

proof, disabling another state's satellite in orbit by polluting the space environment with debris should trigger a fault-based liability under the Outer Space Treaty and the Liability Convention.

But the broad interpretation of these provisions has been resisted, and pollution of the space environment *per se* has not been recognized as triggering state responsibility.[58] It remains the unchallenged understanding of the United States, for example, that the harmful contamination prohibition of Article IX is spatially limited, obliging states to conduct their activities in space "in such a manner so that the *atmosphere of the earth* is not contaminated by any experiments that are conducted in space."[59] And even pollution of the atmosphere must be of a particular type before state responsibility is engaged.[60] The scope of liability is further narrowed by the difficulties of determining responsibility as a matter of fact, defining "space object" for purposes of the Liability Convention, and establishing who (or what) has standing to protect the space environment *per se* in the absence of direct damage.

As a result of the apparent discrepancy between the text of these treaty provisions and their interpretation or implementation, states have identified a range of environmental issues in space, including the problem of space debris[61] and nuclear-powered satellites (NPS).[62] It seems likely that these

---

beyond the limits of national jurisdiction," including presumably outer space. Declaration of the United Nations Conference on the Human Environment, UN Doc. A/CONF.48/14 & Corr.1 (1972), at Principle 21 (emphasis supplied). Some scholars have suggested that the Stockholm Declaration restates customary international law. See A. Kiss, *Droit International De L'Environnement* 81 (1989).

[58] Compare the Moon Agreement, note 1 above, art. 7:

In exploring and using the moon, States Parties shall take measures to prevent the disruption of the existing balance of its environment, whether by introducing adverse changes in that environment, by its harmful contamination through the introduction of extra-environmental matter or otherwise. States Parties shall also take measures to avoid harmfully affecting the environment of Earth through the introduction of extra-terrestrial matter or otherwise.

[59] Treaty on Outer Space, Hearings before the Comm. on Foreign Relations, S. Exec. Doc., 90th Cong., 1st Sess. 42 (1967).

[60] According to the Senate report accompanying consent to ratification, "Article VII pertains only to physical, nonelectronic damage that space activities may cause to the citizens or property of a signatory state." Treaty on Outer Space, S. Exec. Doc. No. 8, 90th Cong., 1st Sess. 5 (1967). The United States apparently wanted to reserve the power to jam unfriendly broadcasting and to ensure that such electronic "pollution" would not create liability under the Treaty.

[61] See generally H. Baker, *Space Debris: Legal and Policy Implications* (1989); Office of Technology Assessment, US Cong., Orbiting Debris: A Space Environmental Problem – Background Paper, OTA-BP-ISC72 (Sept. 1990). The problem of space debris has been discussed in numerous international fora, including the ITU, COPUOS, INTELSAT, the Conference on Disarmament, and the negotiations surrounding the space station.

[62] In 1992, the General Assembly adopted Principles Relevant to the Use of Nuclear Power Sources in Outer Space, but discontent regarding the principles has led to periodic calls for their reexamination. Jose Alvarez, "Legal Issues," in *A Global Agenda: Issues before the 50th General Assembly of the United Nations* 273 (J. Tessitore & S. Woolfson eds., 1995).

issues will be the next focus of attempted law-making within the United Nations, potentially expanding the regime of liability for ultra-hazardous activities to include obligations *erga omnes* for the protection of the space environment.

C. The regime of freedoms

1. Presumptive powers

The regime of freedoms in space refers to those presumptive powers of states to use outer space without interference by other states or international organizations. The Outer Space Treaty explicitly recognizes the freedoms of "exploration and use" as well as "scientific investigation,"[63] and it is clear that these terms are to be broadly construed. But the activities that qualify as freedoms cannot be exhaustively enumerated *a priori* and so are defined only by reference to what is *not* allowed: a state can explore and use space in any way so long as its acts are peaceful, do not establish or presuppose a claim of title, and do not evade state responsibility. Space freedoms are "presumptive" in other words because they are defined not by their substantive content but by their limits.

In this, the regime of space freedoms resembles the regime governing the high seas: exemplary freedoms are enumerated by treaty without the implication that the examples exhaust the field.[64] To the contrary, the limit on such freedoms is the requirement that they be exercised consistently with international law and the correlative rights of other states. They may not be exercised in such a way as to discriminate against the equal freedoms of another state or in violation of international law.[65]

---

[63] The Outer Space Treaty, note 1 above, art. I, provides in part that:

> Outer space, including the moon and other celestial bodies, shall be free for exploration and use by all States without discrimination of any kind, on a basis of equality and in accordance with international law, and there shall be free access to all areas of celestial bodies. There shall be freedom of scientific investigation in outer space, including the moon and other celestial bodies, and States shall facilitate and encourage international cooperation in such investigation.

[64] 1982 United Nations Convention on the Law of the Sea, UN Doc. A/CONF.62/122 (Oct. 7, 1982), Corr. 3 (Nov. 23, 1982) & Corr. 8 (Nov. 26, 1982), art. 87, identifies six explicit freedoms, *inter alia*, including the freedoms of navigation, overflight, research (subject to other provisions of the treaty), and fishing (also subject to other provisions of the treaty). *Ibid.*, at ¶1. In exercising these freedoms, states are obliged to act "with due regard for the interests of other States in their exercise of the freedom of the high seas." *Ibid.*, at ¶2.

[65] The United Nations has recognized the *erga omnes* obligations with respect to the space environment. See, e.g., N. Jasentuliyana, "Space Activities and International Environmental Protection: Perspectives on the United Nations Role," *Proceedings of the 33rd Colloquium on the Law of Outer Space* 152–54 (1991).

2. Remote sensing

invasion of national privacy [handwritten marginal note]

Perhaps the best example of this dialectic is the controversy over remote sensing from space, a satellite technology for collecting detailed information about conditions on the surface of the earth, including the location and condition of natural resources. *A priori*, such a use of space might be considered a freedom, protected by Article I of the Outer Space Treaty, but, because of the high resolution of remotely sensed data (including photographic images), it has been challenged as an invasion of national privacy, potentially compromising a state's national security and its sovereignty over the disposition of its resources.

It took the United Nations almost twenty years to resolve the tension between a conception of sovereignty that would allow remote sensing as a freedom of space and a conception of sovereignty that would give the sensed state the right of prior consent. In 1969, the United Nations General Assembly resolved that "earth resources survey satellite programmes be available to produce information for the world community as a whole,"[66] but the circumstances under which that information would be gathered or disseminated, and especially the necessity *vel non* of the sensed state's prior consent, remained controversial. Two years later, following discussions in the Legal Subcommittee of COPUOS, the General Assembly convened a special Working Group on Remote Sensing of the Earth by Satellites,[67] which surveyed the legal principles in conflict and considered a range of institutional arrangements for overseeing the collection and distribution of remotely sensed data. There followed fifteen years of debate on the rules governing remote sensing, a time during which the technology improved dramatically and the remote sensing industry became internationally competitive.[68]

Finally, in late 1986, following consensus within COPUOS, the General Assembly formally adopted fifteen principles relating to remote sensing of the earth from space. These principles reaffirm that remote sensing, like other space activities, "shall be carried out for the benefit and in the interests of all countries, irrespective of their degree of economic, social, or

---

[66] GA Res. 2600 (XXIV) (Dec. 16, 1969).

[67] GA Res. 2778 (XXVI) (Nov. 29, 1971).

[68] For a midflight assessment of the tortuous path to the principles on remote sensing, see C. Q. Christol, *The Modern International Law of Outer Space* 720–64 (1982). Throughout the 1970s, treaty developments outside the United Nations affected the evolution of those principles. In particular, various bilateral agreements were adopted providing for cooperation in the collection and dissemination of remote sensing data. See, e.g., Memorandum of Understanding between the National Remote Sensing Agency, Government of India, and the United States National Aeronautics and Space Administration, Jan. 3, 1978, reprinted in S. Comm. on Commerce, Sci. & Transp., *Space Law: Selected Basic Documents* 593 (2d ed., 1978). Significantly, these bilateral agreements did not generally recognize a right of prior consent in the sensed state.

scientific development, and taking into particular consideration the needs of the developing countries";[69] that remote sensing, like other space activities, must be conducted in accordance with international law,[70] and that sensing states should promote international cooperation[71] and environmental protection on earth.[72]

But the relatively innocuous text of the principles is perhaps most significant for what was *not* there, namely that remote sensing or the dissemination of data can occur only with the prior consent of the sensed state. States that had insisted on such a requirement ultimately accepted a right to be consulted for the purpose of enhancing their "participation" in the exercise,[73] to receive data "that may be useful to States affected by natural disasters" as promptly as possible,[74] and to receive data on a nondiscriminatory basis and at reasonable cost, "taking particularly into account the needs and interests of the developing countries."[75] As a result, although the less developed countries are entitled in principle to special (unspecified) consideration, the text leaves little or no room for a norm of prior consent as to either the collection of data or its distribution. Irrespective of whether these principles are ultimately adopted by treaty, remote sensing should continue to emerge as a presumptive freedom of space.

3. Direct broadcast satellites

Related to but distinct from the gathering of information by remote sensing is the dissemination of information by direct broadcast satellites (DBS), a technology that allows *inter alia* the direct transmission of television images to individual receivers in countries around the world. As it had with respect to remote sensing, the United Nations early on convened a working group to develop legal principles governing DBS, and it similarly confronted the tension between freedom of use and prior consent. Unlike the principles governing remote sensing, however, the asserted regime for DBS tends toward the requirement of prior consent, i.e., some agreement by the receiving state before the signals may be broadcast. But the United States and others have consistently rejected such a requirement on human rights grounds, and the preliminary question arises whether (and how) a resolution within the United Nations Organization purporting to articulate norms governing DBS affects the legal position of nations that voted against it.

On the merits, the case for a prior consent requirement is not baseless,

[69] GA Res. 41/65 (Dec. 3, 1986), Principle II.   [70] *Ibid.*, at Principles III, IV, IX, & XIV.
[71] *Ibid.*, at Principles V & XIII.   [72] *Ibid.*, at Principles X & XI.
[73] *Ibid.*, at Principle XIII.   [74] *Ibid.*, at Principle XI.   [75] *Ibid.*, at Principle XII.

though the whole of the argument seems greater than the sum of its parts. For example, regulations of the International Telecommunications Union oblige states to minimize "the radiation over the territory of other countries unless an agreement has been previously reached with such countries,"[76] and early resolutions of the United Nations condemned war propaganda, a content-based restriction incorporated by reference in the Preamble to the Outer Space Treaty. That principle assertedly vitiates the objection to prior consent based on free speech or the free flow of information. But the legal force of the ITU regulation is undermined to the extent that it was designed to reduce radiomagnetic interference, i.e., "spill-over," and was not intended to control direct broadcasting, and the anti-propaganda resolutions were arguably superseded by the Universal Declaration of Human Rights and other human rights instruments.

As a consequence, the "norm" of prior consent with respect to DBS is manifest only in a series of nonbinding resolutions, adopted by the majority of states but rejected by a group of states which owns and uses the technology. In these circumstances, it cannot be said that prior consent has emerged as a rule of international space law, though there is little doubt that there is more support for such a norm in the DBS context than there is in the remote sensing context, presumably because direct broadcasting has been perceived as the greater intrusion on domestic sovereignty. Of course, the demise of totalitarian governments since 1989 may eventually loosen even this equivocal regulation, bringing DBS more clearly into the regime of space freedoms.

D. The regime of relative normativity

The previous discussion suggests that space law, like other elements of modern international law,[77] consists in a gradient of norms, ranging from binding obligations under treaty and customary law through the "soft law" of declarations, resolutions, and authoritative interpretations. Although these latter, prenormative, acts are clearly not obligatory, they are equally clearly not irrelevant. They may suggest tendencies in the law or areas of agreement that may crystallize into binding law. They may provide meaningful guidance in a political world only partially committed to law.

In particular, three types of sub-treaty norms should be recognized. First among these are authoritative interpretations of the UN Charter, including the extension of general international law into outer space. The obligations of states under the UN Charter and customary international law are

---

[76] Final Acts of the World Administrative Conference for Space Telecommunications, 23 UST 1648, TIAS No. 7435, Reg. 428A (*entered into force* Jan. 1, 1973).

[77] P. Weil, "Towards Relative Normativity in International Law?," 77 *AJIL* 413 (1983).

auth. interpretations

357

applicable in the space environment, meaning that states are obliged to resolve space-related disputes peacefully, to forgo the threat or use of force in space, and to respect the principles of *pacta sunt servanda, sic utere,* and other principles of state responsibility, as well as human rights. Of course, the applicability of customary law may be rebutted by a special space treaty intended to alter preexisting custom (so long as that custom does not rise to the level of *jus cogens*), and some provisions of the specialized treaties have become customary in the regimes of principles identified above. But there is no doubt that interpretations of the Charter and of customary law by the United Nations presumptively apply in space as well.

Second, at least some of the resolutions and declarations identified above should qualify as *de lege ferenda,* especially with respect to remote sensing and the use of nuclear power sources in space. State positions on these issues have increasingly reaffirmed the regimes of freedom in the former case and state liability in the latter. Similarly, that part of the redistributive equity agenda which includes the definition of outer space (and the broader related issue of LDC entitlements) has been accommodated somewhat, particularly in the 1988 World Administrative Conference governing the geostationary orbit. That disposition – though it is unlikely to yield an enforceable common heritage principle in space generally – nonetheless represents a genuine incremental commitment to fairness. By contrast, the prospects seem remote altogether for consensus on an expansive interpretation of the peaceful uses principle that includes the total demilitarization of space, in the absence of a treaty requiring it. Plainly then, we can distinguish between the authentic and the spurious prospects for legal development.

Third, the ICAO, the ITU, and some of the ITU's common user organizations possess legislative or quasi-legislative powers that have been used to create meaningful norms of international space law. These regulations under existing international instruments are generally technical, pertaining to harmonization of standards and procedures, or dividing the limited natural resource of the geostationary orbit or the electromagnetic spectrum. Taken together, these norms (or prenorms) undermine the traditional distinction between binding and nonbinding law, suggesting a middle range of authority that channels disputes and offers grounds for resolution and closure.

IV. CONCLUSION AND PROSPECTIVE

The Charter of the United Nations, with its multiple statements of purpose, provides some initial criteria for assessing the role of the

Organization in the development of international space law. Under Article 1, for example, the United Nations is designed in part to "maintain international peace and security," to "achieve international cooperation in solving international problems of an economic, social, cultural, or humanitarian character," and to serve as "a centre for harmonizing the actions of nations in the attainment of these common ends." Under Article 13, the General Assembly "shall initiate studies and make recommendations for the purpose of . . . encouraging the progressive development of international law and its codification." Judged by these admittedly generous standards, the United Nations has had a profound impact on the international law of space, offering a dominant forum for the rapid articulation of principles by consensus and assuring that humankind's activities in space would be subject to law in the first place. The accomplishment is especially remarkable if we consider the centuries it took to develop a regime for the high seas.

If the space principles seem flawed in retrospect, there may be many reasons. If they seem modest or even trifling, for example, it may be because they cannot of their own force resolve the more conspicuous causes of discord between states, causes in which legal principles may serve as tokens. It may be especially unrealistic to expect space, an obvious national security resource, to become amenable to significant international regulation. But it is not meaningless to have laid out the framework for resolution and incremental regulation; indeed, the fact that principles which were contentious at the beginning seem now inevitable or trivial may count as evidence that the United Nations has been at least partially successful in its efforts. It seems pathological to fixate on the hard case and to miss the surprise in the realization that easy cases exist at all.

If by contrast the space principles seem now indeterminate or even self-contradictory, that may reflect our increasing impatience with the positivist conception of law, with its understatement of law's indeterminacy. Perhaps we invite disappointment by expecting international legal principles to serve as something other than touchstones in an international discourse that is irreducibly political. Inevitably, the space principles will change shape as the world order changes, and, if that includes a greater concern for the less developed countries, for example, the norms of sharing or nonappropriability will more dramatically circumscribe the norms of freedom. Similarly, liability and dispute-resolution issues will become more pronounced with the wide-scale commercialization of space. But, because the four regimes of principles noted above reflect broadly held notions of self-interest at some level of abstraction, they are unlikely to be abandoned, only developed through concrete applications.

If, finally, the United Nations seems an unlikely institution for further development of these principles, it may be because, ironically in an increasingly multilateral world, other groupings of states have proved to be more workable. These may include bilateral arrangements or institutions organized by region or function. But even these organizations will operate within a legal world defined by the efforts of the United Nations and its specialized agencies.

The success of the next round of space law-making within the United Nations will depend on members' ability to anticipate problems arising out of some dynamic other than the competition between superpowers: in addition to the issues that are the recurring fare of COPUOS, especially demilitarization and distributional equity, the new concerns will include commercialization, space transportation, and environmental protection. But the broader issue will continue to be how states choose to define "sovereignty." Sovereignty itself has resolved none of the debate, for example, in DBS or remote sensing. Indeed, the debate is between two sides, both of which take sovereignty as a starting point: sovereignty as freedom (an expansive and permissive notion) versus sovereignty as privacy (an exclusive notion limiting the freedoms of other states).

That traditional dialectic will doubtless continue, especially as issues of distributional equity come to dominate the international agenda. But a new dimension has been added to the problem of sovereignty by the rise of nonstate actors in international legal life. The blurring of the distinction between "public" and "private" international norms is especially striking in space law because of the increasing state–private cooperation in the exploitation of space. Public and private actors are intrinsically linked legally and operationally, especially in space telecommunications and liability law. New forms of international organization have already emerged, as intergovernmental institutions assume a corporate form or include both sovereign and private actors. In this respect, space law reflects the overall move in international law away from the classical statist orientation and toward a new paradigm for a new century.

SELECTED BIBLIOGRAPHY

Annual Proceedings of The International Institute of Space Law
Benko, M., W. De Graaf & G. Reijnen, *Space Law in the United Nations* (Martinus Nijhoff, 1985)
Christol, C., *The Modern International Law of Outer Space* (Pergamon, 1982).
Jasentuliyana, N. & R. S. K. Lee, *Manual on Space Law:* Travaux Préparatoires *and Related Documents* (Oceana, 1981)
Lachs, M., *The Law Of Outer Space: An Experience in Contemporary Law-making*

(Sijthoff, 1972)

Marchan, J., *Derecho Internacional Del Espacio: Teoria Y Politica* (2d ed., Civitas, 1990)

Matte, N., *Aerospace Law* (Carswell, 1977)

Merges, R. & G. Reynolds, *Outer Space: Problems of Law and Policy* (Westview, 1989)

Senate Committee on Commerce, Science, and Transportation, *Space Law: Selected Basic Documents* (3d ed., US GPO, 1990)

Smith, M., *International Regulation of Satellite Communication* (Martinus Nijhoff, 1990)

Space Law: Development and Scope (N. Jasentuliyana ed.; Praeger, 1992)

United States Space Law (S. Gorove ed.; Oceana, 1990)

CHAPTER THIRTEEN

INTERNATIONAL CRIMES

John F. Murphy

I. INTRODUCTION

Before considering the United Nations' role in combating terrorism, drug trafficking, and other international crimes, it should be stressed that this is an area of considerable definitional ambiguity. The eminent British international law scholar Georg Schwarzenberger, writing in 1950, concluded that "international criminal law in any true sense does not exist."[1] Defining international law narrowly to cover only rights and obligations of states and not those of individuals, Schwarzenberger was of the opinion that "an international criminal law that is meant to be applied to the world powers is a contradiction in terms. It presupposes an international authority which is superior to these states."[2]

Turning to piracy and war crimes, the examples most often "adduced as evidence *par excellence* of the existence of international criminal law,"[3] Schwarzenberger denied that these actions constitute crimes under international law. Rather, in his view:

The rules of international law both on piracy *jure gentium* and war crimes constitute prescription to States to suppress piracy within their own jurisdiction and to exercise proper control over their own armed forces, and an authorization to other States to assume an extraordinary criminal jurisdiction under their own municipal law in the case of piracy *jure gentium* and of war crimes committed prior to capture by the enemy.[4]

Most other commentators have arrived at a different conclusion.[5] With respect to piracy the International Law Commission (ILC), a subsidiary organ of the United Nations General Assembly, in drafting the articles on

---

[1] G. Schwarzenberger, "The Problem of an International Criminal Law," 3 *Current Legal Problems* 263, 295 (1950).　　[2] *Ibid.*　　[3] *Ibid.*, at 268.　　[4] *Ibid.*, at 27.
[5] See, e.g., Mueller & Besharov, "Evolution and Enforcement of International Criminal Law," in *International Criminal Law*, I, 59 (M. C. Bassiouni ed., 1986).

piracy that ultimately helped constitute the 1958 Geneva Convention on the High Seas,[6] adopted what Alfred Rubin has termed the "naturalist" model, that is, the view of "'piracy' as a crime against international law seeking only a tribunal with jurisdiction to apply that law and punish the criminal," as opposed to the "positivist" view of piracy "as solely a municipal law crime, the only question of international law being the extent of a state's jurisdiction to apply its criminal law to an accused foreigner acting outside the territorial jurisdiction of the prescribing state."[7] As to war crimes, the decision of the International Military Tribunal at Nuremberg and subsequent action by the UN General Assembly have arguably supported the "naturalist" view, as will be shown.

Another dimension of "international criminal law" involves international cooperation in the enforcement of municipal criminal law. Even for those crimes arguably constituting crimes under international as well as municipal law, it is necessary – in the absence of an international criminal court – to employ national law enforcement officials and national courts for purposes of prosecuting and punishing offenders. Although most efforts toward international cooperation in the enforcement of municipal criminal law have been on a bilateral or regional basis, the United Nations has played an increasingly important role in this area as well.

II. DEFINING "INTERNATIONAL CRIME": THE ROLE OF THE UNITED NATIONS

A. "Traditional" international crimes: the Nuremberg Principles

Volumes have been written about the Nuremberg trials.[8] Our focus is on the contribution, if any, they have made to the development of a substantive international criminal law.

Georg Schwarzenberger has contended that they have made no contribution. In his view, although the Nuremberg Tribunal explicitly applied customary and treaty international law in the trial of the defendants, it was sitting as a *municipal* war crimes court rather than as an *international* tribunal, because

the signatories to the Charter of the Tribunal only did jointly what each of them, if in sole control of Germany, could have done alone. In the exercise of their *condominium* over Germany, the occupying Powers were not limited to the

---

[6] For a discussion of the ILC's efforts, see A. Rubin, *The Law of Piracy* 319–37 (1988).
[7] *Ibid.*, at 328.
[8] For a recent effort, see *The Nuremberg Trial and International Law* (G. Ginsburgs & V. N. Kudriavtsev eds., 1990).

application to Germany of the customary laws of warfare. In their capacity as co-sovereigns of Germany they were free to agree on any additional legal principles which they cared to apply.[9]

It is debatable whether the Nuremberg Tribunal is viewed accurately as a municipal or an international tribunal. Certainly the Tribunal's judgment stated that the making of the Charter was the "exercise of the sovereign legislative power by the countries to which the German Reich unconditionally surrendered," and concluded that these countries had the "undoubted right" to legislate for occupied Germany.[10] On the other hand, the London Charter, which established the Tribunal, was an international agreement and, as previously noted, the Tribunal applied international law as the basis for its decision. Assuming *arguendo*, however, that the Tribunal is properly viewed as a municipal court, it does not follow that its decision made no contribution to the development of international criminal law, as Schwarzenberger posits.

On the contrary, the Tribunal's judgment may be viewed as a truly landmark step in the progressive development of international law. Albeit controversially, the Tribunal proclaimed the existence of two "new" crimes under international law – crimes against peace and crimes against humanity. With respect to the more traditional concept of war crimes, the Tribunal declared that they had evolved from their initial status as treaty law, binding only on states parties, to the status of customary international law binding on all nations. In 1947, moreover, the UN General Assembly adopted a resolution affirming "the principles of international law recognized by the Charter of the Nuremberg Tribunal and the judgment of the Tribunal,"[11] thereby further supporting the proposition that proscription of the Nuremberg crimes has been recognized broadly as international customary law. The Nuremberg Principles also endorsed the controversial propositions that individuals as well as states have obligations under international law and that the proscriptions of international law prevail over national laws that authorize or at least allow such acts.

The concept of crimes against humanity was affirmed further when the General Assembly adopted, on December 9, 1948, the Convention on the Prevention and Punishment of the Crime of Genocide.[12] The Convention declares genocide, as defined therein, to be a crime under international law, and directs that persons charged with genocide shall be tried "by a

---

[9] Schwarzenberger, note 1 above, at 290–91.

[10] The text of the Judgment of the International Military Tribunal may be conveniently found in 6 FRD 69, 107 (1946).   [11] GA Res. 95 (I), UN Doc. A/64/Add.1, at 188 (1947).

[12] Convention on the Prevention and Punishment of the Crime of Genocide, GA Res. 260A (III), UN GAOR 3d Sess. (1), at 174, UN Doc. A/810 (1948) (hereinafter Genocide Convention).

competent tribunal of the State in the territory of which the act was committed, or by such international penal tribunal as may have jurisdiction."[13] As of March 1990 the Convention had 102 states parties. Although the Convention has not established an operative framework for the prosecution and punishment of those who have committed genocide, it is nevertheless widely regarded as a critical step in establishing genocide as a crime under international law.

B. "Modern" international crimes

Since the General Assembly affirmed the Nuremberg Principles and adopted the Genocide Convention, the United Nations and its specialized agencies have taken a number of other steps toward the development of a substantive international criminal law and the creation of a legal framework for its enforcement. We turn first to a consideration of the Draft Articles on the Draft Code of Crimes against the Peace and Security of Mankind.

1. Draft Articles on the Draft Code of Crimes against the Peace and Security of Mankind

It should be noted that the status of the Draft Articles on the Draft Code of Crimes against the Peace and Security of Mankind as "law" of the United Nations is problematic at this stage of its development. Although the ILC adopted the Draft Articles on a first reading, many provisions remain controversial, and there were numerous critical comments forthcoming from the governments to which they were submitted.[14] Moreover, it has not yet been determined whether these Articles will be adopted in binding legal form – perhaps as part of a treaty or as a model law – or in a nonbinding mode along the lines of the Helsinki Accords. This issue is closely linked with the question of whether the Code should serve, in whole or in part, as the statute for an international criminal court – an issue examined later in this chapter.

To be sure, even if it is adopted in nonbinding form, the Code could be instrumental in the development of law or result in expectations on the part of member states that they would be enforced as if they were law;[15] adoption of the Draft Articles on first reading thus is a significant development worthy of consideration.

[13] *Ibid.,*, art. VI.
[14] For examples, see *Commentaries on the International Law Commission's 1991 Draft Code of Crimes against the Peace and Security of Mankind* (M. C. Bassiouni ed., 1993).
[15] For discussion, see O. Schachter, "The Twilight Existence of Nonbinding International Agreements," 71 *AJIL* 296 (1977).

Space limitations preclude an exhaustive examination of the Draft Articles in this chapter. Rather, the goal here is to offer an overview of them, while highlighting some of the more salient provisions in terms of possible law development. First and foremost, it should be noted that the Draft Articles are limited in their coverage to crimes that threaten the peace and security of mankind. Because of this bedrock test, Article 21 of the Draft Articles covers "systematic or mass violations of human rights" but not human rights violations that do not rise to this level of magnitude, on the rationale that the latter are unlikely to cause disputes that would threaten the peace. The international nature of the crimes covered by the Draft Articles is highlighted by Article 2, which provides in pertinent part that the "characterization of an act or omission as a crime against the peace and security of mankind is independent of internal law," and which goes on to state that the presence or absence of punishment for such acts or omissions under internal law "does not affect this characterization."

It should first be realized that the Draft Articles both codify and develop the law of international crimes. For example, some of the acts covered clearly constitute international crimes under current law, including aggression, threat of aggression (probably), genocide, international terrorism (at least as defined by the Commission), and illicit traffic in narcotic drugs. Other acts, although arguably already constituting international crimes and in some cases covered by international conventions, are more debatable. Many developed Western countries in particular would deny some are currently established as international crimes, for example, intervention; colonial domination and other forms of alien domination; apartheid; and the recruitment, use, financing, and training of mercenaries. With respect to still other acts the Commission would seem to be proposing new categories of international crimes. Systematic or mass violations of human rights, for example, is a new crime against the peace and security of mankind. Some of the human rights violations covered – torture, slavery, and deportation or forcible transfer of population – are already established as international crimes when committed on a nonsystematic or nonmass basis. Others, namely murder and persecution on social, political, racial, religious, or cultural grounds, are not generally regarded as international crimes absent the higher level of magnitude.

Similarly, although war crimes, including "grave breaches," have long been established as international crimes, the concept of "exceptionally serious war crimes" as a crime against the peace and security of mankind is new.

Finally, although there are some provisions in treaties and conventions on the law of armed conflict regarding damage to the environment, the provision on willful and severe damage to the environment is an exercise in law development. Deliberate and widespread damage to the environment during the Gulf war, with global repercussions, has helped generate support for such a provision.

A number of general questions regarding the Draft Articles should be noted briefly. Some definitions of the crimes differ from those found in other legal instruments; for instance, the definition of aggression deviates in some possibly significant respects from that of the General Assembly's resolution defining aggression. Some commentators have suggested that such inconsistency is undesirable. On the other hand, in some cases, genocide, for example, it may be appropriate to improve upon the definition found in the applicable international convention or instrument.

The historical record indicates that many, perhaps most, of these crimes against the peace and security of mankind will prove difficult to prosecute and punish. Aggression and genocide have long been established as among the most severe of international crimes, yet since the Nuremberg and Tokyo trials, there have been no prosecutions – much less punishments – for their commission. The crime of aggression is not even listed among the crimes covered by most national criminal codes and statutes.

We now turn to other efforts of the United Nations and its specialized agencies to develop substantive international criminal law and to create a legal framework for its enforcement. They have been particularly active with respect to international terrorism.

2. International terrorism

Despite efforts to do so, neither the United Nations nor its specialized agencies have been able to agree on a definition of "international terrorism." Partially because of this, the United Nations has also been unable to agree on a single convention on the legal control of terrorism.[16] Rather, the United Nations has adopted a piecemeal approach to the problem through the adoption of separate conventions aimed at suppressing aircraft hijacking,[17] unlawful acts against the safety of civil aviation,[18] or of airports serving international civil aviation,[19] unlawful acts against

---

[16] For background, see J. Murphy, "Defining International Terrorism: A Way Out of the Quagmire," 19 *Isr. Y. B. Hum. Rts.* 13, 14–18 (Y. Dinstein ed., 1989).

[17] Convention on Offenses and Certain Other Acts Committed on Board Aircraft, Sept. 14, 1963, 20 UST 2941, TIAS No. 6768, 704 UNTS 219; Convention for the Suppression of Unlawful Seizure of Aircraft (Hague Convention), Dec. 16, 1970, 22 UST 1641, TIAS No. 7192, 860 UNTS 105, reprinted in 10 *ILM* 133 (1971).

[18] Convention for Suppression of Unlawful Acts against the Safety of Civil Aviation (Montreal Convention), Sept. 23, 1971, 24 UST 564, TIAS No. 7570, 974 UNTS 177, reprinted in 10 *ILM* 1151 (1971).

[19] Convention for Suppression of Unlawful Acts of Violence at Airports Serving International Civil Aviation, Feb. 24, 1988, reprinted in 27 *ILM* 627 (1988).

internationally protected persons, including diplomatic agents,[20] the taking of hostages,[21] unlawful acts against the safety of maritime navigation[22] and, most recently, the use of plastic explosives. On March 1, 1991, at the International Conference on Air Law, sponsored by the International Civil Aviation Organization, forty-one delegates signed the Convention on the Marking of Plastic Explosives for the Purpose of Detection. Among other things, this Convention requires states parties to prohibit and prevent the manufacture in their territories of unmarked explosives, as well as the movement of such explosives in to or out of their territories. It also requires that all plastic explosives be marked by manufacturers with any one of four "detection agents."[23]

Although these treaty provisions are often loosely described as "antiterrorist," the acts themselves that they cover are criminalized regardless of whether, in a particular case, they could be described as "terrorism." Whether the crimes covered by the anti-terrorist conventions may be classified as "international crimes" is debatable. At the least, they establish a legal framework for states parties to cooperate toward punishment of the perpetrators of these crimes. They also create a system of universal jurisdiction over these crimes for states parties and, in the case of those conventions that have been ratified by a large number of states,[24] they may have contributed to the establishment of a system of universal jurisdiction available to all states. In no case do the conventions establish an international criminal court as a forum in which alleged offenders could be tried.

3. International drug trafficking

Although international drug trafficking was at one time supported by governments – the British fought two "opium wars" with China when the

---

[20] Convention on Prevention and Punishment of Crimes against Internationally Protected Persons, Including Diplomatic Agents, Dec. 14, 1973, 28 UST 1975, TIAS No. 8532, 1035 UNTS 167 (hereinafter New York Convention).

[21] International Convention against the Taking of Hostages, Dec. 17, 1979, UN GAOR, 34th Sess., Supp. No. 39, at 23, UN Doc. A/34/39 (1979), reprinted in 18 *ILM* 1456 (1979) (hereinafter Hostages Convention).

[22] Convention for the Suppression of Unlawful Acts against the Safety of Maritime Navigation, March 10, 1988, reprinted in 27 *ILM* 672 (1988); Protocol for the Suppression of Unlawful Acts against the Safety of Fixed Platforms Located on the Continental Shelf, reprinted in 27 *ILM* 685 (1988).

[23] See "International Controls to Regulate Plastic Explosives Adopted in Montreal," *UN Chronicle* 32 (June 1991).

[24] The number of parties to the anti-terrorist conventions varies greatly. As of early 1989, for example, the Hague Convention had 141 states parties and the Montreal Convention had 140. By contrast, the New York Convention, as of the same period, had only 78 states parties and the Hostages Convention only 56. See J. Lambert, *Terrorism and Hostages in International Law* 48 (1990).

latter tried to ban the inflow of opium from British India in the late 1830s – attitudes changed dramatically in the late nineteenth and early twentieth centuries. Increasingly intense efforts to combat the trade were undertaken, with early efforts focused on limiting the manufacture and distribution of drugs.[25] The 1936 Convention for the Suppression of the Illicit Traffic in Dangerous Drugs,[26] the last treaty to be concluded under the auspices of the League of Nations, added a criminal dimension. Specifically, it called for drug traffickers to be punished by all governments, regardless of the criminal's nationality or the place where the crime was committed. The goal of the drafters of the Convention was to raise drug trafficking to the level of an international crime.[27]

For its part, the United Nations was the forum for the conclusion of several protocols that transferred to the United Nations the functions exercised originally by the League of Nations under the various narcotic treaties concluded before World War II and that expanded the scope of coverage of these treaties. In 1961 the United Nations adopted the Single Convention on Narcotic Drugs,[28] which unified most of the earlier treaties into one comprehensive document. This was followed a decade later by the Convention on Psychotropic Substances,[29] which brought additional substances under international control. Because of various deficiencies in these conventions, pressures built up during the 1980s for the conclusion of still another convention. The result was the 1988 Convention against Illicit Traffic in Narcotic Drugs and Psychotropic Substances.[30]

The final text of the 1988 Convention was adopted by consensus by the 106 states represented at the conference. In its Preamble, the Convention recognizes that illicit drug trafficking is an international criminal activity and that "eradication of illicit traffic is a collective responsibility of all States and that, to that end, co-ordinated action within the framework of international cooperation is necessary." In light of this and the other earlier multilateral efforts a good argument can be made that international drug

---

[25] Some of this background material is taken from a paper by Ethan A. Nadelmann, Assistant Professor of Politics and Public Affairs, Woodrow Wilson School of Public and International Affairs, Princeton University, Global Law Enforcement Regimes: Their Evolution, Fate and Future (unpublished paper, on file with author).

[26] 1936 Convention for the Suppression of Illicit Traffic in Dangerous Drugs, 198 LNTS 229.

[27] Nadelmann, note 25 above, at 40.

[28] Single Convention on Narcotic Drugs, Mar. 30, 1961, 18 UST 1407, TIAS No. 6298, 520 UNTS 204.

[29] Convention on Psychotropic Substances, Feb. 21, 1971, 32 UST 543, TIAS No. 9725, 1019 UNTS 175.

[30] Convention against Illicit Traffic in Narcotic Drugs and Psychotropic Substances, UN Doc. E/Conf. 82/15/Corr. 1 & Corr. 2, *adopted by consensus* Dec. 20, 1988, reprinted in 28 *ILM* 493 (1989).

trafficking is a crime under customary international law as well as under municipal law.

4. Other international crimes

Apartheid and torture are two "international crimes" that have been a focal point of UN activity.

(a) Apartheid

Apartheid, that is, the official racial policies of South Africa, has been sharply criticized in the political organs of the United Nations since the early days of the Organization, and in its advisory opinion on Namibia,[31] the International Court of Justice concluded that South Africa's extension of apartheid to that territory violated treaty and customary international law. Several General Assembly resolutions, moreover, declare that apartheid is a "crime against humanity,"[32] and Security Council resolutions proclaim it to be "a crime against the conscience and dignity of mankind."[33]

On November 30, 1973, the General Assembly adopted the International Convention on the Suppression and Punishment of the Crime of Apartheid.[34] It did so over the opposition of the United States and the Western European states, and as a consequence, although as of August 1987 eighty-five states were parties to the Convention, neither the United States nor any Western European states have ratified, and few Latin American states have become parties. The representatives of those states that voted against the Convention, moreover, including the US and British representatives, made statements strongly opposing the concept that apartheid – though deplorable as a violation of fundamental human rights – could be made a crime against humanity.[35] In light of this opposition it is problematic whether apartheid has been established as an international crime or not.

(b) Torture

Although torture has been widely practiced throughout the ages and, according to reports, continues to be employed extensively,[36] there appears

[31] Advisory Opinion on the Continued Presence of South Africa in Namibia (SW Afr.), 1971 ICJ 16.
[32] For discussion of these resolutions, see R. Clark, "The Crime of Apartheid," in *International Criminal Law: Crimes*, I, 299, 300 (M. C. Bassiouni ed., 1986).   [33] *Ibid.*, at 300.
[34] GA Res. 3068 (XXVIII), UN GAOR, 28th Sess., Supp. No. 30, at 75, UN Doc. A/9030 (1973).   [35] Clark, note 32 above, at 312–15.
[36] See Bassiouni & Darby, "The Crime of Torture," in Bassiouni ed., note 32 above.

to be a general consensus today that it constitutes both a tort and a crime under international law. In the development of this consensus, the United Nations has played a key role.

Numerous UN documents implicitly or explicitly prohibit torture. The UN Charter provisions on human rights are cast only in general terms, but the Universal Declaration of Human Rights,[37] which arguably has binding effect as its principles have achieved such a degree of acceptance that they now constitute general principles of international law recognized by all civilized nations,[38] expressly states that: "No one shall be subjected to torture or to cruel, inhuman or degrading treatment or punishment."[39] A similar provision is found in the widely ratified International Covenant on Civil and Political Rights.[40]

Several unanimously or near-unanimously adopted General Assembly resolutions categorically reject the use of torture for any purpose whatsoever.[41] Perhaps the most important of these is the Declaration on the Protection of All Persons from Being Subjected to Torture and Other Cruel, Inhuman or Degrading Treatment or Punishment[42] which, *inter alia*, takes the vitally important steps of defining "torture," calling upon states to ensure that all acts so defined are criminal offenses under their criminal law, and providing for redress and compensation for the victims. This declaration was followed by the General Assembly's adoption in 1984 of the Convention against Torture and Other Cruel, Inhuman or Degrading Treatment or Punishment (Torture Convention).[43] As of this writing, seventy-two states are parties to the Torture Convention.

As US Circuit Court Judge Irving Kaufman concluded in the landmark case of *Filartiga* v. *Pena-Irala*, UN actions, coupled with provisions in regional human rights treaties and court decisions, national constitutions and laws, and the writings of jurists, establish that "the torturer has become – like the pirate and slave trader before him – *hostis humani generis*, an enemy of mankind."[44] Although Judge Kaufman's holding was limited to a finding that torture constituted an international tort under customary international law, developments since then, especially the conclusion and

37 Universal Declaration of Human Rights, GA Res. 217A (III), UN GAOR, 3d Sess., at 71, UN Doc. A/810 (1948).
38 For discussion, see E. Schwelb, "The Influence of the Universal Declaration of Human Rights," 1959 *Am. Soc'y Int'l L. Proc.* 217.
39 Universal Declaration of Human Rights, note 37 above, art. 5.
40 International Covenant on Civil and Political Rights, art. 7, GA Res. 2200 (XXI), UN GAOR, 21st Sess., Supp. No. 16, at 52, UN Doc. A/6316 (1966).
41 See Bassiouni & Darby, note 36 above, at 379–80.
42 GA Res. 34/52 (XXX), UN GAOR, 30th Sess., Supp. No. 34, at 91, UN Doc. A/10034 (1975).
43 GA Res. 39/46, UN GAOR, 39th Sess., Supp. No. 51, at 197, UN Doc. A/39/51 (1984).
44 *Filartiga* v. *Pena-Irala*, 630 F.2d 876, 890 (2d Cir. 1980).

widespread ratification of the Torture Convention, would appear to have confirmed that torture is an international crime as well.

(c) Attacks against United Nations and associated personnel

With the great expansion in UN peacekeeping operations following the end of the Cold War and the collapse of the Soviet Union, the number of UN peacekeepers and other personnel who were being attacked, injured, and killed increased at an alarming rate. In particular, the killing of UN peacekeepers in Somalia led to efforts in the fall of 1993 to take steps to criminalize attacks against peacekeepers and to apply to UN operations the prosecute-or-extradite principles employed in a number of existing multi-lateral conventions on international crime. The result was the approval by the General Assembly on December 9, 1994, of the Convention on the Safety of United Nations and Associated Personnel.[45]

Article 9 of the Convention defines a series of new international crimes – "Crimes against United Nations and associated personnel." Parties to the Convention will be required, where sufficient evidence exists, to either prosecute persons suspected of these crimes, or extradite them to another party willing to prosecute. The terms "United Nations personnel" and "associated personnel" are broadly defined to include all persons engaged or deployed in support of a United Nations operation, regardless of whether they are military, police, or civilian. The Convention excludes from its scope Chapter VII enforcement actions "in which any of the personnel are engaged as combatants against organized armed forces and to which the law of international armed conflict applies."[46] The Convention would not, therefore, have applied to United Nations authorized combat operations in Korea or Kuwait and Iraq.

III. THE LEGAL FRAMEWORK FOR SUPPRESSING INTERNATIONAL CRIME: PARADIGM AND PRACTICE

Although many of the treaties and conventions discussed contain provisions requiring states parties to cooperate in efforts to *prevent* the crimes covered, their primary focus is on international cooperation to prosecute and punish the perpetrator(s) of these crimes. This focus is not misplaced because it is difficult to codify the various measures that might be taken to prevent these crimes (often these measures consist of informal and loose

---

[45] GA Res. 49/59, UN Doc. A/RES/49/59 (Feb. 17, 1995), reprinted in 34 *ILM* 482 (1995). The United States became a signatory to the Convention on December 19, 1994. The Convention is expected to be submitted for ratification in 1996. [46] *Ibid.*, art. 2.

arrangements between law enforcement and intelligence officials). As a consequence, the provisions on prevention in these treaties are drafted in general terms.

The treaties primarily establish a system whereby a state party is obligated, if it apprehends an alleged offender in its territory, either to extradite him to the country where he allegedly committed his crimes or to some other country with an interest in seeking his prosecution or, if it decides not to extradite, to submit the case to its competent authorities for the purpose of prosecution. The goal of this arrangement is to strengthen the prospects that the perpetrators of international crimes will be prosecuted and punished in accordance with procedures that safeguard an accused's fundamental human rights.

The next section examines the extradite-or-prosecute arrangement, as well as the closely related practice of mutual legal assistance. We shall also attempt to evaluate how well the system has worked in practice, identifying gaps in coverage and examining the institutions established to implement these arrangements. The section then turns to a consideration of the prospects for an international criminal court, a concept that, after a long hiatus, has recently regained the attention of the world community.

A. Extradite or prosecute

It is worth noting that, with respect to the "classic" international crimes such as piracy, the slave trade, crimes against peace, and crimes against humanity or genocide, the United Nations has not established an extradite-or-prosecute regime. With respect to piracy, pertinent provisions of the Geneva Convention on the High Seas merely require states parties to "cooperate to the fullest possible extent in the repression of piracy on the high seas or in any other place outside the jurisdiction of any state,"[47] and authorize a state party on the high seas or in any other place outside the jurisdiction of any state to "seize a pirate ship or aircraft"[48] and arrest the persons on board. The Convention further provides that the "courts of the State which carried out the seizure may decide upon the penalties to be imposed."[49] Not surprisingly, in view of its focus on the high seas, the Convention makes no provisions for what a state may or must do if it apprehends a "pirate" on land.

As to crimes against peace or the "planning, preparation, initiation or waging of a war of aggression, or a war in violation of international treaties," the UN response, other than passage of the previously mentioned

[47] Geneva Convention on the High Seas, April 29, 1958, art. 14, 13 UST 2312, TIAS No. 5200, 450 UNTS 82.   [48] *Ibid.*, art. 19.   [49] *Ibid.*,

General Assembly resolution endorsing the concept, has been nonexistent.[50]

The Genocide Convention, while defining the crime of genocide and requiring states parties to enact legislation imposing "effective" penalties for persons found guilty of genocide, does not establish an extradite-or-prosecute requirement. The Convention instead strongly encourages the extradition of persons accused of genocide by providing that genocide shall not be considered a political crime for purposes of extradition and by requiring states parties "to grant extradition in accordance with their laws and treaties in force."[51] The Convention is not itself an extradition treaty, however, and does not create a system of universal jurisdiction. On the contrary, by its terms, it limits the trial of a person charged with genocide to "a competent tribunal of the State in the territory of which the act was committed"[52] (or an international penal tribunal should one be established with jurisdiction over the crime). The negotiating history of the Genocide Convention indicates that the state whose national is the accused may also exercise jurisdiction, and the United States has expressly reserved its right to do so.[53]

The Convention has been inoperative in practice, since no person has been prosecuted in accordance with its terms. The Convention also provides that states parties may "call upon the competent organs of the United Nations to take such action . . . as they consider appropriate for the prevention and suppression of acts of genocide"[54] and that disputes between states parties regarding the "interpretation, application, or fulfillment of the present Convention, including those relating to the responsibility of a State for genocide . . . shall be submitted to the International Court of Justice at the request of any of the parties to the dispute."[55] These provisions have been invoked only once in *Bosnia and Herzegovina v. Yugoslavia (Serbia and Montenegro).*[56] Moreover, some states, including the United States, have made reservations to the jurisdiction of the ICJ that preclude their calling another state party to account for the commission of genocidal acts.[57]

The law of war crimes, arguably already well established as part of international criminal law by the time of the Nuremberg trials, has largely been developed outside the United Nations, in conferences held in Geneva

---

[50] For further discussion, see J. Murphy, "Crimes against Peace at the Nuremberg Trial," in Ginsburgs & Kudriavtsev eds., note 8 above, at 141, 153.

[51] Genocide Convention, note 12 above, art. VII.   [52] *Ibid.*, art. VI.

[53] For the full text of the US resolution of ratification, see S. Res. 347, 99th Cong., 2d Sess., 132 Cong. Rec. 137778 (daily ed. Feb. 19, 1986).

[54] Genocide Convention, note 12 above, art. VIII.   [55] *Ibid.*,, art. IX.

[56] See 32 *ILM* 888 (1991) and 32 *ILM* 1559 (1993).

[57] See US resolution of ratification, note 53 above.

and sponsored by the International Committee of the Red Cross. The Geneva Conventions of 1949,[58] in particular, designate certain "grave breaches" as universal and extraditable offenses within the criminal jurisdiction of each state party. Each of the four 1949 Geneva Conventions obligates states parties: (a) to enact any legislation necessary to impose effective criminal sanctions on persons committing, or ordering to be committed, any grave breaches of the conventions; (b) to search for alleged offenders and to submit them for prosecution before their own courts, whatever their nationality, or, alternatively, and in accordance with their own legislation, to extradite them to another state party, provided the requesting party has made out a prima facie case; and (c) to ensure to accused persons a fair trial with judicial safeguards specified in the Third Convention on prisoners of war.

The United Nations has taken some steps to develop further the law on war crimes. In 1953 the General Assembly adopted a resolution on "Principles of International Co-operation in the Detection, Arrest, Extradition and Punishment of Persons Guilty of War Crimes and Crimes against Humanity."[59] The resolution, *inter alia*, reaffirms that war crimes and crimes against humanity are subject to universal jurisdiction, calls upon states to assist each other in "detecting, arresting and bringing to trial persons suspected of having committed such crimes and, if they are found guilty, in punishing them," and provides that, "as a general rule," persons accused of war crimes and crimes against humanity should be tried in the countries where they committed their crimes, that states shall cooperate on questions of extraditing such persons and that states shall not grant asylum to any person who is suspected of having committed a "crime against peace, a war crime or a crime against humanity." Also, in 1968, the General Assembly adopted the Convention on the Non-Applicability of Statutory Limitations to War Crimes and Crimes Against Humanity.[60] The Convention has not been widely ratified, however, in part because apartheid is listed as an example of a crime against humanity.

[58] Geneva Convention for the Amelioration of the Condition of the Wounded and Sick in Armed Forces in the Field, 6 UST 3114, TIAS No. 3362, 75 UNTS 31; Geneva Convention for the Amelioration of the Condition of Wounded, Sick and Shipwrecked Members of Armed Forces at Sea, Aug. 12, 1949, 6 UST 3217, TIAS No. 3363, 75 UNTS 85; Geneva Convention Relative to the Treatment of Prisoners of War, Aug. 12, 1949, 6 UST 3316, TIAS No. 3364, 75 UNTS 135; Geneva Convention Relative to the Protection of Civilian Persons in Time of War, Aug. 12, 1949, 6 UST 3516, TIAS No. 3365, 75 UNTS 287. See also Protocol I Additional to the Geneva Conventions of August 12, 1949, *opened for signature* Dec. 12, 1977, UN Doc. A/32/144 Annex I; Protocol II Additional to the Geneva Conventions of August 12, 1949, *opened for signature* Dec. 12, 1977, UN Doc. A/32/144 Annex II.

[59] GA Res. 3074 (XXVIII), UN GAOR, 28th Sess., Supp. No. 30, at 78, UN Doc. A/9030 (1973).

[60] GA Res. 2391 (XXIII), UN GAOR, 23d Sess., Supp. No. 18, at 40, UN Doc. A/7218 (1968).

Although most authorities agree that war crimes may be punished by any state that obtains custody of alleged offenders under the principle of universality, war crime cases tried by national tribunals of states other than those of the nationality of the victim, the accused, or the locale of the crime have been quite rare. The obligation to exercise jurisdiction over grave breaches of the Geneva Conventions of 1949 extends to neutral states, yet they have been reluctant to fulfill this obligation. Their reluctance to become involved in the trial of war criminals hampers efforts to provide an impartial tribunal for the trial of these crimes.

As the preceding discussion indicates, the goal of prosecution has been supported with varying intensity by the various conventions on international crime. The Geneva Conventions of 1949 appear to require that an alleged offender actually be brought to trial. In contrast, the provision commonly found in the anti-terrorist conventions – that a state party which does not extradite an alleged offender must turn the case over to its competent authorities for the "purpose of prosecution" – does not require that he actually be brought to trial.[61] Although many states, including the United States and Russia, have argued during negotiations on these conventions that the obligation should be to bring an alleged offender to trial, this view did not prevail, because a majority of states insisted that such an obligation would infringe upon the discretion of their prosecutorial authorities.[62]

The conventions do contain provisions that limit the discretion of prosecutorial authorities. For example, Article 8 of the Hostages Convention requires that "those authorities shall take their decision in the same manner as in the case of any ordinary offence of a grave nature under the law of that State." In other words, prosecuting authorities must handle the offenses under the Convention in the same manner as they would any ordinary – as compared to political – crime. Article 8 would also seem to prohibit (although this is less clear) political authorities of a state party from intervening in the prosecution so as to prevent the trial or conviction of the alleged offender.

The most obvious case where such a provision would allow prosecutorial discretion would be where the evidence was not strong enough to justify prosecution. Other examples would include a decision not to prosecute an alleged offender in exchange for his agreement to testify against his co-defendants, or one based on humanitarian considerations. An exercise of prosecutorial discretion is subject to the normal requirement of treaty law – that the decision be taken in good faith in light of all the circumstances involved.

---

[61] For discussion, see Lambert, note 24 above, at 198.　　[62] *Ibid.*, at 198–200.

With a view to strengthening extradition as a method of combatting international crime, the United Nations completed work recently on a Model Treaty on Extradition. Specifically, the Eighth United Nations Congress on the Prevention of Crimes and the Treatment of Offenders, held in Havana, Cuba, from August 27 to September 7, 1990, recommended to the General Assembly the passage of a Draft Resolution whereby the Assembly would adopt a Model Treaty of Extradition annexed to the resolution.[63] For its part the General Assembly passed a resolution on December 14, 1990, adopting the Model Treaty on Extradition recommended by the Congress,[64] wherein the General Assembly recognizes that "in many cases existing bilateral extradition arrangements are outdated and should be replaced by modern arrangements taking into account recent developments in international criminal law," and adopts the Model Treaty on Extradition "as a useful framework that could be of assistance to States interested in negotiating and concluding bilateral agreements aimed at improving co-operation in matters of crime prevention and criminal justice."

The extradite-or-prosecute framework established by the UN conventions on international crime has some significant gaps in coverage. The area most often identified in this connection is terrorism, especially deliberate attacks against the civilian population. Such attacks clearly constitute an international crime if committed under circumstances covered by the law of armed conflict but remain largely outside the realm of international law in noncombat situations unless the attack falls within one of the specific manifestations of international terrorism covered by the anti-terrorist conventions.

A more serious problem, however, is that few UN conventions on international crime establish institutional arrangements to ensure an effective system to oversee their implementation. In this respect they stand in sharp contrast to at least some of the human rights treaties.

The major exception to this lack of supervision would appear to be the Convention against Illicit Traffic in Narcotic Drugs and Psychotropic Substances. Continuing a supervisory system established by the two predecessor conventions, the Narcotic Drugs Convention assigns the International Narcotics Control Board overseeing responsibilities for the provisions of the Convention related to illicit manufacture of narcotic drugs and psychotropic substances, material and equipment, commercial

---

[63] Report of the Eighth United Nations Congress on the Prevention of Crimes and the Treatment of Offenders, UN Doc. A/Conf. 144/28, at 71 (1990). For a helpful discussion of the Model Extradition Treaty, as well as of other recently adopted UN model treaties on international cooperation, see R. Clark, "Crime: The UN Agenda on International Cooperation in the Criminal Process," 15 *Nova L. Rev.* 475 (1991).
[64] Model Extradition Treaty, GA Res. 45/116 (1991).

documentation, and labeling of exports.[65] The United Nations Commission on Narcotic Drugs is given supervisory responsibility to review the operation of the Convention, to make suggestions and general recommendations based on the information transmitted by the states parties, and to take action on matters referred to it by the Board.[66] Unfortunately, this supervisory mechanism has not resulted in the gathering and analysis of reliable data regarding the extradition, prosecution, and punishment of drug traffickers. Indeed, with the exception of data on the extradition and prosecution of aircraft hijackers and saboteurs, compiled by the International Civil Aviation Organization and the US Federal Aviation Administration, reliable data on the extradition, prosecution, and punishment of those who commit international crimes are not available.[67]

B. An international criminal court

Proposals to create a permanent international criminal court predate the United Nations.[68] The Treaty of Versailles, for example, provided for prosecution of Kaiser Wilhelm II by an international tribunal, but the Kaiser escaped to asylum in the Netherlands and was never prosecuted.[69]

The United Nations produced a Draft Statute for an International Criminal Court in the early 1950s. However, it did not resume work on the Draft Statute when the International Law Commission again took up the Draft Code of Offences against the Peace and Security of Mankind in 1982.

By the mid-1990s, however, the situation had changed dramatically. Specifically, the General Assembly has established a preparatory committee on an international criminal court, which is scheduled to meet during 1996 from March 25 to April 12 and from August 12 to 30. The task of this preparatory committee will be to discuss further the major substantive and administrative issues arising out of a draft statute for an international criminal court prepared by the International Law Commission. The aim here is to prepare a widely acceptable consolidated text of a convention for an international criminal court that eventually will be considered by an international conference for possible adoption.

[65] See Convention against Illicit Traffic in Narcotic Drugs and Psychotropic Substances, note 30 above, art. 22.   [66] Ibid., art. 21.

[67] See, e.g., J. Murphy, *Punishing International Terrorists* (1985).

[68] For a discussion of the history of attempts to create an international criminal tribunal, see M. C. Bassiouni, Report on: A Comprehensive Strategic Approach on International Cooperation for the Prevention, Control and Suppression of International and Transnational Criminality, Including the Establishment of an International Criminal Court, Annex I, pt. B, prepared for the United Nations Crime Prevention and Criminal Justice Branch (Feb. 1, 1990, amended April 20, 1990).   [69] Ibid.

Moreover, on February 22, 1993, the Security Council decided by resolution[70] "that an international tribunal shall be established for the prosecution of persons responsible for serious violations of international humanitarian law committed in the territory of the former Yugoslavia since 1991." A similar tribunal was established by the Council for the trial of such crimes committed in Rwanda in 1994. Both tribunals issued indictments in 1995 and 1996, and the trial of an accused person is scheduled to take place before the tribunal of the former Yugoslavia in the summer of 1996. Many (but not all) of the issues involved in the creation of *ad hoc* international criminal tribunals differ from those surrounding a permanent international criminal court, but a discussion of those lies beyond the scope of this chapter.

The issues that the proposal for an international court has raised are manifold, albeit beyond the scope of this chapter.[71] At a minimum, however, it should be noted that the primary goal of any civilized criminal process is to punish criminals for their crimes in a manner consistent with the protection of the fundamental rights of an accused. Fulfilling this goal with respect to those who commit international crimes has not been an easy task. All too often persons who have committed their crimes have effectively escaped any threat of punishment. In some cases where they have been returned to the requesting country, and have been prosecuted and punished, the method of rendition employed, or the proceedings at trial, have raised serious questions about violations of human rights.

A primary argument, perhaps *the* primary argument, in favor of the establishment of an international criminal court is that it would facilitate prosecution of international criminals in accordance with fundamental principles of human rights. On the other hand, some contend that the presence of an international criminal court would do no such thing. While admitting that unwillingness on the part of requested countries either to extradite or prosecute persons accused of international crimes has been a problem, the contention is that, in such instances, governments unwilling to extradite or prosecute would also be unwilling to turn the accused over to an international criminal court. It is also contended that efforts spent to

---

[70] SC Res. 808 (Feb. 22, 1993).
[71] For discussion of some but by no means all of these issues, see Report of the Ad-Hoc Committee on the Establishment of an International Criminal Court, UN GAOR, 50th sess., Supp. No. 22, UN Doc. A/50/22, (1995); Final Report of the American Bar Association Task Force on an International Criminal Court (Jan. 1994); Report of the American Bar Association Task Force on the International Tribunal to Adjudicate War Crimes Committed in the Former Yugoslavia (July 8, 1993); International Meeting of Experts on the Establishment of an International Criminal Court, Vancouver, Canada (March 22–26, 1993); Preliminary Report to the House of Delegates of the American Bar Association's Task Force on an International Criminal Court (Jan. 17, 1992); M. Scharf, "The Jury Is Still Out on the Need for an International Criminal Court," 1991 *Duke J. Comp. & Int'l L.* 135.

create an international criminal court, or even the actual creation of such, could undermine the progress that has been made in strengthening the extradite-or-prosecute approach and the integrity and effectiveness of national systems of justice.

A plethora of other issues need to be resolved before an international criminal court is created. How broad should the scope of the court's jurisdiction be? Should it, as some have proposed, encompass the crimes set forth in the Code of Crimes against the Peace and Security of Mankind plus other crimes covered by international conventions? Or should it be more limited, perhaps covering only war crimes, crimes against humanity, and genocide? Should the court be established on a global or a regional basis? How should the judges on such a court be selected so as to insure the highest professional competence and integrity? What rules of evidence and procedure would the court apply? What mechanisms would it employ for obtaining evidence, access to witnesses, and custody over offenders and for conducting investigations and prosecuting the accused? Where would alleged offenders be incarcerated prior to, during, and after trial? What penalties would be appropriate for the specific crimes? How would the court be funded? Much work consequently remains to be done before an international criminal court can be transformed into an international juridical reality.

SELECTED BIBLIOGRAPHY

A. Official sources

As the footnotes to this chapter indicate, there is a rather large number of treaties, General Assembly and Security Council resolutions, reports of various commissions, committees, and rapporteurs as well as of the Secretariat, and decisions and opinions of the International Court of Justice relevant to the subject of the United Nations and the control of international crime. Copies of these treaties, resolutions, reports, decisions, and opinions can be obtained from sources identified elsewhere in this study. In addition, some special UN reports may be of interest. Most of these can be obtained from the UN Department of Public Information and include:

The United Nations and Drug Abuse Control (1987)
A series of reports prepared by the UN Department of Public Information on the
    1990 Special Session of the General Assembly on Drug Control
A summary of the Vienna Conference that adopted the Convention against Illicit
    Traffic in Narcotic Drugs and Psychotropic Substances, *UN Chronicle*,
    March 1989, at 83
Declaration of the International Conference on Drug Abuse and Illicit Trafficking

and Comprehensive Multidisciplinary Outline of Future Activities in Drug Abuse Control, UN Doc. ST/NAR14 (1988)

Annual reports of the International Narcotics Control Board, established on March 2, 1968 by UN ESCOR 1106 (XL), pursuant to the Single Convention on Narcotic Drugs of 1961

The Yearbook of the International Law Commission; Summary of the Convention on the Suppression and Punishment of the Crime of Apartheid, *UN Chronicle,* May 1973, at 61–62

Reports of the United Nations Congresses on the Prevention of Crime and the Treatment of Offenders, sponsored by the United Nations Committee on Crime Prevention and Control, and held by the United Nations every five years beginning in 1955

B. Unofficial sources

One of the best sources of current news about the United Nations, including legal developments, is the *Interdependent,* published by the United Nations Association of the USA. An excellent publication for developments regarding international criminal law, including UN activities, is the *International Enforcement Law Reporter.* A leading treatise, which includes discussion of the UN's role, is *International Criminal Law* (M. C. Bassiouni ed.; 2nd ed., Transnational, 1996). Some other books on various subjects covered in this chapter include:

Murphy, J. F., *Punishing International Terrorists: The Legal Framework for Policy Initiatives* (Rowman & Allanheld, 1985)

Paust, J. J. & A. Blaustein, *War Crimes and Due Process* (1974)

Rubin, A. P., *The Law of Piracy* (Naval War College Press, 1988)

Wijngaert, C. V., *The Political Offense Exception and Extradition* (Kluwer, 1980)

PART III

INTERNAL LAW

CHAPTER FOURTEEN

LAW OF THE INTERNATIONAL CIVIL SERVICE

Robert S. Jordan

I. INTRODUCTION

In addressing principles of internal law in the United Nations system, the central issues are the specified and implied powers of the Secretary-General and the concept and character of the international civil service. Internal law derives its source primarily from the Charter of the United Nations which, similar to a constitution – although it has the force of a treaty – defines and demarks the powers of the various organs. In particular, for purposes of internal law, the Charter defines the administrative aspects thereof. The administrators may be categorized as: (a) the Secretary-General of the UN and somewhat analogously the heads of the UN agencies; (b) the international staff, including career staff and seconded personnel; and (c) experts, mediators, and others who are agents of the Organization but not officials or staff in a legal sense.

The relationship of law to authority as applied to the international civil service can be ranked as follows: (a) the United Nations Charter and other constituent instruments (generally similar to the Charter); (b) treaties, in particular the two general conventions on privileges and immunities that apply, respectively, to the United Nations and to the specialized agencies; (c) bilateral host state agreements with states having UN activities giving special privileges and immunities; (d) resolutions and regulations of the General Assembly and other governing bodies; (e) general principles of law and equity (e.g., abuse of power, nondiscrimination, due process) that have been identified mainly by the administrative tribunals in appeals by staff members and are also applied, as a rule, in administration; (f) decisions of the three administrative tribunals interpreting and applying applicable principles and rules – of the United Nations, the International Labour Organization (ILO), and the World Bank; (g) advisory opinions of the International Court of Justice (ICJ) relating directly to personnel; (h) rules promulgated by the Secretary-General (or agency head) that are subsidiary to regulations; and (i) legal opinions of Secretariat legal staffs or advisory panels.[1]

The General Assembly performs the function of a legislative body, and the UN administration as a whole is accountable for the performance of its duties to that body and/or, as appropriate, to the Security Council. In the latter case, the activities of the international civil service, when acting as "international agents," bring into play what are characterized here as principles of "external law," since such law involves principles of privileges and immunities and other aspects of international law concerning diplomatic relations. This situation is distinct from what may be characterized as international public law, or the law of international public administration.[2] In both cases, however, the willingness of member states to act in support of, or in conformity with, such principles is essential.

II. THE EXCLUSIVELY INTERNATIONAL CHARACTER OF THE SECRETARY-GENERAL AND THE INTERNATIONAL SECRETARIAT

As with most constitutional offices, the character of the office of the Secretary-General is formed largely by the incumbent's use of the powers given to him or her – both as specified (in the Charter) and as implied. The foremost practitioner of the implied-powers approach was the second Secretary-General, Dag Hammarskjöld. As former Under-Secretary-General Brian Urquhart commented: "Hammarskjöld had pushed his powers of independent initiative to a new limit . . . leaving behind him a vacuum of constitutional authorization."[3] In contrast, former Secretary-General Javier Perez de Cuellar stated at the outset of his tenure: "I think that perhaps we could very much insist on the necessity of respecting our United Nations Charter as a kind of constitution, as any country, and then the less we innovate on the Charter, the better it is."[4] But all the Secretaries-General have had to define the extent of their powers according to the inherent nature of the office itself.

This is, of course, only half of the story, since all the Secretaries-General

---

[1] For an elaboration of the legal rights of the United Nations, see Y. Beigbeder, *Threats to the International Civil Service* 121 (1988). The United Nations' Conventions on Privileges and Immunities is contained in ICJ Acts and Documents, No. 3, 1977.

[2] A recent book reflecting this distinction is *International Public Administration* (H. B. Kruger comp., 1992).

[3] B. Urquhart, *Hammarskjöld* 286 (1972). See also R. Khan, *Implied Powers of the United Nations* (1970).

[4] Quoted in *Diplomatic World Bulletin*, Feb. 7, 1983. See also "The Secretariat under Perez de Cuellar," in G. Berridge, *Return to the UN: UN Diplomacy in Regional Conflicts* 12 (1991).

have taken initiatives that, if set against the Charter, would have placed them on uncertain legal ground. This especially can be so when fulfilling what they regard as their responsibilities in regard to dispute settlement. The legal framework, therefore, is important, but only as a basis for, and not as an irrefutable guide as to how far, any particular Secretary-General will actually go in carrying out the duties of his office as he perceives them. Nonetheless, in principle, the Secretary-General can be overruled by either the Security Council or the General Assembly since, as pointed out earlier, he is always subject to their authority under the Charter. With respect to Security Council matters, however, that authority is limited by the veto, since an action by the Secretary-General under a Security Council resolution may not be overridden by the Council majority if a permanent member casts a veto.

The relevant Charter provisions with respect to the role of the Secretary-General are Articles 97–101. Article 97, harking back to the League of Nations precedent, makes the Secretary-General the chief administrative officer of the Organization; this provision allocates to him the key "internal" role, and has the potential for permitting him to take independent action. In his "external" role, Article 99 is considered the key, and most controversial, mandate: "The Secretary-General may bring to the attention of the Security Council any matter which in his opinion may threaten the maintenance of international peace and security." In this respect, it follows that in order to "bring [any matter] to the attention of the Security Council," the Secretary-General must be able to acquire information on his own initiative. Thus, citing Article 99 or suggesting its possible relevance has enabled the Secretary-General in some cases to use it as a legal prop to support an action where his initiative had been criticized. An outwardly less controversial mandate, but nonetheless possessing possibilities, is Article 98, which requires the Secretary-General to perform "such other functions as are entrusted to him."

Almost as important as the Charter in a discussion of the powers of the Secretary-General is Dag Hammarskjöld's famous lecture, "The International Civil Servant in Law and in Fact," delivered at Oxford University in 1961.[5] As Oscar Schachter eloquently put it in his discussion of this speech:

The questions raised were perhaps most difficult in their philosophical and psychological aspects. Is "objectivity" possible in applying political principles? Is personal integrity adequate to reconcile deep differences in perspective and values? Is legitimacy grounded in consensus or in transcendent principles? Can any individual be entrusted to rise above personal and social conditioning?[6]

[5] D. Hammarskjöld, *The International Civil Servant in Law and in Fact* (1961).
[6] O. Schachter, "The International Civil Servant: Neutrality and Responsibility," in *Dag Hammarskjöld Revisited: The UN Secretary-General as a Force in World Politics* 40–41 (R. Jordan ed., 1983).

However one may respond to these important questions, which form the framework for much of the following discussion, the Secretary-General was clearly made subject to the authority of the General Assembly. The Assembly is responsible under the Charter for adopting regulations relating to personnel and other administrative matters that the Secretary-General is expected to implement. For example, under Article 98, he is required to report to the General Assembly annually on the success of, or on the extent of, his efforts to carry out the wishes of the main political organs – the Security Council and the General Assembly. But, as mentioned earlier, he is more likely to become embroiled in disputes among the member states if he chooses to refer to Article 99 as a source of authority for action.

The first Secretary-General, Trygve Lie, set the pattern when he referred to this provision to justify bringing to the Security Council the invasion (or perhaps more accurately, incursion) of South Korea by North Korea in June 1950. To say that this was not an administrative matter would be begging the issue because the consequences for the United Nations as a whole were profound in that, as discussed next, the superpowers' rivalry at that time was so intense that it threatened both the office of the Secretary-General itself and the integrity of the Secretariat.[7]

In contrast, with the Lebanon crisis of 1958, after encountering a Soviet veto of his efforts to strengthen the UN Observer Group (UNOGIL), Hammarskjöld asserted that he could, on his own authority, act whenever it appeared to him "necessary in order to help in filling any vacuum that may appear in the systems which the Charter and the traditional diplomacy provides for the safeguarding of peace and security."[8] There could be no clearer assertion of "implied powers" than this statement, and interestingly, in this instance the Security Council adjourned without objection.[9]

When Hammarskjöld used Article 99 to explain his interest and authority regarding the intervention of the United Nations into the post-independence civil war in the Congo, the Council did not initially oppose him; he was, however, later attacked by the Soviet Union, both in

---

[7] Lie justified his intervention by claiming that he had to speak as the "conscience of mankind," but the Soviet Union did not agree. Already, in 1946, he had claimed that he had the power to investigate a threat to the peace and make whatever initiative to the Council that he thought appropriate. As he said at that time: "I hope that the Council will understand that the Secretary-General must reserve his right to make such enquiries or investigations as he may think necessary, in order to determine whether or not he should consider bringing any aspect of this matter up to the attention of the Council under the provisions of the Charter." UN SCOR, 1st Sess., 70th Mtg. (Sept. 20, 1948), quoted in T. Franck, "The Prerogative Powers of the Secretary-General," in *The Nonaligned and the United Nations* 271–72 (M. Rajan *et al.* eds., 1987). In addition to Franck, see L. Gordenker, *The UN Secretary-General and the Maintenance of Peace* (1967), for a full discussion of this claim of authority – if it is not forbidden then it can be done.

[8] UN SCOR, 837th Mtg. (July 22, 1958). UN Doc. S/PV 1360, at 1 (1958).

[9] See Franck, note 7 above, at 273.

terms of his office and the exercise of its powers. This is what gave rise to his Oxford lecture – a riposte to the so-called "Troika" proposal by Nikita Khrushchev.

Through Article 99, which empowers the Secretary-General to perform a clearly political role, members of the Secretariat of which he is the administrative head, by extension, share that political role when acting as international agents.[10] In its advisory opinion on reparations for injuries suffered in the service of the United Nations, the International Court of Justice (ICJ) defined an international agent as: "Any person who, whether a paid official or not, and whether permanently employed or not, has been charged by an organ of the Organization with carrying out or helping to carry out one of its functions. In short, any person through whom it acts."[11]

All international agents are subject to the general rule that, under Article 100, in the performance of their duties they must show complete independence of any "other authority external to the Organization." On the other hand, they enjoy the functional protection of the Organization if they are injured in the line of duty.[12] Efforts at protecting these privileges and immunities form a large body of case law that strikes at the heart of the UN's capacity to carry out its responsibilities, whether on behalf of the Organization as a whole or on sole behalf of the Secretary-General.

In fact, the issue of privileges and immunities has been at the forefront of international administration for some time. Article 105 of the Charter states flatly that "representatives of the Members of the United Nations and officials of the Organization shall similarly enjoy such privileges and immunities as are necessary to the independent exercise of their functions in connection with the Organization."[13] The Secretary-General is regularly called upon to report to the General Assembly on violations to this article. For example, in 1990 Perez de Cuellar submitted to the General Assembly his report, "Personnel Questions: Respect for the Privileges and Immunities of Officials of the United Nations and the Specialized Agencies and

---

[10] This point is made in R. McLaren, *Civil Servants and Public Policy: A Comparative Study of International Secretariats* 21 (1980).

[11] Quoted in P. Reuter, *International Institutions* 243 (J. M. Chapman trans., 1958). This book is a useful brief survey of the historical antecedents of the contemporary international civil service.

[12] *Ibid.* See also note 33 below and its citation as a further reference to the "functional" protection of members of the international staff.

[13] League of Nations Covenant, art. 105, para. 2. The League Covenant provides in art. 7, para. 4, that: "Representatives of members of the League and officials of the League when engaged on the business of the League shall enjoy diplomatic privileges and immunities." In fact, it can be traced as far back as the Convention of Contingents of the Panama Congress of 1826 and the European Danube Commission of 1856. See J. Kunz, "Privileges and Immunities of International Organizations," 41 *AJIL* 828 (1947).

Related Organizations."[14] The Secretary-General, however, assisted by the UN Security Coordinator in dealing with these problems, can be successful in his efforts on behalf of the staff only if governments will cooperate. This obviously affects the Secretariat's sense of being "international" in a nonpolitical sense.[15]

Aside from arrest and detention, in the early days of the UN the case of Count Folke Bernadotte is cited as playing a controlling role in defining the legal rights of international agents. Bernadotte was assassinated while serving on a mediatory mission to Palestine authorized by a resolution of the General Assembly of May 15, 1948. As a consequence, in 1949 the ICJ was asked to rule on the question of reparations to the United Nations. The United Nations sought direct reparations for damage to the institution and indirect damages for the members of the Bernadotte family. The Court unanimously upheld the right of an international organization to sue for damages in its own name, signifying that an international institution possesses at least some measure of legal personality – a status otherwise reserved for states. This measure of protection of its agents has had a vital place in the "pure" concept of an international civil service.[16]

Robert Rhodes James, a distinguished British historian and at one time a senior UN official, has pointed out that one of the striking aspects of the concept of internationality is its "essential novelty."[17] In fact, prior to the advent of the League of Nations there are almost no examples of truly international secretariats.[18] The "novelty" was the fact that the men and

[14] 45 UN GAOR, 45th Sess., Supp. No. 49, UN Doc. A/C.5/45/10, at 9 (1990). See also UN Doc. A/C.5/48/5 (1993) for a report by Secretary-General Boutros Boutros-Ghali.

[15] Reparations for Injuries Suffered in the Service of the United Nations, 1949 ICJ (advisory opinion of April 11). See also Yuen-Le Liang, "Reparations for Injuries Suffered in the Service of the United Nations," 37 *AJIL* 460 (1949); S. Tarassenko & R. Zacklin, "Independence of International Civil Servants (Privileges and Immunities)," in *International Administration: Law and Management Practices in International Organisations*, pt. III.1/1–15 (C. de Cooker ed., 1990). It should be pointed out that it has not been proposed that functional immunity be expanded to diplomatic (or absolute) immunity. See C. M. Crosswell, *Protection of International Personnel Abroad: Law and Practice Affecting the Privileges and Immunities of International Organizations* (1952).

[16] See R. Jordan, "'Truly' International Bureaucracies: Real or Imagined?," in *Politics in the United Nations System* 424–45 (L. Finkelstein ed., 1988). Searching farther back in time than the Charter for the guiding principles of the international civil service, as with the administration of international political organizations in general, one finds the UN system's cadre of civil servants derives its conceptual basis from the tradition of the British civil service. Specifically in regard to the settlement of disputes through multilateral means, it looks to the tradition established by the British Committee of Imperial Defence just after the turn of the century. See R. Jordan, "The Contribution of the British Civil Service and Cabinet Secretariat Tradition to International Prevention and Control of War," in *The Limitations of Military Power* 896 (J. B. Hattendorf & M. H. Murfett eds., 1990).

[17] R. James, "The Concept of the International Civil Servant," in *International Administration: Its Evolution and Contemporary Applications* 53 (R. Jordan ed., 1970).

[18] While it is true that in the nineteenth century there were public international unions that sometimes had permanent staffs to carry out research or to coordinate the circulations of papers, these persons were almost entirely drawn from nationals of the host country.

women of the various nationalities who composed the civil service of the League were drawn from all the member states. They composed an international Secretariat whose primary responsibilities were to prepare and present to the League Council (and other bodies) objective papers for their consideration and discussion. They were also entrusted with the execution of any decisions made by the member states.[19] The Secretary-General would act as the coordinating center of the activities of the Secretariat, whose members would be responsible to him alone as the League's chief administrative officer. As a further precaution against national pressure, the Secretary-General and his staff would be remunerated from the general funds of the League only. It is this attempt at immunizing the international Secretariat from national pressures that is at the core of the concept of an international civil service.

III. RECRUITMENT, LOYALTY STANDARDS, TYPES OF CONTRACTS, AND STAFF RULES AND REGULATIONS

Thomas Weiss wrote somewhat idealistically nearly two decades ago:

International administrators were intended to form a nucleus of international forces around which a global community would develop. While no one seriously expected sovereign states to subordinate what they perceived as their national interests to the good of a wider community, theorists reasonably hoped that the international civil service might transcend nationalism.[20]

Essentially the basis of legal standing for an international civil servant is the contract of employment, which establishes those rights and obligations that

---

[19] More recently, M. B. Akehurst has observed:

In the days when international secretariats were small and had only routine functions to perform, it was customary to entrust them to the management of a member state. The secretariat might include officials seconded from other states or even foreigners recruited independently, and the officials in charge of it were often given a free hand by the host state; but in principle the officials' legal position was that of civil servants of the host state, which ran the Secretariat as part of one of its Government departments.

M. B. Akehurst, *The Law Governing Employment in International Organizations* 4 (1967), quoted in C. Amerasinghe, *The Law of the International Civil Service*, IV, 4 n. 3 (1988).

[20] T. Weiss, *International Bureaucracy: An Analysis of the Operation of Functional and Global International Secretariats* 149 (1975). Other earlier citations are E. Phelan, "The New International Civil Service," *Foreign Affairs* 307–14 (Jan. 1933); P. Jessup, "The International Civil Servant and His Loyalties," 9 *Colum. J. Int'l Aff.* 55 (1955); and *The International Civil Service: Changing Role and Concepts* (N. Graham & R. Jordan eds., 1979). It is, however, often assumed that some staff members are influenced by their governments and in some cases are instructed by them. There appear, however, to be no cases in which an international official has been dismissed or disciplined for violating this principle. Although assertions have been made that governments have sought to influence staff in performance of duties, none has been officially reprimanded for doing so.

can be enforced, if necessary, before tribunals. In 1953, the UN Administrative Tribunal (UNAT) asserted that

there were contractual elements in addition to statutory elements governing the legal position of a staff member, the contractual elements being all matters affecting the personal status of the staff member . . . the contract of employment is a source of rights and duties for the parties to it and is, thus, a source of law.[21]

The relevant Charter provisions in regard to personnel matters are Articles 100 and 101. From the former, the following should be noted; point number 3 is from the latter:

1. In the performance of their duties the Secretary-General and the staff shall not seek or receive instructions from any government or from any other authority external to the Organization. They shall refrain from any action which might reflect on their position as international officials responsible only to the Organization.

2. Each member of the United Nations undertakes to respect the exclusively international character of the responsibilities of the Secretary-General and the staff and not to seek to influence them in the discharge of their responsibilities.

3. The paramount consideration in the employment of the staff and in the determination of the conditions of service shall be the necessity of securing the highest standards of efficiency, competence, and integrity. Due regard shall be paid to the importance of recruiting the staff on as wide a geographical basis as possible.

These provisions are intended to provide the staff with the freedom to develop what C. W. Jenks has termed an "international outlook," which he considered as "something quite different from the attitude . . . of 'a friend of every country but his own.'" In Jenks's view:

The international outlook required of the international civil servant is an awareness made instinctive by habit of the needs, emotions and prejudices of the peoples of differently-circumstanced countries, as they are felt and expressed by the peoples concerned, accompanied by a capacity for weighing these . . . elements in a judicial manner before reaching any decision to which they are relevant.[22]

---

[21] See Amerasinghe, note 19 above, at ch. 7, for an elaboration on the legal place of contracts, which can be considered as part of international administrative law.

[22] C. W. Jenks, "Some Problems of an International Civil Service," *Pub. Admin. Rev.* 95 (1943). A landmark work is H. Guetzkow, *Multiple Loyalties: A Theoretical Approach to a Problem in International Organization* (1955).

In Article 101, pursuit of the "highest standards" in recruitment was intended to be paramount over due regard for "geographical distribution." But this provision has been honored more in the breach, certainly before but especially after decolonization understandably generated intense political pressures on the Secretary-General and the executive heads of the various UN agencies to make room in their secretariats for nationals of the new member states.

In fact, the geographical distribution of the staff has been an important item on the annual agenda of the Fifth Committee since at least 1960. During this period numerous efforts have been made to achieve a more balanced representation of nationalities, in large part through the elaboration of increasingly complex criteria and national quotas – or "desirable ranges." For example, by Resolution 3417B (XXX) the General Assembly requested the Secretary-General to take all necessary measures to recruit staff members subject to geographical distribution from countries unrepresented and underrepresented in the Secretariat, in particular from developing countries. By Resolution 31/26 (November 1976) the General Assembly revised the method of calculating desirable ranges of posts for member states to ensure equitable geographical distribution of the staff. The allowance of posts for the factor of membership (which together with population and contributions make up the three factors on which the desirable range of posts is calculated) was increased from 1–6 to 2–7 for each member state. This, of course, reduced the weight attached to the factor of budget contributions, which favored the older member states.[23]

The most obvious relevant consideration with regard to recruitment thus has to do with this dramatic change in the nature of the United Nations' membership since its founding. During the 1960s and 1970s especially, there was sharp disagreement as to whether or not the principle of geographical distribution (sometimes called "representation") should, at times, dominate over the principle of merit as regards personnel recruitment. Today, even if one's perspective is limited to the top echelons, the picture is not good. As a recent report observed:

This senior UN echelon [USGs and ASGs] has responsibilities at a very high level, yet very few reached these top positions through the UN's equivalent of monitored and prescribed civil service performance and promotion procedures . . . The member-governments, whose delegations spend so much time and energy

---

[23] Taken from Graham & Jordan eds., note 20 above, at 34ff. Other requirements of recruitment that have tended to weaken the principle of merit have been to favor women and younger persons. For a look during the decolonization period, see L. Goodrich, "Geographical Distribution of the Staff of the UN Secretariat," *Int'l Org.* 465–82 (1962). A good general discussion can be found in S. Bailey, *The Secretariat of the United Nations* 80–101 (1962).

elaborating the UN's actual work programmes, devote little or no time or energy to ensuring that these programmes will be executed by the best possible managers. The incumbents are not accountable to a monitoring body of any kind.[24]

It can, of course, be debated whether this situation has any relationship to the fact that the General Assembly has requested the Secretary-General to take effective measures to increase the number of staff from all developing countries in senior and policy-making posts in the Secretariat.

As to the fate of Article 100, in 1952 the United States uncharacteristically raised the issue of the "national loyalty" of its citizens employed as international civil servants when President Harry S. Truman issued Executive Order 10422. This Order, which appeared to violate paragraph 2 of Article 100 (quoted earlier) required a full field security investigation, not only of all United States nationals under consideration, but also those already working for the Organization. Not unexpectedly, this political "means test" aroused strong opposition. This matter came to a head when an American who was under investigation invoked the Fifth Amendment provision that a person shall not be compelled in any criminal case to be a witness against himself. Lie clearly was unhappy with being placed in this position. As he said later in self-justification to the General Assembly: "Permit me to say simply that I have done the best I could in political circumstances that were not of my making. I have done my best to maintain the Charter inviolate and to uphold the basic principles of an independent, international Secretariat."[25] As indicated earlier, Cold War pressures bore down upon Lie, not only in his "external" role but also in his "internal" role as he attempted to carry out the duties of his office, which meant balancing the political pressures brought by the member states on the international civil service with regard both to the issue and to the definition of loyalty.

Lie concluded, rightly or wrongly, that by invoking the Fifth Amendment – the constitutional privilege against self-incrimination – those

---

[24] B. Urquhart & E. Childers, *A World in Need of Leadership: Tomorrow's United Nations* 37 (1990). Secretary-General Boutros Boutros-Ghali has put into effect an extensive regrouping of functions, and hence personnel, primarily in order to respond to the sharply increased responsibilities put on the Organization in fulfilling the various Security Council resolutions with regard to peacekeeping.

[25] Quoted in A. Rovine, *The First Fifty Years: The Secretary-General in World Politics, 1920–1970* 255 (1970). The United States loyalty program did not involve an "instruction" as such by the United States to the Secretary-General. Rather, the information obtained relating to "loyalty" was simply presented to the Secretary-General and may have resulted in applicants being rejected even though no one was terminated on grounds of loyalty as such. In May 1986 the United States informed the UN that "the investigative program for US citizens being considered for . . . employment with international organizations has been suspended as a result of a judicial decision concerning the constitutionality of Executive Order 10422." Quoted in Beigbeder, note 1 above, at 55–56.

Americans under suspicion were acting inconsistently with their obligations as international civil servants. Consequently he insisted that UN
officials had to waive particular constitutional rights when they joined the
Secretariat; otherwise, as he put it, their actions could "discredit the
Secretariat as a whole, to cast suspicion on all the staff – and, still more
serious, it imperiled the position of the Organization with the host
country."[26]

Although Lie could dismiss immediately persons serving on temporary
fixed-term contracts, he could not do so as easily with regard to those
holding career (or permanent) contracts. For the latter, the provision was
that dismissal could be due only to misconduct, unsatisfactory service, or
physical incapacity.[27]

Lie thereupon formed a three-man international Commission of Jurists
as advisers. In November 1952 they rendered their opinion: Refusal of
Americans on permanent contract to testify on the basis of the Fifth
Amendment was a breach of the Staff Regulations. Therefore such persons
could be dismissed. Lie thereupon allowed them to withdraw their pleas,
but when they refused, he dismissed them.[28]

This general question of loyalty to the Organization, quite obviously, is
neither simple nor easily applied legally. What might appear as selfless
(politically speaking) devotion to duty can appear also to the civil servant's
national state as conduct bordering on the disloyal.[29] To guard against
pressures to compromise their political integrity – especially from the
member states – the United Nations codified the principles of conduct and
of administration applicable to members of the international civil service.

---

[26] T. Lie, *In the Cause of Peace* 397 (1954).

[27] As T. Young reported:

> The Fifth Committee of the sixth session of the General Assembly upheld the view that the
> Secretary-General should have discretionary power over termination of appointments of staff
> members with temporary contracts if the interests of the United Nations so required; but he
> should have no such power over staff members with permanent or fixed-term contracts, as
> their termination could only be based on certain facts which could be tested.

> T. Young, *International Civil Service: Principles and Problems* 161–62 (1958). The Secretary-
> General could, of course, abolish the post in question, a practice familiar in national civil
> services.

[28] These dismissals were later condemned by the UNAT, which granted them compensation. It
was the United States' opposition to the UNAT's decision that led to a further appeal
procedure, which provides that a case can go beyond the UNAT to the ICJ when approved by
a committee of member states. Obviously, as was true later when the United States used the
pressure of withholding its assessed contributions in order to achieve certain policy objectives,
the issue of "loyalty" was a pressure tactic as well as a reflection of domestic politics.

[29] For example, during the League, the Fascist states, Germany and Italy, had put pressure on the
Secretary-General to accept only those of their nationals who were politically acceptable to
them. For a discussion of the influence of the Fascist states on the League's second
Secretary-General, Joseph Avenol, see Rovine, note 25 above, at 105–72.

They are contained in the Staff Regulations and Staff Rules.

The Staff Regulations embody the fundamental conditions of service and the basic rights, duties and obligations of the UN Secretariat. They represent the broad principles of personnel policy for the staffing and administration of the Secretariat. The Secretary General, as the Chief Administrative Officer, shall provide and enforce staff rules consistent with these principles as he considers necessary.

They are, in sum, a source of law to which the UNAT can turn; paragraph 1 of Article 101 of the Charter by implication attributes to the General Assembly the power to make Staff Regulations and thereby allowing the General Assembly to "legislate." It has, in turn, delegated this power with regard to setting down the rules of administration to the head of the administration, who is the Secretary-General. As provided by the UNAT, Staff Regulations

empower the Secretary General to amend and establish the Staff Rules within the limits laid down by the Staff Regulations. The Secretary General has the duty to report to the General Assembly on the exercise of his rule-making authority, which is derived from the Charter and from the Staff Regulations, but the bringing into force of the provisions established by the Secretary General, on a date fixed by him, is not subject to the approval of the General Assembly.[30]

Article 1.1 contains the definition of an international civil service whose "responsibilities are not national but exclusively international"; Article 1.2 establishes the exclusive authority of the Secretary-General in matters concerning personnel; Article 1.3 eliminates any source of authority over officials other than that of the Organization; and Article 1.4 specifies the type of individual behavior (particularly political and religious) that is forbidden on the grounds that it would compromise the autonomy of the international administration: "As international civil servants, UN staff representatives have an obligation of reserve and 'utmost' discretion."[31]

---

[30] Quoted in Amerasinghe, note 19 above, at 146, for Nortished UNAT Judgement No. 273 (1981). They are essentially the same regulations that guided League officials. See also Akehurst, note 19 above; T. Elias, in de Cooker ed., note 15 above. Elias discusses the major cases concerning the UNAT that have come before the ICJ. Dag Hammarskjöld discussed issues raised by the Fifth Amendment cases and by the loyalty investigations in his 1953 Report to the General Assembly, see 8 UN GAOR, UN Doc. A/2533, at 10–20 (1953). This report led to a clarification of the Staff Regulations in regard to activities of members of the Secretariat that might be considered political. With regard to alleged "political activities" of staff members, the Staff Regulations were amended in 1953 to declare that "staff members may exercise the right to vote but shall not engage in any political activity which is inconsistent with or might reflect upon the independence and impartiality required by their status as international civil servants."

[31] Beigbeder, note 1 above, at 139. He went on to comment: "They must avoid any kind of public pronouncement which may adversely reflect on their status, integrity, independence and impartiality." *Ibid.*

Article 1.5 requires confidentiality, even after an official's departure. Article 1.6 prohibits the accepting of national honors or decorations by an active international official. Article 1.7 provides that officials may vote but may not engage in any other activity inconsistent with the independence and impartiality required of international administrators. Article 1.8 permits a limited amount of part-time work with the stipulation that such work must not compromise the employee's commitment to international service. Article 1.9 concerns the oath of office by which international officials commit themselves to uphold the standards of conduct set by their appointment.[32]

The ICJ issued an advisory opinion in April 1949 that established that the United Nations Organization's right of "functional" protection to its staff is also an obligation. It is worth quoting at length:

In order that the agent may perform his duties satisfactorily, he must feel that this protection is assured to him by the Organisation, and that he may count on it. To ensure the independence of the agent, and, consequently, the independent action of the Organisation itself, it is essential that in performing his duties he need not have to rely on any other protection than that of the Organisation (save of course for the more direct and immediate protection due from the State in whose territory he may be). In particular, he should not have to rely on the protection of his own State. If he had to rely on that State, his independence might well be compromised, contrary to the principle applied by Article 100 of the Charter. And lastly, it is essential that – whether the agent belongs to a powerful or to a weak State; to one more affected or less affected by the complications of international life; to one in sympathy or not in sympathy with the mission of the agent – he should know that in the performance of his duties he is under the protection of the Organisation. This assurance is even more necessary when the agent is stateless.[33]

IV. ADJUDICATION OF GRIEVANCES AND EFFORTS AT REFORM OF THE ADMINISTRATION OF THE INTERNATIONAL CIVIL SERVICE

There has thus grown up a body of internal law dealing with aspects of the recruitment and the conditions of service of those employed by the UN and its various agencies. The most transparent example of individual governments exerting influence (and even direction) to the international staff and the Secretary-General relates to the appointment and promotion of

---

[32] This is drawn from Weiss, note 20 above, at 40–41. See also Amerasinghe, note 19 above, at ch. 6.
[33] 1949 ICJ 183–84 (advisory opinion of Apr. 11), quoted in Beigbeder, note 1 above, at 122.

officials.[34] As C. F. Amerasinghe put it: "It has come to be generally accepted now that it is the internal law of the organization that governs the employment relationship of international civil servants with the international organization for which they work."[35] In other words, "Internal rules, as a class, have the attributes of law."[36]

As Oscar Schachter has commented, however: "The international civil service, by and large, operates under a far more limited conception of delegated authority than do national civil services."[37] This would include, *inter alia*, rules for budgeting, program planning, and expenditure of funds, as well as for personnel management and administration. These rules are considered as having a "binding effect."[38] They are generally considered to be part of the *corpus* of public international law in that internal law is considered as "having a special character as a system akin to municipal law."[39]

A legal approach to problems relative to what has been termed "international public service" began with the Monroe case of 1925. The League Council had reduced the salary of its officials, and was challenged. The Council asked a committee of three persons for an advisory opinion and later a committee of five jurists examined the question. As a result,

---

[34] For a more general but useful discussion of the means of applying international law to international organizations, see F. Morgenstern, *Legal Problems of International Organisations*, ch. 3 (1986). For a more specific treatment of the recruitment issue, see R. Bulkeley, "UN Recruitment," 22 *NYU J. Int'l L. & Pol.* 749 (1990). The Secretary-General is normally "informed" of a government's recommendation of an applicant, but at times this can appear to be an "instruction" because a government's approval can weigh heavily if not decisively.

[35] Amerasinghe, note 19 above, at 9. Amerasinghe further posits that

this internal law has a number of sources. It is directed to ensuring the preservation and fullest expression of the integrity of international organizations as an essential idea. It is a special system of law which is both an individual and organizational necessity and aims at formulating those rules for conduct which will ensure that an international secretariat will be able to function efficiently. It places the relationship between administration or management and staff concerning the latter's assuming, occupancy, and termination of position in the secretariat in the domain of law. In this sense, irrespective of whether there are courts to decide disputes relating to the employment relationship in the organization, it is a real system of law.

Ibid.

[36] R. Riggs, "The UN and the Politics of Law," in Finkelstein ed., note 16 above, at 47.

[37] O. Schachter, "Some Reflections on International Officialdom," in *International Organisation* 56 (J. Fawcett & R. Higgins eds., 1974).

[38] Weiss, note 20 above, at 49. That budgeting can have a direct bearing on conditions of service can be seen in the so-called Kassebaum Amendment (named for US Senator Nancy Kassebaum, Republican of Kansas), which limits the US contribution to no more than 20 percent of the assessed UN budget, beginning with the 1987 UN fiscal year, until such time as voting on budgetary matters is made proportional to each member state's contribution. This led to pay and hiring freezes and forced reductions in staff. For a further discussion, see M. Bertrand, "Can the United Nations Be Reformed?," in *United Nations, Divided World: The UN's Role in International Relations* 193 (A. Roberts & B. Kingsbury eds., 1988).

[39] Amerasinghe, note 19 above, at 25.

individual administrative tribunals were established.⁴⁰ As Manley O. Hudson explained:

A new situation arose when much larger staffs began to be created by certain organizations, recruited on an international basis and maintained independently of national control. The interpretation and application of contracts of service required an exercise of the judicial function, and as the organizations themselves were not subject to the jurisdiction of any national courts, need arose for vesting competence in special international tribunals.⁴¹

The legal status of the UNAT originated with the League of Nations when, in the Supervisory Commission report, it was stated that the League's proposed Tribunal

is to be exclusively a judicial body set up to determine the legal rights of officials on strictly legal grounds . . . The function of the Tribunal will be to pronounce finally upon any allegations that the Administration has refused to give an official treatment to which he was legally entitled or has treated him in a manner which constitutes a violation of his legal rights. The Tribunal will be the final authority for the interpretation of the terms of an official's appointment, and the regulations applicable to the official.⁴²

Decisions of the UNAT can be appealed to the ICJ for an advisory opinion under certain circumstances. Article II, paragraph 1 of the UNAT Statute, as amended in 1955, provides that a member state, the Secretary-General, or the person in regard to whom a judgment has been rendered by the Tribunal, or the successor to such a person's rights on his death, can object to a judgment. Possible grounds are that: (a) the Tribunal has exceeded its jurisdiction or competence; or (b) the Tribunal has failed to exercise jurisdiction vested in it; or (c) it has erred on a question of law relating to the provisions of the Charter; or (d) it has committed a fundamental error

---

⁴⁰ Reuter, note 11 above, at 244. See League of Nations, 6th Yr, 10 *Official J.* 1441; 107 *Official J.* 206 (Spec. Supp.) (both cited in Reuter, *supra*).

⁴¹ M. Hudson, *International Tribunals: Past and Future* 220 (1945). See also C. Amerasinghe, *Documents on International Administrative Tribunals* (1989). As Amerasinghe observed: "International administrative tribunals have accepted the applicability of this system of law and have agreed in characterizing it as the 'internal law' of the organization." *The Law of the International Civil Service*, note 19 above, at 9–10. For more on this point, see S. Bastid, "Have the UN Administrative Tribunals Contributed to the Development of International Law?," in *Transnational Law in a Changing Society* (W. Friedmann ed., 1972). See also B. Koh, *The United Nations Administrative Tribunal* (1966); H. Wriggins & E. Bock, *The Status of the United Nations Secretariat: Role of the Administrative Tribunal* (1954).

⁴² League of Nations, 8th Ass., 4th Comm., 58 *Official J.* 250–51 (Spec. Supp.). The concept was modeled on the French *Conseil d'Etat*. There are two administrative tribunals which accept appeals from United Nations staff members. The UNAT deals with cases concerning the United Nations, ICAO, and IMO, as well as questions involving the UN Joint Staff Pension Fund. The ILO Administrative Tribunal deals with cases for the other organizations of the Common System. The World Bank and the IMF have their own appeals procedure.

in procedure that occasioned a failure of justice.[43] The Tribunal uses concepts of law followed in most legal systems, e.g., procedural rights, equality of treatment, *res judicata*, and equity.

This review procedure, in the view of T. O. Elias, "is a significant and important contribution to modern public international law."[44] Obviously the General Assembly cannot negate an advisory opinion of the ICJ because such opinions are not binding, even though an argument was made that the General Assembly could because of its responsibility for the budget of the Organization (and hence could withhold or award compensation).

A significant effort at establishing standards of equity in international administration was the creation of an International Civil Service Commission, which was recommended by the UN Preparatory Commission and was adopted by the First Session of the General Assembly on February 13, 1946. The provision reads:

An International Civil Service Commission shall be established by the Secretary-General after consultation with the heads of the specialized agencies brought into relationship with the United Nations, to advise on methods of recruitment for the Secretariat and on the means by which common standards of recruitment in the Secretariat and specialized agencies may be secured.[45]

Instead, an International Civil Service Advisory Board (ICSAB) was created in 1948 concerned primarily with recruitment, remaining in existence until 1974.[46] The International Civil Service Commission (ICSC), created at that time, was thought to have the potential for ameliorating, if not reversing, some of the negative trends just discussed. The exact motivations for creating the ICSC have been given as follows:

Different preoccupations have influenced the parties in favouring the establishment of the Commission. For Governments, the overriding concern was to provide the common system with more effective controls over the pay-setting procedures than seemed possible under the [ICSAB] regime of co-ordination by consent. For the administrations, the most pressing problem was the need to obtain objective assessments of the special conditions affecting employment in an international organization. For staff associations, in turn, the aim was to have a

[43] T. Elias, "The International Court of Justice in Relation to the Administrative Tribunals of the United Nations and the International Labour Organisation," in de Cooker ed., note 15 above, at pt. V.4/1.

[44] *Ibid.*, at pt. V.4/29. A special committee must be established, according to the UNAT Statute, "to decide whether or not there is a substantial basis for the application." UNAT Stat. art. 11, para. 2.

[45] Quoted in J. Renninger, *Can the Common System Be Maintained? The Role of the International Civil Service Commission* 19 (1986).

[46] *Ibid.* See Young, note 27 above, at 60, for the ICSAB's terms of reference.

forum where their representatives could participate, on a footing of equality, with administrators, in the process of arriving at decisions of interest to the staff.[47]

The Commission at first set for itself the task of expending serious effort to deal with questions of recruitment and career development; indeed, both subjects have been continuously active parts of the Commission's agenda. That said, however, it is also true that the Commission allowed itself to be overburdened by other personnel policy and administrative questions that have detracted from its ability to give adequate attention to recruitment and career development.

The membership of the Commission is intended to be a balance of national positions and political interests which, of course, can differ widely at times, though as Article 2 of the Statute provides:

1. The members of the Commission shall be appointed in their personal capabilities as individuals of recognised competence who have had substantial experience of executive responsibility in public administration or related fields, particularly in personnel management.

2. The members of the Commission, no two of whom shall be nationals from the same State, shall be selected with due regard for equitable geographic distribution.

In addition, the Commission is constrained by the apparent reluctance of the specialized agencies to pursue questions relating to the "career concept" within the framework of the UN common system. One of the recurring debates in the ICSC, in fact, as also in the General Assembly's Fifth Committee, has been an agreement as to what exactly *is* a "career concept."[48] Some governments, for example, have favored fixed-term appointments over permanent contracts; other governments have favored the opposite, citing as justification the "traditional" concept of an international civil service.

Whether or not a high turnover of staff meets the long-term interests of the Organization, pressure to create opportunities for women, underrepresented countries or regions, overrepresented countries or regions, underrepresented developing countries, etc. appears to weaken the sense of bureaucratic self-identity that should undergird a career system. To others, turnover appears to strengthen the diversity of a career service that should draw on the talents of virtually all countries.

---

[47] Quoted in Renninger, note 45 above, at 28.
[48] For FICSA comments on this issue, and also that of the matter of pensions which follows, see UN Doc. A/C.5/45/23 (Nov. 5, 1990). See also F. Morgenstern, "Social Security Problems in International Organisations," in de Cooker ed., note 15 above, at pt. IV.1.

As to the legal implications of that part of employment contracts dealing with remuneration, more recently the Commission has been concerned with the impact of the US Federal Employees Pay Comparability Act of 1990, which provides flexibility in setting salaries and annual raises. Specifically, a portion of a federal employee's annual raise is now linked to the wage or salary scales of his/her local labor market (i.e., the economy of New York City [or state] or Washington, DC.) Since UN salaries are set on a basis of comparability with the US federal civil service wage structure, this may not have an adverse effect on UN salary scales due to the difference in cost of living, for instance as between Washington, DC and New York City. Adding to the uncertainty is the fact that the President is authorized to reduce the amount of federal employees' annual adjustments in serious national circumstances, such as if a war were to erupt or if a negative GNP growth were to occur for two consecutive quarters.

The Coordinating Committee for Independent Staff Unions (CCISU) has suggested that salary comparisons be carried out periodically with other employers of international staff, such as the European Communities (EC), the Organization for Economic Cooperation and Development (OECD), World Bank, etc., that compete with the UN system for staff as well as with expatriate nondiplomatic staff and the expatriate diplomatic staff of the US federal civil service. Such periodic comparisons could presumably be used as a barometer of trends. This might be one way out of the dilemma of linking UN salary scales with US federal civil service scales, which has resulted in UN employee pay freezes. In fact, the General Assembly asked the ICSC to undertake a study to determine which, in effect, is the "best paid national civil service."[49]

A very real concern has also arisen for the stability of the UN's pension system. Even though the system is, by its nature, worldwide in scope, pension stipends are expressed in the local currency of the retiree. It is, for example, not assured that guaranteed replacement income can be maintained for retirees from strong-currency member states, since this guarantee may not have been reflected in preretirement contributions. The specific cause of this concern is fluctuation in the value of the US dollar (in which the UN budget is denominated) relative to other major currencies. This situation contributes not only to lower staff morale and rising staff discontent, but also to uncertainty as to the eventual prospects of and need for a post-UN career. Furthermore, if the potential retiree's official duties involved sensitive political activities, the anxiety can be that much greater.

Another problem has been a practice by an increasing number of more affluent member states of violating the principle of equity by paying additional allowances and compensation to their nationals while, according

---

[49] See Report of the International Civil Service Commission for the Year 1995, 50 UN GAOR, 50th Sess., Supp. (No. 30), UN Doc. A/50/30 (1995).

to FICSA, most of these same countries remain strongly opposed to any improvement in staff conditions.[50] This practice can be detrimental to the independent character of the Secretariat and was once considered to be contrary to Article 100 of the Charter. Today, however, it is accepted.

V. INTERNAL JUSTICE AND ALTERNATIVE CAREER CONCEPTS

On a broader plane, there have been serious attempts in recent years to upgrade the United Nations' "internal justice system." In October 1990, for example, the Secretary-General was asked by the General Assembly, in reference to its resolution of December 19, 1989, to continue reforms, "in particular with regard to improving the informal procedures for amicable settlements of staff grievances."[51] This reform program had been initiated in 1987 to streamline the appeals procedure, and responsibility for its process has rested with the Office of the Under-Secretary-General for Administration and Management, working in close coordination with the Office of Human Resources Management; the Office of Program Planning, Budget and Finance; and the Office of Legal Affairs. Many of the cases come before the Joint Appeals Board (JAB), or in cases of misconduct, before a Joint Disciplinary Committee (JDC). In 1995, Secretary-General Boutros Boutros-Ghali recommended that the JDC be replaced by a Disciplinary Board comprised of qualified professional staff members, appointed to serve on each case. The Secretary-General also recommended the creation of an Arbitration Board to replace the JAB, hoping thereby to encourage efforts at conciliation.[52] Significantly, the UN Administrative Tribunal did not agree with the Secretary-General's assertion that the JAB had been ineffectual, nor did the Staff Union.[53]

One related development is an increased resort to a Panel of Counsel, composed of volunteer staff members who have been authorized to represent colleagues who have cases before the JAB, the JDC, and/or the UNAT, and their use has steadily increased. They can advise with regard to staff grievances and disputes as well; thus, by settling disagreements through the intervention of the Coordinator of the Headquarters Panel of Counsel, formal litigation can often be avoided.[54]

Another reform, initiated in 1976, was the creation of grievance and conciliation panels. The purpose of these panels is to investigate allegations

---

[50] 45 UN GAOR, UN Doc. A/C.5/45/23 (1990).

[51] 45 UN GAOR, Supp. (No. 30), UN Doc. A/45/30 (1990). See also 50 UN GAOR, UN Doc. A/C.5/50/2 (1995).   [52] See 50 UN GAOR, UN Doc. A/C.5/50/2 (1995).

[53] See 50 UN GAOR, UN Doc. A/C.5/50/2/Add. 1 (1995), and *UN Staff Report*, November 1995.   [54] 45 UN GAOR, Supp. (No. 30), UN Doc. A/45/30 (1990), para. 22.

of discriminatory treatment and therefore to provide an informal procedure to supplement the formal recourse procedures of the JAB, the specialized appeals bodies, and the UNAT.[55] Grievance panels have handled about a hundred cases a year since their establishment, excluding informal advice on complaints that the Panel did not consider serious enough to constitute grievances necessitating investigation and/or further action.[56]

Alternative concepts of what the international civil service should be have been widely discussed as the political/cultural basis of the United Nations has expanded, resulting in various grievance and appeals procedures. More recently, these have centered around the advantages and disadvantages of secondment – serving on loan from one's own government with the understanding that the loanee can return to his/her previous position with promotion and retirement rights intact. As the late Paul Reuter put it:

Each national system of law lays down rules governing its agents. Each international organisation does the same. Nevertheless we can distinguish three broad groups of agents. The first group hold[s] permanent posts to the exclusion of any other professional activity. They are in the position of civil servants. The second hold[s] temporary posts, full-time, to the exclusion of any other professional activity. Unlike the first group they are not on the permanent staff of the organisation. The last group are employed part-time and they continue to exercise another profession.[57]

The second and third categories are appointments made with fixed-term contracts. The customary method of appointment, stemming from the League, was to make career appointments after an initial probationary period. The reason given is that probation primarily serves the interest of the organization determining suitability of employment. Consequently tribunals have recognized that the United Nations (and other international organizations) have considerable discretionary authority with regard to the disposition of probationary appointments.[58] By 1952, it was generally agreed that security of tenure "was not only indispensable to the maintenance of staff morale, but also closely related to the interests of the Organization."[59]

---

[55] 45 UN GAOR, UN Doc. A/C.5/45/11, para. 1 (1990).

[56] *Ibid.* Departmental panels are also being established to see if this decentralized approach to resolving grievances quickly could eventually replace the Secretariat bodies on discrimination and other grievances. *Ibid.*, para. 17.   [57] Reuter, note 11 above, at 243.

[58] See Amerasinghe, II, note 19 above, at 776: "Tribunals in practice merely reviewed and controlled the exercise of this discretionary power." *Ibid.*

[59] Young, note 27 above, at 161. See also earlier discussion of the Fifth Amendment dilemma.

VI. CONCLUSIONS

It is clear from the foregoing that the precedent of the League of Nations played an important part in the evolution of the policies and practices of the UN's civil service. The forthright example of the League's first Secretary-General, Sir Eric Drummond, of how to organize and administer an international civil service representative of the interests of all member states, enabled the United Nations to organize its civil service much more quickly and effectively than would otherwise have been the case. As Arthur Rovine said: "The world community was convinced in a relatively brief time that an international secretariat was highly functional in the complex arena of continuous transnational negotiation and bargaining."[60] The United Nations has, of course, gone far beyond the League pattern.

The legal basis stems clearly from the General Assembly's power to "legislate," and from the authority granted to the Secretary-General as chief administrative officer of the Organization. M. B. Akehurst expressed the essential point succinctly: "The unique character of employment in an international organization can best be emphasized by subjecting it to a unique system of law."[61] The legal basis for the United Nations presumably rests in Chapter XV of the Charter.

The right of appeal to redress grievances is firmly established, in a legal sense, not only by the creation of the Administrative Tribunal and the Joint Appeals Board, but also in other, more informal methods of conciliation and dispute settlement (and also perhaps dispute avoidance) authorized by subsequent resolutions of the General Assembly. Trygve Lie's creation of an international Commission of Jurists to provide advice might perhaps be considered useful (although held subsequently to be illegal by the UNAT). Recourse to advisory opinions of the ICJ, or to other adjudicatory bodies, is also well established. The Secretary-General has used these methods at times to buttress his position under highly sensitive political circumstances, or to obtain clarification of contractual relationships that can become, within the Organization, highly contentious.

By the same token, expectation that the ICSC could relieve some of this pressure, first in its work on recruitment (also undertaken by the ICSAB) and then in attempting to create a so-called "common system," has so far not been fulfilled. Not only has the ICSC encountered a generally uncooperative attitude throughout the UN system to such an attempt, but it has also run afoul of the same political abuses and ambiguities that it was charged to devise ways to avoid. When the ICSC's own procedures are called into question, and the General Assembly feels constrained to call for

---

[60] 29 UN GAOR, UN Doc. A/9980 (1974).
[61] Quoted in Amerasinghe, I, note 19 above, at 7.

an investigation, then the "legality" or "legitimacy" of its work is bound to be questioned as well.[62]

The right of members of the Secretariat to organize into staff unions (or staff associations), and to demonstrate (as well as remonstrate) in order to obtain more favorable treatment, is also recognized. Although the Staff Association (or Staff Union) remains a bargaining agent that represents the collective interests of UN employees, the Statute of the UNAT has not given the Staff Association (or Staff Union) *locus standi* to bring actions before it. Nonetheless, as Amerasinghe observed: "Strikes are in principle not illegal and cannot usually be regarded as a cause for terminating employment or imposing disciplinary sanctions."[63] Strikes and work stoppages, although arousing at times strong resentment from member states, are considered as legally authorized even though not necessarily acknowledged as such by the Administration.[64]

Finally, it should be pointed out that conditions of service, not only questions of recruitment, emoluments, promotions, etc., but also the general climate in which the civil service performs its duties, can affect the broad question of its "international" character directly. Recourse to legal instrumentalities, however well embedded in the judiciary fabric of the Organization, can only be effective if the culture of the Organization is receptive.[65]

SELECTED BIBLIOGRAPHY

Akehurst, M., *The Law Governing Employment in International Organizations* (Cambridge University Press, 1967)

---

[62] The ICSC came under sharp criticism in 1995, to the extent that the CCISU withdrew from the work of the ICSC in August. See 50 UN GAOR, UN Doc. A/50/30 (1995), Annex I; *UN Staff Report*, November 1995. There has also been increased interest lately in performance appraisal, which is a report by the joint Inspection Unit concerning UN management.

[63] Amerasinghe, II, note 19 above, at 1003 & 1010, respectively. See also R. Jordan, "The Fluctuating Fortunes of the International Civil Service: Hostage to Politics or Undeservedly Criticized?," *Pub. Admin. Rev.* 353–57 (Jul./Aug. 1991).

[64] See Beigbeder, note 1 above, especially ch. 7: "In contrast to national trade unions, international staff associations have a built-in limitation: their statutory loyalty to the organization. As international civil servants, the staff representatives are committed to accept and promote the objectives of their organization, to discharge their international functions and regulate their conduct with the interests of the organization alone in view, as required by their oath of office." *Ibid.*, at 139.

[65] I am especially grateful to Oscar Schachter for his meticulous editing, and to Christopher Joyner for making the other aspects of my participation both easy and pleasant. Theodor Meron, John Renninger, and Richard Van Wagenen provided comments, for which I am grateful. Responsibility for the results, rests, of course, with me, and not the Air War College/Air University. Tristan Greene, a graduate student in the Department of Political Science at the University of New Orleans, assisted in preparing the manuscript for publication, as did my wife, Jane.

Amerasinghe, C., *The Law of the International Civil Service* (Clarendon Press, 1988)

Documents on International Administrative Tribunals (The Clarendon Press, 1989)

Beigbeder, Y., *Management Problems in UN Organizations, Reform or Decline?* (Frances Pinter, 1987)

Threats to the International Civil Service (Pinter Publishers, 1988)

Berridge, G., *Return to the UN: UN Diplomacy in Regional Conflicts* (St. Martin's Press, 1991)

Bettato. M., *Le Droit des organisations internationales* (Presses universitaires de France, 1987)

Bowett, D., *The Law of International Institutions* (Stevens & Sons, 1982)

Crosswell, C., *Protection of International Personnel Abroad: Law and Practice Affecting the Privileges and Immunities of International Organizations* (Oceana, 1952)

Dag Hammarskjöld Revisited: The U.N. Secretary-General as a Force in World Politics (R. Jordan ed.; Carolina Academic Press, 1983)

Elmandjra, M., *The United Nations System: An Analysis* (Faber & Faber, 1973)

Fact-Finding before International Tribunals (R. Lillich ed.; Transnational Publishers, Inc., 1992)

Finger, S. & J. Mugno, *The Politics of Staffing the UN Secretariat* (The Ralph Bunche Institute on the United Nations, 1974)

Franck, T., *Nation against Nation: What Became of the United Nations Dream and What the US Can Do About It* (Oxford University Press, 1985)

Judging the World Court (Priority Press Publications, 1986)

Gordenker, L., *The UN Secretary-General and the Maintenance of Peace* (Columbia University Press, 1967)

Guetzkow, H., *Multiple Loyalties: A Theoretical Approach to a Problem in International Organization* (Princeton University Press, 1955)

Hammarskjöld, D., *The International Civil Service in Law and in Fact* (Clarendon Press, 1961)

International Administration: Its Evolution and Contemporary Applications (R. Jordan ed.; Oxford University Press, 1970)

International Administration: Law and Management Practices in International Organisations (C. de Cooker, ed.; Martinus Nijhoff, 1990)

The International Civil Service: Changing Role and Concepts (N. Graham & R. Jordan eds.; Pergamon Press, 1979)

International Organization: Law in Movement (J. Fawcett & R. Higgins eds.; Oxford University Press, 1973)

James, R., *Staffing the United Nations Secretariat* (Institute for the Study of International Organisation, University of Sussex, 1970)

Koh, B., *The United Nations Administrative Tribunal* (Louisiana State University Press, 1966)

Langrod, G., *The International Civil Service* (Oceana Publications, 1968)

Loveday, A., *Reflections on International Administration* (Clarendon Press, 1956)

407

McLaren, R., *Civil Servants and Public Policy: A Comparative Study of International Secretariats* (Wilfrid Laurier University Press, 1980)

Meron, T., *The United Nations Secretariat: The Rules and the Practice* (Lexington Books, 1977)

Status and Independence of the International Civil Servant (Sijthoff & Noordhoff, 1981)

Morgenstern, F., *Legal Problems of International Organisations* (Grotius Publications, Ltd., 1986)

The Nature of United Nations Bureaucracies (D. Pitt & T. Weiss eds.; Croom Helm, 1987)

The Non-Aligned and the United Nations (M. Rajan ed.; Oceana, 1988)

Politics in the United Nations (L. Finkelstein ed.; Duke University Press, 1988)

Renninger, J., *Can the Common System Be Maintained? The Role of the International Civil Service Commission* (United Nations Institute for Training and Research, 1986)

Reymond, H. & S. Mailick *International Personnel Policies and Practices* (Praeger, 1985)

Rovine, A., *The First Fifty Years: The Secretary-General in World Politics, 1920–1970* (A. W. Sijthoff, 1970)

Russell, R. & J. Muther, *A History of the United Nations Charter* (The Brookings Institution, 1958)

Schermers, H., *International Institutional Law* (A. W. Sijthoff, 1972)

United Nations, Divided World: The UN's Roles in International Relations (A. Roberts & B. Kingsbury eds.; Clarendon Press, 1989)

US Department of State, *United States Participation in the UN: Report by the President to the Congress for the Year 1990* (Department of State Pub. 9880, Released September 1991)

Weiss, T., *International Bureaucracy: An Analysis of the Operation of Functional and Global International Secretariats* (Lexington Books, 1975)

CHAPTER FIFTEEN

FINANCIAL RESPONSIBILITY

Jose E. Alvarez

UN system organizations have relied on a variety of methods for financing, not all of which are specified in their constituent instruments. These financing methods have been canvassed elsewhere and need only be briefly summarized here.[1]

All UN system organizations rely on assessed contributions from member states, although the method of apportionment varies. None apportion these assessments in equal shares and most use scales of assessment on which a certain percentage is assessed to each member.[2] The United Nations Charter leaves the formula for determining assessments, as well as the actual level, to be determined by the political will of the UN's plenary organ, the General Assembly, which is charged with the power to approve the budget.[3] The General Assembly, through its Committee on Contributions, has varied the percentage of the regular UN budget assessed to individual states over the years but has adhered, at least in principle, to "capacity to pay" as the basis for assessment.[4] It has also adopted both minimum and maximum assessment levels.[5] The UN assessment scale has been adopted by many of the other UN system organizations, including the

---

[1] See especially: H. Schermers, *International Institutional Law* (1980), ch. 7; J. Stoessinger, *Financing the United Nations System* (1964); G. Schwarzenberger, *International Constitutional Law* (1976), ch. 27; D. Williams, *The Specialized Agencies and the United Nations* (1987), ch. VII; P. Szasz, *The Law and Practices of the International Atomic Energy Agency* (1970), ch. 25; S. Ogata & P. Volcker, *Financing an Effective United Nations* (Ford Foundation Report, 1993).
[2] Schermers, note 1 above, at 472, 475.   [3] See UN Charter, art. 17.
[4] For discussion of the origin and early development of the "capacity to pay" formula, see Stoessinger, note 1 above, at 82–90. While the "capacity to pay" approach violates the principle of sovereign equality and is inconsistent with the parity of voting rights in the General Assembly, it has traditionally drawn widespread support on the basis of fairness, although giving content to this formula has proved troublesome. *Ibid.* See also Schermers, note 1 above, at 476–77.
[5] The current floor is 0.01 percent; the maximum, since 1972, is 25 percent. Schermers, note 1 above, at 484–85.

ILO, FAO, WHO, UNESCO, UNIDO, and the IAEA.[6] Other organizations, such as ICAO and the WMO, base their scale of assessments at least in part on the interest individual members have in the work of the organization.[7] Changes in individual members' percentage assessments have varied in response to institutional changes such as the withdrawal of members, as well as to political pressure.[8]

While the UN Charter and some of the constituent instruments of other UN system organizations say nothing about them,[9] voluntary contributions are the second primary source of funds. Voluntary contributions provide an increasing portion of the total source of funds for UN system organizations for a number of reasons. They are a cost-effective way for major donors to achieve influence since these funds, unlike assessed contributions, usually can be earmarked for the donor's favored projects or consist of aid in kind, such as training scholarships, which can also serve to tailor the assistance to a donor's policies.[10] Major donors, such as the United States, can use voluntary contributions to reward some programs or agencies and penalize others.[11] For the UN, reliance on this seemingly unauthorized source of funds accords with the established practice of several League of Nations-era organizations which had also turned to such contributions from both governmental and nongovernmental sources.[12]

---

[6] *Ibid.*, at 477 n. 133. UNIDO's constitution, for example, provides, at art. 15:

Equal budget expenditures shall be borne by the Members, as apportioned in accordance with a scale of assessment established by the Conference by a two-thirds majority of the Members present and voting, upon the recommendation of the Board adopted by a two-thirds majority of the Members present and voting on the basis of a draft prepared by the Programme and Budget Committee.
    The scale of assessment shall be based to the extent possible on the scale most recently employed by the United Nations. No member shall be assessed more than twenty-five percent of the regular budget of the Organisation.

Constitution of the United Nations Industrial Development Organization, Apr. 8, 1979, TIAS No. 1985, 18 *ILM* 667 (1979).

[7] Both ICAO and the WMO use the UN scale for 75 percent of their respective expenditures, with the other 25 percent assessed according to the interest of individual members in their respective work. See Schermers, note 1 above, at 478.

[8] *Ibid.*, at 482. According to the formula for assessments formulated by the General Assembly in 1946, the US assessment at that time would have been 49.89 percent. The US opposed this level and it was lowered to 39.89 percent. The US level is now 25 percent. See *ibid.*, at 484; L. Goodrich & E. Hambro, *Charter of the United Nations* 184–85 (1949).

[9] Some specialized agency constitutions do provide for them. See, e.g., UNIDO's constitution, whose Article 13.2 specifically provides that the expenditure of the organization may be met "from voluntary contributions . . . and such other income as may be provided for in the financial regulations." UNIDO constitution, note 6 above, art. 13.2.

[10] M. Imber, *The USA, ILO, UNESCO and IAEA* 123 (1989); Schermers, note 1 above, at 503, 506–9; Williams, note 1 above, 85–94.

[11] See, e.g., Imber, note 10 above, at 124; Statement by Ambassador Richard S. Williamson, Assistant Secretary for International Organizations Affairs, US Department of State, UN Agencies and the Budget, 88 *Dep't St. Bull.* 81, 83–84 (Apr. 1988).

[12] Schermers, note 1 above, at 502.

The capacity to create separate trust funds for the administration of such funds has been accepted as inherent when not specifically authorized by constitutional provision.[13] Such contributions are, by definition, nonmandatory but have become a customary source of funds. Thus, the IAEA, for example, engages in systematic solicitation of voluntary contributions, in which members are requested to meet specific "targets," to be used to support its "operational programme" (principally technical assistance).[14] "Pledging conferences" at which members announce their voluntary contributions have become common in many UN system organizations.[15] The allocation as well as any restrictions on the receipt of such funds, such as with respect to gifts tendered with conditions from both governmental and nongovernmental sources, is sometimes the subject of direct provision in the organization's financial regulations.[16]

Generally speaking, income generated from other sources is not as significant a source of revenue as assessed and voluntary contributions.[17] Nonetheless, certain organizations, such as the IAEA, derive some revenue from equipment, facilities or materials furnished or services rendered to members, individuals, or other organizations.[18] Some, such as the UN Postal Administration and UNICEF, sell products directly to the public, while several have raised money from investments or secured commercial or other loans.[19] Since generally UN international civil servants pay no national taxes but US nationals in the Secretariat do pay US taxes, many UN system organizations attempt to equalize the situation by raising gross salaries for their personnel while imposing a differential salary levy or "staff assessment." For the UN this additional source of revenue constitutes approximately 16 percent of all regular income.[20]

Most of the controversy surrounding the financing of UN system organizations results from the decision of the drafters of the UN Charter to attempt to rectify the "pitfalls which had so hamstrung the financial activities of the League."[21] Thus, Article 17 of the Charter establishes the principle that members of the Organization bear a collective financial responsibility to the Organization. In the words of Article 17(2), the "expenses of the organization shall be borne by the Members as appor-

---

[13] See *ibid.*, at 508–9.   [14] Szasz, note 1 above, at 864–66.
[15] Schermers, note 1 above, at 511–12.
[16] See, e.g., Schermers, note 1 above, at 518; Szasz, note 1 above, at 863–64 (discussing the IAEA regulations on point). These Financial Regulations, such as the Financial Regulations and Rules of the United Nations, UN Doc. ST/SGB/Financial Rules/1/Rev.3 (1985) (hereinafter UN Financial Regulations), also deal with such issues as rules for internal audits and for acceptable currencies.   [17] Schermers, note 1 above, at 518.
[18] See, e.g., Szasz, note 1 above, at 869–70; Schermers, note 1 above, at 522–24.
[19] Schermers, note 1 above, at 525–26.   [20] *Ibid.*, at 528.
[21] J. Singer, *Financing International Organization: The United Nations Budget Process* 8 (1961). On the financial starvation of the League of Nations, see C. W. Jenks, "Some Legal Aspects of the Financing of International Institutions," 28 *Grotius Soc'y Transactions* 87, 91 (1943).

tioned by the General Assembly." In contradistinction to the original League of Nations Covenant which did not specify which organ was responsible for setting the budget, required unanimity on budgetary matters, and established an inflexible basis of apportionment, the Charter provides that the General Assembly can approve the budget by a two-thirds vote, leaves the level of assessment open to flexible determination, and states that members overdue in their payments for two full years "shall" have no vote in the General Assembly unless the Assembly determines otherwise.[22] The constituent instruments of all UN system organizations, with the exception of those financial organizations, such as the IMF, which permit weighted voting, follow a similar approach.[23] The result is that two-thirds of the members of these organizations can impose a budget which is not to the liking of as many as one-third of their members. This potential "tyranny of the majority" is exacerbated by the fact that whereas voting in the plenary or general conference of the organization is typically on the basis of one state, one vote, UN system assessments vary from the US's 25 percent to the minimum of 0.01 percent.

UN system organizations have attempted, within the framework of their own constituent instruments and financial regulations, to deal with the potential "tyranny of the majority" problem with varying degrees of success. Some, like the IAEA, turn to two-tier budgets: "administrative" expenses (covering the costs of running the organization, including personnel and buildings) are covered by assessed contributions, while "operational" expenses (costs of projects performed by the organization) are covered by voluntary contributions or on a fee-for-service basis.[24] Since for most UN system organizations, administrative expenses constitute by far the largest part of their overall budgets,[25] this approach diffuses the "tyranny of the majority" problem only to a limited extent. The UN itself has, particularly

---

[22] See UN Charter, arts. 17, 18, & 19.

[23] UN Charter, art. 17. See also Const. of the Food and Agriculture Organization, Oct. 16, 1945, arts. XVIII, XIX, 12 UST 980, TIAS No. 4803; Constitution of the International Atomic Energy Commission, Oct. 26, 1956, art. XIV, 8 UST 1093, TIAS No. 3873; Convention on International Civil Aviation, Dec. 7, 1944, art. 61, TIAS No. 1591, 15 UNTS 295; Constitution of the International Labour Organization, Oct. 9, 1946, art. 13, TIAS No. 1868, 15 UNTS 35; Convention of the International Maritime Organization, Mar. 6, 1948, art. 41, 9 UST 624, TIAS No. 4044; International Telecommunication Convention, Nov. 6, 1982, art. 15, reprinted in G. Wallenstein, *International Telecommunication Agreements*, Binder, pt. 3 (1985); Constitution of the United Nations Educational, Scientific and Cultural Organization, Nov. 16, 1945, art. IX, 4 UNTS 275; Constitution of the Universal Postal Union, July 10, 1964, art. 21, 16 UST 1291, TIAS No. 5881; Constitution of the World Health Organization, July 22, 1946, art. 56, 62 Stat. 2679, TIAS No. 1808; Convention of the World Intellectual Property Organization, July 14, 1967, art. 11, 21 UST 1749, TIAS No. 6932; Convention of the World Meteorological Organization, Oct. 11, 1947, art. 24, 1 UST 281, TIAS No. 2052; Statutes of the World Tourism Organization, Sep. 27, 1970, art. 25, 27 UST 2211, TIAS No. 8307.

[24] See, e.g., Szasz, note 1 above, at 820–25 (discussing the "two-budget system in the IAEA"); Schermers, note 1 above, at 458–60.   [25] Schermers, note 1 above, at 459–60.

since 1962, sometimes turned *de facto* to a similar approach, despite Article 17 of the Charter which provides only that the Assembly "consider and approve the budget," without limitation to administrative expenses.[26] A variety of operational projects, including some peacekeeping activities, have been funded through voluntary contributions.[27]

Despite these attempts, the UN, like the League of Nations, is no stranger to financial crises.[28] Withholdings of particular peacekeeping expenses included as part of the regular budget led to the Assembly's nineteenth (1964) session which, rather than confront the question of whether the Article 19 loss of vote sanction should be applied to defaulting states, conducted all business without benefit of vote.[29] In that same year the spiraling budgets of some UN specialized agencies led major donors to form an intergovernmental group, the Geneva Group, to press for reduced expenditures and greater financial accountability.[30] In more recent times, concern over the growing dominance of third-world states over UNESCO's budget led the US Congress to withdraw from that organization.[31] In addition, starting in 1978, the United States Congress and/or its Executive enacted a series of specific restrictions on the payment of US assessed contributions to particular UN programs, including threats to withhold a progressively higher proportion of US annual assessments unless UN system budgets are adopted on the basis of "weighted voting."[32] Such deliberate withholdings by the United States and at one point as many as seventeen other members, delays in making assessed contributions, and threats to withhold either portions of or the entirety of assessments continue to plague the UN and many of its specialized agencies.[33]

The result, for much of the 1980s, were periodic warnings by the UN Secretary-General that the UN was in imminent threat of bankruptcy.

---

[26] By contrast, UN Charter art. 17(3) provides that the General Assembly examine the "administrative" budgets of the specialized agencies.

[27] See, e.g., Secretary-General, Report on the Status of Contributions as of March 31, 1991, ST/ADM/SER.B/354.

[28] See, e.g., Singer, note 21 above (enumerating the UN's problem in collecting payments of assessed contributions from the first report by the Secretary-General in 1948 through 1960); K. Simmonds, "The UN Assessments Advisory Opinion," 13 *Int'l & Comp. L. Q.* 854, 856–57 (1964) (writing of financial problems in 1956–64); H. Barber, "The United States vs. The United Nations," 27 *Int'l Org.* 139 (1973) (on the 1970s); J. Alvarez, "Legal Remedies and the United Nations à la carte Problem," 12 *Mich. J. Int'l. L.* 229 (1991) (on the 1980s through the present). On the arrearages and other financial problems which the specialized agencies have periodically faced, see Stoessinger, note 1 above, at ch. 9; Williams, note 1 above, ch. VII; Imber, note 10 above, at chs. 6 & 7. For more recent dilemmas prompted by expensive peacekeeping burdens, see Ogata & Volcker, note 1 above.

[29] M. Whiteman, 13 *Digest of International Law* 320–27, 330–32 (1968).

[30] Williams, note 1 above, at 85–88. On the rapid growth of UN budgets through 1980, see, e.g., Schermers, note 1 above, at 454.   [31] Imber, note 10 above, at ch. 6.

[32] For a summary of these, see Alvarez, note 28 above, at 232–42.

[33] See, e.g., Report of the Secretary-General on the Current Financial Crisis of the United Nations, UN Doc. No. A/45/830 (1990).

"Budgetary reforms" were instituted, including, in 1986, the "gentleman's agreement" contained in GA Res. 41/213 which, while it reaffirmed that the provisions of the Charter on budget-making prevail, opted for decision-making by consensus in budget-making committees.[34] These reforms placated those calling for a change in the "one state/one vote" budget-making scheme without amending the Charter but have not resolved underlying legal and practical difficulties. In the 1990s many member governments, including the United States, continue to fail to pay their annual assessed contributions to the regular budget within the time period for payment required in the Financial Regulations,[35] thereby causing uncertainty, cash shortages, and increasing resort to alternative, and possibly expensive, sources of funds within affected agencies.[36] As of March 1996, arrearages for member countries were $3.3 billion – $1.6 billion in the regular budget and $1.7 billion for the peacekeeping budget. About one-third of that total is owed by the United States, which is obligated to pay one quarter of both budgets.[37] US pledges to repay its accumulated arrears and future assessed contributions remain contingent, however, on the UN's continued progress in achieving "budgetary restraint" and on the Organization's continued adherence to consensus-based budget-making.[38] Indeed, recent developments have led many to suggest that major contributors to UN system organizations are now exercising or threatening to exercise a financial veto never anticipated by the drafters of the UN Charter –

[34] UN Doc. No. A/41/49 (1986); see E. Zoller, "The 'Corporate Will' of the United Nations and the Rights of the Minority," 81 *AJIL* 610, 633 (1987). For a third-world perspective on the crisis and the "budgetary reforms," see H. Choudhury, "United Nations Reforms: Some Reflections," 2 *Ethics & Int'l Aff.* 155 (1988).

[35] UN Financial Regulations, note 16 above, regs. 5.3 & 5.4 (providing that contributions are due within thirty days of notification of assessments or as of the first day of the calendar year to which they relate, whichever is later).

[36] See, e.g., US General Accounting Office, Delaying US Payments to International Organizations may not be the Best Means to Promote Budget Restraint (Feb. 15, 1983) (hereinafter GAO Report). This report examined the effects both on the United States and on international organizations of deliberate delays in the US payments to international organizations, a policy designed in part to demonstrate US concern over increasing budgets. The US government report advised against this policy since international organizations were reacting to the cash shortfalls by, for example, resorting to commercial borrowing, or turning to peacekeeping and other special accounts, without specifically affecting those programs to which the US objected or the general level of program activities. The report also concluded that the US policy undermined the very goals it was designed to achieve since, among other things, US savings were illusionary and undermined the cohesion of the Geneva Group. On the tendency to turn to the Working Capital Fund in case of need, see Schermers, note 1 above, 497–502; Szasz, note 1 above, at 858–62.

[37] John M. Goshko, "To Help Ward Off Bankruptcy, UN May Lay Off More Than 1,000 Staff," *Washington Post,* Feb. 3, 1996, at A-16.

[38] Thus the Foreign Relations Authorization Act for fiscal years 1994 and 1995, Pub. L. No. 103–236, tit. IV, 108 Stat. 382 (1994), among other things, threatened a 20 percent withholding of US assessments to the regular budget unless the UN established an "Inspector General's Office" to ferret out mismanagement and corruption.

often in addition to the Security Council veto given permanent members.[39] By 1994 the Organization's finances had come under such severe strain that there was serious discussion of a revision to the scale of assessments.[40]

The ICJ's 1962 Advisory Opinion in Certain Expenses of the United Nations is the necessary starting point to an understanding of the scope of the General Assembly's appropriations power under Article 17. In that instance, France and the Soviet Union challenged the validity of certain peacekeeping expenses. France argued that the General Assembly was not a world legislature or a "super-state" but had only the limited power to impose on members the legal obligation to pay for "administrative" expenses; the costs for peacekeeping were not among the "expenses" included in Article 17.[41] The Soviets contended that such expenses could "be determined only on the basis of special agreements to be concluded by the Security Council and the Member States of the Organization" and that, in any case, since all General Assembly resolutions are hortatory in nature, they "cannot establish legal obligations for the Member States of the Organization."[42] The United States argued by contrast that Article 17 had been intended to state a "general principle . . . applicable to all associations, that legally incurred expenses of an association must be borne by all its members in common"; that both the terms of the Charter and subsequent practice confirmed the "exclusive character of the fiscal authority of the General Assembly"; and that the power of the General Assembly to create "legally binding financial obligations" was not limited to "administrative" expenses but extended to peacekeeping. To the US, Article 17 was a clear statement that "the United Nations can pay for what it is empowered to do" and "what the United Nations can do, it can pay for."[43]

The ICJ's majority advisory opinion essentially affirmed the legally binding nature of General Assembly budgetary resolutions, rejecting the French and Soviet positions with respect to the specific peacekeeping expenses at issue as well as their more general arguments with respect to the

---

[39] Particularly with the advent of a Republican-controlled Congress in 1994, US payments to the UN regular and peacekeeping budgets fell dramatically such that the US in early 1996 was the UN's largest debtor, with over $1.5 billion in arrears. See John Goshko, "Boutros-Ghali Proposes Cut in US Dues," *Washington Post*, Feb. 7, 1996, at A-16. These arrears threatened to accumulate even more given the Foreign Relations Authorization Act for 1994 and 1995, note 38 above. Under that Act, the US Congress unilaterally reduced the share of peacekeeping expenses from approximately 31 percent to 25 percent, prompting US demands that the Organization establish a new scale of peacekeeping assessments.

[40] See Goshko, note 37 above, at A-16; *A Global Agenda: Issues Before the 50th Assembly of the General Assembly of the United Nations* 294–305 (J. Tessitore & S. Woolfson eds., 1995).

[41] 1962 ICJ Pleadings (Certain Expenses of the United Nations) (UN Charter art. 17, para. 2), 133–34 (Feb. 15, 1962 letter to the Court).   [42] *Ibid.*, at 273 (Soviet Pleadings).

[43] *Ibid.*, at 193–97, 202–3 (Written Statement of the United States), 424 (Oral Statement of Mr. Chayes).

meaning of Article 17. Although the Court refused to define "expenses of the organization" for purposes of Article 17, it stated that "such expenditures must be tested by their relationship to the purposes of the United Nations in the sense that if the expenditure were made for a purpose which is not one of the purposes of the United Nations, it could not be considered an 'expense of the Organization.'"[44] The Court noted that

[the Charter] purposes are broad indeed, but neither they nor the powers conferred to effectuate them are unlimited. Save as they have entrusted the Organization with the attainment of these common ends, the Member States retain their freedom of action. But when the Organization takes action which warrants the assertion that it was appropriate for the fulfillment of one of the stated purposes of the United Nations, the presumption is that such action is not *ultra vires* the Organization.[45]

In response to the contention that General Assembly resolutions are only hortatory under Article 10 of the Charter, Fitzmaurice, in a separate concurring opinion, argued that the rule *generalis specialibus non derogant* applies and "the special obligation to contribute to the expenses incurred in carrying them out prevails, and applies even to Member States voting against."[46] To Fitzmaurice, the duty to contribute to the regular expenses of the organization would have arisen "as a matter of inherent necessity" since

even in the absence of Article 17, paragraph 2, a general obligation for Member States collectively to finance the Organization would have to be read into the Charter, on the basis of the same principle as the Court applied in [the Reparations case], namely, "by necessary implication as being essential to the performance of its [i.e., the Organization's] duties." Joining the Organization, in short, means accepting the burden and the obligation of contributing to financing it.[47]

On this view, a legal duty to pay for at least the administrative expenses of the organization would have arisen, even in the absence of Article 17, based on customary international law.

The General Assembly's subsequent acceptance of this advisory opinion[48] did not lead to any immediate change in either France's or the Soviet Union's position with respect to the questioned expenses.[49] It also did not

---

[44] Certain Expenses of the United Nations, 1962 ICJ 16 (hereinafter Expenses case).

[45] *Ibid.*, at 168. [46] *Ibid.*, at 212 (Fitzmaurice). [47] *Ibid.*, at 208–9 (Fitzmaurice).

[48] Whiteman, note 29 above, at 319; Stoessinger, note 1 above, at 153–54.

[49] Whiteman, note 29 above, at 320–44. Soviet policy to refuse to pay for peacekeeping expenses to which it objected changed in October 1987 when it announced payment of its outstanding debts to the UN, including $197 million for peacekeeping expenses. These did not include the expenses challenged in the Expenses case. *NY Times,* Oct. 16, 1987, at A1, col. 6. For its part, France later paid a token lump sum and began paying for the amortization of the bond issue that had largely financed the Congo operation which it had challenged in 1962. See R. Hottelet, "$ and ¢ and the United Nations," *Commonweal* 347 (Jan. 19, 1973); *Christian Science Monitor,* Oct. 22, 1971.

lead to the application of Article 19 which provides that members in arrears

shall have no vote in the General Assembly if the amount of its arrears equals or exceeds the amount of the contributions due from it for the preceding two full years. The General Assembly may, nevertheless, permit such a Member to vote if it is satisfied that the failure to pay is due to conditions beyond the control of the Member.

The United States had urged that this loss of vote sanction was "mandatory and automatic" in the absence of a General Assembly vote to the contrary; the Soviets had argued otherwise.[50] The result was the announcement by US Ambassador Goldberg that, while the US still adhered to its views on the binding nature of Article 17 and the automatic loss of vote sanction of Article 19, the US would not seek to frustrate the consensus of the General Assembly in not applying the sanction in this instance. Instead he indicated that:

if any Member State could make an exception to the principle of collective financial responsibility with respect to certain United Nations activities, the United States reserved the same option to make exceptions if, in its view, there were strong and compelling reasons to do so. There could be no double standard among the Members of the Organization.[51]

Despite the enforcement difficulties, the ICJ's advisory opinion had an immediate effect on subsequent Security Council practice. Eventually, the Security Council felt free to assess particular peacekeeping expenses as part of assessed, obligatory contributions.[52]

While the legal status of the US's so-called "Goldberg Reservation" has been repeatedly questioned,[53] more significant ambiguities have emerged in the wake of the Court's acknowledgment that the General Assembly's apportionment power, and presumably members' duties to pay, are limited by the Charter. The opinions rendered in the Expenses case, as well as pleadings in that case, have led most commentators to conclude that members have no legal duty to pay for *ultra vires* acts, that is, those involving "manifest" violations of the Charter, such as an expense that is

---

[50] See, e.g., Whiteman, note 29 above, at 324–25.

[51] Quoted in Whiteman, note 29 above, at 330–32.

[52] Since the Expenses case, the UN has adopted a special formula for determining obligatory assessments for peacekeeping operations under which Permanent Members such as the US are assessed at a higher rate than for the regular budget. This is described in S. Mills, "The Financing of the United Nations' Peacekeeping Operations: The Need for a Sound Financial Basis," in *International Peace Academy, Occasional Papers on Peacekeeping* (No. 3, 1989). See Whiteman, note 29 above, at 330. See also 1974 *UN Jurid. Y. B.* 159 (legal opinion of Oct. 23, 1974 concluding that UNEF and UNDOF expenses were obligatory under Article 17(2)). See also Schermers, note 1 above, at 463–64.

[53] See, e.g., Zoller, note 34 above, at 617.

not in accord with the substantive purposes of the Charter or has been enacted in violation with the procedural requirements established by the Charter, as, for example, an expense authorized by the wrong organ or by a less than two-thirds vote of the General Assembly.[54] Nonetheless, the consequences that flow from this conclusion are far from clear. In particular, does "manifest" illegality render the Organization's action void *ab initio* such that a member can unilaterally withhold payment corresponding to such action or is the action merely voidable if the Organization or some third party, such as the World Court, makes a determination that the action is *ultra vires?*

This question has reemerged in the wake of repeated challenges to UN authorized expenses, particularly by the United States. Even at the height of US withholding in the mid-1980s, US officials usually continued to adhere to the US position before the ICJ in 1962 that there is a legally binding duty to pay assessed contributions.[55] To the extent that legalities were raised, US officials characterized many US withholdings as appropriate responses to *"ultra vires"* acts by the UN. US officials condemned expenditures on behalf of the PLO, SWAPO, or the Decade of Racism or GA Resolution 33/79 as violations of the Charter or contrary to international law.[56] Similarly, expenses for the Law of the Sea Preparatory Commission were branded as "illegal" because the Commission was not a "subsidiary organ" answerable to the UN.[57] Alleged "kickbacks" by seconded UN officials allegedly violated Articles 100–101 of the Charter providing for independent international civil servants.[58]

With the possible exception of US withholdings regarding the Law of the Sea Preparatory Commission, scholars have not found the threadbare US legal justifications for these withholdings convincing.[59] Thus, commentators found at most political, not legal, justifications for those withholdings designed to effect budgetary reforms such as Kassebaum, withholdings for the Ethiopian Conference Center, and other across-the-board

---

[54] See, e.g., Zoller, note 34 above; Stoessinger, note 1 above, at 3; R. Russell, "United Nations Financing and the 'The Law of the Charter,'" 5 *Colum. J. Transnat'l L.* 68, 90 (1966); ASIL Special Working Comm. on UN Rel., Report and Resolutions (Aug. 1989), reported in *ASIL Newsletter*, July–Sept. 1989, at 4; T. Franck, "Unnecessary UN-Bashing Should Stop," 80 *AJIL* 336–37 (1986); H. Lauterpacht, "The Legal Effect of Illegal Acts of International Organizations," in *Cambridge Essays in International Law* 88 (1965).

[55] Compare Alvarez, note 28 above, at 242–54 to *ibid.*, at 259 n. 115.

[56] Alvarez, note 28 above, at 242–54.

[57] Statement by President Ronald Reagan on the Withholding of United States Funds from the Law of the Sea Preparatory Commission, 2 Pub. Papers 1652 (1982).

[58] See, e.g., Statement by Sen. Moynihan, 125 Cong. Rec. 10, 434–35 (1979).

[59] Compare Note, "United Nations Financing of the Law of the Sea Preparatory Commission: May the United States Withhold Payment?," 6 *Fordham Int'l L. J.* 472 (1982–83) (hereinafter Note, UN Financing) with Alvarez, note 28 above, at 296–98.

cuts.[60] Frederic Kirgis found US threats growing out of the possibility of a change in status of the PLO not justified under treaty law and "disproportionate" as a legitimate reprisal.[61] Further, the factual or legal premises underlying other US withholdings have been or remain questionable.[62] Finally, there are difficulties squaring withholdings with the UN's internal law since nothing in the UN's Financial Regulations authorizes the organization to accept "earmarked" contributions; as the US government repeatedly argued prior to 1980, the Secretary-General is "not authorized to finance some programs in the regular budget and not finance others."[63] Thus, shortfalls in members' contributions to the regular budget, however intended to "target" allegedly *ultra vires* activities, affect all UN programs equally, and not solely the targeted activity. Similar objections have been raised in connection with US withholdings to other UN system organizations.[64]

Nonetheless, these withholdings by the US as well as by others,[65] have led to more general arguments concerning the legality of unilateral withholding of assessed contributions to international organizations in

---

[60] See, e.g., Zoller, note 34 above, at 633; R. Nelson, "International Law and US Withholding of Payments to International Organizations," 80 *AJIL* 973 (1986).

[61] F. Kirgis, "Admission of 'Palestine' as a Member of a Specialized Agency and Withholding the Payment of Assessments in Response," 84 *AJIL* 218, 224 (1990) (hereinafter Kirgis, "Palestine"). [62] See, e.g., Alvarez, note 28 above, at 300–1.

[63] GAO Report, note 36 above; Opinion of the Legal Adviser of the Department of State on Legal Issues Arising in Respect of the Issuance of Bonds and the Contracting of Loans by the United Nations, Exh. No. 14 to US Dept. of State, Information on the Operations and Financing of the United Nations 27 (June 25, 1962) (hereinafter 1962 Legal Opinion). US Assistant Secretary of State Charles William Maynes once indicated why earmarked contributions were "constitutionally unacceptable" to UN agencies:

The funds provided through assessments by a particular state are commingled with the contributions of others and lose their national identity. Consequently, the UN agencies have no way of guaranteeing that the contributions of a particular country are not used for a specific purpose. If they attempted to do so, not only would UN finances become chaotic but the ability of the agencies to carry out programs approved by the membership would be badly crippled. The financial viability of the individual UN agencies – and possibly the future of the UN system itself – would be seriously challenged if not destroyed.

79 *Dep't St. Bull.* 54 (June 1979).

[64] See, e.g., Imber, note 10 above, at 114–15 & ch. 7. See also letter of Nov. 24, 1979 from the Director General of the IAEA to the United States denying the validity of any "limitation or condition imposed by Member States on the use of [assessed contributions] . . . under principles of law common to international organizations in general" (extracts on file with author).

[65] For example, the People's Republic of China, once it gained membership to the UN, refused to pay for the financing of certain peacekeeping expenses. See *NY Times*, Oct. 10, 1972, at A4, col. 4. See also Schermers, note 1 above, at 494–95; Imber, note 10 above, at 126–27. According to a June 12, 1986 Memorandum by the UN's Legal Counsel, Carl-August Fleischhauer, Financial Crisis at the United Nations (hereinafter Fleischhauer Memorandum) (on file with author), approximately eighteen members were withholding at least part of their assessed contribution as of that time. Fleischhauer Memorandum, at 6.

response to allegedly *ultra vires* acts. Three basic approaches have emerged, based on: (a) the law of treaties; (b) doctrines of state responsibility; and (c) international institutional law.

First, the question can be seen as arising out of the interpretation of a multilateral treaty, i.e., from the perspective of the Vienna Convention on the Law of Treaties or the similar Vienna Convention on the Law of Treaties between States and International Organizations or between International Organizations.[66] Unilateral withholding of assessed contributions might be justified under established treaty law if regarded as a "suspension" arising from an unforeseen, fundamental change of circumstances constituting an "essential basis" of the parties' consent to be bound which "radically transform[s] the extent of obligations still to be performed under the treaty."[67]

Problems with this justification abound. First, unless one accepts, for example, the dubious notion that the increase in the number of third-world members, together with the one-state, one-vote budget-making basis of most UN organizations, constitutes such a "fundamental change of circumstances," none of the actions by the UN which members are apt to challenge present an arguable "radical transformation" of the Organization.[68] Second, even if a particular UN activity constitutes such a fundamental change from what members could have anticipated, treaty law does not "contemplate suspension of only a nonseparable part of a party's obligations. The obligation to pay assessed dues would not be separable from the remainder of the constituent instrument."[69] Third, the permissible treaty remedy is only "suspension" which clearly anticipates a "temporary withholding of performance with a view to eventual resumption, if possible."[70] A financial withholding cannot be a "termination clothed as a suspension."[71] Since at least some of the US withholdings purport to be permanent and are not included in any plans by the US to pay arrears, some of them appear to violate this condition. Fourth, there are doubts about the procedural steps a state needs to take under relevant treaty law prior to suspension of its treaty obligations. On one view, applicable treaty law obliges states to notify other treaty parties prior to suspension, indicating the measures "proposed to be taken with respect to the treaty and the

---

[66] Vienna Convention on the Law of Treaties, May 23, 1969, 1155 UNTS 331, reprinted in 8 *ILM* 679 (1969) (hereinafter Vienna Convention); Vienna Convention on the Law of Treaties between States and International Organizations or between International Organizations, Mar. 20, 1986, UN Doc. A/CONF.129/15, reprinted in 25 *ILM* 543 (1986) (hereinafter International Organizations Convention).

[67] Vienna Convention, note 66 above, art. 62; International Organizations Convention, note 66 above, art. 62.   [68] Compare Kirgis, "Palestine," note 61 above, at 224.

[69] *Ibid.*, at 224. See also Zoller, note 34 above, at 628–29 (to similar effect).

[70] F. Kirgis, "Some Lingering Questions about Article 60 of the Vienna Convention on the Law of Treaties," 22 *Cornell Int'l L. J.* 549, 573 (1989) (hereinafter Kirgis, "Article 60").

[71] *Ibid.*, at 569.

reasons therefor."[72] At least one commentator has argued, by contrast, that this does not preclude a state from partially and unilaterally suspending its performance of a treaty obligation by way of reciprocity or reprisal and that procedural preconditions apply only if a state is suspending its performance of the entire treaty, and not merely a part.[73]

Justification under another treaty doctrine, "material breach," permitting suspension of a treaty obligation if there is a "violation of a provision essential to the accomplishment of the object or purpose of the treaty"[74] is also a possibility, albeit a dubious one for this purpose. Whether any of the challenged actions to date rise to the level of violations of essential provisions of the UN Charter is questionable. As Kirgis has argued with respect to US threats to withhold on the PLO, "respect for the efficient operation of treaty regimes . . . suggests that relatively isolated departures from the strictures of even an essential provision are not material breaches if they do not threaten to defeat the purpose of the treaty."[75] Further, the right to suspend the treaty "in whole or in part" under this doctrine belongs only to states "specially affected by the breach."[76] Neither the US nor any particular UN members (with the possible exceptions of Israel and South Africa) usually can claim to be specifically affected by challenged UN actions.[77] Further, withholdings cannot be justified on the grounds of reciprocity, i.e., as a permissible response to others' failures to pay, since withholdings do not specifically injure the "responding" member more than others (since its own contribution is not raised as a result) and each member's withholdings affect the organization as a whole and not solely those other states which withhold.[78] In any case, the duty to respond in a proportionate manner, presumptively applicable from the law of state responsibility, presents problems to the extent the withholdings exceed the degree of any prior breach.[79]

---

[72] See Vienna Convention, note 66 above, art. 65; International Organizations Convention, note 66 above, art. 65.

[73] See Kirgis, "Article 60," note 70 above, at 559. The express permission to forgo notification in cases of "special urgency," see Vienna Convention, note 66 above, art. 65(2); International Organizations Convention, note 66 above, art. 65(2), would not appear applicable in the context of UN actions since typically states are on notice, through voting on the underlying GA resolution authorizing the action, long before expenses are assessed.

[74] Vienna Convention, note 66 above, art. 60; International Organizations Convention, note 66 above, art. 60.   [75] Kirgis, "Palestine," note 61 above, at 225.

[76] Vienna Convention, note 66 above, art. 60(2)(b); International Organizations Convention, note 66 above, art. 60(2)(b).

[77] Compare Kirgis, "Palestine," note 61 above, at 225. South Africa refused to pay at least some contributions to UN organizations to which its representatives had not been admitted. See Schermers, note 1 above, at 495.   [78] Zoller, note 34 above, at 623.

[79] Thus, Kirgis argues that the US threat to withhold, should "Palestine" be admitted as a member of a UN organization, its full 25 percent assessment is "manifestly out of proportion to a breach that would not significantly increase the burdens of membership or go very far toward defeating accomplishment of the organization's goals." Kirgis, "Palestine," note 61 above, at 226–27.

A final treaty argument, that unilateral withholdings constitute "reservations" to impermissible action, is even more farfetched. Even assuming what many scholars have denied – that a member upon acceptance of UN membership can attach a reservation to its acceptance[80] – reservations must be timely, accepted by the competent organ of the Organization, and compatible with the object and purpose of the constituent instrument.[81] Neither the US's Goldberg "Reservation" nor any other members' assertion of a similar right to unilaterally withhold fulfills these requirements.

The law of state responsibility, or more specifically, the doctrine of nonforcible reprisals, provides the second potential avenue for legal justification of unilateral withholdings. Commentators and at least one arbitration award support the view that a party may proportionally suspend performance of a treaty for a nonmaterial breach.[82] But apart from the requirement of proportionality (already discussed), nonforcible reprisals are lawful only if (a) directed in good faith at "obtaining redress for the wrong committed" and not at "producing an outcome extraneous to the violation and the situation created by the illegal act"; (b) are previously notified to affected parties; and (c) are not designed to "avoid third party settlement."[83] Such reprisals are illegal when they frustrate the judicial process or are designed to terminate the dispute without regard to judicial settlement.[84] Judged by these standards, withholdings of UN financial obligations would only be justified if necessary to prevent irrevocable harm to the member and are accompanied by a good faith effort to seek redress through third-party settlement. Recent withholdings by the US and others would appear to fall far short of these criteria.[85]

The third conceivable approach relies on international institutional law. Some US officials as well as some legal scholars have sought refuge in the idea that "tolerance developed over time" provides a legal justification for the failure to pay.[86] One problem with this approach is that neither the International Court of Justice nor the International Law Commission has ever endorsed the concept that institutional or state practice can modify a

[80] See, e.g., M. Mendelson, "Reservations to the Constitutions of International Organizations," 45 *Brit. Y. B. Int'l L.* 137, 146–48 (1971).
[81] International Organizations Convention, note 66 above, arts. 19, 20.
[82] Kirgis, "Article 60," note 70 above, at 572 (and cites therein); Kirgis, "Palestine," note 61 above; O. Schachter, "International Law in Theory and Practice, General Course in International Law," 178 *RCADI* 170 (1982) (citing, *inter alia*, the Arbitral Decision in the Dispute between the US and France Concerning the Air Transport Services Agreement).
[83] Schachter, note 82 above, at 170; see also O. Elegab, *The Legality of Non-Forcible Counter-Measures in International Law* 64–79 (1988). Thus, the US self-help measures in the US–France Arbitral case were upheld because they were necessary to preserve the respective rights of the parties and because they encouraged resort to judicial settlement. Schachter, note 82 above, at 173–74.   [84] Schachter, note 82 above, at 174.
[85] See Alvarez, note 28 above, at 160.
[86] Compare Zoller, note 34 above, at 615 with T. Franck, *Nation against Nation* 259 (1985).

clear obligation set forth in the Charter.[87] In fact, under treaty law, subsequent practice may only be "taken into account" when it "establishes the agreement of the parties regarding its interpretation."[88] On at least two occasions the ICJ has distinguished the use of state practice to interpret a vague provision from its use to revise a clear provision.[89] A second problem with this approach is that it is not clear that UN system organizations have in fact "tolerated" members' failure to pay assessed contributions by failing to apply constitutionally authorized sanctions.[90] The UN Legal Counsel has never opined that the Article 19 loss of vote sanction does not apply to assessed contributions (as opposed to voluntary contributions) or that the duty to pay norm has fallen into desuetude.[91] In fact, the UN Legal Counsel has taken the position, consistent with the US position in 1962, that the Article 19 loss of vote sanction applies automatically; for these reasons the names of members with two years' accumulated arrears on assessed contributions are not called out during votes in the General Assembly.[92] Thus, the UN General Assembly has not acquiesced in the evisceration of the legal duty to pay since the UN has applied the Article 19 sanctions to states in default of their financial obligations.[93] For this reason, Elisabeth Zoller concludes that the so-called "practice" of withholding has not become legally meaningful and has never ceased to be a "sequence of departures from the Charter."[94]

Professor Zoller does, however, conclude that international institutional law within the context of the UN Charter scheme sanctions unilateral withholdings by UN members where, in the views of member states, such withholdings are "compelling" and necessary to protect members from the "tyranny of the majority" since such withholdings are "necessitated through the need" to keep the organization from turning into "a super-State."[95] While this view has drawn at least general support,[96] a

---

[87] See Zoller, note 34 above, at 616.

[88] Vienna Convention, note 66 above, art. 31(3)(b); International Organizations Convention, note 66 above, art. 31(3)(b).

[89] See Interpretation of Peace Treaties (second phase), 1950 ICJ 221, 229 (advisory opinion of July 18); Judge Dillard's separate opinion in the Namibia case, 1971 ICJ at 15354 (suggesting subsequent practice is relevant to Charter interpretation only in the absence of "precise prescription").

[90] See, e.g., "Contemporary Practice of the United States," 58 *AJIL* 752–58 (1964).

[91] Zoller, note 34 above, at 617–18. As Zoller points out the Goldberg Reservation merely "reserved" US rights pending resolution of the payment problem. It did not "acquiesce in exceptions to the principle of collective financial responsibility." *Ibid.*, at 617.

[92] See, e.g., 1968 *UN Jurid. Y. B.* at 186–88 (legal opinion justifying the UN's practice of not calling out names of members which are two years in arrears during roll-call votes).

[93] See Zoller, note 34 above, at 618–20; D. Bowett, *The Law of International Institutions*, at 386 n. 7 (4th ed., 1982).   [94] Zoller, note 34 above, at 617.   [95] *Ibid.*, at 631–32.

[96] See, e.g., Stoessinger, note 1 above, at 3; Russell, note 54 above, at 68, 90; *ASIL Newsletter*, note 54 above, at 4; Franck, note 54 above; see also Schermers, note 1 above, at 495.

contrary approach, grounded in the "presumptions" of validity found by the Court's majority in the Expenses case and in other advisory opinions rendered by the Court, appears more plausible.

Under this alternative view, international institutional law, viewed from the perspective of the majority and concurring opinions in the Expenses case, licenses in the context of the legally binding duty to pay a reversal of the traditional presumption in the *Lotus* case that international law will not presume prohibitions on state action.[97] By agreement among its members, the legal order of the Charter imposes certain limitations on unilateral withholding designed to uphold rights of the Organization, including its international legal personality.[98] Implicit in the Court's presumptions of validity in the Expenses case, as well as in the legal preconditions on nonforcible reprisals, are the requirements that at a minimum, prior to withholding, a member state must establish a prima facie case for invalidity and seek judicial or third-party resolution of the question. If the majority opinion in the Expenses case is taken seriously, unilateral withholding in response to *ultra vires* action is, at most, an option of last resort,[99] to be taken only after the complaining member has given the organization the opportunity to correct any error.

This conclusion is only strengthened by the seemingly obvious point that an organization has "no alternative but to honor" commitments made to third parties.[100] Were members free to withhold unilaterally, third parties to whom the organization owed debts could be left without a remedy – unless such parties were free to bring claims directly against members of the organization once the organization defaults on payment.

---

[97] See L. Gross, "Expenses of the United Nations for Peace-Keeping Operations: The Advisory Opinion of the International Court of Justice," *Int'l Org.* 1, 5 (1963); Stoessinger, note 1 above, at 154. For a more detailed version of the argument summarized here, see Alvarez, note 28 above, at 278–90.

[98] See Reparation for Injuries Suffered in the Service of the United Nations, 1949 ICJ 182 (advisory opinion of Apr. 11) (finding that the UN had international legal personality). But see Gross, note 97 above, at 31.

[99] Commentators differ on whether a right to treat organizational decisions as a nullity exists as a right of last resort. Compare E. Osieke, "The Legal Validity of Ultra Vires Decisions of International Organizations," 77 *AJIL* 239, 254 (1983), with M. Reisman, "Has the International Court Exceeded its Jurisdiction?," 80 *AJIL* 128 (1986).

[100] See Expenses case, note 44 above, at 204 (Fitzmaurice), 182–7 (Spender), 216–26 (Morelli); Effects of Awards of Compensation made by the UN Administrative Tribunal, 1954 ICJ 59 (advisory opinion of July 13). Even critics of the Expenses case have acknowledged that the "good faith, credit, and future of the United Nations is at stake" and that the "interests of third parties must be protected." Gross, note 97 above, at 34. See also M. Herdegen, "The Insolvency of International Organizations and the Legal Position of Creditors: Some Observations in the Light of the International Tin Council Crisis," 35 *Neth. Int'l L. Rev.* 135 (1988). The UN's Financial Regulations, note 16 above, providing, *inter alia*, at 4.1, that the Secretary-General is authorized to incur obligations and make payments once appropriations are voted upon by the General Assembly, also confirms the Organization's obligation to pay third parties.

Yet the possibility that members of an international organization are concurrently or secondarily liable for the obligations of the organization is in itself dubious.[101]

The next question that naturally arises is how does the organization go about enforcing the duty to pay on members such that it can meet its obligations. Interpretative disputes may arise in connection with those sanctions contained in constituent instruments. Most UN system organizations contain a provision similar to Article 19 of the UN Charter providing for loss of vote for failure to pay, but some provide for loss of vote in more than one organ and some are more permissive in language than the seemingly "automatic" loss of vote sanction of Article 19.[102] The scope of suspension of voting rights for failure to pay – whether throughout the organization or only in one organ – may give rise to controversy where it is not expressly stated.[103] The triggering event for suspension may be less

---

[101] Although the question has not arisen very often, C. F. Amerasinghe has argued that under international law, in the absence of provision in a constituent instrument specifically indicating an intention to impose concurrent or secondary liability on members for the organization's obligations, members are presumptively not so liable. Amerasinghe notes that constituent instruments of UN system organizations, with the exception of financial institutions such as the IBRD, make no reference to liability or nonliability of members but that commentators have differed as to the consequences of such an omission. C. F. Amerasinghe, "Liability to Third Parties of Member States of International Organizations: Practice, Principle and Judicial Precedent," 85 *AJIL* 259, 265–73 (1991). Amerasinghe's persuasive analysis of the issue, which includes a review of a British case in point, concludes that member liability arising out of organizations' treaties, contracts, quasi-contracts, or delicts cannot be presumed absent constitutional provision or institutional practice suggesting that members have accepted such liability. *Ibid.* (reviewing the judgments involving the International Tin Council [ITC] by the British Court of Appeals in *Maclaine Watson & Co. Ltd.* v. *Department of Trade & Indus.*, [1988] 3 All ER 257 and in its House of Lords in *J. H. Rayner Ltd.* v. *Department of Trade & Indus.*, [1989] WLR 969). This conclusion, he argues, is supported by broader principles, namely (a) the international legal personality of organizations that, as with municipal corporations, seeks to limit the liability of "shareholders" (members); (b) the risk that would otherwise exist of "undue member interference" in the day-to-day activities of the organization; and (c) the need to put third parties on notice. See Amerasinghe, cited above, at 277–79. To the extent that Amerasinghe is correct, third parties' only recourse is against the organization.

[102] The constituent instruments of most UN system organizations contain provisions for automatic loss of vote for failure to pay unless an exception is made. See IAEA const., note 23 above, art. XIX ("no vote in the agency"); ILO const., note 23 above, art. 13(4) (same); IMO Convention, note 23 above, art. 42 (no vote in Assembly, Council or Maritime Safety Committee); ITU Convention, note 23 above, art. 15(8) (no vote in Union, Committees, and Administrative Council); UNESCO const., note 23 above, art. IV(c) (no vote in General Conference); WIPO Convention, note 23 above, art. 2(5) (no vote in any organ); WTO Statutes, note 23 above, Financing Rule 13 (no vote in Assembly or Council). Other constitutions provide that voting privileges "may" be suspended when a member is in arrears. See Convention on International Civil Aviation, note 23 above, art. 61 (in the Assembly and Council); WHO const., note 23 above, art. 7; WMO const., note 23 above, art. 31. Neither the UPU nor the FAO charters contain suspension provisions.

[103] See, e.g., Szasz, note 1 above, at 857–58 (indicating some question about whether the sanction applies in all organs of the IAEA).

precise than Article 19's two-year rule, as where the possibility of sanction applies for failure to discharge financial obligations "within a reasonable period."[104] Moreover, Article 19's presumptive distinction between deliberate withholdings and those that occur "due to conditions beyond the control of the Member"[105] may suggest that deliberate withholdings could lead to a greater willingness to apply sanctions where discretion is possible. Perhaps more significant than these questions, however, is whether organizations are limited to enforcement through constitutionally sanctioned remedies such as Article 19, or whether they can, as in a particularly flagrant case, take other action. While it has been suggested that an organization has no power to expel or suspend members in the absence of constitutional provision providing for such possibilities,[106] neither this issue nor the related issue of the possibility of imposition of progressively higher sanctions on defaulting members – loss of vote, suspension, followed by expulsion under provisions such as Articles 19, 5, and 6 of the UN Charter – is clearly settled. Repeated and deliberate failure to pay assessments may even constitute a "persistent" violation of the Charter sufficient to trigger expulsion under Article 6 of the UN Charter.[107]

If the principle of collective financial responsibility is regarded as imposing a duty on members to make real the financial independence of the organization and there is an inherent right on the part of the organization to enforce such a duty – some of these interpretive issues regarding en-

---

[104] Compare, for example, UN Charter, art. 19 (prescribing suspension of vote in the event of arrears equal to or exceeding contributions due for two years); ILO const., note 23 above, art. 13(4) (same) with Convention On International Aviation, note 23 above, art. 62 (for failure to discharge financial obligations "within a reasonable period"), WHO const., note 23 above, art. 7 (simply for failure to "meet . . . financial obligations"), WMO Convention, note 23 above, art. 31 (same). At least some of the specialized agencies have, like the UN, exercised the suspension option for failure to pay. See, e.g., Szasz, note 1 above, at 856–57; Stoessinger, note 1 above, at 231 (all discussing IAEA); Stoessinger, note 1 above, at 220, 236 (discussing the ILO and ICAO). Some of the constituent instruments in addition provide for the possibility of expulsion, usually for "persistent" violation. See, e.g., UN Charter, art. 6. Exercise of this sanction by the UN may have broader repercussions since a member expelled by the UN may *ipso facto* cease to be eligible for membership to some UN specialized agencies: see UNESCO const., note 23 above, art. II(4). See N. Singh, *Termination of Membership of International Organizations* (1958); Schermers, note 1 above, at 496–97, 720–32. 740.

[105] The full text of Article 19 is as follows:

A Member of the United Nations which is in arrears in the payment of its financial contributions to the Organization shall have no vote in the General Assembly if the amount of its arrears equals or exceeds the amount of the contributions due from it for the preceding two full years. The General Assembly may, nevertheless, permit such a Member to vote if it is satisfied that the failure to pay is due to conditions beyond the control of the Member.

[106] See, e.g., Bowett, note 93 above, at 389. The constitutions of the UPU and FAO, for example, do not have such provisions.

[107] See UN Charter, arts. 5 (suspension) & 6 (expulsion). Compare Fleischhauer Memorandum, note 65 above, at 9 (suggesting the possibility of application of suspension and expulsion provisions for defaulters).

forcement of the collective financial principle might be resolved in favor of a more flexible response by UN system organizations. The Article 19 loss of vote sanction obviously has not prevented withholdings and untimely payments at the UN. As the UN Legal Adviser has noted, Article 19

is not an effective weapon; Member States facing the Article 19 sanction may pay the minimum required to bring them just above the line drawn by that Article, without, however, living up to their full commitments. Besides, by the time the Article 19 penalty becomes applicable in respect of the largest contributors, the Organization could no longer survive financially.[108]

Thus, various members of the US Congress argued in 1986 for continuing US withholdings on the premise that since, at the then-current withholding rate, the United States would not lose its General Assembly vote for five to seven years, the United States could continue to keep the Organization "one step ahead of bankruptcy" by paying "as little as we can without losing our standing."[109] But if the loss of vote sanction does not constitute a "self-contained" regime that is "entirely efficacious,"[110] the doctrine of necessity or effectiveness would appear to authorize the organization to take other measures, not otherwise contrary to its constituent instrument or international law, required to protect the financial needs of the organization which are therefore part of the inherent powers of the organization.[111] The organization could seek to enforce any procedural preconditions on withholding if these apply, such as the need to make a prima facie case to a third party. It could also attempt to take measures in addition to those specifically authorized by its charter for failure to pay, including charging interest on arrearages,[112] assessing user fees or suspending organizational services,[113] setting off sums which the organization otherwise owes to defaulting members, and most boldly, bringing enforcement actions, if these are possible, in domestic courts to compel payment.[114] The organization might be deemed to have such inherent powers even where no sanction for failure to pay is otherwise specified in the constituent instrument or where the remedy specified is ambiguous either in scope or application, for the same reasons the UN was found to have the power to bring claims on behalf of its personnel in the Repar-

---

[108] Fleischhauer Memorandum, note 65 above, at 2.
[109] Impact of Gramm–Rudman–Hollings on US Contributions to International Organizations: Hearings before the Subcomm. on Human Rights and International Organizations and the Subcomm. on International Operations of the House Comm. on Foreign Affairs, 99th Cong., 2d Sess. 28 (1986).   [110] Zoller, note 34 above, at 621.
[111] Alvarez, note 28 above, at 301–10.
[112] See, e.g., Stoessinger, note 1 above, at 235 (discussing the UPU's and ITU's practice of charging interest).   [113] See, e.g., Schermers, note 1 above, at 726–28.
[114] Jenks, note 21 above; Alvarez, note 28 above, at 305–7. See generally, Schermers, note 1 above, at 750–69. For additional suggestions on ways to reform the UN financing scheme, including ways to improve the financing of peacekeeping, see Ogata & Volcker, note 1 above.

ations case: as a necessary attribute of legal personality essential to insuring organizational survival. Institutional practice by UN system organizations would appear to support this. Thus, the UN's Financial Regulations, containing rules regarding, for example, the UN's power to undertake revenue-producing activities or internal audits, or stipulating a date certain for payment of assessed contributions, already constitute modest precedents for implied revenue-enhancing (or revenue-protecting) powers.[115]

Application of sanctions against defaulting members may not be merely a means to secure payment from particular members but may involve matters of broad principle. If the doctrine of desuetude threatens the principle of collective financial responsibility as some have contended,[116] persistent failure to enforce this principle undermines the legal duty to pay. Should this occur and withholdings or delays become the rule and not the exception, the very survival of the organization may be called into question.

As was evident in the Expenses case, an organization's decision to include a particular expense as part of the "regular" (or "administrative") budget such that a portion of that expense is assessed to every member of the organization has other legal consequences. It constitutes a determination that the particular activity giving rise to the expense is encompassed by the organization's "purposes" as regarded by the membership. Depending on the effect such institutional practice is given in the subsequent interpretation of the organization's charter, such a determination, if made by the proper organ in accord with the proper procedures and particularly if part of a series of similar determinations over a period of time, may serve to estop members or other organs from challenging the legitimacy of that type of activity in the future. Thus, institutional practice, as well as other factors, made it difficult for the US to contend successfully, in 1978, that "technical assistance" was improperly part of the UN regular budget.[117]

---

[115] UN Financial Regulations, note 16 above.   [116] See Franck, note 86 above, at 259.

[117] Departments of State, Justice, and Commerce, the Judiciary and Related Agencies Appropriations Act, 1979, Pub. L. No. 95–431, 92 Stat. 1021 (*approved* Oct. 10, 1978). President Carter signed the law under protest, stating that if allowed to stand this restriction would cause the US to "violate its treaty obligations" and is "contrary to the policy of collective financial responsibility." 79 *Dep't St. Bull.* 48 (Jan. 1979). In response, the UN Administrative Committee on Coordination stated:

Member States do not have the right to designate those parts of the regular budget or program which are to be, or are not to be financed by their assessed contribution, and the secretariats do not have the right to earmark assessed contributions in such a manner as to prevent their being used to finance any specific activity or program.

Ibid. When Congress passed its short-lived restriction withholding that portion of US payments to the UN's regular budget which would be used for technical assistance, approximately 19 percent of UN technical assistance was funded from assessed contributions. *Ibid.*, at 41 (Mar. 1979); *Ibid.*, at 54 (June 1979).

For similar reasons, absent resort to a doctrine of "improper delegation,"[118] it may prove difficult for the US today to claim that the expenses of subsidiary bodies in charge of the implementation of a multilateral treaty drafted under UN auspices, charged with implementation of activities within broad Charter purposes, such as the Preparatory Commission for the Law of the Sea, cannot generally be included in the UN's regular budget.[119]

The appropriation and collection of assessed contributions may, in turn, have other effects on an organization's internal law and practice. Decisions on remedies for withheld or delayed payments may affect the permissible scope of discretion accorded or the inherent or implied powers of the Secretary-General or the Secretariat.[120] They may also create precedents for the scope of permissible actions by the organization as a whole or by an organ or have an impact on other interpretative disputes. Thus, the General Assembly's decision to adopt a regulation, pursuant to its power to adopt such resolutions within the Headquarters District, to limit its tortuous liability and therefore its indemnity insurance premiums, created a modest precedent for what Paul Szasz has called "territorial legislation."[121] A decision to levy assessments for the period of a member's absence from an organization, when that member purports to withdraw from the organization and later seeks to return, may have an impact on whether the organization has accepted in general the possibility of withdrawal in the absence of express Charter provision[122] and may also help determine doubtful issues of representation or succession.[123] Indeed, the process of adopting and executing budgets has generated a body of institutional practice concerning such issues as, for example, the authority of one organ to review decisions taken by another.[124]

---

[118] See, e.g., Note, UN Financing, note 59 above, at 472.

[119] Alvarez, note 28 above, at 296–99.

[120] For example, in reaction to cash shortages, the UN General Assembly authorized the Secretary-General to issue bonds. See 1962 Legal Opinion, note 63 above; Schermers, note 1 above, at 499, 527. For a summary of the Secretary-General's initiatives in the face of the 1980s financial crisis, see Y. Beigbeder, "La Crise financière de l'ONU et le groupe des 18: perspectives de reforme," *Ann. Français de Droit Int'l* 426 (1986).

[121] P. Szasz, "The United Nations Legislates to Limit Its Liability," 81 *AJIL* 739 (1987).

[122] Compare E. Schwelb, "Withdrawal from the United Nations: The Indonesian Intermezzo," 61 *AJIL* 661 (1967); M. Akehurst, "Withdrawal from International Organisations," in *Current Legal Problems* 143 (1979); Bowett, note 93 above, at 390–92.

[123] See, e.g., the IAEA's rescission of Chinese assessed contributions to the IAEA for the period before and immediately after the Board expelled the representatives of Taiwan, IAEA Doc. GC (XIII)/527, pt. III, paras. 12–13 and Schedules F.2 & 3, section 6.2.1 para. (a)(iii); and its division of assessments for Bangladesh and Pakistan, IAEA Doc. GC (XVIII)/528, App., table 3, note b. See also Schermers, note 1 above, at 495–96.

[124] See, e.g., Schermers, note 1 above, at 544–54; Szasz, note 1 above, at 834–62; Y. Beigbeder, *Management Problems in United Nations Organizations: Reform or Decline?* ch. 4 (1987) (discussing financial/auditing controls).

At present each UN agency experiments with a mix of voluntary contributions, consensus-determined obligatory assessments, and a small stream of self-generated income. In doing so they walk a tightrope between organizational cohesion/fidelity to the principle of collective financial responsibility and a realpolitik need to encourage timely payments. More grandiose "fixes" for the UN system's perennial financial problems have been proposed, including such possibilities as a UN "tax" on international commodities or services, a more centralized UN-budgetary scheme for the UN and all specialized agencies, or various forms of weighted voting.[125] Since some of these involve Charter amendment, while others threaten either sovereign rights or the independence of existing organizations, such changes remain (for now) unlikely. In any case, radical reforms may be both unnecessary and unwise. They may be unnecessary because international organizations may already possess, through their inherent powers to enforce collective financial responsibility, basic legal remedies to encourage members to abide by the duty to pay. They may be unwise because they fail to address the basic reason for perennial financial crises: lack of political willingness on the part of organizations and/or their members.

In the face of political constraints, the duty to pay remains an evolving and, like much of international law, an imperfect legal obligation. The UN system does not have a perfected power to tax – even though, under Chapter VII, it has exercised, ironically enough, the power to destroy.

SELECTED BIBLIOGRAPHY

Alvarez, J., "Legal Remedies and the United Nations à la carte Problem," 12 *Mich. J. Int'l L.* 229 (1991)

Franck, T., *Nation against Nation* (Oxford University Press, 1985)

The Power of Legitimacy among Nations (Oxford University Press, 1990)

Kirgis, F., "Admission of Palestine as a Member of a Specialized Agency and Withholding the Payments of Assessments in Response," 84 *AJIL* 218 (1990)

Nelson, R., "International Law and US Withholding of Payments to International Organizations," 80 *AJIL* 973 (1986)

Note: "United Nations Financing of the Law of the Sea Preparatory Commission: May the United States Withhold Payment?," 6 *Fordham Int'l L. J.* 472 (1982–83)

Ogata, S. and P. Volker, *Financing an Effective United Nations* (Ford Foundation Report, 1993)

[125] See, e.g., Stoessinger, note 1 above, at 244–46; Williams, note 1 above, at 110–18; E. Steinberg & J. Yager, *New Means of Financing International Needs* (1978); GAO Report, note 36 above, at 163–78.

Schemers, H., *International Institutional Law* (2d ed., Sijthoff & Noordhoff, 1980)

Steinberg, E. and J. Yager, *New Means of Financing International Needs* (Brookings, 1978)

Stoessinger, J., *Financing the United Nations System* (Brookings Institution, 1967)

Williams, D., *The Specialized Agencies and the United Nations* (St. Martin's Press, 1987)

Zoller, E., "The 'Corporate Will' of the United Nations and the Rights of the Minority," 81 *AJIL* 610 (1987)

CHAPTER SIXTEEN

CONCLUSION: THE UNITED NATIONS AS INTERNATIONAL LAW-GIVER

Christopher C. Joyner

I. INTRODUCTION

The United Nations functions as a political organization and forum where representatives of states convene to discuss and negotiate issues involving international political, social, and economic concerns. The world body is sometimes viewed as an arena where accusations are traded by governments involved in a dispute; or where disparities in socio-economic situations between various countries are rhetorically lamented and sometimes addressed; or where the merits of international sanctions are deliberated and applied by the Great Powers on the Security Council against lesser countries whose activities are condemned as posing threats to the peace. From a more cynical perspective, the United Nations has been depicted in recent years as an ineffective international bureaucracy hobbled by waste, inefficiency, and mismanagement.[1] While certain degrees of truth obviously reside in each of these impressions, none of them accurately reveals the whole picture, purposes, or activities of the United Nations or its successes. Nor do they suggest the broad truth that the United Nations has emerged since World War II for nearly all states as the preeminent institutional source of international law.

The main purposes of the United Nations as set out in the Charter are to "save succeeding generations from the scourge of war"; develop friendly relations among states; cooperate in solving international economic, social, cultural, and humanitarian problems; and promote respect for human rights and fundamental freedoms.[2] To accomplish these objectives, member states over the past five decades have persistently resorted to using

---

[1] See, e.g., John M. Gosho, "Beleaguered UN Struggles to Maintain Peacekeeping Role," *Washington Post*, Oct. 22, 1995, at A24; Thomas W. Lippman, "Florida GOP Freshman Moves to Scuttle the UN," *Washington Post*, Nov. 6, 1995, at A9.

[2] UN Charter, art. 1.

UN institutions and processes to create new international law to address problems accrued from changing circumstances and political developments. This chapter examines the ways and means employed by the United Nations for creating norms, rules, and processes of international law that affect the behavior of states in their interstate relations. In so doing, the purposes and functions of the world body as an international law-giver, as well as the institutions that perform those roles, are highlighted and evaluated. The chief aim of this study then becomes to point out how the United Nations has contributed to the corpus of international law. Some suggestions are also proffered regarding what roles the United Nations might play in the future development of international rules and legal norms.

II. THE ESSENCE OF UNITED NATIONS LAW

The United Nations plays an extensive and sophisticated role as law-giver to the international community. It creates, amends, and implements international law from a variety of sources for its member states. Yet scant appreciation acknowledges that contribution. The fact is that the United Nations is a complex institutional arrangement comprised of six main organs and numerous agencies, many of which constantly remain engaged in making, codifying, or revising international law. This law is often pragmatic and highly utilitarian. It can be negotiated, adopted, adapted, and implemented more easily into the mainstream of international intercourse through the universal forum afforded by the United Nations. Often, too, this role of law-giver evolves into the creation of new legal norms, i.e., those legal principles that are agreed upon as "right" and proper actions, which have become binding on members of the international community and which serve to guide, control, or regulate proper and acceptable conduct among international actors.

III. FORMS OF UNITED NATIONS LAW

The United Nations contributes substantially to making international law by serving as a source, forum, and facilitator of the law-creating process. The rules, principles, and norms generated by UN bodies and processes primarily take the form of public international law, i.e., that law which concerns the structures, powers, and relations of international actors, most directly, its member states.

Rather than being merely procedural, public law created by the United

Nations is mainly substantive. UN-created law in large part has been expressly designed to influence the essence and scope of the rights and obligations of states, with the purpose of influencing the conduct of interstate actions. In this regard, UN law can be broken down into three distinct forms.

First, the United Nations serves as a source of *constitutional or regulatory law*. The Charter, in effect the constitution of the United Nations, embodies the fundamental law of the Organization. It is the Charter that furnishes the body of rules and norms in accordance with which the powers of the world body and its member states have been exercised for five decades. The Charter is intended to give lawful form to the United Nations, to set out the Organization's legal structure, and to provide a legal framework through which the process of international organization might function authoritatively and more effectively.

A second type of law created by the United Nations is *prescriptive, or remedy* law. Such prescriptive law generally aims to lay down authoritative rules, or set out written directives, or establish customary norms that must be followed. It consists of laws that impose obligations to do or forbear from doing certain things, the infraction of which is considered to be an offense not only against the United Nations, but also against international society as a whole. Prescriptive laws may be backed up by punitive sanctions, which have been applied on occasion by the United Nations when certain UN Charter norms and principles have been egregiously breached.

Third, the United Nations supplies a source for varieties of *administrative law*. International administrative law, as the name suggests, aims to manage or supervise the execution of international affairs. Such administrative law includes the rules and regulations governing the operation of the United Nations and its various agencies, the substantive and procedural rules that these agencies formulate and apply pursuant to their regulatory and other administrative functions, and relevant court decisions involving public agencies and states. Though little appreciated outside the United Nations, the body of law for administering internal UN affairs is sophisticated and complex. This should not be surprising, however, since that internal administrative law for the United Nations must oversee more than ten thousand permanent employees,[3] working in over forty agencies,[4] located in sixty-seven states.[5]

---

[3] John M. Goshko, "UN Chief Plans Large Staff Cut to Avert Crisis," *Washington Post*, April 2, 1996, at A10, col. 4; Catherine Toups, "UN Prepared to Do Much Less if Money Woes Aren't Resolved," *Washington Times*, Feb. 22, 1996, at A6.
[4] *Yearbook of the United Nations: Special Edition UN Fiftieth Anniversary*, at x (Boston: Martinus Nijhoff, 1995). [5] *Basic Facts About the United Nations* 223–54 (1992).

It is important to realize that none of these three general forms of UN law are exclusive to any organ or agency alone. Each body in the United Nations contains various rules and procedures that might be construed as being either constitutional, or prescriptive, or administrative in content. Moreover, most bodies in the UN system have their own capabilities to generate new law that might be construed as constitutional, prescriptive, or administrative in effect. The basic point here is that the United Nations in its various capacities can act as an international law-giver. That potential for law-giving is real and frequently realized. The kind of law produced, however, remains dependent upon the context, circumstances, and purposes of that law being created.

IV. THE UNITED NATIONS AS CONSTITUTIONAL LAW-GIVER

The Charter of the United Nations is an instrument of international law.[6] As a multilateral agreement articulating principles and rules for the conduct of states, the UN Charter has become a viable contributor to the development of modern international law. The Charter is significant for its profound influence upon the dynamics of the international process for legal development. More than this, the lasting significance of the Charter lies in its scope and capacity for generating new legal principles and functional agencies which in turn can produce further additions to international law.

The UN Charter establishes a general, multipurpose organization.[7] It also affirms the legally binding quality of key rules for international state conduct, among them principles of nonintervention, peaceful settlement of disputes, decolonization, respect for human rights, the sovereign equality of states, and the duty of cooperation. But the Charter goes far beyond being a statement of agreed principles and rules. It actually authorizes creation of an elaborate system of major organs and subsidiary agencies, numerous committees and commissions, and a nexus of cooperation between the central body and a network of specialized agencies, regional organizations, and nongovernmental organizations throughout the world. The UN Charter furnishes the fundamental constitutional law for

---

[6] Charter of the United Nations with the Statute of the International Court of Justice annexed thereto. *Signed* at San Francisco June 26, 1945, *entered into force* Oct. 24, 1945, 59 Stat. 1031, T.S. 993, 3 Bevans 1153. By 1996 at least 185 states were parties to the UN Charter. As a unique actor, the United Nations Organization also enjoys certain special privileges and immunities under international law. See Convention on the Privileges and Immunities of the United Nations, *done* at New York Feb. 13, 1946, *entered into force* Sept. 17, 1946. 21 UST 1418, TIAS No. 6900, 1 UNTS 16, 90 UNTS 327 (corrigendum). www.un.org/Depts/Treaty/bible/ Part_I_E/III_III_I.html.

[7] See UN Charter, art. 7 and Chapters IV, V, X, XIII, XIV, and XV.

operating the only general purpose, near-universal organization operating in the world today.

Each major organ in the UN family makes significant contributions to fashioning the rule of law among states. Indeed, the United Nations itself is the product of international law. The UN Charter is a multilateral agreement – an international convention – to which 185 member governments have pledged their obligations, with attendant rights and duties.[8] The United Nations is comprised of six major organs: the General Assembly, Security Council, International Court of Justice, Trusteeship Council, Secretariat, and Economic and Social Council. Each of these organs, to varying degrees, makes salient contributions to the international rule of law. As a constitutional instrument, then, the Charter legitimizes the authority, structure, and functions of these various UN components.

A. The International Court of Justice

The UN organ perhaps most visible for its role in affecting the international legal process is the International Court of Justice (ICJ). This court is the principal juridical arm of the United Nations, and its Statute remains an integral part of the Charter. By ratifying the Charter, governments perforce become obligated to accept the Statute as well.[9] In its deliberations, the ICJ clarifies the rule and role of international law. In the process, the Court may interpret the legal implications of the UN Charter for the Organization as well as its membership and also contributes to facilitating application of that constitutional law internationally.

The World Court performs juridical duties independently of other UN organs and reaches decisions on the basis of international law, not international political considerations. Only governments of states may appear before the Court, and decisions by the Court apply only to the governments involved. Importantly, ICJ decisions do not constitute or rely on precedents that bind the Court's subsequent decisions. That is, the ICJ does not abide by the practice of *stare decisis*. Rather, each decision rendered by the Court is deliberated on an *ad hoc* basis, as determined by the facts of that particular case, without binding implications for future cases. Even so, ICJ decisions are widely recognized as important statements of existing international law, and they are often cited as authority to support fundamental principles or precepts of international legal development.

[8] The United Nations, "United Nations Member States," www.un.org/Overview/unmember.html (Apr. 4, 1996).

[9] Interestingly enough, more governments have subscribed to obligations under the Statute of the ICJ than to the UN Charter itself. In 1996, there are 187 parties to the Statute, whereas only 185 states had accepted membership in the UN. The two non-UN parties to the Statute are Switzerland and Nauru.

Decisions of the ICJ are final and binding, with no possibility of appeal. Such finality of the Court's decision no doubt has dissuaded governments from rushing to seek its deliberations in settling longstanding disputes. Persistent political stalemate has been viewed by states as preferable to the possibility of losing in court. As a consequence, the ICJ historically has assumed less than a notably active role in the international juridical process. Since 1946, a total of ninety-six cases have been submitted to the tribunal. Of those, the Court has rendered sixty judgments, of which thirty-nine have been on the merits. The ICJ has rendered twenty-one advisory opinions since its creation.[10] That amounts to the Court hearing an average of less than two cases each year. Yet, since 1993, the Court has experienced a redirection in course, as it has become particularly active. There are in 1996 at least eight contentious cases on the ICJ docket, as well as two requests for advisory opinions.[11] This development suggests that governments are coming to recognize the value of impartial judicial settlement over the frustration produced by protracted nonresolution of international disputes.

The Court contributes directly and indirectly to international law-making. Many cases pertain to boundary disputes, or disputes over jurisdiction in given areas (e.g., maritime claims and continental shelf delimitation). An ICJ decision effectively determines the legal status of that territory. Hence, the Court furnishes a means for settling bilateral disputes lawfully, peacefully, with formal adversarial procedures. States are offered the opportunity to resolve their differences through the rule of law, rather than through resort to armed force. Importantly, each World Court decision directly contributes to the body of law regulating the specific behavior between the disputants. Moreover, to the extent that certain principles set out in ICJ cases become adopted in state practice generally, international law can be affected in broader scope.[12]

B. Other United Nations tribunals

The United Nations has recently expanded its juridical functions by creating special international tribunals that deal with violations of humanitarian law in the former Yugoslavia and in Rwanda. Coming in reaction to genocidal atrocities and ethnic cleansing perpetrated by Bosnian Serbs against Muslims in Bosnia–Herzegovina, in 1993 the Security Council

[10] Letter from Eduardo Valencia-Ospina, Registrar, International Court of Justice, The Hague, to the author, dated April 17, 1996.
[11] Peter H. F. Bekker, "Recent Developments at the World Court," *ASIL Newsletter* (Jan.–Feb. 1996), at 2.
[12] For a recent appraisal of the Court, See generally Robert Y. Jennings, "The International Court of Justice after Fifty Years," 89 *AJIL* 493 (1995).

created the war crimes tribunal for the former Yugoslavia.[13] In the aftermath of the massacre of 500,000 Rwandans in 1994, the Security Council acted similarly to set up a special tribunal to deal with persons accused of committing crimes against humanity and genocide in that tribally instigated bloodbath.[14] Both juridical bodies are *ad hoc*, criminal courts created by Security Council resolutions. Modeled after the 1945 Nuremberg Military Tribunal, the decisions of both tribunals are legally binding. No death penalty can be imposed, however. Although the jurisdiction and prosecutorial purposes of both the Bosnian and Rwandan tribunals are limited to criminal activities in those states, the success or failure of their performance may be viewed as an indication of the real prospects for the successful establishment of an international criminal court.[15] No question exists that should an International Criminal Court eventually be established, the administrative function and scope of the United Nations would be authoritatively enhanced. Similarly, the experience of the Bosnian and Rwandan tribunals are likely to weigh heavily in determining the prospects for such an international criminal court.

V. THE UNITED NATIONS AS PRESCRIPTIVE LAW-GIVER

The UN Charter codifies certain principles of international law to regulate relations among states. The most fundamental obligations among these principles for all members are, first, to refrain from the threat or use of force against other states or in any manner inconsistent with the purpose of the Charter (as contained in Article 2(4)) and second, to settle their disputes by peaceful means (as contained in Article 33). These obligations are departures from international law's traditionally more permissive – or at least more ambiguous – attitude on the use of force. The Charter aims to make those obligations universal among the UN membership.

While the means for UN enforcement and degrees of state compliance with the United Nations' use-of-force provisions have been uneven and at times ineffective, these principles have been applied by the United Nations (in particular, the Security Council) in considering disputes and attempting to minimize violence in interstate behavior. Despite remarkable growth in the number of states, increased frequency of state contact, and expanded sources of interstate tension over the past five decades, the scale and scope of international conflict has not approached the level of world war. While the

---

[13] UN Doc. S/RES/808, at para. 1 (1993). For discussion, see Christopher C. Joyner, "Enforcing Human Rights Standards in the Former Yugoslavia: The Case for an International War Crimes Tribunal," 22 *Denv. J. Int'l L. & Pol'y* 235 (1994).

[14] UN Doc. S/RES/955, annex (1994).

[15] See generally James Crawford, "The ILC Adopts a Statute for an International Criminal Court," 89 *AJIL* 404 (1995).

United Nations' contribution to this trend is debatable, the prescriptive principles in the UN Charter have delineated more clearly the permissible legal perimeters for using force in interstate relations.

A. The Security Council

Under the United Nations system, responsibility for maintaining international peace and security falls to the Security Council. As provided for in the Charter, the Security Council has as its main functions the responsibility to settle disputes peacefully (under Chapter VI) and to meet threats to or breaches of the peace with concerted action by the Organization (Chapter VII). In carrying out these functions, the Security Council is clearly empowered with the authority to make decisions binding upon the entire UN membership. In accepting the Charter, each member state agrees that the Security Council can act on its behalf and that it will carry out certain decisions as stipulated by the Security Council.[16] This means in legal effect that certain Security Council resolutions are binding upon all members of the United Nations, specifically those resolutions that contain action statements averring that "the Security Council decides that . . ." Such resolutions are considered to be fiats from the Security Council, endowed with the binding force of legal obligation on member states as a whole.

Security Council resolutions that pertain to international disputes, threats to the peace, breaches of the peace, or acts of aggression are prescriptive and often carry the force of law, and members are expected to abide by those fiats. The scope of Security Council resolutions has been dramatized since 1990 by a number of sanctions measures enacted by the United Nations against transgressor states.[17] Legally binding sanctions measures adopted by the Security Council remain in force against several states, including Iraq,[18] Libya,[19] Liberia,[20] Somalia,[21] Angola,[22] and until

---

[16] In full, Article 24, paragraph 1 of the Charter provides that:

In order to ensure prompt and effective action by the United Nations, its Members confer on the Security Council primary responsibility for the maintenance of international peace and security, and agree that in carrying out its duties under this responsibility the Security Council acts on their behalf.

UN Charter, art. 24(1).

[17] See generally Christopher C. Joyner, "Collective Sanctions as Peaceful Coercion: Lessons from the United Nations Experience," *Austl. Y. B. Int'l L.* 241–70 (Australia National University: Centre for Public and International Law, 1996).

[18] SC Res. 660 (Aug. 2, 1990).

[19] SC Res. 748 (Mar. 31, 1992). See the discussion in Christopher C. Joyner & Wayne Rothbaum, "Libya and the Aerial Incident at Lockerbie: What Lessons for International Extradition Law?," 14 *Mich. J. Int'l L.* 222 (1993).

[20] SC Res. 788 (Nov. 19, 1992).

[21] SC Res. 733 (Jan. 23, 1992).   [22] SC Res. 864 (Sept. 15, 1993).

1995, against the former Yugoslavia[23] and Haiti[24] as well. Earlier sanctions measures were directed against the white minority regimes in Rhodesia from 1968 to 1980[25] and more diversely, against South Africa from 1977 to 1994.[26]

An admittedly important distinction exists between the obligation of a state to abide by a mandatory Security Council measure and that state's resultant compliance with it. Obligations flowing from certain Security Council resolutions are legally binding. They are deemed compulsory under international law. Yet, at times governments have resisted complying with those obligations. The reasons for such reluctance vary – from adverse international political pressures, to domestic economic considerations, to social or cultural inhibitions, and perhaps even to outright indifference. The fact remains, though, that the Security Council possesses the authority to create international law – to impose binding obligations acknowledged by all members – and that it has often done so over the past five decades. From its first meeting in 1945 through mid-1996, the Security Council has adopted 1,049 resolutions, of which 409 qualify as binding law for the international community.[27] That is undoubtedly an impressive accomplishment, albeit one still underappreciated in the modern development of international law.[28]

B. The General Assembly

While the General Assembly somewhat resembles a global parliament, it clearly is not a legislature *per se*. Except for budgetary or membership questions, the General Assembly does not have explicit authority to fashion, adopt, and implement binding legal norms or fiats upon any of the United Nations membership absent each government's sovereign consent. The power to issue legal norms is not supplied to the General Assembly by the UN Charter, nor by any binding declaration, nor by state practice. Still, the General Assembly evokes a certain "quasi-legislative" capability that can directly influence the nature and substance of contemporary international law in a number of ways. In this way, the General Assembly

---

[23] SC Res. 713 (Sept. 25, 1991). [24] SC Res. 841 (June 16, 1993).

[25] SC Res. 221 (Apr. 9, 1966) and SC Res. 232 (Dec. 16, 1966).

[26] SC Res. 418 (November 8, 1977). See the discussion in Louis B. Sohn, "Interpreting the Law," in *United Nations Legal Order* 169–230. (O. Schachter & C. Joyner eds., 1995). (hereinafter cited as O. Schachter & C. Joyner).

[27] This figure was arrived at by perusing every Security Council resolution since 1945 to determine whether the Council "decided" that an action should be taken by member states of the organization. UN *Security Council Decisions & Resolutions*, 1945–1996. Thanks are due to George Little for assistance in this effort.

[28] For a recent assessment of the Security Council, see Frederic L. Kirgis, Jr., "The Security Council's First Fifty Years," 89 *AJIL* 506 (1995).

contributes to the corpus of prescriptive law furnished by the United Nations.

The legal competence of the General Assembly to contemplate legal matters flows from the UN Charter. Article 10 gives the General Assembly the authority to discuss and make recommendations on any matter within the scope of the Charter, either to the United Nations membership generally, or to the Security Council in particular.[29] The General Assembly is also given the duty to initiate studies and make recommendations for purposes of promoting international political cooperation and encouraging the progressive development of international law and its codification. Other studies and recommendations undertaken by the General Assembly should be aimed at promoting international cooperation regarding economic, social, cultural, educational, and health matters, and assisting in the realization of human rights and fundamental freedoms, without distinction as to race, sex, language, or religion.[30] Thus, the General Assembly's powers to recommend actions that enhance the norm-creating process of international law plainly serve a prescriptive purpose.

Formal consideration of international law within the United Nations falls mainly to the General Assembly, which uses two principal institutions to encourage the progressive development and codification of the law of nations, namely, the Sixth (Legal) Committee of the General Assembly and the International Law Commission (ILC). The Sixth Committee is entrusted with the consideration of legal issues that are of concern to the Assembly. Other topics with which the Sixth Committee is currently concerned include, *inter alia*, measures to eliminate terrorism, nonnavigational uses of international waters, activities of the UN Commission on International Trade Law, jurisdictional immunities of states and their property, and the safety and security of United Nations personnel.

The Sixth Committee makes its own reports on each of these topics. In addition, it has the responsibility of examining reports on legal matters to the General Assembly from other UN bodies. The Sixth Committee, moreover, can draft texts of international conventions, which are then presented to member states in the General Assembly for approval. Perhaps most notable among the products of this drafting process is the 1948 Convention on the Prevention and Punishment of the Crime of Genocide.[31]

---

[29] UN Charter, art. 10. The right of the General Assembly to make recommendations is explicitly circumscribed if those recommendations concern disputes then being debated by the Security Council, unless the Council so requests. UN Charter, art. 12(1).

[30] *Ibid.*, art. 13(1)(b).

[31] Convention on the Prevention and Punishment of the Crime of Genocide, *done* Dec. 9, 1948, *entered into force* Jan. 12, 1951. 78 UNTS 277.

The International Law Commission (ILC), comprised of thirty-four jurists, has been prominent in the General Assembly's efforts to foster codification of international law. The ILC acts as a study and composition group to discuss, design, and draft international conventions. These conventions are then submitted for debate in the General Assembly, and if deemed necessary and appropriate, are presented to the international community for ratification as multilateral agreements.

While the ILC's "codification" endeavors are certainly laudatory, they are often criticized for being tedious and overly ponderous.[32] The treaty-drafting process alone may often be prolonged a decade or more, which is an inordinately protracted period for considering an international instrument given the modern era of spectacular and rapid scientific and technological advancement. For example, the question of state responsibility has preoccupied the ILC's attention since 1953, albeit only with mixed success at producing agreed-upon conclusions on the law and its relevant implications for state behavior.[33] Similarly, for nearly five decades the ILC has considered and worked on a draft code of offenses against the peace and security of mankind,[34] as well as a draft statute for an International Criminal Court.[35] Still, the ILC has produced a number of successful draft instruments, among them the four 1958 Geneva Conventions on the Law of the Sea,[36] the 1961 Vienna Convention on Diplomatic Relations,[37] the 1969 Vienna Convention on the Law of Treaties,[38] and the 1973

---

[32] For commentary on recent ILC activities, see Robert Rosenstock, "The Forty-sixth Session of the International Law Commission," 89 *AJIL* 390 (1995).

[33] See International Law Commission, Draft Articles on the Origin of State Responsibility, II (II) *Y. B. Int'l L. Comm.* 30–34 (1980).

[34] In 1991 the Commission adopted a Draft Code of Offenses upon its first reading. See Twelfth Report on the Draft Code of Crimes against the Peace and Security of Mankind, submitted by Doudou Thiam, UN Doc, A/CN.4/460 (1994). For an insightful assessment, see M. Cherif Bassiouni, Commentaries on the International Law Commission's 1991 Draft Code of Crimes against the Peace and Security of Mankind (Nouvelles Etudes Penales No. 11, 1993). Also compare Draft Code of Offences against the Peace and Security of Mankind, UN GAOR, 9th Sess., 504th plen. mtg., Supp. No. 7, UN Doc. 898 (IX) (1954).

[35] International Law Commission Revised Report of the Working Group on the Draft Statute for an International Criminal Court, UN Doc. A/CN.4/L.490 (1993). For an appraisal, see James Crawford, "The ILC's Draft Statute for an International Criminal Court," 88 *AJIL* 140 (1994).

[36] Convention on the High Seas, *done* at Geneva Apr. 29, 1958, *entered into force* Sept. 30, 1962, 13 UST 2312, TIAS 5200, 450 UNTS 82; Convention on the Continental Shelf, *done* at Geneva Apr. 298, 1958, *entered into force* June 10, 1964. 15 UST 471, TIAS 5578, 499 UNTS 471; Convention on the Territorial Sea and the Contiguous Zone, *done* at Geneva Apr. 29, 1958, *entered into force* Sept. 10, 1964. 15 UST 1606 516, TIAS 5639, UNTS 205; and Convention on Fishing and Conservation of Living Resources of the High Seas, *done* at Geneva Apr. 29, 1958, *entered into force* Mar. 20, 1966. 17 UST 138, TIAS 5969, 559 UNTS 285.

[37] *Done* Apr. 18, 1961, *entered into force* Apr. 24, 1964. 500 UNTS 95, 23 UST 3227.

[38] *Adopted* May 22, 1969, *opened for signature* May 23, 1969, *entered into force* Jan. 27, 1990. UN Conference on the Law of Treaties, 1st & 2nd Sess., UN Doc. A/CONF. 39/27 (1969), at 289.

Convention on the Prevention and Punishment of Crimes against Internationally Protected Persons, Including Diplomatic Agents.[39] The ILC also produced the 1978 Convention on the Succession of States in Respect of Treaties[40] and its companion instrument, the 1978 Convention on the Succession of States in Respect of State Property, Archives, and Debts,[41] although neither of them yet is in force.

Perhaps the General Assembly's most salient role in shaping prescriptive law derives from its right to formulate and adopt international resolutions as delegated by Article 10 in the Charter. Since 1945, at least 9,229 resolutions spanning a vast and varied range of international issues have been adopted by the General Assembly.[42] While this record of the General Assembly's formal concern, deliberation, and articulation of views is indeed impressive, the fact remains that, except for budget and membership questions, General Assembly resolutions are *not* legally binding on member states. These resolutions are only recommendations – and thus only advisory and hortatory measures – without any specific legally binding authority attached. The General Assembly may draft, approve, and recommend international instruments for multilateral agreement. That body can not, however, compel them as binding obligations upon member states. The General Assembly performs as a political organ in its deliberations. It was never intended to be a world legislature for authorizing resolute actions or for imposing legally binding remedies on its membership.

Although the legal status of General Assembly resolutions is unmistakably nonbinding, these instruments have frequently served as the genesis for subsequent multilateral treaties drafted and promulgated under UN auspices. General Assembly "declarations," largely because of their bold assertive quality, have demonstrated the greatest likelihood of evolving into conventions adopted by the international community. Prominent among the many conventions dealing with the use of force that have grown out of UN General Assembly declarations are the 1967 Outer Space Treaty,[43] the 1968 Treaty on the Nonproliferation of Nuclear Weapons,[44] and the 1971

---

[39] TIAS No. 8532, reprinted in 13 *ILM* 41 (1977), *adopted* Dec. 14, 1973 by GA Res. 3166 (Annex), 28 GAOR, Supp. 30, UN Doc. A/9030), *entered into force* Feb. 20, 1977.

[40] *Done* Aug. 23, 1978, not yet in force. UN Pub. Sales No. F.79.V. 10.

[41] *Adopted* Apr. 7, 1983, *opened for signature* Apr. 8, 1983. UN Doc. A/CONF.117/14, 36 UN GAOR, Supp. (No. 51), 243.

[42] This figure was complied by comprehensively searching the *UN General Assembly Official Records* from 1945 to 1996. Thanks are due to George Little for this research effort.

[43] *Done* Jan. 27, 1967, *entered into force* Oct. 10, 1967. 18 UST 2410, TIAS 6347, 610 UNTS 205. See Declaration of Legal Principles Governing the Activities of States in the Exploration and Use of Outer Space, GA Res. 1962 (XVIII) (Dec. 13, 1963), 18 UN GAOR Supp. (No. 15) 15–16, UN Doc. A/5515 (1963); Resolution Regarding Weapons of Mass Destruction in Outer Space, Oct. 17, 1963, UN GA Res. 1884 (XVIII), 18 UN GAOR Supp. (No. 15) 13, UN Doc. A/5515 (1964).

[44] *Done* July 1, 1968, *entered into force* Mar. 5, 1970. 21 UST 483, TIAS 6839, 729 UNTS 161.

Seabed Arms Control Treaty.[45] Also noteworthy is that practically all of the international law pertaining to outer space has evolved from resolutions deliberated upon and produced by the General Assembly's Committee on the Peaceful Uses of Outer Space (COPUOS), which were then adopted by the General Assembly, and subsequently gave rise to appropriate international conventions.[46]

Agreements on human rights have also been generated by General Assembly resolutions. Concern by the General Assembly for human rights is long standing and clearly evident in the Universal Declaration on Human Rights, adopted without formal opposition in 1948.[47] Similarly, General Assembly resolutions were legal catalysts for producing in 1966 two other cornerstones of modern human rights law, the International Covenant on Civil and Political Rights[48] and the International Covenant on Economic, Social and Cultural Rights.[49] No less impressive, though, is the panoply of additional human rights law to which the General Assembly has contributed over the past two decades. Promoted by General Assembly resolutions, major international conventions have been promulgated to prohibit all forms of racial discrimination,[50] suppress and punish the crime of apartheid,[51] eliminate discrimination against women,[52]

---

[45] Treaty on the Prohibition of the Emplacement of Nuclear Weapons and Other Weapons of Mass Destruction on the Seabed and Ocean Floor and in the Subsoil Thereof, 23 UST 701, TIAS No. 7337, reprinted in 10 *ILM* 146 (1971).

[46] Other basic instruments pertaining to activities in outer space include the Agreement on the Rescue and Return of Astronauts, and the Return of Objects Launched into Space, *done* Apr. 22, 1968, *entered into force* Dec. 3, 1968, 19 UST 7570, TIAS No. 6599, 672 UNTS 119; Convention on International Liability for Damage Caused by Space Objects, *done* Mar. 29, 1972, *entered into force* Sept. 1, 1972, 24 UST 2389, TIAS No. 7762, 961 UNTS 1187; Convention on Registration of Objects Launched into Space, *done* Jan. 14, 1975, *entered into force* Sept. 15, 1976, 28 UST 695, TIAS No. 8480, 1023 UNTS 15. See the discussion in Ralph G. Steinhardt, "Outer Space," ch. 12 in this volume.

[47] G.A. Res. 217 (III), (Dec. 10, 1948). 3 UN GAOR, Res. UN Doc. A/810, p. 71.

[48] *Opened for signature* Dec. 10, 1966, *entered into force* Mar. 23, 1976. 999 UNTS 171. See also GA Res. 2200 (XXI), 21 UN GAOR, Supp. (NO. 16), 52, UN Doc. A/6316 (1967).

[49] *Opened for signature* Dec. 19, 1966, *entered into force* Jan. 3, 1976. 993 UNTS 3. See also UN GA Res. 2200 (XXI), 21 UN GAOR, Supp. (No. 16), 49, UN Doc. A/6316 (1967).

[50] Convention on the Elimination of All Forms of Racial Discrimination, *opened for signature* March 7, 1966, *entered into force* Jan. 4, 1969, 660 UNTS 195, reprinted in 5 *ILM* 352 (1966). As of 1996, at least 140 states were parties to this agreement.

[51] International Convention on the Suppression and Punishment of the Crime of Apartheid, *done* Nov. 30, 1973, *entered into force* July 18, 1976. GA Res. 3068 (XXVIII). This Convention was promoted by GA Res. 3068 (XXVIII), 28 UN GAOR, Supp. (No. 30) 75, UN Doc. A/9030 (1974), reprinted in 13 *ILM* 50 (1974).

[52] Convention on the Elimination of All Forms of Discrimination against Women, GA Res. 280 (XXXIV), *opened for signature* Dec. 18, 1979, *entered into force* Sept. 3, 1980, reprinted in 19 *ILM* 33 (1980). See Declaration on the Elimination of Discrimination against Women, Nov. 7, 1967, GA Res. 2263 (XXII), 22 UN GAOR (Supp. No. 16 35, UN Doc. A/6880 (1968). By 1996, 151 states had become parties to the Women's Convention. See the analysis on "Women" by Rebecca J. Cook, ch. 7 in this volume.

protect the rights of the child,[53] prohibit hostage-taking,[54] and outlaw torture.[55]

General Assembly resolutions have contributed also to defining more clearly certain general principles of international law for state practice. Indeed, perhaps the most detailed expression outlining the international legal obligations of states is supplied by General Assembly Resolution 2625, the 1971 Declaration of Principles of Law Concerning Friendly Relations and Cooperation among States.[56] General Assembly resolutions, moreover, have articulated and reified important legal principles that specifically aim to keep pace with the transforming nature of the international system and the emergence of nearly 120 new independent states since 1960. Little question exists that resolutions adopted by the General Assembly have contributed substantially to affirming the legitimate authority of nondiscrimination, nonaggression, self-determination, and decolonization as acknowledged principles of international law. Also significant is that General Assembly resolutions have been used by developing countries as vehicles to introduce new concepts to the international community that eventually aim at attaining the status of general principles of international law. Outstanding among such principles that have been recently developed are the common heritage of mankind,[57] criminalization of apartheid,[58] and permanent sovereignty over natural resources.[59]

---

[53] Convention on the Rights of the Child, *opened for signature* Nov. 20, 1989, *entered into force* Sept. 2, 1990. See GA Res. 1386, 14 GAOR, Supp. (No. 16) 19-20, UN Doc. A/4354 (1959). By March 1996, at least 187 states had become parties to the Rights of the Child Convention.

[54] International Convention against the Taking of Hostages, *adopted* by the General Assembly on Dec. 17, 1979, GA Res. 34/14b (XXXIV), *entered into force* June 3, 1983. reprinted in 18 *ILM* 1456 (1979). TIAS 11081, 1316 UNTS 205. By March 1996, at least seventy-two states were parties to this instrument.

[55] Convention against Torture and Other Cruel, Inhuman or Degrading Treatment or Punishment, *adopted by* GA Res. 39/46/Annex (Dec. 10, 1984), 39 UN GAOR Supp (No. 51), 197, UN Doc. A/39/51. *Entered into force* June 26, 1987. By March 1996 at least ninety-four states had become parties to the Convention. See also Declaration on the Protection of All Persons from Being Subjected to Torture and Other Cruel, Inhuman or Degrading Treatment or Punishment, GA Res. 3452 (XXIX) (Dec. 9, 1975). For a general assessment of human rights law promulgated by the United Nations, see Hurst Hannum, "Human Rights," ch. 5 in this volume.

[56] Declaration of Principles of Law Concerning Friendly Relations and Cooperation among States in Accordance with the Charter of the United Nations, GA Res. 2625 (XXV) (Oct. 24, 1970), 25 UN GAOR (Supp. 28), UN Doc. A/8028, at 121 (1970).

[57] See GA Res. 2749, 25 UN GAOR, Supp. (No. 27) 24, UN Doc. A/8027 (1970). Significantly, this resolution was adopted by 108 in favor to none opposed, with 14 abstentions.

[58] Adopted by UN GA Res. 3068 (XXVIII), 28 UN GAOR, Supp. (No. 30) 75, UN Doc. A/9030 (1974).

[59] See GA Res. 1803 (XVII), 17 UN GAOR, Supp. (No. 17) 15, UN Doc. A/5217 (1963).

The General Assembly thus is not a world legislature. It does not make international rules or statutes as such. It does not codify international laws or norms through its resolutions, even if they are adopted unanimously, repeatedly, or without any formal opposition. General Assembly resolutions are merely recommendations. But in several instances declarations by the General Assembly can function as instruments to distill and crystallize into tangible form the international community's consensus regarding a customary norm. Through such a distillation–crystallization procedure, the resolution is presented to the international community for its acceptance or rejection. State practice, then, becomes the main factor determining whether General Assembly resolutions give rise to new norms of international law, or remain merely recommendations for action. Such new norms subsequently are codified into recognized principles of international law through the promulgation of special conventions adopted by the General Assembly and ratified by the requisite number of parties.

VI. THE UNITED NATIONS AS ADMINISTRATIVE LAW-GIVER

Administrative law is generally thought of as law concerning the powers and procedures of administrative agencies, especially law governing judicial review of administrative action. Administrative law thus aims at several objectives: to resolve particular controversies over discretionary administrative powers; to search for means to obtain justice; to reconcile desires for freedom with demands for good governance; and to formulate policies that reflect the democratic will. In essence, then, within the UN system, administrative law treats that law concerning powers, procedures, and judicial review affecting United Nations administrative agencies.

In these regards, the United Nations has contributed to the formulation of international administrative law in three special ways: first, through the administrative duties and operation of the Secretariat generally and the person of the Secretary-General in particular, as the coordinator of internal UN law and a good officer for international dispute settlement; second, through the successful administrative experience of the Trusteeship Council in preparing nonself-governing territories for their eventual independence; and third, through the Economic and Social Council and administration of its appended specialized agencies. Clearly, though, it is the Secretariat that performs the hallmark administrative legal function for the UN system.

A. The Secretariat

Administrative legal functions affecting the entire United Nations Organization are performed substantially by the Secretariat. The role of the UN

Secretariat in creating international law is multifaceted. Headed by the Secretary-General, the Secretariat generally engages in promoting agreement among governments through quiet diplomacy, good offices, and reconciliation of national differences over international legal concerns. For example, establishing and maintaining UN peacekeeping missions requires the Secretary-General to play pivotal roles as both administrator and diplomat.

The Secretariat remains constantly involved in numerous international negotiations having legal purpose or intent. For example, peacekeeping, refugee relief, humanitarian aid programs, and technical assistance projects are all processed through and administered by offices in the Secretariat, with legal accountability devolving to the respective supervisory agencies. Also of great significance, the Secretariat is responsible for planning and coordinating more than 5,000 meetings and international conferences sponsored annually under UN auspices. These conferences, which nearly always involve scores of governments negotiating issues of international legal concern, can generate new hard international law in the form of binding international conventions negotiated and opened for signature.[60] Or, as is often the case, these UN meetings produce new "soft" international law in the form of formal declarations, action plans, or conference statements.[61] While not legally binding, such instruments still retain normative value by demonstrating the range of international opinion and strength of consensus on a particular issue, as well as the degree of state behavior affecting it.

A chief function of the Secretariat is to facilitate resolution of controversies and disputes between governments of member states. In performing this role, Secretariat personnel are often called upon to serve as mediators, conciliators, or consensus builders – all processes that can contribute to the peaceful settlement of international disputes and hence the rule of law. By way of example, the Secretariat (and Secretary-General) actively worked to negotiate a cease-fire for the Iran–Iraq war, as well as to end recent conflicts in Afghanistan, Cyprus, Namibia, the Falkland Islands, Lebanon, Cambodia, and the former Yugoslavia. Clearly the Secretary-General through

---

[60] For example, at the 1992 UN Conference on the Environment and Development, international conventions were produced on climate change and biodiversity. See United Nations Framework Convention on Climate Change, *done* May 9, 1992, *entered into force* March 21, 1994. By April 1996, at least 155 states were party to this Convention. See Convention on Biological Diversity, *done* June 5, 1992, *entered into force* Dec. 29, 1993. In April 1996, 146 states were party to the Biodiversity Agreement. More recently, in August 1995, a special UN Conference produced an international fishery agreement on straddling stocks and migratory species.

[61] For example, Agenda 21, the Statement on Forestry Principles, and the Declaration on the Environment and Development which came out of the 1992 United Nations Conference on the Environment and Development. See the discussion in Ved P. Nanda, "Environment," ch. 10 in this volume.

quiet diplomacy has the opportunity to play a pivotal role in international dispute settlement. By so doing, he can contribute to peaceful relations between states and thereby permit international law more effectively to affect the mutual relations of both former disputants.

As regards international law, the Secretariat serves as an officially designated world depository for international agreements. More than 45,000 international treaties, conventions, and other international instruments are registered with the UN Secretariat – a realization that highlights both the scope and depth of international legal relations today. Further, the *United Nations Treaty Series* is an authoritative registry of international legal agreements, and for most governments that fact contributes to the authoritative legitimacy of those instruments.

As an administrative legal body, the Secretariat supplies information and advice to member governments on a variety of subjects. That power of information can have substantial influence on shaping the attitudes of member states toward international legal questions and issues. It is not surprising, then, that the General Assembly often requests that the Secretary-General prepare reports, studies, or policy analyses of particular questions under consideration. Such reports carry the weight of institutional legitimacy and political impartiality.

The Secretariat is also responsible for administering the rule of law inside the UN Organization. The United Nations has nearly 10,000 employees. Such a high degree of interpersonal contacts cannot help but create conflicts, grievances, and at times even criminal activities among the population. It falls to the Secretariat to administer internal law throughout the organization – law that aims at ensuring due process is carried out, with hearings, prosecutions, and penalties imposed to fit the crime.[62]

B. The Trusteeship Council

The Trusteeship Council was created as an original UN organ in the Charter to administer and supervise nonself-governing territories for which the United Nations was given responsibility after World War II.[63] In the five decades since the Trusteeship Council began functioning, all of these trusteeship territories either gained their independence or were assimilated into other states. The last remnant of the UN Trusteeship system, the small island of Palau which had been part of the United States Strategic Trust

---

[62] See Robert Jordan, "Law of the International Civil Service," ch. 14 in this volume.
[63] See UN Charter, Chapters XII and XIII.

Territory in the Pacific,[64] gained its independence in 1994 and is now itself a member state of the United Nations. As a consequence, by its very success the Trusteeship Council has been rendered defunct, as its main purpose has been fully accomplished.

Though often slighted among UN institutions, the Trusteeship Council was responsible for actually carrying out a cardinal function of international law – the creation of new international legal actors. Responsibility was assigned to the Trusteeship Council for preparing former colonies and mandates left over from the League of Nations to be new states – states with the capability of participating in the international legal system as independent, sovereign, self-governing polities. The Council successfully performed that mission, as patently evidenced by the impressive list of states that came as the direct product of its administrative legal supervision: Jordan, Israel, Syria, Cameroon, Rwanda, Burundi, Tanzania (with Zanzibar), Togo, Nauru, Papua New Guinea, Somalia, Namibia, the Marshall Islands, Micronesia, Northern Marianas, and Western Samoa – all formerly were trust territories that attained independence under the administrative legal supervision of the Trusteeship Council.

C. The Economic and Social Council and specialized agencies

The Economic and Social Council (ECOSOC), composed of fifty-four members elected by the General Assembly, focuses concern on international economic, social, cultural, educational, and health matters. The ECOSOC consequently engages in a broad range of studies dealing with international legal issues including, *inter alia*, narcotic drug control, water use, trade, refugees, the environment, status of women, and so forth.[65] Importantly, though, the ECOSOC only has the power to recommend. It reports and makes recommendations to the General Assembly. The real law-making significance of the ECOSOC therefore rests in its administrative links to the specialized agencies. It is through these sixteen functional agencies, as well as the International Atomic Energy Agency and General Agreement on Tariffs and Trade, that a tremendous wealth of international law is proposed and codified for member states. In this regard, the ECOSOC acts as a coordinating agent for much of the UN system, with attendant administrative and supervisory legal responsibilities.[66]

Significantly, each functional agency operates under its own interna-

---

[64] As a special "strategic" trust territory, Palau was actually placed under the administrative aegis of the Security Council, which cooperated with the Trusteeship Council in overseeing the area. See UN Charter, art. 83.   [65] See UN Charter, Chapter IX.

[66] See UN Charter, Chapter X.

tional charter or constitution. In acting as an independent body, each agency has its own institutions, membership, rules, procedures, and law-making capability. Consequently, each agency functions lawfully as a separate administrative organization, with responsibility over its own internal affairs and legal dealings. Some specialized agencies are technical organizations and convene their own meeting sessions, deliberate policies, take decisions, and often negotiate and draft international legal agreements that address particular problems of concern. For each functional agency, however, the ability to create and administer international law is essential. Some brief comment on each agency, therefore, reveals the broad scope and reach of their international law-making capacity.

The Food and Agriculture Organization was established in 1945 to raise nutritional level and living standards and to secure improvements in production and distribution of food and agricultural products. With a membership of 171 states, the FAO has negotiated numerous international agreements and institutional arrangements to deal with the changing place of food and agriculture in international relations.[67]

The International Bank for Reconstruction and Development (World Bank) was established in 1945 to provide loans and technical assistance for economic development in developing countries.[68] The World Bank facilitates capital investment and co-financing of projects from public and private sources. Agreements made between the IBRD and its present membership of 179 states are legally binding and often place conditions on recipient states.[69]

The International Development Association, created in 1960 and affiliated with the World Bank, provides funds for development on concessional terms to developing countries. Transactions between the IDA and recipient states are treated as legally binding agreements.[70]

Established in 1956 as a separate legal entity, the International Finance Corporation aims to promote economic development by encouraging the

[67] Constitution of the United Nations Food and Agriculture Organization, *done* at Quebec Oct. 16, 1945, *entered into force* Oct. 1945, 12 UST 980, TIAS No. 4803. For a comprehensive assessment, see Jean Pierre Dobbert, "Food and Agriculture," in O. Schachter & C. Joyner, note 26 above, at 907–92.
[68] Articles of Agreement of the International Bank for Reconstruction and Development, *done* at the Bretton Woods Conference July 1–22, 1994, *opened for signature* Dec. 27, 1945, *entered into force* Dec. 27, 1945. 60 Stat. 1440, TIAS No. 1502; 3 Bevans 1390, 2 UNTS 134.
[69] The World Bank, "The World Bank: A Global Partnership for Development." www.worldbank.org./html/glance.html (Apr. 1, 1996). See generally the discussion in Stephen Zamora, "Economic Relations and Development," ch. 9 in this volume.
[70] Articles of Agreement of the International Development Association, *done* at Washington, DC on Jan. 26, 1960, *entered into force* Sept. 24, 1960. 12 UST 2284, TIAS 4607, 439 UNTS 249. In 1996 at least 157 states are members of the IDA. CIA, World Fact Book. "International Organizations and Groups." www.odci.gov/cia/ publications/95fact/appendxc.html (Apr. 5, 1996).

growth of productive enterprise and private capital investment in developing countries.[71]

Formally established in 1947, the International Civil Aviation Organization promotes standards and regulations for international civil aviation.[72] ICAO has done much to produce standards for safety and operation measures, as well as uniform regulations affecting meteorological services, traffic control, communications, radio beacons, and search and rescue operations. In so doing, ICAO has contributed to simplifying customs, immigration, and public health regulations as they apply to international air transport. Among its vast array of international legal activities, ICAO has drafted more than 140 international air law conventions and other agreements.[73]

The International Fund for Agricultural Development since 1976 has worked to mobilize additional funds for agricultural development projects in developing countries through projects and programs that benefit the poorest rural populations.[74] In 1996, at least 158 states were formally participating in the Fund's activities.[75]

The International Labour Organization strives to promote employment and improve living standards to obtain greater social justice. The ILO was actually created in 1919 as part of the League of Nations under the Treaty of Versailles and was incorporated into the United Nations in 1946.[76] At least 174 international conventions and more than 180 formal recommendations have been promulgated by the ILO over the past five decades.[77]

The International Maritime Organization, formerly known as the Intergovernmental Maritime Consultative Organization, was established

[71] Articles of Agreement of the International Finance Corporation, *done* in Washington on May 25, 1955, *entered into force* July 20, 1956. 7 UST 2197, TIAS 3620, 264 UNTS 117. In 1996, 161 states are party to the IFC. CIA, World Fact Book. "International Organizations and Groups." www.odci.gov/cia/ publications/95fact /appendxc.html (Apr. 5, 1996).

[72] Convention on Civil Aviation, *done* at Chicago on Dec. 7, 1944, *entered into force* April 4, 1947. 61 Stat. 1180, TIAS 1591, 3 Bevans 944, 15 UNTS 295. By 1996, 184 states had become parties to the ICAO Convention. ICAO. "Memorandum on ICAO." www.cam.org/ ~icao/memo.txt (Apr. 5, 1996).

[73] ICAO, *Aeronautical Agreements and Arrangements: Tables of Agreements and Arrangements Registered with the Organization*, ICAO Doc. 9460 LGB/382 (1990). See Frederic L. Kirgis, Jr., "Aviation," in O. Schachter & C. Joyner, note 26 above, at 825–58.

[74] Agreement Establishing the International Fund for Agricultural Development, *done* at Rome June 13, 196, *entered into force* Nov. 30, 1977. 28 UST 8435, TIAS 8765, 1059 UNTS 191.

[75] International Fund for Agricultural Development. www.un.org/Dept/Treaty/bible/ Part_I_E/X_/X_.html (Apr. 1, 1996).

[76] Instrument for the Amendment of the Constitution of the International Labour Organization, *dated* Oct. 9, 1946, *entered into force* Apr. 20, 1948. 62 Stat. 3485, 4 Bevans 188, 15 UNTS 35.

[77] By 1996, at least 171 states are participating as parties in formulating these ILO agreements. CIA, World Fact Book. "International Organizations and Groups." www.odci.gov/cia/ publications/95fact/appendxc.html (Apr. 5, 1996). See Virginia A. Leary, "Labor," ch. 8 in this volume.

in 1958 expressly with the purposes of providing advisory and consultative assistance, as well as international cooperation, in maritime navigation.[78] Considerable efforts have been aimed by IMO's 152 member states at fostering the highest possible standards for safety and navigation, and devising and implementing international restrictions on vessel-source pollution of high seas.[79]

The International Monetary Fund was established in 1945 and works to promote international monetary cooperation, expansion of trade, and currency and exchange stability.[80] Much of the IMF's activity since 1990 has involved loans and rescheduling of debt payments to member states, often with strict conditions of austerity and reform measures. Significantly, each international agreement made between the IMF and the 181 states that in 1996 are parties to it constitutes a set of specified binding legal obligations.[81]

The International Telecommunication Union, oldest among the specialized agencies, began in 1865 and was formally integrated into the UN system in 1947.[82] Its purposes are many: to establish international regulations for radio, telegraph, telephone, and space radio-communications, as well as to allocate radio frequencies among the 184 states parties to it and its numerous ancillary agreements.[83]

The United Nations Educational, Scientific, and Cultural Organization was established in 1946.[84] UNESCO has as its lofty ambition to promote collaboration among its 185 member states through education, science, and culture in order to further justice, the rule of law, and human rights and freedoms without distinction as to race, sex, language, or religion.[85]

---

[78] Convention on the Intergovernmental Maritime Consultative Organization, *done* at Geneva Mar. 6, 1948, *entered into force* Mar. 17, 1958; 9 UST 621, TIAS No. 4044, 289 UNTS 48. The title of the Convention was changed to the Convention on the International Maritime Organization by amendment on Nov. 14, 1975, effective May 22, 1982.

[79] For analysis of IMO, see the discussion in Frederic L. Kirgis, Jr. "Shipping," in Schachter & Joyner, note 26 above, at 715–52.

[80] Articles of Agreement of the International Monetary Fund, *formulated* at the Bretton Woods Conference July 1–22, 1944, *opened for signature* at Washington Dec. 27, 1945, *entered into force* Dec. 27, 1945; 60 Stat. 1401, TIAS 1501. 3 Bevans 1351, 2 UNTS 39.

[81] International Monetary Fund, "General information on the IMF." gopher.imf.org (Apr. 1, 1996). See Stephen Zamora, "Economic Relations and Development," chapter 9 in this volume.

[82] International Telecommunications Convention, with annexes and protocols, *done* at Nairobi on Nov. 6, 1982, *entered into force* Jan. 1, 1984, replacing International Telecommunications Convention, with annexes and protocols, *adopted* at Malaga-Torremolinos on Oct. 25, 1973, *entered into force* Jan. 1, 1975 (28 UST 2495, TIAS 8572).

[83] The International Telecommunications UN., "What is the ITU?" www.itu.ch/publications/itupub_b.htm (Apr. 1, 1996). See Francis Lyall, "Post and Telecommunications," in O. Schachter & C. Joyner, note 26 above, at 789–824.

[84] See the discussion in Stephen P. Marks, "Education, Science, Culture and Information," in O. Schachter & C. Joyner, note 26 above, at 577–630.

[85] UNESCO, "Member States." www.unesco.org./ch-extern/about/ members.html (Apr. 1, 1996).

Since 1985, the United Nations Industrial Development Organization has existed as the specialized agency designated to promote and accelerate the industrialization of developing countries.[86] By 1996 at least 135 states had formally become parties to UNIDO's development activities.[87]

The Universal Postal Union, established in 1874, became a specialized agency in 1947 and operates to facilitate reciprocal exchange of correspondence by setting uniform procedures and speeding up mailing procedures.[88] This international agency is truly universal, claiming among its membership at least 189 states in 1996.[89]

The World Health Organization was established in 1948 to aid the attainment by all peoples of the highest levels of health.[90] Much of WHO's effort aims at coordinating disease control and proffering medical assistance to those needy countries among its 190 members.[91] Considerable attention since 1990 by WHO has focused on controlling spread of the deadly AIDS and Ebola viruses.

The World Intellectual Property Organization was created in 1970, although its origins trace back to the International Bureau of Paris Union (1883) and the Berne Union (1886).[92] WIPO's aim is to promote international cooperation among its 128 member governments for the legal protection of intellectual property, which includes artistic and scientific works, sound recordings, broadcasts, invention, trademarks, industrial designs, and company names.[93]

The World Meteorological Organization aims to improve and coordinate international meteorological work.[94] WMO does this by promoting international exchange of weather reports and greater standardization of observations among its 181 member states, as well as by offering special

---

[86] Convention of the United Nations Industrial Development Organization, with annexes, *adopted* at Vienna Apr. 8, 1979, *entered into force* June 21, 1985, TIAS 23432, 1401 UNTS 3.

[87] Constitution of the United Nations Industrial Development Organization, *done* Apr. 8, 1979, *entered into force* June 21, 1985, 1401 UNTS 3. www.org/Depts/Treaty/bible/Part_I_E/X_/X_9.html (Apr. 14, 1996).

[88] Constitution of the Universal Postal Union, with Final Protocol. *Done* at Vienna July 10, 1964, *entered into force* Jan. 1, 1966. 16 UST 1291, TIAS 5881, 611 UNTS 7.

[89] CIA World Factbook. "International Organizations and Groups." www.odci.gov/cia/publications/95 fact/appende.html (Apr. 1, 1996).

[90] Constitution of the World Health Organization, *done* at New York on July 22, 1946, *entered into force* Apr. 7, 1948. 62 Stat. 2679, TIAS 1808, 4 Bevans 119, 14 UNTS 185.

[91] For a critical assessment of WHO, see Katarina Tomasevski, "Health," in O. Schachter & C. Joyner, note 26 above, at 859–906.

[92] Convention Establishing the World Intellectual Property Organization, *done* at Stockholm July 14, 1967, *entered into force* Apr. 26, 1970; 21 UST 1749, TIAS 6932, 828 UNTS 3.

[93] WIPO, "WIPO: Description of Organization." ananse.irv.vit.no/trade_law/i_p/wipo/art/wipo.html (Apr. 1, 1996).

[94] Convention of the World Meteorological Organization, with related protocol. *Done* at Washington, DC on Oct. 11, 1947, *entered into force* Mar. 23, 1950. 1 UST 281, TIAS 2052, 77 UNTS 143.

weather services to developing countries for their own economic needs.[95]

Though not a specialized agency, the International Atomic Energy Agency was established in 1956 to promote the peaceful uses of atomic energy and to insure that assistance provided by it is not used for military purposes.[96] The IAEA has been used recently as an enforcement agent to inspect facilities in its 122 member states in order to prevent proliferation of nuclear weapons.[97]

Also outside the family of UN functional agencies, the General Agreement on Tariffs and Trade was established in 1947 to set rules for world trade and provide a forum for discussing trade-related issues.[98] As revised in 1994 and now in force, the GATT operates to facilitate negotiation of liberalized trade policies and resolution of trade disputes through the World Trade Organization.[99] By 1996, at least 128 states have become legally bound to these new dispute-settlement provisions.[100]

VII. FUTURE TRENDS

The United Nations' activities have clearly influenced the establishment of international legal order over the past five decades, and they will no doubt do so in the future. As regards the progressive development of constitutional law, efforts by the United Nations are likely to create a considerable body of soft law for guiding state behavior in global environmental matters. The likelihood is that the United Nations will aim to ground certain concepts more firmly as general principles of law, through the repeated adoption of General Assembly and special *ad hoc* conference resolutions. Among concepts that seem ripe for such attention are the "polluter-pays" principle, the principle of good neighborliness, and the notion of sustainable development. States clearly have manifest national interests in protecting and conserving the earth's environment for future use, and the

[95] WMO, "World Meteorological Organization." www.wmo.ch/web/ wmo-text.html (Apr. 1, 1996).

[96] Statute of the International Atomic Energy Agency, *done* at New York on Oct. 26, 1956, *entered into force* July 29, 1957. 8 UST 1093, TIAS 3873, 276 UNTS 3.

[97] IAEA, "The IAEA and the United Nations." www.iaea.or.at/ uniaea.html (Apr. 1, 1996). IAEA inspections have been used since 1991 to monitor nuclear activities in Iraq and North Korea.

[98] General Agreement on Tariffs and Trade, with annexes and schedules attached to the Final Act of the United Nations Conference on Trade and Employment, *signed* in Geneva Oct. 30, 1947, *entered into force* Jan. 1, 1948. 61 Stat. (5), (6), TIAS 1700, 4 Bevans 639, 55–61 UNTS.

[99] 1994 GATT/WTO. For assessments, see Thomas J. Dillon, "The World Trade Organization: A New Legal Order for World Trade?," 16 *Mich. J. Int'l L.* 349 (1995) and Zamora, ch. 9 in this volume.

[100] See the discussion in Zamora, ch. 9 above, in this volume.

United Nations can be readily employed to formulate international legal norms toward those ends. Nonetheless, transformation of these concepts from soft law to principles of law is not tantamount to states implementing them. That will require a much higher ambition.

Another future constitutional law consideration likely to confront the United Nations is the composition of the Security Council. Political pressures are mounting for the Security Council's membership to be expanded, in particular the number of permanent members on that organ. A number of candidates for permanent status have been suggested, ostensibly states which since 1960 have acquired a certain preeminent status in the international community. Included in this group are Germany and Japan, as well as Brazil, India, Indonesia, and Nigeria from among the developing countries. The argument put forward is that the world community has changed appreciably since 1945, but the composition of the Security Council has not kept pace with those developments. Certain Great Powers are now not-so-great, and certain other states have ascended to power "greatness." Hence, the conclusion follows that the time has come to alter the composition of the Security Council by adding more members with the veto power. This would be done by amendment of the UN Charter.

Whether such a change can take place depends on the political will of the present permanent members. Amendment of the Charter constitutes a substantive question. Accordingly, for such a change to pass, a two-thirds majority of the Security Council (i.e., nine of fifteen votes) must be secured, in which no permanent member casts a negative vote on that question. Whether such a majority can be secured seems dubious, particularly since by doing so the current Great Powers would be diluting their very power on the Council.

The future course of United Nations-derived prescriptive law for member states' conduct seems more problematic. In the area of prescriptive law, issues likely to command the future attention of the United Nations, in particular the Security Council, include imposing measures against governments violating the nonproliferation of nuclear arms, setting prohibitions against chemical and biological weapons, and fixing controls on the export of missile technology. No doubt, too, the Security Council will remain concerned with transnational threats to the peace and breaches of the peace. But the Council is likely to exercise more restraint in voting to authorize sending UN peacekeeping missions to resolve internal conflicts. Such missions are too costly for the United Nations in financial terms: In 1996, at least $1.6 billion remained unpaid by member states for peacekeeping efforts since 1990, a sum that threatens to bankrupt the entire UN Organization. Perhaps even more ominous are the political costs associated with the loss of men and national treasure, particularly by the Great Powers on the Security Council. The latter burden erodes the domestic support necessary to portray support of the United Nations as being in the national interest of those states.

While there is no question that the United Nations will attempt to establish more prescriptive norms to meet new threats to the peace, the critical issue still hinges on compliance and enforcement. When certain states fail or refuse to comply with punitive norms affecting peace and security, how should the United Nations react? The key of course lies in the composition and political will of the Security Council and the ability of the Great Powers to act resolutely, in concert, to enforce sanctions against a state committing threats to or a breach of the peace. If the past is prologue, reaction by the Security Council is likely to be calculated more on political considerations than as a resolute response to a grave breach of international law. Such is the price of having five potential vetoes on the Council.

Also in the area of prescriptive law-creation, the increasing trend of national governments to use the International Court of Justice to resolve bilateral disputes is a positive indication of the rule of law. This trend seems likely to persist, so long as governments perceive that the Court has acted fairly and impartially in reaching its decisions.

Finally, the administrative law generated by the United Nations seems likely to expand as international trade and commerce continues to grow. The GATT, augmented by activities of its World Trade Organization and expanding international commercial dealings, is sure to necessitate constant attention by the United Nations in the formulation and implementation of international rules and norms. Similarly, greater resort to using UN bodies may well occur to curb massive human rights violations in internal conflicts. Grave concern over genocidal atrocities, gross deprivation of fundamental human rights, and the plight of refugees and internally displaced persons will no doubt remain high priorities on the United Nations' agenda. The outcomes of the Bosnian and Rwandan tragedies, as well as the search for international justice through their respective tribunals, should indicate the prospects for long-term success or failure in these regards.

VIII. CONCLUSION

The United Nations has contributed substantially to shaping the international legal order throughout the last half of the twentieth century. The UN Charter provides a set of values for the international system in its Preamble where "we the people" reaffirm their "faith in fundamental human rights" and "in the equal rights of men and women and of nations large and small," with the determination "to promote social progress and better standards of life in larger freedom." The fundamental "purposes and principles" in the Charter express international concern over the need to suppress acts of aggression, to support principles of international law, peaceful settlement, and international cooperation. In sum, the Charter codifies normative constructs into hard legal principles for guiding interstate behavior. Even so, at times critical problems remain regarding the political will of states to comply with and enforce those legal principles.

The United Nations surely will maintain its impressive record as a seed bed for developing new rules and norms of international law. The Organization provides a global forum for negotiating and drafting international agreements that address emerging problems of international law. It furnishes opportunities for states to exchange ideas and positions on almost any issue affecting interstate relations, and it offers lawful channels for national governments to seek peaceful redress for any grievances that might be inflicted by some other government.

In the end, however, the contributions made by the United Nations Organization to a just and lasting international legal order ultimately depend upon the political will of its member states to make the law work. States create the law through the United Nations, states break the law in spite of the United Nations, and states often must enforce the law through the United Nations. But the United Nations is not a magic bullet capable of producing international justice and rectitude. Rather, the United Nations is a political organization that operates through political means often for political purposes. Hence, international law created through the United Nations can only be as strong as its member states – especially the Great Powers on the Security Council – are willing to make it be.

Law developed through the United Nations system is manifestly intended to function for the benefit of member states. But this law can only function with the genuine cooperation and diplomatic perseverance by the governments of those same states. For the United Nations as an organiz-ation, as well as for each of its 185 member states, that basic political fact will remain the predominant challenge in determining the effectiveness of the United Nations legal order in the years to come.

INDEX

458